ALSO BY NEIL SHEEHAN

A Bright Shining Lie

The Arnheiter Affair

After the War Was Over

A FIERY
PEACE IN A
COLD WAR

NEIL SHEEHAN

A FIERY PEACE IN A COLD WAR

Bernard Schriever and the Ultimate Weapon

RANDOM HOUSE ☖ NEW YORK

Published in the United States by Random House, an imprint of
The Random House Publishing Group, a division of
Random House, Inc., New York.
RANDOM HOUSE and colophon are registered trademarks of Random House, Inc.

Library of Congress Cataloging-in-Publication Data
Sheehan, Neil.
A fiery peace in a cold war : Bernard Schriever and
the ultimate weapon / Neil Sheehan.
p.   cm.
Includes bibliographical references and index.
ISBN: 978-0-679-42284-6
eBook ISBN: 978-1-58836-905-5
1. Schriever, Bernard A.   2. United States. Air Force—Officers—Biography.
3. Generals—United States—Biography.   4. Military engineers—United States—
Biography.   5. Intercontinental ballistic missiles—Design and construction—
History.   6. Intercontinental ballistic missiles—United States—History.
7. Nuclear weapons—United States—History.   8. Cold War.   9. Aeronautics,
Military—Research—United States—History.   10. Astronautics—
Research—United States—History.   I. Title.
E745.S34S44 2009
355.0092—dc22
[B]
2009002247

Printed in the United States of America on acid-free paper

www.atrandom.com

2   4   6   8   9   7   5   3   1

First Edition

Book design by Caroline Cunningham

For Susan—who else?

For Maria and Catherine

For Will

And for my grandson, Nicholas Sheehan Bruno

FOREWORD

When the Space Age is mentioned, most people think of Sputnik, the launching into orbit of the first man-made satellite by the Soviet Union on October 4, 1957, or the race between Russia and the United States to land men on the moon. Sputnik was a psychological thunderclap. It set off a paroxysm of fear that the Soviet Union had gained a commanding technological lead over the United States. The moon landing by Neil Armstrong and Edwin Aldrin on July 20, 1969, was its reverse: a spectacular feat of American technology with little in the way of practical benefits. This book is concerned with a quite different space race. This other race initiated America's exploration and exploitation of space and was for the highest stakes—preventing the Soviet Union from acquiring an overwhelming nuclear superiority that could tempt Soviet leaders into international blackmail and adventurism with calamitous results for human civilization. Its outcome thus directly affected the security of the United States and the non-Communist nations of Europe, as well as the preservation of the fragile equilibrium between the two superpowers during the Cold War. The story of this other race, of the man who led it, an Air Force officer named Bernard Schriever, of those who labored with him, of the times in which they grew up and came of age and the challenges and obstacles they had to overcome, forms the narrative of this book.

CONTENTS

PROLOGUE:
A Rite of Succession

General Henry Harley Arnold, known as "Hap" because of his unusual smile, was in a hurry in January 1946. During the Second World War, which had ended the previous August with the surrender of Japan, he had created and led the greatest air armada ever assembled, the U.S. Army Air Forces. The stress of the war had exacted a toll on a fragile heart. He had suffered two heart attacks during the war and a third shortly after its conclusion. (He was to die of heart failure on January 15, 1950, at the age of just sixty-three.) He knew he would have to retire soon and turn command of his Army Air Forces over to his trusted friend and second man, Carl "Tooey" Spaatz.

While the outcome of the war was still in doubt, Arnold had, with a couple of exceptions, held innovation to what was practical and could be committed rapidly to combat. The one entirely new aircraft he had decided to build and nurtured to completion during the conflict was the B-29 Superfortress, because it had been necessary for the long-range strategic bombing campaign against Japan. Not that he had neglected to avail himself earlier of civilian scientific talent whenever he thought that it could help him solve particular problems. Back in 1939 with the conflict in Europe just beginning, he had invited General George Marshall, then the new chief of staff and a friend of Arnold Army since they were lieutenants together in the Philippines prior to the First World War, to join him at lunch with a group of scientists with whom he was conferring. Marshall was a believer in the efficacy of air power, but respect born of the friendship was another reason he was to treat Arnold, officially subordinate to him, as an equal. During the war he made him a member of the Joint Chiefs of Staff and allowed him to organize the Army Air Forces with an autonomy that would prepare the way for postwar independence. Marshall was, however, an infantryman by profession. He was not accustomed to the company of "long hairs," as the regular military pejoratively referred to the scientific community. "What on earth are you doing with people like that?" he asked Arnold afterward. Arnold explained that he was using their original minds to create instruments "for our airplanes . . . that are far too difficult for the Air Force engineers to develop themselves."

As 1944 wore on, with the defeat of Hitler's Third Reich not long off and Imperial Japan's demise certain to follow, Arnold could afford to look ahead and set free the evangelist of technology that dwelt within him. He intended to leave to his beloved air arm a heritage of science and technology so deeply imbued in the institution that the weapons it would fight with would always be the best the state of the art could provide and those on its drawing boards would be prodigies of futuristic thought. Above all, he was determined to avoid a return in the postwar period to those disheartening years of the early 1930s when, as he put it in a letter to another old friend, Dr. Robert Millikan, president of the California Institute of Technology, "just a relatively small group of enthusiastic officers [were] struggling against ignorance and indifference as to the importance of aviation and air power to the security and the very existence of the nation." Apparently with the Soviet Union in mind, he was also convinced that the downfall of Germany and Japan did not mean an enduring peace. It was "axiomatic," he wrote, that because the United States would emerge from the conflict as "one of the predominant powers . . . we will no doubt have potential enemies that will constitute a continuing threat to the nation."

The Second World War had also wrought a change in the military cosmos as transforming as the one it was bringing about in the geopolitical universe. The nation could no longer look to the seas as the protective barrier around it, nor to the U.S. Navy as the bulwark to stop an enemy from breaching that barrier. The air was now the space that mattered and the safety of the nation depended upon the ability of the

U.S. Army Air Forces, soon to become the independent U.S. Air Force, to reign supreme in the skies. Hiroshima was also to make the new air arm first among equals where the other services were concerned, because it could deliver that most cataclysmic of weapons—the atomic bomb.

Ever since the early fall of 1944, Arnold had been commissioning studies and funding experimental weaponry. Now, with his retirement impending and his preparations for the future nearing completion, Arnold summoned to his Pentagon office a young colonel named Bernard Schriever. "Bennie" Schriever had grown up in San Antonio, Texas, and acquired his nickname from the sportswriters there. He had been a champion amateur golfer as a youth and they had wanted a snappy moniker for their articles about his exploits on the links. They had dubbed him "Benny," and the nickname had stuck during his military years but had acquired the somewhat inelegant spelling above. Schriever had spent the war out in the Pacific and had reported to the Research and Engineering Division of the Air Staff only a few days before. When he was told that Arnold wanted to see him as soon as possible, he hurried over to the River Entrance on the outer, or E Ring, corridor of the Pentagon overlooking the Potomac, where the high panjandrums like the general had their domain. After the usual wait in the outer office in which the aides and secretaries worked, he was shown into the ample inner one, where Hap Arnold sat behind a large desk. Each of the shoulder tabs of his olive drab uniform jacket held a ringlet of five silver stars, General of the Army, the highest rank to which an officer could aspire. Arnold was the only airman ever to achieve it. He beckoned Bennie to one of the easy chairs in front. What ensued was the classic passing on by an older man of the final mission of his life and career to a young disciple.

There would come a day, Arnold told Schriever, when scientists and scientifically trained officers would be just as important to the Air Force as the "operators" who currently ran it, AAF parlance for the men who had risen to general officer commands by their ability to wield bomber and fighter forces in combat. Nurturing the process that would lead to this day was crucial because of the difference it would make in the potency of American air power. To emphasize his point, the general stressed to Schriever the same parting message he was leaving with Spaatz and others: it was the civilian scientists, not the military engineers, who had been the technological innovators during the war. "They are the ones who made the breakthroughs," he said. He predicted that those breakthroughs—in radar, in jet propulsion, in rocketry, in nuclear weapons—would prove to be the catalysts for further innovation that would radically alter the nature of war. The First World War had been decided by brawn, he said, the Second by logistics. "The Third World War will be different. It will be won by brains." There was no need for him to mention Joseph Stalin's Soviet Union as the threat. Both men understood it. "All of us, at least those of us in the military, thought that we were in for a long siege with Communism," Schriever was to say years later in recounting the meeting.

The rub was that with the end of the war, the scientists responsible for these accomplishments were returning to their universities. The laboratories at which they had worked were either shutting down, like the Radiation Laboratory at MIT, or being drastically shrunk, as at Los Alamos, where the atomic bomb had been created. To try to preserve the relationship with these scientists, Arnold was ordering the formation of a new Scientific Liaison Branch within the Research and Engineering Division. He wanted Schriever to head it. Schriever's task would be to provide staff backup for projects civilian scientists undertook at the behest of the AAF. He was also to help with similar staffing in the establishment of a new network of research and testing centers for which Arnold had laid out plans, and to contribute to any other opportunities that arose to draft science and technology into air power's service.

Had the officer sitting across the desk from Arnold been of more ordinary mind-set, the job he was being given would have been an interesting but hardly inspiring one. Perhaps Arnold sensed that Bernard Schriever was different and that was why he had sent for him. Perhaps he sensed it from their long relationship, which went back to the 1930s, or from the postgraduate degree Schriever had gained in aeronautical engineering; or from his stellar performance as an engineer officer in the Pacific; or from the fact that he had asked for research and development as a postwar assignment. Whatever his reasons, Arnold had summoned the right man. Schriever had the intellectual bent and the foresight to see the implications for the future that Arnold saw. He also shared Arnold's vision. And there was more to it than that. There was a chemistry between the two men. Arnold had been his first chief when Schriever had been a novice second lieutenant pilot at March Field near Riverside, California, in 1933, fresh from the Flying School at Kelly Field next to San Antonio. Arnold had been the man who had later rescued him from the humdrum of an airline pilot's life and set him forth on the surpassing adventure of the Second World War. Arnold had been the leader who had fought so hard and so well to transform their ludicrously antique biplane Air Corps of the 1930s into an invincible host of the skies. In one of the last acts of his career, this man of whom Schriever stood in awe was appointing him to a task that Schriever knew meant more to Arnold than any other. Bennie Schriever said goodbye and left Arnold's office not just as an airman with an assignment. He left as an apostle with a calling. What he would accomplish in the years to come he would do for himself, but in his mind he would also be doing it because Hap Arnold had entrusted him with the mission. He would not fail his chief. He would go on to become the father of the modern, high-technology Air Force and play a pivotal role in preserving peace during the grim years of the Cold War by building the first weapon in the history of warfare that was meant to deter rather than to be fired in anger—the intercontinental ballistic missile.

BOOK I

BECOMING AN AMERICAN

ELLIS ISLAND AND
A TRAGEDY IN TEXAS

The men in the Schriever family were venturesome types who immigrated to America to better themselves or took to the sea. Schriever's paternal grandfather, Bernhard, after whom he was named, had jumped ship as a young German sailor in the port of Norfolk, Virginia, in 1860 and volunteered for the Confederate Army during the Civil War. Afterward, he had made his way down to New Orleans and gone to work on the railroads, building watering towers for the steam locomotives of the time, before returning to Germany in 1870 to pursue the trade of a rigger for sailing ships.

Schriever's mother, Elizabeth Milch, a pleasing dark brunette with bright blue eyes and a strong will, had left Germany as a teenager to work in the household of a German family who owned a pharmacy in lower Manhattan. She had initially dated Schriever's paternal uncle, George Schriever, who had immigrated to Union City, New Jersey, and become a prosperous baker and delicatessen owner there. But George was a bon vivant determined to remain a bachelor ("He played the field," his nephew recalled) and so he introduced Elizabeth to his brother Adolph, a tall stalk of a man with blond hair and a neat mustache who was an engineering officer on the passenger liners of the North German Lloyd Company. They were married at a Lutheran church in Hoboken in 1908, when she was twenty-two. Adolph took her back to Germany. Her first son, Bernhard Adolph, was born in the north German city of Bremen on September 14, 1910, and her second boy, Gerhard, followed two years later just before Christmas. The outbreak of the First World War in August 1914, while Adolph's ship, the *George Washington*, was in New York Harbor, suddenly separated the family, now living in his home port of nearby Bremerhaven. (The German line had apparently built the ship in 1909 for service to the United States and originally named it in honor of America's first president.) Adolph was stranded in New York, Britain's Royal Navy standing by to seize the vessel the moment the liner ventured out.

By the end of 1916, Elizabeth had had enough of waiting for the war to end and her husband to come home. Holland was neutral during the First World War. She booked passage to New York for herself and her two boys out of Rotterdam. They left in January 1917 on the Dutch liner *Noordam*. The English Channel was closed to neutral shipping because of the war and they had to sail north around Scotland. It took them more than two weeks. The North Atlantic was rough sailing in this winter season. Looking at the heaving waves, Schriever remembered thinking that the ocean must be a series of mountains. His mother had a scare when a British gunboat hailed the ship and an inspection party came aboard. She was afraid they would be seized as German nationals and taken off, but fortunately Gerhard had the mumps, a dangerous disease for an adult. When the Dutch crew warned the British sailors, the boarding party avoided the Schrievers' cabin. The next fright came in the intimidating immensity of the Great Hall at Ellis Island. It was a cavernous structure, 189 feet long and 102 feet wide with a 60-foot-high vaulted ceiling. Thousands of immigrants off the ships lined up within it each day to be processed, either accepted as physically fit and freed to go ashore or rejected and sent back to wherever they had come from with now vanished hope. Elizabeth spoke English well, with merely a slight accent, but her boys had only German. Anti-German feeling was reaching war pitch in much of the United States. She feared that if the immigration officials overheard a word of German, she and the boys might be turned away. "Be quiet," Schriever remembered her whispering, taking them by the hand. "Don't say anything." They were cleared and released as landed immigrants on February 1, 1917. Elizabeth Schriever had given her sons an American future just in time. The United States declared war on Kaiser Wilhelm's Germany only two months later.

Adolph was allowed to join his family. Before leaving the ship, he and the rest of his engineering crew, patriotic German men, had done their best to wreck the engines of the vessel they knew was soon to be confiscated. Schriever remembered learning of it because his father appeared with a bandaged thumb, injured while smashing machinery. (The wrecking was to no avail. The *George Washington* was repaired and converted into a troopship to haul American soldiers to France to kill Germans and, after the Armistice of November 11, 1918, had the honor of carrying President Woodrow Wilson to and from the peace conference at Versailles. It survived through the next two decades to again serve as a troop transport during the Second World War.)

To escape the anti-German hysteria of the Northeast, the family moved to the Texas Hill Country between Austin and San Antonio on the advice of John Schriever, another of Adolph's brothers, who had immigrated there years earlier and made his living at cattle ranching and speculating in land and oil properties. The region had been heavily settled by Germans since the wave of exiles created by the failure of the liberal revolutions in Germany in 1848. Adolph found work as superintendent of the machinery in the local brewery at New Braunfels, still a German-speaking community in 1917. School was taught in English and Bernhard and Gerhard learned the language quickly, but they had less trouble than they otherwise might have had because the teacher could always translate when they encountered a problem. With the United States now in the war and its industries going full bore, there was a demand for engineering talent. Adolph took a job as quality control engineer at a factory in San Antonio that was making large gasoline-driven engines. The Schrievers shifted to the city. One day in September 1918, Adolph had his head down inspecting an engine. Someone accidentally flipped the starter. The flywheel fractured his skull in two places. He never recovered consciousness and died on September 17, 1918, sixteen days after his thirty-fifth birthday.

2.

A BENEFACTOR AND THE HOUSE
ON THE TWELFTH GREEN

Elizabeth Schriever and her two boys suddenly confronted a stark existence. There was no compensation for an accident like this in those years and she was a widow with a modicum of education and no particular skills she could call upon to support her sons. They were taken in by an uncle of Bernhard's father, Magnus Klattenhoff, who had immigrated a generation earlier and gone into ranching at Slaton, near Lubbock in West Texas. Schriever got a start on a nickname and Americanization there. A Klattenhoff cousin of his age had been baptized with a good Texas first name—Ben. When another boy of the same age arrived at school with the Klattenhoffs, the teacher decided she was not going to be bothered addressing him by his German first name of Bernhard. She dubbed the cousin Ben One and the arrival Ben Two. The locals also had trouble pronouncing Gerhard for some reason, and so he gradually acquired the nickname of Gerry. Life was mostly outdoors and healthy—helping with the cattle, picking cotton—but the trauma of their father's loss was always with them and charity is not a livelihood. After a year they moved back to New Braunfels, where friends rented them a small house and their mother worked part-time in a butcher shop and at a minor housekeeping job.

Neither brought in enough to sustain herself and her boys and so Elizabeth Schriever made a grim decision. She put her sons in an orphanage in San Antonio while she set about finding a housekeeping position in the city that paid a respectable wage. The next six months were desolate ones for her children. They were at an age, approximately ten and eight, when boys need their mother. In the span of just a few years, they had also been taken from a solid, familiar place to a strange land where they had lost their father and been repeatedly uprooted. "We never felt we'd been abandoned," Schriever said later, because Elizabeth visited often and explained why she'd had to put them in the orphanage. The staff also treated them well and the hardship was mitigated for Gerry because he had an older brother to give him support. But Schriever had no one to whom he could turn. Nothing could compensate for the loneliness. He did not complain. Ever since his father's death he had felt a sense of responsibility not to make things harder for his mother than they already were. In the end what sustained the boys' faith in their eventual rescue was, as Schriever put it, "the great confidence we had in our mother."

Even after she found a job and took them out of the orphanage, there was still the bar to acceptance for two German boys when all things German were unpopular in the hangover animosity from the war. Felix McKnight, who grew up to become a prominent Texas newspaperman—co-publisher and editor of the *Dallas Times Herald*—met Schriever in the third grade. Elizabeth took to McKnight when Schriever brought him home to the house she had rented and became a kind of second mother to him. The two boys began a close and lifelong friendship. McKnight remembered how hard the other boys were on the German kid who spoke with a bit of a guttural accent. He was taller than his schoolmates and so they were afraid to take him on individually, but they would ring him around in a gang, ragging him and yelling that he was Kaiser Wilhelm. Most of the time he kept his temper and endured the taunts, but every once in a while he would make for a couple of the taunters and McKnight would restrain him, afraid that Schriever would get into deeper trouble by being blamed for fistfighting by a teacher who also had an animus toward Germans. His thirst to be adopted by this new land, however, gradually won over the other boys. Every day the class would stand at attention, put their right hands over their hearts, and recite the Pledge of Allegiance. Schriever recited the pledge with far more emotion than any of his schoolmates and it was not long before his voice was the one leading the daily recital. The German accent faded and so did the ragging.

The job Elizabeth finally found also soon transformed their lives. A wealthy and elderly mortgage banker, Edward Chandler, and his wife had a three-story, sixteen-room, gray brick mansion on West French Place in Laurel Heights, at the time the most fashionable section of San Antonio. The mansion required a staff of about half a dozen. The Chandlers recognized in Elizabeth Schriever an efficient, take-charge woman who could run the place for them—supervising the other servants, making the household purchases, relieving them of any worries as head housekeeper.

Within a year Chandler built her a home for herself in which to raise her boys on a lot he owned at 217 Terry Court on the edge of the Brackenridge Park Golf Course, then within the residential section of a San Antonio of roughly 160,000 persons and now at the center of a city of approximately 1,150,000. The house was a small but adequate wood-frame affair with a white clapboard exterior, set under the immense spreading branches of one of the lot's four antique live oak trees, said by local legend to date from the original Spanish settlement in the early eighteenth century. It had two bedrooms, a large dining-living room area, a kitchen and pantry, and a screened-in porch off to one side. Elizabeth occupied one of the bedrooms; her mother, who had come over from Germany to look after the boys while Elizabeth worked (they called her "Oma," the German equivalent of "Grandma" or "Granny"), slept in the other; and the two young men had their beds out on the porch. In winter they slept under heavy, old-fashioned eiderdown comforters from Germany, the sort that were common before central heating. Neither remembers ever being cold.

The rear of the house lot bordered the green of the twelfth hole. Chandler, who had no children of his own, became a bighearted uncle to the Schriever boys. He had a refreshment stand built under the enveloping tent of the branches of another of the live oak trees so that they could earn pocket money by selling lemonade and Cokes and the like to passing golfers. When Chandler and his wife died in the early 1920s, Elizabeth struck out on her own. She transformed the soda pop stand at the twelfth green, which the boys had never made much of, into a business profitable enough to support her family. She had a small white structure built with serving windows on one side and in front set wooden benches next to picnic tables. She called her stand, appropriately, "The Oaks," in gratitude for the shade the venerable trees provided her little building and the bench seats and picnic tables, and she featured homemade sandwiches and cookies, along with lemonade and other soft drinks. She charged fifteen cents for a sandwich and a nickel for a glass of lemonade. Several nights a week she would bake hams to slice for the sandwiches. She soon had a flourish-

ing business not only from the many golfers but also from other locals
seeking a hearty bite and out-of-towners who had heard about her
stand.

Elizabeth Schriever kept her boys under a strict regimen. Even
when in high school, they had their homework done and were in bed
by 9:00 P.M. Yet she did so with persuasion and self-control. Schriever
could not recall her ever striking them, nor did she shout when they
crossed her. "She talked you into it," he said. "She reasoned with you."
Without health one had nothing, she would tell them, and eating well
and sleeping well were vital to maintaining health. Not that they caused
her much trouble. They could see how hard she was working to give
them a good life and the sense of responsibility that had descended on
Schriever with his father's death never left him. Gerry later suspected
that her total devotion to raising her sons was the principal reason she
did not remarry until she was past sixty. She made certain that they
went to catechism class at a church in the Lutheran faith of their father,
Friedens Evangelical. She was not a churchgoer herself. She was a lapsed
Catholic who had rebelled at harsh discipline from the nuns at a con-
vent school in Germany as a girl. She also had no time for church, as
weekends were her busiest days at the stand.

3.

THE VIRTUES OF GOLF

The boys settled into the not unpleasant task of growing up in
San Antonio, Texas, in the 1920s and 1930s. Schriever was the
star pitcher on the Friedens Evangelical baseball team, yet the all-
American game did not attract him as much as it did most other
boys. Golf became his passion. His obsession with it first brought out
the relentless competitiveness, the fierce desire to emerge as number
one that was behind the friendly, restrained exterior of his personality. The generosity of Edward Chandler was responsible for getting
him started. An enthusiastic golfer himself, Chandler had decided

that Schriever and Gerry should be taught the game. After Elizabeth had gone to work for him, he took them out to the San Antonio Country Club (he was its president), and instructed the golf pro there to shorten some clubs (golf clubs had wooden shafts in those days) and to give them lessons. The boys had a ready supply of golf balls from the San Antonio River, then a relatively shallow, free-flowing stream that ran through the middle of Brackenridge Park Golf Course, where they could play for a minimal fee because it was public. They would simply wade in and fish stray balls from the river bottom. Gerry became a quite competent golfer, but never the dazzler on the links his older brother, Bernard, was to become. Schriever was off on his first quest.

Golf is a social game and yet it is also an intensely solitary one. A golfer plays on the course alongside others, but he wins or loses on his own performance. There is virtually no margin for error. A tournament can be won or lost by a single stroke. The game requires enormous and sustained powers of concentration and self-control, because it is as much mental as it is physical.

Much later in life, after the immigrant boy from Bremerhaven wore stars in the U.S. Air Force and was charged with creating America's intercontinental ballistic missile force, Schriever was renowned for his staunchness under stress and the deliberate fashion in which he would thread his way through multiple obstacles to a solution. When test missiles exploded in flames and thunder on the launching pads, fizzled out and crashed back to earth, or strayed wildly off course and had to be blown up in midair by the range safety officer—to ridicule in the press and irritation and impatience at the Pentagon and the White House—others would begin to lose their nerve. Not Schriever. He would remain calm and press on with the searching and questioning, he and his people learning from each failure until the rocket flew straight and true.

At school and on the links of Brackenridge Park Golf Course, he made a small number of close friends like McKnight and he had casual friendships as well, but beneath the affable surface he was a loner. He did not consciously try to distance himself from others or to set himself apart, yet he noticed that others always seemed to sense a distance and to treat him accordingly. His casual friends, for example, usually addressed him as "Schriever," rather than as Ben or Bennie. Others sensed a distance because the distance was there. There was a kind of Teutonic quality about him. Reserve was his most natural state. He was little given to small talk and the jocular exchanges that make for easy friendships. His conversations usually focused on what interested him, and what interested him he took seriously. Part of this introverted personality was undoubtedly in his genes, but whatever his genes gave him had clearly been magnified by the uprooting from Germany, the bolt-from-the-sky death of his father, the striving to be accepted as an American, and the painful, uncertain years before his mother found her position with the Chandlers. The experiences had taught him that to deal with adversity he had to look for strength within himself, a lesson he also learned from his mother, who set an example and of whom he was in awe. In the complexity that is the human personality this introverted side did not diminish in the least his drive to compete and to prevail, initially in golf and then in matters of greater moment later in life. He was insightful enough to be conscious of the need. As he would put it with his wry sense of humor, "I hate to lose."

Right after graduation in June of 1927, still sixteen, he demonstrated that he was a youngster to watch in the sport. The first Texas state championship tournament for juniors was held at the difficult Willow Springs course right outside San Antonio. The dark horse of the tournament, as one local newspaper put it, led the field of fifty-four in the qualifying round to win a pair of golfing shoes from the Broadway Sporting Goods Store and a silver medal from the *Light,* a San Antonio newspaper that was one of the sponsors of the tournament. He was defeated in the semifinal round by another sixteen-year-old, from Dallas, but not before winning more praise from the local press as the "courageous" young golfer who "made a powerful comeback on the last nine holes as the count stood against him." The self-control Schriever displayed in tournaments did not mean that he lacked a temper. When he was playing badly for some reason, he would curse vehemently and fling whatever club he happened to have in his hands a remarkable distance.

His failure to attain the starting lineup on the freshman baseball team at the Agricultural and Mechanical College of Texas, popularly known as Texas A&M, which he entered that fall of 1927, confirmed him in his focus on golf. As always, it was Elizabeth who made it possible for him to go to college, paying the approximately $1,000 a year cost for his room, board, and tuition with the accumulated nickels and dimes from her sandwich stand and with some help from Uncle George back in Union City, New Jersey, who had branched out from the bakery and delicatessen business to acquire a local bus company as well. A shoulder broken the next year in a sophomore touch football game ironically helped. He had always been relentless about practice. Gerry remembered how his brother would spend an hour working on a single stroke. He bore down harder in the course of rebuilding the shoulder muscles after the bone had healed. His golf score went from the low 80s into the low 70s. By his senior year at A&M, again captain of the golf team, he was a scratch player: he had to maintain a consistent average of playing up to par. He gained a mention in *Ripley's Believe It or Not* for three times driving more than 300 yards to the same green on the Brackenridge course and one-putting for an eagle. The year he graduated, 1931, he won the Texas state junior amateur championship and the city championship in San Antonio, where he had become a local golf celebrity.

Now approaching his full adult height of six feet, three inches, but still trimmer than the 180 pounds of muscle and bone he was eventually to weigh, he was a figure of angular elegance on the course, wavy dark brown hair over slim, well-cut features with the bright blue eyes he had inherited from his mother. Most young Texas golfers played in slacks. They considered the British-style golf outfit that the pros then favored as sissified. Bennie, who had a sense of style, did not. The light tan or gray plus fours he wore above long socks, two-tone brown and white golf shoes, a fancy cloth and leather belt at the waist, and a white short-sleeve shirt worked well on his frame and made him stand out still more from the pack.

Decision time came during his senior year at A&M. He was offered the pro's position at the golf course at Bryan, Texas, just north of the college. The job paid $200 a month, more than he could make doing anything else and a lot of money in 1931, the third year of the Great Depression. He had no chance at all after graduation of employment in his major—structural architecture as his degree called it, con-

struction engineering in a more plainspoken description—because the
jobs simply did not exist. Professional golf competition did not have
the social status it was later to acquire, however, and the tournament
purses bore no resemblance to what they were to reach. Elizabeth
was also opposed. She wanted her sons to become men worthy of respect, and professional athletes did not hold a place of respectability in
the German middle-class world from which she drew her standards.
Schriever made up his own mind, however. He reasoned that he hadn't
gone to college for four years and acquired a bachelor of science degree
to devote the rest of his life to golf. He decided he was going to do
what had begun to attract him most and become a flier in the U.S.
Army Air Corps.

4·

WHITE SILK SCARVES AND
OPEN COCKPITS

San Antonio was a military town in the 1920s and 1930s and Bennie Schriever had grown up in its aura. The Alamo is located
there, and during the Spanish-American War at the turn of the century, Theodore Roosevelt and the officers of his 1st U.S. Volunteer
Cavalry Regiment, better known as the Rough Riders, had hung out
in the bar of the old Menger Hotel before departing for fame in
Cuba. The tank had not yet replaced the horse in Schriever's youth,
although in a harbinger of what was to come a squadron of slow,
lumbering First World War tanks was stationed at Fort Sam Houston. Bennie and Gerry would gather with crowds of other children to
watch the tanks and the horses of the cavalry maneuver against each
other on the expanse of the fort's parade ground. The officers of the
cavalry participated in the polo matches regularly staged there and at
the municipal polo field next to Brackenridge Park Golf Course. In

choosing Texas A&M, Schriever had also chosen to attend a military school. The college was all male then, and except for a few youths who were physically unqualified, every student wore an Army uniform, was enrolled in the Reserve Officers' Training Corps, and marched to and from the mess hall for breakfast and dinner. Bennie's ROTC unit was B Battery of the Field Artillery, traditionally a San Antonio organization. After graduation, he was commissioned a Reserve second lieutenant in the artillery of the day, also still drawn by teams of horses. Howitzers and horses held no interest for Schriever. He would later joke that his legs were too long for the stirrups.

Above all, San Antonio was an Army fliers town. Schriever had grown up in a place where technology had literally flown past the horse. Kelly Field on the edge of the city was the Air Corps' main center for advanced pilot training. As a boy, Schriever would sit on the fence out there and watch the First World War–era biplanes take off and land, their Liberty engines emitting so much thick black exhaust that they were called "coal burners." Golf had also played its part in attracting him to flying because he had first caddied for and then played with and against the Air Corps officers who frequented the Brackenridge Park course. Schriever looked up to them as an elite. This was the romantic era of flying, of white silk scarves, leather helmets and goggles, and open cockpits, the First World War exploits of the German knight of the sky, Baron Manfred von Richthofen, and the American Ace of Aces, Edward V. "Eddie" Rickenbacker, fresh in memory. "The gals sure liked it. It was better than owning a convertible," Bennie would laugh and say in his old age. His mother dated a pilot who was subsequently one of his instructors.

In late 1931, after he had reached the minimum age of twenty-one, he applied for Flying School, as it was then called, as a cadet and was chosen for the entering class of July 1932. The course was a year, with Primary and Basic training at recently completed Randolph Field, also adjacent to San Antonio, and then Advanced at Kelly. Even if he survived the 50 percent washout rate and won his wings and a Reserve commission as a second lieutenant in the U.S. Army Air Corps, he still could not have high expectations of turning the Air Corps into a career because he probably would not be able to convert his commission into a Regular, i.e., permanent, one. He could look forward with certainty only to a year of active service before he was tossed back to civilian life and unemployment. In the midst of the Depression, the Air Corps was being kept on a bare-cupboard budget by Congress. It had no funds to take in more than a few new Regular officers annually or to give its Reservists more than a year of flying experience. But at twenty-one, a man could always hope that he might beat the odds.

To pass the time and earn what he could before Flying School, he played a number of exhibition tournaments with other amateurs against pros in the area, worked behind the counter at the clubhouse shop at Brackenridge, and in June 1932, just before going to Randolph Field, won the San Antonio city championship for a second time. His opponent in the final round, Lieutenant Kenneth Rogers, was a pilot instructor there who was to serve as a brigadier general during the Second World War. "City Golf Champ Will Enter Flying Service July 1," the *San Antonio Evening News* bragged in a headline. Schriever paid for the headline and the rest of his local media acclaim with some special hazing: the more senior cadets in an earlier class at Randolph ordered him to stand at attention in the mess hall and read his golf clippings to them while they ate.

He managed to solo successfully after his first half dozen hours of instruction in Primary, when most washouts occurred, despite a badly sprained ankle, which he taped securely in order to work the rudder pedals. Of the approximately 200 aspiring airmen who had entered Randolph on July 1, 1932, Bennie was among the ninety or so who went on to Advanced training at Kelly eight months later. That ever-present risk of an airman's profession, death in a fatal crash, claimed two of his classmates, but his steady temperament made him a good if not a spirited pilot, which may be why he was assigned to bombers rather than pursuit aircraft, as fighters were then designated. He graduated on June 29, 1933, was awarded his wings and second lieutenant's commission, and was sent for his year of active duty to the 9th Bombardment Squadron at March Field near Riverside, California.

5

ENTERING THE BROTHERHOOD

Elizabeth and Gerry went with him to Riverside. The grimly worsening Depression had severely reduced her business at the sandwich stand on the twelfth hole. People were not playing golf in nearly the numbers they had been and the number of visitors coming to San Antonio on vacation had also declined drastically. So she closed the stand before departing. Gerry had been forced to leave A&M in the middle of his sophomore year in January 1933 because of Elizabeth's straitened circumstances. Her bank had failed and taken all of her savings with it. Bennie was now their source of support with his second lieutenant's pay of $125 a month, an additional half again of $62.50 as flying pay, and an allowance of roughly $30 a month to rent a house off base because there were no quarters available at the field for the families of Reservists. His salary and flying pay were soon reduced, however, when the new president, Franklin D. Roosevelt, decreed a 15 percent pay cut for the entire military, which remained in effect into 1935.

In entering the officer ranks of the U.S. Army Air Corps, Bennie Schriever thought of himself as having joined an elite group of flying men. He could not know precisely how important to the destiny of the nation that elite was to be. At the end of 1938, when the menace of Hitler's Germany and Imperial Japan at last began to awaken Congress, there were only about 1,650 officers, including Reservists, in the entire Air Corps. From these 1,650 officers would come the men who were to create and lead the mighty fleet of the skies during the Second World War.

The commanding officer at March Field that summer of 1933 was the man who was to shape and command that armada, Henry "Hap" Arnold, then just a lieutenant colonel. He would subsequently cast a long shadow of influence over the nature of American air, missile, and space power during the Cold War and the arms race with the Soviet Union that followed. Arnold's principal deputy at March Field in 1933 was a trim, mustachioed man, Major Carl "Tooey" Spaatz, who wore his uniform cap crushed in on the sides in rakish fashion as if he were sitting in a cockpit with his earphones on. At bachelor social occasions, he played the guitar and sang risqué songs, and he was fond of late-night poker games at which he would while away the hours sipping Scotch whiskey with soda and chain-smoking cigarettes. Lieutenant Schriever was soon initiated into these nocturnal gatherings. Spaatz's carefree exterior concealed a relentless determination whenever the needs of his profession required it. He was an accomplished fighter pilot. During the First World War he had shot down three German aircraft in just a few weeks and returned with the nation's second-highest decoration for valor, the Distinguished Service Cross. During the Second World War, he would command the air forces of the European theater as a four-star general and oversee the strategic bombing campaign against Nazi Germany. When the independent U.S. Air Force was finally established in 1947, Spaatz would become its first chief of staff. The other officer at March Field on whom Arnold depended was a captain named Ira Eaker—short, balding, and round-faced, with penetrating eyes. In the war to come, Eaker would lead the famous Eighth Air Force out of England and then command the Mediterranean air forces under Spaatz in the task of pummeling the Third Reich into bits and pieces.

Of the three, Arnold was the man who was to matter the most for Second Lieutenant Schriever. Arnold went back to the origins of American aviation. A West Point graduate in the Class of 1907, he had aspired to the cavalry and instead had been sent to the infantry, which he detested. To escape, he had volunteered for the Signal Corps' nascent Aeronautical Division, from which the Air Corps was eventually to evolve, and became one of the first half dozen Army pilots when he was trained to fly in 1911 at the factory the Wright brothers had established at Dayton, Ohio, to profit from their invention. A solidly proportioned man of medium build, Arnold was a complicated figure, always impatient to accomplish any task at hand, yet long-enduring of the frustrations of military life and the struggle to build a modern air force. During the First World War he had been denied a combat assignment in Europe until it was too late to see any action; instead, he had been posted to Washington to monitor the effort to gear up American industry for the mass production of aircraft. The program had been a failure, from which Arnold had learned what not to do when it was his turn to take charge and organize industry for the production of hundreds of thousands of planes during the Second World War. In 1925, he had displayed the moral courage to ignore warnings from his superiors and place his career in peril by testifying in defense of Brigadier General William "Billy" Mitchell, the crusader for an independent air force, at Mitchell's court-martial. Afterward, Arnold had barely evaded court-martial himself for using military printing facilities to lobby congressmen and the press on Mitchell's behalf. His punishment was exile to Fort Riley, Kansas, the nation's largest cavalry post, to take charge of a small detachment of observation aircraft attached to the horse soldiers.

When Schriever met him in 1933, Arnold's career was back in motion. March Field was the Air Corps' West Coast tactical operations center. At forty-nine, Arnold had matured as an adept organizer and commander. In his search for ideas to create a modern air force he had formed a friendship with Robert Millikan, who headed the California Institute of Technology in Pasadena. Millikan had in turn introduced him to Theodore von Kármán, the Hungarian aeronautical engineering genius whom Millikan had recruited for Caltech in 1930. Von Kármán, who had been teaching and directing an aeronautical engineering laboratory at Aachen, was among the first of the distinguished European intellectuals of Jewish ancestry driven across the Atlantic by the rise of Hitler and the growing national madness consuming Germany. Reaching out to such a man was a natural consequence of Arnold's urge to employ science and technology to develop an effective air arm, an urge that was eventually to transform him into a technological visionary. He had every reason to be dissatisfied with the aircraft in his force. The planes with which the Air Corps was then equipped were essentially throwbacks to the First World War era. The B-3 and B-4 Keystone bombers that Bennie and his mates in the 9th Bombardment Squadron flew were big, ungainly biplanes with highly flammable cloth and wood-frame wings and fuselages. The cockpits were open. Some of the Keystones had two-way radios. Others had only receivers—the pilot could not reply. Top speed was a little more than 100 miles per hour and range was just 400. Safe flying was restricted to fair weather because the only instruments were an airspeed indicator, an altimeter, a horizontal needle-and-ball device that mimicked the attitude of the plane when turning or banking, and a compass. The fighters were better—Boeing P-12s with 500-horsepower Pratt & Whitney engines—but they too were old-fashioned biplanes with wood and fabric wings and had no radios at all. Lack of operating funds also affected training. Pilots were restricted to four hours of flying a month, which meant that the younger aviators like Schriever could not get enough time in the air to become proficient.

Golf was one of the ways in which the lieutenant drew himself to the attention of the older man who was to so affect his destiny. Again for lack of operating funds, Air Corps officers usually worked only half a day, at most until 3:30 P.M., after a leisurely lunch, leaving plenty of time to play. Schriever's prowess on the links at the nearby Victoria Country Club at Riverside, where he won two amateur tournaments and set a new club record of 63, received local newspaper coverage that quickly made him stand out among the new pilots. Elizabeth Schriever also helped because of the military social customs of the day. As Schriever was a bachelor, his mother substituted for a wife during social events at the base. Arnold's wife, Eleanor, or "Bee" as she was nicknamed, was roughly the same age as Elizabeth. She had spent three years in Germany as a young woman and enjoyed speaking the language. The two women became friends. Their friendship led to Bennie becoming well acquainted with his commanding officer.

6.

A FIASCO AND REFORM

The air mail fiasco was the beginning of the end to stagnation. In February 1934, President Roosevelt suddenly canceled the air mail contracts between the Post Office and the new-fledged commercial airlines because a Senate investigation had discovered evidence of fraud. Roosevelt had not acted, however, without first having postal officials ask Major General Benjamin D. Foulois, chief of the Air Corps, if his pilots could temporarily fly the mail until honest arrangements could be made with the airlines. Foulois regarded the president's inquiry as an order. He also saw it as an opportunity to gain more appropriations for his strapped Air Corps by generating a lot of favorable publicity from a successful operation. "We have had a great deal of experience in flying at night, and in flying in fogs and bad weather, in blind flying, and in flying under all other conditions," Foulois told the House Post Office Committee. Given the state of his aircraft and the amateurishness of his pilots, Foulois's recklessness in accepting the mission and his false testimony to Congress bordered on the criminal.

To meet the schedule set by the Post Office did require flying at night and in bad weather. Commercial airline pilots were flying at night by the mid-1930s. They had two-way radios to obtain information on weather conditions ahead and at airfields where they intended to land and some rudimentary instruments to fly by when the weather was marginal. Air Corps pilots were not only unaccustomed to flying at night, they couldn't talk to anybody from many of their aircraft, and they lacked both instrumentation and training for dicey weather. The weather that February and March of 1934 would have daunted the best of airline pilots, however, and certainly forced delays in mail delivery. It was some of the worst late-winter weather—blizzards, dense fog, frigid gales, heavy rains—since records had been kept and it struck much of the country, but especially the West, where Schriever and his comrades were operating.

Arnold was put in charge of the Western Region, with his headquarters at Salt Lake City. He broke his squadrons down into detachments so that they could be parceled out along the various routes. Every available aircraft, from the P-12 pursuits, to the observation planes, to the awkward Keystones, was thrust into the task. To keep from freezing in the open cockpits, the pilots wore leather face masks and flying suits, both lined with sheepskin. Bennie's detachment was assigned portions of two routes, from Salt Lake City to Boise, Idaho, and from Salt Lake to Cheyenne, Wyoming, via Rock Springs. Schriever remembered the eagerness with which he and his fellow pilots accepted the challenge, as young warriors so often do when they go into harm's way without knowing the odds. After the miserly four-hours-a-month diet, it was above all finally a chance to do some flying. Bennie's time in the air escalated rapidly and by March and April he was logging nearly sixty hours a month.

On February 19, 1934, just as Foulois had promised, the U.S. Army Air Corps loaded the mail and flew into the breach, night and weather be damned. Three pilots out of Salt Lake were killed in a single day, two of them Bennie's Flying School classmates. One was trying to make it to Boise, pressing on beneath steadily lowering weather, when he ran out of visibility and altitude at the same time and flew into the ground. The two others smacked into the side of a mountain they could not see, apparently while forging on through a snowstorm. On another occasion, Schriever and two other pilots drove out to the airfield at Cheyenne to take a couple of O-38 observation planes from Cheyenne back to Salt Lake at night. The two other pilots were West Pointers who outranked Bennie. They chose to fly together and to take off first in a newer model of the O-38, which had a canopy over the tandem cockpits to protect them from the weather. While Schriever waited behind them in the open-cockpit version, the two West Pointers sped down the runway. What they had neglected to do, because they were too unseasoned to understand the necessity, was to come out and familiarize themselves with the airfield in daylight. They used only part of the runway, pulling up before they had gained enough speed and lift to clear a high-tension wire concealed by the darkness just beyond the end of the field. Bennie watched them die instantly. Twelve pilots were killed in all and there were sixty-six crashes. Although most were obviously not fatal, the wrecks still made for unpleasant photographs in the newspapers. In late March, an embarrassed and angry Roosevelt arranged for the airlines to resume flying the mail as of the beginning of June.

Schriever and many of his fellow fliers came to believe that their comrades did not die in vain, that their deaths helped create an impetus to modernize the country's air force and thus avoid defeat in the new war to come. An investigative board convened under Newton Baker, President Woodrow Wilson's secretary of war during the First World War, recommended important organizational changes in the Air Corps structure and a program of instrument and night flying for pilots as well as enough hours in the air, three hundred per year, to raise them to proficiency. The board did not specifically recommend equipping the Air Corps and Naval Aviation with state-of-the-art aircraft, but the deaths and the shocking nature of the episode made this necessity strikingly apparent. Progress and reform, however, were neither steady nor uninterrupted. The Roosevelt administration and Congress remained stingy until war in Europe loomed in 1938 and hostilities actually began the following year. The Regular Army generals who opposed any independence for the Air Corps used the War Department General Staff, which they controlled, to keep the pace to a slow march. Nevertheless, officers like Hap Arnold kept prodding and cajoling from within and notable advances occurred through the ingenuity and entrepreneurship of the struggling but resourceful American aircraft industry. In 1935, Boeing produced the prototype of the four-engine B-17 Flying Fortress, the first of the long-range strategic bombers that, with the follow-on B-24 Liberator from the Consolidated Aircraft Corporation, were to bring the dark cloud formations of destruction to Germany's skies. With the exception of the B-29 Superfortress, another Boeing triumph that was developed during the war, most of the combat aircraft the U.S. Army Air Forces were to fly during the Second World War were either in production or soon to go into production by the time the Japanese attacked Pearl Harbor in December 1941. Bennie recalled flying the workhorse Curtiss P-40 fighter when he was a test pilot at Wright Field near Dayton, Ohio, in 1939. That same year, the Air Corps purchased the test models of the twin-engine Lockheed P-38, the first of the high-altitude American pursuits to approach the performance of the latest German and Japanese fighters. A rudimentary fighting air force was in place when it was needed. A dozen B-17s on their way to the Philippines were, in fact, preparing to land at Hickam Field in Hawaii when the Japanese arrived on that Sunday morning of December 7. To Schriever, the sequence was clear. Had the alarm not been raised by the air mail disaster, that rudimentary air force would not have existed when the moment of peril came. Another lesson was equally clear to him—technological backwardness meant failure and defeat.

The air mail fiasco also enabled Bennie to extend his flying duty for eight months, in niggardly increments of six months and then an additional two, until he finally was taken off active service in March 1935 and had to return to civilian life in San Antonio. Elizabeth went back with him to resurrect her sandwich stand. The Depression seemed to be easing a bit and she thought she could make a go of it once more. Gerry did stints as a social worker in Los Angeles and then in San Antonio, until he found a night job with an oil field mapping service. It enabled him to take enough classes during the day at what was then called the University of San Antonio to complete the two years of college that was then one of the minimal requirements for Flying School. He entered, as Bennie had, at Randolph Field in February 1938, and won his wings as a pursuit pilot the following February. One of Franklin Roosevelt's programs to alleviate the Depression, the Civilian Conservation Corps, shortly enabled Bennie to return to active duty. Each of the CCC camps had an Army officer in charge. In June 1935, he volunteered to take over a CCC camp on the Gila River along the Arizona–New Mexico border. The camp was four to five miles down a gravel road off a tarmac strip that led to the New Mexico railroad crossing town of Lordsburg.

The CCC was Schriever's first lesson in unorthodox management. While now a Reserve first lieutenant in the Air Corps and theoretically the camp commander, he could not legally apply military discipline to the nearly 200 boys in the place because all of them were civilians. Duty with the CCC ruined a number of freshly begun military careers because the junior officers put in charge did apply ill-suited methods of military discipline and provoked a backlash. The youths, between the ages of sixteen and nineteen, had volunteered to build small water retention dams and do other conservation work in the surrounding high desert country for a nominal salary. Most were whites from impoverished families in Oklahoma, Texas, and New Mexico, with a small number of Hispanics and a half dozen or so blacks. There was no segregation. The young men lived together in barracks. Schriever, at twenty-five not much older than his charges, decided that the only way he could acquire control of the camp was to identify those boys who seemed to be natural leaders and get them to run it for him. As carefully as he could, he chose the six to eight youths who stood out from the others and appointed them group leaders, in effect his top sergeants. They held regular meetings. Bennie urged them to level with him about any problems in the camp. They also held special meetings, in what Schriever called his "kangaroo court approach," whenever one of the inevitable troublemakers among the camp population made a serious nuisance of himself. If the boys decided that the offender, who was not invited to hear his fate, was incorrigible, Schriever would give them the nod to run him out of the camp. There was no violence, simply enough harassment to persuade the nuisance to leave.

The lesson he learned running the CCC camp stayed with Bennie. He was to apply the method again and again throughout his career, ultimately in accomplishing the momentous projects he was given at its height: study a task, identify the right man to solve the problem—no yes-men, you have to know what is really going on and yes-men won't tell you the truth—then win the man's loyalty and back him up while he does the job. Capable people, he observed watching his youth leaders, also have minds of their own and you have to refrain from interfering and let them accomplish a task in their way. He made certain as well that his was a happy camp. He had Army trucks haul the boys into Lordsburg for baseball and basketball games against other camps or just for weekend liberty, showed films for entertainment, bought the best food he could locally, let the boys supplement it with the plentiful pheasants, quail, and doves they shot along the Gila River, and turned the kitchen over to a young man who happened to be a talented cook. When Bennie left in the summer of 1936 at the end of his year, the boys presented him with a .22 caliber Smith & Wesson target pistol and a wristwatch they took up a collection to buy.

7.

STAYING THE COURSE

This time he was off to Panama. As it gradually geared up, the Air Corps had begun accepting applications from Reservists to return to active duty flying status. Schriever applied and was sent to Albrook Field on the Pacific side of the Canal Zone. Before going he had to agree to revert from first lieutenant back to second to save the Air Corps money on his salary. Golf came to his assistance again. The game is, as Schriever once shrewdly observed, "the finest avenue for meeting the right people. . . . It is a friend-making game." Older men who are not particularly adept at golf often like to play with a younger and highly skilled golfer because they can learn from him and a handicap system allots them a set number of strokes in their favor in advance. They can enjoy themselves by participating in some fine golf without being ashamed of their scores at the end of the game.

Brigadier General George H. Brett, the Air Corps commander for the Zone, whose headquarters was at Albrook, was that kind of a golfer. Brett was another of the band of original Army aviators. A 1909 graduate of the Virginia Military Institute at a time when only West Point graduates could obtain direct commissions in the small Regular Army, Brett had accepted what he could get, a second lieutenant's commission in the Philippine Constabulary, a colonial model force manned by Filipino enlisted men and officered by Americans. It had been formed to enforce tranquillity in America's new imperial possession in Asia. Brett had seen quite a bit of action against the independence-minded Moros, the Muslim inhabitants of Mindanao, before he was able to win a commission in the cavalry of the Regular Army and then, in an adventurous move, become a pilot in the Aviation Section of the Signal Corps, the precursor of the Army Air Corps, just as the First World War was erupting in 1914. Over the decades since, he had gradually wound his way up through the officer ranks to the star he now wore as commander in the Canal Zone. He was currently interested in improving his golf game and word of Schriever's aptitude at his avocation had preceded him to Panama. Brett asked Bennie if he would like to serve as one of his two aides. The career opportunity was marvelous because of all a young officer can learn working directly for a general (the job also paid an additional $10 a month).

It led to marriage as well when Brett sent Bennie to the Atlantic side of the Canal one day early in 1937 to meet his twenty-year-old daughter, Dora, who was arriving on an Army transport ship to rejoin the family after staying with friends in Washington. Schriever walked up the gangplank still a bit drowsy because he had risen in the wee hours to cross the Canal Zone and be on time for the ship's 5:00 A.M. docking. His drowsiness dissipated at the sight of the pretty young woman with a figure to remember and curly blond hair. They got acquainted over a breakfast of ham and eggs in the ship's dining room and were soon in love.

In 1935 and again in 1937 Schriever had applied for one of the few Regular Army commissions given out each year and had been turned down both times. A Reserve second lieutenant was in too precarious a position to take on the responsibility of a wife and the family that presumably would follow. He could have been deactivated at any time. And so he requested deactivation himself in order to marry Dora. That August of 1937, he sailed from Panama to take a job as a co-pilot with Northwest Airlines, flying the Seattle to Billings, Montana, run. The aircraft was the Lockheed Electra 10, advanced for its day in that it had an all-metal fuselage and twin radial engines, and was aptly named because it could carry ten passengers. Bennie's additional duties as co-pilot were to load and unload the sacks of mail and hand out sandwiches in box lunches to the passengers. He and Dora were married on January 3, 1938, at Hap Arnold's home in Washington.

By now Arnold was a brigadier general and assistant chief of the Air Corps, soon to become its head when the current chief, Major General Oscar Westover, was killed in the crash of a plane he was piloting that September. Hap and Bee Arnold were close friends of the Bretts. Dora's parents did not come up for the ceremony because there was as yet no airline service from Panama and the journey by ship was time-consuming and burdensome. Arnold gave away the bride.

Schriever was currently making an excellent salary of about $250 a month as a co-pilot with Northwest. The prospect was that he would double that to the fabulous Depression-era salary of $500 a month in the not distant future when he became a reserve lead pilot, or "reserve captain" as the position was designated in the airlines. Dora therefore had every reason to feel content as they set up housekeeping in Seattle.

Then Hap Arnold flew out to Seattle in March to confer with the president of Boeing. He arranged a foursome at golf and invited Bennie as one of the players. Arnold rarely played golf and his purpose in setting up the game became clear as soon as it was over. With war appearing more and more inevitable in Europe, the Air Corps was finally being allowed to award Regular commissions to sizable numbers of Reservists. A competitive examination was scheduled for that August. "Bennie," Arnold said as they were changing in the locker room afterward, "I hope that you'll take the exam for a Regular commission." He explained that he wanted to create an all-weather air arm and therefore needed to get as many airline pilots who were Reservists as possible back into the Air Corps on a permanent basis, because they had the knowledge and experience for instrument flying. Decades later, Schriever remained astonished at Arnold's ability to look into the future. "Arnold was sitting there in 1938, long before we were in the war, saying he wanted an all-weather air force. That was truly visionary. By the end of the war, we had the capability. When the Soviets blockaded Berlin in 1948 and we had to stage the airlift, we had mechanical failures and we had crashes but we rarely had to cancel a flight because of the weather."

Dora was opposed to his taking the examination. If he was accepted as a Regular, he could not reenter at his Reserve rank of first lieutenant. He would have to start all over as a second lieutenant at the bottom of the seniority list. With flying pay and a housing allowance, the cut in income would not be that serious compared to his current salary of $250 a month at Northwest, but it would be half what he would soon be earning there. As a daughter of the regiment, Dora was also acutely aware of the constant moves, the separations, and the dangers of military life. With Northwest there was stability: even when Schriever overnighted in Billings, he was back home the next day in Seattle. She did not make a major issue of her opposition, however, and there was no stopping him in any case. Bennie Schriever was not going to give up the Air Corps to fly to Billings via Spokane.

On October 1, 1938, at Hamilton Field near San Rafael, just north of San Francisco, he held up his right hand again and took the unusual oath that American officers take when they accept their commissions— not an oath of allegiance to the president as commander-in-chief, not an oath of loyalty to the nation, but rather a vow to uphold an ideal of liberty and republican government embodied in law. Schriever swore that, as a second lieutenant in the Air Corps, Regular Army, "I will support and defend the Constitution of the United States against all enemies, foreign and domestic. . . . I will bear true faith and allegiance to the same." Of the 188 men in his group who were accepted, about two thirds were airline pilots. Hap Arnold had apparently passed the word to the examining board as to whom he wanted.

8.

A FORK IN THE ROAD

He was initially assigned to a bomber squadron at Hamilton Field. The Schrievers' first child, Brett Arnold—Brett for his grandfather, Arnold for Hap—was born on March 23, 1939. In the meantime, George Brett returned to the States to take over the Matériel Division, predecessor of the Air Matériel Command, the Air Corps' research and development center, with its testing facilities and laboratories at Wright Field near Dayton, Ohio. Bennie had often told his father-in-law of his ambition to attend the Engineering School there, the Air Corps' senior technical school, which gave those officers selected a year's course in general aeronautical engineering. The school had been temporarily closed, but was due to reopen soon. Brett needed test pilots who could handle the variety of aircraft being evaluated at Wright Field as American industry revved up production. His wife, Mary, also could not enjoy a grandson who was more than half a continent away. Brett contacted Arnold, since promoted to major general and chief of the Air Corps, and asked to have Bennie assigned to him as a test pilot. Arnold assented. To make certain that transfer orders would be issued expeditiously, Brett followed up on August 28, 1939, with a "Dear Duncan" letter to Lieutenant Colonel Asa N. Duncan, one of Arnold's assistants at his office in Washington. He opened by telling Duncan he had just received a note from Arnold saying that Arnold would approve Lieutenant Schriever's transfer from Hamilton to Wright Field:

> As you know, the boy is my son-in-law and Mrs. Brett is very anxious to have them come to Dayton at this time. In addition thereto, Lieutenant Schriever has all the qualifications of one of the officers I am very anxious to get into the Flight Test Section. He is a technical engineer, has had a year with the airlines on one of the toughest runs in the United States, has had about two and a half years' active

duty as a Reserve officer, and has now been on duty at Hamilton Field for approximately one year.

If possible I would like very much to have him sail from San Francisco sometime the first part of October as they have a small baby and we would like to have the baby here before the cold weather sets in.

(Air Corps families moved then by ship and rail, not in aircraft.)

Except for the fact Lieutenant Schriever fits in very well with the qualifications for the Lieutenants I have asked for duty with the Flight Test Section, all the other reasons are on account of a doting grandmother.

The copy of the letter that went into Schriever's personnel file was marked "OK" and initialed by Arnold. The appointment was justifiable enough, but there was one fib, perhaps unintentional. His bachelor's degree in construction engineering from Texas A&M hardly qualified him as "a technical engineer" in any way that related to aircraft. The overt nepotism and easy familiarity of the letter were reflections of the clublike atmosphere in the between-the-wars Army Air Corps, an atmosphere that was soon to dissolve under the hurly-burly of the conflict to come. Schriever was fortunate to have arrived before it did.

He entered the Air Corps Engineering School at Wright Field in July 1940, after nearly nine months there as a test pilot in Brett's Flight Test Section. Schriever had developed an interest in aeronautical engineering to an extent that he was not afraid of being sidelined into technical jobs and deprived of command positions if he pursued it. Air Corps officers of the pre–Second World War period were probably the best-educated group within the entire Army officer corps. Until mid-1941, the two years of college or passage of an equivalent examination remained a minimum requirement for the flying cadet program, and many officers had a full bachelor's degree or were working toward one. A few had gone on to doctorates, the best known of them dauntless James "Jimmy" Doolittle, the accomplished racing pilot who had earned a Ph.D. at the Massachusetts Institute of Technology. He was just being recalled to active duty from an executive position at Shell Oil. A sizable number of others had either obtained master's degrees or attended the Engineering School. One reason higher education did not necessarily shunt an officer off into a technical slot was that almost all were then pilots, "rated officers" as the term went, and so considered potentially qualified to command in the air.

The current commandant of the Engineering School, George Kenney, was an example. Kenney was another figure who later exerted a major influence on Schriever as commanding general of Douglas MacArthur's air forces in the Southwest Pacific. Originally educated as a civil engineeer at MIT, Kenney had become an aviator during the First World War, returned from France after seventy-five missions with a Distinguished Service Cross and a Silver Star for Gallantry, and devoted much of his time in the period between the wars to the study of aeronautical engineeering and its application to combat aviation. He was an earlier graduate of the school himself. That May of 1940, after President Roosevelt had called for a production goal of fifty thousand aircraft a year in a speech to Congress, Arnold had ordered Kenney and a team of officers under him to lay out a plan for the creation of the U.S. Army Air Forces. In those pre-computer years, they had it done with a big roll of butcher-shop paper. As they unrolled the paper they wrote out a two-year program of production schedules, and training schedules, and organization schedules, and airfield construction schedules all meshing with one another—so many trainer aircraft by x date, to train so many pilots by y date, to form so many fighter and bomber groups by z date.

Schriever impressed Kenney, who noted on his efficiency report a year later in July 1941 that he was graduating from the Engineering School with an academic rating of "Superior." He had done so well, in fact, that he was one of those selected to go on to Stanford University in September 1941 for a master's degree in more advanced aeronautical engineering studies. Bennie moved his young family out to Menlo Park, California, right near the university. That June, Dora had given birth to their second child, a daughter, Dodie (after the nickname of Dora's maternal grandmother) Elizabeth (for Bennie's mother).

When the Japanese attacked Pearl Harbor in December, he assumed he would receive immediate orders to drop his courses and go. He heard nothing and after a while grew worried that he had been forgotten in the rush to fight. He called Arnold's office in Washington and spoke to one of the general's assistants. He was told to be patient and that he would be receiving orders. Finally, in March, the orders came. He was to report for further assignment to the headquarters of the U.S. Army Air Services, Southwest Pacific Area, then in Australia, the aviation maintenance and engineering command for the region. To his surprise, the orders stated that he was not to leave until he had completed his course of study and obtained his master's degree, which would keep him at Stanford until June 14, 1942. Schriever thought the orders rather strange. He was an experienced pilot and men like him were needed in cockpits right now. Someone up above had apparently decided, however, that there would be war enough for everybody and that his special knowledge would be put to good use.

9.

"LET'S DIVE-BOMB THE BASTARDS"

He left for Australia from Hamilton Field in the predawn of June 20, 1942, flying west in the diminishing darkness out over the Golden Gate Bridge bound for the first stop in Hawaii. He had not been able to tell Dora, who was staying behind with the two children in the rented house at Menlo Park, when he would return because he had no way of knowing. Bennie did not bid farewell to the great span across the entrance to San Francisco Bay. He was wrapped in a sleeping bag in the back of one of the new B-24 Liberators, the second of the strategic bombers that was entering the inventory of the U.S. Army Air Forces as an alternative to the B-17. Bennie was not saying a sentimental adieu to the Golden Gate because he had stayed up most of the night drinking and playing poker. He had thought he was safe doing so because the weather forecast the day before had said they would not be taking off that morning. There were reports of strong headwinds that would slow them down and possibly run them perilously low on fuel over the 2,400-mile stretch of the Pacific to

Hickam Field on Oahu. The reports turned out to be wrong. He had gone to bed about 4:00 A.M. and slept only an hour or so before someone shook him awake and told him to get out to the flight line for departure. The sleeping bag he had thoughtfully brought for the journey and the solitude in the tail section of the bomber provided a refuge in which he managed to get several more hours of sleep. When he woke he searched his pockets and wallet and discovered that Captain Schriever (he had been promoted that April) had lost his identification card, but was a couple of hundred dollars richer from the poker game, something he had forgotten because of the drinks.

At Hickam he was informed that he was going to have to delay his onward movement until the personnel section could complete the formalities of issuing him a new ID card. He would have had to stay there for a while in any case. B-17s were desperately needed in the Southwest Pacific and he had been tabbed to fly one to Australia. The aircraft had, however, been damaged during the battle of Midway in June, the first Japanese naval defeat of the Pacific war, and was awaiting repair at Hickam. He was patient for the better part of a week, while the mechanics kept saying that parts they needed were on the way from the mainland. Then he told the officer in charge that since no one seemed to know when the B-17 would be ready, he really ought to move on. The man agreed and Bennie climbed into another B-24 for the most perilous segment of the journey, a nearly twelve-hour flight to the first refueling stop at Canton Island, a coral atoll about four miles wide and eight miles long that rises a few feet above the waters of the Pacific 1,650 miles southwest of Hawaii. The Pacific Ocean covers a third of the globe and in a few years Canton Island would once again return to obscurity in the Pacific's 70 million square miles, but in 1942 it was famous, or perhaps one should say infamous, to American airmen. In order not to facilitate Japanese attack, the island had no radio beacon or other navigational aids to guide aircraft to it. The navigators had to resort to celestial navigation and dead reckoning with the compass. If the navigator erred and the plane ran out of gas before the pilots could find the island by "boxing the compass" (flying west for forty-five minutes, then north, east, and south), the water was waiting. (Bennie's crew had no difficulty, but the First World War ace Eddie Rickenbacker was not so fortunate while flying to Australia on a high-level mission in a B-17 that October. The crew missed the island and had to ditch in the ocean. Rickenbacker and six of the other seven men aboard the plane survived when they were rescued in a near miracle after twenty-seven days in a pair of rubber rafts.) The next stops were easier—Viti Levu in the Fiji Islands and New Caledonia—before they finally touched down at Newcastle above Sydney on Australia's east coast.

Schriever arrived in Australia hatless. He had left his officer's cap, through a bit of uncharacteristic absentmindedness this time, not drink, on the hat rack in the club at Viti Levu. He hustled a replacement before reporting for duty in Melbourne, where there was a familiar face, his father-in-law, George Brett, now a lieutenant general commanding Allied Air Forces, Southwest Pacific Area—all U.S. Army and Royal Australian Air Force and Royal New Zealand Air Force aviation in the theater. The reunion was not a happy one. Brett was about to be sacked by Douglas MacArthur, who had reached Australia in March after his escape from the Philippines and been appointed supreme commander of Allied Forces in the Southwest Pacific. Brett had drawn a hard-luck assignment. Hap Arnold had put him in charge of what meager Army Air Forces elements existed in the Far East at the outset of the war when the Japanese advance seemed inexorable and all resistance was collapsing before it. MacArthur was furious that Franklin Roosevelt and George Marshall, the Army chief of staff, had declined to reinforce him in the Philippines, a physical impossibility in any case, given Japanese naval strength at the time. His vanity had been pricked by his defeat there and, although Roosevelt had ordered him to leave, he was full of guilt at having abandoned his troops to their fate on Bataan and Corregidor. On the lookout for scapegoats, MacArthur had lit on Brett as near to hand. He had demanded that Arnold replace him. George Kenney was on the way. Bennie got the impression that his father-in-law, in order to avoid any appearance of personal favoritism, left to subordinates the decision as to where Schriever should be assigned in Australia.

Captain Schriever was sent to the 19th Bombardment Group, a B-17 unit that was in the process of shifting to Mareeba, up toward the northeastern end of Australia across from New Guinea. Bennie did not know it yet because the War Department orders were still in the communications channels to Australia, but while en route he had been promoted to major in another of the mass promotions Hap Arnold was

employing to turn the prewar officer corps into a cadre that would organize and lead the vast U.S. Army Air Forces he was raising. Bennie
and the others of his era were like the foundation and steel beams of a
skyscraper. The hundreds of thousands who were following were to be
the walls and the roof and the interior. The Army Air Forces would
number 2.4 million officers and enlisted men at their height in 1945.

The 19th was the original bomber group in Australia, put together
from the survivors of the Philippines and the battle for Java in the
Netherlands East Indies, the Dutch colony that was to become Indonesia. The Java remnants had fled by plane and ship to refuge in the
southern continent just a week before 20,000 Dutch troops surrendered there in March. A third of the group's officers and most of its enlisted men had been unable to escape and were abandoned to Japanese
captivity. It had since been built back up with replacements to a working strength. Bennie was designated the new engineering officer, in
charge of maintenance. Getting every bomber possible into the air was
vital, as the Americans and their Australian ally were about to go over
to the offensive. By late July 1942, the Japanese were overextended
and vulnerable to a counterstroke. Few yet understood this, despite the
turning-point naval battle of Midway in June, because of the formidable success of the initial Japanese onslaught. Shaken by the Midway
setback, the Japanese had become disjointed in their movements, advancing in too many places at once without concentrating enough
force to be certain of victory at any of them.

One of the endeavors they were pressing forward was a campaign
to seize all of New Guinea as a base from which to launch an invasion
of Australia. The Australian government was in a panic and wanted to
abandon New Guinea and form a defensive line based on Brisbane on
the central east coast. There was also an atmosphere of discourage-
ment within much of the American military in Australia. MacArthur's
staff, in particular, was pessimistic. In a shrewd and brave act of
generalship, MacArthur rejected the fears of the Australians and the
pessimism of his staff. New Guinea was the place to stiff-arm the
Japanese, he decided. He would stymie them there and then begin
pushing them back on the long road of his return to the Philippines. He
reasoned that if they ever got loose in Australia's open spaces it would
be impossible to halt them, but that the "green hell" of New Guinea's
forbidding mountains and rain forests would be just as punishing an

obstacle to the Japanese as it would be to his forces in repulsing them. As a demonstration of his resolve, he moved his headquarters from Melbourne at the southern end of Australia up to Brisbane in the latter half of July.

George Brett was a decent man, but a better administrator than a fighter. George Kenney, who replaced him at the end of July and who was to become another of Bennie Schriever's mentors, was a superb leader of airmen in war. He was an imaginative and innovative air warrior who swiftly perceived his enemy's weak points and found ways to generate the most out of what he had at hand. His aggressiveness and talent quickly won over MacArthur and rightly so, because Kenney contributed more than any other senior officer to the subsequent success of MacArthur's campaign in New Guinea. He solved MacArthur's dilemma of how to get the combat elements of an Australian infantry division and two American divisions that were arriving in Australia across the 600 miles of the Coral Sea to Port Moresby on the southern coast of New Guinea without subjecting them to the risk of having the Japanese navy sink their transports. The engineers built five new airstrips at Moresby and Kenney flew the troops over in C-47s in the first major airlift of the war. He dismantled their jeeps and had the chassis frames of their trucks cut in half with acetylene torches, stuffed the halves into the planes, and then had them welded together again in New Guinea. Port Moresby was transformed from a beleaguered outpost into MacArthur's principal offensive base. Kenney took relatively ineffective B-25 medium bombers and turned them into terrifying machines to strafe Japanese shipping by letting a tinkering genius named Paul "Pappy" Gunn and a technical representative from North American Aviation named Jack Fox install ten simultaneously firing .50 caliber machine guns in the nose, sides, and top turret of the fuselage. He had parachutes attached to twenty-three-pound fragmentation bombs so that an American aircraft could skim low enough over a Japanese airfield to drop the bombs with accuracy on the enemy planes in their protective revetments. Because the parachutes retarded the descent of the bombs, the American attacker could pull up and away before the bombs went off and the explosions destroyed it too.

Although still outnumbered and outclassed by Japanese air strength in the summer and fall of 1942, Kenney decided that he could wrest air superiority from the Japanese over New Guinea by destroying their aircraft on the ground through persistent raids on their bases. He especially wanted to neutralize Rabaul, an air and naval bastion the Japanese had created in a capacious harbor at the northern end of New Britain Island on the other side of New Guinea. In addition to its critical airfields, the Japanese were using Rabaul as a staging point for convoys to supply and reinforce their troops in New Guinea and other Japanese troops who were battling to drive the 1st Marine Division off Guadalcanal, an island near the far end of the adjacent Solomon Islands chain. On August 7, 1942, in the first major offensive action by the United States in the Pacific war, the Marines had sprung from the sea in surprise amphibious landings at Guadalcanal and neighboring Tulagi Island.

Schriever was not content just fixing B-17s for other men in the 19th Bombardment Group to fly. He and Major John Dougherty, a wild streak of an Irishman who was the group operations officer, put together a headquarters strike crew. Daylight raids on Rabaul were halted after the B-17s proved too vulnerable to the Mitsubishi Zeros stationed there. (The Zero was the most advanced fighter in the Pacific in 1942. Only the twin-engine Lockheed P-38, of which Kenney had a mere handful then, came close to matching it.) The 19th switched to night attacks with flares for illumination. The Zero was not originally meant to be a night fighter and for some reason the Japanese never attempted to retrain the pilots and send them aloft after dark. Schriever rigged up a flare-dropping device for the B-17 he and Dougherty flew. They would first drop flares for the other bombers and then they themselves would bomb.

On the night of September 23, 1942, they were after ships assembling in the harbor. Jack Dougherty, who was to end his career as a brigadier general working for Schriever, had had a lot of experience at combat flying and thus was, by mutual agreement, the pilot and aircraft commander. Bennie flew as his co-pilot, even though he was senior by date of promotion. A survivor of the Java disaster, Dougherty was doubly fortunate to have escaped in that he had been shot down and by good luck rescued from a small island off the Java coast. The narrowness of his encounter with eternity had not intimidated him. At Mareeba, in addition to plenty of flares, they loaded four 500-pounders into the bomb racks "to be sure that we had our amount of fun," as Schriever put it in his after-action report. They stopped at Port Moresby to top off their fuel tanks, then headed with the rest of the raiding formation north across the Solomon Sea for Rabaul. They made several passes at 4,000 feet over the wide harbor, formed by the remnant crater of an ancient volcano after it had erupted and exploded, dropping a sequence of five flares to enable the other B-17s to pick out one of the estimated thirty Japanese ships anchored there that night. After they realized the moon was so full and bright that night that flares were unnecessary, they decided to try their own hand at bombing and climbed to 10,000 feet. The new and still top secret Norden bombsight required long minutes of level flight to focus on a target, suicide against antiaircraft fire at 4,000 feet. Unfortunately, a cloud bank right at that lower altitude where they had been dropping flares now obscured the ships and made it too difficult for the bombardier to aim.

In a moment of insane inspiration, Dougherty suddenly said, "Let's dive-bomb the bastards." Although Schriever later admitted he was not the type to have thought of anything so rash and hair-raising, he did not object. "I'll watch the air speed and the altitude," he replied, so that they would not dive too rapidly and tear off a wing. They could not actually dive-bomb a ship with a B-17, but they did the next best thing to it. To keep the Japanese from hearing the noise of the engines as they descended and gain an element of surprise, they cut back the throttles. Then Dougherty pushed the wheel forward and down the big four-engine bomber went, leveling off at 1,500 feet as Dougherty raced straight for four large ships he could see lined up in the middle of the harbor. "To say that AA [antiaircraft fire] was ample would hardly cover the case," Schriever later wrote in his report. "Every ship in the harbor and most ground installations were firing at us. Tracers were converging [from] so many directions that it is a wonder they didn't collide with each other." The Norden bombsight was useless at this speed and altitude. Schriever glanced at the airspeed indicator and it was registering 260 miles per hour. In fact, no one was ever known to have attempted bombing with a B-17 in this harum-scarum manner. But the bombardier, another Irishman, Lieutenant Edward Magee, who had also escaped undaunted from the debacle on Java, had sufficient expertise to be up to the challenge. He eyeballed the bomb release range and angle and, when his instinct said "Now," let a 500-pounder fly. The first bomb turned out to be a dud. With the second, Magee scored a direct hit on a freighter estimated in the 8,000-ton class. The ship was probably destroyed instantly, as a secondary explosion erupted from within the hull right after the bomb struck. Magee then tried for a troop transport in the 12,000-ton class, but had a near miss.

As soon as the third bomb was away, Dougherty threw the B-17 into a series of violent, evasive maneuvers, turning, sliding from one side to another, dancing around the sky while climbing to 4,000 feet to clear the ridge on the other side of the harbor. Schriever was convinced afterward that Dougherty's skill at aerial acrobatics was what saved them from being shot down. As they topped the ridge and were headed back out over the sea they spotted a Japanese destroyer anchored in a bay along the island's shore. They had one 500-pounder left and Magee, crouched in his little compartment under the flight deck in the nose of the B-17 and caught up in the same frenzy of combat that possessed Dougherty, did not want to waste it. "Let's get the son of a bitch," he urged over the intercom. Dougherty turned, dropped to 1,000 feet, and bore down on the Japanese warship. Unfortunately, the bomb hung up in the rack—its release was delayed—and it sailed over the destroyer and exploded harmlessly on the shore.

Back at Mareeba, Schriever and Dougherty were surprised to find only six hits on the B-17 and all by small-arms fire. They also learned they had been doubly lucky. Bennie had not been at Mareeba long enough to know the history of his aircraft. They discovered in the maintenance records that the plane they had exposed to such inordinate stress was what Dougherty called in his after-action report "an old clunk." The main wing spar had nearly been shot away on a mission sometime before. It had been repaired in Australia, but how well was uncertain. It had been sent back to the 19th only because there was such a shortage of B-17s. To prevent the plane from coming apart in the air there was a warning in the records that it was "red-lined"—restricted—to a top speed of 200 miles per hour, clearly a perilous craft in which to undertake an aerial tango. As the pilot and aircraft commander, Dougherty was awarded a Silver Star for Gallantry. Schriever was also recommended for a Silver Star but, as the co-pilot, received an Air Medal instead. "It was a *wild night*. Fun though," Dougherty concluded in his report.

They were back over Rabaul on October 8 in the biggest raid of the war so far. Through his skill as an engineering officer and by motivating and driving his maintenance crews, Bennie managed to put fifty-one B-17s from the 19th Group into the air above the Japanese bastion that night, a record number. (Previously, one third of this number was considered a big raid.) He and Jack Dougherty and the rest of the headquarters strike crew were flying the flare plane again. Suddenly there was a big flash and one of the engines caught fire, its propeller running away out of control. They assumed they had taken a hit from the antiaircraft guns, although they later discovered that the feathering device for the propeller had ruptured and sprayed oil back on the hot engine. Schriever and Dougherty were due to get a few days of combat leave, called R&R for "rest and recreation," down in Sydney, and Schriever's first thought was, "Jesus Christ, we're not going to get to Sydney." Dougherty managed to shut off the engine, the fire went out, and the wind feathered the propeller. They should have headed back to Mareeba immediately, but they hadn't dropped their bombs yet and hated to waste them by jettisoning them into the sea. So they stayed over Rabaul for another forty-five minutes on three engines, first dropping the rest of their flares in one bunch to light up the whole place in what Schriever remembered as "a hell of a 4th of July," then plastering the town where the Japanese garrison was located, starting a number of large fires.

Had they lost another engine to antiaircraft fire or mechanical failure, they probably would not have seen Sydney again. Bennie and the other pilots carried pistols (Schriever wore strapped into a holster the .22 caliber Smith & Wesson target pistol his CCC youngsters had given him in farewell), not for self-defense but to shoot themselves if they had to parachute out over Japanese territory and face capture and the horrors it entailed. As Schriever later noted, "The Japanese were different." During the previous daylight raids on Rabaul, when the Zeros had shot down B-17s, the men in the other bombers had seen parachutes billow as the crews bailed out, but nothing was ever heard of them again. They did not show up on International Red Cross lists nor did the Japanese announce their capture. The Australian troops who repulsed a Japanese landing at Milne Bay on the eastern end of New Guinea in the latter half of August in MacArthur's first counterstroke had afterward found the dreadfully mutilated and tortured bodies of comrades captured during the fighting. Japanese soldiers almost invariably committed suicide or died in banzai charges rather than be captured. An unofficial policy evolved; as the Japanese took no prisoners, the Americans and the Australians took none either. When a Japanese ship was sunk, American and Australian pilots mercilessly strafed the survivors in the water.

Bennie and Dougherty were both awarded Purple Hearts for their valor over Rabaul on the night of October 8, a medal later given only for wounds, but which in 1942 could also be awarded for acts of courage under fire. After they returned to Mareeba that night, Schriever had only a wink of sleep. He was up at first light, inspecting damaged planes and driving his mechanics through the day so that a record-tying fifty-one B-17s from the 19th Group hammered Rabaul for a second night on October 9.

Kenney called Schriever down to his new Fifth Air Force headquarters in Brisbane late that month. (In September, to better utilize his growing American air strength, Kenney had organized the U.S. units into a separate air force, which he commanded. He retained control over the Royal Australian Air Force and Royal New Zealand Air Force elements, however, by keeping his second hat as commanding general, Allied Air Forces.) The 19th was being sent home and replaced, Kenney informed him, because too many of its men had seen their share of comrades falling to an airman's end and the bomber group had become war-weary. Bennie was not going with them, Kenney explained, because he needed all the engineering talent he could get and Schriever had also not flown enough combat missions to qualify, up to that point only ten. Instead, Kenney said, he was transferring Schriever to the Fifth Air Force Service Command as chief of the Maintenance and Engineering Division.

10.

THE TEST OF WAR

War, with its victory-or-defeat, life-or-death dynamic in which there is no excuse for failure or mediocrity, rapidly sets the outstanding officer apart from the ordinary one. This was what was happening to Bennie Schriever. He was starting to move to a level of recognition and responsibility that would distinguish him from his former peers for the rest of his career. On the one hand, his interest in aeronautical engineering was now, in fact, taking him out of a combat cockpit and the ascendancy through regular line positions that most professional aviators craved. He would not become a bomber group commander. On the other hand, in tribute to his performance with the 19th, the commanding general, a man with an eye for talent, was reaching down to pick up a thirty-two-year-old major of barely four months and promote him into one of the most important positions in the organization, in effect chief of maintenance and engineering for the entire Fifth Air Force. Schriever did not mind being taken off the combat cockpit track. He had as much courage as the next man and knew it, feeling no need to prove it to himself or anyone else. He was being given work for which he had a talent and interest and that carried with it great responsibility and meaning. What could be more crucial for an air force than to keep its aircraft battle-worthy and ready to fly? The job also held the promise of promotion. If he did not make a hash of things he would soon be exchanging the gold oak leaves of a major for the silver ones of a lieutenant colonel. He sallied into the work with his usual self-starter attitude. His initiative almost immediately got him into trouble with a terror of an aviator whom no one crossed with impunity—Brigadier General Ennis Whitehead.

Ennis Whitehead was Kenney's right-hand man and deputy for combat operations, which Whitehead ran out of a separate headquarters at Port Moresby. Prior to the appearance of the comic strip *Dennis the Menace,* someone had dubbed Whitehead "Ennis the Menace," and the moniker had taken hold. Whitehead relished it, although no one, of course, dared to repeat it in his presence. A pugnacious man with a ruthlessly forceful nature, which was why Kenney had chosen him as his combat operations deputy, Whitehead even looked the part. He had played professional baseball for a while before joining the Army Air Service, the First World War predecessor of the Air Corps, and had a badly smashed nose from an encounter with a ball. In those days before sophisticated reconstructive nasal surgery, he had to live with the result and tended to snort when he got agitated.

New on the job as chief of maintenance, Schriever inspected a B-17 at Port Moresby that was shot up badly enough to warrant major repairs in Australia. Three of the bomber's four engines were still in working order, however, which made it flyable under the safety rules. The matter seemed simple to Schriever. He issued instructions to fly the bomber over to Townsville, up toward the northern end of the Australian east coast across from New Guinea, where the Fifth Air Force's main supply and maintenance depot was located. What Schriever did not know was that *no one* ordered aircraft about in General Whitehead's domain without his permission. Someone told Whitehead right away, before the plane had been moved. Bennie was invited to lunch at the general's mess, in this case a grass hut with a table and chairs. "Get that son of a bitch in line and bring him in here for lunch," was the way Whitehead's invitation was extended to him by a staff officer. Whitehead's staff sat around the table having their meal with their chief while Schriever became the source of the luncheon entertainment, receiving one of the worst ass chewings of his career. "Goddamn it, I'm the only one who orders airplanes around and I want you to know it," Whitehead said, snorting and firing his words at Schriever machine-gun fashion. "Yes, sir," Schriever said. "Yes, sir," "No, sir," "Yes, sir" remained the totality of Bennie's end of the conversation as Whitehead continued to chew on more than his food. Schriever could see that he had provoked the general into one of his legendary rages and that it was useless to try to explain himself. He also *was* in the wrong. He should have asked permission from Whitehead or his staff as a matter of courtesy. The B-17 was flown to Townsville, later, and with Whitehead's nod.

It was not long before Whitehead was after Schriever again. The P-40 fighters were fitted with an Allison engine that was subject to failure of its bearings. When this occurred, the engine would be removed and flown down to Australia, where Bennie had arranged with Australian machine shops to have the engines overhauled. The rub was that the engines were suffering bearings failures again after only a couple of hours of flying time. Before Schriever could discover the source of the problem, Whitehead flew down to Townsville to complain personally. "God damn it," he berated Schriever, "can't you do a decent job down here in Australia? Your God damn engines are flying two or three hours and failing again." Bennie said he would investigate the problem and fix it.

He did, but before he could report to Whitehead, the general sought him out at the Service Command headquarters in Brisbane to berate him once more. This time Schriever let him rage on for a while and then said calmly, "Well, I've found out exactly what is happening." He explained to Whitehead that when the initial bearings failure occurred, the bearings disintegrated and spewed shards of metal into the P-40's oil cooler, which was separate from the engine itself. The shards of metal from the old bearings thus flowed back into the rebuilt engines and ruined them again. The maintenance crews at Port Moresby had not realized they needed to flush and clean the oil coolers before re-installing the engines. The oil coolers were now being flushed, Schriever said, and the reinstalled engines would last their allotted time. Whitehead snorted and left. When he returned to Port Moresby, however, he checked and learned that Schriever was telling him the truth. From that day onward Bennie, who never let Whitehead down when other obstacles arose to keep planes from flying, was one of the favored people of Ennis the Menace. Whenever he happened to be in Port Moresby, and later at subsequent headquarters Whitehead established as MacArthur progressively drove the Japanese from New Guinea, Schriever would always be invited to lunch or dinner at the general's mess, and Whitehead, who was keenly loyal to those who excelled for him, would always seat Bennie at his right, regardless of the rank of any other guest at the table.

In March 1943, after a little over eight months as a major, he was promoted to lieutenant colonel, and at the end of August he moved up again to become chief of staff of the Fifth Air Force Service Command. In effect, Schriever was now the deputy and chief operating officer of the Fifth Air Force's entire maintenance and supply organization. He was given the job just as MacArthur was unleashing an offensive to seize Lae and nearby Japanese bases about a third of the way up the north coast of New Guinea. More than a hundred new fighter planes were still in crates or various stages of assembly at a depot in Brisbane. Kenney wanted them in the fight—now. Schriever got them assembled and flown to New Guinea at a pace faster than anyone had ever achieved before. The general thanked him with a letter of commendation in September. When his boss, Colonel Ralph Brownfield, who was temporarily heading the Service Command, recommended him that same month for accelerated promotion to full colonel as "the most capable officer known to me," Kenney initialed the request "OK." On December 21, 1943, Bernard Schriever, three months and a week after his thirty-third birthday, received the eagles of a full colonel.

Although his responsibilities would continue to increase, he had gone as far as he could hope for in rank during the war. With the exception of a few who did win a star, the best of the second lieutenants from the Flying School classes of the 1930s became the colonels of the Second World War and saw that the orders of the generals were carried out. The men who won the stars and issued the orders came from the classes of the 1920s and earlier, men like Curtis LeMay, awarded his wings in 1929. LeMay, who was to create and lead the Strategic Air Command at the height of the Cold War, was a first lieutenant as late as 1938 but a major general only six years later.

Kenney's command was doubled in strength in June of 1944, as the destruction of the Japanese empire in the Pacific gathered momentum. He was given a second air force, the Thirteenth. Its deputy commander, Brigadier General Thomas "Tommy" White, became another of Bennie Schriever's mentors in the postwar years, first as vice chief and then as chief of staff of the independent U.S. Air Force, which was to be created in 1947. Ennis Whitehead received his second star as commanding general of the Fifth Air Force, while Kenney, who would gain the fourth star of a full general the following spring, established a higher headquarters, U.S. Far East Air Forces, to control both the Fifth and the Thirteenth. Schriever became chief of staff of the Far East Air Service Command, which supported the combined air forces. Late in the war a third air force, the Seventh, was added to Kenney's sphere and White was given command of it.

MacArthur had devised a strategy of leap-frogging past heavily defended enemy bases to gain time and avoid American and Australian casualties. The bypassed Japanese troops were left to wither. That April he had leapt 400 miles to seize lightly garrisoned Hollandia, more than two thirds of the way up New Guinea's north coast, bypassing heavily garrisoned Wewak farther south, where the Japanese had expected him to attack and concentrated more than 200,000 troops. Hollandia became the new main base. Kenney had a compound built there for himself and his staff. It was as comfortable as one could expect under the circumstances. The bedrooms were located around the outside edges to catch what breezes came off the sea. He invited Bennie to move in with them. Kenney was a rarity among military men in his working and sleeping habits, an owl who liked to work until 3:00 or 4:00 in the morning and then catnap during the day. He did his best brainstorming in the clarity of the predawn hours. He hated staying up alone and so Bennie and the staff took turns staying up with him. For Schriever it was also an opportunity to observe how to run an enterprise on the vast scale in which Kenney operated.

At the beginning of September 1944, as MacArthur was preparing to take Morotai, the northeasternmost island in the Moluccas chain and the stepping-stone to the Philippines, Schriever was given a job that would demand all the energy and improvising skills he could muster. He was put in charge of a new Advance Echelon of the Far East Air Service Command. His task was to solve instantly any supply problems that arose and to oversee the building of new airfields and depots for Kenney's two air forces as fast as MacArthur advanced. When, for example, Whitehead was preparing to launch strikes but was low on aviation gasoline, Bennie had to locate the tankers still at sea with the fuel and get them to the offshore pumping stations to send the fuel in through the lines and fill the tanks at the bases in time for the planes to gas up and take off. There were always shortages, despite the fact that American industry was now producing all-out. The war in Europe continued to receive priority and MacArthur's command, the Southwest Pacific Area, was at the end of the Pacific supply chain. The Navy's zone farther up in the Pacific under Admiral Chester Nimitz and his two fleet commanders, Admirals Raymond Spruance and William "Bull" Halsey, first skimmed off whatever it could. As Schriever put it in a bomber formation metaphor, "We were the tail-end Charlies."

Bennie and his crew of approximately thirty-five officers and men averaged only five to six hours of sleep a night and they were constantly on the move in the B-25s assigned to them for transport. The airfields they had to arrange to rebuild were invariably in ruins—captured Japanese bases with bomb-cratered runways and gutted buildings or former American fields occupied by the Japanese in their initial onslaught and blasted and burned in the retaking. To get a jump start, they would arrange to fly in immediately after the assault troops had cleared the places. Usually there was still plenty of shooting going on as the infantry cleaned out the last of the Japanese snipers and stragglers. In October 1944 it was Tacloban on Leyte, after MacArthur again fooled the Japanese by bypassing Mindanao, the southernmost island in the Philippines chain, and striking at Leyte in the center. In December it was the airstrips on Mindoro, just south of Luzon, the main island at the other end of the Philippines. At the end of February 1945 it was Luzon itself and Nichols Field on the edge of a devastated Manila, where the international airport now stands. One of Schriever's men was killed there by a Japanese straggler hiding in the remnants of a building. In June 1945 it was Naha on Okinawa. The Marines were using flamethrowers to incinerate the Japanese holed up in caves in the hills around the field.

Improvisation was always at a premium. Bennie was ordered to turn Nichols into a new headquarters for the Far East Air Service Command and an air logistics base to support the expected invasion of the Japanese home islands. He lacked cement. He had managed to corner a lot of toilets, which he kept as potential trade goods. The Japanese naval troops who had held Manila to the death, slaughtering 100,000 Filipino civilians in a frenzy at their own defeat and impending end, had also, for some bizarre reason, smashed the toilets in every building still wholly or partially standing. Schriever managed to obtain quite a bit of cement through toilet swapping, but he still did not have enough. He persuaded Major General Leif "Jack" Sverdrup, MacArthur's chief engineer, to give him carte blanche to haul up what cement he wanted from a prewar plant that was still functioning on the island of Cebu, next to Leyte. Sverdrup assumed Bennie would be transporting the cement in C-47s and thus wouldn't be able to take that much. Schriever didn't tell Sverdrup he had rounded up four small ships capable of carrying thousands of tons of cement. But he got too greedy. He loaded so much cement on one of the ships that it could not get across the reef at the outer edge of the harbor and he had to partially unload it to float the ship loose. Sverdrup discovered Schriever's larceny. In later years, after Sverdrup had returned to civilian life, the major St. Louis engineering firm of Sverdrup & Parcel, which he headed, was involved in a number of Air Force construction projects. Whenever he had to introduce Bennie at some public function, he would always amuse the gathering by needling him about the overloaded cement hauler getting stuck on the reef.

About three weeks after the Japanese surrender on August 15, 1945, Bennie flew a B-17 from Nichols Field at Manila to Atsugi near

Yokohama just south of Tokyo, the only usable airfield in the area, ferrying a general and his staff who were to take over all air service and supply functions in occupied Japan. As he came in over Tokyo Bay he was astounded at the destruction Curtis LeMay's B-29s had wrought on one of the great cities of the world. "There was nothing; it was just wasteland," he said later. What was still intact—the moated island of the Imperial Palace grounds and across from it the six-story Dai Ichi Insurance Building, which MacArthur would turn into his headquarters (the name of the building was appropriate for the man who would now rule Japan, as "Dai Ichi" means "number one") and the nearby Hotel Imperial—appeared like a little oasis in the middle of a desert. But he felt no pity. The behavior of the Japanese enemy he had fought had deadened him to any compassion for them and their people. Before flying back to Manila, he stayed for a few days at the Imperial, poking about out of curiosity, and noticed that American officers were already ceasing to carry sidearms. It was obvious there was going to be no resistance from this race, so fierce and fanatic only weeks before. For the Japanese, now that they had lost the war, it was over.

In September, shortly before flying home from Manila, he went to see Kenney to say goodbye. That March the general had arranged for him to be awarded a Legion of Merit for his accomplishments as chief of staff of the Service Command. He did not know it yet, but at Whitehead's insistence and with Kenney's assent, his name had also been submitted for a Distinguished Service Medal, the highest noncombat award an officer can receive, for his singular performance commanding the Advance Echelon. Once Schriever had completed the long leave to which he was entitled with his family and was ready for duty again in the United States, Kenney would make sure that he came into his reward. "You look around and tell me what assignment you'd like to have and I'll see that you get it," Kenney said.

He flew from Manila to Hawaii and there caught a ride on one of the newer four-engine C-54 transports for the final leg home. They took off in the afternoon and it was a long, cold flight through the night because the plane's heater failed. They approached San Francisco just as the sun was rising over the Golden Gate on the clear California morning of September 24, 1945. Schriever wept at the sight and tears came into his eyes again as he recalled it nearly fifty years later. In the fall of 1943, he and a team of other officers had flown back to Patterson Field at Dayton for a couple of weeks to meet with the Air Service Command representatives there and try to alleviate the supply problems Kenney was having. He had stolen one of those weeks to be with Dora and his son and daughter and to fly over to San Antonio to see his mother. Except for those two weeks, he had been at war in the Pacific for three years and three months.

BOOK II

INHERITING
A DIFFERENT
WORLD

II.

ATOMIC DIPLOMACY

While Bennie Schriever was still off in the Pacific in those heady days right after the defeat of Japan, the power relationships of the world in which he had grown up and fought a war were already in motion toward a profound transformation, as great in geopolitical terms as if the plates of the earth underpinning the continents had shifted in some gigantic tectonic movement. The multipolar world of his youth and early manhood was gone. Imperial Japan's far-flung Asian empire was a memory. Japan itself was in cinders, some irradiated from the two atomic bombs the United States had dropped on Hiroshima and Nagasaki. Germany's cities had been made of brick and concrete, not the wooden buildings that would be soft prey to incendiaries from Curtis LeMay's B-29s, but Germany too was in rubble. Hitler's Thousand-Year Reich had endured for twelve, the invincible führer hunkering in his bunker and blowing out his brains with his pistol amidst the flames and ruins of the Wagnerian funeral that was the final battle for Berlin.

France was in moral and physical collapse from its defeat by Germany in 1940, from the shame of Nazi occupation and collaboration by the Vichy regime, and from the devastation wrought by Allied armies after they had invaded at Normandy in 1944 to liberate Western Europe. Great Britain was exhausted by the cost of the victory. The British had been at war since Hitler had invaded Poland in September 1939. They had been drained of a quarter of their national wealth and more than 400,000 lives, including civilians killed by German bombs, out of a population still suffering from the keen memory of the 908,371 men who were supposed to have bought peace with their lives in the trenches of the First World War, that earlier war to end all wars. India, the jeweled keystone of their vast and cherished empire, was about to spin off in independence, initiating an irreversible process of imperial fragmentation and dissolution.

Only the United States and the Soviet Union had emerged from the war with their statures enhanced. Americans had every reason to feel pleased with themselves. With the exception of Honolulu, not a single enemy bomb had fallen on their cities. Their economy, prostrate during the Great Depression, had been turned into a colossus of productivity to arm and equip not only the U.S. forces but also those of Great Britain and the Soviet Union through Lend-Lease. The war spending by the "Arsenal of Democracy" had brought jobs and prosperity to tens of millions. The sacrifice in lives had been large but not beyond proportion—292,131 battle deaths and 115,185 from disease and other causes in an armed forces of 16.3 million men. There was the consolation that all of them had died in the cause of humanity. In contrast to the disillusioning experiences of the Europeans, there had never been a "bad" war in American historical memory. All American wars, beginning with the Revolution to wrest independence from Britain for the Thirteen Colonies, had been unifying ventures, moral crusades in which manhood was proven and glory won. Even the losers in the American Civil War, those who had fought under the stars and bars flag of the Confederacy, had been honored men in their home communities, despite their defeat. Their cause might be a lost cause, but in the white American South it had remained a sacred cause. There had been deviations, of course. The war with Mexico in the 1840s had been a war of conquest and the United States had fought another war of conquest in the Philippines, the first American imperial possession in Asia, at the turn of the twentieth century. These, however, had been pushed out of the American historical consciousness. In this uniquely American perspective the war just concluded had been the ultimate in the long line of good wars, a triumph of American military and industrial genius over the most hideous of enemies. And there was the additional comforting thought that the United States alone had the atomic bomb.

The new president, Harry Truman, who as vice president had succeeded to the office following the death of Franklin Roosevelt on April 12, 1945, was under the impression that the monopoly would last a good many years. Major General Leslie Groves, the Army engineer who had headed the Manhattan Project, the huge, top secret enterprise that created the bomb, predicted it would take the Soviet Union "ten, twenty, or even sixty years" to build one. In October 1947, he was a bit more precise—fifteen to twenty years. Other not so sanguine voices within the scientific community and the intelligence services said the Soviets would probably have a bomb by the early or mid-1950s. Truman paid less attention to them. He assumed that, for the foreseeable future, the United States alone would hold the great destroyer. He and his new secretary of state, James "Jimmie" Byrnes, had devised a scheme of "atomic diplomacy" to wield the bomb as a cudgel to keep the Soviet Union in line in the postwar years.

Franklin Roosevelt, who died before the first mushroom cloud of the atomic era rose over the New Mexico desert on July 16, 1945, in Trinity, the code name for the successful test of the implosion-type bomb dropped on Nagasaki, had hoped to perpetuate the wartime alliance with the Soviet Union into cooperation in the postwar years. In February 1945, he and Winston Churchill, the British wartime leader, had met with Joseph Stalin, the Soviet dictator, at Yalta in the Crimea and ratified Soviet hegemony over Poland, Hungary, Romania, and the other nations of Eastern Europe in exchange for Stalin's commitment to join the war against Japan after the defeat of Germany. While Stalin promised to hold free elections and foster democratic institutions, it was understood that these would be shaped to serve Soviet interests, that Eastern Europe would lie within the Soviet Union's postwar sphere of influence. Roosevelt's Republican opponents would later use Yalta to sully his memory by accusing him of having "given away" Eastern Europe, but Roosevelt could not give away what Stalin, in fact, already possessed. By the end of January 1945 the Red Army had driven Hitler's Wehrmacht from almost all of Eastern Europe and had broken into Germany for the advance on Berlin, which fell on May 2. Short of now going to war with the Soviet Union to wrest Eastern Europe from Stalin, the most that could be done was to try to mitigate his treatment of its peoples.

Roosevelt believed that reason and restraint worked best with Stalin. His scrappy successor had a different attitude. Truman was, to begin with, much more militantly anti-Communist. The day after Hitler invaded the Soviet Union on June 22, 1941, Truman, then a senator from Missouri, had advocated keeping both German and Russian blood flowing: "If we see that Germany is winning we ought to help

Russia, and if Russia is winning we ought to help Germany, and that way let them kill as many as possible, although I don't want to see Hitler victorious under any circumstances. Neither of them thinks anything of their pledged word." Henry Stimson, the elder statesman and holdover secretary of war from Roosevelt's administration, warned him that atomic diplomacy would backfire, that attempting to negotiate with the Soviets with "this weapon ostentatiously on our hip" would only increase Stalin's innate suspicion and distrust. Truman did not believe him. He was convinced that the way to handle the Soviets was with strong words made stronger by the shadow of the mushroom cloud behind them. "If you don't cut out all of this stalling and let us get down to work," Byrnes said to Vyacheslav Molotov, the Soviet foreign minister, at the London meeting of the Council of Foreign Ministers in September 1945, the first major postwar conference, "I'm going to pull an atomic bomb out of my hip pocket and let you have it." The remark was phrased as a joke, but Molotov, and Stalin when it was relayed to him, understood the menace behind it.

12.

SPIES INSIDE THE BARBED WIRE

Truman and Byrnes were living in a fool's paradise. Their atomic diplomacy would only accelerate the postwar arms race Stalin had already initiated to catch up with the United States. On August 20, 1945, just five days after the surrender of Japan, Stalin had secretly ordered an all-out, no-expense-barred program to build a Soviet bomb. That July 24, at the last Big Three conference in the Berlin suburb of Potsdam, Truman, exultant at Groves's awesome description of the Trinity test, had approached Stalin with contrived casualness as the Soviet dictator was leaving the conference room. Truman had said that the United States "had a new weapon of unusual destructive force." Stalin had simply nodded his thanks and left the room. Truman and Churchill decided that Stalin had not understood.

They were wrong. Stalin was well briefed on the Manhattan Project. The latest yield of Soviet espionage, a memorandum he had apparently received a couple of weeks before, had informed him, among other things, that the Trinity test was imminent.

Soviet intelligence had thoroughly penetrated the Manhattan Project. The gumshoes in the U.S. Army Counter Intelligence Corps, fixated on the left-wing connections of J. Robert Oppenheimer, who was in charge of the Los Alamos Laboratory, where the bomb was built, and those of several other scientists, never suspected the real spies. At Los Alamos itself the Soviets had the ideal intelligence setup—two physicists in critical positions reporting independently, neither aware that the other was a spy. Stalin's spymasters at Moscow Center in NKVD headquarters (the initials stand for the Russian words for People's Commissariat for Internal Affairs) at the Lubyanka Prison could thus confirm what they received and pass it on to their own superiors, who in turn passed it to Soviet physicists, confident that the information was accurate. Both spies were "walk-ins," volunteers who approached the Soviets on their own, and both spied out of idealism, not for pay.

A third spy, George Koval, gained wide access to the industrial processes involved in nuclear armament by penetrating plants at Oak Ridge, Tennessee, and Dayton, Ohio, where bomb components were manufactured for shipment to Los Alamos. Born in Sioux City, Iowa, to a family that immigrated in 1932 at the height of the Depression to a secular Jewish colony established in the Soviet Union, Koval was recruited by the GRU, the Soviet military intelligence service, and slipped back into the United States as a mole in 1940. His story did not emerge until 2007, after he died in retirement in Moscow in his nineties and President Vladimir Putin posthumously awarded him the highest post-Soviet decoration, Hero of the Russian Federation.

One of the two spies at Los Alamos, Klaus Fuchs, who had fled to England from Hitler's Germany in the 1930s, is well known, because he confessed in 1950 after U.S. military code breakers had cracked enough of the Soviet wartime espionage cable traffic to lay suspicion on him. By then he was chief scientist at Britain's top secret Harwell nuclear center. He was tried and sentenced to fourteen years in prison, the maximum allowable under British law because the Soviet Union was an ally at the time of his spying. He was released after nine to spend the rest of his years, until his death in 1988, doing research un-related to weaponry at a nuclear institute in East Germany. (Another well-known Soviet spy at Los Alamos was David Greenglass, the brother-in-law of Julius Rosenberg, who recruited him. Rosenberg was himself engaged in industrial spying for the Soviets at war plants on the East Coast, stealing the secrets of such new weapons as the proximity fuse. Greenglass was an Army enlisted man, a machinist by trade, who worked in the conventional explosives division of the Los Alamos complex. He was a man of limited education and none in physics and his often garbled reports, while sufficient to put Julius and his sister, Ethel, in the electric chair, provided Moscow with as much confusion as they did information.)

The second physicist spy for the Soviets at Los Alamos, Theodore Hall, has been little noted because he escaped prosecution and even the embarrassment of disclosure until 1995, when the first fruits of the code breaking, the so-called Venona documents (Venona was the code name of the code-cracking project), were made public. The rest fol-lowed in 1996. Hall was a mathematics and physics prodigy from New York who transferred to Harvard as a junior from Queens College at the age of sixteen, stood out among his peers, and became one of the youngest physicists to work at Los Alamos after he was recruited close to his eighteenth birthday. Hall's case was particularly ironic because, while he aided and protected the Soviet Union by committing treason, his equally brilliant brother, Lieutenant Colonel Edward Hall, devoted himself to threatening its existence as the U.S. Air Force's leading engi-neer in the post–Second World War development of rocket engines. Ed-ward Hall played a vital role in the creation of the first American intercontinental ballistic missile force after Schriever enlisted him as a member of his original ICBM team in 1954. He never knew of the trea-son of his brother, Theodore, until it was revealed forty-one years later when both men were in the evening of their lives.

Fuchs was the more informative of the two spies because he was a senior physicist, in knowledge if not in years, when he arrived at Los Alamos in August 1944 at the age of thirty-three. He was therefore able to furnish Stalin's intelligence officers with a fully detailed de-scription, including drawings with exact dimensions, of the plutonium bomb dropped on Nagasaki. Indeed, Fuchs had been brought to Los Alamos at the initiative of Hans Bethe, another German émigré physicist and subsequent Nobel Laureate, who was in charge of the Theoretical Division, precisely to help solve the most sensitive and secret problem on the laboratory's agenda in 1944—the implosion method required to detonate that same plutonium bomb. And Fuchs had done his work well. "One of the most valuable men in my division," Bethe was later to remark of him with chagrin.

Little Boy, the code name of the atomic bomb dropped on Hiroshima, was a so-called gun type. (The code name was drawn from the relative slimness of the bomb's casing at twenty-nine inches, even though it weighed 9,700 pounds and was ten feet long. The Nagasaki bomb was, in contrast, code-named Fat Man because of the wide girth of its casing. It was not, however, much heavier than Little Boy, weighing 10,000 pounds.) Little Boy had an internal cannon that used a conventional explosive, cordite, to fire a bullet of enriched uranium, an isotope called U-235, into three larger rings of the same isotope stacked one atop another at the muzzle of the cannon. U-235 is so fissionable that when the bullet hit the rings, it set off a nuclear explosion of immense force. The design was simple and Robert Oppenheimer and the other scientists at Los Alamos were so certain it would work that they didn't feel it was necessary to test it.

The rub was that there was a shortage of uranium. Although there were plentiful underground deposits of the naturally occurring substance in the American West and in Canada, exploration for uranium deposits and mining them had hardly begun. The manufacturing process to turn natural uranium into the highly enriched isotope was also so slow that if the scientists relied on U-235 and the gun-type design, the United States would be able to produce only one atomic bomb by 1945. To create more atomic bombs, Los Alamos had to use plutonium as the nuclear core. Plutonium, however, was much more difficult to bring to supercriticality than U-235 because of a phenomenon called spontaneous fission, which resulted from an impurity inherent in the manufacturing process. If it was used in a gun-type weapon, the bomb would fizzle. The method finally decided on was implosion— surrounding the plutonium core with conventional explosives and compressing it with such speed and simultaneousness that the plutonium became supercritical and a nuclear explosion occurred. The concept was simple; designing and executing it was extremely complicated.

The Soviets were to face the same shortage of uranium for the same reason—they had also not yet located and developed mining of natural uranium deposits in Siberia. To create an arsenal instead of just one bomb, they would have to employ plutonium for the cores. And later, after the Trinity test and the dropping of the bombs on Hiroshima and Nagasaki, it was determined there was a second reason to use plutonium. Once the implosion method was mastered, the plutonium weapon yielded considerably greater nuclear force and devastation than the gun type with U-235. The Little Boy bomb that destroyed Hiroshima loosed a nuclear blast equivalent to 12.5 kilotons, or 12,500 tons, of TNT. The Fat Man plutonium bomb dropped on Nagasaki yielded 21 kilotons, or 21,000 tons, of TNT. If the Soviets were going to have spies at Los Alamos, it was most convenient to have them in the sections devising a successful method of implosion.

Klaus Fuchs originally came to the United States at the end of 1943 as a member of a team of fifteen British scientists sent over to help build the bomb. That he made it as far as the Theoretical Division at Los Alamos without arousing anyone's suspicion was evidence of the nadir of British counterintelligence during the Second World War. The British assured General Groves that none of the fifteen was a security risk. At the time Groves accepted this warranty as genuine, the British government had become a dovecote for Soviet penetration agents. The most outrageous example was the "Cambridge Five," so dubbed because they had all been recruited while at Cambridge University. Guy Burgess and Donald Maclean were in the Foreign Office. Harold "Kim" Philby, considered so valuable by the Soviets that he was to be awarded the clandestine rank of colonel in the KGB, the successor to the NKVD, was a fast-rising talent in MI6, Britain's Secret Intelligence Service. John Cairncross was private secretary to Lord Hankey, who in turn was minister without portfolio in Churchill's War Cabinet, with complete access to its secrets and also responsibility for overseeing British intelligence and chairing the cabinet's Scientific Advisory Committee. (It was probably Cairncross who passed the Soviets a complete copy of the important feasibility study on the bomb done by British scientists in 1941, the so-called MAUD Committee report.) The fifth was the renowned art historian Sir Anthony Blunt, surveyor of the Queen's Pictures (keeper of the royal art collection), knighted in 1956 for his services to the Crown, an ardent Marxist and a Soviet spy since he was first enlisted by the NKVD in 1934.

In the case of Fuchs, a simple background check would have disclosed his Communist connections and the peril of placing him in such a sensitive position at Los Alamos. He had entered the Party while a student at the University of Kiel in the early 1930s and openly participated in leading student strikes and other Communist resistance activities against the Nazis until Hitler came to power in 1933. He then had to flee to England via Paris to escape arrest. The family that sponsored him in Bristol had Communist affiliations and so did the professor at Bristol University, a theoretical physicist named Nevill Mott, who gave him an assistantship there. In England, he had also joined a Communist front organization, the Bristol branch of the Society for Cultural Relations with the Soviet Union. When the society staged dramatic readings of the purge trials Stalin was conducting in Moscow to liquidate most of the original Bolshevik leaders on spurious charges, Fuchs would take the part of the prosecutor, the notorious Andrei Vyshinsky. Fuchs subsequently dissembled about his politics, but he had left sufficient tracks for any competent counterintelligence investigator to find. As soon as the British put him to work on preliminary atomic bomb research in Birmingham in 1941, he contacted the Soviet embassy in London and volunteered to spy, turning over copies of all of his research reports.

If Fuchs's entry into the inner temple at Los Alamos reflected a hardening of the arteries in British counterintelligence, Theodore Hall's entrance reflected the incompetence of its American counterpart. The times and his background combined to make Ted Hall into a man who betrayed his country out of principle. His original name was Theodore Alvin Holtzberg, born on October 20, 1925, to a Russian Jewish family on Long Island. Until the stock market crashed in 1929 and the Great Depression that followed bankrupted him, Hall's father, Barney Holtzberg, had prospered sufficiently as a furrier to move the family from an apartment in an immigrant neighborhood in Washington Heights in New York City to a large house in Far Rockaway. With the collapse of the firm, the family moved back to a small apartment in Washington Heights. Barney managed to feed and clothe his family by starting over on a much smaller scale in a niche business in a vastly shrunken fur trade, but the good years and the big home on Long Island were to remain a memory. Adopting the surname of Hall in place of Holtzberg was an idea Ed, eleven years older than his younger brother, came up with. He decided that giving himself an Anglo-Saxon surname would help him evade the widespread anti-Semitism of the period and acquire a job as an engineer. Ted had Ed add him to the court papers and in 1936 he formally became Theodore Alvin Hall.

Left-wing radicalism was common among Russian Jews in the late nineteenth and early twentieth centuries because of the ferociously anti-Semitic policies of Czar Alexander III, a fanatic reactionary who ruled from 1881 to 1894. With the demise of czarism, Fascism became the opposite pole in this ideological universe after its rise, first in Italy in the 1920s under Benito Mussolini, and then with genuine menace under Adolf Hitler in the 1930s in Germany. Ed Hall remembered being attracted by the intense left-wing activity at City College of New York, where tuition was free and where he took his bachelor's degree in engineering in 1935. He lost interest in politics, however, enlisting in the U.S. Army Air Corps as a private in 1939, after a second degree specializing in chemical engineering and the change of his name to Hall still failed to gain him a civilian engineering job amidst the Great Depression.

Not so his younger brother. Ted Hall was far more affected by the world in which he was growing up, perhaps because he was so much younger and more intellectual than the mechanically minded Ed. It was an apocalyptic world, a world of extremes, of war and revolution, of economic collapse and civil unrest, of mass impoverishment. In Spain the forces of darkness, in the person of General Francisco Franco and his backers, the German and Italian dictators, crushed the life out of the Spanish Republic. At home the capitalist system in which Americans had put their faith appeared profoundly flawed, offering nothing for the future beyond interludes of prosperity followed by repetitive plunges into economic and social misery. Extreme times breed a willingness in some to accept extreme solutions. Ted Hall was one of those people. Despite his high intelligence and his gift for mathematics and science, he was also naive enough and ignorant enough not to understand the barbarous nature of Stalin's regime. Communism and the Soviet Union seemed to him to offer hope.

When Ted Hall, the sixteen-year-old prodigy, transferred from Queens College to Harvard as a junior in the fall of 1942, of the 3,494 undergraduates at the university, only about a dozen were active members of the John Reed Society, the Communist organization on campus. (Reed, a 1910 Harvard graduate, was the grandson of an Oregon capitalist who made a fortune manufacturing pig iron. He turned radical journalist and wrote an inspired eyewitness account of the Bolshevik Revolution, *Ten Days That Shook the World*. He died during a typhus epidemic in Russia in 1920 and was buried in the Kremlin wall.) Hall was by chance assigned to room with its chairman and another member and he soon joined. After he and they subsequently moved elsewhere and parted, Hall acquired two new roommates, one of whom was Saville "Savy" Sax, whose Russian Jewish parents had been firm supporters of the Bolshevik Revolution and had passed their Communist convictions on to their son. Although Sax was a literary type with no interest in science (one of his close friends at De Witt Clinton High School in New York had been James Baldwin, who was to become famous as a writer), their shared politics soon made them comrades. When Hall was recruited during his senior year for war work so secret that the recruiter told Hall he could not tell him what it was ahead of time, Sax suggested that if the project turned out to be some superweapon, Hall ought to let the Russians in on it. Hall did not say no.

According to Joseph Albright and Marcia Kunstel, whose book, *Bombshell*, recounts Ted Hall's treachery, he arrived at the new laboratory city 7,200 feet above sea level on the Pajarito Plateau in the Jemez Mountains northwest of Santa Fe, New Mexico—the whole of it surrounded by a fence topped by barbed wire and ringed with guard towers—on January 27, 1944, seven months ahead of Fuchs. Again, as with Fuchs, a simple background investigation would have kept him out. But while the Army Counter Intelligence Corps division charged with protecting the security of the Manhattan Project, under the command of Colonel John Lansdale, Jr., strictly controlled entry and exit through the two gates in the fence on either side of the complex, and had agents planted undercover in hotels and bars in Santa Fe and other communities in the area, it did not bother to conduct background checks on inconspicuous types like Hall and many others it allowed inside those gates.

Within less than six months Hall was at the center of the research to perfect the implosion method for the plutonium bomb. He impressed his immediate superior, Bruno Benedetti Rossi, an émigré Italian physicist who headed one of the sections in the experimental physics division, or P Division, under Robert Fox Bacher, the well-known Cornell professor of physics. In July 1944, Hall was therefore designated a team leader for the so-called Ra-La implosion experiments. Ra-La was an abbreviation for radioactive lanthanum, a tracer isotope that emitted intense gamma rays. In the fall of 1943, Rossi and Philip Koontz, a cosmic ray physicist from the University of Colorado, had come up with an idea for a fast-acting radiation counter. It was called a double ionization chamber.

If a capsule of Ra-La was placed in the center of a metal sphere serving as a dummy plutonium core and the sphere was then crushed with a wrapper of conventional explosives, the pattern of the gamma rays given off by the smashed Ra-La would reveal whether the implosion had been sufficiently symmetrical to detonate an actual plutonium core. Hall's job was to head the team that built the four new ionization chambers normally required for each experiment, as they were destroyed in the explosion, and to rig them to the dummy bomb for the test. Other members of Rossi's group would move the dummy bomb into place and insert the Ra-La pellet into the sphere. All would then move to a blast shelter where Hall had an oscilloscope, an electronic instrument that records a trace reading on the screen of a cathode-ray tube. When the conventional explosive wrapper was detonated, the ionization chambers would pick up the emission of gamma rays from the pulverized pellet of Ra-La and flash a reading to the screen of the oscilloscope in the moment before they too disintegrated in the blast.

Hall's assignment enabled him to see a great deal more than the gamma-ray emission reading on the oscilloscope. Prior to each detonation, he was required to calibrate the ionization chambers so that they would give a correct reading. To do this he had to assemble the dummy core in a small shed erected for this purpose. The test cores were exact replicas of the real thing. While in the shed, Hall had plenty of time to note details, for example to measure the size of the core and thus calculate how much plutonium was required for a bomb.

In addition, there was no impediment to Hall obtaining explanations for everything he observed. As a physicist, and thus a member of the scientific staff at Los Alamos, he had been issued a white identity badge the day he arrived. "White badgers" were cleared to read all of the laboratory's secret technical reports and to attend the weekly colloquia Robert Oppenheimer organized to discuss ongoing work. For security reasons, Groves had wanted at the outset to completely compartmentalize Los Alamos so that a scientist's knowledge would be limited to the task he had been assigned. Oppenheimer had insisted, however, and correctly as it turned out, that they could not get the bomb built by 1945 unless he was free to run the laboratory as an ongoing seminar in which everyone involved could contribute in solving the problems they were bound to encounter. To meet the deadline, Groves let Oppenheimer have his way. Hall thus had no difficulty in learning the design of the implosion wrapper, or the composition of fast-burning and slow-burning explosives being employed by George Kistiakowsky, the émigré Ukrainian chemist who was the wizard of the Harvard chemistry faculty, to make the wrapper work, or the relative velocity required for the implosion to compress the core to supercriticality.

In mid-October 1944, right after the third and still unsuccessful implosion test, Hall left Los Alamos on a two-week leave. He got in touch with Russian intelligence agents operating out of the Soviet consulate in a posh East Side neighborhood in New York at 7 East 67th Street. The NKVD had an intelligence station, or *rezidentura* as it was called in Russian, there. Savy Sax helped him. They made the contact through the New York offices of Amtorg, the Soviet import-export organization, and a New York agency that distributed Soviet films. Sax offered to act as the courier who would travel to New Mexico by bus and train to pick up Hall's reports. Because the mail to and from Los Alamos was censored, the two young men resorted to using Walt Whitman's famous book of poetry *Leaves of Grass* for Hall to signal the date, time, and place of the rendezvous. Whitman numbered each of his poems, so it was not difficult for them to set up a book code, one of the oldest forms of encryption. To make certain no one would overhear them, they rented rowboats on the lake in Central Park for discussions to settle these and other important details.

Hall's motive for committing treason was simple. He believed that his duty did not end with being a good physicist, that he also had an obligation to humanity. His Marxist ideas led him to think that the United States might tumble into another depression after the wartime stimulus to the economy ended with the defeat of Germany and Japan. The social and economic turmoil set off by a renewed economic collapse could bring the triumph of Fascism in America, as it had in Germany. If that happened and a Third World War broke out while the United States still had a monopoly on the bomb, Washington would use it to devastate the Soviet Union. If both nations had the bomb there would be a strategic balance, and thus no nuclear war: both would be afraid of its effects.

Because Fuchs had arrived at Los Alamos but was not yet reporting, the Soviets apparently first learned about the principle of implosion and its implications from a report Hall passed to Sax during a rendezvous in Albuquerque in December 1944. According to David Holloway, the Stanford University political scientist and historian who chronicled the building of the Soviet bomb in a masterly account, *Stalin and the Bomb,* the information reached Igor Kurchatov, the Soviet physicist who was heading Stalin's atomic bomb project, in Moscow in March 1945. Implosion was an idea that had not occurred to him, Kurchatov said in his memorandum commenting on the intelligence report, "but the implosion method is undoubtedly of immense interest, is fundamentally correct, and should be subjected to close scrutiny both theoretically and experimentally."

Hall went right back to the test range on his return to Los Alamos. In three detonations in the first half of February 1945, Rossi's group, employing special quick-firing electrical detonators devised by the Berkeley physicist and subsequent Nobel Laureate Luis Alvarez, finally got the result they had been seeking. The gamma ray reading on the oscilloscope in the blast shelter showed a symmetrical implosion of the core. At the end of the month, Oppenheimer and Groves and other leading figures at Los Alamos settled on the final design of the plutonium bomb, although they ordered continued Ra-La testing right up until shortly before Trinity on July 16 in order to achieve absolute certainty.

When Sax returned to Harvard in early 1945, Hall acquired a new courier, Lona Petka Cohen, an attractive Polish-American woman, then in her early thirties, who, along with her husband, Morris, was to become a legendary operative in the Soviet secret service. (She died in retirement in Moscow in 1992, Morris three years later.) Her second trip to New Mexico occurred after the Hiroshima and Nagasaki bombings, when the secret of what had been going on at Los Alamos was out and the laboratory had become a much publicized place. The Army Counter Intelligence Corps and the Federal Bureau of Investigation had greatly increased security in the whole area. As soon as Hall passed

her his report at a rendezvous on the campus of the University of New
Mexico at Albuquerque, she hurried back to a boardinghouse in the
New Mexican town of Las Vegas, about eighty miles away, where she
had been staying to avoid the attention she might have attracted by
putting up at a hotel in Albuquerque or Santa Fe. She stuffed the papers Hall had given her under the top tissues in a box of Kleenex,
grabbed her suitcase, and headed for the railroad station.

At the station, she discovered that plainclothes security men were
questioning everyone getting on the train and searching their baggage.
She waited inside until just before the train was due to depart, then
walked up to two agents on the platform next to one of the cars. She
put down her suitcase and began to play the helpless female who was
late for her train, fumbling at the zipper on the handbag in which she
had placed her ticket. Making believe she needed to free her hands to
work the zipper, she passed the Kleenex box holding the fruits of Hall's
atomic espionage to one of the agents. After the handbag had been
opened, she displayed her ticket and answered the agents' questions.
They searched her bag and suitcase. She then picked up the suitcase
and proceeded toward the steps into the car, deliberately leaving the
Kleenex box behind with one of the agents. She shrewdly assumed he
would think she had forgotten it and be gallant enough to call this to
her attention and hand it to her, which is precisely what he did. Back
in New York she joked with her NKVD handler from the consulate on
East 67th Street that Hall's report had been "in the hands of the police."

That Hall's information, if less detailed, equaled in importance the
material from Fuchs was something best understood by the agents at
7 East 67th Street and by their superiors at Moscow Center who were
collating it into summary memos for Lavrenti Beria, the chilling figure
who was in charge of the NKVD and the archipelago of slave labor
camps known as the Gulag, an acronym formed from the initial letters
of the Russian words for Main Camp Administration, the bland official term for the camps. Beria was as cruel and as morbidly suspicious
as his master, Stalin. He suspected for a long time that American intelligence might be feeding these reports to his agents in New York in
order to trick the Soviet Union into wasting prodigious resources trying to build a bomb that was a fantasy. Stalin had initiated a small-
scale project to design an atomic bomb in 1943 at the urging of some

of the more farsighted Soviet physicists. Igor Kurchatov had been chosen to head it. The choice was a wise one. A well-built, energetic man
who was liked by his colleagues, Kurchatov was known as "the
Beard," for the one he grew during the war, or as "Prince Igor," for his
self-confident, take-charge manner. Little in the way of resources had
been assigned to the enterprise, however, and it was more in the nature
of a research group than an organization to build a bomb. Other, not
so farsighted Soviet physicists were saying it was impossible to create
such a bomb or that it was something far off in the future. Had the amateurish and frequently incompetent reports from David Greenglass,
the Army machinist who ground sections of high-explosive cast into
solid forms called lenses for the plutonium wrapper, been the only
touchstone against which to compare the materials from Fuchs, the
suspicion of Beria, and in turn that of Stalin, would have been that
much greater and the agents in New York and those in Moscow doing
the collating might have been more hesitant about passing on the fruits
of the espionage. They knew that if they were being hoodwinked, their
lives would be forfeited. Beria had said to one of his senior intelligence
officers as he was being handed a report: "If this is disinformation, I'll
put you all in the cellar." The cellar of the Lubyanka Prison was one of
the places where torture and executions took place. Ted Hall made the
difference. His was the sophisticated spying of another physicist and
Fuchs's information checked out against his.

13.

"THE BALANCE HAS BEEN
DESTROYED"

Hiroshima woke up Stalin. Perhaps because he was preoccupied
with the conclusion of the war against Germany and then a race
to join the war against Japan in order to seize Japanese territory before Tokyo could surrender, Stalin does not seem to have understood

the strategic importance of the atomic bomb, despite the wealth of intelligence information he possessed on the American nuclear weapons program. The flash of atomic fire that destroyed a Japanese city six thousand miles from Moscow destroyed in the same instant the sense of security that Stalin and others in the Soviet leadership thought they had achieved in their victorious struggle against Nazi Germany. Four years of the most devastating war of annihilation in history, a titanic conflict with Hitler's legions in which tens of millions of Soviet citizens, civilian and military, had perished and much of the nation had been laid waste, had ended with security a mirage. They were once more in peril should the Americans, in future years, ever turn on them. What stunned Stalin most was not merely the power of this new weapon, but the fact that the United States had not hesitated to use it against a nation he considered already beaten and on the verge of giving up.

"Hiroshima has shaken the whole world. The balance has been destroyed," he said in a meeting with Kurchatov in the middle of August. There would be no safety now until the Soviet Union had its own atomic bomb. On August 20, 1945, the State Defense Committee, which Stalin chaired, issued a secret decree establishing a special committee, headed by Beria, to oversee the nuclear weapons project. Igor Kurchatov was to continue as scientific director, in effect the Soviet equivalent of J. Robert Oppenheimer in the Manhattan Project, but his organization was no longer to be stingily funded. No expense was too great. "If the child doesn't cry, the mother doesn't know what he needs," Stalin told him. "Ask for whatever you like. You won't be refused."

Making an atomic bomb entails much more than the creation of a laboratory city like Los Alamos, and this is where the industrial espionage of the third major Soviet spy, George Koval, counted. It requires the establishment of an entire nuclear industry, from mines to garner raw uranium ore, plants to process it into metal, and large-scale reactors and gaseous diffusion facilities, such as those General Groves had built at Oak Ridge, Tennessee, and at Hanford, Washington, to enrich uranium into the U-235 isotope and to produce weapons-grade plutonium. The undertaking had cost the United States $2 billion, an enormous sum in 1945. The Soviets would have to spend the rough equivalent, in labor and resources if not in cash, because they would have to replicate what the Americans had done, and Stalin was ordering this accomplished in a land suffering from destruction on a scale difficult to imagine.

What had not been blasted in the fighting, the German invaders had systematically burned down or blown up during their retreat. (Nazi cruelty toward the Russians was deliberate and without limit, emanating from the racial doctrine that all Slavs were subhuman—*Untermenschen*. Hitler had planned to raze Russia's two greatest cities, Leningrad and Moscow, and to turn Russia and its associated lands into a vast new Teutonic colony in which all the Slavic peoples would be reduced to serfs, deprived of education and medical care. The largest group of human beings murdered by the Nazis, aside from the Jews, were Soviet prisoners of war—about 2.7 million of the 4.5 million captured. The Germans did not waste poison gas on them. Especially at the outset of the war, when they were confident of winning and few of their own men had been captured, the Germans either worked Soviet prisoners to death or herded them into barbed wire stockades and gave them the slow death of starvation. Mass shootings of civilians in areas where there was resistance from partisans and looting and rape were commonplace. The Germans were fortunate that they committed crimes like this in the modern era. In ancient times the customs of vengeance would have demanded the dismemberment of the defeated German nation, a pitiless slaughter of the males, and the selling of the women and children into slavery. There was revenge—wholesale rape of German women and uncontrolled looting—after the Red Army, its soldiers enraged by what they saw as they fought their way westward, finally penetrated the Reich. And there was some vengeance killing in Berlin brought on by the ferocity of the fighting there. These were reprehensible war crimes, but hardly equivalent to the killing of millions.) The cities of western Russia and Ukraine—industrial centers as far east as Stalingrad on the Volga—were in ruins. The flaying hand of war had reached out to smash 4.7 million houses, 1,710 towns, and 70,000 villages. Twenty-five million people were homeless. Agriculture and transportation had also been devastated. One hundred thousand collective and state farms had been ravaged, along with thousands of tractor and farm machinery stations. Seven million horses were gone and 20 million of the country's 23 million pigs. More than 40,000 miles of rail line had been torn up and 15,800 locomotives and 428,000 freight cars destroyed or damaged.

The task of reconstruction just to restore the prewar status quo was daunting, and yet Stalin was immediately ordering an immensely expensive project that would detract from reconstruction and delay homes for the homeless and adequate nourishment for the hungry. And he was soon to order other expensive military programs in radar, rocketry, jet-propelled fighter aircraft, and the building of a fleet of long-range bombers copied from the B-29, which would further detract from civilian reconstruction. That he did not hesitate to make the choice told a great deal about the nature of the Soviet state, the character and personality of this man who had fashioned it in his image, and why Americans like Bennie Schriever returned home from one war to find themselves quickly caught up in a new and different confrontation.

14.

THE STATE THAT WAS STALIN

If Louis XIV could say "L'état, c'est moi" ("I am the state") of seventeenth- and early-eighteenth-century France, Joseph Stalin could have said the same of the Soviet Union he created. Vladimir Lenin may have founded the Soviet state, but Stalin shaped it into what it became subsequent to Lenin's death in 1924. Stalin was, after Adolf Hitler, the second great monster of the twentieth century. He cared not a whit for human life, nor did the suffering of the Soviet people ever trouble him. To enforce collectivization of agriculture, he deliberately provoked a famine in Ukraine in 1932–33 that starved millions. The lives of human beings had to him the same value as those of laboratory rats in the historic experiment he was presiding over to build socialism, which would one day transmogrify itself into Communism. (To Stalin, however, there was nothing tentative about his revolutionary society. He believed that he was bringing a new reality to fruition.) The fate of individuals did not matter; the fate of the experiment was everything. He had his best boyhood friend shot. He and Molotov, his closest collaborator after Beria, once signed death warrant lists for 3,187 people and then went to watch Western movies in his private theater in the Kremlin, a favorite nightly relaxation for the Soviet dictator. Yet while the outcome of the experiment provided a rationale for Stalin to justify whatever he wanted to do, his character and personality were the real determinants of his conduct.

Until he adopted a Party pseudonym (Stalin means "man of steel") during his revolutionary youth, he was Iosif Vissarionovich Dzhugashvili, born in 1879 in the then czarist province of Georgia in the Caucasus. A diminutive figure, slim and just five feet, four inches, he had a withered left arm from a childhood injury and a pockmarked face from smallpox. His eyes were hazel, with a dash of yellow that seemed to glint when he was angry. There was nothing diminutive or withered about the man himself. He had a remarkable talent for organizing and manipulating people and bureaucracies and he was a cunning actor with two pronounced traits—suspicion virtually to the point of clinical paranoia and cruelty to the point of sadism. He once remarked that the most pleasant experience a man could have was to lead an enemy into a trap, arrange his doom, and then sleep soundly that night.

In his mind, he and his needs and the Soviet state and its needs were inseparable. Whatever might threaten his security also threatened the security of the Soviet state and therefore amounted to counterrevolution and treason. Whatever he wished to accomplish, the Soviet state needed to accomplish and thus was justifiable in the national interest. No one knows the precise number of his victims. The most authoritative source, Dimitri Volkogonov, a former Red Army general turned historian, had unrestricted access to the Soviet archives while they were still secret and published a biography of Stalin in 1989. He estimated that Stalin's forced transformation of Russian agriculture from private into collective and state-owned farms from 1929 to 1933 cost 8.5 to 9 million peasant lives. Another 19.5 to 22 million persons were arrested for various offenses, real and contrived, between then and his death in 1953. Of these, Volkogonov estimated that more than a third, approximately 6.5 to 7.3 million human beings, were sentenced to death or perished in the slave labor camps of the Gulag.

Leon Trotsky's support within the Soviet Communist Party was virtually nil by the time Stalin exiled him, initially to Turkey, in 1929, but Stalin continued to see "Trotskyist conspirators" and "Trotskyist plots" everywhere and tens of thousands paid with their lives for his obsession. It was a favorite charge during the Great Purge of 1937–38, when 4.5 to 5.5 million people were arrested. He even had the NKVD search the civil war archives for the names of anyone who had served under or been associated with Trotsky when he was Bolshevik commissar for military affairs and chairman of the Supreme War Council. Everyone named was tracked down and arrested and shot. In subsequent years when some of the mass graves were exhumed, the skulls all bore the trademark of the NKVD—a bullet hole in the back of the head.

His suspicion extended to those closest to him. A trick to test their loyalty was to have a member of their family arrested. His factotum was a man named Alexander Poskrebyshev, who worked twelve to fourteen hours a day bringing Stalin documents to read or sign, summoning visitors, and relaying the boss's orders. Stalin gave Beria permission to arrest Poskrebyshev's wife on a charge of Nazi espionage. When the anguished husband several times protested his wife's innocence and pleaded with Stalin to free her, Stalin invariably answered: "It doesn't depend on me. I can do nothing. Only the NKVD can sort it out." The NKVD did sort it out. The woman was held in prison for three years and then shot, undoubtedly with Stalin's consent. All the while, before and afterward, Poskrebyshev continued bringing Stalin his documents. Excessive protest would have condemned him and the rest of his family, and in an example of the bizarre thinking that can develop in a society as twisted as this one was, Poskrebyshev remained personally loyal to Stalin. When Molotov fell out of favor in subsequent years and Stalin replaced him as foreign minister with Andrei Vyshinsky, he arrested Molotov's wife, Polina, for "Zionist connections." (She had Jewish ancestry.) Molotov loved his wife, but at the Politburo meeting where Stalin put the matter of her arrest to a vote, Molotov also voted for it.

It was Stalin's pathological suspicion that his military leaders were plotting against him that was largely responsible as well for the immense losses in the opening months of the German invasion in 1941, including 3 million Red Army officers and men taken prisoner. The purge began in May 1937 with the arrest and subsequent execution on trumped-up accusations of Marshal Mikhail Tukhachevsky, a pioneering exponent of armored warfare and deep, penetrating maneuver.

Tukhachevsky was probably the most talented and resourceful officer in the Red Army, with a sterling record of personal courage and battlefield leadership during the civil war. Stalin then proceeded, in effect, to wipe out the entire command structure of his army. Thousands of officers, the best of the corps, were murdered. Most members of the senior War Council were purged, as were all of the commanders of the military districts, 90 percent of their deputies and chiefs of staffs, 80 percent of the corps and division commanders, and 90 percent of their chiefs of staff and staff officers. Marshal Kliment Voroshilov, an incompetent toady whom Stalin made his defense commissar, reported at the end of November 1938 that the Red Army had been "cleansed of more than 40,000 men." (Many of the lower-ranking officers were sent to slave labor camps rather than being shot.) The purge and its impact encouraged the Germans in their planning for the invasion. "The Red Army is leaderless," Colonel General Franz Halder, the German army's chief of staff, declared at a secret conference in December 1940. A rational ruler would have hesitated to decapitate his army when he faced a potential opponent like Hitler, but in Stalin's sick imagination these men threatened him and therefore they threatened the state.

As a result, when, despite Stalin's concluding of the infamous Non-Aggression Pact with Hitler in 1939 in a futile attempt to avoid war, the führer's armored divisions burst across the Soviet frontier in the opening thrust of Operation Barbarossa on June 22, 1941, the Red Army was commanded by men too young or too inexperienced to know how to handle their units in combat. Seventy-five percent of all officers had held their current assignments for less than a year. Stalin also made the catastrophe worse by placing many of his forces, including aviation units, relatively close to the frontier, where planes were caught on the ground by the Luftwaffe and troops quickly overrun, rather than availing himself of the Soviet Union's depths to hold them farther back until the main lines of the German advance could be identified and powerful and well-organized counterattacks launched. Miraculously, enough talented men like Georgi Zhukov, who was to become the leading Soviet marshal of the Second World War, survived the purge, and Stalin, after additional costly blunders, finally understood the mortal danger in which he stood and had the sense to listen to them. They were able to buy time with those vast Russian spaces and gradually reconstitute an officer corps that, along with the extraordinary courage and fortitude of the ordinary soldier of the Red Army, first halted and then broke the back of the Wehrmacht and drove the Germans all the way to Berlin.

None of this is to say that tens of millions of ordinary Soviet citizens did not follow Stalin enthusiastically. His crimes went unrecognized and the relentless propaganda of the regime constantly extolled the magnificent leadership and genius of Comrade Stalin. Faith in the dream of "building socialism" was also still vibrant in Stalin's time and expressed itself in the 1930s in such herculean projects as the creation of the new steel center at Magnitogorsk, deep in the Urals east of Moscow, which proved indispensable during the Second World War in providing the material for the guns and tanks that defeated the Germans. Ironically, the war could not have been won without the program of heavy industry Stalin had fostered in a backward Russia. The war further enhanced his prestige with the Soviet public. The actor in him reached out cleverly to arouse the wellspring of patriotism for "Mother Russia," whose very existence was threatened by the Germans. His calamitous errors were hidden, and he made certain that he, rather than his generals, received credit for the victories. By 1945 he was widely regarded as a superhuman savior who had led the Russian people to triumph and safety through the most perilous ordeal in their history.

Stalin was proud of the command economy he had created, whereby resources could be channeled into projects he deemed of priority, regardless of deprivation elsewhere. He wanted the bomb as quickly as possible, not because he was worried about any immediate threat of war—relations were only starting to become strained—but because he was concerned that Truman and Byrnes, through their atomic diplomacy, might succeed in imposing a postwar settlement inimical to Soviet interests. Stalin understood the political implications of the atomic bomb. As long as the United States held a monopoly, the bomb gave America an aura of unique technological and military prowess. Once the Soviet Union had its own bomb, that aura would be broken, and Stalin would achieve what amounted to strategic parity with Washington. Kurchatov told Beria, and thus Stalin too, as the information would certainly have been relayed by Beria to his master, that the task would take approximately two and a half years. A plutonium-type bomb was to be tested by January 1, 1948. Kurchatov and the fellow nuclear physicist he had selected as his deputy, Iulii Khariton, a slim, scholarly man who had experimented with nuclear fission prior to the war and whose talent Kurchatov admired, decided that copying the Nagasaki plutonium bomb was the shortest and most certain route. (With perhaps one or two exceptions, they were the only scientists involved who were permitted to read the intelligence information from Fuchs and Hall, and apparently from Koval as well. The other physicists and engineers thought that Kurchatov and Khariton were coming up with these ideas.)

Peter Kapitsa, then the best known internationally of the Soviet physicists, objected. Kapitsa had done research at that home of genius, the Cavendish Laboratory at Cambridge University, for thirteen years until he made the mistake of coming back to the Soviet Union for a visit in 1934 and Stalin blocked his return to England. He was to win the Nobel Prize for physics in 1978. Kapitsa was also privy to the intelligence information as a member of the supervisory Special Committee on the Atomic Bomb chaired by Beria. In letters to Stalin, he argued that mimicking the Americans would place too great a burden on the war-ravaged Soviet economy. Soviet physicists were perfectly capable of coming up with their own, cheaper bomb design and also of building it more quickly. Stalin did not trust his own physicists to better what their American counterparts had already achieved, he was not certain the path Kapitsa was proposing would be faster, and he did not give a damn about the expense.

In a January 1946 meeting with Kurchatov in the Kremlin, Stalin gave the back of his hand to Kapitsa's argument. "It was not worth engaging in small-scale work," he said, according to Kurchatov's notes, "but necessary to conduct the work broadly, with Russian scope." Speed was all that mattered. "It was not necessary to seek cheaper paths," Stalin emphasized. He also held out to the nuclear physicists and engineers the carrot of privileged living that he accorded those who were particularly useful to him. For a nation that supposedly celebrated the equality of its citizens, Stalin's Soviet Union had always been a society riven with inequality. Food, medical care, apartment space, clothing, and luxuries like imported goods were apportioned according to one's rank and position in the Party and the regime. The NKVD was especially pampered, with higher salaries, the best housing, and special shops and canteens. Now Stalin was proposing, if it succeeded, to similarly reward the nuclear weapons community. "Our state has suffered very much," he said to Kurchatov, "yet it is surely possible to ensure that several thousand people can live very well, and several thousand people better than very well, with their own dachas, so that they can relax, and with their own cars." But there was peril in this promise of privileges, because the beneficent emperor who awarded them was also a hangman who rewarded failure with death. In this lay the second explanation for copying the American bomb. Kurchatov and Khariton knew that if they and their colleagues performed the task of copying well, the bomb they produced would go off. If they struck out on their own and sought a different design and it fizzled, the senior physicists and engineers involved would be shot.

Given the nature of Stalin's state, it was logical as well that he appoint Lavrenti Beria head of the committee to oversee the building of his atomic bomb. Stalin had installed Beria, a fellow Georgian whom he had spotted during a trip to the Caucasus in 1931, as head of the NKVD in 1938 when he removed and had shot its previous chief, Nikolai Yezhov, who had carried out most of the Great Purge for him. A round-faced, balding man who wore a pince-nez, Beria was a sadist who sometimes personally tortured and shot his and Stalin's victims and had a penchant for young women that Stalin let him indulge. When he spotted a woman he wanted, he would send his aide to fetch her in one of the dreaded black limousines the NKVD employed to transport its victims to the Lubyanka. The number on which he forced himself ultimately ran into the hundreds. If the young woman refused him, the consequences for her and her family were invariably hideous. At the same time, he was a shrewd and effective administrator who handled a wide variety of projects for Stalin, assuming, correctly, that fear would energize everyone involved. Beria was Stalin's closest collaborator, with privileged access to him, and the NKVD was the keystone in the bureaucratic structure Stalin had fashioned. It secured his position through its ubiquitous network of surveillance and terror and also controlled one of the important economic resources of his state—the millions of prison laborers.

Hundreds of thousands of these labor camp inmates, called *zeks* in Russian slang, were now marshaled to create the atomic industry necessary for the bomb. They worked under a number of Beria's subordinates who had, over the years, become construction managers. Iakov

Rappoport, the man charged with laying out the roads and erecting the buildings for the first large-scale reactor and separation plant to produce plutonium at a secret site called Cheliabinsk-40, because it was located in the Urals northwest of the industrial city of Cheliabinsk, was an NKVD major general. Rappoport had received his initial construction management experience in the early 1930s helping to supervise the creation of the White Sea Canal, a horrendously brutal project in which tens of thousands of prison laborers had died. At Cheliabinsk-40, he was assigned 70,000 *zeks*.

Arzamas-16, the Soviet equivalent of Los Alamos where the bomb would actually be put together under the direction of Iulii Khariton, was also built by prison labor in the village of Sarov, about 250 miles east of Moscow. The site was chosen because it was isolated and on the edge of a large and beautiful forest reserve that allowed for expansion. (It drew its secret name from the city of Arzamas, about forty miles to the north.) The churches and living quarters of an Orthodox monastery closed by the Communists in the 1920s were still standing in the village. The monastery had been a famous one, dedicated to Saint Serafim of Sarov, who had been renowned for his asceticism and concern for the poor. The first laboratories were set up in the cells where the monks had once dwelt, while the prisoners built new laboratories and houses for the physicists and engineers and other technicians. Prison laborers were part of the social landscape of the Soviet Union and the privileged scientists had to get accustomed to seeing them every day. Lev Al'tshuler, a physicist who arrived at Arzamas-16 at the end of 1946, described the sight in an interview published more than forty years later, which David Holloway quotes in *Stalin and the Bomb*: "The columns of prisoners passing through the settlement in the morning on their way to work and returning to the zones [prison camps] in the evening were a reality that hit you in the eyes. Lermontov's lines came to mind, about 'a land of slaves, a land of masters.' "

More, an estimated 80,000 to 120,000, were consigned to the new uranium mines opened in Soviet Central Asia. Little is known of the conditions in those mines, but they were apparently appalling. Those who died were buried in communal graves. Some idea of the conditions can be obtained from those that were observed in the Soviet occupation zone in East Germany, where by 1950 the Russians had 150,000 to 200,000 conscripted German laborers toiling in newly opened uranium mines. Safety measures in these mines were nonexistent, there was no medical care, and the workers were housed in primitive barracks surrounded by barbed wire and guarded by NKVD troops. In what may have been the cruelest twist of all, there are no memoirs of the Soviet prison laborers whose bodies built the atomic industry, because only a few were released at the end of the penal labor terms to which they had originally been sentenced. To preserve the secrecy of the various installations of the atomic complex, once construction was completed Stalin had them shipped to the Gulag's worst camps, the gold mines of Kolyma in the Far East, where they died.

15.

A CONFRONTATION AND
A MISREADING

Looking back, it seems inevitable that there would be a confrontation as soon as the wartime alliance had shed its usefulness with the defeat of Germany and Japan. Even had Franklin Roosevelt lived, it appears doubtful that the policy of accommodation and cooperation he had hoped for could have been maintained, given Stalin's personality and the nature of his state. With Truman's distinctly differing outlook, relations could only deteriorate even more rapidly. The Soviets wanted to be rewarded for defeating Germany and for the price they had paid to do so. That price had been as appalling as the courage of the Soviet soldier had been extraordinary. For every American lost in the Second World War, approximately twenty-seven Soviet servicemen and women died: 11.285 million, including the 2.7 million who perished in German captivity. Because of the extent and nature of the conflict in the East, there are no reliable statistics for civilian deaths in the Soviet Union. What appears to be the most reasonable estimate places the combined military and civilian toll at about 28 million. A second estimate, probably excessive, speaks of nearly 50 million. The statistics are, however, quite clear on who played the major role in winning the war in Europe. Over the entire course of the conflict, Nazi Germany suffered combat losses of 13.6 million killed, wounded, missing, and captured. Of these, approximately 10 million, or about 73 percent, occurred on the Eastern Front.

Contrary to popular American belief, the turning point of the war in Europe was not the Allied landing in France on June 6, 1944, and the ensuing battle of Normandy. The turning point had taken place nearly a year and a half earlier and almost 2,000 miles to the east at Stalingrad on the Volga. There, between September 1942 and February 2, 1943, when the last German elements surrendered, the Red Army had stood and held on in desperate struggle amidst the ruins of the city, rallied, and then encircled and killed or captured, with the exception of 10,000 wounded flown out on Luftwaffe transports, the entire German Sixth Army of well over a quarter of a million men. The victory was a Russian accomplishment, achieved before American and British Lend-Lease supplies and equipment had reached the Red Army in quantity. From that day onward the retreat of the Wehrmacht from Russia had been inexorable, the somber, gray-clad German columns forced back in battle after battle. "The Tigers Are Burning," the headline of one Russian report exulted at the destruction of this most formidable of German tanks during the stupendous battle of Kursk in central Russia in July 1943, when Hitler sought to recoup by going back on the offensive. Instead, the Red Army defeated the Wehrmacht at its own game of firepower and maneuver and the Germans lost approximately 2,000 tanks, well over a thousand planes, and tens of thousands killed in a matter of days.

By the end of 1943, Soviet industry had also recovered to the point where Russia was outproducing Germany in tanks, including thousands of T-34s, universally acknowledged as the best medium tank of the war, and in tracked, or self-propelled, artillery, and other heavy weaponry and aircraft. By June 6, 1944, when the Allies were finally able to open a second front across the Normandy beaches, the Red Army had pushed the Germans out of most of European Russia and was approaching the Polish frontier. Without Normandy the Soviets would have had to fight their way to Hitler's bunker at an even higher cost in blood, but Normandy or no Normandy, the Russians were going to Berlin.

And without Stalingrad and its aftermath, the invasion across the English Channel and the ensuing battle for Normandy would have been far costlier in American, British, and Canadian lives. During that year-and-a-half interval, the Soviets had torn the vitals out of the German army. There were excellent German infantry and panzer divisions in France and they would show their mettle by fighting tenaciously, but taken as a whole the German forces facing the Americans, British, and Canadians were a shadow of the mighty Wehrmacht that had stormed across the Soviet frontier. The savaging in Russia was apparent even in some of the panzer divisions, which lacked their full complement of armor, deploying less than a hundred tanks each, about half what they would face in an armored division of their Allied opponents. A number of the infantry divisions were also second-rate. Six were composed of underage and only partially trained recruits, two more were scrambled together from Luftwaffe ground crews no longer needed in Hermann Göring's shrinking air force, and others were manned by older conscripts (the average age was thirty-seven) organized into static formations considered fit only to garrison trenches and strongpoints along the coast until they were wiped out or relieved. An indication of how desperate the bleeding in Russia had made the Germans for manpower was that 60,000 of the support troops for these overage divisions were Soviet prisoners of war who had volunteered for German service (and been accepted despite being *Untermenschen*!) to avoid slave labor and starvation.

Whether Truman understood any of this is doubtful. Most Americans then and now see the Normandy landing as the decisive event of the war in Europe. If Truman did understand, he certainly did not act as if Soviet casualties concerned him. He viewed the Red Army as a potential threat rather than as a savior of American lives. Stalin and Molotov had hoped for a multibillion-dollar reconstruction loan from the United States after the war. The hope was quickly abandoned in the cooling atmosphere that followed the victory.

The confrontation was also inevitable because both sides were ignorant of or misunderstood the real motivations of the other. A move by one side was invariably misinterpreted by the other. Matters were thus constantly made worse and the animosity rapidly darkened into that long night the world was to call the Cold War. Since the opening of many of the Soviet archives in the wake of the collapse of the Soviet Union in 1991, and the sifting of them by young and open-minded Russian historians like Vladislav Zubok and Constantine Pleshakov, we can discern at last how Stalin actually viewed the world and the true motivations behind his acts.

The most important misreading of him by the Truman administration, the evidence shows, was that while he was a monster, he was not an expansionist monster in the likeness of Hitler. The people threatened by his paranoiac personality were the inhabitants of the Soviet Union and the populations of the East European lands he had placed within his baleful rule by the defeat of Germany, not normally those beyond. Stalin assumed that the post–Second World War period would see a multipolar world resembling that of the interwar years of the 1920s and 1930s. Germany and Japan, he thought, would rise from their rubble during that interregnum to one day become military powers to be reckoned with again. He was also enough of a Marxist-Leninist ideologue to be convinced that capitalist nations like the United States and Britain would fall out with one another in rivalry over markets and imperial possessions (he and Molotov were always hopefully scanning the intelligence reports for rifts between the British and the Americans) and that eventually there would be a Third World War into which the Soviet Union would be drawn as it had been drawn into the Second World War. When that Third World War had ended, Communism, in some unspecified fashion, would triumph throughout the world. His task was to keep the Soviet Union powerful enough to survive and surmount any of these challenges as they arose.

His imperial ambitions were limited. With some exceptions, they were essentially confined to consolidating Moscow's hold over its newly gained security corridor, the occupied nations of Eastern Europe. This was understandable enough, as they had been the invasion route into Russia in two wars in the twentieth century and two of those East European nations, Romania and Hungary, had enthusiastically joined Hitler in his invasion on the promise of capacious segments of Russian territory. In Asia, he wanted to recover the imperial concessions Russia had held under the czars in Manchuria and, with the approval of Roosevelt and Churchill, had wrung them from Chiang Kai-shek's Nationalist government, only to have to give them up a few years later to Mao Tse-tung, the Communist victor in the Chinese civil war. He also wanted to retrieve Russian possession of the southern half of Sakhalin Island off the coast of Siberia north of Japan, which had been lost to Tokyo in the Russo-Japanese War of 1904–05, and, again with the assent of Roosevelt and Churchill, got it on the surrender of Japan. In the Middle East, he wanted to reestablish the pre–First World War czarist dominance of northern Iran and he coveted, as the czars had, the Turkish Straits—the Dardanelles and the Bosporus. These lead from the Mediterranean into the Black Sea, control of which was obviously vital to Russia's security. While he meant to manipulate the large Communist parties in Italy and France in order to weaken and hinder U.S. influence in those and neighboring countries, he had no intention of provoking a war with the United States by invading Western Europe.

George Kennan, who spoke Russian and was, along with Charles "Chip" Bohlen, Roosevelt's interpreter at Yalta, one of the two leading specialists on the Soviet Union within the State Department, cast this misreading of Stalin and the nature of his state into dogma as early as February 1946. Kennan was chargé d'affaires of the U.S. embassy in Moscow at the time. On February 9, 1946, Stalin gave his first major speech since the end of hostilities the year before. He called for a return in economic development to the prewar emphasis on heavy industry through three new and successive five-year plans. The speech caused concern within the administration in Washington, because the emphasis on heavy industry was regarded as an ominous sign of military preparations. In fact, Stalin intended no menace toward the United States in the speech. Indeed, he was careful to praise "the anti-Fascist coalition of the Soviet Union, the United States of America, Great Britain and other freedom-loving countries" that had won the Second World War. He was setting a course to strengthen the Soviet Union to weather the long interregnum that he foresaw in the postwar period and to prepare the country for the contingency of a Third World War in which he thought that interregnum would end. Kennan was asked by Washington to provide an "interpretive analysis" of the speech and what it portended. His response, as Daniel Yergin, the American historian, noted in his study of the Cold War, *Shattered Peace: The Origins of the Cold War and the National Security State,* was aptly named the Long Telegram because it was, at 5,500 words, up to that point probably the longest telegram ever sent in the U.S. diplomatic service. It laid down the doctrinal basis for the hemming in of Soviet power that was to become the U.S. policy of containment.

Kennan's analysis did not reflect the reality of the Soviet Union or of Stalin. Rather, it reflected Kennan's ideological antipathy to both and confused the Marxist-Leninist rhetoric trotted out for ritual occasions with the actual reasoning that lay behind Soviet moves. The Long Telegram was, in a way, evidence of how difficult it was for a foreigner, even one who spoke the language and was as familiar with the Soviet Union as Kennan was, to penetrate beyond the facade of Stalin's closed society. In Kennan's view, Stalin was a fanatical revolutionary, not the complex mixture of genuine Marxist faith, cynicism, Realpolitik calculation, and suspicion and cruelty that history has shown him to be.

The Soviet attitude toward the outside world was not shaped by an "objective analysis of situation beyond Russia's borders," Kennan telegraphed. "At bottom of Kremlin's neurotic view of world affairs is traditional and instinctive Russian sense of insecurity." As a result, Stalin and his associates in the leadership were permanently engaged "in patient but deadly struggle for total destruction of rival power, never in compacts and compromises with it." Marxist dogma reinforced this behavior. The "basic Soviet instinct" was "that there can be no compromise with rival power and the constructive work can start only when Communist power is dominant." In short, coexistence between the United States and the Soviet Union was impossible. "We have here a political force committed fanatically to the belief that with US there can be no permanent modus vivendi, that it is desirable and necessary that the internal harmony of our society be disrupted, our traditional way of life destroyed, the international authority of our state be broken if Soviet power is to be secure." The way to counteract this force, Kennan suggested, was for the United States to draw the Western nations together and systematically block all attempts at Soviet expansion. "Impervious to logic of reason, [the Soviet Union] is highly sensitive to logic of force. For this reason it can easily withdraw—and usually does—when strong resistance is encountered at any point." This last observation was well taken, but it resulted from the caution Stalin frequently exercised in the conduct of foreign policy, from conscious reasoning, not from some auto-neurotic instinct of an ideologically driven power elite.

Preventing further expansion of the Soviet Union was sound policy for the United States to follow in the postwar era, but not from motives of fantasy and in an atmosphere of fear and irrationality that could bring excesses of its own. The idea that a man as respectful of American power as Stalin was would commit his badly wounded nation to a venture as foolhardy as the attempted destruction of the United States was ludicrous, but that is what many men in Washington wanted to hear. Having just triumphed over the expansionist monster Hitler and the forces of Imperial Japan, they seemed, unconsciously, to be seeking a new monster with whom to do mortal combat. The perception of Communism as some sort of international social contagion that could, by almost biological means, infect and destroy society was also widespread in the United States. If Russia was a society with a profound sense of insecurity, as Kennan maintained, America was equally so.

Kennan's Long Telegram was not only the longest in the history of the U.S. Foreign Service, it was also the most enthusiastically welcomed and widely read. H. Freeman Matthews, director of the State Department's Office of European Affairs, who had requested the analysis, telegraphed Kennan that it was "magnificent," saying, "I cannot overestimate its importance to those of us here struggling with the problem." Copies were sent to U.S. diplomatic missions around the world and distributed among the leadership in Washington. James Forrestal, the fiercely anti-Communist secretary of the Navy, soon to become the nation's first secretary of defense with the creation of the Defense Department under the National Security Act of 1947, had hundreds of copies made for circulation within the Navy and, according to an acquaintance, "sent it all over town." It was also leaked to the press to prepare the public for a change, the American people having heard little during the war years except praise for their gallant Soviet ally. *Time,* the magazine of another fervent anti-Communist, Henry Luce, carried a full-page article illustrated by a map entitled "Communist Contagion." The map labeled Iran, Turkey, and Manchuria as "infected" and Saudi Arabia, Egypt, Afghanistan, and India as "exposed." The Long Telegram was also the making of George Kennan. He returned to Washington not long afterward and in April 1947 was made the first chief of the new Policy Planning Staff of the State Department.

From that time on, every move by Stalin was interpreted in the blackest perspective, an attitude his bullying manner and frequently bad judgment did nothing to mitigate. He had shown how bad his judgment in foreign affairs could sometimes be during the first postwar meeting of the Council of Foreign Ministers in London in September 1945, held to decide the question of German reparations to the Soviet Union and the future status of the conquered Reich. This was the conference at which Jimmie Byrnes sought to intimidate the Soviets with the atomic diplomacy scheme that he and Truman had conjured up, quipping pointedly to Molotov, who was representing the Soviet Union at the conference, about the atomic bomb he was going to pull out of his hip pocket. Stalin and Molotov had anticipated the strategy before Molotov left Moscow and had decided how to parry. Molotov proceeded to do so, mocking the American atomic monopoly, belittling the importance of nuclear weapons in general, and clinging stubbornly to irreconcilable positions on the issues the ministers were supposed to negotiate. He was living up to the Party pseudonym he had adopted during the Bolshevik Revolution: Molotov means "Hammer Man" in Russian. (His family surname was Skryabin.) Byrnes had the wit to see that atomic diplomacy was not going to play with the Soviets and after a number of fruitless days privately suggested to Molotov that they get down to business and negotiate a treaty that would keep Germany disarmed for the next twenty to twenty-five years. Molotov cabled Stalin for permission to proceed. Stalin told him to let the conference fail, that Byrnes, and thus the United States, would be blamed in international opinion. The opposite turned out to be the case. The Soviets were blamed because of Molotov's obduracy and Stalin missed his one and only opportunity to keep Germany from rearming.

The initial crisis with the United States occurred over Iran. Prior to the First World War, czarist Russia and Britain had divided Iran between them, with the Russians exercising a sphere of dominance over the north and the British over the south because of the Royal Navy's interest in the huge oil reserves there. A pro forma Iranian government continued to exist in Tehran under the enfeebled Qajar dynasty. The Iranian soldier who replaced the Qajars and declared himself shah in the interwar period, Reza Pahlevi, was a modernist and reformer in his domestic policy, but pro-German in foreign policy. In the wake of Hitler's Operation Barbarossa in 1941, Britain and the Soviet Union had therefore invaded the country to establish a land line of supply to Russia, similarly dividing it north and south. Both nations were supposed to withdraw their troops by March 2, 1946, and turn the country over to a new Iranian government, but Stalin, in the hope of regaining the czarist position, gave every sign of hanging on. He sponsored a separatist regime of Iranian Azerbaijanis, the Turkic people who inhabit the north, and protected it with the Soviet occupation troops.

Oil was the prize. The Soviets assumed that, since Iranian Azerbaijan lies just below Soviet Azerbaijan with its ever-flowing fields at Baku, the Iranian region must hold plentiful resources as well. The United States also had its eye on Iranian oil concessions for American companies. Forrestal and others were worried that the United States was consuming its own reserves with sufficient rapidity that it would become dependent on imported oil in the not distant future. Truman saw Stalin's northern Iran ploy as part of a far bigger scheme of expansion. He feared that if Soviet forces remained permanently entrenched in the north, the Soviets would soon take over the entire country and then threaten the even richer oil reserves the United States coveted in neighboring Saudi Arabia, where the Arabian American Oil Company (Aramco) had held the concession since 1933. The oil motive was never mentioned publicly during the crisis, however. Nor was the influence Washington's London ally continued to exercise in southern Iran through the large, British-owned Anglo-Iranian Oil Company. Instead, the administration hammered away at Soviet "aggression," and insisted on a full airing in the Security Council of the just established United Nations. The crisis became so heated on the American side that at one point Truman told Averell Harriman, who had returned from his wartime tenure as ambassador in Moscow, that "this may lead to war." A resentful Stalin backed down, withdrew his troops in the spring of 1946, and the separatist regime in Iranian Azerbaijan collapsed.

The Turkish Straits, the Dardanelles and the Bosporus, were next. The lengthy passage of the Dardanelles from the Mediterranean into the diminutive Sea of Marmara and the exit from the Marmara into the Black Sea through the short strait of the Bosporus at Istanbul had been an irritant and source of vulnerability for Russia far back into czarist times. The British and French expedition that had laid siege to and subsequently captured the Russian Black Sea naval base at Sevastopol in the Crimea during the Crimean War of 1853–56 had gained entry through the Straits. During the First World War, when Turkey had been allied with Germany, German battleships had used the Straits for raiding forays into the Black Sea. During the Second World War, Turkey had officially been neutral, but had followed its traditional anti-Russian and pro-German proclivity and again allowed the German navy to sail freely through the Straits, this time to inflict considerable damage on the Soviet Union. The issue went beyond the vulnerability of the Black Sea area. Stalin, as had the czars, wanted unhindered access to the Mediterranean for his own navy, although at the time it was just a coastal defense force with no plans for a seagoing fleet.

At Yalta in February 1945, Stalin had said it was intolerable for Turkey to have "a hand on Russia's throat" and denounced the Montreux Convention, the international agreement of 1936 that essentially gave Turkey control over the Straits. Roosevelt and Churchill had agreed that a revision was in order, but Stalin failed to take advantage of the moment to bargain then and there for precisely what he wanted. Instead, he clumsily instructed Molotov in June 1945 to demand a lease from Turkey for a Soviet base in the Straits and the return of two Turkish districts, once conquered by the czars, that Lenin had ceded to Turkey in 1922 when a weak Soviet Union was seeking tranquillity on its southern borders. (The territorial claim was probably just a bargaining gambit, as Stalin later dropped it.) The Turks refused, but Stalin pressed on, apparently assuming that the assent he had received from Roosevelt and Churchill at Yalta still held in Washington and London. In March 1946, he massed a few dozen tanks on the border and in August raised his demand to joint Soviet-Turkish custodianship of the Straits. He was attempting to intimidate the Turks. There is no evidence he intended to actually invade the country.

He does not seem to have understood how profoundly the attitude toward the Soviet Union had changed in Washington and thus the significance of what he was inadvertently provoking—the first show of armed force by the United States against Russia. As early as the end of 1945, Truman was convinced that if Stalin was not deterred, he would invade Turkey and seize the Straits and the United States would have to go to war against the Soviet Union. "Unless Russia is faced with an iron fist and strong language another war is in the making," he told Jimmie Byrnes. As the crisis worsened into August 1946, with the

Americans urging the Turks to defy Stalin, Dean Acheson, the under-secretary of state, convened a study group with the military leadership to recommend a course of action to the president.

The group's report was presented to Truman in an August 15 meeting at the White House. The finding was the first statement of the domino theory that was to so govern and oversimplify and distort American thinking during the Cold War. If Stalin acquired joint control of the Straits, Soviet control of Turkey would inevitably follow. It would then "be extremely difficult, if not impossible, to prevent the Soviet Union from obtaining control over Greece and over the whole Near and Middle East." The recommendation was to send a naval task force to the Dardanelles as a display of American resolve to protect Turkey. Forrestal had assembled a force of five destroyers, two cruisers, the new aircraft carrier USS *Franklin D. Roosevelt,* and the battleship USS *Missouri,* on which, just one year before, the representatives of a defeated Japan had signed the documents of unconditional surrender. Dwight Eisenhower, then chief of staff of the Army, asked Acheson in a whisper if the president understood that the course they were recommending could lead to war. Acheson repeated the question to Truman. The president took a large map of the Middle East and the eastern Mediterranean from his desk drawer and asked those present to gather around him. Spreading out the map, he explained precisely why the falling dominoes finding of the study group was correct. The naval task force, led by the majestic *Missouri* with her sixteen-inch guns, was dispatched to the Dardanelles, and Stalin, still more resentful, again backed down.

16.

CONTAINING THE MENACE

The Turkish crisis was the watershed. Having summoned up the nerve for confrontation once, it was much easier on the second occasion. The British precipitated the next crisis and a policy consensus that had been gradually taking shape in Washington. Under a tactic division of tasks, Britain was supposed to watch over its traditional sphere of influence in the eastern Mediterranean. Virtually bankrupt, the London government suddenly informed the U.S. administration on February 21, 1947, that it was withdrawing from Greece because it could no longer afford to prop up the right-wing government in Athens that was battling Communist-led guerrillas in a civil war. The British also warned that they would be unable to supply the funds Turkey needed for economic and military assistance to buttress itself against the Soviet Union. The response of Dean Acheson, his new superior, General George C. Marshall, now secretary of state, and the president was that the United States would obviously have to step into Britain's place. At a meeting of the congressional leadership, which Truman convened to persuade them to vote the hundreds of millions of dollars he would need, Marshall gave a rather bland presentation that failed to arouse any enthusiasm. With the permission of the general, Acheson stood up to speak.

At fifty-three years of age, Dean Gooderham Acheson, who was to exercise a commanding influence on American foreign policy in the postwar years, was a handsome, commanding figure. His broad-shouldered, six-foot, two-inch frame was elegant in the three-piece suits he favored. His intense eyes were set off by bushy brows and complemented by an equally bushy but always impeccably trimmed mustache turned up at the corners in the fashion of a British officer of the nineteenth century. He was an American statesman and he was also the Anglophile he looked. His father, the Episcopal bishop of Connecticut, was of Scottish and Irish descent and had immigrated to Canada and been educated there at a time when English Canada prided itself on being part of the British Empire. His mother, of similar background, had been shipped off as a girl to be educated in England. At the age of twelve, Acheson had been sent from the family's home in Middletown, Connecticut, to the Groton School when the place was a conscious replica of an English boys school. (Sophomore year, for example, was not sophomore year. It was "the fourth form.") To his credit, Acheson, an outspoken, free-spirited man, had rebelled against the rigid discipline of the school, yet more of Groton had probably rubbed off on him than he was aware. He had frittered away his four undergraduate years at Yale as a campus socialite, getting by with Cs (called "gentleman's grades" in those years), but then the challenge of the law had turned on the engine of his quick and agile mind at Harvard Law School. He had become a protégé of that superlative jurist Felix Frankfurter, then teaching at Harvard, and upon graduation Frankfurter had arranged for him to go to Washington and clerk for another extraordinary jurist with whom Frankfurter was to serve on the Supreme Court, Justice Louis Brandeis.

With the First World War and the growing importance of the federal government, Washington was slowly metamorphosing from a town into a city, and so Acheson had stayed. A highly successful career as an appellate attorney and the prosperity of early partnership in a leading Washington firm followed. Neither was enough for him. Groton had held out an ideal to its boys, public service, an ideal that also happens to attract the kind of man who is drawn by power, who will forsake money and much else for the opportunity to wield authority and take satisfaction from the accomplishments that go with it. In 1941 Acheson had, at the instigation of Franklin Roosevelt, become assistant secretary of state for economic affairs, performing adroitly in helping to create the International Monetary Fund at the Bretton Woods monetary conference of 1944, and then accepted the undersecretaryship of the State Department at the behest of Truman and Byrnes on the death of Roosevelt. His influence had increased after George Marshall had taken over from Byrnes because Marshall, in an adaption of the military line of authority, had insisted that Acheson act as his combined chief of staff and deputy.

A man of no little arrogance, Acheson considered himself highly sophisticated in foreign affairs. Others, including the congressional leaders who were his audience on this fateful day in early 1947, thought the same. This was true where Europe was concerned, but once Acheson got out of Europe, and particularly where Communism and the Soviet Union were involved, he was an intellectual primitive.

At this meeting of the congressional leadership, he was the primitive who flashed fear to these legislators, partly as the shrewd lawyer's tactic to convince, but also because he believed what he was saying. Over the past eighteen months, he said, Soviet pressure on Iran, the Turkish Straits, and now northern Greece, where the guerrillas were strongest, had brought Moscow to the point where it might break through and penetrate three continents. If Greece fell, "like apples in a barrel infected by one rotten one, the corruption of Greece would infect Iran and all to the east. It would also carry infection to Africa through Asia Minor and Egypt, and to Europe through Italy and France, already threatened by the strongest domestic Communist parties." Not since Rome and Carthage had the world been so polarized between two powers, Acheson said. This was not a matter of picking up England's debts, or of being kind to Greece and Turkey. It was the fortifying of free peoples against Communist aggression and thus the safeguarding of America's own security.

(Truman, Marshall, Acheson, the congressional leaders at the meeting, and everyone else in Washington had no way of knowing that Stalin was not backing the Communist-led guerrillas in Greece. In 1944, in a cynical agreement with Churchill dividing up Eastern Europe, he had promised Britain a free hand in Greece because he did not regard the Greek Communist cause of sufficient importance to Soviet interests to warrant the trouble with his former allies that was now, in fact, being aroused. Tito, the Yugoslav leader, was sustaining the Greek guerrillas in defiance of Stalin because he did not want a right-wing Greece on his southern border. He was later to change his mind and abandon them to defeat. The dispute was the first in an increasingly bitter process of estrangement between Tito and Stalin that led to their open break in 1948.)

After a long silence that followed Acheson's exhortation, Senator Arthur Vandenberg of Michigan, the Republican chairman of the Committee on Foreign Relations, told the president that if Truman spoke like this to Congress and the country, the House and Senate would vote him the money. Truman did so in a dramatic, if less hyperbolical, speech, drafted by Acheson, to a joint session of Congress on March 12, 1947. He asked for, and got, $300 million in military and economic aid for Greece (a military advisory mission was to be sent to reform and reequip the Greek army and direct it in a counterguerrilla campaign) and $100 million for Turkey. The president summed up his speech with a call to action that was henceforth to be known as the Truman Doctrine. "I believe," he said, "that it must be the policy of the United States to support free peoples who are resisting attempted subjugation by armed minorities or by outside pressures." There was no need for him to define who these armed minorities and outside pressures were. What was significant about the statement was its universal application. The president's pledge was not confined to Greece and Turkey. He was declaring that the United States would come to the aid of any nation, anywhere, that was threatened by Communism.

What Truman and Acheson and others in the American leadership who thought like them were doing was laying down the moral and intellectual foundation for a new American world system. Acheson reflected their thoughts (and his ego) in the title of his memoirs, *Present at the Creation,* and in its dedication, "To Harry S. Truman, 'The captain with the mighty heart.' " The appeasement policy of Neville Chamberlain, the British prime minister who had, with the assent of the French, delivered Czechoslovakia to Hitler at Munich in 1938, was always in the back of their minds. Now that it was their turn to lead, they were not, like the Europeans, going to lose the peace gained by their victory over Nazi Germany and Imperial Japan through similarly weak behavior toward Stalin and the forces of "International Communism."

Acheson had in his cultural heritage the stabilizing model of the British Empire when the Royal Navy had dominated the seas and "Pax Britannica" had ruled nearly a quarter of the earth's landmass and peoples. The "Pax Americana" that he and Truman and their associates intended to create was not, however, going to be an exploitative system akin to British and European colonialism. Outright colonies were unacceptable to the American political conscience. The one formal colony the United States had possessed, the Philippines, wrested from Spain at the turn of the twentieth century, had been given its independence in 1945. What the United States sought were surrogate governments friendly to American power, free to run their internal affairs as they wished as long as they agreed with Washington in matters of foreign policy. The goal was to contain Communism worldwide by forming as many non-Communist countries as could be persuaded into a system of nations protected by American military might and nourished by American economic and technological prowess.

With a policy consensus reached, the pace quickened. The winter of 1946–47 was a grim season in Europe, a postwar nadir. The economies of Britain, France, and Italy were crippled by inflation, strikes, and worn-out manufacturing equipment. The German population was barely surviving on foodstuffs shipped in by Britain and the United States. To make matters worse, the winter was one of the coldest on record, consuming supplies of coal and power. George Marshall went to Moscow in March 1947 for another meeting of the Council of Foreign Ministers, the venue that had originally been created to negotiate a postwar settlement. The conference quickly stymied over the ever-present and never resolved issue of German reparations to the Soviet Union. Roosevelt had agreed at Yalta that the Germans should be forced to pay $10 billion in reparations for the ruination they had caused in Russia. The British had always been opposed because they assumed that a bricks-and-cinders Germany would never be able to meet the burden and that it would be shifted to them to keep the Germans from starving. The American position also gradually changed to one of opposition after Truman inherited the presidency. By 1947, no matter how persistently Molotov might read off the list of devastated Russian towns and cities, no one in Washington or London wanted to do anything to strengthen the Soviet Union.

When Marshall went to see Stalin shortly before returning home, he noticed how markedly the Soviet dictator had aged—he seemed to have shrunk in his clothes. Stalin said there was no reason to give up trying to resolve such issues as reparations. Difficult matters required time and patience. The evidence indicates that Stalin meant what he was saying, that he hoped to hang on and one day obtain the reparations. Marshall, however, interpreted Stalin's admonition for patience as a ruse. While the United States patiently temporized, conditions in Western Europe might deteriorate to the point where a miserable and disillusioned electorate would vote the local Communist parties, particularly large in France and Italy, into power. And whether or not Stalin was attempting to gull him, Marshall was probably correct in his judgment of where Western Europe was headed. On the way back to Washington, he decided that something drastic had to be done. Acheson had been thinking along the same lines.

That something was the stroke of genius and statesmanship that became known as the Marshall Plan. The United States proposed to donate billions of dollars, $13 billion in all as it turned out, to rebuild completely the economies of Europe and create an environment in which capitalism would thrive. Marshall announced the plan in a speech at the Harvard University commencement on June 5, 1947. To appear evenhanded, he invited all European nations to participate, implicitly including the Soviet Union. He and others in the administration were reasonably certain that Stalin would refuse the offer, because he would reject permitting American engineers and other specialists to move freely about the Soviet Union supervising the projects to make certain the aid was being properly utilized.

Stalin reacted with extreme alarm. He saw the plan as a declaration of economic warfare to undermine his East European security corridor. The command economy he had fashioned was useless in these circumstances. There was no way he could gather sufficient resources to compete with reconstruction on an American scale. His fear for his empire was confirmed when the coalition government in Czechoslovakia, dominated by the big Communist Party under Klement Gottwald, the prime minister, decided that it would take part. The Poles under Wladyslaw Gomulka, the Party general secretary, were willing to join as well. Gomulka was attempting to navigate an independent course, a "Polish way to socialism." This would entail no collectivization of agriculture and freedom for small entrepreneurs to continue to do business. He also needed American largesse to rebuild his wrecked country. (Eighty percent of Warsaw was still in ruins in 1947 and 30,000 Jewish corpses awaited proper burial under the rubble of the Warsaw Ghetto.) Gomulka quickly backed off at Stalin's displeasure, but the Czechs had already announced that they would accept. Stalin summoned Gottwald and Jan Masaryk, the non-Communist foreign minister and son of Thomas Masaryk, the principal founder and first president of the Czechoslovak republic, to the Kremlin and angrily ordered them to reverse course publicly and renounce participation.

The Marshall Plan was a colossal success in Western Europe, an act of generosity, if also self-interest, that was without precedent in history. Entire factories were shipped over from the United States and reassembled in place. The price was to divide Europe into two hostile blocs. The "Iron Curtain" that Winston Churchill had first denounced in his speech at Fulton, Missouri, in early 1946 was now truly rung down by Stalin all along the perimeter of Eastern Europe. As he aged, the Soviet dictator seemed to grow more paranoid. The remnants of the coalition regimes he had permitted in Eastern Europe as facades to please his former wartime allies were swept away. Beria's secret police terrorized non-Communist politicians. Any Communist figures in Eastern Europe suspected of deviating from the Moscow line were also eliminated as Stalin's minions arrested, tortured, shot, and hanged.

Gomulka was to be purged for the sin of "national Communism," but he escaped with his life. The curtain also came down on the precarious neutrality that the non-Communist Czech political groups had been attempting to preserve because of the exposed geographical position of their country, which shared borders with the USSR, Poland, Hungary, and the Soviet occupation zone in eastern Germany. Stalin encouraged the Czech Communists to take full power in February 1948. The takeover was facilitated by the Czech Party's wide public support. The Czech people remembered how Britain and France had delivered them to Hitler at Munich and tended to look to the Soviet Union as a protector. That did not spare Czechoslovakia from Stalin's terror. Jan Masaryk was not as fortunate as Gomulka. The story put out by the regime was that he committed suicide by leaping from a small bathroom window in his living quarters in an upper story of the Foreign Ministry. The probable truth is that he was first murdered and then thrown out the window. In 1952, Czechoslovakia was also to experience one of the worst of the show trials Stalin had a penchant for arranging, with their macabre stagecraft of preposterous accusations of spying and plotting and false confessions elicited by torture. Eleven leading Czech Communists, including the Party's general secretary, Rudolf Slansky, were among those condemned and hanged.

17.

NEITHER RAIN, NOR SNOW, NOR SLEET, NOR FOG

After so many fruitless negotiating sessions over reparations, the administration was now prepared to settle the "German question" by merging the American, British, and French occupation zones into a separate West German state. (The city of Berlin, 110 miles inside the Soviet occupation zone, was separately divided into American, British, French, and Russian sectors.) This would unilaterally abrogate the agreement with the Soviet Union that postwar Germany would be governed by all the victorious powers under general policy direction set by a four-power Control Council. As early as 1946, General Lucius Clay, the U.S. military governor in Germany, had persuaded his British counterpart to merge the economies of their two zones into an entity called Bizonia, but it had been difficult to proceed further toward a unified West German state. The French had been the principal obstacle, as memories of the Nazi conquest were still so raw and fear of German revanchism rife. Other West European countries that had listened to the crunch of German jackboots had also made known their objections. The Marshall Plan helped to remove this opposition. Washington was able to persuade the French and other holdouts that the danger of German resurgence could be controlled by integrating the new German state into the larger European economy. The administration also assuaged French fears by promising to keep U.S. troops in Germany indefinitely as protection against both a renewed threat of German militarism and an aggressive Soviet Union.

At the beginning of June 1948, a conference in London agreed that a German constituent assembly would convene in Bonn that September. The assembly's task would be to write a constitution for a West German state that would be composed of the American, British, and French occupation zones. To begin lifting the Germans out of their economic misery, the process was to start with a currency reform in the western zones—the substitution of a new deutsche mark for the old reichsmark, which inflation had rendered virtually worthless. Clay rebuffed or ignored inquiries and objections to this and other moves by Marshal Vasily Sokolovsky, his Soviet counterpart and Moscow's representative on the Control Council. At Clay's direction, the new currency had already been printed and stored for distribution by the end of 1947.

On June 18, 1948, the American, British, and French authorities announced the currency reform, five days later extending it to their sectors in West Berlin. Stalin was now being confronted with the emergence of a revived German state, in his mind a precursor to the rearmed Germany that he dreaded. On June 24, 1948, the day after the extension of the currency reform to the western sectors of the city, the Soviets, citing vague technical problems, blockaded all road and rail lines into Berlin across the 110 miles of their occupation zone.

Since the Luftwaffe had tried and failed to adequately supply the 270,000 men of the German Sixth Army inside the Stalingrad pocket, Stalin was convinced that, once the rigors of the German winter began, the Americans would never be able to fly in enough food and coal to keep the approximately 2 million people in the western sectors of the city from starving and freezing. Stalin believed he could use land access to Berlin as a bargaining lever to block the creation of the new West German state. Clay wanted to call what he regarded as a Soviet bluff and force open the land routes with an armed convoy. Truman forbade it for fear of precipitating a war. There had never been any written agreement on what constituted the land lines to Berlin through the Soviet zone. They had been established by custom. But there were specific written accords on the three air corridors into the city.

Clay turned to Curtis LeMay, that Cromwellian wielder of bombers who had leveled Japan's cities, now a lieutenant general commanding the U.S. Air Force in Europe, to accomplish what no air force had ever done before. LeMay had anticipated a blockade and when the Soviets closed the land routes on June 24 was ready to begin flying eighty tons of supplies a day into Berlin with the workhorse transports of the Second World War, the C-47 Dakotas that comprised his troop carrier squadrons. Meanwhile, the Teletypes clattered out orders and the newly independent U.S. Air Force and the other services mobilized to back him. The Tactical Air Command and the Military Air Transport Service scoured the United States and Alaska and the Caribbean for more C-47s and the newer four-engine C-54s, which could carry three times as much cargo. The Air Force's airlift specialist, Major General William H. Tunner, who had supervised the flying of supplies from India over the Himalayas to the Chinese Nationalists during the Second World War—over the Hump, as the pilots had named those forbidding mountains—was ordered to Germany to set up a special task force headquarters and conquer this new challenge. The British joined in and LeMay persuaded them to integrate their transports under Tunner, who acquired a Royal Air Force deputy.

Navy tankers ferried across the Atlantic the many additional tons of aviation gasoline required. The trucks of the Army Transportation Corps formed a relay hauling sustenance for Berlin from the ships unloading at Bremerhaven to Wiesbaden and Rhein-Main and the other airfields that were the loading points. The Army Corps of Engineers improved and maintained the runways at the two existing airfields in Berlin, Tempelhof in the American sector and Gatow in the British one, and built a third at Tegel in the French zone. To keep the planes in the air, flocks of military and civilian mechanics were mustered for around-the-clock maintenance depots in Germany and England. Because men tire before aircraft do, relief pilots and crews were dispatched to Germany so that the planes could be flown in consecutive shifts. Tunner soon had a stream of transports moving back and forth along the air corridors to Berlin twenty-four hours a day, landing, unloading, taking off to return to an airfield in the west, and then loading once more for Berlin. By December, the airlift was supplying 4,500 tons a day, 500 tons more than the city's minimum requirement, the biggest portion bulky coal for heating, and the tonnage continued to rise despite the closing in of the German winter.

As Schriever remarked, it was Hap Arnold's technological vision that provided the edge to defeat the blockade. The all-weather air force he had told Bennie he wanted in 1938 had finally come to pass. Arnold had encouraged advances in ground control radar during the Second World War and by the end of the conflict the system had reached near perfection. Whether in day or at night, whether in snow or sleet or rain, the controllers at the Berlin air traffic center would pick out a plane on their radar when it reached the point where it was supposed to start its descent and then talk the pilot down a glide path, giving him heading, airspeed, and rate of descent until the aircraft finally broke out over the illuminated runway. Only fog so dense that it reduced visibility to close to zero forced the cancellation of flights. Throughout that winter the controllers brought in a transport every three minutes. The pilot had one opportunity to land. If he or his co-pilot somehow muffed the controller's instructions and he had to climb back up again, he returned to his airfield of origin and reentered the stream of aircraft once more. Tunner permitted no interruptions. The airlift's accident rate averaged less than half that of the Air Force as a whole, but besting the blockade nevertheless cost lives—a total of thirty pilots and crew members and one civilian in twelve crashes.

Soviet aircraft occasionally appeared in the designated corridors, but there was no serious harassment of the transports, because Stalin apparently decided this would be interpreted as an act of war. Truman reinforced that impression with a show of force by sending sixty B-29s to England in July 1948 and more B-29s and a group of the Air Force's first operational jet fighters, the F-80, to Germany. The bombers were a bluff. Although by now the U.S. nuclear arsenal had grown to about fifty atomic bombs of the Nagasaki type, none of these B-29s was equipped to carry them.

The Berlin Airlift was high drama, an extraordinary achievement that riveted the attention of the West. There was no need to speak of the courage and dedication of the pilots and aircrews. The news films of the transports coming in over the rooftops in the falling snow, as these men held steady course for a runway they could not see, spoke for them. Then there were the grateful Berliners, men and women, unloading the sacks of coal and crates of foodstuffs alongside the American and British and French soldiers who had not long ago been their enemies, and the films of the children cheering and waving at the pilots who tossed them candy. It was heady and emotional and more powerful anti-Communist propaganda than anyone in Washington could have imagined. The blockade and the airlift turned many who were undecided among the peoples of Europe against the Soviets and propelled the nations of Western Europe and Britain and the United States toward closer cooperation. The Russians were laying siege to a city and attempting to conquer it with the weapons of starvation and cold, but the American and British airmen were defeating them by keeping the people of this beleaguered Berlin warm and well fed. As Lucius Clay observed, the blockade was "the stupidest move the Russians could make."

By the spring of 1949, Stalin understood how badly he had miscalculated and was desperate to end the blockade under terms that would not be humiliating, but the administration was in no hurry. With an airlift working this well, there was no need for ground transportation. During one twenty-four-hour period in April, the controllers set a record by bringing 1,398 flights into Berlin, about a landing a minute. The blockade was finally lifted in mid-May 1949 and the land routes reopened. The quid pro quo was an agreement to convene in Paris yet another meeting of the Council of Foreign Ministers. The Soviets attempted to negotiate a return to the original four-power governing system and abort the formation of the new West German state. It was fruitless. Stalin had lost. That same month, May 1949, the constitution of the Federal Republic of Germany, with its capital at Bonn, was adopted.

18.

STALIN GETS HIS BOMB

Then Joseph Stalin got his atomic bomb, although Kurchatov and Khariton and their colleagues were not able to hold to their two-and-a-half-year timetable. Problems with the plutonium production reactor delayed the test for eighteen months. Nevertheless, they moved with a speed unexpected in Washington. At 6:00 A.M. on August 29, 1949, four years and nine days from the date Stalin had signed the order setting the postwar nuclear arms race in motion, they exploded a device identical to the Nagasaki bomb at a spot on the barren steppes of Kazakhstan in Central Asia northwest of the city of Semipalatinsk. The device was subsequently code-named Joe One by American intelligence. Beria, who came to observe this Soviet version of Trinity, and personally report to Stalin on the phone line to Moscow, embraced Kurchatov and Khariton and kissed them on the forehead as the mushroom cloud rose. There were indications later that Beria had been worried about his own fate if the enterprise had been a fiasco.

At the end of October, Stalin signed a secret decree, drawn up by Beria, passing out the rewards. In deciding who received what, Beria is reported to have followed the principle that the highest awards went to those who would have been shot first in case of a fizzle. David Holloway in *Stalin and the Bomb* says that the story may have been apocryphal, but that it accurately reflected the feeling of the scientists involved. Kurchatov and Khariton received the highest honors possible, Hero of Socialist Labor and Stalin Prize Laureate of the first degree; large amounts of cash; ZIS-110 cars, the best the Soviet automotive industry was making at the time; dachas; free education for their children in any establishment; and free public transportation for themselves and their families. In an enticement of what the future could hold, Stalin had already, back in 1946 when tens of thousands of rural families were living in dugouts under the rubble of their homes, built a fancy eight-room house for Kurchatov at his laboratory near Moscow, importing Italian craftsmen to furnish it with parquet floors, marble fireplaces, and elegant wood paneling. A number of the other leading physicists, engineers, and managers were similarly rewarded with the honor of Hero of Socialist Labor and with money, cars, and sundry other privileges in lesser degrees. Khariton was eventually also to be awarded his own private railway car.

In time, through the remaining years of Stalin and during the rule of his successors, Arzamas-16, its sister sites in the atomic industry network, and research centers for other branches of the Soviet military-industrial complex were to grow into self-contained cities, with their own schools, concert halls, hospitals, and, by Russian standards, first-class shops for food and clothing. Although officially secret, they became known as the "white archipelago," and their privileged inhabitants, the scientists and engineers and their families, were referred to as *chocolatniki* by less fortunate Russians. Already by 1953, one of Stalin's henchmen in the Politburo, Lazar Kaganovich, complained that the atomic cities had become like "health resorts."

It would be erroneous, however, to conclude that these Soviet physicists lent their ingenuity to the building of the bomb because a life of privilege was held out before them if they succeeded. On the contrary, their motives were complicated. Imprisonment in a labor camp or execution were ever-present threats in Stalin's Russia for failure to succeed or unwillingness to cooperate. On the other hand, David Holloway discovered in questioning them that they were also motivated forcefully by love of country, by the defense of their motherland. Many of them might not have liked Stalin's system, but they could not change it. The Soviet Union was their country, the only one they had, a conviction ingrained all the more keenly by the war of survival, the Great Patriotic War, as Russians called it, that they had just emerged from with Nazi Germany. The atomic bomb project was, in an emotional way, a continuation of that primeval conflict. Andrei Sakharov was to become a world-renowned figure and to win the Nobel Peace Prize in 1975 because of the persecution and internal exile he suffered in the cause of promoting civil liberties in the Soviet Union. In 1948, however, he was an imaginative twenty-seven-year-old physicist beginning the research that led to Russia's hydrogen bomb. "I regarded myself as a soldier in this new scientific war," he subsequently remarked of those years. "We . . . believed that our work was absolutely necessary as a means of achieving a balance in the world."

Klaus Fuchs and Theodore Hall did not hand Stalin's Russia the bomb, as most of the American public thought that the Rosenbergs and David Greenglass and other Soviet spies unknown and unnamed had done. Kurchatov and those with whom he chose to collaborate were notably competent physicists who, given time, would have created a bomb on their own without any intelligence input. In 1951, they detonated a much improved version of the Nagasaki bomb that weighed only half as much and yielded twice the force, forty kilotons, with a mixed core of U-235 and plutonium. The real secret of the atomic bomb was whether such a hellish device could be devised at all. That secret was exposed in the dawn of the New Mexico desert on July 16, 1945, with Trinity and then dramatized to the world when its monstrous power was unleashed on the inhabitants of Hiroshima.

What Fuchs and Hall did accomplish was to save the Soviet Union time, probably a year to two years, in the race to achieve strategic parity with the United States after the explosion of Trinity a bit more than four years prior to Joe One. Ironically, Stalin initially kept the achievement of his physicists secret for some unknown reason and it was Truman who announced that the Soviets had the bomb. The U.S. Atomic Energy Commission, set up in 1946 to take charge of all things nuclear, had not been unwatchful under its first chairman, David Lilienthal, despite the illusions at the top. It had persuaded the Air Force to cooperate in the Long Range Detection Program, which involved high-altitude flights off the Soviet Union by aircraft equipped with filters to capture nuclear residue from the air. A B-29 flying at 18,000 feet over the North Pacific on September 3, 1949, collected a slightly higher count of radioactive material than would normally be found in the air. Further checks as the high-level winds continued in their stream over the United States, the Atlantic, and Europe confirmed that the Soviets had tested an atomic bomb in the last few days of August.

The Soviet Union still lacked adequate means of striking the United States with atomic bombs. Even the hundreds of copies of the B-29, called Tu-4s (more than a thousand were to be built), that the Soviet aircraft industry was turning out on Stalin's instructions lacked the range to reach most American cities and as propeller-driven aircraft were also vulnerable to the new American jet fighters in daylight bombing.

The practicalities of how the Soviet Union might drop an atomic bomb on the United States did not matter for the moment. The broken monopoly had been replaced by a balance of terror; the threat of nuclear devastation thrust into the minds and emotions of the American public and its leaders. The Berlin Blockade, while a defensive move by Stalin, had been interpreted yet again in the United States as evidence of aggressive intent. In Asia, a new Communist danger was rising as the armies of Mao Tse-tung neared their conquest of all of mainland China. Now the news that Russia had the bomb created a tangible sense of danger, a keener sense of insecurity in a nation already suffering from that malady.

The first response was to end the debate that had been going on over whether to build the hydrogen, i.e., thermonuclear, bomb. Truman reacted to his own apprehension and the clamor from the recently independent U.S. Air Force, the Joint Chiefs of Staff, and their allies in Congress by issuing an order on January 31, 1950, to begin developing this weapon, thousands of times more powerful than the Nagasaki bomb. It was created and detonated within less than two years, on November 1, 1952.

Niels Bohr and other idealistic physicists who had lobbied to place international controls on atomic weaponry and thereby avoid a nuclear arms race after the Second World War were, it has become clear, scholarly Don Quixotes. All the control plans put forward by the Truman administration, such as the Baruch Plan promoted by the financier Bernard Baruch on the administration's behalf in the United Nations, preserved an American monopoly, and Stalin would never have settled for second place. To have satisfied Stalin, Truman would have had to share the atomic bomb with him, a political impossibility.

Similarly quixotic was the attempt earlier in 1949 by Robert Oppenheimer and other physicists who had been involved in the Manhattan Project to stop development of the hydrogen bomb on the grounds that it was "in a totally different category from an atomic bomb" and might become a "weapon of genocide" with "extreme dangers to

mankind." (They also argued that technical problems stood in the way
and higher-yield atomic weapons would serve any military needs, but
it is clear that moral objections most concerned them.) As is now
known, Kurchatov, undoubtedly at the behest of Stalin and Beria, had
organized serious theoretical and design studies for a hydrogen bomb
in 1948. By the end of that year, long before they had broken the American atomic monopoly, the Soviets had a basic design for an intermediate hydrogen weapon, Sakharov's "Layer Cake," which combined
fission (atomic) and fusion (thermonuclear) elements. ("Nuclear fission"
is the term for the explosive reaction that occurs in an ordinary atomic
bomb, while "nuclear fusion" is the term used to describe the vastly
more powerful release of energy that occurs when a hydrogen, or thermonuclear, device detonates.) Advanced design and experimental work
got under way at Arzamas-16 in 1950, along with the creation of manufacturing facilities to produce the thermonuclear fuel, lithium deuteride, and other materials. The Layer Cake device was detonated at
the test site on the Kazakhstan steppes on August 12, 1953, and
yielded 400 kilotons, twenty times the power of the Nagasaki bomb. A
bit over two years later, on November 22, 1955, just three years after
the United States had detonated its first hydrogen bomb, a full-scale
Soviet hydrogen weapon was exploded at the same Kazakhstan site.
Kurchatov, Sakharov, and other Soviet physicists felt none of the moral
qualms of their American counterparts. They saw the development of
thermonuclear weapons as a logical second step to keep pace with the
United States. Years later in his memoirs, Sakharov was certain that
Stalin would not have reciprocated any American restraint in creating
the hydrogen bomb. He would have seen it as either a trick not to be
fooled by or as stupidity of which he should take advantage.

19

THE CONSEQUENCES OF
DELUSION

T he second response to Stalin's acquisition of the atomic bomb was a policy reassessment that was to reinforce, like the domino theory, the oversimplification and distortion of American thinking during the Cold War. Known as NSC-68 after its designation as a National Security Council memorandum, the paper's patron was Dean Acheson and its principal author was a man in the Acheson mold, Paul Nitze. An Easterner and 1928 graduate of Harvard, Nitze was a clever financier who had made a fortune as an investment banker with the tony New York firm of Dillon Read & Co. at a time when others were reaping bankruptcy. He had first been recruited for government service as a high-level economic administrator during the Second World War by James Forrestal, one of his associates at Dillon Read. As he had no need to return to New York and make more money, he decided that he liked the life of a Washington insider and stayed. Nitze was a polished, articulate man with a knack for convincing himself and others that he had knowledge of a subject when he, in fact, had little or none. He also had a talent for sensing and projecting fear of Communism and the Soviet Union, which was to serve him well in a long and distinguished career as a senior Washington official and public figure.

By 1949, George Kennan and Acheson, who had succeeded Marshall as secretary of state, had had a falling out. Kennan had been having second thoughts about the image of a relentlessly militant Soviet Union that he had portrayed in his Long Telegram and was disturbed about the hardening of the attitudes that his famous missive had sanctioned. He had come to believe that Russia did not constitute a military threat to Western Europe. He thought that containment ought to rely on political and economic means rather than a larger military establishment and the increasing militarization of foreign policy that he was seeing. Acheson had in turn come to regard him as naive. "There were times when I felt like a court jester," Kennan said in his memoirs. In January 1950, Acheson replaced him as head of the department's Policy Planning Staff with Nitze, who was of Acheson's way of thinking. Nitze, Acheson said in his memoirs, was "a joy to work with because of his clear, incisive mind."

"The Soviet Union, unlike previous aspirants to hegemony," Nitze's policy paper said, "is animated by a new fanatic faith antithetical to our own, and seeks to impose its absolute authority over the rest of the world." Russia was "inescapably militant because it possesses and is possessed by a world-wide revolutionary movement" and thus this goal of world conquest was inherent in the "fundamental design of the Kremlin." Its "assault on free institutions is worldwide now, and in the context of the present polarization of power a defeat of free institutions anywhere is a defeat everywhere." The United States was being "mortally challenged." The year of maximum danger, Nitze predicted, would be 1954, when the Soviet Union could possess an arsenal of 200 atomic bombs, sufficient for a surprise attack "of such weight that the United States must have substantially increased . . . air, ground and sea strength, atomic capabilities, and air and civil defenses" if it was to survive. The buildup he called for would add about $50 billion to the military budgets that Truman, relying on the U.S. monopoly of the bomb, had been holding to a minimum to keep inflation reined in, just $13 billion in fiscal 1949. Acheson admitted in his memoirs that Nitze had been encouraged to employ scary language in order to spook the administration into action, but there is no indication in his memoirs or elsewhere that he and others at the top doubted the basic positions stated in the paper. Truman signed off on it and the NSC adopted it as national policy in April 1950. The president postponed its costly military buildup, however, again out of concern for inflation and fear that a Republican-controlled Congress would not approve the additional funds.

The two figures in the administration who did not agree with Nitze's masterwork were its two specialists on the Soviet Union, Kennan and Chip Bohlen. Both now believed that Stalin was generally guided by caution in his foreign policy calculations and was sometimes just reacting to Western moves. Their dissent was of no consequence. The men of power were not interested in what the men of knowledge had to say. Their ears were attuned to the skirl of a different piper.

The statesmen of the United States were permitting their exaggerated estimate of the military threat from Stalin's Russia, their preconceived notions of falling dominoes, and a Soviet Union bent on world conquest through an international Communist movement, which it directed, to deprive them of a realistic view of the postwar world they were seeking to manage. The world they created in their minds, and enshrined in dogma through policy pronouncements like NSC-68, was a Manichaean place divided into opposing camps of light and darkness. That world was an illusion. To comprehend the real postwar world, one had to understand that while it was bipolar in terms of the two major powers, within the Communist sphere, as within the non-Communist one, there were national leaders with their own agendas who were prepared to act on those agendas regardless of what Moscow or Washington thought. The clue that the Communist sphere was also a complicated world, a world of varying shades of gray rather than black, was the phenomenon of national Communism, which appeared as early as 1948 when Tito of Yugoslavia openly broke with Stalin and went his own way. He was regarded as an aberration, not as evidence that there might be other Communist leaders like him, authoritarian and socialist in their domestic politics but independent in foreign policy and thus capable of being weaned from Moscow.

The statesmen of one administration after another, from Truman down through Dwight Eisenhower and John Kennedy and Lyndon Johnson, clung to this delusion that they faced an international Communist conspiracy, despite increasingly blatant evidence to the contrary. Acheson departed from the norm in only one sortie in 1949 when he thought he might be able to entice Mao Tse-tung away from Moscow because the Chinese revolutionaries had won their war entirely on their own, without any help from the Red Army. Acheson also tended to regard Mao differently because the United States had wasted so many hundreds of millions of dollars in economic and military aid on the venal regime of the reactionary Chinese dictator, Chiang Kai-shek. The attempt was halfhearted and ended quickly, however, as the right-wing Republicans in Congress brought Acheson under ferocious attack for allegedly "losing China" and Mao turned increasingly anti-American.

Otherwise, the delusion ruled. Years later, after Mao had quarreled openly and bitterly with Stalin's successor, Nikita Khrushchev, and the Chinese and the Russians were close to hostilities in the so-called Sino-Soviet split, American statesmen continued to act as if they faced a Communist monolith. In 1961, as John Kennedy took the United States to war in Vietnam by dispatching military advisers, helicopter companies, and pilots and fighter-bombers to stiffen the regime of Washington's man in Saigon, the South Vietnamese dictator, Ngo Dinh Diem, against the Communist-led guerrillas who were threatening to overthrow him, the U.S. Army security clearance form caught the enduring perspective of American statesmen. The form referred to all the Communist nations as the "Sino-Soviet bloc."

Given these American delusions, Ho Chi Minh, the Vietnamese national leader in Hanoi, had no chance of being recognized in Washington for what he was, an Asian version of Tito. Ho, in particular, held a sad belief that American statesmen were perspicacious enough to distinguish between different Communist regimes. In the fall of 1963, when American deaths in Vietnam were still well under 200, he predicted to a Polish diplomat in Hanoi that the United States was too wise and pragmatic a nation to lavish lives and treasure on a war in his country. "Neither you nor I," he said to his Polish visitor, "know the Americans well, but what we do know of them, what we have read and heard about them, suggests that they are more practical and clear-sighted than other capitalist nations. They will not pour their resources into Vietnam endlessly. One day they will take pencil in hand and begin figuring. Once they really begin to analyze our ideas seriously, they will come to the conclusion that it is possible and even worthwhile to live in peace with us." No American leader with the power to decide ever did take pencil in hand and begin figuring. It would finally take the disillusionment of the tragic and unnecessary war and the lives of the 58,229 whose names would be inscribed on the black granite wall of the Vietnam Memorial in Washington to bring American statesmen up against reality. In retrospect, one wonders why they clung so long to their delusion.

20

GOOD INTENTIONS GONE AWRY

The U.S. military code breakers and the FBI did catch up with Theodore Hall and Saville "Savy" Sax after the Soviet codes were finally broken. The Russians had been careless enough to give the real names of both men in the initial cable from the New York *rezidentura* on November 12, 1944, reporting to Moscow Center that they had volunteered to conduct atomic espionage. Subsequent cables had employed code names—Mlad, taken from an old Slavonic adjective meaning "young," for Hall, and Star, an abbreviation of an adjective meaning "old," for Sax—but there were enough identifying details, even in the cables where code names were henceforth used, to pinpoint them. The FBI was alerted after the initial cable was broken in 1950. By mid-March 1951 the agents thought they had developed the case to the point where they might succeed in getting one or both men to snap during separate but simultaneous interrogations. Hall and Sax had been shrewd enough, however, to foresee that such a day might eventually arise and had rehearsed what they would say. Over three hours of questioning on March 16, 1951, the agents could break neither.

Nonetheless, while they controlled themselves and displayed no trepidation, the interrogations were terrifying for both men and for the young women they had since married and with whom they had begun families. The nation had been at war in Korea, first with Kim Il Sung's North Korean army and then with the forces of Communist China's Mao Tse-tung, since June 1950. The country was in a frenzy of spy fear. Alger Hiss, a senior State Department official, turned out to be a Soviet agent. He had been convicted in January 1950 of perjury for denying that he passed diplomatic reports to Moscow. (He could not be tried for the espionage itself because the statute of limitations had run out.) In February 1951, the Wisconsin demagogue, Republican senator Joseph McCarthy, who was about to launch his madcap witch hunt in which innumerable careers and lives would be ruined, waved a sheet of paper during a speech to the Women's Republican Club in Wheeling, West Virginia. He announced that it listed the names of 205 active Communist Party members in the State Department. (It would be years before anyone discovered that the sheet of paper had been blank.) That same month Klaus Fuchs confessed in England to giving the Russians the plans for the Nagasaki bomb. Julius and Ethel Rosenberg were on trial for their lives in New York for transmitting a great deal less to the Soviets than Hall had through Sax and Lona Cohen. In April the Rosenbergs would be sentenced to death in the electric chair at New York State's Sing Sing Prison. The American public was appalled by these revelations. In these years before the disillusionment of the Vietnam War, it was an article of faith for patriotic Americans that the United States was innately good in motive and deed. We had been justified in using the bomb against Japan to shorten the Second World War and save lives and we would never employ it unjustly. We had been safe and humanity had been safe as long as the secret remained with us. Communists were not to be trusted with anything, least of all with the atomic bomb. Giving it to Stalin's Russia was a monstrous act.

Hall and Sax eluded the hounds. The decoded cables could not be submitted as evidence in court, nor could the FBI agents show them or mention them to Hall or Sax in order to help break them down, because the military cryptologists did not want the Soviets to learn that their code had been compromised. (Moscow already knew. Kim Philby, the mole in the British Secret Intelligence Service, had informed them. He was so highly regarded by his superiors in MI6 that he was considered a candidate to one day become head of the service and in 1949 had been given the extremely sensitive post of liaison to the Central Intelligence Agency in Washington.) Although they had enough information for an interrogation, the FBI investigators could not reach the higher threshold of sufficient independently corroborating evidence for a grand jury indictment. And so the case was placed in bureaucratic limbo and then, as the years went by, dropped.

Ted Hall became bored with nuclear physics by the time he was awarded his Ph.D. at the University of Chicago in 1950. He decided that biology was more interesting and worthwhile and turned to the new field of biophysics. After nine years at Memorial Sloan-Kettering, the cancer center in New York, he gained sufficient recognition in the highly specialized field of X-ray microanalysis, a technique to detect and measure concentrations of chemicals in human tissue, that he was able to seek and receive an invitation to spend the academic year of 1962–63 at the Cavendish Laboratory at Cambridge University in England, which had continued to be a home of genius. (Most recently, James Watson and Francis Crick had won a Nobel for creating their "double helix" model, the first accurate rendition of a DNA molecule, at the Cavendish in 1953.)

The one year turned into twenty-two as Hall and his wife, Joan (she was as intensely left-wing as he was and he had told her everything), and their three daughters settled in at Cambridge and he won international distinction for his work, retiring in 1984 after his research had played itself out. At the request of the FBI, a British counterintelligence officer interrogated him in 1963 in another attempt to crack him, and renewal of his labor permit was held up for a few months. Otherwise, he was left in peace. Nor did anyone ever approach his brother, Ed Hall, the U.S. Air Force rocket engine guru, who held highly secret clearances for his work with Bennie Schriever, including a super-sensitive "Q" clearance that gave Ed access to nuclear weapons designs.

The Halls remained in England after Ted's retirement, occasionally traveling to the United States for scientific conferences, once even to Albuquerque and the University of New Mexico campus where he had passed the atomic secrets to Lona Cohen that went back to New York in her Kleenex box. He assumed that the perilous adventure of his youth would never catch up with him publicly. Then the decoded cables in the Venona documents were published in 1995 and 1996 and brought him precisely the notoriety he had most wanted to avoid. (Savy Sax, who went on to be a teacher and psychological counselor in the Midwest, openly boasted of his role in the spying prior to his premature death from a heart attack in 1980. By that time, however, he had become something of an adult hippie, disheveled in his personal habits and given to LSD and other hallucinogenic drugs. Apparently, no one who heard his stories ever took them seriously enough to tip off the FBI.)

In the few years until his death from cancer in November 1999, Ted Hall would never formally admit in writing to his espionage, apparently fearful that such an admission might still bring prosecution, but neither would he deny it. In 1997, he gave Joseph Albright and

Marcia Kunstel, the two American journalists who wrote a book about his spying, a written statement that, while again making no explicit admission, sought to justify what he had done and expressed no substantial regret. One reflective paragraph said that, given what he knew at the time, he would commit treason again:

> In 1944 I was nineteen years old—immature, inexperienced and far too sure of myself. I recognize that I could easily have been wrong in my judgement of what was necessary, and that I was indeed mistaken about some things, in particular my view of the nature of the Soviet state. The world has moved on a lot since then, and certainly so have I. But in essence, from the perspective of my 71 years, I still think that brash youth had the right end of the stick. I am no longer that person; but I am by no means ashamed of him.

The accomplishment of Klaus Fuchs and Ted Hall in gaining the Soviets a year to two years in their race for an atomic bomb may not, however, have been without a grim postscript. It may have helped to bring on the Korean War in June 1950. There were several causes for the war in Korea and the principal one was undoubtedly the foolish decision by the Truman administration and the American military leaders of the time to place South Korea outside the U.S. defense perimeter in Asia on the grounds that it was of "little strategic interest" to the United States. (Truman and Stalin had divided Korea at the 38th Parallel at the end of the Second World War, with the Red Army occupying the North and U.S. forces the South.) The decision was twice affirmed by the National Security Council and separately by the Joint Chiefs of Staff and publicized in a speech by Douglas MacArthur, then commander in chief of U.S. forces in the Far East as head of the occupation in Japan. In January 1950, Acheson conveyed the same position in a speech before the National Press Club in Washington. Furthermore, the declarations were given credence by American actions. The last of the U.S. combat troops were withdrawn in mid-1949 and Syngman Rhee, the rightist dictator in Seoul, was left with a fledgling army equipped with secondhand infantry weapons, outmoded artillery, and a 482-man U.S. military advisory group to guide it.

Rhee and Kim Il Sung, his Communist rival in Pyongyang in the North, were poles apart in their politics, but identical in the intensity of their nationalism. Each dreamt of reunifying his homeland. Kim was now in a position to persuade Stalin to provide his troops with tanks and other heavy armament and to give him permission to invade the South and unite Korea. Mao Tse-tung also went along. Everything on the Communist side was posited on the assumption that the victory would be quick and that the United States would *not* intervene. Stalin's act in arming a rival claimant to Korea was aggression, of course, but the aim was the attainment of a friendly regime throughout the neighboring Korean Peninsula without the danger of arousing an American reaction.

When what the Truman administration and its military chiefs had invited then occurred, as Kim's freshly armored columns attacked south across the 38th Parallel dividing line in the predawn hours of Sunday, June 25, 1950, the administration reversed itself. Forgetting what they had said and done and misreading their opponent yet again, Truman and Acheson interpreted the invasion as the first bold move by Stalin in the Russian master plan Paul Nitze had warned about just that April in NSC-68, the intent of the Soviet Union "to impose its absolute authority over the rest of the world." This was a challenge they had to meet to preserve the credibility of American power and prestige. If they did not do so Stalin might next attempt to overrun all of Western Europe with the Red Army. Truman ordered MacArthur's troops occupying Japan into South Korea. Acheson described the stakes with high tension to a group of congressional leaders in a briefing six months after the war began: "Since the end of June, it had been clear that the Soviet Union has begun an all-out attack against the power position of the United States. It was clear that the Soviet leaders recognized that their policy might bring on a general war, and it was equally clear that they were prepared to run this risk." (In fact, once the invasion occurred, there was ample strategic justification for reversing what had been a bad decision and frustrating Kim's ambition. Korea had been a Japanese colony until the end of the Second World War and the Japanese were sensitive to what occurred on the peninsula, just eighty miles away across the Korea Strait. A reunified Korea ruled by a pro-Soviet dictator would have shaken their confidence in the United States as a protecting power. The United States had to hold on to South Korea in order to retain that confidence.) The ensuing war dragged on for three years. It took the lives of 54,246 Americans and millions of Koreans, civilian and military, as the entire peninsula was devastated. Untold tens of thousands of Chinese fighting men died as well after Mao joined in when MacArthur rashly pushed U.S. troops into the mountains below the border with China and then all the way up to the Yalu River boundary itself.

Would Stalin have said yes to Kim and provided him with the necessary weaponry for the invasion, despite the assumption that the United States would not intervene, if he had not had the self-confidence provided by the bomb? The question goes directly to the insecurity at the center of Stalin's character, an insecurity that governed so many of his actions. There is thus good reason to think that, with the United States still holding an atomic monopoly, he might well have said no. His subsequent conduct in Korea tends to support this conclusion. As soon as Truman did intervene, a surprised Stalin abandoned Kim. He told the Politburo he was prepared to accept a U.S.-occupied North Korea rather than risk war with the United States. Mao turned out to be of a different mind because he believed that, with Chiang Kai-shek holding on in Taiwan, American troops along China's Korean border would constitute a threat to his newly triumphant revolution. Stalin cleverly maneuvered the Chinese into rescuing Kim. He supported both the Chinese and the North Koreans with arms and equipment and later provided limited air cover along the border itself with the first-generation Soviet jet fighter, the MiG-15, painted with Chinese insignia. Otherwise, he carefully kept his regular forces out of the fight for fear of a clash with the United States.

In the written statement Ted Hall gave Albright and Kunstel two years before his death, the statement in which he sought to justify his espionage, he took pride in the possibility that he might have helped to prevent the use of the atomic bomb against China, presumably for fear of Soviet nuclear retaliation, during the years of Mao's conquest of the mainland and the Korean War. But the stone tossed into the pond has many ripples. It presumably did not occur to him that, while saving lives in China, his actions may have played a part in snuffing out other lives in another place.

The Korean War was a strategic disaster for Stalin. The Truman administration took advantage of it to array Western Europe against him. By fiscal 1953 the American military budget had nearly quadrupled, to $50.4 billion, from the $13 billion of 1949. Some of the additional funds were paying for the war. More were going into the U.S. conventional and nuclear buildup recommended by Nitze's NSC-68 and into rearming, through American military aid, the members of the newly joined North Atlantic Treaty Organization, consisting of the United States, Canada, Britain, France, Belgium, the Netherlands, and Luxembourg. The U.S. aircraft industry rejoiced in the headiness of wartime production, the plants turning out planes at the 1944 level, the peak year of the Second World War. NATO was to confront Stalin and his successors for decades. Worse, by giving Kim Il Sung permission to strike south, Stalin, who was to die in March 1953, had brought to fruition one of his own nightmares. He had made so many West Europeans fearful they might be next that the former victims of Germany were now prepared to accept German rearmament. The Federal Republic of Germany, the new West German state, was being welcomed into NATO, and a new German army, the Bundeswehr, was being formed to march alongside the NATO forces.

BOOK III

THE PERILS OF AN APPRENTICESHIP

21

HAP ARNOLD'S LEGACY

As Kim Il Sung's tanks were crossing the 38th Parallel, Colonel Bernard Adolph Schriever was completing his year as a student at the National War College at Fort Lesley J. McNair in Washington. The War College was a necessary stop for an officer with a future and was part of the apprenticeship Schriever had been undergoing for the momentous role that lay ahead. These years following the end of the Second World War were to be a time of learning and preparation for him and to prove a time of professional peril as well.

After George Kenney had told him just before his return from the Pacific in September 1945 to find himself a job that he liked, Schriever had decided that the place to go was Headquarters, U.S. Army Air Forces, at the Pentagon. This, as he later put it in an old Texas saying, was "where they were cutting the bacon." He wanted to get involved in research and development. Technology and the seemingly limitless possibilities it held for the air arm were an exhilarating prospect for those attuned to grasp it. The Germans had dramatized those possibilities by surprising Allied airmen late in the war with the Messerschmitt 262, the first jet fighter to see combat, and with the V-2, the first ballistic rocket. The V-2 was inaccurate, with an average range of only 180 miles, but terrifying nonetheless when the approximately 1,650 pounds of high explosive in its warhead detonated on impact. Bennie had initially gone back to Wright Field near Dayton, Ohio, still the Army Air Forces' main research and development center. He had been disillusioned. The officers there seemed parochial and, worse, they appeared not to see his colonel's eagles but still regarded him as the lieutenant who had once been a test pilot. The best he could hope for there was someday to run a laboratory. He might, perhaps, be rewarded with the single star of a brigadier before he retired. As always with

Schriever, if he was going to get involved in something, he wanted to do it at a level that mattered, and so he went to the Pentagon. With the endorsement of Kenney, he was accepted by Brigadier General Alden R. Crawford, chief of the Air Staff's Research and Engineering Division. While Crawford hired Schriever on Kenney's recommendation, he did not know at first precisely what he would do with him. Within a few days of Schriever's arrival for duty at the Pentagon in January 1946, Hap Arnold solved that problem by sending for him and starting him on his life's vocation.

When Arnold had been able to begin the process of making science and technology the handmaidens of postwar air power in the early fall of 1944, with the defeat of Germany and Japan now certain, he had turned to an acquaintance from his California days, the renowned Hungarian aeronautical engineer Theodore von Kármán. Robert Millikan, the president of Caltech and Arnold's other California friend in the world of science, had brought von Kármán to Caltech in 1930 as an émigré from the growing threat of Nazism. Von Kármán was an engagingly eccentric man with curly salt-and-pepper hair that was receding, bushy eyebrows, and a prominent nose. No matter how many years he lived in the United States, he would forever speak English with a pronounced accent from his native tongue, turning all w's into v's. He became distinctly American, however, in what he wanted in a glass, Jack Daniel's Tennessee Whiskey, which he drank straight, and he was rarely without a cigar, unless he had put it down to turn his attention to an attractive woman. Yet despite considering himself a connoisseur of the opposite sex, he never married, sharing a large house in Pasadena with his equally eccentric mother and sister.

Von Kármán had been valuable to Arnold on several occasions during the war. On this historic one in September 1944, they met in the back of a staff car at the end of the runway at La Guardia Airport. Von Kármán was recuperating from intestinal surgery at a sanatorium at Lake George, New York, and Arnold was on his way to the second Quebec Conference of Franklin Roosevelt and Winston Churchill and their Combined Chiefs of Staff. After von Kármán had recovered, Arnold said, he wanted him to come to the Pentagon and organize a team of "practical scientists" who would compose for Arnold a blueprint of the future of air power. "What I am interested in is what will be the shape of the air war, of air power, in five years, or ten, or sixty-five. . . . I want to know what the impact of jet propulsion is, of atomic energy, of electronics." After some hesitation and assurances from Arnold that von Kármán would be reporting directly to him and not some intermediary, the Hungarian agreed.

By the end of that month von Kármán was in Washington recruiting his team. When complete, it would consist of thirty-three members, including several Army Air Forces officers assigned as specialists and military assistants. Its star was Lee DuBridge, a Cornell and University of Wisconsin physicist who was then heading the Radiation Laboratory at the Massachusetts Institute of Technology, the Rad Lab as it was called, which had produced remarkable advances in radar for the AAF and the Navy. After the war, he was to succeed Millikan as president of Caltech. In a briefing for the team, Arnold told the scientists to "forget the past; regard the equipment now available only as the basis for [your] boldest predictions." As soon as hostilities diminished enough to permit it, he wanted von Kármán to travel to Europe and scour the Continent for wartime technical secrets that had remained hidden. To provide von Kármán with the status he needed, Arnold awarded him the protocol rank of major general. He also had him officially designated as consultant on scientific matters to the Army Air Forces and he and his team as the service's Scientific Advisory Group.

On May 1, 1945, only five days after Hitler put a pistol in his mouth and pulled the trigger, von Kármán and six members of the team were in Paris on their way to Germany. (One of those he chose to take along was a Chinese-born scientist and protégé of von Kármán named Tsien Hsue shen, a leading rocket expert. Ten years later, partly as a result of the anti-Communist hysteria in the United States, Tsien was to return to China and become the father of its intercontinental ballistic missile program.) The first trove they encountered was a large clandestine laboratory that American troops had overrun in a forest near Braunschweig (Brunswick) in northern Germany. The fifty-six-building complex was managed by a German aeronautical engineer named Adolf Bäumker, who happened to have been von Kármán's assistant when he had directed the aeronautical laboratory at Aachen before immigrating to Caltech. The secret laboratory specialized in advanced research into aircraft design, ballistics, engines, jet propulsion, and guided missiles. The team's interrogations of Bäumker and others on his staff led to caches in nearby salt mines and other hiding places of some 3 million documents, which they ordered microfilmed and shipped back to the United States. A team member from the Engineering Division at Wright Field was so impressed by the swept-back wing, or arrowhead, design used in the Me-262 jet fighter to increase performance that he cabled back to Ohio to have the B-47, then on the drawing boards as the first postwar American strategic jet bomber, changed from straight to swept-back wing.

At Munich, they made more astonishing discoveries. To escape capture by the Soviets, Wernher von Braun, Germany's principal rocket designer, and General Walter Dornberger, the head of its rocket program, had surrendered to U.S. forces, along with about 400 other engineers and technicians who had worked at the rocket center at Peenemünde up on the Baltic. While interrogating these two men and others on the V-2 as well as the V-1—a relatively slow and low-flying cruise missile driven by a pulse-jet engine that had also been used to attack England—team members learned that the Germans had worked out the drawings and computations for a two-stage rocket that would throw a warhead 3,000 miles, the first step in building a missile that could fly even farther to reach the United States. Other surprises followed, including the discovery that the Germans had twelve supersonic wind tunnels in operation or under construction at five different research centers. The best of these were dismantled and shipped home as well. Von Kármán was astounded at the progress German aviation and rocket specialists had made and thankful that Hitler and his generals had failed to take full advantage and transform these discoveries into practical weaponry. Had they done so, he believed that they certainly would have prolonged the war.

The urgency of the team's report was determined by the accelerating decline in Arnold's health with his third heart attack in the fall of 1945. Von Kármán was back in Europe seeking more information that October, and had a trip to Japan planned as well, when Arnold called from his sickbed in Washington and asked him to hurry the report's completion. They agreed on a deadline of December 15, 1945. Von Kármán had already parceled out the work among the team members, each of whom was writing or collaborating in the writing of thirty-two monographs on subjects all across the span of technology from supersonic flight, to heat- and television-guided missiles, to more arcane subjects like terminal ballistics and destructive effects. Now the pace became a quick-step march and then double time to the finish. A few days before the December deadline, the thirty-two monographs, grouped by general subject into twelve volumes, with von Kármán's separate introductory and summary volume, were stacked on a table in the Pentagon office assigned to the group. Von Kármán had entitled his volume *Science: The Key to Air Supremacy,* but no one had given thought to a title for the study as a whole. Major Thaddeus "Teddy" Walkowicz, a team member who was to become a close friend of Bennie Schriever, suggested *Toward New Horizons.* (Walkowicz, like Jimmy Doolittle, was one of the handful of Air Corps officers who had earned a Ph.D., his also from MIT.) Von Kármán liked the suggestion and so Arnold got the blueprint for the future he had requested, prophetic in title and text. The monographs were not how-to-do-its—detailed plans for supersonic planes or missiles or for advanced radars and other electronic devices. Rather, they were guides, elaborate descriptions of what was feasible given further exploration and innovation. In what was to be the most enduring heritage of the report, they pointed the way.

In his letter of transmittal to the general, von Kármán restated the maxim both men shared: the Army Air Forces had become the principal defensive and offensive arm of the nation and the strength of that arm depended on a continuous input of technological and scientific progress for unforeseeable years to come. "The men in charge of the future Air Forces should always remember that problems never have final or universal solutions," von Kármán wrote his friend and patron, "and only a constant inquisitive attitude toward science and a ceaseless and swift adaptation to new developments can maintain the security of this nation through *world air supremacy*" (emphasis added). There was truth in this maxim and there was also a dark side to it that neither man seems to have perceived. Arnold was being given the blueprint he wanted for a high-tech postwar air force. He was also being given the blueprint of the postwar arms race with the Soviet Union. As von Kármán had eloquently stated, there could be no rest if preeminence was to be maintained, and by 1945 technology had reached a liftoff point where, as long as there was fear to provide the money to fuel it, technology would become self-racing. What destructive devices could be created would be created simply because they were possible and the other side might create them if the United States did not. And there would always be more weaponry to create, because technology was now without limits in its inventiveness.

As part of the process of institutionalizing technology within the Army Air Forces, von Kármán recommended perpetuating the Scientific Advisory Group. "A permanent Scientific Advisory Group, consisting of qualified officers and eminent civilian scientific consultants, should be available to the Commanding General, reporting directly to him on novel developments and advising him on the planning of scientific research," he urged. He offered to serve as chairman. He also argued that if science was to be drafted into the service of the AAF, the AAF in turn had to create an infrastructure of well-equipped research and testing centers. The German achievements, he said, were "not the result of any superiority in their technical and scientific personnel . . . but rather due to the very substantial support enjoyed by their research institutions in obtaining expensive research equipment, such as large supersonic wind tunnels."

The AAF's only research and development facilities were those at Wright Field and the proving ground at Eglin Field in Florida. Both were "definitely inadequate," von Kármán said. Wind tunnels require large amounts of electricity to operate. The wind tunnel at Wright Field could be used only an hour a day and then only by prior arrangement with the local power company. With competing demand from the many industries in the Dayton, Ohio, area, electricity was not available in sufficient quantity nor would it be in the future. Von Kármán's discoveries in Germany and the hopelessness of replicating them at Wright Field had already instigated a proposal by the Engineering Division that October for the initial link in the infrastructure von Kármán wanted, a new Air Engineering Development Center at a site with plenty of hydroelectric power. The outcome was the building of a major research and testing center for aerodynamics and propulsion at Tullahoma, Tennessee, named the Arnold Engineering Development Center in honor of the general after his death. Among the first of the facilities installed there were the pick of the German wind tunnels von Kármán's team had dismantled so that they could be put back together at a proper site in the United States. Also constructed was a replica of a high-altitude engine test stand they had run across. It had been de-

THE PERILS OF AN APPRENTICESHIP 123

vised for the Luftwaffe by the Bavarian Motor Works (BMW), whose luxury automobiles were to delight American yuppies decades after the war.

Arnold was extremely pleased. He decorated von Kármán and members of the team with the Meritorious Civilian Service Award. A week after receiving the study he forwarded a copy to General Carl Spaatz, who was now functioning as his deputy, with a memorandum saying he hoped Spaatz would agree with him that "it is an exhaustive report, and one that should be used as a guide for scientific and pre-planning people for many years to come." He also welcomed von Kármán's recommendation to perpetuate the Scientific Advisory Group. In a letter to Spaatz earlier that month he had reiterated his conviction that it was of the utmost importance to retain, in the postwar period, the unhindered access to civilian scientific talent that the AAF had so benefited from during the war years. "We must not lose these contacts," he wrote. He and Spaatz and von Kármán met and agreed that the Scientific Advisory Group would become a permanent organization within the AAF under a new name, the Scientific Advisory Board, with von Kármán continuing to head it.

Von Kármán's patron had also begun to focus that fall and winter of 1945 on ways to implement ideas he was garnering from the professor. He had the staff draw up a plan to initiate twenty-eight different pilot projects in guided missiles in the spring of 1946, from short-range, twenty-mile rockets to intercontinental ones, and set aside $34 million in wartime money to fund them. He allocated as well $10 million to the Douglas Aircraft Company for a one-year program of long-range studies. The first study, completed in May 1946, was on the feasibility of launching a satellite into space for a variety of military uses from photoreconnaissance to weather reporting and communications. The Douglas enterprise, called Project RAND, for "research and development," was separated from the aircraft firm within a couple of years and metamorphosed into the RAND Corporation, located in Santa Monica, California, the think tank that provided the soon to be independent U.S. Air Force with strategic and tactical analyses throughout the Cold War.

Then, in January 1946, with less than a month to go before his retirement to his ranch in Northern California, Arnold had taken his final step. He had summoned Schriever and given him the mission of cultivating relations with the civilian scientific community in the post-war years through a new Scientific Liaison Branch to be established within the Research and Engineering Division.

22.

GETTING ORGANIZED

From the very beginning, however, nothing about von Kármán's and Schriever's mission was easy. Von Kármán's Scientific Advisory Board languished and was nearly abolished. Deciding that it would be beneficial for the combat commanders also to get involved in long-range thinking, Arnold had established the position of assistant chief of the air staff for research and development in late 1945 and given it to his star bomber leader, young Major General Curtis LeMay. The post carried with it a mandate to coordinate all of the AAF's R&D activities. No good deed goes unpunished, as the saying goes, and Arnold's was no exception. Like most of the rest of the bomber generals who were now succeeding to the direction of the air forces, electronics, guided missiles, and other advanced concepts held scant interest for LeMay. He wanted bigger and better bombers that could fly higher and farther and faster and carry as many as possible of the 10,000-pound Mark 3, the Nagasaki-type plutonium bomb that was to become the first standardized U.S. nuclear weapon.

Research and development to a man of LeMay's outlook meant focusing on improvements to these new bombers coming on line. The B-36—a six-engine behemoth that dwarfed the B-29 at more than half the length of a football field, weighed in excess of 160,000 pounds, had a 72,000-pound bomb load, a ceiling of 40,000 feet, and a combat radius of approximately 3,500 miles—was the kind of weapon that got his attention. Moreover, he insisted that because he was head of R&D, the Scientific Advisory Board should report to him and not directly to the chief of staff, now Spaatz, as von Kármán had envisioned and Arnold had agreed in order to give the Advisory Board independence and standing. Spaatz was near the end of his own career and caught up in the interservice squabbling over the passage by Congress of the National Security Act of July 1947 and the emergence of an independent U.S. Air Force that September. He did not intervene.

As a result, no projects of consequence got accomplished by the board. Drastic postwar budget cuts worsened the board's position and also wiped out most of the pilot projects in guided missiles that Arnold had set in train. Only one intercontinental missile project survived. It was code-named MX-774B and was under contract to the Consolidated Vultee Aircraft Corporation (Convair), postwar successor to the Consolidated Aircraft Corporation, which had built the B-24 and was currently the manufacturer of the B-36 in San Diego, California. By 1947, the Scientific Advisory Board had disappeared from the service's organization charts, and the specialists in the laboratories out at Wright Field, jealous of a group of civilian scientists they perceived as rivals, were lobbying for its formal abolition. While von Kármán was away in Paris on vacation, his secretary had to fend off a section of the Air Staff from taking over his office and her desk at the Pentagon.

Salvation occurred that September. LeMay was awarded his third star and transferred to Germany to command all U.S. air forces in Europe. His position on the Air Staff lapsed with his departure, and Major General Laurence Craigie replaced Bennie's boss, Alden Crawford, as head of a newly formed Directorate of Research and Development. Crawford was a somewhat dour individual, but Schriever had won him over with his ability to anticipate what Crawford wanted and take the initiative to get it done. He was more at ease, however, with Craigie. Their acquaintanceship went back to 1923 and the links of the Brackenridge Park course in San Antonio. Bennie was still caddying at thirteen and Craigie played golf at Brackenridge while a student pilot at Kelly Field. They also saw the direction their institution ought to be taking through the same eyes, for Craigie was an officer with a long interest in technology. In 1942, while chief of the Experimental Aircraft Division at Wright Field, he became the first AAF pilot to fly a jet, the test model Bell XP-59A fighter Arnold had ordered built in secret during the war. Its short range, engine problems, and relative lack of speed kept it from going into production, but the knowledge gained resulted in the P-80, subsequently redesignated the F-80, a straight-winged, subsonic aircraft that was the initial American jet fighter of the postwar era. (After the Second World War the prefix for fighter models was changed from P, for "pursuit," a term originating in the First World War, to F, for "fighter.") Recognizing the Scientific Advisory Board's need for renewed stature if its advice was to be heeded, Craigie arranged a formal agreement in May 1948 between von Kármán and Spaatz that the SAB would be considered part of the chief of staff's personal organization and would report directly to him.

The main battle, however, was yet to be won. It was to break research and development away from the stultifying atmosphere of the Air Matériel Command at Wright Field and to set up a separate R&D organization. As matters stood, research and development, and the production of aircraft, as well as the maintenance of the air forces in the field through the supply of spare parts and replacement machines—logistics, as it is called in the military—were all responsibilities of the Matériel Command. One reason the laboratories at Wright Field were, with some exceptions, parochial was that the command they worked for was parochial. The Air Matériel Command had excelled during the Second World War in revving up industry for the mass production of planes. The command had, with commendable success, also seen to it that the air forces deployed in Europe and the Middle East, the cockpit of the war for the AAF, did not want for sustenance. The experience had given the AMC a focus on logistics and on quantity over quality that had carried over into the postwar period. Innovation required separation.

Schriever's role in the campaign was as leader of a group of reformist-minded younger officers. They called themselves the "Junior Indians," because they sat on the sides or at the back of the room, while their chiefs sat at the table during meetings and conferences. His good friend Major Teddy Walkowicz, who, after hitting on the title of *Toward New Horizons* while a member of von Kármán's original team, had then become the first military secretary of the SAB, was a fellow agitator. They thought up ideas and strategies to further the cause and passed these along to their already sympathetic bosses.

Bennie had been putting in a performance at the Pentagon of the kind that had earned him the admiration of his superiors in the Southwest Pacific, earning the unusually fine efficiency reports that point a colonel who stands out from his peers toward a star. He was as much at ease with his third Pentagon boss, Major General Donald Putt, who succeeded Laurence Craigie in September 1948 as head of the Directorate of Research and Development, as he had been with Craigie. Once again, Schriever had a boss with whom he shared a view of what the Air Force ought to be doing. Like Craigie, Putt was another in the tiny band of technology-minded Air Force generals. He had taken his undergraduate degree in electrical engineering and then a master's in aeronautical engineering under von Kármán at Caltech, and the Hungarian professor had remained a mentor and friend.

The campaign began to crest not long before Bennie was to leave in July 1949 for his year at the National War College. The Junior Indians hatched a plot to have von Kármán convene a general meeting of the Scientific Advisory Board that April and invite General Hoyt Vandenberg, who had become the second chief of staff of the U.S. Air Force on Spaatz's retirement the previous year, to address it. Vandenberg's elevation to leader of the Air Force had undoubtedly been assisted by the fact that he was a nephew of Arthur Vandenberg, the Republican power on the Senate Committee on Foreign Relations. It was Senator Vandenberg who had persuaded his Republican colleagues to join him in promoting the bipartisan foreign policy that Harry Truman depended on to sustain his strategy of containment against the Soviet Union. But Hoyt Vandenberg had also long been a favorite of Spaatz and he had acquitted himself well commanding the Ninth Air Force in the battle for France after the Normandy landing. He was considered to have an open mind in the current dispute. The crux of the plot was to have Walkowicz write a speech in which Vandenberg would ask the SAB to conduct a comprehensive study of how research and development should be handled in the Air Force and give him recommendations accordingly. If Vandenberg accepted the text and gave the speech, the hounds would be off and running. Putt and von Kármán approved the scheme and the meeting was scheduled.

Vandenberg agreed and then at the last minute had to cancel his appearance. The speech was delivered instead by his vice chief of staff, General Muir Fairchild. That was good enough. The hounds *were* running. A committee was formed with a swing member who was certain to uphold the plotters' cause—that Renaissance man Jimmy Doolittle. He commanded respect high and low because he had done it all—champion racing plane pilot, the first aviator to take off and land blind on instruments alone, scholar, oil industry executive. His out-of-the-blue air raid on Tokyo in the bleak spring of 1942—Lieutenant Colonel Doolittle at the controls of the lead plane as sixteen bomb-laden B-25s wrestled their way aloft in a forty-mile-per-hour gale from the rolling deck of the aircraft carrier USS *Hornet*—was just the kind of lift in spirit the American public so sorely needed at the time. Hollywood was to make the raid a legend with the wartime film *Thirty Seconds over Tokyo*. Later that year, Hap Arnold had promoted him to brigadier general and given him command of a new air force, the Twelfth, being formed for Torch, the Anglo-American invasion of French North Africa on November 8, 1942, the first offensive action of the war against the Nazis. Then he had gone to England to take over the Eighth Air Force and its strategic bombers. Doolittle had finished the war with the three stars of a lieutenant general and had returned to Shell Oil, but Arnold had persuaded him to become a permanent consultant to the chief of staff and given him an office at the Pentagon. Bennie made a point of getting to know him well, often seeking his help, and Doolittle was to join in pinning Bennie's first star on his shoulder tabs.

Doolittle's presence on the committee was a virtual guarantee that Vandenberg would accept its recommendations, although there were apparently important details still to be worked out. A tale in the Air Force, perhaps apocryphal, says that Doolittle did this final persuading while he and Vandenberg were crouching in a blind hunting ducks. The committee's two principal findings were: (1) the establishment of a separate command to take charge of all research and development (the laboratories at Wright Field, for example, would remain there but no longer be under control of the Air Matériel Command); and (2) the appointment of a deputy chief of staff for development to exercise oversight from Air Force headquarters at the Pentagon and lend R&D equal status with other departments like Operations and Personnel. The Air Matériel Command would retain responsibility for production and supply. On January 23, 1950, a new Air Research and Development Command (ARDC), with headquarters in Baltimore, was established, and Major General Gordon Saville, a combatively forthright man who had shown a gift for destroying columns of German armor with P-47 Thunderbolt fighter-bombers, was named the first deputy chief of staff, development.

Schriever expected to be given a field assignment when he completed his year at the National War College in mid-1950, probably as deputy commander of the proving ground at Eglin Field, now Eglin Air Force Base, in Florida. Instead, General Saville brought him back to the Pentagon and he was soon promoted into a job that seemed ideal for an officer with Bennie's education and temperament. He was made the assistant for development planning. His task was to formulate projections called Development Planning Objectives for each of the Air Force's mission fields—strategic, tactical, air defense, transport, and reconnaissance and intelligence. The projections were not paper exercises. Schriever had to discern the nature of the aircraft and other weaponry, and the related equipment and techniques, required to fulfill each mission in the future. The plans had to be realistic and practical. The aircraft, for example, while next-generation, had to be achievable within what could reasonably be foreseen in the advance of technology. Schriever, of course, lacked the knowledge to complete such projections by himself. To formulate them he had to organize teams of scientists and engineers and other specialists in each area, drawing on the talent pool available to him from the Scientific Advisory Board, the RAND Corporation, and consultants recruited from the universities and industry. The Development Planning job turned out to be excellent preparation for the work that lay ahead of him in overseeing the building of the intercontinental ballistic missile. Because he was always dealing with what was to be accomplished tomorrow and not today, he was learning how to differentiate between what was future-feasible and future-fantasy and to do so in a variety of disciplines, not just in aeronautical engineering, where he had specific competence.

The job, however, soon turned out to be anything but ideal. It put Bennie at grave career risk by running him afoul of "the Cigar," the service nickname for Curtis LeMay, the most prestigious combat officer in the United States Air Force, who was now back from his tour in Europe. His trademark was a stogie, perpetually in hand or clenched defiantly in the side of his mouth, and he had power and influence exceeded only by that of the chief of staff.

23

BOMBER LEADER

He would be remembered as the crazed general who wanted to bomb the people of North Vietnam "back into the Stone Age," as the crank who ran for vice president on the 1968 presidential ticket of George Wallace, the racist from Alabama, and as the inspiration for General Jack D. Ripper in Stanley Kubrick's film *Dr. Strangelove*. But in earlier years there had been a great deal more to Curtis Emerson LeMay. He had been the greatest leader of bomber aircraft in the history of American aviation until his judgment was warped by the advent of nuclear weapons and the fear and fervor of the Cold War. He looked the grim part of a bomber commander. His broad square-jawed face, straight mouth, strong chin, intense eyes, and thick black hair combed back from a high forehead said that this was a man who meant business. The lingering effects on the right side of his face of an episode of Bell's palsy, a type of facial paralysis brought on in his case by flying in the frigid air of unheated cockpits at high altitudes, heightened the impression. So did his taciturn nature and blunt manner of speech.

He began as a fighter pilot, but in 1936, at the age of thirty, he requested a transfer to bombers. He reasoned that the fighter was a defensive aircraft (and this would hold true until the coming of the jet age and the development of powerful fighter-bombers in the late 1950s and 1960s), whereas the bomber was an intrinsically offensive weapon that carried the war to the enemy. His reasoning was infused with the theory on long-range strategic bombardment that had become the central doctrine of the Air Corps in the 1920s and 1930s. As refined and taught at the Air Corps Tactical School at Maxwell Field in Alabama, the doctrine held that air power could win a war alone by bombing an enemy's industry and related infrastructure into rubble and thus destroying his capacity to fight. The bombardment faculty at the Tactical School contended that "a well organized, well planned, and well flown air force attack . . . cannot be stopped." Moreover, the attacks were to be flown in daytime, so that the bombers could be certain of their targets and strike with accuracy.

When LeMay made his decision at the end of 1936, the first of the bombers capable of conducting such long-range raids, the four-engine Boeing B-17 Flying Fortress, was about to enter the Air Corps inventory. The second, the B-24 Liberator, was not far off. Hap Arnold, Carl Spaatz, Ira Eaker, and the other men who were to lead the U.S. Army Air Forces in the Second World War all subscribed to the theory, but evolving a military theory is one thing and carrying it into practice in the furnace of conflict is another. LeMay had the genius of the implementer. While the theory proved too optimistic—air power alone could not win the war—LeMay was the man who demonstrated how it could make a mighty contribution to victory.

The bombsight of the Second World War was called the Norden after Carl Norden, who perfected it over several years during the 1930s. It required a minimum of four and preferably seven or eight minutes of straight and level flight, while the bombardier adjusted it, in order to put enough bombs on a large target, such as a petroleum refinery, a factory complex, or a railway marshaling yard, to inflict serious damage. Sent to England in October 1942, as a colonel commanding a bombardment group of B-17s, LeMay proved that this could be done without losing most of a formation to German antiaircraft fire. Some of the planes would be shot down, others would be damaged, but the majority would get through and the target would be hit hard.

He developed the first practical bomber formation, called the "combat box." He put multiple combat boxes together to form a "combat wing." The aerial gunnery schools in the United States for a bomber's machine gunners were pathetically amateurish in the early years of the war. LeMay lobbied for gunnery schools in England to teach the men how to handle their .50 calibers well enough to knock down German fighters boring in to rake a bomber. He established "lead crew" schools for bombardiers and navigators to familiarize themselves with potential targets. When one of these was designated for a strike at a morning briefing, someone in the room already knew how to fly there and the best approach. As LeMay devised each of these innovations, they were quickly adopted as standard procedure by now Major General Ira Eaker's VIII Bomber Command, the bomber branch of his fledgling Eighth Air Force. And as the struggle in the skies over Germany intensified, the bomber became more than a weapon to Curtis LeMay, it became a fighting machine to which he was deeply wedded emotionally, an arm in which he had unshakable faith.

In September 1943, he received his first star, and then in March 1944, at Eaker's urging, Hap Arnold passed over several more senior brigadiers to give LeMay his second, making him, at thirty-seven, the youngest major general in the U.S. Army. He was also a well-decorated one, with two awards of the Distinguished Service Cross, the nation's second highest award for valor, for LeMay was never shy about taking over the co-pilot's seat in the lead bomber on a mission.

The new long-range B-29 Superfortress was entering the bomber force. Arnold was convinced that if the full potential of the B-29s could be brought to bear on Japanese industry, the transportation system, and other infrastructure, Japan could be forced to surrender without the necessity of an invasion. The seizure of the southern home island of Kyushu, planned for November 1945 at the estimated cost of roughly 300,000 American servicemen killed and wounded, could be averted. Victory through the B-29s would, in addition, demonstrate the efficacy of air power in the most dramatic way possible and strengthen mightily the argument for an independent air force after the war.

In January 1945, Arnold demonstrated the special confidence he had grown to have in LeMay by placing him in command of all B-29s operating out of Guam and its sister islands, Saipan and Tinian, in the Marianas group in the western Pacific. The islands had been seized from the Japanese during the summer of 1944 at the cost of more than 16,000 Marines killed and wounded and nearly 4,000 Army casualties. But LeMay encountered over Japan an enemy he had not met in the German skies. It was a high-altitude jet stream, a wind so strong that it would grab B-29s, whose crews were attempting to line up on a target at 195 miles per hour, and propel them ahead at a speed of almost 450 mph. Accurate calculations with the Norden bombsight became impossible. To make matters worse, the reigning deity of the atmosphere over Japan was a god of the clouds. Clear visibility was infrequent.

LeMay was not a man to persist in a futile exercise and the challenge he faced brought out the ruthlessness in him. In contrast to the brick-and-mortar cities of Europe, Japan's cities, like many other urban centers in the Asia of the time, were wooden and thus highly vulnerable to fire. An estimated 90 percent of the buildings in the wealthier sections of Tokyo were constructed of wood and 99 percent in the poorer districts. Moreover, the streets were narrow and the houses and other buildings close together, so that flames could easily spring from one structure to another and leap the streets, rapidly engulfing an entire area. Tokyo and the neighboring port of Yokohama to its south had experienced devastating fires on several occasions prior to the war, the worst set off by the earthquake of 1923, when much of the metropolitan areas of both cities had been devastated and 100,000 people killed. Since he could not bomb Japan's industries directly, LeMay decided he would burn down the factories by burning down the cities around them.

On the night of March 9, 1945, he staged the most horrendous firebombing in the history of modern warfare. He sent 334 B-29s over the center of Tokyo, each loaded with six tons plus of 100-pound Mark 47 oil-gel bombs, one of which could ignite a major blaze, and Mark 69 bombs of napalm, a jellied gasoline, one of the more terrifying inventions of the war, which had been devised by a Harvard chemist named Louis Fieser. LeMay wanted to head the raid himself, but he had been briefed only recently on the atomic bomb and was thus barred from flying for fear that he might divulge the secret under torture if shot down and captured. He chose as the man to lead the attack his newest wing commander, Brigadier General Thomas "Tommy" Power, a slim, angular Irishman from New York City. His leadership of the attack that night was to begin a long association between the two men, and Power, in a subsequent and quite different role, was also to become a major figure in Bennie Schriever's career in the building of the intercontinental ballistic missile during the 1950s.

"It was a hell of a good mission," Tommy Power shouted down from the cockpit of his Superfortress when LeMay came out to meet him as the bomber taxied to a halt on the airstrip back on Guam at 9:00 on the morning of the 10th. The aerial reconnaissance photographs that afternoon showed that LeMay had razed a wasteland in Tokyo at least fifteen miles square. (The subsequent official Japanese calculation was 16.8.) Hardly anything was left standing amidst the ashes except charred steel beams and the concrete and masonry fragments that had once been parts of buildings. No one knows precisely how many people he killed in that single raid. At the time the Japanese authorities put the number at 83,793 dead and another 40,918 people injured. An official Japanese history of the war later revised the number to 72,489 deaths. A million people were also rendered homeless as the firestorm destroyed more than 267,000 buildings.

While LeMay's willingness to engage in slaughter on such a scale demonstrated the remorselessness of the man, he was not attempting to be deliberately cruel. The firebombings were the only way he could think of to destroy Japan's industry. Balanced against the bloodletting the American infantryman and Marine would have to endure to invade and physically conquer the Japanese home islands, the agony of Japan's civilians had no weight in the scales. No American leader, military or civilian, was going to protect Japanese civilians at the expense of American soldiers.

Two nights later it was the turn of Nagoya, the center of Japan's aircraft industry. Then it was the turn of Osaka, then Kobe. Over a period of ten nights the somewhat stocky man of medium height with the square jaw and the taciturn manner razed thirty-three square miles of Japan's four leading industrial cities. On the night of April 13, 1945, 327 Superfortresses revisited Tokyo, dropping 2,139 tons of incendiaries and torching another 11.4 square miles of the city. The capital's sister city of Yokohama to the south was added to the list. The statistics became a litany of destruction. By the middle of June, LeMay had eliminated 105.6 square miles of Japan's main centers of industry, including 56.3 square miles of Tokyo.

Working his ever-growing fleet of B-29s a record 120 hours a month, LeMay began to drop incendiaries virtually as fast as the Navy transports carrying them reached the Marianas. Japan had become more naked than ever at the end of March 1945, after the assault and seizure of the small volcanic island of Iwo Jima, less than a third the size of Manhattan, from its 21,000 dug-in Japanese defenders at the cost of 6,821 Americans killed from all services, including 4,554 Marines. (For the first time in the war, the assault forces sustained more casualties than there were Japanese on the island—almost 30,000 Americans in all, 23,573 from among the Marines.) Iwo Jima was located just 670 miles south of Tokyo, approximately midpoint from the Marianas. The island was the perfect base for P-51 Mustangs, shifted to the Pacific after the defeat of Germany. From Iwo Jima the P-51s, king of Second World War propeller-driven fighters, could easily rendezvous with the B-29s and escort them on daytime missions. They shot the remaining Japanese fighters out of the sky. The island also served as an emergency landing point for damaged bombers that would never have made it the remaining 625 miles to the airfield at Saipan, north of Guam. Bennie's younger brother, Gerry Schriever, who had also become an Army Air Forces engineering officer in the Pacific, was awarded his colonel's eagles by LeMay for the speed with which the engineer group he commanded repaired these B-29s on Iwo Jima and had them flown back to the Marianas.

By the end of July, LeMay had scorched the greater part of sixty large and medium-sized Japanese cities to cinders with 150,000 tons of firebombs. A total of 670,000 Japanese civilians were to perish in American bombings, most in LeMay's fire raids. In June, Arnold had asked him when he thought he could end the war. LeMay replied that he would run out of targets about the first of October and by then the Japanese ought to be ready to capitulate without the necessity of an invasion. He was wrong about the timing. The awe-inspiring destruction of the atomic bombs dropped on Hiroshima on August 6 and on Nagasaki three days later enabled Japan's emperor, Hirohito, to overrule the fanatical militarist holdouts and announce a surrender on August 15, 1945. Yet LeMay was still the man most responsible for ending the war with such swiftness, for it was he who had reduced Japan to the point where these bolts of nuclear annihilation could immediately snap the will to resist any further.

LeMay's place in the postwar U.S. Air Force as its preeminent combat leader was assured. In determining the way the bomber arm of the U.S. Army Air Forces had fought in Europe and in the Pacific, he had also made the greatest contribution in proving the new preeminence of air power itself. And that preeminence, coupled with the unlimited potency of nuclear weapons, was to be the deciding factor in forming the military strategy of the United States during the early and middle years of the Cold War. LeMay had been the indispensable man. A message from Carl Spaatz to Arnold a week before the surrender of Japan demonstrated in what regard LeMay was now held. In July, with the Eighth Air Force due to transfer out of Europe and join the war against the Japanese, Arnold had persuaded the other chiefs to create a Strategic Air Forces command for the Pacific modeled on the one he had established for Europe in 1944. As in Europe, he put the man in whom he had ultimate faith, Tooey Spaatz, in charge. Spaatz appointed as his chief of staff an officer who had been a captain five years earlier, Major General LeMay, and told him to carry on. His message to Arnold, referring to LeMay's B-29 command with the military message traffic term of Baker Two Nine, explained why:

HAVE HAD OPPORTUNITY TO CHECK UP ON BAKER TWO NINE OPER-
ATIONS AND BELIEVE THIS IS THE BEST ORGANIZED AND MOST
TECHNICALLY AND TACTICALLY PROFICIENT MILITARY ORGANIZA-
TION THAT THE WORLD HAS SEEN TO DATE.

In October 1948, Hoyt Vandenberg had brought LeMay home from Europe, where he had been commanding general of U.S. Air Force units deployed there, and handed him a languishing organization called the Strategic Air Command with instructions to turn it into the formidable nuclear striking force it was intended to be. SAC had initially been formed by Spaatz in March 1946 with precisely this objective in mind. It had been so ill-maintained and badly trained over the two years before LeMay inherited it that the SAC of 1948 literally couldn't hit anything under realistic conditions. The jet fighters the United States and the Soviet Union were both fielding meant that the propeller-driven B-29s, then the mainstay of SAC, and the B-50s then entering service, an improved version of the B-29 more easily rigged to carry an atomic bomb, could not survive in the daytime. (The B-36 colossus just coming on line could still bomb in daylight because Soviet fighters could not reach its 40,000-foot altitude, but that advantage would disappear as Russian jets improved.) The B-29s and B-50s therefore had to strike at night. This was made possible by employing the plane's radar to pick out prominent terrain features or tall buildings, called "target finders," that would show up distinctly on the screen, and then calculating the direction and distance to the drop point.

To demonstrate to the SAC crews precisely how incompetent he suspected they were, LeMay ordered the entire command, approximately 480 B-29s and a sampling of the new B-50s and B-36s, to stage a mock night raid on Wright Field. The nearness of the airfield to Dayton, Ohio, should have given the crews plenty of tall buildings to use as target finders. As they approached Wright Field, the planes would transmit a tone over their radios. It would be picked up by an antiaircraft radar unit at Wright. The bombardier would simulate the release of his bombs by halting the tone. The antiaircraft unit would then calculate from the moment the tone halted and the altitude, speed, and distance of the plane precisely where the bomb would have landed. Shoddy maintenance kept a lot of the bombers from even getting off the ground that night and forced others to abort and turn back. And of those that did make it to the general vicinity of Wright Field and sent the Bombs Away signal, not a single crew hit the target. The details of SAC's assault on Wright were immediately classified secret to try to hide from the Soviets that they faced a sawdust bogeyman. But every crew learned how dismally it had performed. LeMay had made his point and reformation began.

When Bennie Schriever first encountered him in 1951, LeMay was about to gain the fourth star of a full general and had been back in the strategic bombing business for the better part of three years. He was transforming SAC into an organization that inspired dread in Moscow. As of December 1951 he had tripled its manpower to 144,525 officers and men, including civilian specialists and maintenance personnel, and his aircraft, 1,186 of all types, had grown significantly in numbers and striking power. His three heavy bomb wings were approaching their full complement of thirty B-36s each and he had another approximately 550 B-29s and B-50s organized into seventeen medium wings. Within the near future he would also have two more medium wings of the revolutionary B-47 Stratojet, America's first strategic jet bomber, as the Boeing production lines fed them into his force. A svelte-looking aircraft with its slim fuselage and six jet engines slung on pods under the swept-back wings that were the first fruit of the von Kármán team's postwar discoveries in Germany, the B-47 had a top speed of 630 miles per hour, as fast as most fighters of the day, and could climb above 40,000 feet.

Moreover, through a combination of midair refueling from tanker aircraft and overseas staging bases from which his bombers could launch strikes or stop to refuel on the way to raids, LeMay had given his entire SAC force an intercontinental span. The overseas bases encircled the Soviet Union. In most of Stalin's empire, no city or town, no military installation, no industrial plant was beyond the touch of

LeMay's hand of destruction. The first of the staging bases were borrowed RAF airfields in England. Engineers were set to work meanwhile reconstructing into permanent SAC installations other disused fields such as Greenham Common, a former paratroop and glider base west of London near Newbury, or Brize Norton amidst the rolling landscape and stone-roofed cottages of the Cotswold Hills farther west in Gloucestershire. The locations west of London were deliberately chosen so that the RAF jet fighters at fields on the other, eastern, side of the English capital could protect SAC's bombers against attacking Soviet aircraft.

When the B-36 with its 3,500-mile combat radius was counted in, everything from the satellite states like Poland, Hungary, and Romania, and all of western Russia as far as Moscow and beyond to the industrial centers of the Urals, was within reach of these English bases, airfields that recalled those from which the B-17s in which LeMay had learned his craft had risen not long before to humble Nazi Germany. The oil wells and refineries at Baku and elsewhere in Azerbaijan in the Soviet Caucasus were vulnerable to SAC bombers staging out of North Africa from the air base abuilding at Sidi Slimane in Morocco. Any targets worth hitting in the Soviet Far East, like Vladivostok with its air and naval facilities, and much of China, where the Communist leader Mao Tse-tung now ruled, were exposed to attacks staged from Guam and Yokota Air Base in American-occupied Japan.

The U.S. nuclear arsenal, which numbered 549 atomic, i.e., fission, weapons by the end of 1951, did not yet possess quite enough for all of LeMay's bombers, but that shortcoming was being remedied. The Sandstone series of nuclear tests at Eniwetok Atoll in the Pacific in April and May of 1948 had led to the development of a more advanced plutonium bomb, the Mark 4, which, at 31 kilotons, exceeded the blast of the Nagasaki weapon by approximately 10 kilotons. The Atomic Energy Commission geared up its facilities at Oak Ridge, Tennessee, Hanford, Washington, and elsewhere to mass production. LeMay was also hoping that his aircraft would soon be armed with the hydrogen bomb, which, in 1950, President Truman had ordered the AEC to create through the laboratory it now controlled at Los Alamos.

SAC was no longer the bumbling organization LeMay had been given in 1948. He honed his combat crews and subordinate commanders with the training techniques he had devised for use against the Germans and the Japanese. He instituted practice bombing competitions. To further motivate his men, he wangled the authority, a privilege extended only to SAC, to award spot promotions for outstanding performance, as high as lieutenant colonel in the officer grades and technical sergeant and master sergeant in the enlisted ranks. The awards were usually given to an entire crew at once in order to encourage teamwork. For example, a command pilot who was a captain could go to major, his co-pilot from first lieutenant to captain, and everyone else in the crew could also jump one rank ahead of their peers. If their proficiency fell, LeMay would take away the promotions. By 1951, LeMay's force was ready to go. The atmosphere of the time reinforced the motivation. These were the years when anti-Communist fervor ran so high that some of the citizenry did not think it insane to repeat the slogan "Better Dead Than Red!"

LeMay's SAC had, in fact, become the centerpiece of America's national strategy. The concept underlying it had originally evolved out of Truman's short-lived confidence in an American atomic monopoly— the same source of his and Jimmie Byrnes's abortive attempt to intimidate Stalin with their postwar atomic diplomacy—and out of his concern to avoid deficits, curb inflation, and prevent the American economy from being undermined by profligate military spending. If the United States alone possessed the bomb and the means to deliver it through a long-range strategic bomber force, there was no need to burden the American economy with the huge expense of large ground forces to match the Red Army and with major naval forces for a prolonged war with the Soviet Union. The bomb would render any war with Russia short and decisive.

Truman demonstrated his determination to hew to this strategy when it put him on a collision course with the Navy and set off the "Revolt of the Admirals" in 1949. That April he and his secretary of defense, Louis Johnson, canceled the Navy's planned "supercarrier," the USS *United States,* in favor of more adequate funding for the B-36. The Navy had been counting on construction of this imposing ship, the model for the majestic aircraft carriers that were to be built in later decades to handle modern jet aircraft, to keep it on a par with the Air Force. The secretary of the navy, John Sullivan, resigned and Truman and Johnson sacked Admiral Louis Denfeld, the chief of naval operations, to quell further opposition within the senior ranks.

Soviet acquisition of the bomb in 1949 did not negate the economic rationale for the strategy. The end of the monopoly simply meant that the United States would have to outpace the Russians constantly in the size and power of its nuclear arsenal and the means to deliver an annihilating assault. The same economic motivation then led Dwight Eisenhower to adopt and elaborate on the strategy after his election in 1952. The surge in military spending for conventional armaments brought on by the Korean War, and the need to arm the new West German state and rearm Washington's European allies for the North Atlantic Treaty Organization alliance Stalin had clumsily provoked, peaked after his death in 1953 cleared the way for a truce in Korea that July. To achieve what he called "security with solvency," Eisenhower resumed Truman's policy of restricting spending on the conventional military in favor of reliance on the intercontinental reach of LeMay's nuclear bombers.

The Eisenhower administration's official euphemism for the strategy was "The New Look," taken from a women's fashion line exhibited by Christian Dior in the late 1940s. (Some in the administration also favored a catchy phrase for the strategy that was tinged with a bit of gallows humor—"a bigger bang for a buck.") It soon became more appropriately known as Massive Retaliation, after Eisenhower and his stridently anti-Communist secretary of state, John Foster Dulles, made clear that a Soviet assault on West Berlin, for instance, or on any of America's allies, would result not merely in a local defense under NATO, but in an all-out response of America's nuclear might. Eisenhower and Dulles reasoned that the threat would curb military adventurism by the Soviets on the periphery of their empire and deter the Russians from launching a general war with their own growing nuclear arsenal. And if general war did occur, SAC would be the fist that delivered the knockout blow of a nuclear holocaust.

The strategy entailed previously unimaginable civilian casualties, but this does not seem to have bothered anyone in authority. The prospect certainly did not disturb LeMay. Having had to inflict a cruel death by fire on hundreds of thousands of Japanese civilians in order to destroy Japan's industry and render the country prostrate and ripe for surrender appears to have calloused him morally. Taking human life on a horrendous scale once apparently made it easier for him to contemplate taking it on a far more horrendous scale the next time. It was therefore not that difficult for him to go from anonymous Japanese men, women, and children by the hundreds of thousands to the planned killing of tens of millions of anonymous civilians in the Soviet Union, the East European states, and China. The same could be said of the other military leaders of his generation who had not had LeMay's personal experience and of the civilian politicians above them. The RAF campaign of nighttime "city busting," culminating in the slaughter at Dresden in February 1945, when a city filled with refugees was struck by both British and American bombers and from 36,000 to 136,000 civilians killed (no one has been able to estimate the number accurately), along with the incineration of Japan, inculcated the assumption that strategic bombing entailed massive civilian casualties as an unavoidable consequence. By 1954, when LeMay would have 1,500 atomic bombs at his disposal, the estimate was that 60 million people would be killed and 17 million injured within the Soviet Union, Eastern Europe, and China if SAC was unleashed. A chilling phrase began to appear in the lexicon of advocates of strategic nuclear bombing: "to kill a nation."

Massive Retaliation as a national strategy also confirmed the primacy of the Air Force among the services and raised LeMay's Strategic Air Command to ascendancy within the Air Force itself. While Eisenhower reduced the overall strength of the military establishment by nearly a million men, inflicting most of the cuts on the ground forces of the Army but also shrinking the Navy and the Air Force as a whole, he encouraged SAC to grow. By 1957, when LeMay was to depart after nearly nine years to go to Washington as vice chief of staff, his creation would number 224,014 officers, enlisted men, and civilian support personnel. One hundred and twenty-seven of the B-36s would linger, but not for long. The rest of the propeller-driven fleet, the B-29s and B-50s, would have become a memory. In their place, lavish spending would have immensely enhanced the air power they had represented. SAC would field 1,285 B-47 medium jet bombers in 1957 and almost 250, with many more to come, of the new eight-engine B-52 jet Stratofortresses Boeing had begun delivering two years earlier to constitute the heavy bomb wings. (The tanker shortage had also long been solved after hundreds of KC-97s had flowed into SAC's fleet by the end of 1953 and into 1954 to form new refueling squadrons that would meet the bombers going out and coming home.) When LeMay took command of

SAC in 1948 his title was the ordinary one of commanding general. By 1955 the ordinary would be exalted to commander-in-chief. The letters and memoranda LeMay exchanged with his superior, General Nathan Twining, who was to succeed Vandenberg as chief of staff in mid-1953, reflect the unique status he held within the Air Force. It was customary for ranking generals to address each other in the familiar Dear Nate, Dear Curt manner, but LeMay's side of the correspondence, preserved with Twining's in the archives of the Library of Congress, goes one step further. It has the tone of a man addressing an equal, not a senior.

24.

INTO THE LION'S DEN

A general Bennie Schriever once worked for paid him an unusual compliment in an efficiency report: "He is not afraid of anybody." In crossing Curtis LeMay, however, Schriever was placing himself in peril of being crushed by a titan of his profession. And in their first encounter, he looked decidedly foolish. It was one of the few occasions in his life when he came up with a genuinely harebrained scheme. At the time, in early 1951, Bennie was working in a preliminary job General Saville, the deputy chief of staff, development, had given him when he brought him back to the Pentagon after graduation from the National War College. He was made an assistant to evaluate R&D projects, deputy to a remarkably imaginative scientist from MIT named Ivan Getting. An electrical engineer and physicist, Getting had won a Medal of Merit, the highest decoration the president could then award a civilian for military work, for his achievements in radar design at the Radiation Laboratory during the Second World War. After the outbreak of the Korean War, Saville had persuaded Getting to take a leave from MIT and come down to the Pentagon as his principal assistant to sort out R&D enterprises.

LeMay complained that, although SAC was the most important element of the Air Force, it wasn't receiving enough attention from Saville's department. Saville passed the complaint on to Getting, who in turn passed it to Schriever. One of the issues at the moment was how to disperse SAC's bases in order to make them as survivable as possible. Stalin's only long-range bombers, his Tu-4 copies of the B-29, might carry just enough gas for a one-way trip to only some of America's cities, but one still had to guard against the contingency, however remote, that he might order his air force to attack anyway. This was one of the reasons SAC headquarters had been moved from Andrews Air Force Base near Washington, D.C., to Offutt Air Force Base just outside Omaha, Nebraska (the base had originated as a cavalry post during the Indian wars of the nineteenth century), when LeMay assumed command in October 1948.

Schriever took a look at the map and it struck him that all of the waterways running through the American continent and others along its edges like the Chesapeake Bay provided an obvious means of dispersal. If floating SAC bases were established on them the aircraft could be shifted as often as desired. The catch was that the bombers would have to be equipped with pontoon landing gear in order to land and take off on water. This was theoretically possible, but the additional weight would reduce range and the pontoons would create drag that would also reduce speed. Getting should have recognized the proposal as impractical and General Saville certainly should have known that it would appear absolutely wacky to a bomber man like LeMay. Unfortunately, neither had his common-sense radar turned on and Bennie and Getting flew out to Omaha to present the scheme to LeMay.

Getting sat beside the general and his senior staff officers while Bennie set up his charts on an easel in front and flipped through them as he gave his presentation. LeMay reacted with mutterings of disgust and ridicule and, at the end of the briefing, took his cigar out of his mouth, leaned forward, and asked with sarcasm, "Did you say your name was Schriever?" Then he left and Bennie folded his charts and he and Getting left too, right back to Washington.

Later that year Saville retired and Getting went off to take a high-level position in the electronics industry. Donald Putt, the technology-oriented student of von Kármán, stepped into Saville's place as deputy chief of staff, development, and promoted Bennie to be his assistant for development planning. Because the job entailed literally planning the future of the Air Force, Bennie had to deal with LeMay. He found, however, that when he returned to Omaha with sensible advice or proposals, LeMay wouldn't listen on these occasions either.

The obstacle doesn't seem to have been that first silly episode. If LeMay remembered it, he never mentioned it. The problem was that Curtis LeMay had become an altered man. The young colonel who had been so open-minded and keen to learn that he had risked personal humiliation by convening all-ranks, freewheeling criticism sessions in the mess hall after a raid on Nazi-occupied Europe had become the four-star general who was no longer willing to hear anything that did not fit his preconceptions. He was the classic example of a man made arrogant by power. Years of commanding with unchallenged authority had rendered him rigid. He had become a figure of obsessions and had lost his sense of proportion. His former restraint had also been replaced by a quick temper, a short fuse as it was called in the military, which further inhibited his ability to listen.

The change was conspicuously apparent in his correspondence with Nathan Twining in the mid-1950s. Formed as he was by the gruesome, no-quarter-given air battles with the Luftwaffe in 1943, he was fixated in the belief that the Soviets were also going to build an air force powerful enough to challenge his SAC in a similar death struggle for supremacy of the skies. He had such profound and unquestioning faith in the bomber that he could not imagine someone else might resort to an alternative weapon to rain nuclear fire on an opponent. The fixation resonated in a March 21, 1955, memorandum to Twining and in a covering letter of the same date. Both assessed with uninhibited criticism a plan by Twining's headquarters that laid out a proposed structure for the Air Force through 1965. "Before 1965 Soviet Forces will probably attain a delivery capability and a [nuclear] stockpile of sufficient size and configuration to completely destroy any selected target system within the U.S.," LeMay stated on the opening page of his memorandum. Some of this "delivery capability," he conceded, may consist of future Soviet intercontinental ballistic missiles, but he was convinced that the predominant element would be intercontinental bombers. (The prototype of the first strategic bomber of original Soviet design, not a copy of the B-29, had been detected in 1954. It was the Miasishchev Mia-4, dubbed the Bison by NATO intelligence, with swept-back wings and four jet engines.)

Therefore, he emphasized again and again in the memorandum and in the covering letter, the Air Force had to structure itself so that its "primary objective . . . should be to win the battle against Soviet Air Power." This meant a bigger and better SAC because "the bomber airplane is the best delivery vehicle" to triumph in this "battle against Soviet Air Power," a phrase he repeated constantly. He asserted that his bombers would catch the Russian planes on the ground and destroy them and their bases as well as the industries that produced them. He wanted 1,440 of the new B-52s by 1965. To keep this bomber fleet aloft with midair refueling, he asked for 1,140 of the forthcoming Boeing KC-135 four-engine jet tankers, which were to replace the propeller-driven KC-97s. (The KC-135, ample-bodied to carry as much aviation fuel as possible, initiated one of the most spectacularly successful commercial spinoffs from military hardware. The entrepreneurs in Seattle saw in its dimensions a passenger jet and with the installation of seats and other civilian accoutrements it became the famous Boeing 707 jetliner, over a thousand of which were sold to American and foreign airlines. The plane transformed international air travel.) With the cost of this stupendous bomber and tanker fleet in mind, he objected to the number of jet fighter-bombers and air superiority fighters the Air Force planned to buy to fulfill the Tactical Air Command's mission of providing close air support over a battlefield for Army ground troops. Assisting the Army was not a mission that interested LeMay. He even argued that the bomber was the best weapon to neutralize any ICBMs the Soviets might field by 1965 because of its ability "to destroy their launching sites as a matter of high priority." (Since it would take hours for SAC's bombers to reach the launching sites and only half an hour for a Soviet ICBM to reach its target in the United States, the logic of bombing empty launching sites hardly seems to follow.)

LeMay's attachment to the bomber and his fixation on winning the air battle he anticipated with a Soviet version of SAC led him to what was perhaps his most astonishing proposal to Twining. He wanted to abolish conventional armaments and go entirely nuclear. "Atomic and thermonuclear weapons have made conventional weapons obsolete, and the United States should cease stockpiling of conventional weapons," he wrote. "The expense of developing and maintaining a limited conventional capability in the face of the critical need for skilled personnel and resources to man and equip strategic units can no longer be justified." He proposed henceforth to use only nuclear weapons in wars both big and small. In other words, it was just as appropriate to let fly with nuclear weapons in a small-scale war like the recent conflict in Korea as it was in a full-scale one with the Soviets. "The distinction between localized and general war is political rather than military," he said, and the United States should "always use the best weapons available in either general or limited war."

There was a further advantage to moving straight to nuclear weapons in small wars, he maintained. They would bring quick victory and, apparently with the example of Korea in mind, avoid having the war drag out and public opinion turn against it. Therefore, "to insure the favorable outcome of a localized war in a short period of time, it was necessary that any political or psychological restraint in employing atomic weapons be erased." Precisely what Twining thought of LeMay's proposal is unknown and there is no record of a reply in the correspondence. Presumably he understood, as the changed LeMay did not, that for the U.S. Air Force to publicly advocate something like this would set off a political firestorm at home and abroad of nuclear dimensions.

His memory of those terrifying skies over Germany was also the root cause of LeMay's most striking loss of a sense of proportion—his unquenchable desire for more and more megatons of nuclear explosive to drop on his Soviet opponents and more and more bombers with which to loose it. (A megaton is the equivalent of a million tons of TNT.) He feared that when war came, unnerved crews would not strike with the accuracy they attained in practice exercises in peacetime. Some planes would also not find their targets because of navigational errors, others would be shot down, still others would turn back because of mechanical failures. The answer was to make up for these errors and omissions with bigger and bigger bombs and enough planes to double and triple the number of strikes programmed for a single target.

He was extremely pleased in late 1954 to get the first practical hydrogen bomb, designated the Mark 17, a "weaponized" version of a dry thermonuclear device, fueled by lithium deuteride, which the Los Alamos laboratory had set off at Bikini Atoll earlier that year in a test called Romeo. This first "droppable" H-bomb weighed 42,000 pounds, which meant that only a B-36 in the current SAC fleet could carry it, but it exploded with a doomsday blast of eleven megatons, the equivalent of

524 Nagasaki, first-generation plutonium bombs, and 880 times the force of the smaller atomic bomb that had devastated Hiroshima. LeMay began pressing right away for lighter hydrogen bombs of equal or greater megatonnage. With them he wanted to turn his B-47s, which had a 25,000-pound payload, into thermonuclear bombers and fit more than one hydrogen bomb into the new B-52, with its 43,000-pound capacity (soon increased to 50,000), in order to obliterate multiple targets. When the Mark 21 hydrogen bomb, which weighed 15,000 pounds and yielded 4.5 megatons, appeared in 1955, he immediately mated it to the B-52 as the central component of SAC's striking power for the next couple of years. The Mark 21's "bang" did not satisfy LeMay, however, and so he pressed for an upgrade. This was to be the Mark 36, which would be produced the following year. It was somewhat heavier than the Mark 21 at 17,500 pounds, but yielded more than twice the force when it exploded.

In another memorandum to Twining that November of 1955, LeMay raised the ante on bombers. He now said he needed approximately 1,900 B-52s and some 1,300 KC-135 jet tankers to midair refuel these bombers *by 1963*. (Eisenhower was eventually to cap B-52 production at 744 aircraft by the fall of 1962, a decision the Kennedy administration was to uphold, with the comment: "I don't know how many times you can kill a man, but about three should be enough.") Nor did LeMay succeed in persuading the Eisenhower administration to build an H bomb, except for the original Mark 17, beyond ten megatons, but not for lack of trying. In 1953, he asked the Nuclear Weapons Panel of the Air Force Scientific Advisory Board to look into the feasibility of a hydrogen bomb of twenty megatons or greater, an idea Eisenhower is said to have vetoed as beyond common sense. The massive megatonnage and the doubling and tripling on targets was to lead to fantastic overkill. SAC was to end up programming for Moscow alone more than twenty-five megatons. Pressure from LeMay was to be the major impetus in driving the yield of the American stockpile of nuclear warheads up to the record 20,491 megatons peak it was to reach in 1960, enough to provide each of the approximately 180 million inhabitants of the United States at the time with bomb material equivalent in explosive force to 110 tons of TNT.

While LeMay wished to be absolutely certain that enough planes got through with enough big bombs to "kill" every target on his list, it is clear from his correspondence and statements over the years that he also simply wanted to blast the Soviet Union, and any targets he thought worthy of his attention in Eastern Europe and China, with as much explosive force as he could muster. He apparently did not understand how different in nature nuclear weapons were from the conventional explosives he had dropped on Nazi-occupied Europe. He seems to have thought of hydrogen bombs essentially as just vastly more powerful bombs. He had a pitiless, smug vision of what he was going to do to the peoples of the Soviet Union with them, a vision he described in a lecture to the National War College in April 1956:

> Let us assume the order had been received this morning to unleash the full weight of our nuclear force. (I hope, of course, this will never happen.) Between sunset tonight and sunrise tomorrow morning the Soviet Union would likely cease to be a major military power or even a major nation. . . . Dawn might break over a nation infinitely poorer than China—less populated than the United States and condemned to an agrarian existence perhaps for generations to come.

What LeMay did not realize was that if he ever launched the war for which he had prepared, the result would be national suicide. It would hardly matter should the Soviet Union fail to strike the United States with a single nuclear bomb. If he dropped all of this megatonnage on the Soviets, the American people would perish too. And he would also be condemning to an agonizing perdition the peoples of Canada, Europe, and most of the rest of the Northern Hemisphere through the Middle East and Asia. The puny, by comparison, bombs that had shocked the world in demolishing Hiroshima and Nagasaki had been fused to burst in the air. (The Little Boy Uranium-235 bomb dropped on Hiroshima had been detonated at 1,900 feet above the courtyard of one of the city's hospitals.) The air burst technique had been deliberate in order to focus the maximum pressure and heat of the bomb's blast on the buildings and people below, obliterating both in an instant. While there was extensive radiation, it did not extend far beyond the area covered by the blast, because comparatively little dirt and debris was blown up into the atmosphere.

LeMay, however, as he wrote to Twining, was going to fuse a lot of his monster bombs for ground or near-ground bursts to be certain of crushing underground bunkers and so-called hardened targets, such as concrete revetments with thick overhead cover used to protect aircraft. These ground-level bursts would hurl massive amounts of irradiated soil and the pulverized remains of masonry and concrete structures high into the upper atmosphere. The clouds of poisoned soil and debris would spread as they were carried around the earth by the upper atmospheric winds. One result would be a nuclear winter, a catastrophic change in climate of unknown duration, with frigid temperatures at the height of summer, because the dirt in the upper atmosphere would block out the sun's rays. Agriculture, on which human beings depend for sustenance, would become impossible. Most animal and bird life would be extinguished because the plants, shrubs, and trees on which so many of these creatures depend would also die from the cold and lack of sunlight, without which plants cannot perform the photosynthesis process that nourishes them. And as precipitation brought down the irradiated particles, humans and animals and birds would be stricken with fatal radiation sickness. The water resources would be contaminated too as this deadly residue from LeMay's thermonuclear devices was gradually absorbed into them. Civilization as we know it in the Northern Hemisphere would cease to exist.

To give the man his due, he created a force that posed a formidable deterrent to Soviet military adventurism in Western Europe, had the Soviet dictator been so inclined. That Stalin had no intention of launching such adventures, as was revealed with the opening of the Soviet Union's archives after its collapse in 1991, did not negate the fact that the threat was perceived as real by Americans in the early 1950s. And the promise of overwhelming retaliation from SAC undoubtedly kept Stalin's successor, Nikita Khrushchev, from being more rash than he was. LeMay's deterrence mission was thus a legitimate one, given the thinking of the period. Although he would later express regret that the United States missed an opportunity in the early 1950s to unleash SAC and destroy the Soviet Union at what he believed would have been little or no cost to itself, there is no evidence that LeMay actively sought to provoke what was referred to at the time as "preventive war."

He was subsequently to be accused of this because he ran SAC spy flights along the edges of Soviet territory and an occasional flight that deliberately penetrated Russian airspace and flew over outlying regions to conduct photoreconnaissance. The espionage flights along the periphery,

called "spoofing," were a ruse to gather information on Soviet air defenses by tricking the Russians into turning on their radars, scrambling
fighters, and activating their radar jammers. LeMay was perpetually
worried about the Soviets jamming the radar in his bombers, without
which the planes could not bomb at night. The spy flights enabled SAC
to stay abreast of this capability and teach crews to switch the bomber
radar frequencies to alternates the Russians might not be jamming. Time
and the release of secrets also absolved him on the penetrations of Soviet
airspace for photoreconnaissance. Truman and Eisenhower gave permission for the flights because of reports of Soviet aviation buildups.
Both presidents feared a sneak attack, a nuclear Pearl Harbor, from
which the United States would not be able to recover.

LeMay did assume that if war with the Soviet Union appeared imminent, he would be released to launch a preemptive strike with the
bolts of nuclear lightning held in a mailed fist on SAC's unit patch.
"The United States cannot under any circumstances suffer the first
blow of having bombs fall on this country," he remarked in his March
21, 1955, memorandum to Twining. "Therefore, Soviet action short of
general war could force the United States to initiate an offensive."
Again, this position did not differ radically from the presidential one.
While Truman and Eisenhower would have been far more reluctant
than LeMay to order a general nuclear assault, both presidents, and
their successors throughout the Cold War for that matter, consistently
refused to abjure the first use of nuclear weapons.

The bomber gap episode helped confirm LeMay in his conviction
that his opponents were seeking to imitate him. In a fly-past in Moscow
on July 13, 1955, their Aviation Day, the Soviets showed off their new
four-jet Mia-4 Bison bombers. American military attachés counted nine
bombers in the first formation, then ten in the second, then another nine
in the third. Air Force intelligence, eager to create pressure for higher
production of B-52s, immediately concluded that if the Soviets were
willing to display twenty-eight Bisons, they must have twice that many
in service. Citing their estimate of Soviet production capacity, Air Force
intelligence officers also predicted that the Russians would have a fleet
of 600 to 800 Bisons within four to five years. This prediction and reports of Andrei Tupolev's four-engine turboprop Tu-95 Bear bomber,
which was to enter Soviet service in 1956, set off an outcry in the
United States of a bomber gap that would negate SAC.

LeMay made the most of it. In testimony before the Air Force Sub-committee of the Senate Committee on Armed Services in April and May of 1956, he claimed that unless appropriations for B-52s, then coming off the Boeing assembly lines at six aircraft a month, were increased, the Soviet Union would achieve air superiority over the United States. By 1960, he said, "the Soviet Air Force will have substantially more Bisons and Bears than we will have B-52s. . . . I can only conclude then that they will have a greater striking power than we will have." Congress voted an additional $1 billion (in these years before the severe inflation set off by the Vietnam War a substantial sum of money) for the Air Force budget in fiscal 1957 and again in fiscal 1958. While LeMay, who had become adept at manipulating legislators, was hyping his testimony to extort more funds, his top secret correspondence with Twining, where he had no reason to conceal his true feelings, demonstrates that he really did believe the Soviets were attempting to match his SAC. "As you know," he wrote in a June 1956 memorandum to Twining, "the first enemy targets that would have to be destroyed are the bases of the Soviet long-range air force. Destruction of these targets is the number one task of the Strategic Air Command."

The CIA, which had no budgetary interest, discovered that the Russians were turning out far fewer Bisons and Bears than the Air Force contended. The analysts in its economic intelligence section did so by studying the tail numbers on the Soviet bombers and matching these to known Soviet production schedules. The Soviets had apparently displayed all of the Bisons they had on July 13, 1955. Some civilian intelligence analysts also guessed, but could never prove, that the Soviets might have flown the nine-plane formation by twice to further impress the American military attachés watching through their binoculars. Then, in 1958, when the Russians had about 85 bombers of both types and SAC had 1,769, including 380 B-52s, the Soviets curtailed their bomber production. They ended up a few years later with a long-range air force that consisted primarily of 85 Bisons and 50 to 60 Bears.

MOSCOW OPTS FOR ROCKETS

Curtis LeMay could not understand that his bombers were in danger of being undermined as a credible deterrent by the advance of technology. In strategic terms, they were coming to represent the past. He was not heeding von Kármán's warning to Arnold in 1945 that "the men in charge of the future Air Forces should always remember that problems never have final or universal solutions and only a constant inquisitive attitude toward science and a ceaseless and swift adaptation to new developments can maintain the security of this nation through world air supremacy." Stalin's successors after his death on March 5, 1953, initially a committee and then Nikita Khrushchev alone when he overcame his rivals, did not intend to rely on bombers to counter America's nuclear might. Long-range bombing was not part of the Russian military experience. The aircraft they had deployed during the Second World War, such as Sergei Ilyushin's famous Il-2 Shturmovik fighter-bomber, were designed to support the Red Army as flying artillery and tank destroyers. They built bombers, but these were mainly medium-range types, again meant to enhance the fighting power of the army. Tupolev's Tu-4 copies of the B-29 on which Stalin had lavished resources in the immediate postwar period were impractical because of their lack of range. The Soviets would never be able to overcome this obstacle. There was no way, short of going to war, for them to acquire the type of staging bases with which LeMay had encircled their empire and, because of the distances involved, midair refueling was also not an answer. With everything having to take off from the Soviet Union or its satellites, the tankers, to stay aloft, would be using up the fuel they were supposed to pass to the bombers.

The Russians had difficulties as well with the long-range bombers of their own design. As a would-be intercontinental, the Bison was deficient in range at about 5,600 miles and the turboprop Bear was vulnerable to American jet fighters. Neither approached being an equal of the B-52. The designer of the Bison, Vladimir Miasishchev, suggested to Khrushchev that they might overcome the range deficiency by landing in Mexico after bombing the United States. "What do you think Mexico is—our mother-in-law?" Khrushchev replied. "You think we can go calling anytime we want? The Mexicans would never let us have the plane back."

On the other hand, Russia had a long record of experimental rocketry and visionary theories of space travel, beginning with the end-of-the-nineteenth-century writings of Konstantin Tsiolkovsky, a provincial math teacher with dreams and a knowledge of physics. Marshal Tukhachevsky, the star of the prewar Red Army leadership, had an intense interest in rocketry, seeing it as a way to hurl large charges of explosive beyond the range of conventional artillery. He established a flourishing laboratory for military rocketry in Leningrad in the 1920s. One of its inventions, a prototype bazooka, might have proved quite useful against German tanks. But after Stalin had Tukhachevsky purged and executed in 1937 during the Great Purge, the laboratory was suppressed and about 200 of its specialists suffered the marshal's fate. Nevertheless, a number of the more imaginative scientists and engineers, including Sergei Korolev, who was to become the senior Soviet rocket designer in the postwar era, managed to evade an executioner's bullet. The Red Army also employed what rocket artillery it had developed to powerful effect during the conflict. The German soldier had trembled at the whooshing salvos of high explosive from the massed batteries of 122mm Katyusha rockets.

At the close of hostilities, the bombproof V-2 production plant tunneled into a mountain near Nordhausen in north-central Germany and run full-tilt with the lives of thousands of slave laborers turned out to be located within the Soviet occupation zone. So were the V-2 engine test facilities in the Frankenwald Mountains. The U.S. Army got to the Nordhausen plant first, however, and hauled off all the documentation along with as many intact V-2s as it could before the occupation lines were formalized. But there were enough parts and engines left to serve the Russians. The Americans also got the best of the German rocket engineers from the group of 400 rocketeers who, with Wernher von Braun, had fled to them. The Soviets still managed, sometimes willingly and sometimes by force, to assemble their own group of competent German rocket men. The leader was an engineer named

Helmut Gröttrup, a left-winger who came to the Russians voluntarily. He had been one of the ranking guidance and control specialists at Peenemünde. Altogether, about 5,000 German engineers and technicians of various skills were rounded up and transported to the Soviet Union for rocket work. The V-2 blueprints and associated documentation were reconstructed, German-made V-2s assembled and fired, and copies then manufactured by the Soviets themselves.

As the Russians acquired enough expertise of their own, the Germans became superfluous and were sent back home. Steady progress was made in subsequent years devising more advanced ballistic missiles under the direction of Korolev and the rocket engine builder Valentin Glushko. Stalin's heirs set the course of the Soviet Union firmly at the end of 1953. The Politburo of the Communist Party, the highest governing body, formally decided to have Korolev create an intercontinental ballistic missile that would carry as its warhead the hydrogen bomb the Russians were to acquire two years later in November 1955. Andrei Sakharov, the most talented of the young Soviet physicists, had just completed his preliminary design for the Russian hydrogen weapon in November 1953. While the development of bombers continued, as the appearance of the Bison and Bear demonstrated, the Politburo decision held. The pattern of the future had been drawn. The Soviet Union would rely, not on bombers as LeMay continued to think it would, but on intercontinental ballistic missiles to deliver most of its nuclear warheads.

If the Soviets had fielded a considerable force of ICBMs with nuclear warheads before the United States possessed equivalent weapons or had them well in progress, panic certainly would have ensued at home and among America's allies in Europe. LeMay's Strategic Air Command would have been trumped. SAC would have ceased to be, in the minds of much of the American public and among West Europeans, a credible deterrent force. The appearance of the Bison and Bear bombers had already raised worries about the safety of SAC bases beyond the simple one at the beginning of the decade that had prompted Bennie Schriever's inane amphibious bomber scheme. Soviet ICBMs in quantity would have transformed those worries into a genuine fear that SAC could be eliminated in a surprise attack and the United States left with no adequate means of retaliation.

LeMay needed six hours to load nuclear weapons into all of his bombers and get them into the air. The American radars of the day would give only fifteen minutes' warning of an ICBM assault because the radars could not pick up the incoming missile warheads until they had reached their apogee halfway through their flight. Some SAC bombers could be kept on strip alert, as was always being done, and some could be rotated aloft on aerial alert, but this could never be more than a portion of the force. To keep all of SAC permanently on alert twenty-four hours a day wasn't feasible. The task would have required triple manning of the aircraft and doubling or tripling the ground crews and support staff. LeMay would have argued, and with logic, that in real circumstances there would be sufficient warning of imminent war with the Russians for him to prepare his bombers. He would have argued in vain, for many would not have believed him.

(In 1960, three years after LeMay departed to become vice chief of staff of the Air Force, SAC reached a personnel strength of 266,788 officers, men, and civilian specialists and was able to keep a third of its bombers and tankers on fifteen-minute strip alert around the clock. The following year SAC adopted an airborne alert in which some of its bombers were always aloft and on station waiting for a go order, along with a permanent airborne command post, named Looking Glass, under a general officer. The command post planes flew eight-hour shifts day and night in converted KC-135 tankers equipped with communications, radars, and other necessary gear to direct SAC's bombers. But the strategic equation was changing by 1960 and 1961. SAC's bombers were no longer so important. Earlier, when the bombers represented all that the country had, not even a third of the force on perpetual fifteen-minute alert might have been enough to silence the skeptics and alarmists like Paul Nitze who were on a perpetual alert of their own to arouse and batten on fear.)

A NUCLEAR REACTOR IN THE SKY

The precise sequence is hazy in retrospect, but Schriever's slide into an increasingly dangerous confrontation with LeMay probably began over the nuclear-powered airplane. For airmen, the dream of a flying machine propelled by atomic fission meant the possibility of unlimited range. A plane would be able to stay aloft for weeks and even months without refueling. As Theodore von Kármán had told Hap Arnold in *Where We Stand,* his preliminary report to *Toward New Horizons,* nuclear propulsion, if attainable, would "secure us the conquest of the air over the entire globe." Although they ignored almost all the rest of von Kármán's visionary theorizing, the bomber men of the postwar U.S. Air Force, the "operators" like LeMay, paid enthusiastic attention to his thoughts on this subject.

The program for the atomic-powered airplane, subsequently titled Aircraft Nuclear Propulsion (ANP), had begun in 1946. The Air Force and the Atomic Energy Commission were to spend more than $7 billion on the project. Most of the work was conducted in secret, but with unstinting funds and support from the atomic power enthusiasts among the congressmen and senators on the Joint Committee on Atomic Energy, particularly the nuclear weaponry hawks Senators Brien McMahon of Connecticut and Henry "Scoop" Jackson of Washington, both Democrats.

While the entire Air Force hierarchy wanted an atomic-powered airplane, LeMay didn't want just any nuclear-driven bomber that would fly from the United States directly to the Soviet Union, drop its hydrogen bombs, and then return for more without ever having to bother with midair refueling or refueling stops at overseas staging bases. He wanted a supersonic one and had levied this attribute on the Air Staff in Washington as a SAC requirement. He was convinced that supersonic flight gave a bomber a much greater chance of survival against enemy fighters and other air defenses. As assistant for development planning, Schriever was charged with recruiting the scientists and engineers who could build the plane for LeMay. As far as he could determine from the men already working on the project and from other extensive exploration, it was possible to design a reactor light enough to power a subsonic bomber, but a supersonic one was out of the question. Generating enough power within the reactor to achieve supersonic flight would create temperatures so extreme that no materials in existence or foreseeable could withstand them. The reactor would melt. His findings were not welcomed at SAC and he was summoned to Omaha.

The meeting took place in LeMay's office in SAC's original headquarters at Offutt, fashioned by partitioning up an abandoned Second World War aircraft assembly plant on the base. As was his custom, LeMay was chewing on his cigar as he sat behind his desk. In front of it was a large couch with a couple of generals who were ranking members of his staff and Dr. Carroll Zimmerman, a civilian analyst who was chief of SAC's Operations Analysis section. Behind the couch were more chairs with other senior members of the SAC staff. Tommy Power, who had circled over Tokyo assessing the damage for LeMay when they had lit that first horrendous firestorm and killed 72,000 to 83,000 people on the night of March 9, 1945, was now a major general and LeMay's deputy as vice commander of SAC. He sat in a chair close beside the desk. Schriever was beckoned to an empty chair next to him. Bennie was not afraid, but he felt alone, and he was. LeMay pointed a finger at him and said, addressing him coldly by his rank and not by his name, "Colonel, I understand that somebody in the Pentagon is against the supersonic nuclear bomber." Schriever waited, breathed deeply, and said, "Yes, it is me." LeMay's head snapped back a bit at the directness of the answer. Bennie went on to say that he was not opposed to the plane as such, that it was simply a technological impossibility, explaining how subsonic seemed feasible, but that the ferocious heat of supersonic would melt any material they had or could foresee.

They went back and forth for half an hour. LeMay was not going to settle for a subsonic nuclear-powered bomber. Supersonic was what he wanted, that was that. Schriever held his line. "Look," he said, "I am running the Development Planning Office and I have access to all the top scientists and engineers in this country. And I have not had a single one tell me that they could, in fact, build a nuclear-powered engine that will operate at supersonic speeds. And it's not me that's saying that; it is the experts in the country who are saying that." LeMay did not appear convinced. "If you can find someone who is knowledgeable, a scientist or engineer who understands all the technology that is involved in supersonic flight with a nuclear power plant, I will stand corrected," Bennie said. "But that has been my job to look into these things." He was a bit surprised that LeMay did not throw him out of the office right then. Instead, the general appeared to take what had been said in good nature and addressed him by name this time. "Schriever," he said, "I am going down to the gym to do some judo. Would you like to come down?" Power had become an expert at this Japanese art of unarmed combat. He held the highest rank, black belt. LeMay had apparently decided to try it as well. Schriever could see in a flash in his mind's eye what would happen to him in a judo bout with Curtis LeMay after what he had just told the big man. "No, not today, General," he said. LeMay chuckled. The meeting broke up.

Despite what Bennie had learned about the heat barrier, the supersonic nuclear-powered bomber remained a project of extremely high priority for the Air Force, and work on it continued through the 1950s, long after Schriever had moved on. The success of Admiral Hyman Rickover of the Navy in building nuclear-powered attack submarines, the first of which, the USS *Nautilus,* was commissioned in 1954, undoubtedly honed the envy of the Air Force leadership. In his March 21, 1955, memorandum to Twining on the future structure of the Air Force, LeMay posited two wings of supersonic nuclear-fueled bombers, a total of ninety such aircraft, in SAC's inventory by 1965. In January 1955, the Air Force Council, the committee of lieutenant generals at Air Force headquarters under the chairmanship of the vice chief, recommended accelerating the program in order to have an operational atomic-powered bomber by 1963. The idea of airplanes flying around with nuclear reactors in them might seem daft to subsequent generations, given the appalling consequences if one crashed. In the edge-of-battle atmosphere of the Cold War, such risks were rationalized as necessities.

In fact, the Air Force and the AEC secretly installed a three-megawatt, air-cooled nuclear reactor in the aft bomb bay of a converted B-36, designated the NB-36H or Nuclear Test Aircraft, and staged forty-seven flights with it between July 1955 and March 1957.

The objective was to test the feasibility of having a reactor in an airplane and find ways to adequately protect the crew from the radiation it gave off. Accordingly, a twelve-ton lead-and-rubber-shielded compartment, with leaded glass windows almost a foot thick, was built into the nose of the bomber. The pattern was to fly the B-36 from a Convair plant at Carswell Air Force Base outside Fort Worth, Texas, to another base near Roswell, New Mexico. There, the reactor would be turned on and the plane sent up again to test-fly over New Mexico before returning to Fort Worth. The B-36 was always followed by a B-50 carrying a unit of specially trained paratroopers who, in the event of a crash, were to jump and cordon off the impact area from the public until cleanup crews of nuclear specialists could arrive.

The path of its forty-seven flights took the B-36 with its radioactive cargo directly over Lake Worth, Fort Worth's main water supply. Had the plane gone into the lake, the paratroopers could hardly have been of much assistance to the thirsty inhabitants of the city. Schriever became convinced in retrospect that LeMay's supersonic demand helped to sabotage the project by delaying the creation of a subsonic nuclear-powered aircraft until time and cost and the safety issue doomed the idea. It seems likely, however, that other technological Gordian knots may have rendered the vision of an atomic-powered airplane of limitless range a mirage. Fitting a nuclear reactor into an immensely sturdy vehicle like a submarine was one thing; installing one in a comparatively fragile vehicle like an aircraft quite another. President Kennedy put an end to the dream in 1961 by canceling the project as impractical and unnecessary.

LOW-LEVEL TACTICS AND
THE FLYING BOOM

Schriever's subsequent confrontations with LeMay were to become less civil. Not that LeMay was always wrong. While the B-52 was in its early stages of development, Schriever proposed extending the life of the existing B-47s by strengthening their wings and reducing the number of B-52s to be built. He argued that given the rapidity with which the nuclear weapons designers were slimming down the weight of bombs while simultaneously increasing the explosive yield, the Air Force didn't need the 50,000-pound carrying capacity of the big bomber. It could get by with the 25,000-pound bomb load of the smaller B-47 and save billions of dollars. LeMay, in a rage, ridiculed the idea. It was abandoned and Schriever admitted afterward that LeMay had been right: the B-52 was a much better airplane and therefore a much better long-term investment. The problem was not who was right and who was wrong in what was supposed to be a mutually beneficial exchange. The problem was that LeMay was so overcome by hubris, he had turned into a caricature of his former self. He listened now only to Curtis LeMay. He could not sense that what he might least want to hear was what he might most need to know.

An example was the reception he gave Schriever's warning that SAC needed to change its tactics to survive against advances in Soviet air defenses. On the assumption that bombers would always be able to fly higher than fighters, LeMay believed firmly that, after speed, height was the second most important attribute for a bomber's survival. Given the intelligence reports the Air Force was receiving on Soviet air defense innovations, Bennie grew doubtful. The progress in Soviet jet fighters showed gains in altitude. The air defense radars to vector the fighters to engage incoming American bombers were also improving. Most worrisome of all were the reports of intensive efforts to field a surface-to-air missile system, the weapon that was to evolve into the infamous SAM of the Vietnam War. As with so much else, the Germans had devised the first surface-to-air missiles. One might have wreaked havoc with the B-17s and B-24s and with the RAF's Lancasters had it been perfected and mass-produced. It was called the Wasserfall (Waterfall). Twenty-six feet in length with a 674-pound warhead, a speed of 1,900 miles per hour, and an altitude of 42,000 to 52,000 feet, it was radar-guided and designed to destroy an approaching bomber at a distance up to thirty miles. As with the V-2, the Soviets had picked up on this and another German surface-to-air missile called the Rheintochter and improved immensely on the German lead.

The Soviets' first-generation surface-to-air missiles were deployed in batteries around Moscow in 1957. Designated the MK-6 by the Soviets and referred to as the SA-2 Guideline by NATO intelligence, the missiles were steadily upgraded in subsequent years and thousands were emplaced around other Russian population centers and important military sites. Tracking radars at the batteries first picked up the intruding aircraft. The missiles were then guided to their targets by radio control. A proximity fuse detonated the 441-pound warhead as soon as the missile was close enough to destroy or seriously damage the plane. The missile demonstrated its efficacy on May 1, 1960, when the explosion from a near miss caused enough damage to knock down the U-2 photoreconnaissance spy plane being flown by Francis Gary Powers at 68,000 feet over Sverdlovsk in the Urals. What all these innovations in Soviet air defenses added up to for Schriever was that to maximize the chance of a bomber reaching its target, the plane had to come in not high as LeMay thought, where it would display a sharp profile on the radar screens for the fighters and worst of all for the SAMs, but low and under the radar.

Bennie got together with Colonel Delmar Wilson, who, as a major with one of the first groups to come to England in the fall of 1942, had observed bombs flung wildly about, tearing up rutabaga gardens in German-occupied Europe until LeMay arrived and proved that a B-17 could make a straight and level bomb run and survive. By 1952–53, Wilson was a colonel heading up the Strategic Air Requirements Division of the Air Staff. He had been having similar thoughts about how to survive against Soviet air defenses. They contacted Boeing to find out what a B-47 could withstand in low-level flight, where the denser air puts a lot more stress on the airframe, in order to contrive evasive maneuvers that could be added to the low-level approach to heighten survivability. They also gathered information from the Special Weapons Command at Kirtland Air Force Base in New Mexico on low-level delivery of atomic bombs. There were various ways in which this could be done. One was to throw the bomber at the last moment into an Immelmann, a maneuver named for Max Immelmann, the German fighter pilot who originated it during the First World War. This was a half loop upward followed by a half roll away, resulting in a reversal of direction and increased height. While still climbing, the plane would toss the bomb at the target in a parabolic arc and thus be far enough away when the bomb detonated to escape being destroyed by the blast. They designed some charts to illustrate their points and flew out to Offutt to try to convert the man whose bomber crews would want to stay alive and reach their targets against those Soviet antiaircraft defenses.

The session took place this time in the formal briefing room at SAC headquarters. There was a stage a foot or so high and facing it were rows of chairs with folding seats like those in movie theaters. The rows were well filled by about thirty to forty members of the SAC staff, with LeMay and Power up front as would be expected. Bennie mounted the stage first. Wilson, who was to go on to the two stars of a major general before his Air Force career was completed, recalled long afterward what happened next:

> Schriever started our presentation and had no more than introduced the subject of low-level approach and bombing, when LeMay stood up, grunted, stuck his cigar in his mouth, and stomped out of the room. Schriever continued a few minutes more before Power and a few other general officers left. . . . Needless to say, I never had a chance to unfold my briefing charts. We put our tails between our legs and headed for our airplane.

The next confrontation came over midair refueling. There were two methods in use. One was called the probe and drogue. With probe and drogue, the tanker aircraft trailed behind itself a hose with a funnel-shaped device, the drogue, attached to the end. The aircraft needing refueling maneuvered up from behind and plugged the probe, a pipelike fixture attached to the front of its fuselage and connected to its fuel tanks, into the center of the drogue. As soon as a firm connection was made, the pilot of the thirsty plane notified the tanker over the radio and a crewman turned on the fuel. The second method was called the flying boom. A metal fuel pipe that telescoped and was also capable of being turned up and down and from side to side was slung under the tail section of the tanker. This was the boom. The aircraft wanting fuel approached the tanker's tail and moved into station just below. An operator sitting in a control compartment in the tanker's tail, with a Plexiglas window that gave him full view downward, extended and maneuvered the boom until he had succeeded in plugging it into a receptacle built into the front part of the receiving plane's fuselage. He then turned on the fuel and filled its tanks.

The advantage of the flying boom was that it could replenish an aircraft's tanks faster because the pipe had a wider diameter than the hose used in probe and drogue and the fuel was transferred under high pressure. The disadvantage was that it could refuel only one aircraft at a time. The probe and drogue system, on the other hand, could simultaneously refuel up to three aircraft by trailing hoses from near the end of each wing as well as from the tail section. The boom was best suited to bombers. They drank the most, yet because of the size of their tanks usually had a margin of safety. It was normally not that critical if they had to wait in line for the boom to be free. The opposite was true of fighters and fighter-bombers, which was why probe and drogue worked best for them: they needed less in a gulp from a tanker. Their far smaller tanks, however, meant they might not be able to wait in line. The Navy, most of whose carrier aircraft were similar in size to Air Force fighters and fighter-bombers, had standardized on probe and drogue with its tankers for this reason. The admirals wanted the ability to keep a maximum number of planes aloft at any one time and without losing pilots and planes in the sea because tanks ran dry.

The boom was the method in widest use in the Air Force because SAC, which favored it, possessed the most tankers. By the early 1950s, however, the time had come to standardize so that any Air Force plane could fill its tanks from any Air Force tanker. Bennie's Development Planning Office was tasked to do a study. It soon became clear to him that midair refueling had become an absolute necessity, not just for SAC's long-range bombing missions, but for the entire Air Force, and that the measure was not a stopgap but a permanent demand that would persist indefinitely into the future. The need to refuel fighters and fighter-bombers on their way across the Atlantic in support of NATO, to sustain transport aircraft on long hauls, or to keep planes in the air fighting in one area when they were based at a distance in another—as was now occurring with aircraft flying out of Japan to prosecute the war in Korea—all called for midair refueling.

To help with the study, Bennie recruited a colonel working in research and development at Air Force headquarters in the Pentagon named Jewell "Bill" Maxwell, who had conducted a previous inquiry on midair refueling and was considered the expert on the subject. Maxwell had been a bomber pilot, but he favored probe and drogue because of the versatility it would give the Air Force to refuel various types of aircraft in virtually any situation. Pilots, he had discovered, preferred it as well, since it was easier to hold in position behind the tanker, particularly if there was turbulence, when hooked up to a flexible hose that allowed for some movement in contrast to being attached to a stiff pipe. Another characteristic of probe and drogue also made pilots less nervous about the possibility of a midair collision: the hoses were longer than the flying boom and the refueling aircraft therefore did not have to approach as close to the tanker. The objection that the boom fed fuel to bombers faster could be overcome simply by installing wider-diameter hoses and higher-capacity pressure pumps. A memo summing up the study that Bennie sent to Major General George Price, a powerful man as head of the overall Requirements branch of the Air Staff, won him over to the probe and drogue method, principally because of the versatility it offered. He told Bennie he would endorse a recommendation that the Air Force standardize on it. If the recommendation went through, SAC would have to convert. LeMay, apparently alerted to what was happening, summoned Bennie out to Offutt to brief him.

The setting was the same SAC conference room with the stage in front and the rows of movie-theater-style chairs facing it. The audience filling the chairs was also the same, except that this time Bennie seated himself close to the general and let Maxwell, the man with the specialized knowledge, do the briefing. LeMay slumped in his chair, ruminating on his cigar and saying nothing while Maxwell paraded through his charts and viewgraphs projected onto a screen to illustrate the merits and drawbacks of each system toward his conclusion that the probe and drogue method best served the entire Air Force and would work fine for SAC.

As soon as Maxwell was finished, LeMay turned his head around to the rows of SAC staff officers seated behind him. "Well," he said, "we don't want any part of that. We're going to stay with what we've got." Then he asked, "Any difference of opinion around here?" There was silence. If any member of LeMay's staff thought that Maxwell was right, it was a long way from a mess hall in England, where Colonel LeMay would gather all participants in a mission, from officer pilot to enlisted gunner, to thrash out how to fly it better the next time, and would invite anyone to tell the group commander he was "a stupid son of a bitch," provided he gave a reason. LeMay then swung himself back toward Maxwell up on the stage. "Who the hell keeps promoting that probe and drogue stuff?" he asked. "General, I think I can answer that question," Maxwell said. Lieutenant Colonel Benjamin P. "Paul" Blasingame, an aeronautical engineer with a Ph.D. from MIT who had recently joined Bennie's team, watched fascinated as Maxwell, a tall, strapping man with a ruddy complexion who had flown forty-four combat missions in Europe, strode across to the edge of the stage, pointer in hand, and looked down at LeMay, close enough to appear to be confronting the demigod. "Every pilot that ever flew it is promoting it," he said, in a voice that resonated through the room. LeMay stared up at him for a moment, then stood and walked out.

Maxwell got away with his boldness to win two stars before leaving the Air Force, but Bennie received an unpleasant surprise after they returned to the Pentagon. He learned that Major General Price, the Requirements chief, had changed his mind and was now recommending that the Air Force adopt the flying boom method. Bennie had known and admired Price since his cadet days and they had become good friends while serving together as test pilots at Wright Field before the war. It was the end of the friendship and of Bennie's admiration. He marched over to Price's office in a fury. "I went in there and just flew off the handle," he remembered years later. He told Price "that I felt he had pulled the rug out from under me and asked him why the hell he did it." They had agreed that probe and drogue was the method the Air Force needed and Price had told Bennie he was behind him before Bennie had gone out to Offutt. Price did not contradict him nor did he give him a satisfactory answer, but Bennie knew the answer. LeMay had intimidated Price. And Bennie knew LeMay's motive. He wanted to do all he could to keep the Tactical Air Command, with its fighters and fighter-bombers, in check. He had no intention of facilitating its ability to more easily refuel and extend the range of its aircraft and employ smaller nuclear weapons to compete with him in the bombing business. The Air Force standardized on the flying boom system of midair refueling and Bennie Schriever moved on to a larger struggle with Curtis LeMay over what kind of strategic bomber the Air Force ought to build to succeed the B-52.

28.

THE LAST TANGLE AND
AN AMBUSH

While LeMay and the rest of the Air Force leadership were keen to acquire a nuclear-powered bomber as soon as possible, they also intended to create in the meantime an intermediary aircraft that would be the most up-to-date conventionally fueled bomber. The plane was seen as a kind of insurance policy in case there were more technological obstacles to the building of the atomic aircraft than could be anticipated and its production in quantity was delayed. The role of the intermediate strategic bomber would also be to replace the early models of the B-52 when these became a decade old in 1965. This "follow-on bomber," or "HB-X for Heavy Bomber—Experimental," as it was referred to in the planning documents, was intended eventually to supplant all of the B-52s and become SAC's mainstay until the nuclear-powered bomber supplanted it.

In accordance with his convictions about speed and height, LeMay had laid down a SAC requirement for a supersonic aircraft, one capable of several times the speed of sound, and with an extremely high cruising altitude. He also demanded a heavy bomb load and the ability to strike the farthest possible targets and return to base in the United

States with no need for midair refueling. Even the B-36, with its 3,500-mile combat radius, required midair refueling when carrying a full bomb load to strike targets that were deep within the Soviet Union and get back home. LeMay regarded midair refueling as a crutch, not a permanent feature of intercontinental flying as Bennie had concluded, because Schriever could not perceive any way around it short of nuclear power. LeMay felt, however, that SAC should put up with midair refueling only as long as necessary and then do away with it.

The intermediate bomber was the place to start. This meant a bomber with a minimum range of 11,000 miles, and LeMay was compounding the problem with his simultaneous demand for supersonic speed. Aircraft burn fuel at a much faster rate when flying supersonic, even at high altitudes where the air is thin and there is less resistance. And LeMay's requirement for a heavy bomb load made things still worse. Bennie tried to explain to him that they would end up with a mammoth plane, "a battleship," as he later dubbed it, which would be wildly impractical. LeMay would not relent. "He just didn't wish it, that was it," Bennie recalled. "He could say, 'Well, you bastard, you aren't really trying.' He was of the school that 'Goddamn it, I know what I need. This is a requirement, goddamn it, now go out and do it.' "

A lesser man would have humored "the king of the mountain," as Blasingame remembered thinking of LeMay as they sat in the SAC conference room during the flying boom versus probe and drogue episode. A lesser man would have given the king what the king desired, no matter how ludicrous it might be, picked up a promotion, moved on, and left the consequences to his successor. There were plenty of such lesser types in the Air Force, as there are in all major institutions. Price in the Requirements division was an example. It was a measure of Schriever's character, however, and another reason he would accomplish so much when his turn came, that he was constitutionally incapable of caving in to pressure he considered unjust. Attempting to browbeat him into doing something he believed was wrong usually had the reverse effect, as it did in this case.

He formed a Strategic Air team in his office and set it to work on a Development Planning Objective for the intermediate bomber that would reflect reality and the best technology possible to cope with that reality. He knew that the way LeMay wanted to go was absolutely the wrong direction. The growth and the nature of Soviet air defenses made that conclusion inescapable. He would try again to convince LeMay as the team's work progressed. If he did not prevail in the end, he would at least have fulfilled the trust the Air Force had placed in him. He chose Paul Blasingame to head the team. Aeronautical engineers of Blasingame's quality were rare in the Air Force in the early 1950s. He was one of the first of the postwar Ph.D.'s, the result of a decision by the Air Force, again inspired by Hap Arnold, to offer more of its bright and technologically inclined officers an opportunity to obtain advanced degrees at government expense.

Blasingame had gained his Ph.D. in 1950 after three years of study under Professor Charles Stark Draper, the MIT genius who led the way in the use of inertial guidance as the means to navigate ships and aircraft and to guide bombs and missiles to their targets. (An inertial guidance instrument contains data laying out a course to a predetermined destination. The instrument measures the speed and direction of the plane or other vehicle in which it is installed and compares these to the stored data to maintain the correct course.) To recruit disciples within the military who would promote his instruments and techniques, Draper had shrewdly organized a master's and a Ph.D. degree program at MIT for Air Force and Navy officers in what he called Aircraft Instrumentation. Blasingame was one of its earliest graduates. He had an excellent, clear-thinking mind and vision as well. After later serving under Bennie as one of the senior figures in the ICBM project, he would go on to found the Department of Astronautics, the science of space travel, exploration, and use, at the Air Force Academy.

Although Blasingame was still atmosphere-bound in 1953, the bomber he and his team planned under Schriever's guidance was a high jump in aircraft technology. They based their design on the concept that Schriever and Delmar Wilson had earlier conceived of going in under the radar in a low-level attack. If one took LeMay's route, it wouldn't make any difference in the end how high and fast the bomber flew. The promise of rocket technology said that the Soviets could always build a surface-to-air missile that would destroy the bomber by going higher and faster. A bomber flying at approximately 600 miles an hour, something approaching the speed of sound, Mach .85 or .9 in the professional's terminology, would suffice. What mattered most was to approach on the bottom and then, if detected, to immediately adopt evasive tactics while staying down on the deck to prevent the Soviets from locking onto the plane with their radars and taking it under fire.

The team found itself immediately faced with a conundrum. Pure jet engines, the type with which the B-47 and the B-52 were equipped, achieve propulsion, i.e., propel an aircraft forward, by the backward thrust of high-speed jets of gas generated when their fuel, a type of kerosene, is burned. They are notoriously inefficient at low level because the backward thrust is not powerful enough to overcome the denser air and thus they gobble profligate amounts of fuel. The team needed a jet engine that would give them much greater fuel efficiency. The result of their search was a pioneering model called the turbofan or high bypass ratio engine. It has a large turbine-driven fan installed in the front. The fan is turned by diverting some of the gas from the burning fuel. The great whirling blades of the fan create vastly more forceful backward thrust than a pure jet engine does to drive the aircraft ahead. There were other advantages. The big increase in thrust of the turbofan meant that fewer engines would be required for aircraft of equivalent size. The pure jet B-47, for example, had six engines and the B-52 would have eight. Blasingame and his team thought they could get by with four turbofan engines on the strategic bomber they had on their drawing board. The additional lift the turbofans provided through their higher thrust would also allow the bomber to take off from a much shorter runway.

Innovation did not stop with the turbofan engine. Blasingame exploited his Draper education to give the plane the most advanced navigation and bombing system he could imagine. He twinned an inertial guidance navigation instrument with a radar that was not yet in production, but soon would be ready, in order to produce a night and all-weather bomber. The inertial navigation device would keep the aircraft on the essentially correct course while the radar enabled the pilot to adjust it with precision. The radar was a type called rapid forward scanning. Its signal did a constant quick sweep of the terrain ahead of the plane and bounced back the images it encountered at high speed. These images were also much sharper on its screen than on those of the older radars. The pilot or the navigator/bombardier would have to thoroughly familiarize himself beforehand with a map in order to translate what he was seeing on the screen to the actual terrain ahead of him and the features he wanted to follow to his target. But if he did so, he could attack at low level at night and in bad weather and the radar would serve as his eyes. This instrumentation package that Blasingame conjured up for the intermediate bomber was a forerunner of the sophisticated electronic systems, the avionics suites for navigation, bombing, and air-to-air combat, that were to form such a critical feature of warplanes of the future. An example was the next logical step in radar—the terrain-following radar that was to appear in the early 1960s. The pilot cranked the necessary data into a computer and the radar then took over and flew the plane automatically on a ground-skimming course.

The plane was never built. Schriever couldn't sell the proposal to LeMay. He remained adamant against low-level attack. The team's effort got no further than publication as an internal Air Force document in 1954. (It has since been lost.) The aircraft that did emerge from all of this wrangling was America's first supersonic bomber, the B-58 Hustler, a high-altitude, medium bomber with a top speed of approximately 1,300 miles per hour, approaching twice the speed of sound. Schriever had proposed it in an earlier and separate Development Planning Objective in 1952 in an ill-considered attempt at compromise. The Hustler was a boldly handsome aircraft of full arrowhead, delta-wing design, but unfortunately its attributes—high altitude where Bennie soon came to see low as a necessity, shorter combat radius of approximately 1,600 miles, and a medium bomber when LeMay wanted long-range and heavy—satisfied no one.

LeMay was eventually to get his way when Schriever was no longer at the Pentagon to frustrate him. In 1957, the same year LeMay left SAC and moved up to become vice chief of staff, the Air Force gave North American Aviation a contract for the bomber he wanted as the successor to the B-52. It was the B-70 Valkyrie, massive at 500,000 pounds (bigger and more than 50,000 pounds heavier than the B-52); high-flying at 75,000 feet; supersonic at more than three times the speed of sound (Mach 3.2); expensive at $9.2 billion to obtain and test two prototypes; and useless. When decision time came in 1961, LeMay fought as hard as he could to have the plane accepted and put into production. He argued that the B-70 could be used as a reconnaissance-strike bomber to find and destroy Soviet airfields and missile complexes that had escaped an initial American nuclear attack. The trouble was that if the B-70 survived the Soviet surface-to-air missiles, the crew would not be able to see anything on earth while flashing across the stratosphere at more than 2,000 miles an hour and 14.2 miles high. No sensors existed at the time to replace their eyesight and detect the airfields and missile sites below for them. President Kennedy canceled the Valkyrie, except for the two experimental prototypes, as "unnecessary and economically unjustifiable."

(There never was to be a satisfactory successor to the B-52 as a heavy bomber. The Air Force resorted to keeping the last model, the B-52H, in service indefinitely, periodically sending the planes back to Boeing to have them rebuilt. For nine years, from 1965 to 1974, B-52s were to carpet-bomb Vietnam and then Laos and Cambodia, snuffing out many thousands of lives and causing incalculable environmental damage to the forest and agricultural landscape, with the conventional high-explosive bombs LeMay had wanted to abolish in favor of nuclear-only munitions. The SAC staff referred to these ordinary 500-pounders as "garbage bombs." During the Gulf War of 1990–91, the B-52s were to be back at carpet-bombing, this time in a just cause, liberating Kuwait by helping to destroy the army of the Baghdad dictator, Saddam Hussein. The Iraqi soldiery were to find no shelter in desert bunkers that the strings of bombs collapsed into tombs. The B-52's role in the second Iraq war of the second President Bush was to be limited, but the fuel capacity of the massive bombers made them the perfect aircraft to loiter in the skies over Afghanistan and periodically launch one of the latest in precision-guided 2,000-pounders at a redoubt of the Taliban or the al Qaeda terrorists. As of the publication of this book, the B-52s are still flying.)

By 1953, Schriever had begun to suffer an affliction that was new to him, severe headaches from the tension of being repeatedly at odds with the biggest man in the Air Force. Although he was actually accomplishing a lot, he couldn't see the results of his endeavors because they lay in the future. If Boeing's shrewd conversion of the KC-135 jet tanker it produced for SAC into its renowned 707 jetliner was to bring a major surge in international air travel, the introduction of the turbofan engine was to set off a revolution in military and commercial aviation. Blasingame blamed LeMay's attitude for retarding its advent by years, but when the engine builders and aircraft manufacturers caught on to its potential at the beginning of the 1960s, it soon became the universal engine. The H model of the B-52, which emerged from the

Boeing production lines in the final runs in 1961 and 1962, was equipped with an early version of the turbofan in place of the J-57 pure jet engines that had powered previous models. As a result, the turbofan's economy in fuel consumption was to enable a B-52H to establish a new long-distance flying record in January 1962—12,532 miles from Kadena Air Base on Okinawa to Torrejón in Spain with no midair refueling.

While Blasingame and his colleagues were still engaged in their study for the intermediate strategic bomber, Bennie had given another team the task of planning a wide-body cargo aircraft that would utilize the turbofan engine. This study was to bear its first fruit in 1965 in the grand C-141 Starlifter transport. With just four turbofan engines, the C-141 could loft 154 fully equipped troops and their weapons or 7,000 cubic feet of cargo 4,000 miles. In 1968, the mammoth C-5 Galaxy appeared, again with only four hefty turbofan engines, which could lift virtually anything that might be loaded into its astonishing 34,000 cubic feet of cargo space. Standing inside its cargo bay, one had the sensation of being in a flying warehouse. In 1990 and 1991, both transports would perform an indispensable role in ferrying troops, tanks, armored personnel carriers, helicopters, and the rest of the manifold equipment and supplies necessary to deploy an army in Saudi Arabia to drive Saddam Hussein from Kuwait.

The impact on commercial aircraft was even more dramatic when, in 1970, the first of the jumbo jets, Boeing's 747 jetliner, went into service with Pan American and Trans World Airlines. Its four turbofans could fly 400 passengers from New York to Paris and beyond. With the mass market these giants fostered, air fares fell accordingly and millions who might otherwise never have traveled abroad flew off to see the world. It was no small irony that this miraculous engine had first emerged in a search for a low-level nuclear bomber to attack the Soviet Union that was never built. Bennie was even to be vindicated on low-level tactics to counter Soviet air defenses. SAC was to start switching to them in 1959 under LeMay's successor and the crews of the lumbering B-52s would learn how to hug the contour of the earth.

Nevertheless, the premonition that lay behind Bennie's tension headaches was not without substance. On June 23, 1953, he was promoted to brigadier general. The photograph in his study years later would show an excited and happy Bernard Adolph Schriever standing between two men, one of them Jimmy Doolittle, each pinning a silver star onto his shoulder tabs. In a note to Nathan Twining, Bennie thanked the chief of staff for his first stars with Schriever restraint. "My one hope is that I can do the job expected of me," he wrote. LeMay then almost got him. Colonel Schriever had given Curtis LeMay enough trouble. Brigadier General Schriever would give him more. The Cigar reached out to burn him. Bennie suddenly received orders assigning him to South Korea as chief of logistics for the Fifth Air Force units stationed there. His boss at the time, again Laurence Craigie, now a lieutenant general and deputy chief of staff, development, called him at home to warn him that the orders were coming through from Personnel. Craigie told him not to give up, that he was going to intervene and rally others to try to get the orders overturned.

There was no doubt that LeMay was behind the maneuver. No one else had a motive to boot Schriever off into exile. At first, Bennie was stunned and then deeply angry, but he would have tamped down his anger and gone if he had to go, rather than leave the Air Force and make money in one of the military industries, as he might easily have done. Had LeMay succeeded, history would not have been the same. As Curtis LeMay had been the indispensable man in the success of the strategic bombing so important to victory in the Second World War, Bernard Schriever was to be the indispensable man in the creation of the intercontinental ballistic missile during the Cold War and the enormous consequences that were to flow from it—America's penetration of space and an unspoken but permanent truce of mutual deterrence with the Soviet Union. Lieutenant General Earle Partridge, an admirer of Schriever who had given him the funds for a turbofan engine prototype while head of the Air Research and Development Command, had recently been promoted to deputy chief of staff, operations, in effect the third man in Headquarters, USAF. He and Donald Putt, another of Bennie's former superiors, who had replaced Partridge at ARDC, joined forces with Craigie. They apparently went to General Tommy White, the vice chief who had known Bennie slightly out in the Pacific, and to Twining. The orders were rescinded. Schriever had survived and just in time, for he had begun to set in motion the great work of his life.

BOOK IV

STARTING A RACE

29

SEEKING SCIENTIFIC VALIDATION

The thought that propelled the United States into the race for the ultimate weapon—nuclear-armed ballistic missiles hurtling across continents at 16,000 miles per hour through the vastness of space—occurred to Bernard Schriever toward the end of March 1953 at Maxwell Air Force Base, Alabama, nearly three months before his promotion to brigadier general. He was in Alabama to present the concept for the intermediate strategic bomber he was attempting to create for SAC to a meeting of the Air Force Scientific Advisory Board. Many men would have found the thought fantastical, but not Schriever. His mind was receptive because he was so caught up in the opening years of the sinister arms competition between the Soviet Union and the United States, a rivalry that would help to bankrupt and dissolve the immense Soviet empire and bequeath America a national debt of colossal proportions.

Two members of the Advisory Board at the meeting were exceptional men even among the generation of exceptional European minds who had transformed American science and learning in the decades since their arrival in the 1930s. One of the men was John von Neumann, a Hungarian-born mathematical genius, possibly the finest intelligence of the twentieth century after Albert Einstein. The second was another Hungarian, Edward Teller, a physicist of great talent and monomaniacal ambition who claimed to be the sole parent of the hydrogen bomb. The flight of this wealth of intellectual talent across the Atlantic had been a born-in-sorrow gift to America from Europe's economic and social turmoil after the First World War and the rise of Adolf Hitler and his virulent anti-Semitism. Both men had participated in the building of the atomic bomb at Los Alamos, New Mexico, during the Second World War. Both had then taken part in the creation of the awesome thermonuclear or hydrogen weapon that followed the initial unleashing of the atom.

The first of these hydrogen bombs, as they were commonly called, code-named Mike, had been detonated at Eniwetok Atoll in the Pacific on November 1, 1952, only three years before the Soviet Union was to acquire its hydrogen weapon. Mike erupted with a force of 10.4 megatons, 832 times the power of Little Boy at Hiroshima. It vaporized the island on which it was tested and left a crater under the sea. Mike was not really a bomb in the sense that it could be dropped from an airplane, although the Air Force attempted for a time to obtain a lighter version that it could drop. Mike was an eighty-two-ton device, laboriously constructed, of giant metal containers called dewars, after James Dewar, the Scottish physicist who in 1892 had invented the thermos bottle, from which these highly sophisticated receptacles were descended. Mike's doomsday contents were in liquid form, flowing into the dewars through connected piping, and had to be cooled down to cryogenic levels. Von Neumann and Teller had, nonetheless, labored sufficiently long in the devil's workshop of nuclear weapons design to be able to calculate rapidly how to transform unwieldy monsters into practical devices of mass destruction. In their briefings to the Advisory Board meeting, they predicted that by 1960 the United States would be able to build a hydrogen bomb that would weigh less than a ton but would explode with the force of a megaton, i.e., eighty times the power of the simple atomic or fission bomb that had blown away Hiroshima.

Schriever pondered the prediction for a moment and immediately understood its implication. The barrier to the construction of the weapon against which there was no defense had always been the excessive weight of the warhead required. Von Neumann and Teller had just told him that it was now possible to devise a warhead of acceptable weight and thus to build this weapon—a rocket that could catapult up into space, hurl its thermonuclear projectile nearly 6,330 miles, and fling this bomb of eighty Hiroshimas down on any city in the Soviet Union.

On May 8, 1953, the earliest he could obtain an appointment, Schriever went up to the Institute for Advanced Study at Princeton to see von Neumann. He wanted to be certain he had interpreted correctly what von Neumann and Teller had said. He needed to have von Neumann, the mathematician and mathematical physicist wizard who held the research chair in mathematics at the institute, confirm that it really would be possible by 1960 to downsize a hydrogen bomb with a megaton's blast to less than a ton in weight. These two attributes were the sine qua non for the building of a practical intercontinental ballistic missile, or ICBM. If the warhead was a great deal heavier, a rocket of mammoth porportions, difficult to transport and field at dispersed launching sites, would be required to lift the warhead into space and hurl it the approximately 6,330 statute miles that was the desired range. (The Air Force and Navy normally measure distance in nautical miles. One nautical mile is equivalent to approximately 2,025 yards. Civilians, however, measure distance in statute miles, one of which is equivalent to 1,760 yards. Because this book has been written for lay readership, statute miles, with some exceptions, have been used here and throughout.) Yet the yield had to be high, given the relatively primitive guidance technology of the day and thus the difficulty of hitting a target, even one as large as a city, thousands of miles away. A thermonuclear warhead exploding with a million tons of TNT would allow the average accuracy requirement (technically called CEP for circular error probable) to be eased to two to three miles from the center of the target, because the blast would be sufficient to destroy or severely damage anything within that radius and beyond.

No one had told Bennie Schriever to go to Princeton, nor had anyone instructed him to find out how to build an ICBM. His previous initiatives, such as his confrontations with LeMay, had all occurred in the course of carrying out the duties of his job. This time was different. This time, for the first time, he was initiating something entirely on his own. If anyone was responsible for sending him to Princeton to see von Neumann it was Hap Arnold, who, the better part of a decade before, had inspired him to set off down a visionary's road. Schriever had arranged the meeting through his friend Teddy Walkowicz, who knew von Neumann well from his years of working with von Kármán, first on the *Toward New Horizons* task force, then as secretary of the Scientific Advisory Board, and subsequently as executive assistant to Jimmy Doolittle. (During the SAB meeting at Maxwell there had been no opportunity for Bennie to do more than introduce himself briefly to von Neumann.) Worried that he might not be able to understand the intricacies of nuclear physics, a subject with which Walkowicz would have no difficulty, Schriever had asked his friend to join him. Walko-

wicz was by this time a civilian living in New York. He had resigned
from the Air Force in disgust and gone to the big city to work for Lau-
rance Rockefeller in venture capital finance. Despite the Ph.D. he had
gained at MIT at considerable sacrifice, Walkowicz had been unable to
gain promotion beyond lieutenant colonel because he had never gone
to Flying School and become a pilot. In the terminology of the profession, he was a "nonrated officer." As far as the airplane drivers, the
bomber generals who then dominated the Air Force, were concerned,
that barred him from the higher ranks, whatever his technical prowess.
To these men an officer who could not fly lacked the essential qualifi-
cation for admission to the brotherhood—he would never be able to
exercise command in the air.

While they were waiting for their appointment with von Neumann
in a combined lounge and small library at the institute, Schriever was
surprised by an elderly figure who walked in, apparently on the way to
his office. The wildly unkempt mane of white hair and the untidy mustache could belong to only one man—Albert Einstein. Bennie got up
and introduced himself and Einstein shook his hand and said a few polite words before moving on. There was a certain irony in the encounter, however fleeting. Einstein, then in his seventy-fourth year, had
two years left to live and, as he reflected on his extraordinary life, the
act he regretted most was signing the famous 1939 letter to Franklin
Roosevelt that was the genesis of the American atomic bomb project.
He had done so at the behest of fellow émigré physicists out of fear
that the Nazis would build the bomb first and win the Second World
War with it. He had then been horrified when the United States had
used the bomb to massacre the civilian populations of two Japanese
cities. He was now equally upset over the postwar arms race that had
sprung up between the United States and the Soviet Union, because he
regarded the proliferation of nuclear weapons as a threat to the existence of humankind. One wonders what he might have said had he
known he was shaking the hand of a man who was making it his mission to put not a mere atomic bomb, but rather a hydrogen bomb of
eighty Hiroshimas, on the tip of an intercontinental ballistic missile.

At the agreed time, 10:30 A.M., von Neumann's secretary, a friendly,
middle-aged woman named Elizabeth Gorman, appeared and led them
into the eminent Hungarian's office. He was standing behind his desk,
a portly figure of modest height, as ever dressed correctly in a business

suit (he usually wore the full three-piece model with matching vest), white shirt, and tie, and white handkerchief ironed and folded precisely into two points and tucked into his lapel pocket. His hand was held out in greeting and he was smiling, the smile redoubling the double chin in his wide, friendly face. The deep brown eyes also seemed to smile a greeting, emphasized as they and the brows above them were by the high forehead, growing higher all the time because of the receding line of his equally dark brown curly hair. Schriever had come to the right man. "Johnny" von Neumann, as he referred to himself and as his friends called him, was always pleased to welcome members of the American military establishment and to put himself at their service.

30.

WHEN HUNGARY WAS MARS

This genius with the benevolent-seeming exterior, Johnny von Neumann, the epitome of bonhomie, was one of the most ardent of Cold War hawks. In his view of how to handle the Soviets, he surpassed even Curtis LeMay. LeMay advocated "preemptive war," striking first but only when it was clear that the Soviets were about to strike the United States. Von Neumann argued one chilling step further. He advocated what was known at the time as "preventive war." Convinced that hostilities with the Soviet Union were inevitable sooner or later, he believed the United States should strike as soon as possible at the best opportunity. "With the Russians it is not a question of whether but when," he once remarked. "If you say why not bomb them tomorrow, I say why not today? If you say today at five o'clock, I say why not one o'clock?" In 1949, before Truman rendered the argument moot by ordering the building of the Super, as the hydrogen bomb was then called, the number and prominence of von Neumann's wartime associates at Los Alamos who recoiled from the creation of a terror bomb more than 800 times as powerful as the Hiroshima weapon was truly impressive. Among them, in addition to

Robert Oppenheimer, were two Nobel Laureates, the American physicist I. I. Rabi and Enrico Fermi, the émigré Italian physicist. The Super would be, Fermi and Rabi said, "a danger to humanity as a whole . . . necessarily an evil thing considered in any light." Von Neumann shared neither their fears nor their moral qualms. "I don't think any weapon can be too large," he had remarked to Oppenheimer.

While von Neumann still kept his hand in at pure mathematics by doing an occasional proof, he had long since become bored with the abstract realm of mathematical research. He was instead dedicating his nonpareil mind to the practical application of mathematics and mathematical physics in the service of the American state, first during the Second World War and now in its contest with the Soviet enemy. With the exception of the Coast Guard, no American military or intelligence organization existed that John von Neumann did not advise.

He had pioneered the coming of digital electronic computers, played the major role in devising stored programming to run them, and designed and supervised the building of the second electronic computer to exist in the United States, the most advanced in the world at the time, under a project he had organized and the Navy had funded at the Institute for Advanced Study. It was variously called the IAS, Princeton, or von Neumann machine. The electronic computer had initially attracted his interest, however, not primarily for its potential civilian applications, but because of its extreme usefulness in devising nuclear weapons, particularly the hydrogen bomb.

Nuclear weapons could not be made through traditional engineering methods as, for example, new aircraft are built: a model is designed, manufactured, and flown by test pilots, with defects gradually eliminated and improvements added. If a new nuclear weapon was incorrectly designed, there would be a "fizzle," the term for such embarrassing fiascoes in the world of nuclear engineering. The would-be weapon would simply fail to go off or detonate in such a flawed fashion that nothing would be learned or gained from the time and expense of preparation. Vastly complex simulated models therefore had to be constructed and tested mathematically with innumerable computations to determine whether the new weapon was going to perform as hoped. The Mike hydrogen device exploded in November 1952 had, in fact, waited upon—been paced by—the progress von Neumann had brought about in electronic computers on which the equations could be run.

The explanation for what motivated Johnny von Neumann lay, as with LeMay and so many other major figures of the Cold War, in his past. He was one of the "Martians," an extraterrestrial distinction awarded by associates of his day to him and several other Hungarians of scientific renown. Teller, whose obsession with building the hydrogen bomb was eventually and unjustly to gain him the popular reputation he so coveted that he and he alone had fathered the Super, was another Martian, as was von Kármán, of aeronautical fame. The appellation had stuck because their non-Hungarian colleagues had difficulty imagining how so many lustrous minds, of which von Neumann's was the most radiant, could have originated in a country like Hungary. Actually, von Neumann and his fellow Hungarians had come from a kind of Mars, a golden age of Jewish secular life in Central Europe that had flourished and then been snuffed out, vanishing into history as remote as Mars was in the vastness of space.

The von, meaning "of," the German designation of aristocratic status, was an indication of the wealth and prominence of the family in which von Neumann had grown up. His father, Max Neumann, was a banker. In 1913, on the eve of the First World War, which was to begin the destruction of their shining but fragile universe, Max had been granted a Hungarian title of nobility by Franz Josef, the Austro-Hungarian emperor. He became Max Neumann of Margitta. When the eldest son of this newly ennobled family began teaching mathematics at the University of Berlin in 1926 he had accordingly styled himself Johann Neumann von Margitta. The American consul to whom he applied for an immigrant identification card three years later trimmed it to Johann von Neumann, and von Neumann Anglicized the Johann to John after he settled in the United States.

The von Neumann family lived in a capacious apartment in Budapest in a building constructed by von Neumann's maternal grandfather, Jacob Kann, who had gained his fortune in the agricultural equipment business. Max had made a good match for himself by successfully courting Margaret, one of Jacob's younger daughters. Von Neumann was the first of the three sons born to them, three days after Christmas 1903, and was named Janos, Hungarian for John. Hungarians customarily do not address a person by his formal first name. He was thus always called Jancsi, the diminutive of Janos, which is why he quickly turned the John to Johnny after immigrating.

There was a cook and other household servants. Johnny and his two younger brothers, Michael and Nicholas, who eventually followed him to the United States, had nursemaids to care for them when they were toddlers. When they grew older a German governess was hired to teach them German, the second language of their parents and the language in which they were to be educated, and an Alsatian governess to teach them French. They learned English from two Englishmen interned during the First World War who preferred quarters in the family apartment to enforced residence in a camp. In addition, Johnny learned on his own to read Italian.

This tranquil world to which wealth and culture gave a seeming sense of permanence had arisen out of a compromise political settlement in 1867 whereby Hungary acquired self-government and became the equal of Austria in the polyglot Austro-Hungarian Empire. Casting about for allies to buttress their position, the Magyar nobility set aside the previously official anti-Semitism and encouraged Jewish immigration into the country as well as Jewish participation in Hungary's business and professional life. The change coincided with an era of unparalleled growth, industrialization, and prosperity in Hungary's larger towns and cities, especially in the capital. Budapest burgeoned from a city of 280,000 in 1867 to 800,000, the sixth largest in Europe after London, Paris, Vienna, Berlin, and St. Petersburg, by the time von Neumann was born in 1903.

As agents for capitalist growth, Jews contributed enormously to this transformation and benefited enormously from it. Although a mere 5 percent of the population as a whole, by 1910 Jews comprised approximately half of Hungary's lawyers, journalists, and commercial businessmen, nearly 60 percent of its doctors, and 80 percent of its financiers. The Jews of this golden age who managed the climb into the middle and upper-middle classes tended to leave the religious observance of their forebears behind them. By the second or third generation, as was the case with the von Neumann family, they became secularized and casually ecumenical in their customs. At Christmas the family put up a tree and exchanged gifts, and the boys sang Christmas carols with their German and Alsatian governesses.

Perhaps the finest accomplishment of the period was the educational system and perhaps the finest institutions within the system were the secondary schools. They were not public schools. They were elite schools, designed to educate the sons of the middle and upper-middle classes who could afford the high tuition fees. The secular Jewish bourgeoisie contributed to the excellence of these schools as well, out of their inherited love of learning that derives from the rabbinical system and its reliance on study of the Torah. Again, they were ecumenical in their choices. Max sent his boys to the Lutheran Gymnasium (the word is a German one for an academic high school that prepares its students for university). The school was nondenominational in its admissions policy. Its course was rigorous and included eight years of Latin, four of classical Greek, history, physics, and the full range of mathematics through calculus and analytical geometry.

Of all the students who ever attended Lutheran, John von Neumann was by far the most brilliant in the estimation of his peers. When he was six, his parents would amuse visitors and show off their Johnny by having him read a page in the telephone book, then take it back while he reeled off the names and numbers from his photographic memory for the astonished guests. Near the end of his life, as he lay dying of cancer at Walter Reed Army Medical Center in Washington, his brother Michael came to see him and, to distract him from the pain, sat beside the bed and read Goethe's *Faust* in the original German of their school days. As Michael reached the bottom of a page, von Neumann would start reciting the first lines of the next one.

He was a genuine mathematical prodigy. His mathematics teacher at Lutheran had to devise special advanced courses for him because he quickly worked his way through the school's regular math curriculum. The proofs he wrote in subsequent years for publication in journals of higher mathematical studies resemble Mozart's musical scores. The original drafts, written with a fountain pen in von Neumann's firm, clear hand, go on for twenty to thirty pages with hardly anything ever crossed out. As Mozart could hear the music in his head while he composed his scores, so von Neumann could see in his mind the steps leading to the solution of the mathematical challenge. "He wrote last drafts first," his daughter and only child, Marina von Neumann Whitman, who became a prominent economist, remarked. At Los Alamos during the making of the atomic bomb he was renowned for solving in a few minutes in his head defiant equations that took other physicists and mathematicians nights of toil with slide rule and mechanical calculator.

The first cataclysm struck in 1918 with the defeat of Austria-Hungary and Kaiser Wilhelm's Germany by the Allies. The Austro-Hungarian monarchy fell and the empire disintegrated. The second cataclysm occurred in March 1919 when Johnny was fifteen and still attending the Lutheran Gymnasium. Béla Kun, a Hungarian socialist who had absorbed Bolshevik ideas while a prisoner of war in Russia, staged a Communist revolt with the support of Hungarian soldiers home from Russian prison camps, who had been similarly radicalized by the success of Vladimir Lenin's revolution there. Kun's regime was marked by a utopian ineptness at governing and a Red Terror in which about 500 opponents were executed. The chaos ended after 133 days when Admiral Miklós Horthy, who was to become the right-wing dictator of Hungary, enlisted Romanian troops to oust Kun and launched a White Terror in which as many as 5,000 may have died. And the Jews got the blame.

The von Neumann family fled to Austria about a month into the revolt, when Max saw that it was too dangerous to stay. The Hungary to which they returned was a different land. Eight of Kun's eleven senior commissars had been Jews and so had a goodly number of lesser figures in his regime. The backlash was a powerful resurgence of traditional anti-Semitism. Anti-Semitic laws that had been in abeyance since the grant of self-government and the creation of the Dual Monarchy in 1867 were reenacted. One struck at education for Jews at the University of Budapest and other higher schools. Henceforth, they were to be restricted in admission to the 5 percent Jews represented of the population as a whole. But the worst consequence of the backlash was the loss of the secure place Jews had known in Hungarian society. Even families like that of Max von Neumann, who had plotted with the right-wing Magyars to rid the country of Kun's regime, were now outsiders with an uncertain future.

John von Neumann had imbibed Russophobia in his Hungarian culture. It was as much a part of his heritage as paprika goulash, inculcated by generations of confronting the Bear along the eastern frontier of the Austro-Hungarian Empire. The upheaval of Béla Kun's revolution and its aftermath immensely reinforced that attitude within him. He saw Russia as the font of this menacing new radicalism and became, in his words, "violently anti-Communist."

Von Neumann wanted to take his university degree in mathematics in Budapest (he would obviously have no trouble qualifying no matter how high the bar was set) and to teach the subject, but Max was convinced he could not earn a decent living that way. There was virtually no chance of gaining a post in mathematics at the university level in Hungary. They settled on chemical engineering as a compromise. Von Neumann obeyed his father, but had his own way too by designing a unique higher education career for himself. He went off to Germany in 1921 to study chemistry at the University of Berlin, moving on two years later to the prestigious Federal Institute of Technology in Zurich, where he took a chemical engineering degree in 1925. All the while, at both institutions, he continued his studies in mathematics and physics. Then he came home and enrolled in the University of Budapest. In a single academic year he whizzed through the remaining courses required, wrote his doctoral thesis in mathematics, and in 1926, at the unprecedented age of twenty-two, was awarded his Ph.D. with highest honors.

He never worked a day as a chemical engineer. Rather, he returned to the University of Berlin as an assistant professor of mathematics soon after gaining his Ph.D. Germany's economic troubles and the shortage of funds at all institutions prevented him from turning the Berlin post into something permanent. In 1929, the year his father died, Princeton offered him a visiting lectureship for the following year. He accepted it, to begin with less out of apprehension over the growth of Nazism in Germany and the drift from old-fashioned authoritarianism toward Nazi-style Fascism in Hungary, than out of simple lack of opportunity there. He was still bound to Europe, but the ever more looming menace of Nazism gave him pause. When Princeton held out a visiting professorship in mathematics and mathematical physics at the end of his initial lectureship, he responded and kept renewing it until Hitler made up von Neumann's mind for him by rising to chancellor of Germany in January 1933, quickly establishing an absolute and stridently racist dictatorship. There was no alternative now but America.

In a letter to a friend around this time, von Neumann predicted that if the Nazis managed to hold on to power they would destroy creative science in Germany. German science and technology remained formidable until the ruination of defeat in 1945, but von Neumann was essentially right about the creative aspect. The 1928 volume of the German edition of the *Annals of Mathematics,* found among his papers at the Library of Congress, provides a sampling of the scientific talent that the Nazis hounded out of Germany to inadvertently enrich science in the United States. Theodore von Kármán is listed as one of the editors. Albert Einstein is among the contributors. Another is John von Neumann, with a paper on a mathematical model of economics he had just devised. He elaborated the theory in his new home and, in collaboration with a colleague at Princeton, Oscar Morgenstern, published it as a book, *Theory of Games and Economic Behavior.* The theory became widely influential on everything from nuclear strategy and arms control negotiations to economic analysis and race relations. In 1933, von Neumann was also made an offer he could hardly refuse. The Institute for Advanced Study, independent of the university, had been founded at Princeton. He was appointed its first research professor of mathematics at the then generous salary of $10,000 a year. The post was ideal for a man of von Neumann's temperament. While he could and did accept protégés in mathematics as temporary fellows at the institute, he had no classes to teach, indeed no fixed duties at all. He was expected simply to follow his bent and break new ground in his field.

31.

A FASCINATION WITH EXPLOSIONS

It was hardly surprising that a man of von Neumann's background and experience would be afflicted with a profound sense of insecurity, which sometimes manifested itself in comic ways. One was his obsession with proper attire. A unique photograph exists of him walking down a sidewalk in Santa Fe in 1949 with his daughter, Marina, then fourteen, in business suit but with his shirt collar open and no tie. It seems to have been a singular occasion, for no friend's camera appears to have caught him ever again in such disarray. More typical of the lengths to which he would go to maintain sartorial decorum is a photograph taken in the late 1940s of a group on a break from work at Los Alamos for an excursion into the Grand Canyon. They are about to start the descent, astride the mules that will carry them down. All, including von Neumann's second wife, Klara Dan, who was called Klari, are wearing casual clothes and some have broad-brimmed hats to protect them from the sun. Von Neumann brings up the rear. His balding head is exposed to the sun and he sits astride his mule in business suit and tie with white handkerchief tucked into his lapel pocket. For some reason, his mule is also headed in the wrong direction.

The insecurity manifested itself as well in his concern for money. There was no need for it. His salary at the institute was ample. He also held a couple of civilian consultantships, one with IBM, which paid him thousands more. He lived in the manner of the wealthy European he had been born, sailing the Atlantic in first-class cabins each summer for international mathematical conferences in Europe, and seeking out the best hotels. He drove the best of American cars, a snappy Cadillac coupé. Yet this willingness to treat himself to luxury never stopped him from chasing down the last penny to which he felt he might be entitled. In 1955, while a member of the Atomic Energy Commission, he dictated a letter to his secretary for the management of the Nassau Tavern in Princeton. It was typed on official stationery and dispatched by government postage. Enclosed were unused vouchers for the restaurant's parking lot. Von Neumann requested reimbursement, by check or credit. The total amounted to seventy-five cents.

He also had an identity problem. He couldn't seem to decide whether he was a Christian or a Jew. His first wife, the daughter of a Budapest physician, was a Gentile and a Roman Catholic. The child of that marriage, Marina, was by prior agreement raised in the Roman Catholic faith. Three days before she was baptized in 1935 at Saint Mary's Cathedral in Trenton, New Jersey, von Neumann had himself baptized at the same place. He never practiced Roman Catholicism in subsequent years, however, and his Jewish friends assumed he considered himself a secular Jew because he acted like one when he was with them. One of his closest Jewish friends, the highly talented Polish-born mathematician Stanislaw Ulam, recalled in his memoirs how von Neumann liked to tell a joke mocking the "goyim," a derogatory Yiddish term for Gentiles. (Ulam, who also immigrated to the United States during the 1930s, was in 1951 to make the hydrogen bomb feasible by coming up with a new idea for detonating the thermonuclear core. Teller would never subsequently acknowledge the contribution because it detracted from his claim to sole parentage.) Not until death confronted him would von Neumann make up his mind.

Von Neumann displayed the same sort of intensely emotional patriotism Schriever did, the patriotism of the immigrant who is deeply grateful to a land that has been good to him. He had a fierce desire to defend this society that had given him shelter and that embodied values he cherished in the rule of law and the freedom of scholarly inquiry. The traits also made him eager to cooperate with the U.S. military. He found the relationship fulfilling, a measure of his acceptance by American society. Systematic mobilization of scientific talent then got under way at the outset of 1941. Roosevelt recruited Vannevar Bush, an electrical engineer and mathematician who was president of the Carnegie Institution and one of the country's most eminent scientific figures, to oversee the effort as his science czar. Bush established the National Defense Research Committee (NDRC), with himself as chairman. That February 26, he wrote von Neumann notifying him that he was being made a consultant to a section of the committee under Bush's friend James Conant, a chemist who was president of Harvard.

By now von Neumann was eager to give the slip to his scholar's tower at the institute. His was not the contemplative genius of Einstein. His mind was quick and restless and this was an opportunity to dedicate his extraordinary talent for mathematics and mathematical physics to a cause that had such intense and personal meaning for him. He quickly developed a fascination with explosions. The subject is called hydrodynamics because of the similarity between the expanding waves of an explosion and fluids in motion. The section of the National Defense Research Committee to which he had been assigned was focused on the subject, using a laboratory at Princeton. Soon his correspondence was filled with such terms as "gas dynamics," "shock collisions," "shock waves in several dimensions," and "oblique shock reflection." He studied explosions through every technique available, including flash photography with high-speed film, and composed mathematical models for the various types, phases, and effects. By the spring of 1942 he had begun to make himself an authority on the subject, evolving a theory on explosions that he laid out in a secret report entitled "Detonation Waves." Unaware as he sometimes was that lesser mortals had difficulty keeping pace with his mind, his initial report was composed almost entirely of mathematical models and equations. At the request of some of his colleagues, he wrote a second report, "a more 'popular' version," as he called it, which contained enough of the English language so a technically qualified person could comprehend his mathematics.

His reputation for expertise on explosives became sufficiently widespread within the military and scientific communities that the Navy sent him to England for six months to advise on the effects of detonations underwater, apparently for use in antisubmarine warfare. After his return from England in the summer of 1943, Robert Oppenheimer summoned him out to Los Alamos. He wanted von Neumann's advice on the implosion method the laboratory was attempting to develop to set off the Fat Man plutonium bomb that was to be dropped on Nagasaki. The two men had been acquainted since the late 1920s, when they had met while Oppenheimer was studying in Germany. Von Neumann endorsed the implosion concept and provided some ideas for it, but Oppenheimer then made the mistake of assigning to an American physicist from Caltech the task of perfecting it. The job was light-years beyond the man. Even Hans Bethe, the gifted German Jewish physicist who was to win a Nobel for his research on the energy production of stars, at the time chief of the Theoretical Division at Los Alamos, tried and failed to design a workable method.

Early in 1944, "Oppie" summoned von Neumann back to Los Alamos. Other developments on the plutonium bomb had rendered imperative the creation of an implosion method that would succeed. Wrapping the plutonium core of the bomb with conventional explosives and detonating them to crush the plutonium with enough force and simultaneity to drive it to the supercritical stage of a nuclear explosion was a simple idea. The details, however, were extraordinarily complex. Enlisting his friend Stanislaw Ulam to help him with the mathematics, von Neumann set out to solve the riddle. To prevail, von Neumann needed all the knowledge of explosions he had acquired from past experiments.

His first task was to determine precisely how and at what speed the detonation waves from the wrapper of conventional explosives should converge in order to force the plutonium to supercriticality. To find the answers to this part of the problem, von Neumann and Ulam had to perform an exhaustive number of mathematical calculations. Once they had the results and had put together a mathematical model of the correct convergence, von Neumann moved on to his second task—diagramming the detonation wrapper by delineating the arrangement of fast-burning and slow-burning explosives required. He had to diagram to nearly perfect exactness. The calculations showed that an error of more than 5 percent would make the difference between a conventional explosion followed by a nuclear detonation and a conventional bang followed by a nuclear fizzle. The diagram was then turned over to George Kistiakowsky, the ingenious Ukrainian-born chemist, to transform it into reality, which he so brilliantly did.

And as the bombs were dropped on Hiroshima and Nagasaki, the fruit of John von Neumann's mind was at work again to enhance their destructiveness. It was he who had discovered in the course of his experiments that large bombs had a greater blast effect if detonated at an optimal height above their targets rather than at ground level. At both Hiroshima and Nagasaki, therefore, the bombs had been set for air bursts to maximize the obliterative effect on the cities and their inhabitants.

When Bennie Schriever went to Princeton to seek his help, von Neumann was near the height of his influence and prestige. His role in the making of the atomic bomb and then the Super were widely known within the upper reaches of government and the scientific community. His initiative in advancing the electronic computer had also brought him public recognition and the luster of his reputation for mathematical genius was undimmed. Von Neumann was liked as well as admired by his colleagues. With his wide erudition and a trove of ribald jokes, he was always an interesting and amusing companion. The militancy of his attitude toward the Soviet Union was not regarded as wild and totally irrational at the time, even by those who did not share its intensity. Fear of a Soviet invasion of Western Europe had been brought to a peak by the Korean War, and no matter how mistaken in retrospect that fear may have been, it was all too real at the time. (In 1952, von Neumann had proposed persuading the best mathematicians in West Germany to immigrate to the United States in order to deprive the Soviets of their talents when the place was overrun.)

The death of Stalin in March 1953 and the negotiations that were to bring a truce in Korea that July did not lessen the fear because the Soviet Union, rather than the person of Stalin, was now perceived as the menace. At bottom, von Neumann's contemporaries liked and trusted him as much as they did because they sensed the fundamental decency of the man. He was to display it conspicuously in 1954 by testifying in defense of Robert Oppenheimer, who was wrongly accused of disloyalty and deprived of his security clearance because of his opposition to creating the hydrogen bomb when the issue was still open to debate before Truman had made his decision. Von Neumann's defense of Oppenheimer was all the more striking for its moral courage because his political patron happened to be the financier Lewis Strauss, the man who, as chairman of the Atomic Energy Commission, was stage-managing the conspiracy against Oppenheimer. Despite this conflict of opinion, Strauss apparently appreciated von Neumann's sincerity because he subsequently arranged his appointment to the commission.

———

Schriever recalled years later that, as he had anticipated, the technical details of the conversation between von Neumann and Teddy Walkowicz were beyond his ken. Von Neumann was generous with his time—the meeting lasted several hours. Von Neumann explained, with occasional resort to chalk and blackboard, the process by which one progressed from the eighty-two-ton, liquid-fueled Mike device exploded the previous November to the warhead Schriever needed by the end of the decade for a practical ICBM—a dry hydrogen bomb of less than a ton in weight and one megaton in yield. Von Neumann based his findings on radiation flow and other data from the Mike test, which gave him confidence that much lighter dry bombs of lesser yield could be built in the future. He said he expected more data from the Castle test series scheduled for the spring of 1954 at Bikini Atoll in the Marshall Islands of the central Pacific, when the United States was to set off its first dry thermonuclear devices fueled by lithium deuteride.

Bennie left the meeting well satisfied. He now had more than the simple confirmation for which he had originally gone to Princeton. He had scientific validation and, coming from von Neumann, perhaps the nation's foremost authority on nuclear weaponry, that validation was unchallengeable. He also recalled returning to Washington with something else that gave him additional satisfaction. Earlier that year, von Neumann had agreed to head the recently created Nuclear Weapons Panel of the Air Force's Scientific Advisory Board. Ironically, it was Schriever who had lobbied Jimmy Doolittle to set up the panel during the March gathering at Maxwell, so that they could obtain better information on what to expect in the size and yield of nuclear weapons to come. (Among his other roles, Doolittle served as a vice chairman of the SAB.) In the course of this meeting at Princeton, von Neumann now told Bennie he would see that the panel included in its reports a hydrogen warhead light enough for a missile to carry. When attempting to drive a project as big as the ICBM through the Air Force bureaucracy, having as much scientific judgment as possible in your favor was a key component in succeeding. Von Neumann's ultra-hawkish views, the widespread esteem in which he was held, and his ability to marshal the talents and support of his fellow scientists were to provide assistance of the utmost importance in bringing Schriever's vision to fruition.

32.

FINDING AN ALLY

Schriever understood that as a mere colonel—even though on the list for promotion to his first star in approximately a month and a half—he could not possibly carry a project of this magnitude forward by himself. He needed a leader much higher in the Pentagon aviary, someone with the imagination to see the strategic necessity to build an ICBM force and with the energy, verve, and daring—and the bureaucratic and political clout—to prevail against the entrenched opposition. As it happened, for the past several months he had known just such a man, Trevor Gardner, the new special assistant to the secretary of the air force for research and development. In the story of how the ICBM came into being, Gardner was to soar briefly across the firmament like a Roman candle. While he burned, he burned brightly.

Gardner was, like Schriever and von Neumann, another immigrant to America. He was a Welshman, born in Cardiff in 1915. His father was a boilermaker who worked for a firm in Wales that built boilers for steam electrical generating plants. While Gardner was still a child, his father obtained a position as manager of one such small plant in South America and took the family off with him. The precise country and town has been lost to family memory. All that is remembered is that the place was somewhere up in the Andes. Whatever the location, the job did not last and by 1928, when Gardner was thirteen, the family had shifted to Southern California. Despite the empty-pocket years of the Great Depression, Gardner managed to cobble together enough odd jobs to take full advantage of California's magnificent educational opportunities. He took his bachelor's degree in engineering with honors from the University of Southern California in Los Angeles in 1937 and then taught freshman mathematics at USC while he gained a master's in business administration two years later.

By 1942, soon after Japan's Sunday morning surprise at Pearl Harbor, he was running the developmental engineering section of the California Institute of Technology at nearby Pasadena as a protégé of Charles Lauritsen, Caltech's senior and highly respected physicist. Under Lauritsen, he helped to fabricate explosives for George Kistiakowsky to use up at Los Alamos. The work earned him a Presidential Certificate of Merit at the end of the conflict. When Bennie Schriever met him in 1953, Gardner had five years of prosperity behind him running a company he had started in Pasadena, Hycon Manufacturing, which produced electronic components for aircraft and for short-range, air-to-ground rockets for Navy fighter-bombers. Hycon brought him to the attention of Harold Talbott, a wealthy New York businessman, investment banker, Republican Party fund-raiser, and acquaintance of the new president, Dwight D. Eisenhower. Ike believed that prosperous businessmen and bankers would make sound government executives and so appointed a goodly number to his cabinet and the higher levels of the administration.

Talbott happened to have had extensive experience in aircraft manufacture during earlier years. Eisenhower therefore named him secretary of the air force and Talbott in turn summoned Gardner to Washington to be his special assistant for research and development.

Colonel Vincent "Vince" Ford, who was to serve as Gardner's executive assistant and became his closest friend and confidant, remembered the day in March 1953 when he glanced up from his desk in the outer room of the office suite on the fourth floor of the Pentagon and saw a figure standing in the open doorway. The man was looking at Ford intently through thick rimless glasses held in place by narrow gold frames. He was large, about six feet tall and a couple hundred pounds, with big shoulders and dark, reddish-brown hair trimmed close. He was attired fastidiously in a navy blue suit with the points of a crisply pressed and folded white handkerchief protruding from the breast pocket, a silk tie of steel gray, and a white shirt. In his left hand he held a gray felt fedora, which was, like the suit and the silk tie and the white shirt, part of the dress code of a successful business or professional man of the era. When he put his right hand forward to shake Ford's, Vince noticed the flicker of one of the gold cuff links that held the French cuffs of the shirt in place. "Hi," the man said in a resonant voice. "My name's Gardner. I've been told this is where I come to work." As Ford shook the proferred hand, he felt it grip his firmly. "My name is Ford," he replied. Gardner gestured toward the open doorway of the large inner office that was to be his. "Let's go in here and talk," Gardner said.

Ford assumed the conversation was meant as an employment interview so that Gardner could decide whether to hire him. Then a lieutenant colonel, Ford had been executive assistant to the previous special assistant for research and development during the Truman administration, William "Bill" Burden, the first to hold the position and like Talbott a New York investment banker. After Burden had left, Ford waited on in the office to see whether Burden's successor would want him to continue. He wasn't certain he would be kept. Technically, Ford was physically unfit for active duty. A flying accident in his youth had left him with a grotesquely twisted left foot and ankle. In order to be able to walk, Ford had to encase the foot in a specially fashioned boot with steel braces on both sides of the ankle. He was able to move reasonably nimbly, without crutches or cane, but that did not change the fact that he was still a cripple. In 1948, Schriever, not a man to let a technicality deprive him of the services of a capable officer, had hired Ford and got him restored to active duty. Ford had then worked for Schriever for two years before moving up to become Burden's executive assistant. He was an ambitious, highly intelligent, and complicated man, capable of being extremely devious.

As it turned out, Gardner paid no more attention to Ford's disability than Schriever had. He never did tell Ford he was hired. They simply picked up where they were that day. "My name is Trev," Gardner said, after Ford had addressed him as Mr. Gardner, "and that's the way I like it. No formalities. Okay?" Gardner then did something during that first conversation which told Ford that informality was not the only thing that was different about this man. As Ford was speaking, Gardner suddenly reached across to a yellow legal pad that was lying between them on the conference table. He tore off a corner of the top sheet, rolled it into a wad with his thumb and forefinger, and, tossing it into his mouth, began chewing it, all the while continuing to listen and to fix Ford with those intense hazel eyes behind the glasses. It was a clue that, as Ford was later to concede, Trevor Gardner was "not the sort of man with whom one ordinarily made friends."

Whatever contradictory traits could exist in one man, Gardner had them. He was a good listener, but he was also extremely impatient. The ponderousness of the Air Force bureaucracy provoked particular ire. When he inquired about some matter he considered urgent and was told that the subject would have to be "staffed" and that he could expect a memo in three days, he would bark back over the phone, "I don't want a memo. I want a decision—in an hour!" He could be offhanded and informal and polite, as he was in Vince Ford's first encounter with him, and he could be abrasive and profane. Gardner did not hesitate to tell some important man that what he was doing "isn't worth a good goddamn." And he once snapped, "Shut up, Tommy!" at Lieutenant General Thomas Power during a meeting in a room filled with other bestarred men. Power had annoyed Gardner by talking while Gardner wanted to think. Since leading LeMay's first firebombing of Tokyo on March 9, 1945, Power had become one of the Air Force's most prominent generals. He did not appreciate the humiliation, especially in the presence of his contemporaries. Like encounters led much of the senior Air Force leadership to detest Gardner. And

Gardner had a serious drinking problem. He kept it under control during the day, although a couple of double-shot Old Forester bourbons with ginger ale, his standard potion at lunch, made him more aggressive back at the office in the afternoon. The night was another matter. Ford grew accustomed to calls from him at all hours, the voice sometimes so slurred that he could barely understand him. The nocturnal bouts affected his personal life by worsening a troubled marriage, but seemed not to interfere with his work because he had extraordinary recuperative powers. After a few hours of sleep, a shower, and breakfast with strong black coffee, he was fit and alert.

Yet for all his disdain for bureaucracy when it got in his way, he was a canny bureaucratic operator himself. He had an excellent sense of when and how to maneuver. His own memos, always "staffed" for him by Ford and frequently by Schriever or others with special knowledge, were trenchant and to the point. He was apt at recognizing the talents of other men and at exploiting those talents to further his objectives. He had the ability to gain the confidence of those above him who mattered. Harold Talbott had complete trust in him. He was also a man of extraordinary determination, utterly ruthless about accomplishing his goals. The determination showed in his walk, the powerful shoulders hunched forward slightly, the head inclined in thought. And, like Schriever and von Neumann, Gardner was motivated by the intense patriotism of the immigrant to whom America has been good. All of these qualities were to make him the man for the hour.

Schriever and Gardner met through Vince Ford. In one of his first moves on Gardner's behalf, Ford had taken Gardner around the Pentagon and introduced him to anyone in the research and development field he thought might be useful. Jimmy Doolittle had been one; Schriever had been another. Gardner shared Schriever's vision of technology as the means to maintain American military superiority. He also shared Schriever's interest in ballistic missiles. In an article published in *Air Force,* the magazine of the semiofficial Air Force Association, the same March of 1953 that Gardner arrived at the Pentagon, he argued that the United States and the Soviet Union were in a race to build long-range missiles. "The fate of the free world may well depend," he wrote, on which nation won. A keen strategic sense was another of Gardner's many qualities. He understood how the credibility of LeMay's Strategic Air Command as a deterrent would be undercut in the public mind and among America's European allies if the Soviets achieved an ICBM first and the United States had none of its own in the works to match. What he did not know was that the ultimate weapon had at last become feasible.

Hoping that Gardner might be able to initiate the ICBM program that was beyond him for the moment, Schriever went to see him soon after returning from Princeton. He passed on the information he had obtained from von Neumann, explaining how the ability to size down a thermonuclear warhead made the missile feasible. Gardner hardly needed encouragement. On May 20, 1953, twelve days after Schriever's and Walkowicz's visit, he was in von Neumann's office at the Institute for Advanced Study, seeking and receiving the same briefing and the same scientific validation that a one-megaton hydrogen bomb less than a ton in weight would be available as a missile warhead by the end of the decade. Gardner returned to Washington and began the campaign.

Charles "Engine Charlie" Wilson, the president of General Motors, had become secretary of defense after Eisenhower's inauguration in January 1953. He was one of the "eight millionaires" in the new cabinet. (The dollar still held sufficient purchasing power then for the term to signify wealth equivalent to that of a billionaire at the end of the twentieth century.) The assumption behind his appointment was that a man who ran the largest private corporation in the world, which General Motors then was, could use his skills as an industrial manager to oversee and reform the biggest of government departments. That June, in one of his efforts to try to bring efficiency to the military-industrial complex, Wilson instructed Harold Talbott to form a committee to review the confused and confusing array of missile projects the Army, Navy, and Air Force had under way. These encompassed air-to-air, surface-to-air, and both short-range surface-to-surface tactical and long-range surface-to-surface strategic weapons. The point was to eliminate duplication and boondoggle projects that would never result in anything useful. Talbott in turn assigned the task to Gardner. His enterprising special assistant for research and development proceeded to use the committee not as a means of saving money, but rather as a cover for a scheme Gardner was evolving to spend a lot more money

on a crash program to build an intercontinental ballistic missile. As
Gardner was wont to gleefully exclaim to Ford when he had a project
in play that particularly appealed to him: "We've got a live one."

33.

MARSHALING THE EXPERTISE

In directing the committee's work, it soon became apparent to
Gardner that the big aircraft companies, whose colossal production of flying machines had won the skies of the Second World War,
were incapable by themselves of meeting the demands of the missile
age. They lacked the scientific and engineering talent to chart the unknown and untie the myriad technical knots involved in creating an
ICBM. There was, for example, the reentry problem. Once the missile had been launched and the warhead containing the hydrogen
bomb was hurtling through the vacuum of space, how was one to
bring the warhead back down without burning it up from friction
when it struck the resistant air of the earth's atmosphere? The major
aircraft manufacturers were also unlikely to acquire the talent they
needed by recruiting the best graduates of the technical schools, particularly the California universities. The management of these old-
line firms was too conventional, the atmosphere too stultifying, to
attract these young minds seeking technological adventure. In short,
the United States had an aircraft industry, but the nation was yet to
acquire an aerospace industry. To get the ICBM built, Gardner would
have to find the genesis of one.

He encountered what he was seeking in Culver City, California, in
a firm owned by Howard Hughes, the exceedingly neurotic and reclu-
sive multimillionaire. Hughes Aircraft Company was a subsidiary of
Hughes Tool, the main source of drilling equipment for America's oil
fields, which Howard Hughes had inherited from his father when he
was just eighteen years old. He rarely appeared at his Culver City
property, knew little of what went on there, and understood less.

Hughes Aircraft had been transformed into something quite different from an ordinary aircraft company by two men, Simon Ramo and Dean Wooldridge, who were to become immensely wealthy princes of the American military-industrial complex as co-founders of one of its preeminent firms, TRW, Inc. And the ICBM project, for which Ramo was to serve as Bennie Schriever's chief technical director and engineer, was to launch them.

Simon Ramo was a technological entrepreneur. He had an eye for the main chance of the future and understood how to exploit it. A trim man of medium height with dark hair and angular features, Ramo had one of those effervescent minds that are never still. He was born in 1913 in Salt Lake City, Utah, the son of Jewish immigrants from Russia and Ukraine who ran a small store. His parents encouraged their children in both education and the arts. Salt Lake City was then a center of culture in the West with its own opera company, ballet corps, symphony orchestra, and the renowned Mormon Tabernacle Choir. Ramo, whose brilliance at mathematics and science sent him skipping grades through school, also became an accomplished amateur violinist.

Family funds for higher education were limited. In 1929, a senior in high school intent on entering the University of Utah that fall to study electrical engineering, Ramo engaged in his first risk taking based, as he later wrote in an autobiography, "on cool calculation." If he could walk off the stage with most or all of the prizes in a forthcoming interstate music contest, he could claim a full scholarship to the university and a considerable amount of cash. Otherwise, he faced the drudgery of four years of after-school work to get through. He reasoned that he had sound hope of winning because of his skill with the violin, but that he would measurably improve his chances if he invested in an instrument with much better sound quality than the rudimentary $25 Japanese model he was playing. Withdrawing all his savings from the bank, he bought an Italian violin for $325. He swept the contest and took his bachelor's degree in electrical engineering in 1933, the youngest in his class by two years, and with the highest grade point average. Had he left his money in the savings account he would have lost it, as the bank collapsed in October 1929 right after the stock market crash. As with so many other college graduates in 1933, there was no employment to be had in the midst of the Depression. His scholastic attainment, however, gained him a graduate fellowship to

Caltech in Pasadena, where he received his Ph.D. in electrical engineering and physics in 1936 with high honors.

His Italian fiddle now got him a job. When the General Electric Company recruiter came out to Caltech that spring of 1936, Ramo did not expect to be hired. The country was still in the trough of the Depression and there were too many other qualified candidates in California for the handful of positions the recruiter would be able to offer. Robert Millikan, the Nobel Laureate in physics and friend of Hap Arnold who was president of Caltech at the time, had Ramo play a couple of violin selections at a lunch he gave for the GE recruiter prior to an afternoon round of interviews. Ramo had performed uncomfortably, believing the performance would hurt his already meager prospects; the recruiter would regard him not as a sound and pragmatic engineer but rather as a dreamy musician. At his turn for an interview, Ramo had hardly sat down before the recruiter told him that there was a symphony orchestra in Schenectady, the upstate New York city where GE's main facilities were located, that the company was the orchestra's principal sponsor, and that most of its members were GE employees. "Ramo, you will enjoy the orchestra," the recruiter said. Ramo was puzzled at the remark and then surprised as the recruiter consulted a notebook and gave him a date to report for work that August at the firm's General Engineering Laboratory. On his first day at the laboratory, the conductor of the Schenectady Symphony phoned to tell him the time and place of the orchestra's next rehearsal. It turned out that with so many engineers of prowess to choose from, the recruiter had taken Millikan's bait and decided he might as well have a violinist in the bargain. And he chose well, as Ramo became the orchestra's first violinist, or concertmaster.

Ramo was thrilled to be assigned to research and development in the then virginal field of electronics, but disappointed to discover that General Electric's laboratories were not the powerhouses of pioneering electrical science they were reputed to be. Some of his research in generating high-frequency electromagnetic waves that are the basis of radar brought him to the attention of the U.S. Navy. Nothing came of his work, however. To his chagrin, British scientists had already accomplished the same research independently and were applying it to their radars. Near the beginning of the war, he also made the mistake of declining an invitation to push aggressively the frontiers of radar by going on a leave of absence from GE and joining the staff of a laboratory forming at MIT in Cambridge under the distinguished Cornell and University of Wisconsin physicist Lee DuBridge. He let the director of his laboratory in Schenectady talk him out of accepting with the argument that this laboratory of "professors" would never amount to anything. The important research in radar would be done at major institutions like GE, the director said, and Ramo should stay where he was, positioned to accomplish the maximum. He stayed and he accomplished the minimum, missing his opportunity to become one of the heroes of the MIT Rad Lab, renowned for their wartime achievements in radar. General Electric's contribution to the war effort was its cornucopia of equipment for the armed forces. Its laboratories provided no innovation of consequence to military technology. The pattern held, in general, for the other big corporations. The corporations produced and wartime innovations came from the academics gathered into high-spirited, fertile-minded communities like the Rad Lab and the atomic bomb laboratory at Los Alamos. Too late, Ramo realized that the men who ran GE's laboratories had become unimaginative bureaucrats, comfortable in their positions, content in their outmoded ways.

By the end of the war, he was determined to leave as soon as he could. In addition to his professional discontent, Ramo was suffering from an ailment he described as "Californiaitis." So was his wife, the former Virginia Smith, an Easterner by birth who had gone to college in California, where she and Ramo had met and married. After the chill of nine upstate New York winters in Schenectady, they wanted to feel the sun of Southern California again. His eye for the main chance had also given Ramo an insight into the future that he hoped would enable him to start a company of his own in California. He foresaw the military consequences of the bipolar world that emerged from the Second World War. The alliance between the United States and the Soviet Union would not survive for long. The societies were too different, there was too much potential for rivalry and conflict, he reasoned. As soon as American airmen perceived the Soviet Union as a future opponent, they would seek means to defend the United States against the long-range bombers they would assume the Soviets would build. (In fact, they already had. Planners within the U.S. Army Air Forces had singled out the Soviet air force as a postwar rival as early as 1944.)

In the jet age that had arrived in the skies over Germany in the fall of 1944 with the appearance of the Messerschmitt 262, the world's first jet fighter, machine guns and fast-firing aerial cannon were also being rendered obsolete. Intercepting fighters would need air-to-air guided missiles to knock down fast, jet-powered bombers. The interceptors would also need radars and fire-control computers compact enough to fit into a cockpit, yet powerful enough to lock onto the bombers at night and in foul weather and send the missiles flashing to their targets. On the ground, the air defense system would require better long-range warning radars and advanced communications in order to detect the bombers while they were still far out and direct the fighters toward them. Unlike Lieutenant General Leslie Groves, who had headed the Manhattan Project, Ramo also did not believe it would take the Soviet Union twenty years to acquire its own atomic bomb. He suspected that a few years would suffice to end the American monopoly. And when that first Russian bomb did explode, American air defense preparations would accelerate feverishly. Billions would be spent to create a continent-wide network. A company in position to provide technology for this system could profit most handsomely. But where was Ramo to find the millions to start such a firm?

In early 1946, while on an assignment in Southern California for GE, he ran into some men who said they were working at what they described as the "hobby shop" of Howard Hughes, an aircraft organization recently set up with capital from Hughes Tool. They persuaded Ramo to come over to Culver City for a look. What he found hardly merited the term "organization." Hughes Aircraft had a general manager, but he was an accountant who existed mainly to sign checks. Yet enough money to keep things together did flow in from Houston, where Hughes Tool had its headquarters, and the people employed at Culver City seemed to have a free hand to be creative. Rather than struggling to raise money on his own, Ramo decided he could instead use this place as a base on which to start. That April of 1946 he said goodbye to frosty Schenectady and arrived in Culver City to establish a center for high-technology military research and development.

His original plan had been to keep the enterprise small, at about a hundred physicists and engineers skilled in a spectrum of disciplines. They would furnish the military with innovative concepts, research, and information, but not hardware. The furthest they would venture would be hand-built prototypes. When the time came to actually go into production, they would farm out the task to one of the large and established firms. The plan didn't work. Ramo had been more perspicacious than he realized in foreseeing the military consequences of the bipolar postwar world. As relations between Moscow and Washington deteriorated, the demands of the military for air defense grew apace.

He acquired a partner in the summer of 1946, a classmate and close friend from Caltech, Dean Wooldridge, who was to become the W in TRW, Inc. A physicist, Wooldridge had grown up in Oklahoma, the son of an independent oil broker. He had graduated from high school at the age of fourteen, taken the University of Oklahoma at Norman in his stride, and moved on to Caltech, where he had been granted his Ph.D. summa cum laude. He quit a job at the prestigious Bell Telephone Laboratories to join Ramo. The two men were contrasting types. Both were spare-time musicians, but Wooldridge, a tranquil, introspective man, relaxed by playing not a lively instrument like the violin, but the organ. The ebullient Ramo's other extracurricular passion was tennis. But they complemented each other. Wooldridge's strength lay in the business and administrative side, while Ramo oversaw the research and engineering. Together, they recruited hundreds more of the technologically adept to staff their operation. There was no shortage of candidates. Ramo had suspected correctly that a lot of the nonacademic technical experts who emerged from the universities early enough to serve their apprenticeship on exciting wartime projects would prefer to continue pursuing the challenge of military innovation rather than turn to less interesting civilian work. There was also no difficulty recruiting many of the best postwar graduates of California's technologically strong universities. In these immediate postwar years, long before the Vietnam conflict, there was no stigma attached to employment in military industry.

When the Soviet Union exploded its own atomic bomb on the steppes of Kazakhstan in Soviet Central Asia on August 29, 1949, the money spigot turned into a fire hose. After SAC, air defense was now the major preoccupation of the U.S. Air Force. And the electronics section of Hughes Aircraft under Ramo and Wooldridge became the Air Force's preponderant source by far for air defense equipment. Virtually every first-line jet interceptor in the new Air Defense Command's squadrons was equipped with a Hughes airborne radar and fire-control computer. Ramo and Wooldridge discovered that they could not farm out their prototypes for production by one of the major air-craft firms. The older companies, ensconced in their Second World War–era ways, either would not or could not retool and reorganize a production facility fast enough to meet Air Force deadlines.

Ramo and Wooldridge tore down unused airplane hangars on the Hughes property at Culver City, erected factories of their own, and hired and trained a labor force. Their organization was so proficient that it never lost a competition for a contract. Ramo emphasized a relatively new concept known as systems engineering, which he defined as "the discipline of the design of the whole, to realize a harmonious and effective ensemble, as distinct from the design of the parts." What he meant in layman's English was to design everything in advance with the end result in mind, so that when the individual parts were put together the whole would function smoothly. There might well be, of course, the usual malfunctions when the weapon was tested because the engineers had overlooked or not foreseen something, but the objective was to anticipate and eliminate as many of these bugs as possible beforehand.

The Falcon, the Air Force's first air-to-air guided missile, was an example of systems engineering and perhaps Ramo's finest achievement of these early years. The missile was a sleek six-and-a-half-foot-long aluminum tube, six and a half inches in diameter, with a rounded radar guidance device at the nose, seven pounds of high-explosive warhead tucked underneath, and three stabilizer fins that emerged at midsection and flared out wide as they swept back to the tail, where the rocket motor was located. It had originated in a contract Ramo won from Wright Field in 1947 for a study of air-to-air missiles. The initial flight test in 1950 was a complete success. Two missiles were launched by an interceptor plane and each struck and destroyed one of two drones, remotely controlled aircraft, being used to simulate a pair of approaching Soviet bombers. The Falcon itself, however, was only a part of the weapon or, to use the proper and more accurate term, the weapon system. The airborne radar and the fire-control computer in the interceptor were of equal importance. When the interceptor drew within the five-mile range of the missile, the radar "painted" the bomber with its electromagnetic waves and "locked on." The fire-control computer connected to the radar automatically calculated converging speed and angle. At the most opportune moment, the computer then ignited the missile's rocket engine. As the Falcon streaked toward the bomber at two to three times the speed of sound, the guidance node in its tip picked up the impulses from the radar in the interceptor and held the missile true to course. In the perspective of microcircuitry and the miracles of electronics to come by the turn of the century, the Falcon system was primitive, but by 1953, when Trevor Gardner came calling at Hughes Aircraft, it was state-of-the-art indeed. The modest research and development center Ramo had set out to create in 1946 had also by then been grown by him and Dean Wooldridge into a high-technology powerhouse, with 3,000 employees and $200 million in business annually, an enviable sum in those years.

34.

THE TEA POT COMMITTEE

Gardner and Ramo had known each other since 1937. They had happened to live in the same apartment house in Schenectady while Gardner was doing a brief stint as a student engineer for General Electric. He too had soon decided that GE was not for him and returned to the University of Southern California to teach freshman mathematics and earn his M.B.A. Gardner also had some knowledge of Ramo's and Wooldridge's accomplishments at Culver City because his own firm, Hycon Manufacturing, was located in nearby Pasadena. But he apparently did not fully appreciate how far they had gone until he visited Hughes in the course of the Department of Defense guided missile survey he was heading. He realized then that he had found two men who had fostered the beginnings of an aerospace industry. They could marshal and wield the scientific and engineering expertise necessary to overcome the technological obstacles inherent in the building of an ICBM. He complimented them on the "forceful and focused" manner in which they developed a weapon system and picked Ramo's brain for ideas on how to proceed with an ICBM project. Ramo urged him to start by setting up a blue-ribbon committee to study the problem and issue a judgment on the ICBM's feasibility. He should select its chairman and members with care, Ramo advised, because if he managed to form a committee with sufficient academic and scientific gravitas, Secretary Wilson and others Gardner wanted to impress at the Pentagon would be unable to ignore its findings. Gardner had divided the Defense Department's overall guided missile review committee into panels, each to study and report on a category of missiles. He had reserved leadership of the panel on intercontinental strategic missiles to himself. Its recommendation, naturally, was to convene precisely the sort of all-star committee Ramo advocated.

And so Gardner and Vince Ford set off for Princeton once more in Gardner's green Cadillac convertible. (Gardner and the Hungarian genius he was going to see shared a taste for expensive automobiles.) The conversation in von Neumann's office at the Institute for Advanced Study was briefer this time. "I vill do it," Ford recalled von Neumann immediately replying to Gardner's request that he chair the committee, turning the w into a v with his Hungarian accent. Gardner was elated on the way back to Washington, driving at his usual madcap speed, whipping around every car ahead of his on a rain-slick road while he called out to Ford the names of prospective members of the committee. Ford had observed that, figuratively speaking, Trevor Gardner seemed to know only two speeds in an automobile—zero when the car was stopped and seventy miles per hour when it was on the move. They took a break in Maryland for a couple of drinks and a steak dinner.

Ramo and Wooldridge had meanwhile been preparing all that summer to leave Hughes Aircraft after seven years and found their own firm. They were too ambitious to work forever for a company owned by another man and, if they stayed, with the loony Hughes in possession they believed they would never be able to break the aircraft company away from Hughes Tool and acquire the authority they needed to further expand and diversify. To get to see Hughes was extremely difficult and time-consuming. When Ramo did succeed, he could never get a coherent response out of the man, who at one point shifted his residence from a set of frostily air-conditioned hotel rooms in Las Vegas to an old and bare mansion in Santa Monica with a folding camp cot to sleep on, two milk cartons on the floor beside it. Howard Hughes was so bizarre he would not allow himself to be fingerprinted for a security clearance, which meant that he could not participate in decisions involving classified military projects. He could not even enter the research laboratory of his own company. In September 1953 they submitted their resignations, confident that with the reputations they had gained from their accomplishments at Hughes Aircraft, they would have no trouble attracting investment capital and talent to their own enterprise. They envisioned a computer and electronics firm that would focus on the civilian rather than the military market, a version of what the civilian side of IBM (International Business Machines Corporation) became.

Now it was Ramo who was to be surprised. On Monday, September 14, 1953, he and Wooldridge, their resignations submitted to Hughes the previous Friday, flew from Los Angeles to New York and conferred with attorneys from a Wall Street law firm who were handling the formalities of establishing a company to be called the Ramo-Wooldridge Corporation. That Monday evening they took another plane for Cleveland. On Tuesday, they met there with executives of Thompson Products Company, a manufacturer of automotive and aircraft engine parts with an interest in electronics. In return for a share of forthcoming Ramo-Wooldridge stock, Thompson Products agreed to become their financial backer. At noon on Wednesday, they signed the agreement with Thompson Products; in the afternoon they learned from their New York attorneys that they were the owners of a corporation newly registered in Delaware, a practice common for legal and tax reasons; and the same evening they boarded a night flight home to California. (In 1958, Ramo-Wooldridge merged with Thompson Products to become Thompson Ramo Wooldridge, Inc. The corporation's name was then abbreviated in 1965 to TRW, Inc. Because much of this narrative occurred before 1958, the firm will usually be referred to as Ramo-Wooldridge.)

The scene on Thursday in the one-room office on West 92nd Street in Los Angeles, which they had rented as a temporary headquarters (the place was later to be the site of a barbershop), was a kind of barebones bedlam. A secretary sat on a folding chair and typed on a rented typewriter at a folding card table. There were two telephones, ringing constantly with calls from scientists and engineers who wanted to join the enterprise. Suddenly, an Air Force major walked in and said he had a message from Secretary Talbott, who had been unable to get through on either of their phones. They were to report to his office at the Pentagon at noon on Friday to meet with him and his special assistant for research and development, Trevor Gardner. That Thursday evening Ramo and Wooldridge were flying through the night back east again toward the dawn.

Gardner, along with Secretary Talbott, was waiting for them when they arrived. He explained that, with Talbott's assent, he had decided to form the study committee on intercontinental strategic missiles that Ramo had suggested. He wanted Ramo and Wooldridge, and however much of their new organization as they needed, to act as the committee's staff. They were to locate specialists in the various fields where the technological obstacles lay, arrange for them to brief the committee members, keep the record of the meetings, and write the final report with the committee's findings and recommendations. They were also to serve as full members of the committee themselves. Although, at least in the short run, this hardly accorded with their plan to focus their firm on computers and other electronic gear for the civilian market, they felt they had no choice but to accept.

Bennie Schriever offered to provide the funds for Ramo's and Wooldridge's work and the other expenses of the committee out of the $10 million budget he controlled through his Development Planning Office. He had wide discretion in the use of the monies. Gardner accepted and Bennie immediately issued a letter contract to the fledgling firm of Ramo-Wooldridge. He also volunteered to serve as the committee's military representative and Gardner accepted that as well. Ramo and Wooldridge left for Los Angeles at the end of the afternoon pleased that, while the contract was modest, their enterprise was already in the black. They had no sense, as Ramo was later to write, that Trevor Gardner had a great deal more in mind for them, that the committee assignment was just "the tip of the iceberg."

The committee was as blue-ribbon as Ramo had advised Gardner to make it. In addition to von Neumann, its chairman, the eleven members included some of the most respected figures in American science. There was Clark Millikan, son of Robert Millikan and head of the Guggenheim Aeronautical Laboratory at Caltech; Charles Lauritsen, Gardner's patron; Jerome Wiesner, the electrical engineer who had specialized in the advancement of airborne radar at the Rad Lab during the Second World War, and who would one day serve as science adviser to John Kennedy and later as president of the MIT Corporation; and George Kistiakowsky, who was back on the Harvard chemistry faculty. Gardner chose them after consulting with von Neumann and Ramo. When Vince Ford put the call through to Kistiakowsky, the assembler of the explosive wrapper for the Nagasaki bomb was out blowing up the stumps of some trees he had cleared away near his house in a suburb of Boston. No one refused. The mention of von Neumann's name was sufficient to overcome any conflict with teaching or research schedules. Enough years had also elapsed since the end of the Second World War to dissipate the guilt many scientists had felt over their community's role in opening the nuclear Pandora's box. In the interval, a renewed spirit of patriotic urgency had emerged. Stalin's brutality, his disastrous foreign policy, and the Korean War had returned the United States to the climate of fear and danger it had known when Nazi Germany and Imperial Japan had threatened.

Ramo pointed out that they needed a code word for the committee, as he and Gardner and the others would inevitably be discussing its progress on the phone. He proposed to honor its instigator with Tea Garden for Trevor Gardner, but Gardner thought that would make it too easy to guess at his identity and thus the subject of the inquiry, because his interests were known. Ramo came back with Tea Pot. The group was later given the dignified title of Strategic Missiles Evaluation Committee, but Tea Pot Committee was how it was to go down in history.

Ramo and Wooldridge proved as adept as Gardner had suspected they would be at rounding up specialists to brief the committee members on the technological problems that would have to be overcome. Von Neumann thrust himself into the task as an enthusiastic chairman, probing and insightful in his questions at the meetings. The rest of this distinguished group were hardly bashful at asking their own. The Air Force currently had three long-range strategic missile projects. Two were cruise missiles designed to fly within the earth's atmosphere. One, the Snark, was to head for its target at an altitude of ten miles on a turbojet engine. The other, Navaho, was to have a large rocket booster to lift it fifteen miles in altitude, where its twin ramjet engines were to take over. Snark went into production and was deployed in 1959 in small numbers before being withdrawn from service. Navaho was subsequently canceled. The Tea Pot Committee report examined both of these programs, but it focused on the third, the Air Force's only intercontinental ballistic missile project—Atlas.

Atlas was another example of futuristic weaponry that owed its origin to the farsightedness of Hap Arnold. It was one of the twenty-eight pilot projects in guided missiles he had ordered the Army Air Forces to initiate in the spring of 1946 with the $34 million he had earlier skimmed off the bountiful stream of Second World War funds and set aside for this purpose. As a result, in April 1946, the laboratories at Wright Field awarded the leading California aircraft firm that was to build the B-36 for SAC, Convair, a $1.4 million study contract for two missiles capable of 5,750 miles. One, a subsonic cruise type, was dropped, but work went forward on the other, a ballistic missile that was to soar into space. In June 1946, Wright Field added another $493,000 to bring the contract close to $2 million and agreed to let Convair fabricate ten smaller, scaled-down test missiles so that knowledge could be gleaned from actual firings.

A Belgian-born engineer named Karel J. Bossart was put in charge of the project, code-designated MX-774 (the initials stand for "Missile Experimental"). "Charlie" Bossart had graduated from the University of Brussels in 1925 as a mining engineer and then decided that the upper atmosphere interested him more than the subterranean. He won a fellowship to study aeronautical engineering at MIT and stayed on this side of the Atlantic. His specialty was aeronautical structures, which turned out to be a blessing, but he had virtually no experience with missiles, other than a brief acquaintanceship with an early Navy antiaircraft missile called the Lark. This too turned out to be a blessing, as he was sufficiently detached not to begin by using the wonder of the day, the German V-2, as a model on which to improve. Instead, he set himself and his team the task of creating a distinctly different and better missile.

The V-2 was a sturdy missile. It had double walls of sheet metal welded and riveted into place and supported by internal braces. The casing of the warhead was steel plate. The whole weighed 27,376 pounds when fueled with its alcohol and liquid-oxygen rocket propellants. Wernher von Braun and the other originators of the V-2 conceived this design because it did not occur to them to have the warhead separate itself from the rest of the missile at some point in flight. Instead, the V-2 flew up into space and then the entire missile—warhead filled with 1,650 pounds of high explosive, the by now empty fuel tanks, the guidance system, rocket engine, and all—came back down through the earth's atmosphere to its target. The V-2's rocket engine, which generated only 56,000 pounds of thrust, limited the missile to an average range of 180 miles. (A maximum of 220 miles could be attained by lightening the warhead.) Bossart and his team confronted a challenge of far greater magnitude. They had to propel a warhead thirty-two times farther than the V-2's. And it would probably be thousands of pounds heavier. In these years before the thermonuclear breakthrough in the Mike test of 1952, the assumption was that the warhead would be the atomic, or fission, type, which exploded with considerably less force than a hydrogen, or fusion, bomb. To make the missile as potent as possible, the fission bomb constituting the warhead would therefore have to be a big one weighing well beyond 2,000 pounds. The weight of the missile thus became a critical factor. If Bossart followed the V-2 design pattern, he would end up with a missile so huge and so heavy that it was difficult to imagine any rocket engine or cluster of rocket engines powerful enough to lift it off and send the warhead 5,750 miles.

Bossart's first conclusion was that it was a foolish waste of rocket engine power to propel the entire missile all the way to the target. He could gain range relative to thrust if he built a missile with a warhead that broke free of the main body. The moment of separation would occur when the rocket was at the correct angle and speed so that its momentum would, in effect, hurl the warhead through space in a trajectory that would carry the bomb to its target. He then turned to the body of the missile. The lighter the missile body, the potentially heavier the warhead could be, because more of the thrusting power of the rocket engines could be devoted to lifting the bomb rather than spent getting its delivery vehicle into the air. His answer was to create a missile body that was simply a tank for the rocket propellants. The tank was made of thinly rolled aluminum alloy. (Later stainless steel rolled as thin as a wafer would be employed.) In a further saving of weight, there were no internal supports to prevent this balloon tank from collapsing. Instead, the tank was filled with inert nitrogen gas to keep it pressurized to full extension until the time came to pump in the propellants. The bottom of the tank was attached to a bulkhead strong enough to hold the rocket engines.

The fourth and extremely important contribution Bossart and his teammates made to American rocketry was to invent an effective technique to steer the missile in flight. The Germans had been able to steer the V-2 after a fashion by installing movable vanes in the thrust opening at the base of the rocket engine, fabricated from graphite so that they would not melt in the furnace of the rocket's flame. These did not work that well and reduced the engine's power. The Bossart group's approach to the steering problem was to mount the four rocket engines in the cluster that would power their test missile on swivels. The swivels were connected by rods to an autopilot and gyroscope mechanism, which could be programmed to guide the missile on a given course. There was a limitation. The swivels could swing each of the four engines in the cluster in only one preselected direction. Nevertheless, this was a marked improvement over the vanes in the V-2 and pointed the way toward the later mounting of rocket engines on gimbals, which could swing in any direction.

By 1947, the armed services were strapped by peacetime money rationing. That July 1, just as the first test missile was almost finished, Project MX-774 was canceled. The newly independent U.S. Air Force did, however, allow Convair to use the funds in the contract still unspent to construct two additional research rockets and to test-fire all three at the Army's White Sands Proving Ground in New Mexico. They were trim rockets, shimmering in the New Mexico sun, thirty-one feet tall from the fins at the base to the pencil point tip at the top of the nose cone. The four-engine cluster provided 8,000 pounds of thrust. The hope was that the missiles would reach an altitude of about one hundred miles so that Bossart and his fellow engineers could fully test all their ideas. None did, however, because of engine burnout. The third and last MX-774, launched in December 1948, reached an altitude of thirty miles before it too failed and started down to destruction on the desert floor. Nevertheless, enough was learned, from earlier static tests of the swiveling system for the engines as well as from these live firings, to conclude that the innovations would work.

Convair invested its own funds in further research directed by Bossart and on January 23, 1951, after the scare provoked by the war in Korea had replenished its coffers, the Air Force revived the project by giving Convair a new study contract. The specifications were outlandish. They reflected the abiding dilemma of the weight inherent in a fission bomb warhead and a consequent accuracy requirement precise enough to ensure massive destruction of the target by a weapon with far less bang than a hydrogen bomb. The Air Force wanted a missile that would throw an 8,000-pound warhead 5,750 miles and strike its target with an average accuracy (CEP) of just 1,500 feet. Convair responded with equally outlandish specifications for the ballistic missile that would loft this mammoth warhead. Code-named Atlas by Convair, the rocket was to measure 160 feet in height and twelve feet in diameter. By October 1953, new specifications had been worked out that were supposed to be a compromise. They were still outlandish. The warhead weight had been reduced to 3,000 pounds, but the wishing-well accuracy requirement of 1,500 feet lingered. And the missile itself remained a monster. It was to be 110, rather than 160, feet in height, but still twelve feet in diameter, would weigh 440,000 pounds fully loaded with fuel, and needed a cluster of five rocket engines putting out a combined thrust of 656,100 pounds to lift it. This was where the project stood when the Tea Pot Committee, organized in late September and early October 1953, took it up.

Approximately four months later, on February 10, 1954, the committee's inquiry was complete and its final recommendations forwarded to Trevor Gardner with a covering letter from Simon Ramo. Gardner could not have asked for a better outcome if he had written the committee's report himself. What he had essentially wanted was validation by these eminent scientists that an ICBM was technically feasible. He got this and he got a great deal more. The committee said that not only was the unstoppable weapon feasible, the first ready-to-fire ICBM could be produced by 1960–61 and enough missiles to constitute a deterrent threat to the Soviet Union could be fielded by 1962–63. However, this goal was contingent, the committee said, on the Air Force conducting a "radical reorganization" of the project. The measures it recommended for this reorganization were also just the sort that Gardner had in mind. The scientists came to the same conclusion he had that the nation's Second World War–era aircraft industry was incapable of bringing to fruition a project as technologically challenging and complex as this one. They too sought the creation of an organization that would constitute the seed of an American aerospace industry.

To begin with, the committee recommended that, except for some limited additional research, the Air Force halt all further work by Convair. "The most urgent and immediate need," the committee said, was for the Air Force to set up a "new IBMS development group, which . . . should be given directive responsibility for the entire project." (IBMS were the original initials for Intercontinental Ballistic Missile System, later changed to ICBM to avoid confusion with the initials for the International Business Machines Corporation, IBM.) This command group was also to exercise its "overriding control" with a unique independence and freedom from bureaucratic harassment and was to be composed of "an unusually competent group of scientists and engineers." (Gardner thought he already knew how to find this scientific and engineering talent and so did Schriever. Shortly after the submission of the Tea Pot report, Schriever and Gardner put the Ramo-Wooldridge Corporation on hold with another letter contract from Schriever's Development Planning Office, this one for further missile research.) "Within a year" of study and experimentation, the committee predicted, a group of this quality would be "in a position to recommend in full detail a redirected, expanded, and accelerated program" that would meet its beginning of the 1960s deployment schedule for the missiles.

The report also lent assurance to von Neumann's pronouncement to Schriever and Gardner that a hydrogen warhead weighing less than a ton, yet with a megaton's blast, could be readied by the end of the decade. "The warhead weight might be reduced as far as 1500 lbs," the committee said, and its diameter scaled down as well. Given the advent of thermonuclear weaponry, the committee said that the impossible accuracy requirement of 1,500 feet, tied to a lower-yield fission warhead, should be extended to a CEP of "at least two, and probably three, nautical miles [2.3 to 3.4 statute miles]." (For some reason, von Neumann had been unable to persuade his colleagues on the Nuclear Weapons Panel of the Air Force Scientific Advisory Board, which he also headed, to predict a one-megaton bomb of less than a ton in an October report on the panel's deliberations. The closest they got was a three-ton bomb yielding two megatons.)

The Tea Pot Committee said that the final decision on the warhead should be left to the results of the Castle series of thermonuclear tests at Bikini Atoll that von Neumann had spoken of in his meeting the previous May with Schriever and Walkowicz. A 23,500-pound dry thermonuclear device, fueled with lithium deuteride and misnamed Shrimp, was set off on March 1, the first day of the tests. The physicists from the Los Alamos Laboratory discovered they had miscalculated somewhat the forces they were about to liberate. They had predicted that Shrimp would go off with a detonation of five megatons. Instead it ran amuck to fifteen megatons, one for every 1,566 pounds. The 1,500-pound, one-megaton missile warhead indispensable to the building of a practicable ICBM was now a certainty. Gardner, and Schriever always working closely with him through these developments, could count on substantially trimming the dimensions of the 110-foot-high monster ICBM most recently proposed by Convair and reducing its 440,000-pound weight by roughly half.

Johnny von Neumann tipped the issue decisively in their favor by injecting a clincher argument into the committee's report. It was once again based on the fear that drove American military technology, in this case fear that the United States was already caught in a race with the Soviet Union to determine which of the two great powers would be the first to build an ICBM. As Schriever recalled many years later, there was no firm evidence at the time that America confronted such a race; in fact, no hard intelligence at all on Soviet missile work. Nor would there be for another year and a half. Not until mid-1955 would Gardner succeed in setting up a long-range radar installation and electronic eavesdropping posts in Turkey to monitor missile firings at the Soviets' then main testing range at Kapustin Yar in southern Russia, on the dusty, dismal Astrakhan steppe about seventy-five miles east of where Stalingrad (subsequently renamed Volgograd) lies in the bend of the Volga River.

The Air Technical Intelligence Center at Wright-Patterson Air Force Base (Wright Field had been amalgamated with neighboring Patterson Field into a single installation after the Air Force was proclaimed independent in 1947) believed the Soviets were making swift advances in a number of guided missile types, but there was no proof. In late 1951 and early 1952, the center also received reports that the Soviets had built a super–rocket engine producing 265,000 pounds of thrust, twice as powerful as any American counterpart, and precisely the sort of engine most useful for an ICBM. The engine reports proved to be false. Senior Air Force intelligence officers were, in any case, focused mainly on Russian progress in bombers. At the time, no one who mattered in the U.S. intelligence community was concerned about the possibility of a missile gap, which John Kennedy was to make one of the main slogans of his successful run for the presidency in 1960. The National Intelligence Estimate for 1953 put out by the CIA, an annual top secret report that collates and summarizes the collective judgment of all the nation's intelligence agencies on subjects of importance, does not even mention Soviet missile activities.

What intelligence did exist had mostly been gleaned from interviews with the German rocket specialists whom the Russians had released and allowed to go home, the last sizable group returning to Germany in November 1953. Once the Soviets had milked the Germans of their expertise, however, they had been careful to isolate them from more advanced missile designs and experimentation. As early as the fall of 1950, most had been excluded from secret work. The existence and location of Kapustin Yar had first been learned from a Red Army general and rocket expert named Gregory A. Tokady (also known as Tokaty-Tokaev), who had defected to the British in 1948. But an attempt to photograph it in late August 1953 by a British twin-jet Canberra bomber, with a large, oblique-looking camera fitted into its aft fuselage by RAF and U.S. Air Force photoreconnaissance technicians, had nearly ended in disaster. As the plane was approaching Kapustin Yar, it was intercepted and shot up by Russian fighters and was vibrating so badly from damage when it reached the test range that the photographs were useless. Fortunately for the crew, the Canberra was battle-worthy enough to hold itself together while they turned south along the Volga and across the Caspian Sea to land safely in Iran. The RAF did not try any more daytime spy flights deep into Russia.

No one in the United States knew that on March 15, 1953, the better part of two months before Bennie Schriever ventured up to Princeton to see von Neumann, the first Soviet medium-range ballistic missile (MRBM), the R-5, had been test-fired from Kapustin Yar without a hitch and had flown its full 800-mile range. Subsequently named the SS-3 Shyster by NATO intelligence officers, the R-5 was designed to carry a nuclear warhead. Through espionage or through their own high competence, Soviet missileers had gained and were employing some of the same ideas, like separating warheads and swiveling engines to steer their rockets, that Charlie Bossart and his crew had brainstormed in 1946 and 1947 for the MX-107B. The men who led these Russian missile advances, men like Sergei Korolev, the chief rocket designer, and Valentin Glushko, the principal rocket engine maker, were still anonymous figures hidden behind the high wall of a closed society. Their identities were regarded as high secrets, officially to protect them from assassination by American agents, but actually because of the Soviet state's obsessive concern with security. Most important, nothing was known of the decision by the Politburo at the end of 1953 to base the Soviet Union's nuclear strategy on long-range missiles, rather than on an imitation of SAC's bombers, and to commence the building of an ICBM to carry the hydrogen bomb Moscow was to acquire in two years. The United States was indeed caught in a missile race, a strategic competition of profound importance of which it was quite unaware, and in which it was behind.

The Russophobia ingrained in von Neumann by his Hungarian youth led him to perceive the danger, as did the incisive logic of his mind. The committee had been briefed on currently available intelligence on Soviet missile activities. Because the information was so sparse and inconclusive, there was a dispute within the committee about what to believe. In his initial draft of the committee's report, Ramo wrote that "the Russians are probably significantly ahead of us in long-range ballistic missiles." After about half the committee members objected, he came up with fuzzy compromise language to try to bridge the gap. Von Neumann would not hold for this fence straddling. In a statement he insisted on appending to the report, he argued, in effect, that however imprecise the evidence, responsible men should err on the side of caution and conclude that a race was on and that the Russians were leading.

He began by focusing on another reason Ramo had raised for building an ICBM with "unusual urgency." This, von Neumann noted, was "a rapid strengthening of the Soviet defenses against our SAC manned bombers." He was referring to an integrated air defense system of radars, jet interceptors equipped with air-to-air missiles like Ramo and Wooldridge's Falcon, and batteries of surface-to-air missiles. The Soviets were indeed busy putting together such an air defense system, as Schriever had already discovered, though he had been rebuffed by Curtis LeMay when he had sought to persuade LeMay to have SAC's bombers adopt evasive tactics in a low-level approach rather than the high-level one LeMay favored. This reason alone was sufficient for proceeding with an ICBM project, von Neumann said in a prophetic comment, because one could expect the Soviet air defense system to be in place "during the second half of this decade." And so it was when the Russians demonstrated what formidable air defenses they had deployed by shooting down the U-2 in 1960 at a moment the Soviet leadership must have savored, news of it arriving while Nikita Khrushchev and the rest of the Soviet chieftains were assembling atop Lenin's mausoleum in Moscow's Red Square to review the annual May Day Parade of armed might. As for information on Soviet progress toward an ICBM, von Neumann conceded it was true that "available intelligence data are insufficient to make possible a precise estimate." Nevertheless, he argued, "evidence exists of an appreciation of this field" by the Soviets and there was "activity in some important phases of guided missiles" connected with development of an ICBM. "Thus," he concluded ominously, "while the evidence may not justify a positive conclusion that the Russians are ahead of us, a grave concern in this regard is in order." When a scientist of von Neumann's reputation spoke this solemnly, who could fail to pay attention?

35.

GETTING STARTED

Having obtained a scientific validation "which those narrow-gauged bastards in the Pentagon couldn't back away from," as Gardner triumphantly told his assistant, Vince Ford, he now set about convincing the authorities in the Air Force and the Department of Defense to launch a crash program to create an ICBM. On February 16, 1954, six days after Simon Ramo had sent him the final draft of the report, the "wild Welshman," as Ford affectionately referred to his boss, forwarded a copy to Donald Quarles, an engineer and physicist whom Secretary of Defense Wilson had chosen as his assistant secretary for research and development. In his covering memorandum,

Gardner told Quarles that the Air Force could build and be ready to launch the first ICBMs within just about four years, by mid-1958. Although the Tea Pot report had specified 1960–61 as the earliest possible goal for operational missiles, Gardner said it was his belief, confirmed by talks with von Neumann, Kistiakowsky, and Jerome Wiesner of MIT, that "a 'Ph.D. type' operational capability" was attainable by mid-1958. What he meant by this self-coined term was the ability to deploy and threaten the Soviets with the initial few missiles off the production line, using civilian test-launch crews from the rockets' manufacturers to form the firing crews. (There would not be enough missiles available this early to train regular Air Force launch crews.) Gardner brought von Neumann, Kistiakowsky, and Wiesner down to the Pentagon to make the rounds of senior officials and talk up the report. He spoke of the scientists as his "influence matrix." He already had his own superior, Air Force Secretary Harold Talbott, on board.

Talbott instructed him to draw up a detailed plan. The memorandum spelling out the scheme was ready as early as March 11. Stamped top secret, it was addressed to Talbott and to General Nathan Twining, who had taken over as Air Force chief of staff after Hoyt Vandenberg was felled by cancer the previous June. Schriever and Vince Ford pitched in with substantial contributions to help Gardner compose the memorandum, but he was its principal author and the credit must go to him. The document was a masterly example, concise and flexible, of preliminary planning for an enterprise of surpassing scope. After a brief paragraph referencing the Tea Pot report as the practical basis for his plan, Gardner specified two primary objectives. The first was to attain his "Ph.D. type" capability, which he now defined as having "two launching sites and four operational missiles" by June 1958. The second was a full-bore deterrent to a Soviet nuclear attack—the creation of "20 launching sites with a stockpile of 100 missiles" by June 1960. To achieve these goals, Gardner proposed forming what amounted to a separate organization within the Air Research and Development Command. It would be headed by a major general who was ostensibly a vice commander of the ARDC, but whose "sole responsibility" would be leadership of the ICBM program.

The purpose of placing the new organization within the ARDC was to enable it to draw on the larger resources of its parent. The major general was to be "backed up by a brigadier general of unusual competence to work directly with the contractors in supply of top level support and technical supervision." Gardner named the two generals he had in mind. The first was Major General James McCormack, an Air Force intellectual with a specialty in nuclear weaponry who was already vice commander of the ARDC. The brigadier "of unusual competence" who was to back him up was Brigadier General Bernard Schriever. Both "should be prepared to remain with the program until it is satisfactorily completed." Attached to their organization would be a "systems management scientific group of the highest competence" to provide the know-how necessary to overcome technological obstacles like reentry. His preference, he said, was "the Ramo-Wooldridge Corporation." He estimated the total cost over the next five fiscal years at $1.545 billion, an enticingly reasonable figure that would prove to be a gross underestimate.

Wasting no time, Gardner took the paper in hand and strode off to a meeting with Secretary Talbott and General Twining the same day the memorandum was completed to brief them on his plan. Both reacted favorably, but Twining could not render a firm decision until, in courtesy to his staff, he had received a recommendation from the Air Force Council. The council was the highest advisory body to the chief of staff. It was chaired by the vice chief, currently Lieutenant General Thomas White. The other members of the council comprised the next tier down, the deputy chiefs who headed the various staff sections at Air Force headquarters. After briefing Talbott and Twining on March 11, Gardner briefed the Air Force Council too, returning for a second session on the 15th. "We've just introduced the Air Council to the nuclear missile age," he announced to Vince Ford.

Another threat nearly as dire as the Russians in Air Force eyes was also now prompting construction of the ICBM—the Army. Interservice rivalry was particularly acute during the late 1940s and the 1950s. Among other disputes, the Joint Chiefs of Staff had never been able to agree on which service was entitled to build what missiles. Furthermore, the Army had "the Germans," as Wernher von Braun, Nazi Germany's chief scientist on the V-2, and his team of rocketeers were referred to wryly within the Pentagon. They were currently working at the Army Ordnance Department's Redstone Arsenal near Huntsville, Alabama. Twining and White were being warned by the handful of officers who sided with Gardner and Schriever that if the Air Force did not build the ICBM, the Army, claiming superior expertise in von Braun's group, would snatch the mission from it. With this threat in mind, the council accepted Gardner's plan and on March 23 recommended directing the Air Research and Development Command to obtain an operational ICBM as early as possible, "limited only by technical progress." Twining quickly signed off on the recommendation.

In the meantime, the ever impatient Gardner had moved to preempt the decision making. He persuaded Talbott to order Twining on March 19 to speed up immediately the process of putting his plan into effect. Talbott also appointed Gardner his "direct representative in all aspects of the program." But Gardner's blowtorch methods had their limits. He could not build the missile by himself. He had to get the Air Force to do that for him and so he chafed and fretted while the struggle resolved itself within the service bureaucracy. LeMay was vociferously opposed because the ICBM would divert funds from aircraft production, and his allies among the bomber generals on the Air Staff were with him. He predicted that the Atlas would turn out to be an extravagant boondoggle. It would never perform as anticipated.

April went by and nothing much got done by the Air Staff. Gardner, however, did not let the month pass entirely idle. He wanted a means to overcome future naysayers by continuing to provide the program with the prestigious scientific imprimatur he had achieved through the Tea Pot Committee. At his suggestion, von Neumann volunteered to chair a permanent Atlas (later ICBM) Scientific Advisory Committee. Seven of the original Tea Pot members, including Kistiakowsky and Wiesner, agreed to stay on and nine new members were added. One was Norris Bradbury, director of the Los Alamos Laboratory, which would be designing the warhead. Another, apparently chosen for fame rather than his scientific knowledge, was Charles "Lucky Lindy" Lindbergh, the hero of the first transatlantic flight to Paris in 1927. Lindbergh had been declared a pariah by President Roosevelt for his isolationist and anti-Semitic agitation on the eve of the Second World War. Talbott, who was prepared to forget all of this in remembrance of Lindbergh's transatlantic exploit, had resurrected him, awarding him a reserve rank of brigadier general.

In mid-May, General White, with the assent of Twining and Defense Secretary Wilson, who had been brought into the discussion, assigned Project Atlas the Air Force's highest priority and ordered its acceleration "to the maximum extent that technology would allow." In White, Gardner and Schriever had won an advocate for the ICBM within the hierarchy. White was an urbane man, thoughtful and open-minded, and his route to the top was an unusual one for the time. He was an intellectual and linguist who had spent four years studying Chinese in Beijing in the 1920s and served in intelligence posts as air attaché in Stalin's Russia and Mussolini's Italy during the 1930s, rising to become assistant chief of staff for intelligence in 1944. Hap Arnold had then recognized his all-round talents and given him senior command posts in the Pacific during the last year of the war. Schriever had known him slightly after White had been designated deputy commander of the Thirteenth Air Force in September 1944 for the New Guinea campaign and then promoted to chief of the Seventh Air Force in the Marianas not long before the surrender of Japan. Colonel Ray Soper, who subsequently served as an ally for Schriever in a pivotal position on the Air Staff, remembered White lecturing the assembled deputy chiefs in the Air Force Council. Ballistic missiles were here to stay, he told them, and the Air Staff had better realize this fact and get on with it. Nevertheless, the opposition had not yet exhausted stalling tactics. It was not until June 21, 1954, three months after Twining had said go, that Lieutenant General Thomas Power, who had just completed his six years as LeMay's vice commander at SAC and taken charge of the Air Research and Development Command at Baltimore in mid-April, received a directive from Air Force headquarters. It ordered him to get things moving by establishing "a field office on the West Coast with a general officer in command having authority and control over all aspects of the program."

36

"OKAY, BENNIE, IT'S A DEAL"

Napoleon is said to have remarked that a man makes his own
luck. There is also an old Marine Corps maxim that may express the thought more precisely: "Luck occurs when preparation and
opportunity coincide." So it was to be with Bernard Adolph Schriever.
Major General James McCormack, Gardner's choice to lead the
building of the ICBM as vice commander of the ARDC, had a heart
attack that spring and would have to retire soon. The number of stars
an officer wore on his shoulder tabs could matter in an enterprise like
this, because he would have to hold his own against civilian contractors who might try to bully or hoodwink him and against other generals who had competing interests. Gardner had the choice of going
with Schriever, who was to have served as McCormack's backup in
the field but who had only the single star of a brigadier awarded the
year before, or finding another major general qualified to replace
McCormack. He hesitated, scanning the records of potential candidates. Vince Ford urged him to give the command to Schriever alone.
Schriever and Ford were friends and Ford owed Schriever a professional and moral debt for bringing him back on active duty.

Their relationship was not, however, the reason for Ford's recommendation. Ford had seen Schriever manage one high-tech study project
after another. He knew how pragmatic yet tough and independent-
minded Schriever could be and what moral courage he had displayed in
taking on the mighty LeMay. Ford was convinced that Schriever was
precisely the man for the job, that the lack of a second star would prove
no handicap. But Schriever and Gardner had not hit it off at all well during Gardner's initial weeks at the Pentagon in the winter and early spring
of 1953. Gardner had at first mistaken Schriever's controlled manner for
lack of imagination and written him off as another careerist. "He felt
that Bennie ran too long in one spot," was how Ford put it with a smile
of remembrance. Gardner had also offended Schriever by one of those
acts of alcohol-induced boorishness to which Gardner was prone. Ben-

nie and his wife, Dora, had given a welcoming cocktail party for Gardner at their home in the Belle Haven section of Alexandria, Virginia, south of Washington. The guest of honor had arrived pre-stoked for an evening of inebriation with a couple of his double-shot potions of Old Forester and ginger ale already under his belt. After several more, he had picked up a newspaper, sat down, and expressed his scorn for host and hostess and the rest of their Air Force company by burying his face in the paper for most of the party. It had taken Gardner a while to discern the knowledge and character Ford knew so well beneath Schriever's restrained exterior. And it took time for Bennie to understand that despite Gardner's abrasiveness and occasionally outrageous behavior, this was a man who cared about the same things he did and who possessed the daring and influence to accomplish them. Nevertheless, the memory of that inauspicious start to what was to become an extraordinary collaboration and abiding friendship seemed to linger with Gardner as he skimmed the records of possible two-star replacements for McCormack. It did not linger for long.

Early one morning in May 1954, the telephone rang in Schriever's office. His secretary picked it up to find Gardner's secretary on the line. She said that she was calling for Gardner, who wanted to speak to Schriever. His secretary replied that he was out at a meeting. Gardner's secretary said he wished to have lunch with Schriever that day at Restaurant 823, a German rathskeller located in a basement at that number on 15th Street in downtown Washington. Would Schriever please call back when he returned to say if this was possible? In the meantime, Vince Ford arrived at Gardner's office on the fourth floor of the Pentagon. He heard Gardner talking to someone on the phone behind the oak door to the inner office. "What's up?" Ford asked the secretary, with whom he shared the outer room. "He's talking to Mr. Talbott and he's trying to locate General Schriever," she said. Ford had noticed that Gardner somehow "had a way to look and listen in four different directions at once." He apparently overheard Ford. The busy light on the telephone line Gardner was using suddenly went out on the console on his secretary's desk and his door opened. "Hi," he said to Ford. "Come on in a sec." He told the secretary to try again to reach Schriever. Ford took a chair at the conference table opposite Gardner. "The job is Schriever's—if he wants it," Gardner said, raising his eyebrows, his face softening into a half smile in recognition of Ford's successful lobbying. Just then the secretary appeared in the doorway. "General Schriever will be at the River Entrance at noon," she said.

Bennie was waiting for them when they arrived precisely at noon. The River Entrance facing the Potomac was the status entry to the Pentagon. The chiefs of staff and the secretary of defense and other civilian VIPs had their offices on that side of the building. Officials of Gardner's rank were allowed to park their cars in the small lot there. They climbed into Gardner's Cadillac convertible, Schriever in the passenger seat in front and Ford in the back, and, as Ford described Gardner's speed-limits-be-damned driving, "boomed across" the 14th Street Bridge into Washington. Ford observed that the fancy auto "would be a wreck—finished ahead of its time, like one day he would be. He was as hard on his cars as he was on himself." Swinging down I Street, Gardner suddenly turned sharply at a parking lot near the intersection with 15th, bounded over the curb, and stopped just in front of a "Lot Full" sign. The Cadillac straddled the sidewalk at an angle. Schriever smiled and shook his head. Gardner got out and tossed his keys at the outstretched hands of several parking attendants. They were used to him and were grinning. He was a generous tipper.

The "823," as its habitués called it, was a short way down the block on 15th. "It's always gemütlichkeit at Restaurant 823," the ad in the yellow pages of the telephone book promised, and so it was. The rathskeller had an old fashioned imitation Bavarian atmosphere with a violinist and two pianists on back-to-back grands, draft beer in steins, and the heavy, hearty German food that patrons happily consumed in these years before cholesterol frights. Gardner had discovered the "823" during business trips to Washington in earlier years while he was running Hycon Manufacturing. The moment they walked down the steps to the basement level and entered the restaurant, it was clear that the waitresses and barmen knew and liked him. As he passed through he called to them by their names. His favorite waitress, a woman named Helen, pointed them to a booth and then came over with a smile and asked, "Know any new dirty stories, Mr. G?" "No, but I could use one," Gardner responded in kind. She leaned forward, cupped her hand, and whispered into his ear, both laughed, and Gardner, no beer drinker, ordered his double Old Forester and ginger ale.

"Bennie, what'll it be?" he asked Schriever. "I'll have a martini, very dry, Beefeater's with a twist," Schriever said. He quickly and uncustomarily added, "Better make it a double."

Ford had a Scotch and watched Schriever's face. He could see that from the sudden invitation to lunch, Bennie knew something was up, but did not appear to have guessed what it was. He was wrong. Schriever had guessed precisely what was up and was prepared. As soon as his martini arrived, he circled the bell of the glass with his right hand and looked straight at Gardner, who now wasted no time. "Bennie," he asked abruptly, "how'd you like to run the new missile organization we're setting up in California?" The eyes behind the thick rimless glasses fixed on Schriever. The wheel had come full circle. Schriever had needed Gardner to launch the ICBM enterprise and Gardner now needed Schriever to carry it to fulfillment. Bennie desperately wanted the opportunity, but was determined to have it on his terms because he was convinced that was the only way he would succeed. And so he deliberately kept Gardner waiting to raise suspense. He slid his long fingers up and down the stem of the martini glass for several seconds while he glanced down in thought. At last he looked up at Gardner.

"I'll take the job, but only on one condition," he said.

"Like what?" Gardner responded aggressively.

"I'll take the job," Schriever said, speaking slowly so that each word came through distinctly, "provided I can run it—completely run it—without any interference from those nitpicking sons of bitches in the Pentagon."

Gardner seemed pleased by this Gardner-like response. "Okay, Bennie, it's a deal. The job is yours," he said.

Schriever ordered a middle European dish that his German ancestors had appreciated, pig's knuckles, for lunch.

BOOK V

WINNING A PRESIDENT

37

A SCHOOLHOUSE AND A RADICAL
NEW APPROACH

He set up shop in a former Roman Catholic boys school in Inglewood, a suburb of Los Angeles out near the city's international airport. An Air Force lieutenant colonel, the West Coast representative of the Air Research and Development Command, had run across the place while searching for a house that Bennie could rent or buy for his family. Bennie had asked him to look for a house in Santa Monica, farther north, but had specified that it had to be close to a parochial school. While Bennie remained a nominal Lutheran, he had agreed when he married Dora, a devout Roman Catholic, that the children would be raised in her faith. The lieutenant colonel had decided that the logical way to proceed was first to locate a good parochial school, since it was an absolute requirement, and then to find a house. In the course of exploring, he had learned that Saint John's Catholic School for boys had outgrown its space on East Manchester Boulevard in Inglewood and moved elsewhere. A quick reconnaissance had convinced him that the vacated buildings would make excellent start-up quarters for the new missile organization, to be called, for purposes of anonymity, the Western Development Division (WDD).

The Los Angeles Archdiocese had wanted to sell the buildings rather than rent them, but in the spirit of patriotism agreed to let the Air Force have a lease. The address of the main two-story classroom and administration building was 401 East Manchester, just at the intersection with Locust Street. Space was not at such a premium in the Los Angeles area in the mid-1950s and the school was laid out leisurely. Next to the main building back down the boulevard was a modest chapel, then a single-story classroom structure, and beyond it a large, fenced-in parking lot. In July, Schriever and the initial members of his missile band, to be known ever afterward as the Schoolhouse Gang, began moving into the buildings.

Again in the hope of preventing Soviet spies from discovering what was to go on in this decidedly unmilitary-appearing, onetime educational complex, Bennie and everyone else wore civilian clothes, or mufti, the military term for civilian garb. The desire for clandestinity was unrequited. A couple of weeks after the Schoolhouse went into operation, a member of Schriever's crew walked to the bank a short way down Manchester Boulevard to cash his government paycheck. The teller, a tall and quite attractive brunette, smiled at him, compared the signature on his government ID card with that on the check, and then counted out the $20 bills he requested. As he turned to go, she said in a quiet voice, still smiling, "Don't blow us up over there, will you?"

They decided to make the chapel their briefing room. The priests had desanctified the chapel, but had otherwise left the interior intact. When it was put to its first important use, a two-day meeting on July 20–21, 1954, of the enlarged and now permanent ICBM Scientific Advisory Committee (soon to be commonly referred to as the Von Neumann Committee), there had been no time for remodeling. Bennie had not yet even officially taken charge of the fledgling Western Development Division, something he would not do for nearly another two weeks, until August 2, when he issued General Orders No. 1, formally assuming command.

And so on this opening morning of the meeting he stood on the step before the altar rail, where the students had knelt to receive the Communion wafer, and updated his prestigious audience on what had transpired since the formation of the new committee by Gardner and its initial meeting in Washington in April. Johnny von Neumann, Kistiakowsky, Wiesner, Norris Bradbury, and Charles Lindbergh sat on the pews in front of him with the other members new and old. Running down the walls on both sides of the chapel were windows of stained glass with portraits of saints and depictions of religious scenes. These were subsequently covered with plasterboard when the pews were ripped out and replaced by seats. The altar was also removed and a small briefing stage erected in its place. Technically, the plasterboard was nailed over the windows for security reasons, but some of Bennie's subordinates also found themselves uncomfortable devising a weapon of such terrible proportions amidst the stained-glass reminders that this had once been a holy place.

Obstinately attempting to hang on to the entire project, a Convair team sent up from San Diego to brief the committee now proposed that the firm continue development of its five-rocket-engine, 440,000-pound behemoth missile while it studied the feasibility of a 250,000-pound ICBM. Von Neumann and the other members of the new committee rejected this, as had the original Tea Pot group, and focused where the Tea Pot report had led—on the precise nature of the managerial and technical organization required to put ICBMs on launching pads. By this time it was assumed, as Gardner had schemed to arrange, that the new Ramo-Wooldridge firm would provide the engineering and scientific expertise required. The question now was how they would relate to Schriever's Air Force organization.

Donald Quarles, the assistant secretary of defense for research and development, was attending the meeting as an observer to contribute whatever he could. An electrical engineer and physicist, Quarles had run the Sandia Laboratory in Albuquerque, New Mexico, before entering the Pentagon. The laboratory devised the techniques required to transform nuclear devices produced by Los Alamos, and later by Livermore, the second nuclear weapons laboratory established at Livermore, California, in 1952, into useful weapons for the Air Force. In the lingo of the service, it weaponized the devices. Quarles suggested that instead of setting up the Ramo-Wooldridge team as a separate staff of advisers, it would be more effective to integrate them with Schriever's Western Development Division by placing them in a "line position" right under it. General Power, who was also attending, ordered Bennie to study the matter and come up with a recommendation. As WDD was a field office of Power's Air Research and Development Command, Power was Bennie's immediate superior in the Air Force chain. Schriever had a report ready by the latter half of August. He proposed that the Air Force act as its own prime contractor through his WDD organization and employ the Ramo-Wooldridge firm as a "deputy" responsible for systems engineering and technical direction of the project. (In practice, although the Air Force was to retain final authority, the men of the two groups were to work side by side and Schriever and Ramo to form a close partnership.)

The radical approach that the Tea Pot Committee had first propounded and Schriever was now advocating would amount to a revolution in the Air Force's relationship with the aviation industry. The prime contractor system, under which one firm was given responsibility for the entire development, testing, and production of a new aircraft, including any elements it might decide to subcontract out to other companies—engines, for example, were always subcontracted—was time-honored and immensely profitable. And the method had succeeded reasonably well in the evolution of aircraft. It was not that great a bound in technology from the Air Force's first swept-back-wing, jet-powered bomber, the Boeing B-47 Stratojet, to Boeing's next and far more formidable swept-back-wing, eight-jet-engine offspring—the B-52 Stratofortress. Guided missiles were quite another matter due to the much more intractable technological challenges. The Tea Pot Committee had seen this in the multitude of modifications, delays, and failures in the histories of the other two strategic missiles it had examined, Snark and Navaho. Schriever planned to give Convair a contract only to manufacture the fuel tank and other sections of the body of the Atlas, what was referred to as the airframe. The contract would also include assembling the entire missile once all the components were ready and participation in the subsequent test firings.

Simon Ramo would, in effect, become chief engineer and chief scientist of the enterprise. Except for the hydrogen bomb itself, which Los Alamos would build and test, the Ramo-Wooldridge task force under him would oversee the design of virtually everything else, such as the guidance and control mechanism, and the warhead, or reentry vehicle as it was called, which would house the bomb. The actual manufacture of these subsystems would then be done by organizations the Ramo-Wooldridge and WDD teams would have worked with in the design and prototype phases. These would often be subsidiaries of larger firms, but they would have already established a reputation in a specialized field and would be selected for their expertise. Convair was not among the candidates. (To avoid conflict of interest, Ramo-Wooldridge would be forbidden under its contract with the Air Force to manufacture any ICBM components. Dean Wooldridge was in the process of exiting the scene in order to seek and manage separately other non-ICBM business for the firm.) If Schriever's newfangled approach prevailed, Convair stood to lose a great deal of money, hundreds of millions and possibly even billions of dollars in business, on a program with the potential of the ICBM. Bennie had no alternative if he was to succeed, but he had been warned that the course he was taking would ensnare him in a nasty power struggle right at the outset of his venture.

38.

THE GURU OF ROCKETS

In the meantime, Schriever had been recruiting his own missile-building task force. Because Atlas had been given the Air Force's highest priority, he could pick whomever he wished and their commands had to release them. To give Bennie's team continuity, Gardner had also arranged with White and Twining that once an officer was selected, unless Bennie subsequently relinquished or fired him, he was assigned to WDD for the duration.

No missile could fly without rocket engines. It was thus understandable that the first name on a list Bennie had been compiling was that of Lieutenant Colonel Edward Hall, the expert on rocket propulsion at the laboratories of the Air Development Center at Wright-Patterson. Hall had been the man who had briefed the Tea Pot Committee on rocket engines. Schriever and Ed Hall could not savor the irony involved when Schriever summoned Hall to a meeting at his office in the Pentagon that July of 1954, explained the project to him, and invited him to become WDD's chief of propulsion. At the time, neither knew that Ed Hall's younger brother, Ted, had been, along with Klaus Fuchs, one of the Soviet Union's two invaluable physicist spies at Los Alamos.

Edward Nathaniel Hall was, in fact, considerably more than an expert on rocket engines. He was the U.S. Air Force's guru on rocketry. He was also well known to devotees of the subject outside the Air

Force. In the following year, 1955, his achievement in improving liquid rocket fuel was to earn him the American Rocket Society's Robert H. Goddard Memorial Award, commemorating the American rocket pioneer who had first attempted to interest the Army in the military utility of rockets near the close of the First World War in 1918. While Ed Hall did not share Ted's politics, he did share the brilliance of mind and the largeness of ego of the brother who was his junior by eleven years. He also had a trait distinctly his own that would serve him ill—a flash-pan temper.

His road to recognition as a rocketeer had not been an easy one. Born Edward Nathaniel Holtzberg in New York City on August 4, 1914, three days after the First World War broke out, his sense of security had not been improved by the socioeconomic roller coaster on which his father, Barney Holtzberg, had taken the family in the rise and crash of his fur business. That sterling quality in Jewish culture, the sense by both parents and child of the value of an education, had been Ed Hall's salvation. He won his way into Townsend Harris, one of New York's elite high schools, where entrance was by competitive examination, and went on to the City College of New York. Tuition at CCNY was free in the 1930s. In 1935, he acquired a bachelor's degree in chemical engineering and then, to improve his chances in the job-scarce environment of the Depression, took a professional degree, the equivalent of a Ph.D. without the thesis, in the subject the following year.

But he couldn't find a steady job as an engineer. Hall knew that the difficulty was not simply the lack of opportunity posed by the Depression. When an opportunity did come along, someone else less able was hired and he was turned down because of the anti-Semitism that was also so prevalent at the time. His more advanced degree in chemical engineering didn't help, nor did a disguise he sought to adopt by filing court papers to change Holtzberg to Hall. A tall, husky man with an aquiline nose, deep-set brown eyes, a high forehead, and dark curly hair, Ed Hall looked much too East European to pass for an Anglo-Saxon. He had to be satisfied bouncing about earning his living as an auto mechanic, a steamfitter, a plumber, an electrician, a radio repairman, whatever he could scrounge. And so he finally gave up on the civilian world. In September 1939, as Hitler's armies invaded Poland and the Second World War began, Hall joined the U.S. Army Air Corps as an enlisted man. The Air Corps was not yet awarding commissions to engineers. A man had to become a pilot first and then go into engineering, but Hall reasoned that this would change with the world situation becoming more perilous and the Air Corps thus bound to grow. He opted for the mechanics school at Chanute Field south of Chicago. Familiarizing himself with the service's flying machines seemed the obvious way to get started.

At his first posts—March Field, California, where, not that many years before, Bennie Schriever had served his initial stint as a novice pilot under Hap Arnold, and then at a new airfield in Alaska, Elmendorf, near Anchorage—Hall's skill at repairing aircraft and correcting the mistakes of the ordinary mechanics gained him quick promotion to sergeant. He succeeded so well at Elmendorf that he became a captive there. In 1941, with war approaching and the Air Corps on the edge of a breakneck expansion into the Army Air Forces, Arnold realized that he would require a lot of competent engineer officers to keep his planes in the air. An announcement went out that enlisted men with the requisite qualifications could apply for commissions. Hall immediately did. The airfield commander had no intention of losing him. He threw Hall's application for a commission into his wastebasket. A fellow sergeant who ran the Elmendorf radio shack rescued him, surreptitiously transmitting the application to Sacramento, where it was routinely forwarded to Washington.

Hall entered the war as a freshly commissioned second lieutenant right after Pearl Harbor. It was a measure of his capacity to get himself into jams and to irritate people that despite membership in a burgeoning organization where promotions came faster than paymasters could keep track of them, and his heroic contributions as an aircraft repair and engineering fireman for the air forces in England, he managed to finish the war in 1945 just four grades up. (And passage from second to first lieutenant is, barring serious misconduct, virtually automatic, not really counting as a promotion.) He did not make major until June 1, 1945, after Germany had surrendered and Japan was two and a half months from collapse.

At the beginning of 1943, when Hall was given his first emergency assignment, he was up one grade to first lieutenant. His task was to organize and operate a mobile repair service for B-17s that had crash-landed at airfields, in meadows, and in other open spaces all over southern England and the Midlands after being shot up on bombing raids into the Nazi-occupied continent. Squadron mechanics were qualified for routine maintenance; major fixes were beyond most of them. The original scheme for handling seriously damaged bombers had been to dismantle them and send them to a central depot for repair, but this had proven impractical. The brigadier general in charge of the maintenance and repair division of the Eighth Air Force's service command came up with the mobile repair idea as a way to attack the problem. With losses to the Luftwaffe's fighters and German flak rising and promised replacement bombers being diverted to the campaign in North Africa, the need to get these wounded Boeing warriors fit for the air once more was literally desperate. Hall was chosen for the job because of the reputation for energy and effectiveness he had established while engineer officer for a transport group that supplied the way station airfields built at Goose Bay, Labrador, and on Greenland and Iceland to ferry aircraft to Britain.

The brigadier gave Hall a letter authorizing him to take charge of any battle-damaged aircraft anywhere in the British Isles and carte blanche to organize his repair teams. He interviewed other junior engineer officers until he found six he thought reasonably competent. They in turn each rounded up four or five enlisted mechanics for their teams. Even though he was repairing aircraft manufactured by a competitor, civilian engineers from the Lockheed company stationed over in Northern Ireland were kind enough to ship him half a dozen trucks. Hall outfitted them as on-the-road machine shops with drills, riveting equipment, and other tools and spare parts. The Lockheed group also sent him some of their expert civilian aircraft mechanics to train his men and tackle the really complicated jobs. He finagled a Ford station wagon that had once belonged to the British to transport himself around. It had the RAF's roundel insignia on one side and the American star on the other, allowing Hall to gas up at any fuel point run by either service. He also requisitioned enough radio equipment to set up a network that kept him in touch with all of his teams and enabled him to receive warnings of where downed aircraft were located. As soon as he got a report, Hall would whisk to the scene in the station wagon, write up a repair plan for the aircraft, and dispatch a team. He and his men were soon reviving "splashed down" bombers, the English euphemism for a crash landing, hither and yon.

Then one day he was notified of a B-17 down in bad condition at an airfield under LeMay's command. He arrived to discover a mechanic from an English civilian repair crew on a ladder making what the Englishman seemed to think was an acceptable fix to a spar, the main support for the span of a wing. The spar had been shot nearly in two at a point where it bore a particularly heavy load. Hall looked at the repair the English mechanic was attempting and asked where his foreman was. Hall found the foreman and asked him who had designed this fix. "Oh, it was done by Boeing," the foreman replied. Hall could see that this had to be false. Under the proposed repair the wing would have snapped in two under the stress of flight. He told the English foreman to cease work. "Go to wherever you live or whoever runs you, but no more work on this airplane," Hall said. "Oh, I can't do that. We are under contract," the foreman said. "Contract, bontract! Get out of here," Hall shouted. He gestured at the .45 caliber semiautomatic service pistol he carried in a holster on his hip. "Look, I have a gun here," he said. "I am going to take it out, point it at you, and count to five," and proceeded to do just that. The Englishman, as Hall told the story, "took off like a scared cat," his mechanics with him.

Not long afterward, while Hall was inspecting the B-17 for more battle damage, he was called to the telephone. In the hurly-burly of the buildup, the usual had occurred—incompetents had snookered their way into rank and place. The caller was a colonel at the central depot. Hall had run across him in earlier years and knew that he had sparse engineer training. The man had somehow convinced the authorities otherwise, been given a colonel's eagles, and put in charge of the depot's engineering section. He had then apparently hired some Englishman with a crew of self-styled aviation mechanics to repair bombers. The colonel said he understood Hall had dismissed the crew from a job and ordered Hall to put them back on it right away. Hall refused and said the colonel's hired mechanics had no idea what they were about. "What they were doing would have guaranteed that the airplane would have crashed," Hall said. The colonel asked by whose authority Hall was acting. Hall read him the letter of blanket authorization from the brigadier general commanding the maintenance and repair division. "It doesn't make any difference," the colonel said. He once again ordered Hall to put his English crew back on the job. Instead of simply hanging up, informing the brigadier of what was going on, and taking satisfaction as the brigadier brought his heel down on the colonel, Hall did something that he subsequently reflected "wasn't very wise." He let loose the spring of his temper. "You son of a bitch!" he yelled into the phone. "I'm not about to put anybody back and kill people and ruin airplanes." And then he hung up.

A couple of weeks later he received a notice to report for a court-martial hearing at Eighth Air Force headquarters at Bushy Park, up the Thames from London, near Hampton Court Palace, where Henry VIII had held sway. When he arrived at the appointed office, a major sitting behind a desk read him a charge sheet the colonel had sworn out against Hall. To Hall's further anger and insult, the colonel did not accuse him of insubordination or conduct unbecoming an officer and a gentleman. Rather, he charged Hall with gross technical incompetence in the performance of his duties as an engineer. The major handed Hall a copy and instructed him to return in two days with a response. Hall went immediately to the Boeing office in London. He knew the engineers there because he had been consulting regularly with them on how best to repair the B-17s. He told them what had happened, showed them the charge sheet, and asked if they would write a letter affirming his competence. They were happy to oblige. The letter said that not only was Hall an extremely accomplished engineer, his mobile group was far better at repairing B-17s than any other organization in the United Kingdom and its disbandment would be a disaster.

The next morning, Hall presented the letter to the major. He could see the man's face color with anger as he read it. He asked Hall if there were any other copies and, if so, to hand them to him. Hall replied that that was impossible because he had mailed the copies to friends in the United States, with instructions to give the letter to their local newspapers if they did not hear from Hall within two weeks. The major ordered Hall to take a seat and strode off, letter in hand. About fifteen minutes later, a general appeared. Hall subsequently decided that the bestarred figure was probably Ira Eaker. It may well have been, as Eaker was then commanding the Eighth while Carl Spaatz was off in the North African theater as Eisenhower's deputy for air. The general grinned at Hall as he rose from the chair where he had been sitting, shook his hand, slapped him on the back, and said, "Ed, get out of here and keep them flying," which was what Hall did. He kept his teams at it until, as more trained engineering personnel arrived from the United

States and more and better repair depots were established, they worked themselves out of a job and were disbanded.

(Hall's quickness to reach for his pistol was not limited to professional crises. Shortly after his arrival in England in late 1942, while he was briefly stationed at Oxford, Hall met a young Englishwoman named Edith Shawcross. She was a niece of a prominent English jurist, Hartley Shawcross, later awarded a life peerage as Baron Shawcross of Friston for his accomplishments as senior British prosecutor at the war crimes trial of the leading Nazis at Nuremberg in 1945–46. An independent woman with a will that was strong, if not quite as strong as Hall's, Edith was an honors graduate in botany from St. Hilda's, one of the women's colleges at the university. She had joined the Civil Defence Corps and in 1942 was driving an ambulance in Oxford. While she was standing in line to buy a drink at a hotel bar there one evening, an American officer walked up and asked if she would step aside so that he could pass through. Thinking he was trying to jump the line, she said, "No, I was here first." Hall pointed to a bartender farther down the bar who had gone unnoticed. There was no line in front of him. "That's all right, baby," Hall said, "I'll buy you a drink." He did and they were married nine months later.

In early 1944, while Hall was momentarily stationed near Bournemouth on the south coast, he received a phone call that Edith was giving birth to their first child and having an extremely troublesome time. He tore up the roads to Oxford in the Ford station wagon he had not yet surrendered. At the hospital there, Edith's obstetrician told him that she had been in labor for about fifty hours, that the heart of the child still within her was weakening, and that she was also failing rapidly. The obstetrician seemed confused, as if he had lost his nerve, and, in any case, Hall decided, time was critical if either mother or child or both were to survive. He drew his .45, pressed the muzzle into the doctor's chest, and ordered him to deliver the baby immediately. This the obstetrician, who seemed relieved at being forced to take action, did in a procedure using a forceps. Edith rallied. As an infant, the child was weak from the almost certain deprivation of oxygen he had suffered during his prolonged birth, but he lived. The Halls named him David and he went on to gain a Ph.D. in physics from Caltech.)

Hall's achievement with his mobile repair teams should have

brought him immediate promotion to captain. In March 1943, the brigadier in charge of maintenance and repair presented him with a letter of commendation praising his "intelligence, initiative and industry" and his "quick grasp of the requirements of field maintenance" for the success of the project. The letter was endorsed by the major general heading the entire Service Command and a copy was filed in Hall's records. Furthermore, he received a Legion of Merit for his next major accomplishment between May and August 1943, while still a first lieutenant: keeping the bombers flying during that critical year when the Eighth Air Force was so beleaguered. The citation praised the "long hours and untiring efforts" he had devoted "to the invention and development of special tools" that made it possible to repair the fuselages of damaged bombers much more rapidly. The award of such a high decoration to a man at the bottom of the officer ranks was a rarity and spoke for the importance of Hall's contribution. But he had to wait until mid-October 1943 for his captaincy.

The problem was that for every equal or superior whose admiration Hall aroused, he raised the hackles of others. He was the classic smart aleck with a chip on his shoulder, the wise guy who could not resist preening his cleverness, or needlessly pushing too far a confrontation with a more senior officer, as he had with the incompetent colonel over the repair of the B-17. He could be vindictive too. Hall did not turn in the Ford station wagon he had managed to acquire for the mobile repair team job, as he should have done. Instead, he held on to it as a personal vehicle. A motor pool officer demanded that Hall hand it over for general service use. Hall refused. He finally turned in the station wagon, but only after pouring enough of the solvent carbon tetrachloride into the gas tank to ruin the engine.

After another contribution to the Allied war effort in organizing the last-minute assembly of scores of gliders to ferry airborne troops behind German lines in Normandy on D-Day, Hall found the inspiration for his life's work amidst the ruins of the Third Reich. Hap Arnold would have approved, as he had a distant if unknowing hand in Hall finding his métier. In addition to recruiting Theodore von Kármán for the major expedition to glean the best of German technology, which resulted in *Toward New Horizons*, Arnold had also ordered the formation in England of a small air technical intelligence team called the Directorate of Technical Services. The team was a joint venture with the

RAF, about a dozen American engineers and a handful of British. Operating first in England and France, the team then followed the Allied armies into Germany, garnering whatever it might discover as they advanced. Hall was assigned to it and charged with gathering intelligence on all sources of aerial propulsion, from ordinary reciprocating engines to jets, ramjets, and rocket engines. While still in London, where the team was put together, Hall had collected pieces of the V-1 ramjet cruise missiles, dubbed buzz bombs by the Londoners, and the V-2 ballistic missiles the Nazis were launching against the British capital, to see what clues these shards might provide. He had, in fact, nearly been killed by a V-2. One evening, just as he was closing the blackout curtain in the room where he was sleeping, a five-story structure across the street was suddenly lifted into the air before disintegrating and crashing into rubble. The V-2 apparently penetrated right down through the building and then the 1,650 pounds of high explosive in the warhead detonated, lofting it upward.

In his unpublished autobiography and in an interview, Hall claimed he was sent on a secret mission to the Satan's lair where the V-1s and V-2s were being manufactured. It was a bombproof factory tunneled into a mountainside in a lonely valley of the Hartz Mountains, near Nordhausen in north-central Germany, by slave laborers. Thousands died blasting and burrowing out the chambers and thousands more were then worked to death running the factory around the clock. The place bore the banal name of Mittelwerk (Central Factory). His orders, which he said he successfully carried out, were to arrange for U.S. Army trucks to remove several samples of both V-1s and V-2s for shipment back to the United States and to sabotage the plant by destroying the master drawings and data settings for the machines. The purpose of the sabotage was to prevent the Soviets, in whose preagreed occupation zone the Mittelwerk would lie, from using the plant to manufacture any of the rockets or the jet engines that were also being produced there.

Hall did get to Germany and was later awarded a Bronze Star for his intelligence work there, but whether he ever reached the V-2 factory is unclear, as details of his account are contradicted by other known historical facts. Ed Hall's ego was sufficiently large to make him prone to elaborating the facts in his favor or even wish-thinking something out of whole cloth. As the Air Force's foremost rocketeer, which he was subsequently to become, he certainly would have wanted others to believe that he had gone to the home of the V-2. What is clear is that its creation inspired him to devote his life to rocketry.

Back in the United States in the late summer of 1946, with Edith and their first and hard-born child, David, Hall was ordered to the Air Development Center at Wright. He hoped he was being sent there with an assignment to design and develop rocket engines. To his chagrin, he was instead designated chief propulsion officer in the Technical Intelligence Department (later renamed the Air Technical Intelligence Center), tasked, as he had been in London, with gathering information on all new means of aerial propulsion being devised at home and abroad. While a handful of far-seeing air warriors like Hap Arnold had been impressed by the potential the V-2 heralded, most American airmen had regarded it as an expensive curiosity. Given its limited range of 180 to 220 miles and lack of accuracy, it might unnerve the citizens of London with its random death dealing, but it could accomplish no military purpose. To alleviate his frustration with intelligence work, Hall wrote a series of papers arguing that this dismissal was premature and a serious error. Rocket-propelled missiles possessed, he pointed out, the possibility of infinite range. When rocket engines were built with enough power to hurl a warhead into space with extreme velocity, as they someday would be, and guidance systems of high accuracy were also devised, targets anywhere on earth could be destroyed.

In the fall of 1947, Hall thought he had escaped the intelligence types. He and the family moved out to Pasadena after the newly independent U.S. Air Force approved his request for a year's grant to obtain a master's degree in aeronautical engineering at Caltech, concentrating on jet propulsion systems, as there were no courses on rocket engines available at the time. Hall was not only to be the Air Force's leading rocket specialist, he was also to be a self-taught one. He would have stayed another two years at Caltech to gain a Ph.D., but Air Technical Intelligence needs stymied him once more. He was dispatched to England to determine whether jet engines a British firm had been allowed to sell the Soviets for their new MiG-15 fighters could be altered for high-altitude performance. Unfortunately, Hall discovered, they could be. On May 22, 1950, just a month and three days before the outbreak of the Korean War, he was at last given the opportunity to demonstrate what he was really capable of achieving. He was transferred back to the Air Development Center and assigned to the Power Plant Laboratory as assistant chief of the nonrotating engine branch, i.e., ramjets and rockets.

While all aspects of rocketry fascinated Hall, the straight-to-the-point logic of his mind led him to focus on first things first—the engine. The most powerful created up to that time was the V-2 engine, with its 56,000 pounds of thrust. North American Aviation in Los Angeles was one of the few aircraft firms with the foresight to get into the rocket business after the Second World War, soon establishing a separate rocket division, appropriately called Rocketdyne, at Canoga Park north of Burbank. With funding from the Air Development Center, it built several copies of the V-2's power plant. About half blew up on test firing. It was decided that the German engine was seriously defective and, in any case, greatly underpowered for Air Force purposes. Hall arranged funding for a new and bigger engine fabricated to his design ideas and those the North American engineers contributed.

Rocket engines in this early period were notoriously fickle devices, even when put together with care. What occurs within a rocket engine, as soon as the ignition button is pushed, is a controlled explosion, and "controlled" is a hoped-for attribute. Because the chain reaction is so volatile, a minor malfunction or small design flaw in the engine is enough to send the explosion out of control with an enormous flash and bang that blasts engine and rocket into bits. To improve reliability, Hall therefore pestered Rocketdyne to adopt strict quality control of components and uniform procedures when testing the engines by bolting and clamping them to concrete stands for static firings. The result of his initiative was an engine of 75,000 pounds thrust, an improvement but neither reliable nor potent enough for what Hall had in mind. Hall regarded the engine as a way station, but it did not go to waste. Wernher von Braun showed up at Hall's laboratory one day and asked if he could have the few test engines North American had produced for a new missile he and his team were putting together at the Army's Redstone Arsenal near Huntsville, Alabama. Hall consented readily and had von Braun sign the appropriate transfer form. Hall's beginning venture in rocket enginery thus ended up as the power plant for Redstone, a 200-mile-range tactical missile, an upgraded V-2, which von Braun launched for the Army in 1953.

Hall meanwhile pressed on with the single-mindedness and ruth-

less determination so characteristic of the man. When his goals were
endangered, scruples that might have deterred others aroused no hesitation in Hall. Rather, he displayed at such moments the ultimate and
imaginative form of gall known as chutzpah in Yiddish. After the
budget for his rocket engine program was initially "decimated" in mid-
1950 by the more immediate needs of the Korean War, he wrote in his
unpublished autobiography, he decided to fake an intelligence report
of a monster Soviet rocket engine to frighten the Air Force into leaving
his money alone. He approached a friend who was an officer in Technical Intelligence, explained how desperate his plight was, and asked
the friend to help him pull off the con. He would provide a design, he
said, drawn in what was known of Russian style, of an engine rated at
one hundred metric tons (220,500 pounds) of thrust. The friend was
then to slip it into intelligence channels as a genuine report picked up
in the Soviet Union. The man refused to be part of such a hoax. Sub-
mitting fraudulent reports is a serious offense under military law.

If caught, Hall and his friend could both be court-martialed and
dismissed from the service. Hall pestered the friend for weeks, pleading
that the trick was the only way to save his endeavors. The man finally
relented and a drawing of Hall's bogus Soviet whopper engine was
duly submitted. The report caused a sensation at the Air Development
Center. A special briefing was laid on and ranking officers invited. Hall
cannily stayed away. As he recounted in his autobiography, early that
evening, right after the briefing, the chief of the Power Plant Laboratory, where Hall worked, a senior colonel, "entered my office and cas-
tigated me for failing to press hard enough to retain my budget for
large rocket development. The program was saved!"

Faking the report of the Soviet engine was not the only confidence
game Hall played. The budget funds he drew on for his rocket engine
advancement program were designated for a project he was supposed
to further, the development of the Navaho intercontinental cruise missile. It was one of the three strategic missiles the Tea Pot Committee
was to examine. A big multiengine rocket booster putting out more
than 400,000 pounds of thrust, and weighing 300,000 pounds, was
planned to lift the Navaho to the point fifteen miles in the air where the
twin ramjet engines were supposed to kick in and propel the missile
6,330 miles to its target. Hall had no faith in the Navaho. He regarded
ramjet engines as more difficult to fabricate and less reliable than rock-

ets. He was also convinced that the Navaho's inertial guidance system would not prove sufficiently accurate to carry the missile to its target over the relatively long flight time. His game was to use the requirement for adequate engines for the Navaho booster as a cover to acquire a rocket engine for an intercontinental ballistic missile. He believed that an ICBM's much shorter flight time over the same distance, about half an hour, would allow for correspondingly more accurate guidance, particularly given the advances then occurring in guidance technology. (And Hall was proven correct where Navaho was concerned. Despite the later availability, thanks to Hall, of rocket engines of sufficient power, the Air Force could never get the contraption to fly properly and it was finally canceled in 1957.)

At the Air Development Center, Hall was in a milieu where he could shine and where his talents were appreciated. His colleagues were other engineers caught up like himself in the exploration of uncharted technology that could enhance the reach and power of the U.S. Air Force. His difficult personality made enemies, of course, as it always did. But there were others who saw beyond his flaws to the imaginative and insightful cast of his mind and admired and befriended him. One was Major Sidney Greene, a fellow New Yorker, although Brooklyn-born, and like Hall a graduate of the Townsend Harris competitive-entrance high school and the City College of New York. Greene had been forced to take his B.S. at CCNY in premedical studies, because his mother had been intent on him becoming a doctor. But after spending the Second World War in the Army Air Forces, mostly as a communications officer, he had set out on his own road. He discovered that he liked military life, applied for and received a Regular commission, and obtained a B.S. in electrical engineering from the Air Force Institute of Technology (a larger and more advanced postwar version of the Engineering School Schriever had attended at Wright in 1940). He followed it up with a master's in the subject through university extension courses. By 1952, Greene was in charge of the New Developments Office at the Air Development Center. He had a myriad of study projects on his agenda, from a reconnaissance satellite, for which the Air Force as yet had no rocket to launch it into space, to a radar decoy for the B-52 named Green Quail. Everything was on paper; no prototypes had been produced.

One of the studies in Greene's cupboard was Atlas, still in its original monster missile incarnation to carry a huge fission warhead, which the Air Force had revived the previous year by granting a new study contract to Convair. The funds for the Convair study were channeled through Greene's office. Hall learned this and approached Greene with a proposition. "Look, let's not throw away more money on paper. What we need is a rocket engine. Why don't we take $2 million, you transfer it over to me, and we will modify the Navaho booster." Hall explained that he would use the $2 million to get North American's Rocketdyne to build a prototype with enough thrust to give them a real ballistic missile engine. Greene knew Hall well by this time. He was subsequently to work under Hall at Schriever's Western Development Division. He understood all of Hall's kinks. He also regarded Hall, he was to remark years later, as "one of our geniuses." The proposition made eminent sense to him. "Great idea," Greene said, "I'll give you the money." After Greene's immediate superior, a colonel, also assented, he let Hall have the funds. The action was legal, but they were supposed to clear a transfer involving this much money with the commander of the center, Major General Albert Boyd, whom Greene remembered as a tough-minded, grim-looking man who had been a famous test pilot in his younger years. Convair apparently complained over the shortfall of $2 million in revenue it had expected to receive and Secretary Talbott wrote to Boyd demanding an explanation. Greene and his boss were summoned to the general's office. Greene thought Boyd "was going to rip me apart." He and his superior explained why they had made the transfer. The general focused his gaze on the apprehensive Greene. "If I were in your place, I would have done the same thing," Boyd said to Greene's surprise. "Get out. I'll take care of it."

Combining their talents, Hall and the Rocketdyne engineers produced a prototype engine that generated an unprecedented 120,000 pounds of thrust. Hall then had an insight that further enhanced the engine's force. It came to him from his research into liquid rocket fuels. The traditional liquid rocket fuel, the one used in the V-2 engine and in the two more powerful ones for which Hall had since been responsible, was alcohol and liquid oxygen. The two substances were mixed as they flowed into the combustion chamber of the engine, the liquid oxygen serving as a burning agent to draw maximum energy from the alcohol while it was being consumed at an extremely high temperature. Hall soon realized from his research that a hydrocarbon fuel would release considerably more energy than alcohol when burned. He experimented until he hit on what seemed to be the optimal substance. It was a re-fined petroleum much like the Pearl Oil kerosene that John D. Rocke-feller had grown wealthy selling to millions of Chinese. (In one of the early twentieth century's more memorable marketing ploys, Rocke-feller had thoughtfully provided, free of charge, the kerosene lamps in which to burn it.) Hall gave an appropriately terse military designation to his variation, RP-1, for Rocket Propellant-1. Adjustments had to be made to the engine to burn the hydrocarbon fuel, but when the RP-1 was substituted for the alcohol, Hall got an increase in thrust from 120,000 to 135,000 pounds, a remarkable accomplishment for the time. Hall's initiative also led North American to construct bigger con-crete stands, called "hard stands," for static testing of large rocket en-gines at Santa Susana in Southern California.

As Ed Hall drove out to Inglewood from Ohio that August of 1954 with Edith and David and their second son, Jonathan, to join the Schoolhouse Gang, he was bringing Schriever a jump start for the en-tire enterprise. The hurdle of a suitable engine had not yet been fully overcome. They would need one generating 150,000 pounds of thrust to lift the Atlas ICBM they were to design. Developing and perfecting this still more powerful engine would require time and trial and error and heartache. But Ed Hall had already brought them a long way toward attaining that without which they could never reach into the sky.

39.

A PROBLEM WITH TOMMY POWER

Until three days before the Los Angeles meeting of the new Von Neumann Committee on July 20–21, 1954, Bennie did not re-alize how much peril he was in over the decision to abandon the prime contractor system and use the Ramo-Wooldridge organization for engineering and technical expertise. He had assumed that Power, as head of the Air Research and Development Command, supported him and the ICBM program as he and Gardner and von Neumann and the rest of their associates had conceived it. In a meeting with Power at ARDC headquarters in Baltimore on the afternoon of July 17, he was stunned to learn otherwise: Power privately frowned on virtually everything that was being done and let Bennie know it in direct and brutal fashion. Schriever was so upset by what he heard that he wrote out an account of the meeting, something he rarely did because he was so busy, and placed it among the pages of the sparsely noted diary he kept each day on the long, lined yellow paper of legal pads.

At forty-nine years of age with twenty-six years of service in the Army Air Corps and the U.S. Air Force, Thomas Sarsfield Power was a man whose ambition was as wide as his frame was lean. He had been born at a time when Irish-American families often named a son for an Irish patriot and his middle name was an apt one for a military man. General Patrick Sarsfield, the Earl of Lucan, had been one of Ireland's most renowned soldiers, holding off the forces of William III at the siege of Limerick in 1691 longer than was thought humanly possible in the last major battle before the enveloping darkness of English colonialism closed over the Irish. Power had come up the hardscrabble way, studying civil engineering in night classes at Cooper Union in New York City until he had enough credits to join the Army Air Corps and qualify for Flying School. He had graduated from Kelly Field in 1929, seven months ahead of LeMay. Flying B-24 Liberators out of Italy, Power had gained a reputation as a hard-tasking, innovative commander, which is why Arnold had given him one of the B-29 wings and a star. He was cold-blooded in judgment and shrewd at his craft. LeMay had taken to him right away after his arrival in Guam and had sent him to lead that first night firebombing raid on Tokyo because he trusted him more than any of his other wing commanders. Power had just received his third star on appointment as commander of ARDC that April. Having served LeMay for the previous six years as his deputy at SAC, Power was intent on adding a fourth star to the row on his shoulder tabs and succeeding LeMay as commander-in-chief of the world's mightiest aerial striking force. He saw Schriever and this ICBM burden he had been handed as a threat to his dream. It had been naive of Schriever to assume that Power would approve of him and his project, given the contrasting nature of their careers. Power personified the operational Air Force par excellence. LeMay had maneuvered him into command of ARDC precisely because he wanted to keep the research and development organization out of the hands of technological visionary types like Schriever. As an operator, Power naturally tended to view the Air Force world in conventional terms. Not having participated in the work of the Tea Pot Committee and its sequel, he also understood virtually nothing of the nature of the task Schriever faced. Furthermore, had the choice been his, as the former vice chief of SAC and a witness to LeMay's repeated clashes with Schriever, he certainly would not have chosen this independent-minded colonel, now sporting a single star, for the ICBM job.

With White and Twining behind the project, Power was too shrewd to oppose it openly, but that did not stop him from letting Schriever know how he felt. The first thing he hit Schriever with was his objection to tossing the prime contractor tradition overboard in favor of this newfangled approach. He was obviously alarmed over the repercussions that were certain to follow when the aircraft industry fought back. Power was being drawn against his will into the middle of a fight in which he did not want to be involved and his ignorance of the technological obstacles inherent in building an ICBM prevented him from understanding why this revolution in contracting and program management was necessary. The B-52 Stratofortress, he told Schriever, was just as complex a weapon as the Atlas ICBM would be, yet Boeing had nurtured it to success. Why didn't they just let the aircraft industry handle the ICBM? "He inferred," Schriever wrote in his memo of the encounter, "that we were attempting to tie [a] can to Convair and R&W [Ramo-Wooldridge] would grab off the prize." Power also objected to the nature of the directive he had received on June 21 from Air Force headquarters. He was carrying out the directive because it was an order, but he didn't like it, Power said. The whole arrangement was unfair. He was being instructed to create a separate ICBM organization out on the West Coast run by a general officer who was to have complete authority over every detail of the program. Yet the directive also made Power responsible for the ultimate outcome. In short, he was to be held responsible for what he could not control. (His objection here was understandable, given the justly venerated military principle that there can be no responsibility without command.)

Schriever was still his subordinate, of course, but how was Power supposed to adequately supervise him from the East Coast? The field office ought to be located in Baltimore with his headquarters so that he could direct its actions. The argument that scientific and engineering expertise was most easily recruited in California and that many of the industries they would need were also situated there did not sway Power. "Only with inward reluctance does he go along with my moving west," Schriever wrote. Moreover, out there in California an officer as junior as Schriever would be "a country boy among the wolves," Power said. The aircraft industry would devour him at its leisure. His eventual discrediting could rebound on Power, and Power, allowing his ego and his ambition to flash, "made a point that he was senior to me and had much more at stake than I." The necessity Schriever had stated so baldly to Gardner that momentous afternoon at the rathskeller on 15th Street, that to get the missiles built he had to be free to operate "without any interference from those nitpicking sons of bitches in the Pentagon," had backfired when he had mentioned it to Power. "By his several allusions to my making big decisions on my own . . . he must feel that I am motivated by a personal desire for power," Schriever noted. Worst of all, "He obviously does not trust me nor have confidence in me—very important factors when undertaking a job of this magnitude." Bennie left Power's office a shaken man. He had been put on probation. If he did not succeed in allaying Power's worries, no amount of intervention from Gardner would suffice to protect him. Power would find a way to sack him in order to save his own hide.

Seeing the unity of the Von Neumann Committee at the July 20–21 meeting and the additional support from as ranking a figure in the Pentagon hierarchy as Donald Quarles, Power hid his misgivings. He played along by instructing Schriever to give him the memorandum on the proposed management structure, knowing in advance what it would say. But he also took out some insurance by playing a game known in the military as "cover your arse," or "CYA" for short. Whenever a matter was up for decision, or some sensitive point had been discussed, he demanded a written proposal from Schriever or a memorandum for the record. He was preparing a defense for the investigation that would be certain to follow if the project failed—men eminent in their fields had urged these actions on him and he had had no logical recourse but to accept their advice.

Schriever now launched his own "win over Tommy Power" campaign. He became the most attentive subordinate any general could desire. He wrote Power a report every week and shot off a message by Teletype or called on the phone in between whenever the occasion seemed to warrant it, made certain Power was invited to all significant meetings, and traveled to Baltimore frequently to personally update the boss. Judo wasn't Power's only sport. He was a keen golfer as well and Bennie turned on the charm here too, arranging the schedule so that their get-togethers were also an opportunity for the general to play with a partner in top form.

40.

HOW GREED CORRUPTS

The men who ran Convair were not interested in being reasonable, nor were they amenable to charm. Schriever stood between them and the pot of gold they were hungry to possess and that was all that mattered. Long months of wrangling with them ensued. They refused to accept Schriever's offer of a contract limiting them to manufacture of the airframe—the fuel tank and elements of the missile body; to assembling the entire Atlas once the other components (the subsystems) from different firms were ready; and to participation in the testing. They held out doggedly for everything except the engines, which it was agreed would come from Rocketdyne—in short, for the traditional prime contractor role.

The president of Convair was a retired general named Joseph McNarney. He was typical of those former senior officers who had built large reputations during the Second World War and then cashed in those reputations and the connections they entailed for the large financial rewards awaiting those who could help the military industries take advantage of the demands of the Cold War. McNarney was an old-timer in the Army Air Corps, having led an observation squadron in France during the First World War, a friend and collaborator of

Arnold's, and one of the best minds in that unique brotherhood. In 1938–39, Arnold had put him to work with Spaatz and Eaker to help plan the expansion of the Air Corps in preparation for the combat that loomed. McNarney's most important patron, however, had been the forbidding and demanding General George Catlett Marshall, chief of staff of the Army. Marshall had understood that he could not fulfill the enormous task of managing the war on his own and he believed, in any case, in delegating authority. He sought staff officers who were strong, able, and decisive men, who could correctly analyze problems and then implement solutions on their own authority, without constantly referring matters back to him. McNarney, a somewhat aloof, self-confident man, fit Marshall's requirements nearly perfectly. In December 1941, shortly after Pearl Harbor, Marshall had entrusted him with direction of a committee that had recommended the most important reform to ready the Army for its role in defeating Nazi Germany and Imperial Japan—reorganization along strikingly simple, functional lines into Army Ground Forces, Army Air Forces, and the Services of Supply, subsequently renamed Army Service Forces. Marshall had then appointed McNarney his deputy chief of staff, a position he had held until the end of the war, rising to lieutenant general. In 1952, with the aircraft industry surging under the demands of the Korean War and the anti-Soviet buildup in Europe, Convair had needed leadership. Its parent company, General Dynamics, had offered McNarney the presidency and he had accepted.

McNarney's point man on Atlas, Thomas Lanphier, Jr., had made his mark by participating in the shooting down of a Mitsubishi bomber carrying the commander-in-chief of the Imperial Japanese Navy, Admiral Isoroku Yamamoto, one Sunday morning in April 1943. The U.S. Navy had broken the Japanese code and, learning Yamamoto's precise schedule for an inspection tour of Japanese defenses in the Solomons, arranged an aerial ambush by Army Air Forces P-38 Lightning fighters flying out of Henderson Field on Guadalcanal. Lanphier was a captain and leader of the killer team designated to destroy Yamamoto's bomber, while the other Lightnings in the group fended off its escort of Zero fighters. As it turned out, there were two Japanese bombers in the flight. One Mitsubishi was ferrying Yamamoto and some of his aides, while the second bomber held other members of his staff. And two P-38s, one piloted by Lanphier and a second by a lieutenant named Rex Barber, did the shooting that brought both bombers down. Which P-38 pilot got which bomber was impossible to tell, but Lanphier claimed to be the man who had sent the legendary Japanese naval warrior, the inspirer of the surprise attack at Pearl Harbor on another Sunday morning two years earlier, plummeting to his end.

Like Teller's contention that he was the sole parent of the hydrogen bomb, Lanphier's claim somehow stuck. An operator in the wily, human sense of the term, he turned his exploit into a ticket to a living after the war. Ingratiating himself with W. Stuart Symington, who was to become the first secretary of the Air Force with the creation of an independent air arm in 1947, Lanphier served as his aide. By the 1950s, he had shifted to Convair. When Atlas became a potential money-maker in 1954, McNarney appointed Lanphier vice president for the project. One reason Lanphier was given the job was that he had maintained his political connections in Washington. Symington was now a Democratic senator from Missouri and a figure to be reckoned with on the Senate Armed Services Committee.

McNarney and Lanphier had gotten their way in the past by intimidation and they saw no reason why they should not get their way again. They regarded the insignificant brigadier general who opposed them exactly as Power had predicted, as a "country boy" they could run over. They started a campaign against Ramo and Wooldridge in the trade press, accusing them of stealing technicians for their new firm from Hughes Aircraft in order to corner the ICBM business. (Ramo and Wooldridge had, in fact, taken some of the best of their staff at Hughes with them when they left and stopped enticing away more at Schriever's request after the matter became an issue.) "Aircraft Industries Assn. is considering a strong protest to the Pentagon," an article in the November 8, 1954, issue of the magazine *Aviation Week* warned. "Big battle on upper Pentagon levels looms between the established missile contractors and the Johnny-come-latelies in the field." McNarney and Lanphier, apparently thinking that Bennie would heed one of the idols of his youth, set Ira Eaker on him. Eaker, who was drawing, by the measure of the day, a lavish salary of $50,000 a year from the Hughes Tool Company as its liaison to Hughes Aircraft, warned Schriever not to put his faith in Ramo and Wooldridge. They were upstarts who were not well regarded by the major aviation industries, he said. He invited Schriever to an Aircraft

Industries Association convention in Phoenix, allegedly to clarify questions members of the association had. Bennie saw the invitation as a
ploy to pressure him and declined.

He was convinced that McNarney and Lanphier's motive was simple greed. Their argument that Convair could handle the missile by itself contradicted the opinion of some of the best scientific brains in the
country on the Von Neumann Committee. They were not stupid
enough, he believed, to think that they possessed superior technical
judgment. What mattered to them was profit. In the last analysis, they
did not give a damn whether the ICBM got off the ground or not, as
long as they harvested the taxpayers' treasure in the meantime. One
proof of this was the absurd proposal they had kept pushing to go
ahead with production of their impractical five-engine, 440,000-pound
ICBM design. "They *don't want* to understand," Schriever wrote in
notes for a briefing he gave at the Air Matériel Command in Dayton on
October 28, 1954, underlining his frustration at his fruitless attempts to
reason with McNarney and Lanphier. "Efforts to discredit AF approach
selfishly motivated—don't stand close scrutiny," he added. He drafted a
letter of protest for Power to send McNarney. Power signed it despite
his misgivings. Under the circumstances, he had no choice but to back
his subordinate for now. Schriever and Gardner also persuaded Twining
to telephone McNarney to tell him that he, the chief of staff, stood behind everything McNarney was hearing from Schriever and to urge him
to accept the terms.

Still, McNarney and Lanphier held out. They tried more intimidation by also setting Symington on Schriever, but the ploy again failed.
The senator flew out to California for briefings by Bennie and his team
at the Schoolhouse in Inglewood and then by McNarney and Lanphier
and their Atlas team at Convair headquarters in San Diego. After his return to Washington, Symington indicated he was going to start making
trouble over the way the ICBM program was being handled. Schriever
and Gardner took the initiative and confronted him together in order,
as Bennie put it in his diary, to "lay cards on table with Symington."
Charles Lindbergh also intervened, persuading Talbott to call the senator. The counterattack seems to have been effective. Symington apparently decided he did not want to get involved. He did nothing.

At the end of November, McNarney and Lanphier convened a

meeting in San Diego to present what they apparently regarded as a compromise. Gardner flew out from Washington to attend, joined by Lindbergh on behalf of the Von Neumann Committee. Schriever arrived with an attitude growing ever more suspicious. He had had lunch the day before with Jimmy Doolittle. Friends like Teddy Walkowicz had been warning him that Convair had by no means slackened its lobbying campaign on Capitol Hill and wherever in the Pentagon McNarney and Lanphier thought they might get a sympathetic hearing. Doolittle described their attitude and that of other major aircraft makers with grim succinctness: "AIA [Aircraft Industries Association] wants to see us fail," Schriever recorded in his diary. At San Diego, Charlie Bossart handled the main briefing, McNarney or Lanphier occasionally interrupting with additional information they thought might help to sell their offer.

Bossart said Convair had abandoned the assumption of a 3,000-pound warhead that had been the basis for its earlier monster missile design. His team was now laying out a far lighter model based on a 1,500-pound hydrogen bomb. He also briefed on what Convair was doing to design the nose cone that would house the bomb and its ideas for the guidance and control system. The company wanted to hang on to both of these subsystems. Lanphier said the firm was prepared to hire 250 consultants and to put 1,600 engineers to work on Atlas in 1956. The meeting settled nothing. McNarney and Lanphier continued to refuse to accede to Schriever's demand that they confine themselves to manufacturing the airframe and assembling the missile.

By mid-December, Schriever was so exasperated that he drew a cartoon in his diary entry of December 14. It showed a bloated figure labeled "Industry," which exuded "Politics" and "Pressure," and had an arm reaching out toward a bulging sack of money to satisfy the "Ravenous appetite accustomed to." Underneath were the words "Motive Big Profit." Bennie had then written "(Pat)," an apparent abbreviation for "Patriotism," followed by the words "Small Thought." What Schriever had run up against was the moral corruption that had become endemic to the U.S. military industry as a result of the Cold War and its demand, year, upon year, upon year for new weaponry. The behavior of McNarney and Lanphier epitomized the vice. The offer he was making to them might not be nearly what they wanted, but it would provide Convair with a reasonable profit. This was particularly true at a time when the overall military budget was diminishing because of the end of the Korean War and the determination of President Eisenhower to hold down military spending. Schriever also alluded to this in his cartoon by sketching a shrunken sack of money for the fiscal year to come. A decent return, however, was not enough to satisfy McNarney and Lanphier. They wanted the whole kit and caboodle.

While American industrialists had reaped stupendous profits during the Second World War, patriotism had also been a motive for many. Andrew Higgins, the New Orleans boatbuilder, had, along with several pioneering Marine Corps officers, developed the ubiquitous amphibious assault craft of the Second World War, the LCVP (Landing Craft Vehicle and Personnel). It, and a larger version to ferry tanks, carried men and equipment ashore on innumerable contested beaches. Both boats were produced in the many thousands, yet Higgins declined to exercise his patent rights. He passed his designs freely to any other company that would agree to build them. By 1954, men such as Higgins were extinct. U.S. military industry, particularly the aircraft industry, had been coddled for so long that its leaders were like spoiled children. They had come to expect high profits as a virtual right. The firms were heavily subsidized. North American Aviation, for example, had by 1954 invested $33.8 million of its own funds in building its plants, while the Air Force and the Navy had furnished it with additional facilities worth roughly twice as much, $61.6 million, free of charge. In this atmosphere of government largesse, greed had become institutionalized. McNarney and Lanphier might fear advances in Soviet strategic weaponry as Schriever, Gardner, and von Neumann did, but if so, their fear was overmastered by their desire for lucre.

Gardner had also become sufficiently exasperated to ask Schriever what he thought about cutting off negotiations with Convair and finding another firm to build the missile's airframe and perform the final assembly. Bennie was opposed. They would lose a year's time, he said. As it was, to hold to schedule they would have to release designs for the airframe and the other components in the spring of 1955. He told Gardner that they had no choice but to keep hammering at Convair. Fortunately for Schriever, McNarney and Lanphier apparently did not realize how tight Schriever's deadlines were. Perhaps fearing an outcome such as the one Gardner had proposed, they caved in to the "country boy" and on January 6, 1955, agreed to a contract on his terms. Bennie made one concession. In addition to manufacture of the airframe, assembly, and participation in the testing, Convair would also provide the control mechanisms that steered the missile during liftoff and the first stage of flight. (The long-range guidance system to direct the warhead to its target remained a separate element to be awarded to a source with specialized expertise. Convair had come up with a radio-controlled system called Azusa, but like all radio schemes, it was vulnerable to interference. Von Neumann and the members of his committee favored an inertial guidance mechanism that would be integral to the missile and thus beyond the reach of the Soviet Union's defenses.) Given the innovation of swiveling rocket engines that Bossart had introduced in his work on Atlas's progenitor, the experimental MX-107B back in 1946–47, it was reasonable to assume the firm could perform this task adequately. Whatever the case, under the contract the specifications for everything would be those laid down by the Western Development Division and Ramo-Wooldridge. In turn, Schriever exacted a pledge from McNarney to create a distinct work force devoted only to Atlas at Convair's San Diego plant. There was to be no dual tasking with Convair's other enterprises, which could result in delays.

The signing of the contract did not put an end to Schriever's distrust of McNarney and Lanphier and their allies in the Aircraft Industries Association. He feared that they had not truly given up. Near the end of February, he wrote Power a secret fourteen-page memorandum recounting the flawed performance of the old-line aircraft companies in missilery and defending the unique organization that he and Simon Ramo had formed. Nor did the signing of the contract put an end to Schriever's troubles with Convair's performance. Ramo reported to him that Convair was not hiring the right kind of engineers in such specialties as metallurgy. More unpleasant exchanges followed with McNarney and Lanphier. It was not until May 1955, with Roger Lewis, the assistant secretary of the Air Force for matériel mediating, that Schriever and Ramo sat down with McNarney and Lanphier and settled on procedures that satisfied Bennie.

In the meantime, Schriever's relations with Power had undergone a transformation since their unnerving conversation of the previous July.

Despite his years of association with LeMay and the conventional attitudes of the senior Air Force bomber general that his career had ingrained in him, Power had a mind of his own. Months of listening to
scientists as prestigious and as persuasive as von Neumann discuss the
ICBM had given him an appreciation of its strategic importance. He
was by now a convert and saw it as a necessity in the nuclear arms competition with the Soviet Union. Those same months of listening had also
brought him around to an understanding of why the special management arrangement with Ramo-Wooldridge was needed. Tommy Power
was a tough and decisive man and, as he valued those qualities in himself, so he also admired them in others. The persistent, unflinching manner in which Schriever had stood up to and eventually won out over
McNarney and Lanphier made him realize how badly he had misjudged
this younger officer in assessing him as a naive amateur.

The first fitness report on Bennie that Power rendered at the end of
April 1955 demonstrated the dramatic reversal of attitude. Schriever
has "excellent staying qualities when the going gets rough," Power
began. "Professionally, he is characterized by his thoroughness. He has
a brilliant mind and can be depended upon for outstanding work. He is
highly respected by his associates, both senior and junior. His management ability has been demonstrated in the organization and operation
of the highly classified special project for which he was hand-picked."
Power recommended Schriever for a second star, promotion to major
general. In short, Power had perceived that Bernard Schriever was made
of the stuff that bred success and his success would shine on Power,
which is above all what Power wanted. From this point on Schriever no
longer had to worry about the wary three-stars in Baltimore. Power was
now behind him.

AN ASSAULT FROM AN
UNEXPECTED QUARTER

Having bested McNarney and Lanphier, Bennie was astonished in mid-February to find himself suddenly involved in a totally unexpected fracas with Air Force Secretary Harold Talbott. He had been looking forward to Talbott's scheduled visit to the Schoolhouse on February 16 as a "Happy to Have You" occasion, as he had written at the top of the outline for his briefing on the progress they were making. Instead, he subsequently recorded in his diary, "It was indeed a painful meeting." Schriever and Ramo had, with the concurrence of Gardner and von Neumann and the other scientists on his committee, decided on a management strategy that was a dual approach. One side was called concurrency. On this side, work on every part of the missile—airframe, engines, long-range guidance, nose cone or reentry vehicle—was to go forward simultaneously. The objective was to gain time. They assumed that if each of these parts was adequately tested beforehand and Ramo and his colleagues did their job of systems engineering competently to make certain that everything would fit together, they would have a ready-to-fly ICBM much sooner than if they developed each part in sequence.

The other aspect of the strategy was fail-safe redundancy. They were going to build not one, but two different ICBMs. And they were going to create a complete second set of the subsystems that went into an ICBM. If the Atlas or any of its components proved a failure, they would always have a fallback. Schriever already had his staff sizing up which other aircraft companies were the best candidates to design and manufacture the airframe for the second ICBM. He intended to launch a competition as soon as possible. And, on Hall's advice, he had also just negotiated a contract for the rocket engines that were to power this alternate ICBM. The firm was Aerojet General, a full-grown descendent of a seedling company started in 1942 by von Kármán and a number of his students with Hap Arnold's assistance to build small rockets that would give heavily laden aircraft an extra boost to take off. Aerojet had agreed to develop the new engines in collaboration with a less well-known firm called Reaction Motors, Inc., another pioneer in the rocket business.

Bennie cheerfully recounted all of this good news to Talbott and got a reaction he least expected. As with his unnerving session with Power the previous July, he was so upset by it that he again wrote a long memorandum, this time eight pages, for his diary. Talbott paid no attention to what had been accomplished. Instead, he was solely concerned with stopping any additional work on the project in California. To render military industries less vulnerable to attack, President Eisenhower wanted to start dispersing them inland, rather than leaving them concentrated, as they were, on both coasts. He was also particularly concerned about the extent to which California's economy was based on military industry. The state's dependence on the military made California, he felt, highly vulnerable to future cutbacks. Talbott had obviously left Washington freshly briefed on the president's wishes. He should have explained to Eisenhower that the ICBM project was so dependent on scientific and industrial resources virtually exclusive to California at this point in American history that an exception would have to be made if the program was to move ahead at an acceptable pace. But he had not done so. Instead, he had flown out a somewhat frightened man, determined to enforce what he interpreted as the boss's orders.

He told an amazed Schriever, and Gardner and Ramo, who were also present at the meeting, that he wanted no additional work assigned in California, or at least none that would enable a California firm to enlarge its organizational or industrial base. He ordered Schriever to cancel the contracts with Lockheed and Aerojet General. When Bennie replied that carrying out those orders would severely impair the project, Talbott lost his temper and threatened to fire him on the spot and reduce him in rank. "Before this meeting is over, General, there's going to be one more colonel in the Air Force," he shouted at Schriever with a menacing look on his face. He yelled that he expected his orders to be obeyed. Other people might lose their jobs for failure to carry out the president's wishes on this issue, but he was not going to be one of them, Talbott said. Bennie could also lose his temper on occasion, but never when he was under assault. He grew cold and deliberate then. He replied quietly, yet pronouncing each word with unaccustomed precision, that he could not accept the order "because I have a prior and overriding order. On being handed this assignment, I was directed to run this program so as to attain an operational ICBM capability in the shortest possible time." Talbott also regained control of himself and began speaking calmly, but he did not back down.

Ramo and Gardner came to Schriever's defense. So did Roger Lewis, Talbott's assistant secretary for matériel, who had also apparently flown to Los Angeles for the gathering. They pointed out to Talbott that if the president wanted industry dispersed, production facilities could be found inland once research and development of the prototypes was completed. The R&D, however, had to be done in California. Otherwise, they would lose a year. Lewis said he had read the agreement with Aerojet and that creation of new rocket engines for the alternate ICBM with this firm in California was the way to go. The solution of development in California and production elsewhere did not satisfy Talbott. He lost his temper again at a remark by Gardner and then said that the Aerojet General contract should have gone to General Electric. With its headquarters in upstate New York, GE was presumably far enough away from the coast to satisfy Talbott's understanding of the dispersal criterion. The company had never previously manufactured rocket engines. In a reflex search for new business, however, it had competed for the alternate engine contract and lost because of its lack of qualifications. To his listeners, Talbott's championing of GE now smacked more of politics and favoritism than obedience to the president's dispersal policy. Gardner snapped a Gardner retort at his chief and patron. Bennie recorded it in his diary. "This would have been a big mistake because GE was a shitty outfit." Ramo was glum and grim. Bennie also recorded his warning. "If no R&D is done in Calif., you might as well scrub the [whole] program." Talbott waffled somewhat, but he left still refusing to rescind his instructions and aimed a parting shot at Schriever. The secretary told him that whatever contractor he chose for the airframe of the second ICBM, it would have to be a company "east of the Rockies."

Horatio Viscount Nelson, the British naval genius who brought his country a century of command of the seas and thus the freedom to build its extraordinary empire by destroying the combined French and

Spanish fleets in the battle of Trafalgar in 1805, was once ordered by a superior to break off an action in which he believed he would prevail. In an account of the incident that may be apocryphal but which is entirely within character, Nelson put his telescope to an eye blinded in an earlier fight. He pointed it at the signal flags waving from his superior's flagship and declared, "I really do not see the signal." Bennie Schriever had not come this far in the United States Air Force to fail to learn the lesson that when a foolish order is issued, a wise officer ignores it. "The only way in which a development can be accomplished in the shortest period of time is when all other considerations are subordinate to time," he observed in his diary. He canceled neither contract, instead forwarding both for approval. He ordered his deputy, Colonel Charles "Terry" Terhune, a redheaded Dutchman and one of the most accomplished engineers in the Air Force, who had been present at the meeting, not to tell anyone what had occurred. He also instructed Terhune to get the search for a second airframe contractor moving. He was careful with Power. The next morning, before leaving for Patrick Air Force Base in Florida to start planning for the launch pads and other missile test facilities they would have to construct on nearby Cape Canaveral, he telephoned Power in Baltimore, filled him in on the tumult of the previous day, and told Power what he intended to do. Power did not object.

The contracts went through and the ICBM project was eventually granted a complete exemption from the dispersal policy. Ironically, Harold Talbott, who had predicted that someone was going to lose his job but that it was not going to be he, was forced to resign that August because of a conflict of interest imbroglio. He had been using Air Force stationery and his phone and office to further the fortunes of a former business partner. Some of the companies he had contacted on behalf of his friend were Air Force contractors whom he had to have known would feel themselves under obligation to him. He had also retained his partnership in a New York investment group and had accepted more than $132,000 from them, he claimed for services not performed while he was secretary of the Air Force.

42

A SENSE OF ADVENTURE

Despite these traumas, Schriever and Ramo and their associates at the Schoolhouse in Inglewood were by no means discouraged. On the contrary, they were filled with the stir of adventure. They were giving birth to a "New Era," two words that appear repeatedly in Bennie's diary entries at this time. The ballistic missiles they were fashioning would lift the Air Force out of the atmosphere and carry it off into the world of outer space. In these chilling years of the early Cold War, fear of the Soviet Union was a constant and powerful stimulant. The probability that they were in a race with unnamed and unknown but nonetheless all too real rivals hard at work to destroy the United States from within the dark, closed society behind the Iron Curtain was pervasive, and Schriever never let anyone forget this. "If we don't push into it [this New Era], we have failed our country and seriously endangered our security," he told the Schoolhouse gang in a pep talk.

Yet anxiety for the security of their nation and a race against opponents who would endanger it were only half of what drove them. These men were engineers. They built things. Theirs was a different ethos from that of operators like Power and LeMay, who got their adrenaline rush from the lure of aerial combat. The engineers' fulfillment came from creating the new, from bringing into being that which no one else had yet achieved. And in building their lethal rockets, they were simultaneously opening the realm of space that had so far been beyond the reach of man. Their rockets would be more than weapons. They would also become launch vehicles to penetrate this unexplored vastness. If they could acquire the means to send a hydrogen bomb into space and bring it back down again, they could do so with other things and, although they were military men to whom human exploration of space was not a priority, they could do so too with man. The technology that applied to sending the bomb up and bringing it back down again intact applied to virtually everything else. The first American astronauts to venture into space were, in fact, to ride up on military missiles and to return in capsules that were modified versions of the initial hydrogen bomb warhead.

Bennie imparted some of the exhilaration of this adventure in a secret briefing he gave to the staff of the Air Force's think tank, the RAND Corporation, in nearby Santa Monica on January 31, 1955. He spoke of a warhead flashing through space at the previously unimaginable speed of 20,000 feet per second, of the "invulnerability" of this nuclear spear point to Soviet defenses. And yet, he said, the real objective of the adventure was to contribute to the preservation of peace. The ICBM was not being built to be used as a weapon. Rather, as an instrument of war the ICBM would have the "highest probability of *Not* being used." The thought was an idea he had absorbed from Gardner and was to reiterate over and over in the years to come. Once the missile existed the Soviets were "unlikely to miscalculate our capability to retaliate" and would be afraid to attack. The ICBM would thus achieve its highest purpose. It would have "*deterred Total War.*" Schriever was articulating a concept that would subsequently become known as Mutual Assured Destruction. And once they had attained the means to penetrate what he called the "New Environment—outer space," they could move on to the next contribution to "preserve the peace." They would power their rockets to even higher speeds than 20,000 feet per second in order to fling into orbit around the earth the spy satellites Arnold and von Kármán had envisioned. The "constant surveillance," the regular flow of information on "enemy intentions" provided by these spy satellites, would deny the Soviets the possibility of a surprise attack, of a nuclear Pearl Harbor, the dread of which haunted many, including Eisenhower.

43

NO TIME FOR FAMILY

Schriever found a house for his family in a neighborhood in Santa Monica with the Roman Catholic schools that Dora wanted. There were three Schriever offspring now. Brett Arnold, their son and firstborn, was a fifteen-year-old high school student when his father took command of the Western Development Division on August 2, 1954. Their second child, Dodie Elizabeth, who had arrived in June 1941, in time to be bundled off to California on that earlier trip when Schriever had spent a year studying for his master's degree in aeronautical engineering at Stanford University in Palo Alto, was a thirteen-year-old in junior high. Another daughter and the last of Dora and Bennie's children, Barbara Alice, who had been born in June 1949, was just five.

The family had grown accustomed to seeing a great deal of Schriever while he was stationed at the Pentagon and they lived in Alexandria. Although he might work late, as he often did, he came home at night. On weekends, there was the Belle Haven Country Club, where he played golf, but Dora and the children had the pleasure of the swimming pool and tennis courts. And periodically he would take leave. Dora and the children would climb into the car, the luggage would go into the trunk, and with Bennie at the wheel they would set off for a visit with General and Mrs. Brett, who had retired to Winter Park, a suburb of Orlando in central Florida. All of this ended with the move to California and Bennie's new responsibilities. When he was home he was preoccupied and he was away as much as he was at home, shuttling between Los Angeles and Washington and Baltimore or off on trips like the one to Patrick Air Force Base to start planning for the missile test range on Cape Canaveral.

As soon as the conference at Patrick was over, he left for a two-day tour of the Bahamas to try to get some idea of the tracking system they would need to establish in order to monitor the flight of the mock warheads over the Caribbean and into the South Atlantic after the missiles had been launched from the Cape. The islands were still a British colony then, but London had already given the Air Force permission to set up some tracking stations there for test firings of the Snark and earlier missiles. Although his relationship with Dora began to come under strain from his lack of attention to her and the family, Bennie was energized by this relentless quick-step regime of shuttlecock travel, decisions under pressure, and a workload that seemed to be forever expanding. This was the mission for which, it seemed, he had spent his life preparing himself, and now he was living it. He was ruthless at keeping himself organized and he prevented himself from becoming exhausted by a trick he had of suddenly putting aside whatever he was doing in an office or on a plane and going off on a catnap.

44.

GETTING TO IKE

Even prior to the confrontation with Talbott and the additional complication it had raised with the policy to disperse military industries, Gardner and Schriever had decided they had to make an end run around the Air Force and Department of Defense bureaucracies. They were going to have to do what Gardner had said all along would be necessary. They had to reach President Eisenhower and convince him to underwrite the project with his personal support. Despite the advances Schriever and Ramo and their teams had made, they were not moving nearly fast enough to meet Gardner's June 1958 deadline for a "Ph.D. type" capability of two launching sites and four operational missiles, let alone his major deterrent of twenty launching sites and a stockpile of one hundred missiles by June 1960. Dealing with the Department of Defense and Air Force bureaucracies meant navigating an obstacle course. Bennie had his staff count up the number of agencies or offices from which, depending on the nature of the request, they had to seek prior approval. The total came to forty-two. Merely to obtain an air-conditioning unit to protect a

Elizabeth Milch, Schriever's mother, as a young woman in New York not long before she met his father, Adolph Schriever. She had left Germany as a teenager to work for a German family who owned a pharmacy in lower Manhattan and moved back to Germany after marrying Adolph. COURTESY OF BARBARA SCHRIEVER ALLAN

The street-corner building in Bremen, Germany, where, in one of the apartments above the shop, Bernard Adolph Schriever was born on September 14, 1910. COURTESY OF BARBARA SCHRIEVER ALLAN

Adolph Schriever, in his engineer officer's uniform on board the North German Lloyd Company's passenger liner *George Washington*. During a cruise in 1914, the ship was trapped in New York Harbor by the outbreak of the First World War that August. The United States was then neutral, but Britain's Royal Navy waited outside the harbor to seize German ships. COURTESY OF BARBARA SCHRIEVER ALLAN

A strong woman who would not wait for the war to end to be reunited with her husband: Elizabeth Milch Schriever with her two sons, six-year-old Bernard (left) and four-year-old Gerhard (middle). Holland remained neutral throughout the war, so they boarded the Dutch liner *Noordam* at Rotterdam in January 1917, just a little more than two months before a U.S. declaration of war against Germany would have blocked their coming. COURTESY OF BARBARA SCHRIEVER ALLAN

Pluck and enterprise: "The Oaks," the soft drink and homemade ham sandwich stand, erected under the shading branches of a grove of venerable live oak trees next to the twelfth green of the Brackenridge Park Golf Course in San Antonio, which Elizabeth Schriever established to support herself and her two boys. A sandwich cost fifteen cents and a glass of lemonade a nickel. COURTESY OF JONI JAMES SCHRIEVER

"Champ Gets Hot," boasted a headline in one San Antonio newspaper: Bennie Schriever in 1931 as a senior at Texas A&M, playing a long shot while stylishly attired in the plus fours and two-tone golf shoes of the era. That year he won the Texas state junior amateur championship and the San Antonio city championship for the first of two times. Schriever's prowess at golf not only would give him great pleasure but would also be a valuable asset in his military career. COURTESY OF JONI JAMES SCHRIEVER

Shiny boots and riding breeches: Schriever, in his senior year at Texas A&M, in the spit-and-polish uniform of an officer cadet in the horse-drawn field artillery. He would later joke that he chose airplanes because his legs were too long for the stirrups. COURTESY OF GENERAL BERNARD SCHRIEVER

Reaching for the sky: Bennie in the open cockpit of a trainer aircraft at Flying School at Randolph and Kelly Fields near San Antonio in 1932 or 1933. The washout rate was more than 50 percent, but he survived and received his wings and a second lieutenant's commission in the Air Corps Reserve on June 29, 1933. COURTESY OF GENERAL BERNARD SCHRIEVER

A white scarf, goggles, and a leather helmet, the romantic regalia of the early 1930s, the open-cockpit era, when Schriever was a young pilot. "The gals sure liked it," he said. "It was better than owning a convertible." COURTESY OF JONI JAMES SCHRIEVER

The future General of the Air Force: Schriever's idol, Henry Harley "Hap" Arnold, then a lieutenant colonel, about to take off in a Boeing P-12 biplane fighter with a load of mail during the air mail catastrophe of 1934. Arnold was commander of the operation's Western Region, with Salt Lake City as his headquarters. Schriever was one of his pilots. ARMY AIR CORPS PHOTO COURTESY OF GENERAL BERNARD SCHRIEVER

Bennie with his prize: Dora Brett and Bernard Schriever aboard a ship traveling from the Panama Canal Zone to San Francisco in August 1937, he to head for Seattle to begin flying for Northwest Airlines, she to proceed on to Washington, where they were to be wed at Hap Arnold's home on January 3, 1938. "Wonderful trip," Dora wrote in her scrapbook. COURTESY OF BARBARA SCHRIEVER ALLAN

The daring of the young: Major Bernard Schriever and Major John "Jack" Dougherty, back at their home base in northeastern Australia after their wild "dive-bombing" attack in a B-17 on Japanese shipping in Rabaul Harbor on New Britain Island on the night of September 23, 1942. COURTESY OF GENERAL BERNARD SCHRIEVER

Keeping 'em flying, New Guinea, 1943: Schriever, as chief of maintenance and engineering for General George Kenney's Fifth Air Force, supervising the repair of an engine. Schriever's honesty and efficiency won over Kenney's irascible deputy for combat operations, Brigadier General Ennis "Ennis the Menace" Whitehead. ARMY AIR CORPS PHOTO COURTESY OF GENERAL BERNARD SCHRIEVER

A wartime reunion: Bennie and Gerhard (right), who had acquired the nickname "Gerry" in his boyhood, visiting their mother in San Antonio during Bennie's brief trip home in the fall of 1943. Both were lieutenant colonels by then, Gerry commanding an engineering unit at Tinker Field in Oklahoma. Behind is the little white house on Terry Court in which they grew up. COURTESY OF JONI JAMES SCHRIEVER

Where it all began: the Schoolhouse, the vacant Roman Catholic boys' school in the Los Angeles suburb of Inglewood, as it was when Schriever and his band of rocket pioneers began secretly assembling there in July 1954 to launch the project to build the intercontinental ballistic missile. The former chapel, the small structure in the middle with stained-glass windows depicting the saints, was the site of their briefing room. U.S. AIR FORCE PHOTO COURTESY OF THE SPACE AND MISSILE SYSTEMS CENTER

"The wild Welshman": Trevor Gardner, the brash, brave visionary to whom Schriever first turned to get the enterprise started. COURTESY OF TREVOR GARDNER, JR.

Gardner, left, being briefed on another of his secret high-technology projects. Looking over Gardner's shoulder is his then assistant, Lieutenant Colonel Vincent "Vince" Ford, dubbed "the Gray Ghost" by Schriever's staff because of his capacity for behind-the-curtain maneuvering. His talent for it was crucial in arranging the White House briefing that won Eisenhower's backing for the missile program. The briefer is unidentified. COURTESY OF GENERAL BERNARD SCHRIEVER

A future cardinal of the military-industrial complex: Simon Ramo, center, who would rise to become the R in TRW, Inc., conferring with Schriever. On the right is Dr. Louis Dunn, Ramo's deputy for the missile effort. Both Schriever and Gardner knew Ramo was indispensable for assembling the array of engineering and scientific talent needed to overcome the technological obstacles. COURTESY OF GENERAL BERNARD SCHRIEVER

Cold War forgiveness: John von Neumann (right), a Jewish exile from Hitler's Europe, conferring with Wernher von Braun, a former SS officer, Nazi Party member, and the führer's V-2 missile man, during a visit to the Army's Redstone Arsenal in Alabama. A mathematician and mathematical physicist with a mind second only to Albert Einstein's, von Neumann headed the scientific advisory committee for the ICBM and lent the project his prestige. JOHN VON NEUMANN PAPERS, MANUSCRIPT DIVISION, LIBRARY OF CONGRESS

The heartlessness of an early end: Seven months after immensely impressing Eisenhower at the July 28, 1955, White House briefing on the missile project, "Johnny" von Neumann had been driven to a wheelchair by the ravages of his cancer. Ike awarded him the Presidential Medal of Freedom in February 1956. "I wish I could be around long enough to deserve this honor," Johnny said to the president. He died approximately a year later, on February 8, 1957, at the age of fifty-three. WHITE HOUSE PHOTO, JOHN VON NEUMANN PAPERS, MANUSCRIPT DIVISION, LIBRARY OF CONGRESS

A powerful opponent: Curtis LeMay, the formidable bomber leader who created the Strategic Air Command and directed it for nearly nine years, was a relentless foe of the ICBM program. Nicknamed "the Cigar" for the stogie he had perpetually in hand or clenched between his teeth, LeMay mocked the first of Schriever's ICBMs, the Atlas, as "a fucking firecracker." Courtesy of the National Museum of the U.S. Air Force

An essential ally: General Thomas "Tommy" Power (right) gives a souvenir handshake to Technical Sergeant Anderson in December 1957 at the "Thor Show" Major Jamie Wallace staged in Los Angeles, under the guise of a Development Engineering Inspection, to promote the Air Force's intermediate-range ballistic missile. Initially alarmed by Schriever while heading the Air Force Research and Development Command, Power, who succeeded LeMay as commander in chief of the Strategic Air Command, was won over and became a staunch supporter. U.S. Air Force photo Courtesy of Jamie Wallace

Going public in style: Schriever makes the cover of *Time*, then the nation's leading news-magazine, in April 1957. *TIME* MAGAZINE

Bennie in his element: testing missiles at Cape Canaveral in 1958. U.S. AIR FORCE PHOTO COURTESY OF JONI JAMES SCHRIEVER

The guru of rockets: Lieutenant Colonel Edward Hall, the rocketry genius who devised Minuteman, the missile that crowned the mission to deter the Soviets from any attempt at a surprise attack. U.S. AIR FORCE PHOTO COURTESY OF SHEILA HALL

Theordore A. Hall

The younger brother who betrayed: the Los Alamos identification badge of Theodore Hall, the Harvard physics prodigy who, along with Klaus Fuchs, was one of the Soviet Union's two important spies at the atomic bomb laboratory. Hall apparently did not bother to have the mistake in the spelling of his first name corrected. COURTESY OF LOS ALAMOS NATIONAL LABORATORY

All systems go: the first successful training launch of an Atlas D–model ICBM by a Strategic Air Command crew at Vandenberg Air Force Base, on April 22, 1960. The missile is raised from its protective concrete shelter, fueled, and fired into space. U.S. Air Force photo

Try and try again to put a spy in the sky: After the thirteenth attempt, Lieutenant Colonel Charles "Moose" Mathison presents the first capsule retrieved from a would-be photoreconnaissance satellite, Discoverer XIII, which had been flung into orbit around the earth, to a jubilant Schriever and General Thomas White, chief of staff of the Air Force, at Andrews Air Force Base, August 13, 1960. LOCKHEED MISSILES AND SPACE DIVISION PHOTO COURTESY OF GENERAL BERNARD SCHRIEVER

Fulfillment: Bennie Schriever with four stars amid his missiles, circa 1962. HISTORY OFFICE, U.S. AIR FORCE SPACE COMMAND

BEFORE RETIREMENT

The Schriever family at Barbara's "sweet sixteen" birthday party at Andrews Air Force Base on June 11, 1965. Left to right: Brett, an Air Force navigator, with his captain's bars; Barbara; General Schriever; Dora; Dodie; and Dodie's pilot husband, Theodore Moeller, then also a captain. U.S. AIR FORCE PHOTO COURTESY OF BARBARA SCHRIEVER ALLAN

HAPPINESS IN THE EVENING

The Schriever luck holds: Joni James and Bernard Schriever on honeymoon in southern France after their wedding, which took place on October 5, 1997. COURTESY OF JONI JAMES SCHRIEVER

A LAST SALUTE

The Generals of the Air Force salute Schriever's coffin on July 12, 2005, as it is carried up the slope of a knoll at Arlington National Cemetery to rest, as he wished, near Hap Arnold. He was buried with the honors due a chief of staff. U.S. AIR FORCE PHOTO COURTESY OF JONI JAMES SCHRIEVER

computer the Ramo-Wooldridge team was purchasing from the Southern California heat became a hassle.

Having been awarded the Air Force's highest development priority was fine, but it turned out that this did not absolve them from competing against other high-priority projects for funds. Their overall budget for each fiscal year also had to be approved by, in turn, the budget committees of the ARDC and the Air Matériel Command, and then by the Air Staff, the Air Force Budget Advisory Committee, the Air Force Council, the secretary of the Air Force, the Office of the Secretary of Defense, and the Bureau of the Budget. What they needed was a streamlined decision-making process, their own separate budget, and a designation of the highest national—not just Air Force or Department of Defense—priority, which would enable them to override everything else. Only Eisenhower could give them these privileges. The question was, how were they to get to him?

It was a task made for Vincent Thaddeus Ford, a man to whom duplicity was second nature, an adept backdoor operative whom Schriever's staff was to nickname "the Gray Ghost." He was an odd, neurotic man. He had been born in Winstead, Connecticut, in 1907 and grown up there until, in his mid-high-school years, his father had developed chronic chest problems of colds and pneumonia and been warned by a doctor that if he wanted to live, he had better move to a warmer and dryer climate. The family had shifted to the community of Alhambra in Southern California southeast of Los Angeles, where Vince had completed high school and studied engineering for two years at UCLA. To support himself, he also worked part-time as a meteorologist for one of the original airlines, Western, which had a contract to fly the mail. He got to know a number of the pilots and discovered that they were all college graduates, some from prestigious schools like Stanford and the University of California at Berkeley, who had taken up flying for the sheer love of it. One pilot, he recalled, always tossed in his bag of golf clubs along with the mail sack so that he could play at stopovers.

This, Vince decided, was a pretty good way to earn a living, and he became fascinated with flying himself. With the two years at UCLA to qualify him, he was accepted by the Army Air Corps and reported to Randolph Field, Texas, in the fall of 1931, just as Schriever was to do in July of the following year. He survived the 50 percent washout rate, received his wings and the gold bars of a second lieutenant in the Air Corps Reserve, and in 1932 reported for a year of active duty, again as Bennie was subsequently to do, at March Field, California. Hap Arnold was already there as base and overall wing commander. Unlike Schriever, however, Ford managed to avoid bombers and to gain a coveted assignment to one of the pursuit, or fighter, squadrons. His was the 34th, commanded by then Captain Ira Eaker and equipped with Boeing P-12 biplane fighters.

On April 14, 1933, while the 34th was practicing formation flying for its part in an air show the March Field units were to stage at the forthcoming annual air races at Santa Monica, turbulence either flung Ford's plane down on the aircraft below or tossed the plane below up into his. They had been flying at about 10,000 feet, so Ford had plenty of time to unbuckle his seat belt, push away from the tumbling plane, and pull the rip cord on his parachute. Then he passed out. His left leg was shattered by the propeller of the plane below, which had ripped right through the skin of the P-12's fuselage. He was flown to the Letterman Army Hospital at the Presidio of San Francisco and spent the next two years and two weeks there. The leg also became infected. The infection was ultimately cured, a lengthy process in these years before antibiotics, but bone grafts were then required to get the fragmented leg to calcify and knit back together again. By the time this had occurred, the left ankle, so long in a cast and with the foot turned off at a crazy angle to the outside, had also frozen and calcified, and so in order to walk on it he had to wear a custom-made boot with steel braces at the ankle.

Over the next few years, however, the leg itself, which had healed fairly straight, strengthened and the knee was fine. Friends would later urge him to have the ankle and foot amputated, so that a false foot could be fitted to the stump of the leg and he could lead a normal life. Edward Teller, for example, had lost a foot when he slid under a Budapest tram as a youth, but no stranger would ever know it watching him walk. Ford always refused, preferring to hop about on the dreadful souvenir of his accident. Acquaintances decided that he clung to the deformed foot because he thought it elicited sympathy.

The Second World War saved him from an empty life back in Alhambra. Contemporaries from his Air Corps days were suddenly lieutenant colonels and colonels. He hitched a ride to Washington aboard a plane being flown there from the Douglas Aircraft plant and went to see a Flying School mate who was now a full colonel in charge of all filmmaking for the Army Air Forces. He had Ford assigned as a lieutenant to the 1st Motion Picture Unit at the old Mack Sennett studios in Culver City, California. Ronald Reagan, who had obtained a lieutenant's commission in the Cavalry Reserve after he discovered that he liked riding horses while a young radio sportscaster in Iowa, had also been assigned to the unit and promoted to captain. Ford offered to take him out to a nearby airfield on weekends to hitch rides on planes for fun, but Reagan declined. He said that the sixteen hands measurement of an average horse's height was as high as he wanted to go.

For a man who had known the company of serious airmen, making movies in Culver City was not a satisfactory way to spend the war. Ford returned to his catalogue of classmates and one of them arranged an assignment to the Air Transport Command in England and a post as assistant operations officer for a C-47 transport squadron at Bovingdon, just northwest of London. The work was hardly exciting, but it was worthy. The surrender of Japan in August 1945 soon brought banishment to civilian life once more. By 1948, an unhappy Ford was again banging on the gate. A persistent effort led from connection to connection until a Colonel Bernard Schriever hired him. Bennie had heard of Ford's accident after his own arrival at March Field in 1933, but the two had never met until a mutual acquaintance introduced them fifteen years later. It was the beginning of a relationship that was to last the rest of their long lives.

Although Schriever and Ford became friends and Ford felt indebted to Schriever for a renewed professional life, he had no intention of becoming Schriever's Sancho Panza. Ford had his own agenda. He was a shrewd man who enjoyed wielding power and influencing events. He was zealous to promote causes in which he believed. But because of the limitations life had imposed on him, he had to do this through other men with rank and status. Lacking both himself, had he sought center stage, his ambition would have been regarded as ludicrous and he would have found himself back in Alhambra. His personality and character fitted him for his behind-the-scenes role. He had a smile that disarmed and great capacity for charm. He rarely showed irritation or anger and was never confrontational. The rub was that the affability might mean he was in sympathy with someone or it might mean that he was just putting them off, for Ford wore it as a mask in all seasons.

His initial move upward from being just another member of Schriever's staff came in September 1950, when William Burden was appointed the first special assistant to the secretary of the Air Force for research and development. Through Teddy Walkowicz, who was then working for Doolittle, Vince gained an introduction to Burden and the job as his executive assistant. This had put him in position for the meeting with Gardner and the adventures that followed after Gardner appeared in the office doorway on that fateful day in March 1953.

Beginning in December 1954, Gardner and Schriever set Ford to work secretly briefing Henry Jackson, the Democratic senator from Washington State, on the impediments the ICBM program was encountering. Ford met Jackson in restaurants that were not frequented by other politicians or military officers, who might get curious. The objective was to gain Jackson's assistance in reaching Eisenhower. They would have been hard put to find a senator more willing to help them. Scoop Jackson was not merely anti-Communist, he was ferociously anti-Soviet and, like von Neumann, a believer in "maximum armament." He was also well placed to assist because he held the chairmanship of the Military Applications Subcommittee of the Joint Committee on Atomic Energy, the joint Senate and House committee that oversaw the Atomic Energy Commission and all nuclear activities, including the manufacture of nuclear weapons. In addition, he was a member of the Subcommittee on the Air Force of the Senate Armed Services Committee. Schriever and Gardner had invited him out to WDD the previous fall and he had been impressed. It was common in the 1950s for the military to surreptitiously appeal to friendly legislators with an end-run play like this when the need arose. There was risk, but Bennie was hardly risk-averse when the goal was worthy of the danger, and he would also have been a moral coward to have let Gardner assume sole responsibility for the plot.

He sent his executive officer, Lieutenant Colonel Beryl Boatman, to join Ford at the clandestine rendezvous with Jackson and to regularly pass the senator copies of his latest classified reports. Had the gambit gone awry, Gardner's authority would not have saved Schriever, particularly given the antipathy toward Gardner within much of the senior ranks of the Air Force. Years later, LeMay accused Bennie of sneaking around behind the chief of staff's back. Schriever called the accusation "a goddamn lie" and claimed that he had kept Twining informed of everything. This is doubtful. Both Twining and White, the vice chief, were supporters of the missile program. What probably happened is that they learned something of what was occurring through the grapevine—such covert maneuvering is always difficult to keep entirely hidden within the armed services—and tacitly approved by not interfering. Twining later showed his hand by invariably protecting Bennie whenever he did get into trouble. Power also apparently learned what was going on and said nothing. The unobtrusive briefings of Jackson continued for six months. The senator used the ammunition Ford and Boatman provided to hold fifteen closed hearings by his subcommittee. Gardner naturally appeared as a witness and von Neumann, ever prepared to pitch in, volunteered to testify as well. From March 1955 onward, Johnny carried the additional prestige of being one of the five commissioners on the Atomic Energy Commission, the first foreign-born scientist to be nominated to the post.

All the while, Ford had been boring another tunnel into the White House. Near the end of March 1954, Eisenhower met with a group of eminent scientists who constituted the Presidential Science Advisory Committee, PSAC for short. Its chairman was Lee DuBridge, by then president of Caltech. Eisenhower asked them to undertake a study of the nuclear Pearl Harbor nightmare that was always foremost in his mind. He was convinced, the president said, that modern weapons had increased the danger of such a surprise attack on the nation and wanted them to suggest measures through which science and technology might reduce the peril. A subcommittee subsequently entitled the Technological Capabilities Panel, and commonly known as the Killian Committee, was formed under James Killian, the president of MIT. Gardner gave the panel its first briefing, focusing on the ICBM. And Ford got himself appointed a member of the Killian Committee staff.

He managed this maneuver through a friendship he had struck up with another unsung, toiling-in-the-wings figure like himself, David Beckler, the executive director of PSAC. When the subcommittee officially began its inquiry in August 1954 after Eisenhower had reviewed and approved its agenda—which Gardner and Ford also helped to draft—Beckler needed an experienced staff man to assist the panel and to act as its liaison with the Air Force. With Ford prompting, Gardner offered the services of his executive assistant. The offer was not accepted without second thoughts. While the panel members admired Gardner, they were also wary of his zealotry and thus of Ford as his agent. Beckler's private investigation through his own sources at the Pentagon elicited the response that, although Ford might work for Gardner, he was by nature loyal, honest in reporting, and invariably discreet. Ford did not disappoint Beckler, and Killian and the other panel members praised his "exceptional" contribution to their report. He received a letter of commendation on behalf of the president as well. But in retrospect there is also no doubt that, character reference notwithstanding, Ford never wavered from what had become his central mission in life. He did his best to put his finger on the Killian Committee's scale.

The panel's report, delivered in mid-February 1955 to the president and the National Security Council, did address Eisenhower's concern with a surprise attack. It urged reducing SAC's vulnerability by dispersal of its bombers and the creation of a substantial airborne alert. In a separate and ultrasecret recommendation, it also urged the building of the U-2, which, through the lenses of its spy cameras when it began overflights on the Fourth of July 1956, was to ease Eisenhower's worry by providing the first good look into the closed interior of the Soviet Union. The most striking element in the panel's mid-February report, however, was its warning of the strategic consequences if the Soviets achieved an ICBM capability before the United States. "The intercontinental ballistic missile can profoundly affect the military posture of either country," the report said. The panel recommended something without precedent. The NSC had never previously lent its endorsement to a specific weapon system. The panel urged that this now be done, that the council single out the ICBM project "as a nationally supported effort of highest priority." Gardner, Ford, von Neumann, and Schriever were elated, but then nothing happened. Nobody at the top did anything to rescue them from their plight. They learned to their chagrin that it was not enough to lay a report before the president and the National Security Council. One had to follow up by persuading the council and the president that the matter was sufficiently urgent to warrant an NSC Action Memorandum, signed by the president, and spelling out a specific measure or measures, in order to shake the bureaucracy out of its complacency. Otherwise, the system continued on in its blithely obstructionist fashion. Killian and his associates had failed to do this and Eisenhower, apparently still unaware that the Soviets would beat the United States to the launch if corrective steps were not taken, was content to leave ICBMs to the Air Force and the Department of Defense.

The crafty Ford was undaunted. He set in motion his third clandestine campaign. His new friend David Beckler helped him. With Gardner's assent, he remained on Beckler's PSAC staff in the Executive Office Building next to the White House. He had more freedom of action that way. The goal now was to get the subject of the ICBM itself placed on the agenda of the National Security Council so that the president could be fully informed on what needed to be done. The question was how to accomplish this. Arranging for a subject to be placed on the NSC agenda might sound like a trifling formality, but in the world of government bureaucracy, such formalities counted. It was a sine qua non if Schriever, Gardner, and von Neumann were ever to reach Eisenhower.

The NSC was the apex of the elaborate military-style staff system that Eisenhower had constructed to undergird his presidency. The council had originated with the National Security Act of 1947, which had also established the Department of Defense and reorganized the armed forces to provide for an independent U.S. Air Force. Truman had used it, as Paul Nitze's famous NSC-68 policy paper of 1950 on the Soviet threat attests, but in limited fashion. Eisenhower transformed the council, making it his paramount body to formulate, evaluate, and guide military and foreign policy. The president was its chairman and its principal members were the heads of relevant cabinet departments, such as the secretaries of state, defense, and the Treasury, and those at the top of other concerned government organizations, like the chief of the CIA, the chairman of the Atomic Energy Commission, and the chairman and members of the Joint Chiefs of Staff. The staff director was the president's special assistant for national security affairs. Under him was a beehive of sections dealing with the multitude of subjects and issues of interest to the council. The most important element was the NSC Planning Board, because it set the council's agenda. A representative of each of the NSC's principal members sat on it. The Planning Board was, in effect, the back door to the council's deliberations.

One of the board's unwritten but long established rules was that a subject had to be referred to it by the department concerned, in this instance the Department of Defense. That was impossible in the case of the ICBM because Defense Secretary Wilson was opposed to singling out the missile project for special attention to the possible detriment of other high-priority projects. Beckler suggested that Ford resort to a flanking movement to get around this obstacle—going though the State Department's Policy Planning Council, the new, more elegant name for the old Policy Planning Staff. Assistant Secretary of State Robert Bowie was chairman of the Planning Council and also sat on the NSC Planning Board as the representative of John Foster Dulles, Eisenhower's secretary of state. Beckler introduced Ford to a civil servant who proved immensely helpful—Carlton Savage, executive secretary of State's Planning Council. Tall, slim, and courtly, Savage was an old-timer at the State Department, a friend of Cordell Hull, Franklin Roosevelt's secretary of state during the Second World War. He differed from many in the civil servant tribe, however, in that he had imagination and courage. As soon as he understood the importance of what Ford was about, he gave him his full support. At Ford's request, he arranged a briefing by Gardner and von Neumann for his own superior, Robert Bowie, and a number of other senior State officials, including Robert Murphy, the deputy undersecretary of state for political affairs; Loy Henderson, the deputy undersecretary for administration; and Chip Bohlen, the Soviet specialist and current ambassador to Moscow, who happened to have been called home to assist with preparations for Eisenhower's first summit meeting in Geneva in July with Stalin's successors to the leadership of the Soviet Union. The objective was to make the diplomats realize the psychological and political repercussions on America's European allies if the Soviets were able to threaten with a weapon like the ICBM and the United States had no equivalent to deter them. The briefing went extremely well and the State Department was won to the cause.

Ford was enjoying himself immensely at all of this maneuvering. Years later, he was to write of "the fun and excitement and challenge of roaming the Washington jungle when you're hot on the trail of a major blow for freedom." Throughout the period, unbeknownst to Beckler or

Savage, Ford kept working the Senate angle, arranging more furtive meetings with Scoop Jackson. He saw to it that the senator always had a supply of fuel for his subcommittee hearings from Schriever's classified reports delivered by Boatman. To cover his movements, Ford adopted various tricks, including the use of public telephone booths for calls he did not want anyone to be able to trace back to Beckler's or Gardner's offices. He jokingly referred to these afterward as "my many carefully staked out field offices around Washington—a telephone booth in the Pentagon, or over at State, or in the nearest bar, or perhaps my favorite field office on the lower deck of the Army-Navy Club—the phone booth right at the bottom of the stairs, not the other one." (The anonymity of public phones in the 1950s appealed to others besides Ford. They were a favorite communications system of the Mafia.)

In addition to Savage, Beckler also introduced Ford to another figure who was to be of considerable aid in placing the ICBM on the agenda of the NSC. He was William Yandell Elliott, a professor of government at Harvard, who was in Washington on a temporary stint with a relatively unknown but influential organization called the Office of Defense Mobilization. It too was housed in the Executive Office Building. The Presidential Science Advisory Committee was, in fact, subordinate to it. The ODM was a successor to the Second World War's Office of War Mobilization. During the Truman era it had become another of those skeletal formations to which Eisenhower was to give flesh and vitality. Its stated mission was to centralize management of mobilization activities in the event of conflict, but Eisenhower used it to provide him with general advice on a range of policies. Its head, Arthur Flemming, was a presidential confidant. He saw Eisenhower once a week for lunch, served on the president's four-man Committee on Government Reorganization (an attempt at reform at which Eisenhower and his committee were not successful), and held a seat as a full member of the NSC.

Professor Elliott was Flemming's representative on the NSC Planning Board. To impress Elliott, and a civil servant named Vincent Rock, who was Elliott's alternate on the board, Ford brought to bear his full battery—briefings by Gardner, von Neumann, and Schriever. He had shied away from including Schriever in the State Department briefing, thinking the danger of exposure there too great for a military man. The EOB was less conspicuous. Elliott and Rock became com-

mitted partisans and in turn recruited James Lay, the executive secretary of the NSC. The result was that when the critical meeting of the
NSC Planning Board took place that June of 1955, the Pentagon representatives found themselves outweighed by Bowie from the State Department, Elliott and Rock from the Office of Defense Mobilization,
and Lay in the Secretariat. They backed down, the ICBM was placed
on the NSC agenda, and the way was now open to speak directly to the
president.

Had the road to the NSC on which Beckler had set Ford been
blocked, he and Schriever, and Gardner and von Neumann, had another and so far hidden path prepared. On June 30, 1955, Eisenhower
received a five-page letter signed by two senators. One was Jackson.
The other was Clinton Anderson, a Democrat from New Mexico. If
Jackson had clout, Anderson had a lot more. He was chairman of the
Joint (House and Senate) Committee on Atomic Energy, to which Jackson's Subcommittee on Military Applications belonged. He had also
visited Schriever's California organization in the fall of 1954 and reacted sympathetically to what he had seen and heard. He had then followed Jackson's hearings and volunteered to co-sign the letter with
him. There was no way the president could ignore the letter, even if he
had wanted to do so. It described the obstacles the missile enterprise
was encountering and recommended a series of radical changes to remove them. Among these were a separate budget for the ICBM independent of all other Air Force needs and an exemption from any
Pentagon procurement regulation that hindered advancement. It also
recommended that Eisenhower designate the program as carrying the
highest national priority and that he arrange to be briefed on the project at the first opportunity. In short, the letter to the president contained all that Ford, Schriever, Gardner, and von Neumann could have
wished, and with good reason. In a final act of legerdemain, Ford,
Schriever, and Gardner had drafted it for Jackson and Anderson to
sign. Eisenhower instructed Arthur Flemming to organize a briefing at
the next meeting of the NSC. The briefing would have to wait until the
end of July because Eisenhower was readying himself for his first summit confrontation in Geneva on July 18 with Stalin's heirs.

A DIFFICULT DIALOGUE AT GENEVA

By 1955, the Cold War had persisted for the better part of a decade. The attitudes initially formed among the policy-making elite in Harry Truman's time had congealed into an American theology that purported to explain the dynamics of Communism worldwide. The consensus among the few at the top had become the consensus of the nation. The beliefs were taken for granted and were shared by virtually all Americans, from President Eisenhower down to a worker on an automotive assembly line in Flint, Michigan. One can hear these beliefs repeated mantralike in Eisenhower's memoir of his first four years in the White House, *Mandate for Change*. Such phrases as "the dangers of international Communism," "the international Communist conspiracy," "Communist subversion," "the Marxist theory of world revolution and Communist domination," and "the never-ending struggle to stem the tide of Communist expansionism" are replete throughout the text. No one yet understood the extent to which this theology got in the way of perceiving reality and would thus lead to the disastrous consequence of the war in Vietnam.

It was a tribute to Eisenhower that where his Soviet opponents were concerned he managed to get past enough of this truth-obscuring dogma to deal with them on a human basis. His secretary of state, John Foster Dulles, had been opposed to a summit meeting in Geneva with the Soviet Union's post-Stalin leadership. He was afraid that the inevitable news photos of Eisenhower shaking hands with Nikita Khrushchev, who had risen to general secretary, that is, chief, of the Soviet Communist Party, since Stalin's death, might destroy the image of America's moral integrity, resonate badly with the public, and "lull" America's allies into a dangerous complacency. Eisenhower had appointed Dulles to head the State Department because he and Senator Arthur Vandenberg had been the recognized foreign policy spokesmen of the Republican Party. A prominent figure in the New York legal establishment, Dulles was a rigid ideologue. "The Soviets have a world plan to overthrow capitalism wherever it may be and to substitute police states," he said in a speech to the influential Council on Foreign Relations in New York in April 1947, and never changed his lyrics. But when, in the spring of 1955, the Soviets suddenly announced that they would join the United States, Britain, and France in signing a peace treaty with Austria, ending military occupation of that country and restoring its independence and territorial integrity in exchange for some reparations to Russia and other nonpunitive conditions, Eisenhower overruled Dulles. He decided there might be some hope for compromise agreements or at least an easing of tensions. He instructed Dulles to inform the Russians that he was interested in a summit and in mid-June 1955 they agreed. Prime Minister Anthony Eden of Britain and Edgar Faure, serving his second term as one of the revolving prime ministers in the chronically unstable French Fourth Republic, would also attend, making the meeting a "Big Four" conference in the newspaper parlance of the day.

Looking across the negotiating table in the Council Chamber of Geneva's Palais des Nations, a vast classical structure erected between 1929 and 1938 to house the ill-starred League of Nations that had emerged from the First World War, Eisenhower wondered which of the five members of the Soviet delegation facing him was the boss. Ostensibly, the delegation was being led by the portly Nikolai Bulganin, the equivalent of prime minister in the Soviet hierarchy as chairman of the Council of Ministers. He might, however, be performing to a score composed by one or a combination of the other three big men: Eisenhower's acquaintance from the Second World War Marshal Georgi Zhukov, currently the Soviet Union's minister of defense; Vyacheslav Molotov, the minister of foreign affairs; or Khrushchev. Only the fifth member, Andrei Gromyko, deputy foreign minister, was junior enough to actually rank as advertised. Before the conference had concluded, Eisenhower would find out.

On the afternoon of the fourth day, July 21, 1955, Eisenhower opened the box on his surprise arms-control proposal—Open Skies. The plan amounted to legalized aerial arms inspection. The United States, the Soviet Union, and any other participating nations would provide one another with blueprints locating and fully describing all of their military installations at home and abroad. The participants would then be allowed to station aircraft at fields within reach of these facilities and to conduct photoreconnaissance and inspection flights to verify the information they had been given. The stationing of the aircraft and the frequency and nature of the flights would be subject to reasonable conditions, which Eisenhower spelled out, but otherwise Soviet and American fliers would have open skies before them to detect any cheating.

The heavens did not react auspiciously to Eisenhower's proposition. As soon as he had finished speaking, there was a deafening clap of thunder from an electrical storm outside the *palais* and the Council Chamber was flung into darkness. Eisenhower broke the amazed silence of his audience by remarking that he had never dreamt he would be "so eloquent as to put the lights out." Everyone laughed and the Swiss engineers managed to restore the lights and air-conditioning in a few minutes. Then, after Anthony Eden of Britain and Edgar Faure of France had endorsed the plan warmly, the delegates hung on the Soviet response. The day before, the Soviets had proposed their arms control monitoring scheme. It consisted of fixed ground inspection posts on main highways, and at railway junctions, airfields, and the like. Eisenhower had rejected it, pointing out that a similar scheme had been tried in Korea under the armistice there and the Chinese and North Koreans had taken advantage of it to cheat blatantly because the inspectors could not move about. There was thus considerable suspense as to what Bulganin would say. His reply, as Eisenhower wrote, was unexpected. He said that "the proposal . . . seemed to have real merit, and the Soviets would give it complete and sympathetic study at once." And the Soviet who mattered did give it immediate if unsympathetic study.

At the end of each day's formal session, there was a cocktail hour. Eisenhower favored it because he thought it would help the leaders to relax and do business informally. He always mingled with the Soviet delegation. On this particular afternoon, he found Khrushchev walking beside him to the lounge. Referring to Bulganin by his title, Khrushchev suddenly said through an interpreter, "I don't agree with the chairman." He smiled as he spoke, but "there was no smile in his voice," Eisenhower recalled. "I saw clearly then, for the first time, the identity of the real boss of the Soviet delegation." It was the first encounter between a president of the United States and the man who was to rule the Soviet Union for the next nine years: Nikita Sergeyevich Khrushchev, short, pudgy, balding, with ears that stuck out too far and little eyes that fixed one with their gaze, maddeningly complicated, of boundless energy, Stalinist henchman turned reformer, seeking to put a human face on Soviet Communism and then having to ruthlessly quell the turmoil his liberalizing unleashed, truth teller and yet addict of the dangerous gamble and the perilous bluff. With Bohlen interpreting in the cocktail lounge, Eisenhower pressed on, attempting to persuade Khrushchev of the merits of the scheme. It was mutually beneficial and entirely trustworthy. Everything would be out in the open, he argued. Khrushchev kept claiming that the NATO countries were planning aggression against the Soviet Union, Eisenhower said. Now he could satisfy himself by tracking all of NATO's movements.

Khrushchev wanted none of it. He told Eisenhower, as Bohlen remembered, that he did not question the president's motives, "but in effect whom are you trying to fool? In our eyes this is a very transparent espionage device, and those advisers of yours who suggested it know exactly what they were doing. You could hardly expect us to take this seriously." Bohlen had predicted that the Soviets would reject the proposal. They would see it as exposing their weaknesses, that they did not have the fleet of long-range bombers the Americans thought they had and they had reduced the size of the Red Army for economic reasons. Like Stalin, they would also fear the possible introduction of Western influences into their closed society and they shared his fetish for internal secrecy. Years later Khrushchev told his son Sergei that he thought the United States would have used the proposal to refine its nuclear targeting plan for the Soviet Union.

Eisenhower was sincere in proffering his Open Skies idea. He was not simply seeking the public relations benefit he reaped from its announcement. He was convinced that eliminating the possibility of surprise attack for both sides would dramatically lessen the possibility of nuclear war. In contrast to LeMay and others who thought like him, Eisenhower was also conscious of the lethal aftereffects of nuclear weapons. He said at the Geneva meeting that fallout alone from a nuclear war between the United States and the Soviet Union would destroy the entire Northern Hemisphere. He kept strengthening the Strategic Air Command and building more and more powerful nuclear weapons because that seemed to be the only possible military edge over the Soviets, given the estimates at the time of their ground strength facing Western Europe.

What Khrushchev did not know was that if he said no, Eisenhower was going to open the Soviet Union's skies anyway. As the delegates met in Geneva in July 1955, the first U-2 was, in conditions of utmost secrecy, being completed and readied for flight testing from a dry lake bed amidst the desolate mountains and wild, arid country northwest of Las Vegas, Nevada. Within a year, this odd-looking aircraft, in reality a long-winged glider propelled by a jet engine and carrying a special high-altitude, high-resolution camera, would make its first spy flight over Russia. And Khrushchev was to rage at each subsequent flight the U-2 was to make over the following four years, until the Soviets finally fielded an antiaircraft missile capable of shooting it down, because he would know that Eisenhower would know when he was bluffing. "I'll give it [Open Skies] one shot," Eisenhower said just before the Geneva summit to the minuscule circle of aides who knew of the plane's existence. "Then, if they don't accept, we'll fly the U-2."

Except for Eisenhower's Open Skies surprise, little of moment occurred at the July 1955 Geneva summit. Major issues, such as the status of postwar Germany, that might once have been susceptible of negotiation, were by now glacialized into the same frozen forms as the theology of the Cold War. The United States was not about to agree to demilitarize what Stalin's strategic disasters, the Berlin Blockade and the Korean War, had helped bring to birth in the increasingly prosperous and rearmed West German state, which was a member of the new West European Union and in the front line of NATO. Nor were the Soviets about to march out of their former occupation zone, the East German state their troops were now propping up, and accept a reunified and remilitarized Germany. Eisenhower and Dulles were determined to bring up the position of the Baltic and East European nations, even though they knew the Soviets would refuse to negotiate on the subject. In fact, the Soviets now had no space to maneuver there either because they soon faced revolt, not conditions for relaxation, in what they regarded as their sensitive security zone, the invasion route in 1914 and again in 1941.

Stalin's tyranny had stoked ferocious anger and resentment among

the populations of the East European nations. Khrushchev's liberalizing actions within the Soviet Union, his release of thousands of victims
from the labor camps of Siberia, his moves to posthumously rehabili-
tate innocent Party members who had been purged and shot, and, most
seismic of all, the secret speech he was to give on February 25, 1956,
at the Twentieth Congress of the Soviet Communist Party denouncing
Stalin's crimes—soon not so secret as copies were distributed within
Russia and Eastern Europe—were like gasoline thrown on the glowing
coals of this pent-up fury.

     The first eruption was to be a dramatic strike by workers in the
Polish city of Poznan in June 1956 crying for "Bread and Freedom."
Poland's Communist leaders put down the strike with their own army
and Interior Ministry troops, killing at least fifty-three of the workers
and wounding hundreds. That October, however, desperate to hold on,
they moved to make Wladyslaw Gomulka the new prime minister. Gomulka was the national Communist who had wanted to take Poland
into the Marshall Plan in 1947. He had escaped an NKVD bullet but
only recently emerged from the prison in which Stalin's agents had put
him. This and the ouster of Konstantin Rokossovsky, a Polish-born
Red Army marshal and hero of the Second World War whom the Russians had imposed on the Poles as their minister of defense, led
Khrushchev and others in Moscow to conclude that Poland was about
to divorce the Soviet Union. He ordered Soviet troops based there to
begin moving on Warsaw. The Poles started mobilizing their own
forces. A madcap confrontation occurred at Warsaw airport and continued into the city after Khrushchev landed on October 19 with a delegation that included a dozen ranking Soviet military men in dress
uniform and began shouting about Polish traitors. An equally tense
Gomulka convinced him that the Polish Party could rule in its own
house and would remain a Soviet ally, but that if Russian troops entered Warsaw "it will become virtually impossible to control events."
In other words, the Poles would fight. Khrushchev decided to trust him
and called off the troops, and Gomulka proved as good as his word.

     But that same month, events did become impossible to control in
Hungary. Despite juggling Hungarian Communist politicians and dispatching thousands of Soviet troops and tanks to Budapest to try to intimidate the rebels, a full-scale revolution broke out across the country.
Hungarian secret policemen were lynched from lampposts, Hungarian

army units defected, and Russian tanks were assailed with Molotov cocktails—bottles filled with gasoline and set alight to engulf the armored vehicles in flames. Khrushchev vacillated and then smashed the rising at the beginning of November 1956 because, given the Soviet Union's sense of its own security, he had no choice. Approximately 20,000 Hungarians and 1,500 Red Army troops were killed or injured.

The Geneva summit did result in the first cultural, educational, and scientific exchanges between the United States and the USSR and brought, for a time, a lessening of tensions in what was called "the Spirit of Geneva." The summit also gave Eisenhower an opportunity for a private and, it was hoped, productive luncheon chat with his old military associate from the victory days in Germany Marshal Zhukov. They met alone at the villa where Eisenhower was staying, their interpreters, Bohlen for Eisenhower and Oleg Troyanovsky for Zhukov, the only other participants in the lunch. Georgi Zhukov had been the greatest of the Soviet military leaders of the Second World War—physically and morally courageous and a bold and imaginative strategist. Zhukov was the man to whom Stalin had always turned when the situation was most despairing. It was he who had held Moscow in the stand-and-die, there-is-no-room-to-retreat battles in the fall and early winter of 1941, when the Wehrmacht's panzers had penetrated the suburbs of the capital and German officers could see the towers of the Kremlin in the distance. And once more in August 1942, when Stalin's military blundering had brought the Germans to the verge of capturing Stalingrad, crossing the Volga, and driving south to sever the link to the precious oil fields of Azerbaijan, without which Russia could not survive, Stalin had taken the extraordinary step of appointing Zhukov deputy supreme commander to rescue the situation. In the summer of 1945, at Stalin's invitation, Eisenhower had stood with Zhukov and Stalin on the Lenin Mausoleum in Moscow's Red Square to witness one of the victory parades. To Zhukov had been given the honor of leading the first and grandest of these parades earlier that summer astride a prancing white horse. Eisenhower remembered him from their time together in Germany as a self-reliant, confident, and cheerful man, so certain of his position in the Soviet hierarchy that on one occasion he had dismissed from the room Andrei Vyshinsky, the infamous prosecutor at the 1930s purge trials, who was serving as Zhukov's political adviser and coincidentally as Stalin's spy, so that the two men could discuss a problem alone with their interpreters.

In his memoir, Eisenhower's comments about Zhukov reveal how difficult it was for the leaders on both sides of the Cold War to comprehend conditions in each other's societies. He wrote of Zhukov as having been in their Germany days "a great personal friend of Stalin's," a figure "perhaps second only to Stalin himself." Friendship, of course, was as foreign to Stalin as Greek, and it was precisely Zhukov's prominence and popularity as a war hero that put him in grave peril from Stalin's paranoia once Hitler had been defeated and Zhukov's talents were no longer needed. As soon as he could, later in the 1940s, Stalin, with Beria's assistance, had concocted the usual treason charges. Several officers who had served under Zhukov were arrested and false confessions beaten out of them in the cellars of Lubyanka Prison. Zhukov had been saved because the other ranking Red Army marshals and generals who sat on the Military Council had said emphatically that they did not believe the accusations. (Perhaps recalling the fate of their predecessors, who had mistakenly thought to save themselves by acquiescing in the condemnation of Marshal Mikhail Tukhachevsky in 1937, they had reasoned that if the foremost among them again went down, they would all go down one by one.) Stalin had contented himself by demoting Zhukov to command of the Odessa military district. The marshal had recovered his career with Stalin's heirs by joining the plot, cunningly guided by Khrushchev, to accomplish the arrest and execution of Beria in 1953. The chief of the secret police was the one heir of Stalin whom the other heirs could not allow to live. They had feared, probably correctly, that if he gained paramountcy he would liquidate them all.

Not knowing the decade-long interregnum through which his acquaintance had passed, Eisenhower observed at the lunch in Geneva that "Zhukov was no longer the same man he had been in 1945." The Soviet marshal now seemed "subdued and worried." When the president shifted the talk from wartime reminiscences at the outset of the lunch to serious discussion of the issues of the summit, Zhukov simply reiterated, "in a low monotone," what Eisenhower had been hearing from the other Soviet participants. "He spoke as if he was repeating a lesson that had been drilled into him until he was letter perfect . . . devoid of animation, and he never smiled or joked, as he used to do," Eisenhower wrote. "My old friend was carrying out orders of his superiors. I obtained nothing from this private chat other than a feeling of sadness." And so Eisenhower abandoned serious subjects and asked Zhukov near the end of the lunch what he planned to do for a vacation. Zhukov replied that he was going to fish for trout in European Russia. It turned out that he did not favor fly-fishing, to which Eisenhower was addicted, but preferred a spinning reel and rod to cast a lure. The president promised to send him a set of American spinning equipment through Bohlen's embassy in Moscow. He was true to his word and accompanied the fishing gear with a note saying that he hoped Zhukov would catch "a lot of big ones." The West German intelligence service learned of the existence of the note, but not its harmless contents, and informed the elderly and prickly chancellor of the Federal Republic, Konrad Adenauer. He, for some bizarre reason, suspected that Eisenhower might be attempting to sabotage his efforts to make West Germany robust and independent. He complained privately that his American ally was conducting secret talks with the Soviets, using Zhukov as a channel. But by this time Eisenhower was long back at the White House, in a mood to listen to a briefing on how to build an ICBM.

46.

DAZZLING THE MONARCH

Bennie Schriever arrived at the White House at 9:30 A.M. on July 28, 1955, half an hour before the scheduled briefing for the president. Trevor Gardner and Johnny von Neumann were with him in the back seat of one of the Pentagon's long black Cadillac limousines as the car entered the rear gate to the White House grounds and made its way slowly up the circular drive. Schriever had been informed on July 11 that the briefing would take place on the 28th and they had been readying themselves ever since, most intensively after

Bennie flew in from California on the 22nd. It had been decided that Schriever would anchor the briefing by wrapping up at the end. Gardner would go first with an introduction on the strategic significance of the ICBM. Von Neumann would follow with an explanation of how the invention of the hydrogen bomb and the ability to size it down, the "thermonuclear breakthrough," had made an ICBM practicable. Bennie would conclude with a description of the unique organization the Air Force had formed with Ramo-Wooldridge to overcome the technological hurdles, and lay out the deadlines set for the building of the missile and its costs. Then they would run a short reel of 16mm film depicting fiery scenes of the rocket engines Ed Hall was experimenting with being tested on concrete stands across the continent in California. The film would constitute a bit of showmanship at the end if the president seemed inclined to let them take the additional time for it.

They had been told by the NSC staff that they were restricted to half an hour in all for the three presentations. Power, who participated in the planning and rehearsals, did not think this would be nearly enough time to get across a subject of such strategic and technical breadth to a lay audience, but Gardner, von Neumann, and Schriever believed that if they compressed hard enough and kept things simple, they would be able to get their main points across.

The worst restriction had been laid on them two days earlier by Dillon Anderson, Eisenhower's special assistant for national security affairs and as such head of the NSC staff, at a meeting in his offices in the Executive Office Building. Anderson had warned them that they were to confine their presentations to "straightforward and factual" descriptions of the project, that there was to be no attempt to "sell" the president on their needs or "pressure" him. "In particular, you will not comment on, or make any reference to, or use in any way," he said, the letter Eisenhower had received on June 30 from Scoop Jackson and Clinton Anderson. (Dillon Anderson obviously had no idea he was addressing its ghost authors, or they might not be briefing the president two days hence.) Any recommendation to the president to order the radical changes advocated in the letter—a separate budget for the ICBM exclusive of all other Air Force needs, exemption from any Pentagon procurement regulation that might impede its progress, and a designation of the highest national priority—should come from Secretary Wilson on behalf of the Department of Defense, not just from the Air Force through them.

In an indication that he did not view with favor this wish list the plotters were hoping would emerge from their briefing for the president, Anderson remarked that "there are other important areas—in addition to the ICBM—which bear heavily on the national security and which warrant Presidential support." He mentioned SAC, the Air Defense Command, and a new early warning radar system under construction on the Aleutian Islands off Alaska, on Alaska's north coast, and thence through the Arctic regions of Canada to Greenland and Iceland. It was called the DEW Line, for Distant Early Warning. "If we set up one project for high Presidential priority, then we are, in effect, downgrading the others," he said. His listeners surmised that Secretary Wilson's delegates on the NSC Planning Board had preceded them to Anderson. "Termites in the woodwork," Schriever wrote in his diary that night. The best hope the plotters had of getting around this restriction was to convince the president that the ICBM was not just another parochial Air Force project, but rather an issue of the most acute national and international significance. They had to arouse sufficient enthusiasm in him, win him so thoroughly to their cause, that he would see the need for these extraordinary measures himself when he took another look at the Jackson-Anderson letter after their briefing.

Vince Ford and Beryl Boatman had preceded them to the White House much earlier with the paraphernalia for the briefing. Their blue Air Force staff car had pulled up to the guard cubicle just inside the northwest gate to the White House off Pennsylvania Avenue at precisely 7:30 A.M. They had been instructed by the NSC staff to arrive two and a half hours beforehand in order to have plenty of time to complete their preparations. In the trunk behind them were the briefing charts, easels to set the charts on, a blackboard and a box of white chalk for illustrations, a pointer, and the reel of 16mm film displaying Ed Hall's rocket engine experiments. Vince told the White House policeman inside the cubicle who they were and why they were there. The policeman glanced at a sheet of paper and said, "Just a moment, please," while he turned, picked up a telephone, and apparently called someone inside for clearance. "Okay," he said into the phone, "I'll send them in." He turned back and, addressing them politely as "Gentlemen," instructed them to proceed along the drive and bear to the right until they saw a ramp that would take them to the lower level of the West Wing of the White House. Someone would meet them at the doorway there.

Ford and Boatman set to work swiftly, setting up the easels, the blackboard with the chalk within easy reach, and the small, roll-down screen on which they were to show the film. It was placed on the podium at the front of the room, behind and to one side of the lectern that was already there, so that the president and others in the briefing audience could see it without obstruction. They left nothing to chance. They had not brought a 16mm film projector with them because they had been told that the White House had one. As their first move, Boatman ran a segment of the film to check out the machine and be certain it was in good order. They had calculated that if the machine malfunctioned, they would have plenty of time to send to the Pentagon for a substitute. The site of the briefing was a comparatively small room with a shallow arched ceiling on the lower level of the West Wing known as the Broadcast Room. It was often used for briefings and on this humid Washington morning in July it was filled with rows of straight-back wooden chairs. The one exception to this austere seating was a capacious, plumply stuffed red leather armchair in the center of the first row for the comfort of the president.

Ford was familiar with the place. He had been there in mid-February when James Killian, the president of MIT, and his committee had briefed Eisenhower and the NSC on reducing the vulnerability of SAC by dispersing its bombers and increasing the number on airborne alert. The silence of the room and the rows of chairs "had a strange kind of eloquence," Ford thought, because of the importance of the men who would soon be sitting in them and the importance to the nation of what they would soon be hearing. This was the era when the freshness of the triumph over Nazi Germany and Imperial Japan and the enormous power and paramountcy of the United States among the non-Communist nations had endowed the president and the surroundings in which he lived and worked with a monarchical aura. Ford had been conscious of "mixed feelings of awe" from the moment the staff car had passed through the White House gate. As he and Boatman went about their work in the Broadcast Room "electricity filled the air all around us."

They were done before they knew it. The time was still only 8:20

A.M. The big men of the land would not start gathering in the Broadcast Room for more than an hour at the earliest and so they went in search of a caffeine lift. A policeman in the corridor outside the room directed them to a small coffee bar in the West Wing basement that the White House police used. The cups of hot black liquid helped "calm the butterflies we knew we had but wouldn't admit," Ford recalled.

After the limousine from the Pentagon arrived at 9:30 A.M., Schriever, Gardner, and von Neumann walked down the corridor toward the briefing room. They were an unusual threesome, the portly von Neumann flanked by the long-stem figure of Schriever on one side and the big-shouldered Gardner on the other. They were talking in lively fashion, but von Neumann was apparently dominating the conversation, as both Schriever and Gardner had their heads turned in toward him. As soon as he spotted them, von Neumann said, in his pronounced Hungarian accent and with jovial mock ignorance of the occasion, "Hello Veence, hello Boat, vat iss cooking?" Then his irrepressible curiosity took him over to the door to the briefing room, where he peeked inside. Gardner greeted Ford with a roar, "Dr. von Ford!" in more mock joviality to ease the tension of the occasion, instantly elevating Ford to genius rank in rocketry with Wernher von Braun. "Got any hot coffee?" he asked. When Ford and Boatman returned ten minutes later cups in hand, they found Gardner and Schriever talking to Dillon Anderson and James Lay, the executive secretary of the NSC, apparently about the procedure for the briefing. Johnny von Neumann was sitting in a chair next to the far wall making notes on a small white pad. Von Neumann didn't need notes. Everything he was going to say was already concisely arranged in his head. Perhaps the note making helped him to focus and calm himself.

Gardner, von Neumann, and Schriever would be addressing, in addition to Eisenhower and Vice President Richard Nixon, approximately twenty of the most important civilian and military leaders in the country. The lesser figures like Tommy Power, who was there because the program officially belonged to him, arrived early, not long after 9:30. At 9:50, with just ten minutes to go, the weighty men began strolling into the room in groups of two and three, chatting to one another as they took their seats—Vice President Nixon; Admiral Arthur Radford, chairman of the Joint Chiefs of Staff; John Foster Dulles, secretary of state; his brother, Allen Dulles, head of the CIA. They had been attending a prior meeting of the NSC in the Cabinet Room of the

White House and it had just broken up. At 9:55, with only five minutes to go, Dillon Anderson walked to the podium to make sure that any laggards got themselves seated quickly. "Gentlemen," he said, "if you will please find chairs so that everyone will be in place and seated when the President arrives." Eisenhower, the military man, wanted his meetings to begin with precision.

But then 10:00 A.M. came and passed and 10:05 and 10:10 and the president still did not come. As unobtrusively as he could, Ford got up from his seat in the separate row of chairs arranged against the far wall where von Neumann, Gardner, and Schriever were also sitting. He and Boatman, who had been on station next to the projector at the back of the room, sidled over to the entrance and stepped just outside so that they could spy down the corridor toward a double set of French doors through which the president would emerge. They had not waited long when suddenly the doors swung open and Eisenhower appeared striding at a fast pace down the corridor. He seemed angry about something, his face flushed. Whatever it was apparently concerned Defense Secretary Wilson, who was walking beside him, hurrying to keep up as the two men swept past Ford and Boatman and into the briefing room.

Everyone in the room was standing. The president stopped, glancing around. He spotted his favorite cabinet member, George Humphrey, a Cleveland banker who was secretary of the Treasury, standing next to a chair in the second row. Eisenhower availed himself of the amenities offered by his rich friends and subordinates to take frequent vacations, too frequent in the opinion of his critics. He was obsessed with golf—he had a putting green constructed on the White House lawn—but also enjoyed hunting quail, fly-fishing for trout, and playing bridge. He often spent a week at Humphrey's 13,000-acre Milestone Plantation near Thomasville in south Georgia, shooting quail with Humphrey and golfing at the neighboring Glen Arven Country Club. "Hello, Gawge," he said in a drawl, the anger disappearing as his face metamorphosed into the famous slightly off-center Eisenhower grin. Then he seated himself in the well-padded red leather chair in the first row, rested his elbows on its arms, cupped his big bony hands together, and looked up at Anderson on the podium. The moment had come.

Gardner was out of his chair and halfway to the podium by the time Anderson had finished announcing the subject of the briefing and identifying the three briefers. He laid down on the lectern a couple of white three-by-five-inch cards on which he had jotted notes in red pencil, then stepped off to one side so that he was standing directly in front of the president, about eight to ten feet away. He was at his natty best in dark suit, fashionable tie, and starched white handkerchief crisply folded into the lapel pocket. Nathan Bedford Forrest, a much feared Confederate cavalry leader, boasted that one of the ways he won battles was to put the "sceere" into his opponents. Gardner wasted no time putting the "sceere" into his audience. He explained briefly how the invention of the hydrogen bomb and its projected downsizing had made possible the creation of the intercontinental ballistic missile.

Then he hit them with the consequences. "This breakthrough," he said, "caused an irreversible change in the world power equation, in the waging of war. It says loudly and clearly that not only is it now technically feasible to develop a nuclear-armed ICBM but, more importantly, it is now of overriding importance to the security and survival of the United States that we do it first—ahead of the USSR." He waited a moment or two for his words to register and then he hit them again harder. "Because, gentlemen, this technology is also known to the Soviets—and our intelligence tells us that they are going full out to develop it. It means, gentlemen, that it is now possible to send a ballistic missile armed with a nuclear warhead from the continental United States to Soviet Russia—or vice versa—in roughly thirty minutes." He paused again. The room was absolutely silent. There was no clearing of throats, no shuffling of feet or shifting of chairs. Everyone in the room, including the president, had their eyes fixed on Gardner. That was all he would have to say for the moment, Gardner said, as if half an hour to annihilation was not enough. He then took the time to describe what von Neumann and Schriever would cover in their presentations and turned the briefing over to Johnny.

Von Neumann walked in an unusual sort of toed-in fashion, but there was no lack of dignity in the slightly stout man in the three-piece suit who made his way forward to the podium. He did not mount it. Instead, he took his stance a few feet directly in front of the president and, looking out over his audience, began to speak. He held no notes in his hands. Everything he had to say had been set out with precision in his mind. He had no intimation that on this, one of the most eventful days of his life, he had less than nineteen months in which to live, that a cancer was coursing through his body. He would not learn of it until the following month. But at the moment there was nothing else he could be doing that could give him more contentment. He had arrived finally and fully in his adopted land. He was addressing the most august body in the nation and speaking as the nation's preeminent scientist in matters of nuclear weaponry. His political patron, the financier Lewis Strauss, Eisenhower's appointee as chairman of the Atomic Energy Commission, was sitting in that audience, pleased that he had made Johnny the first foreign-born member of the commission. And everything he had to say would be credible, precisely because he spoke with the gravitas of a scientist whose judgment on these esoteric but utterly important matters had been proven correct again and again over the years.

Johnny now took his audience on a journey into the relationship between weight and yield in hydrogen bombs and the nuclear engineering processes through which these were achieved, on the speed of reentry vehicles—the missile warheads—plunging from space through the atmosphere to carry the bomb to its target on earth, on the latitude to dispense with pinpoint accuracy in the missile because the radius of destruction to be expected from a one-megaton thermonuclear explosion, equal to eighty Hiroshima bombs, was so great. Von Neumann had a knack for making nuclear intricacies comprehensible to laymen and it did not desert him on this morning before the NSC. Bennie's staff out in California had helped by providing him with a chart showing the Atlas as it had been reconfigured into a lighter, more easily transportable ICBM with the one-megaton warhead. Another chart illustrated the flight of the rocket from the flame of its launch to the release of the warhead and the warhead's trajectory through space and then down onto its target. Von Neumann interspersed his technical exegesis with some of the grim phrases that were never far from his mind: "nuclear blackmail" if the Russians got the ICBM first, "no known defense against it," and a fact Gardner might have used to telling effect but had somehow overlooked, only "fifteen minutes' warning" of incoming missiles. (Given the limitations of the American radar system in 1955, Soviet missiles would not be detected until they had reached their apogee halfway through their flight.) Ford, who was again watching the faces, was convinced that von Neumann had lost no one. Indeed, Ford thought, he had "knocked the ball out of the park."

Gardner was on his feet once more striding for the podium the moment von Neumann finished speaking.

"Thanks, Johnny," he said, and then turned to Eisenhower. "Mr. President, General Schriever will now give you a quick rundown on how we are set up to run this thing. Bennie," he said, glancing toward Schriever, who was up and moving. It was already five minutes after 11:00 A.M. Von Neumann had talked far longer than he was supposed to do, long enough to already put them twenty minutes over the half hour they had been allotted in all and Schriever was just beginning. Yet there seemed to be no restlessness, no desire on the part of anyone to leave, certainly not the president, who was all attention.

It did not hurt, in this carefully crafted effort to impress Eisenhower, that Bernard Schriever was without a doubt the handsomest general in the United States Air Force. A *New York Times* reporter would later compare his appearance to that of James "Jimmy" Stewart, the "Slim Jim" Hollywood actor of the period who inevitably played the hero in Westerns and other screen dramas in which he starred. At forty-four, there was still not a wisp of gray in the dark curly hair combed up in a wave above his forehead. The blue eyes looked ahead confidently, the mouth and chin were firm. The litheness of his six-foot, three-inch frame was accentuated by the long, tailored uniform jacket and immaculately pressed trousers in the light tan that officers then wore in summer. The silver wings with the star in the middle encircled by the wreath of a command pilot and the rows of ribbons representing his Purple Heart and Distinguished Service Medal and his other medals and awards for the victorious campaigns in the Pacific were pinned above the left breast pocket. He wore two stars on his shoulder lapels now. On Power's recommendation, he had been promoted to major general seven months earlier. The ever careful Schriever did have notes from which to speak. He placed them on the lectern, his fingers curled around its edge, as he turned to the president, acknowledged the rest of his audience with a sweeping glance, and began.

"My job out in Inglewood," he said, after recapitulating in a couple of sentences Gardner's and von Neumann's remarks, "is to make sure . . . that the United States will have an operational ICBM in the quickest time technology will allow." Then he paused, smiled at Eisenhower, and adroitly plumbed the president's patience. He said he realized they had exceeded their allotment, that he would keep what he had to say as brief as possible, but they also had the eight-minute film of Hall's engine firings to show at the end. Did the president still wish to see it? Everyone in the room understood the gesture. Schriever was deliberately giving Eisenhower an opportunity to cut off or shorten the briefing then and there.

The president did not accept it. He nodded at Schriever to continue and the nod signaled that time was no longer a problem, that Schriever could take whatever time he needed to make his own points.

In describing the organization of the project and what was occurring out in California, Bennie cleverly attributed everything that was being done to the Tea Pot Committee and its recommendations. Furthermore, to capitalize on the credibility of von Neumann and the other distinguished scientists, like Kistiakowsky, who had served on it, he always referred to the group as the Von Neumann Committee. The ploy also enabled him to get around at least partially Dillon Anderson's stricture on not attempting to "sell" or "pressure" Eisenhower. When he described the "radical reorganization" that entailed integrating the Ramo-Wooldridge group into his WDD command and the requirement, once the program got moving, as it now was, for "increased financial support and high project priority," he invariably cited the Von Neumann Committee and its report. He spoke of an imperative need for "the operation of the new group [to] be relieved of excessive, detailed regulation by existing government agencies," meaning streamlined management, as another conclusion drawn from the Von Neumann Committee's findings. Schriever occasionally broke the seriousness of his talk with light detail. "Our first field office, Mr. President," he said, smiling and turning toward Eisenhower, and Vice President Nixon and Secretary of State Dulles, who were sitting on each side of the president, "was an abandoned parochial grammar school in Inglewood, California." Eisenhower nodded once more and gave Bennie a light smile in return.

But the breaks for humor were few as Bennie drove home repeatedly the utter seriousness of the challenge. "Today we are not at war," he said, "at least not in the conventional sense, and yet the importance

and urgency of this project requires the same dedication and competence and all-out effort one would expect to find in wartime." He
forged on, explaining the abstruse, to laymen, management technique
of concurrency he and Ramo had adopted "in the interest of compressing time—our most critical commodity." It was "simply . . . the
development, testing, and perfecting of all major components simultaneously . . . at the right time all [of] this will come together, flow inward, converging finally at a central point in San Diego where it will be
assembled to produce the final product—the ICBM."

He told the president of the plan to develop a second ICBM (it was
to be called Titan) as a hedge in case the Atlas did not fulfill expectations. A fresh chart placed on the easel laid out for Eisenhower the proposed test launch schedule at the Air Force's Eastern Test Range at Cape
Canaveral. He replaced it with yet another chart estimating how much
this investment in rocketry was going to cost the United States, from
$150 million in the current fiscal year to $538 million in Fiscal Year
1958. (As might have been expected, given the pressure Schriever and
Gardner must have felt not to frighten the economy-minded Eisenhower, all of the future estimates turned out to be far below actual
costs.) As Schriever concluded his presentation, Eisenhower was no
longer sitting back relaxed in his commodious armchair. He had shifted
forward and was sitting up straight, intent on what Bennie was saying.
Boatman rolled the film and the briefing climaxed in the roar and flame
of the engine firings.

"Thank you, General Schriever," Eisenhower said warmly when
the film had ended. He turned in his chair to von Neumann and Gardner, who were seated along the far wall. "And my thanks also to you,
Dr. von Neumann, and Mr. Gardner. This has been most impressive,
most impressive!" he said. "There is no question this weapon will have
a profound impact on all aspects of human life, not only in the United
States but in every corner of the globe—military, sociological, political." He turned all the way back, searching down the rows of chairs
behind him. "Where's Radford—is he here today?" Eisenhower asked,
seeking his chairman of the Joint Chiefs of Staff. The president spotted
the admiral almost as soon as he inquired. "Radford, let's war game
this—these long-range missiles—what they will do to the force structure. Do it right away. Let me know what answers you come up with."
He leaned over to say something to Vice President Nixon, then rose

from his chair, smiled, and said, "Thank you once again, General Schriever, Dr. von Neumann, Mr. Gardner." He gave another of his quick nods to recognize everyone else in the rows of seats who rose simultaneously in respect, then walked out of the Broadcast Room alone.

The half-hour ration of the president's time had stretched on into an hour and thirty-five minutes. Gardner, von Neumann, and Schriever "had done the job," Ford thought. "We had introduced the President and the National Security Council to the nuclear missile age." Virtually everyone stopped on the way out to thank Schriever, von Neumann, and Gardner, who had gathered in front of the podium. Twining was among them. He told Bennie how well he had done. Ford had spotted the older general sitting amongst other members of the Joint Chiefs with a satisfied "That's my boy" smile on his face as Eisenhower had complimented Schriever. Nixon and CIA chief Allen Dulles lingered. "Why haven't we started this sooner? What's been the holdup?" the vice president said, tapping the palm of his left hand with the stiffened fingers of his right in a gesture of emphasis that was peculiar to Nixon. Schriever took on the answer and explained once more why, until the thermonuclear breakthrough and the imminence of a relatively light hydrogen bomb warhead, nothing practical had been possible. In Nixon and his concern they clearly had won an advocate at the top of the administration. Allen Dulles then asked what Ford called "cops and robbers" questions. Despite Gardner's opening statement to the gathering that the Russians were "going full out," Ford noted that none of the three men could provide detailed factual answers to Dulles's questions "mostly because of what our intelligence people *didn't* know about Soviet missile progress" (emphasis in the original text of Ford's memoir).

Eisenhower may have been personally won over, but the bureaucratic struggle wasn't at an end. At 3:00 that afternoon Gardner, von Neumann, and Schriever repeated their briefing to the NSC Planning Board. It would be up to the Planning Board to submit an NSC action directive for the president to sign, and in the wording of the directive would lie the key to what action ensued. Schriever recorded the reaction of the board members in his diary. He noted that William Yandell Elliott, the Harvard professor who represented the Office of Defense Mobilization on the board and who had been so helpful in getting the ICBM on the NSC agenda in the first place, was still "a friend in court." And be-

cause of Wilson's opposition, the Pentagon representative, Brigadier
General Charles Bonesteel, the defense secretary's military aide, was still
"reasonably negative." Again by custom the Pentagon, as the department concerned, had the privilege of drafting the directive. Its draft was
an exercise in sophistry. The proposed directive for the president to sign
proclaimed the ICBM "a program of the highest priority," and then fizzled into language that would entail nothing more than what was already being done. But as the maneuvering walked its slow pace on
through August, others with clout in the administration saw the gambit
and moved to negate it. The most important was Richard Nixon, who,
with Eisenhower away on a trout-fishing vacation in Colorado, chaired
a September 8 meeting of the full NSC that would decide the issue. He
invited von Neumann to the meeting to lend a hand and Johnny waded
in with more unnerving talk of nuclear blackmail and only fifteen minutes' warning of incoming Soviet missiles.

NSC Action No. 1433, the presidential directive that emerged and
that Eisenhower signed on September 13, 1955, in offices he and his
staff had taken over as a Summer White House at Lowry Air Force
Base, near Denver, stated that "there would be the gravest repercussions on the national security and on the cohesion of the free world" if
the Soviet Union acquired an ICBM before the United States did. The
president was therefore designating the ICBM project "a research and
development program of the highest priority above all others." He ordered the secretary of defense to build it with "maximum urgency."
The plotters had won none too soon. Ten days later Eisenhower suffered his first heart attack. It would be two months before he was able
to preside over a gathering on the scale of the July 28 missile briefing,
and that was a cabinet meeting under controlled circumstances at the
presidential retreat at Camp David, Maryland.

47

NO MORE NITPICKING

Those words, "highest priority above all others" and "maximum urgency," were what Gardner and Schriever had been scheming and hoping for so long. They lost no time seizing the momentum a president's pronouncements could release. With forty-two potential naysayers in their path, Bennie and his staff at WDD in California had been driven to distraction by the hurdles races they constantly had to run to get anything accomplished. One day at the Pentagon, Schriever had grown so exasperated with an Air Force functionary called the deputy assistant secretary for logistics that his habitual self-control had shattered like a glass hitting the floor. "You son of a bitch," he had abruptly shouted at the man, "you are holding up the whole goddamn program." His surprise loss of temper had intimidated the bureaucrat and won the argument for him on this occasion, but obviously one could not do business like this on an everyday basis and survive.

In late August, Schriever had begun to document precisely how this bureaucratic octopus held the ICBM project in its tentacles. Bennie had his staff draw up a dozen flip charts listing the multitude of offices and agencies involved and illustrating, with lines going here and there in a bewildering, crisscrossing maze, how many had to be contacted to approve what and how long the tortured process was taking. When they were completed, Schriever dubbed them his "spaghetti charts," and headed off to Washington to brief Gardner. As he went through one chart after another even Gardner, who had heard so often from Schriever of what an incredible tangle they were encountering, was astonished. "Let's go down and see Quarles," he said as soon as Schriever was done, taking him by the arm and marching to Quarles's office. The secretary was about to leave for a meeting, but Gardner was insistent. "Don, you've got to listen to this," he said. With Quarles standing behind his desk, Bennie propped his charts up on an armchair in front and repeated his briefing, this time to Quarles's astonishment. "Is that really what you have to do?" he asked Schriever. Assured that it was, Quarles said, "Well, we've got to do something about this." Turning to Gardner, he said, "Trev, you set up a study effort and come up with some recommendations on how to do it." With this license in his pocket, Gardner proceeded to settle the argument once and for all.

On the same day, September 13, 1955, that Eisenhower signed the NSC directive with the magic words, Gardner named a civilian official to head such a study who was both a supporter of the ICBM enterprise and familiar with the obstacles it was encountering. His name was Hyde Gillette and he was the deputy for budget and program management in the Office of the Assistant Secretary of the Air Force for Financial Management. Gillette formed a twenty-five-member committee and allowed Gardner and Schriever to select its members and to seed it with their own people. Schriever, Ramo, and Ford were members, along with ten of Schriever's officers from WDD. Gillette divided the committee into seven panels to cover all aspects. It met both in Washington and out at WDD. Within five weeks, the work was done. Gardner swiftly approved the committee's report and sent it to Wilson's office on October 21, 1955.

Wilson abandoned his opposition in the face of Eisenhower's decision. He approved the reforms in a memo to Quarles on November 8. Subsequently called the Gillette Procedures, they were a dramatic and drastic streamlining of the decision-making process. Three quarters of the forty-two reviewing agencies and offices were jettisoned and the remaining ten consolidated into two committees. At the top was the Ballistic Missile Committee of the Office of the Secretary of Defense, chaired by Wilson's deputy. Beneath it at the Office of the Secretary of the Air Force level was the Air Force Ballistic Missile Committee. Quarles chaired this committee, but Gardner managed to have himself appointed its vice chairman and liaison with its OSD counterpart. The Gillette Procedures pushed authority downward to those who were doing the work. Schriever was to decide how the job was to be done. His WDD command was to draw up and present to Quarles's committee on December 1, 1955, a comprehensive five-year plan covering everything from missile design to trial launches at Cape Canaveral. Gone were the days of piecemeal requests and incessant bureaucratic tussles to obtain permission for each and every element of the project. Everything would be included in one document. Authorization to proceed would be granted by Quarles's committee in one-year increments for the year currently under consideration. This was subject to review by the higher committee at Wilson's level, but approval was virtually automatic. Once authorization had been given, the plan for that year's work became the equivalent of a directive that Schriever could use as a shield to ward off interference by anyone.

He and Gardner did not succeed in getting a separate budget for the ICBM. Missile funds would continue to be included within the overall Air Force appropriation. But they got the next best thing to it. A budget annex accompanied the comprehensive development plan submitted to Quarles's committee and, once approved, the funds became the WDD budget for that year. No other Air Force organization could touch them. As a fillip to their achievement, Gardner and Schriever arranged for scientific advice that would be critical when necessary but unfailingly supportive. The ICBM Scientific Advisory Committee that von Neumann had helped them to organize under his chairmanship for WDD was named the scientific advisory body for both the Wilson and Quarles committees. The same November 8 memo from Wilson to Quarles approving the Gillette Procedures stated that "the Air Force ballistic missile programs [would] be subject to no other outside scientific consultant review." Bennie Schriever's troubles were by no means at an end. In some ways, they were just beginning. But two and a half years after his pilgrimage to von Neumann's office at Princeton, the road ahead of him was finally open.

48.

A RADAR IN TURKEY

One day in September 1954, at General Electric's facilities in Syracuse, New York, a retired Air Force officer who had worked in R&D at the Pentagon and then been hired by GE's marketing department walked into the office of Burton Brown. A genial man who towered six feet, six inches, Brown was a specialist in long-

distance radar. "Is there any way you could build a radar that would
see a missile at a thousand miles?" the retired Air Force officer asked.

"Well, I don't know. Maybe. What have you got in mind?" Brown
replied. The retired officer had become acquainted with Trevor Gardner while still on active duty and would stop by to see Gardner whenever he happened to be in Washington. He had done so on his latest
sales-generating trip. He said Gardner had told him that the Soviets
were test-launching guided missiles from a site near the port of Odessa
on the Ukrainian coast of the Black Sea. Gardner wanted to intercept
and track the missiles in order to learn as much as possible about their
capabilities. "Let me think about it a little bit," Brown said.

When he saw the man the next day, Brown said he might have a solution. Radar works by sending out pulses of high-frequency electromagnetic waves. The waves bounce off the targeted object or objects
and are picked up by a receiver. Depending on how the receiver is designed, the radar operator can detect the distance, direction, and speed
of moving objects like aircraft or ships, or the location of stationary
objects like buildings. The difficulty in this case was that radar waves
are sent out on line-of-sight beams. The curvature of the earth over the
roughly 1,000-mile distance between possible sites in West Germany
and Odessa might be sufficiently great so that the beams would over-
shoot the missiles, and the rockets would fly under the beams. Brown
did not see the problem as insurmountable. He proposed to overcome
it by constructing an extremely large transmitting station in Germany
that would direct huge electromagnetic waves down toward Odessa.
He would then put the receiver that was to pick up the reflection of the
radar waves off the missiles much closer to Odessa, on the coast of
Turkey across the Black Sea just south of the Soviet Union. The proximity of the receiver to the launching ground should enable them to
pick up enough reflections of the radar waves to track the missiles.

The following Monday, a visitor from the Pentagon appeared in
Brown's office, identified himself as Dr. Chalmers Sherwin, chief scien-
tist of the U.S. Air Force, and said, "Let me hear your proposal."
Brown described it. The visitor listened and then thanked Brown and
left. There were no questions. Brown assumed that meant the end of
the matter. But on Tuesday he got a telephone call from someone in
Trevor Gardner's office. Mr. Gardner wanted Brown to fly down to
Washington the next day and brief him on the proposal. Brown and an

associate prepared some charts and dutifully appeared in Gardner's office at the Pentagon on Wednesday. Gardner, like the scientist, listened quietly during the briefing, saying little, which surprised Brown. Gardner's reputation for aggressiveness had reverberated to Syracuse and Brown had expected to be handled roughly. As he put it in an interview in his modular retirement home in Florida forty-three years later, Brown had heard that Gardner was definitely "not a deadpan-type guy." Gardner also raised no questions or objections when Brown told him that the work would take two years and cost about $5 million. At the end of the briefing, Gardner said, "Let me have what you said in writing on Friday." He explained that he was going out of the country and wanted to study the proposal before he left. And so Brown and his associate rushed back to Syracuse, hurriedly put their ideas down on paper, and had a memorandum typed and in Gardner's office by courier on the last day of the week.

On Monday, Burton Brown got another telephone call he was not expecting. It was from an acquaintance of many years who happened to be the senior civilian technician at the Air Force's main electronics facility, the Air Development Center at Rome, New York, about forty miles east of Syracuse. "Hey, what have you been telling Trevor Gardner?" his acquaintance asked. "We have an order from Gardner's office to put you people under contract right now for some kind of radar. What the hell are you talking about? Come on down tomorrow and tell us about it." When Brown arrived at Rome, he found about twenty people assembled in the conference room there to hear him. Two of them, he was to discover, were officers from the Air Technical Intelligence Center at Wright-Patterson Air Force Base near Dayton, the organization Hap Arnold had created to uncover the secrets of German technology, now targeted on the Soviet Union. At the end of Brown's presentation, one of the officers stood up and introduced himself. He was Lieutenant Colonel James Manatt, chief of the guided missiles section at ATIC. "Mr. Brown, that is very interesting, but there are two things wrong with this," he said. "Number one, the launch point is not Odessa." Taken aback, Brown asked where it was. Manatt explained that it was a place called Kapustin Yar, near Stalingrad at the bend of the Volga River. Apparently, the fact that Air Force intelligence knew of the mere existence of Kapustin Yar was considered such a big secret in 1954 that he had previously been deliberately misled. He called for a map and measured off the distance from Odessa to Stalingrad. It was more than 650 miles. He could not possibly pick up missiles being launched that far away with a radar transmitter situated in Germany, no matter how big. The curvature of the earth definitely fell off sufficiently between Germany and Stalingrad so that the missiles would fly under the beams. Despite being misled, Brown felt exceedingly foolish. He regarded himself and GE as under a verbal contract at this point to deliver a radar that could detect and track the Soviet missiles and "here we are sitting with an invalid proposal . . . and it's just all nuts." Manatt had more bad news for him. "The second thing," he announced, "this two-year delivery schedule you have got, that's for the birds. We have to have a radar on the air to see what goes on at the beginning of the next Russian firing season, June first next year [June 1, 1955], not two years from now."

Brown formed a steering committee of radar experts from the Air Development Center at Wright-Patterson, the Lincoln Laboratory at MIT, and elsewhere in academia to puzzle out the problem. They decided to begin with the fact that they were going to have to abandon any attempt at secrecy, such as clandestine radar receiving stations on Turkey's Black Sea coast. To get close enough to observe what was going on at Kapustin Yar, they would have to build the biggest radar installation in the non-Communist world in eastern Turkey. This would put them on the most direct line south from their target. They would still be roughly 800 miles away, however, and so they would have to construct an antenna the size of a football field.

In between committee sessions, Brown studied earthquake maps. Turkey and the entire surrounding area are notorious for violent earthquakes, which pose an obvious threat to a radar installation, particularly one of these gargantuan dimensions. The maps were covered in red to indicate earthquake zones, but Brown noticed one spot about twenty-five to thirty miles in diameter that was relatively earthquake-free. It was just below the city of Diyarbakir, on the upper reaches of the Tigris River in southeastern Turkey, approximately 430 miles southeast of the capital of Ankara. The region is one of the most ancient in the inhabited world, the scene of peoples and empires succeeding one another over many centuries, the land worn down by man and the uses and abuses to which he puts the earth. Antique Diyarbakir is itself built on the ruins of the still more ancient city of Amida. Mount Ararat, the solitary 16,496-foot mountain where the Bible says that Noah's ark landed after the Deluge, rises from the dismal landscape off to the east where Turkey meets Armenia and Iran. The Diyarbakir region is currently known as Turkish Kurdistan, because it is peopled by the Kurds, an originally nomadic, mountain race whose spread of habitation extends over into Armenia and Iran and down into Syria and Iraq. They are Muslims, but neither Arab nor Turk, speak a language of their own, and have struggled unsuccessfully over the more recent centuries to form an independent Kurdistan. Besides being earthquake-safe, Diyarbakir held another advantage for Brown. The Turkish air force had a fair-sized airfield there with a small contingent of U.S. Air Force advisers. Brown could use the airfield as a base from which to scout.

In November 1954, he flew to Turkey with three colleagues from GE, a young geologist, and two officers from the Air Force Security Service's headquarters in San Antonio. The AFSS is the Air Force's electronics spying agency. It listens to the communications and eavesdrops on anything else it can profitably glean on the military activities of opposing nations, in 1954 obviously the Soviet Union and its allies. GE was going to supply the technicians to operate the radar installation, but the AFSS would administer it. They landed in Ankara and then headed down to Diyarbakir in two twin-engine C-47 transports of Second World War vintage. One carried them and a Turkish interpreter and the other a pair of jeeps in which to explore for a site. They bunked at the small compound at the airfield where the U.S. Air Force advisers lived. Brown and the others then went in search of an American Protestant missionary whom they heard had lived in the area for a long time. Brown assumed the man would be familiar with the countryside around the city and thus could help them select a site. Somehow, they left the Turkish interpreter back at the advisers' compound at the airfield. But, spotting some children in the city they thought might help them, they stopped the jeeps and were soon surrounded by a flock of about fifty curious Kurdish youngsters. One of the Americans took out a Turkish/English dictionary and pronounced as best he could the Turkish word for "church." His pronunciation apparently made the word sound to the children like the Turkish one for children's playground.

As Kurds, the children did not speak good Turkish in any case. They all nodded assent and beckoned to the Americans to follow them.

Parking the two jeeps, Brown, the two Air Force officers, the other GE men, and the geologist walked for what seemed about a mile through a labyrinth of dirt streets until they came to a dead end. There was no church nearby. The place looked like a handball court and was clearly a children's play yard. One of Brown's colleagues resorted to sign language. He clasped his hands together and raised them as in prayer. Then he made the sign of the cross. The children understood that immediately and, being militant Muslims, picked up stones and anything else that lay to hand and pelted the Americans, who ran for their lives back down through the dirt streets. They were rescued by some adults who emerged from mud houses at the tumult and stopped the youngsters.

The Turkish interpreter managed to locate the missionary the next day through the local authorities. Brown invited the man and his wife to dinner at the best of the town's hotels. They were a forlorn couple. They had been laboring in Diyarbakir for twenty years and their congregation still numbered only ten people. The wife said the atmosphere was so hostile to the conversion of people to Christianity that she feared they would one day be attacked. The dinner was also Brown's first experience with Turkish food. The hotel was attractive and clean, but the meat and vegetables tasted to him as if they had been cooked in rancid butter. He was glad to get back to the canned American military rations served at the little Air Force compound. The missionary was also of no help in locating a site for the radar installation.

And so Brown and his contingent set off to scout the region about ten miles south of the town. He was appalled at the poverty and desolation. The Kurdish farmers were dressed in baggy pants and sheepskin coats, but went barefoot, despite the November cold. Even the village chief had no shoes. They had few cattle, mainly camels, and their plows, drawn by oxen, were crude wooden contraptions that bit only about three inches into the hard soil as the farmers maneuvered them around the many boulders. Brown thought the fields resembled rock orchards with sprigs of winter wheat showing here and there. He noticed that about one out of every four of the dirty, tatterdly clad children was blind and diseased in one eye. The Turkish interpreter from Ankara regarded these people, with whom he was barely able to communicate, with scorn. (Turkish abuse of the Kurds was to provoke a rebellion in the area during the 1980s that took 30,000 lives.) He told

Brown that the blindness came from filth and indicated that in his opinion the Kurds were a subspecies of humanity. Brown had the interpreter question the farmers about earthquakes. Had the houses ever shaken? Did their fathers ever speak of the houses shaking? What about their grandfathers? He noticed that despite the poverty, the houses had electricity. Ice storms can impose great weight on a radar antenna. Had the farmers ever seen ice build up on the electric wires?

When the responses to all the questions were negative, he foraged for a site, setting up his surveyor's transit theodolite on tripod legs at various likely places and pointing it in the direction of Stalingrad to measure the horizon. To achieve optimal results in sending the radar's electromagnetic waves beaming into the Soviet Union, he needed as low a horizon as possible, less than a degree and a half. After he had found a field with the horizon he wanted, he had one more check to make as a precaution against earthquakes. He needed to know how far down the bedrock was on which he could rest the foundations for the antenna and the rest of the station. The young geologist he had brought along assured him it was only about three feet below. How did he know that? Brown asked. The geologist pointed at a nearby mound and explained that it was an extinct volcano. The eons since its extinction would have deposited a covering of soil and debris above its once molten rock, but about three feet down they ought to run into solid basalt. Brown didn't believe him. He had twenty laborers with picks and shovels brought from the town. Marking off a fifteen-foot square in the dirt with a stick, he told them to dig. Soon he had a fifteen-foot-square hole in the ground, roughly three feet deep, with basalt rock at the bottom.

"The rug does not shake," Brown telegraphed his superiors at GE in Syracuse. He assumed from all of the talk about the threat of earthquakes before he left that they would understand he was signaling he had found a safe site. He asked the Turkish interpreter how much land they could have for the radar station. The interpreter said as much as they wanted. Brown calculated they would probably need about ten acres for the huge antenna, the transmitter and receiver, and housing for the approximately one hundred GE technicians who would be required to operate the facility. The Air Force Security Service intended to add a detachment of ten officers and men and they would also obviously need housing. Someone on high reached an agreement with the Turkish authorities to turn the land over to the Air Force. Whether the Kurdish farmers were compensated is unknown.

After Brown returned to the United States, he discovered that the word had been put out in the Air Force, probably by Gardner through Twining and White. No matter what he wanted, everyone was eager to cooperate. He had originally intended to ship the monster antenna, assembled in pieces at Syracuse, and the related equipment by sea and then to put everything together on the site. It was not until mid-January 1955 that all was ready to go, however, and he was afraid that sea shipment, followed by overland transport to Diyarbakir, would be too slow to meet the June 1 on-air deadline. During a steering committee meeting at the Pentagon, he asked, "How's chances for an airlift?" An Air Force colonel down at the end of the table said, "Let me see." He picked up the phone, dialed a number, and spoke to an officer at the other end. "How much stuff have you got?" he asked Brown. "Four hundred and fifty tons," Brown said, expecting to be told this was a ridiculous imposition on the Air Force and he would have to find himself a ship. The colonel relayed the figure over the phone and returned to Brown, "Okay, you're in. Can you have it at Dover [Dover Air Force Base in Delaware, the Military Air Transport Service center] in ten days?" Brown said yes he could, and he did. Prefabricated barracks type housing for the hundred GE technicians and ten-man AFSS contingent, along with generators, a water purification system, and a sewage treatment plant, were also airlifted in pieces to Diyarbakir. The airfield there turned out to be long enough to handle the big American transports coming into service, like the mammoth Douglas four-engine C-124 Globemaster, with two massive doors at the front of the fuselage that swung open to roll cargo, vehicles, or machines on and off.

The Turkish Radar, as Brown's and also Trevor Gardner's creation was henceforth to be known within the Air Force, was on the air by June 1, 1955. Its football-field-sized antenna boomed a whopper of an electronic signal out over the southeastern end of the Black Sea, across the Caucasus Mountains of the Soviet Republic of Georgia, and into southern Russia toward Kapustin Yar approximately 800 miles away. The Soviets could not fail to detect it, nor fail to understand that electronic missile espionage was under way. Another radar specialist on

Brown's steering committee predicted that it would enjoy a life span of one week. The Soviets would then jam it. Brown noted they could easily have done so, either permanently with a ground jamming station or selectively when they were testing missiles by having an aircraft equipped with jamming gear circle over the Black Sea. They never did jam the Turkish Radar or interfere with it in any other way during the many years it was on the air. Brown was uncertain why. Lieutenant General Forrest McCartney, who left a country town in northeast Alabama for an Air Force life that saw some of its most memorable days working for Schriever, had what was perhaps the best explanation. There were, he said, certain "implied rules of engagement" that both sides adhered to throughout the Cold War, unspoken but carefully observed modes of conduct based upon common sense. Sending spy planes like the U-2 over the Soviet Union was unacceptable to the Russians, but electronic spying and later espionage from space were something else. They wanted to do their own. If they jammed an American radar in Turkey spying on their missile launchings, the Americans would jam the radars on the Soviet trawlers that lurked off Cape Canaveral, Florida, to monitor American missile firings.

About a week or two after the Turkish Radar went on the air, Brown got a telephone call from Lieutenant Colonel Manatt of the Air Technical Intelligence Center at Wright-Patterson. When he devised the radar, Brown had also created a system whereby a camera constantly filmed the radar's viewing scope, called an oscilloscope. The oscilloscope was connected to the receiver and showed what the radar was detecting. Because of the way the radar operated, the electromagnetic waves reflected off the flying missile and back to the receiver would appear on the oscilloscope not as an unbroken streak but as a series of images, contacts with the missile, separated by empty spaces between them. They would thus appear the same way on the film of the camera photographing the scope. Brown had calibrated the film so that one could calculate the speed of the missile by measuring the distances between the contacts. Manatt said the radar had achieved an intercept and he was sending a copy of the film to Brown by an armed Air Force courier. Would Brown please study the film and give him a reading?

Brown laid a straight edge ruler on the film and measured the distances between the contacts. The warhead of a ballistic missile that is launched into space at the optimal fifteen-degree angle and is traveling a mile a second is capable of going approximately 1,100 miles. That was the angle and speed at which the warhead of this Soviet missile was flying. Brown called Manatt back and told him what the film revealed: "You've got an eleven-hundred-mile missile." There was hesitation at Manatt's end of the line. "Are you sure?" Manatt asked. Brown replied that that was what the film said. Manatt thanked him and hung up. For some reason, the information percolated slowly up through the Air Force intelligence bureaucracy. Schriever, Gardner, and von Neumann do not seem to have received this first "hard evidence" of Soviet missile progress by the time they briefed Eisenhower on July 28, 1955. The news apparently reached them a bit later. The Soviets were clearly testing an intermediate-range ballistic missile, or IRBM. It was certain now that they were in a race.

BOOK VI

BUILDING THE UNSTOPPABLE

A COMPETITOR

Trouble, always trouble, came from a new quarter. In the fall of 1955, Eisenhower decided—formalizing his decision in another National Security Council Action Memorandum that December 1—to order the building of an intermediate-range ballistic missile with a reach of 1,725 miles. The creation of an IRBM, the president further ordered, was to have equal priority with that of the ICBM. The Killian Committee had first recommended an IRBM to the president in its February 1955 report, not with the same urgency as the committee's advocacy of an ICBM, but with a similar strategic argument. The committee had reasoned that if the Soviets acquired an intermediate-range ballistic missile first, Moscow could wield nuclear blackmail over the West European nations within the missiles' range and undermine the fledgling NATO alliance. The president's concern grew with evidence, such as that provided by the Turkish Radar, that the Soviets were striving for such a weapon. He seems to have been influenced as well by another State Department study concluding that should the Soviet Union attain an ICBM before the United States did, repercussions among the Western allies could be mitigated if Washington had IRBMs based in England and Europe. Intermediate-range missiles poised there would have all of western Russia, including Moscow, within their range. The British government had already expressed interest in such a basing scheme and there was hope of persuading other West European nations to accept the missiles.

If the IRBM project, like the ICBM, had its genesis in fear of Soviet advances in missilery, the impetus to build the weapon, as in the case of the ICBM, also arose from the profound rancor between the U.S. Air Force and the U.S. Army. The Army's chief of staff, General Maxwell Davenport Taylor, who had won his reputation for courage in battle by leaping from a C-47 to lead the 101st Airborne Division into Normandy on D-Day (he was given an assist by a boot in the buttocks from the jumpmaster when he hesitated at the door), was embittered by Eisenhower's policy of Massive Retaliation. It held down military spending by starving the Army of funds in order to foster SAC and the Air Force in general. (Just a year after his retirement in 1959, Taylor was to publish a widely read book, *The Uncertain Trumpet,* which denounced Eisenhower's neglect of conventional forces as dangerously shortsighted.) Although long-range strategic bombardment was supposed to be the province of the Air Force, Taylor refused to accept any limit on the range of guided missiles the Army might build. When, in the summer of 1956, he defiantly told Senator Symington, then chairman of the Subcommittee on the Air Force of the Senate Committee on Armed Services, that "the role of the Army is . . . the destruction of hostile ground forces and the 1,500-mile [1,725-statute-mile] missile will do just that," the Army was already well along in the acquisition of just such a missile. Army officers contended that all missiles, no matter what their range, were simply "guided artillery." Studies for an Army intermediate-range ballistic missile had started at the Redstone Arsenal in 1954 under Wernher von Braun and his German rocket technicians. It was to be called Jupiter and to be a leap forward from the 200-mile-range Redstone missile, which von Braun had already devised using Hall's 75,000-pound-thrust engine as a power plant.

By May of 1955, the Air Staff was sufficiently nervous over what the Army was doing at Redstone to urge Power to solicit industry proposals for an Air Force IRBM. Power passed along the Air Staff memorandum to Schriever, instructing him to explore but not to commit himself. There was no need for Power's injunction of caution. Schriever, with Gardner's backing, had already been engaged for months in attempting to ward off the building of an IRBM. He was convinced it would interfere with the progress of the intercontinental ballistic missile, the one that really mattered, by draining off time and engineering and scientific expertise, along with component parts common to both. For example, he already needed for Atlas all of Hall's 135,000-pound-thrust engines, being upgraded to 150,000 pounds thrust, that he could obtain from North American's Rocketdyne. If he was now tasked with an IRBM, he would have to part with engines for it. He argued that it was best to go forward at maximum speed with the ICBM until they had learned enough to spin an IRBM off from the bigger rocket.

As the fall of 1955 approached, he could hold out no longer. In October, with Eisenhower's mind virtually made up, Secretary Wilson asked the Joint Chiefs of Staff to meet and decide which service should build the intermediate missile. The JCS deliberations foundered on the shoals of interservice rivalry. Their report, referred to in military bureaucratese as a "split paper," recommended that Wilson approve the development of two IRBMs. One, which bore alternative code names, XSM (Experimental Strategic Missile)-75 and WS (Weapon System)-315A, was to be the province of the Air Force, while the other, XSM-68, was to be a joint Army-Navy project. The IRBM was not so vital to the nation's security that it required such duplication, but surprisingly, Wilson, undoubtedly with Eisenhower's approval, accepted this squandering of money and effort. The president's reasoning is unknown. He may have believed he would get an IRBM faster this way or he may have thought he could not slight the Army further without provoking a rebellion by Taylor and other senior Army generals.

On November 8, 1955, Wilson instructed both services to proceed. His memorandum specified that the IRBM was to be given "a priority equal to the ICBM but with no interference to the valid requirements of the ICBM program." Eisenhower's subsequent NSC directive of December 1 abandoned this mealymouthed equivocation and assigned a straightforward "joint" highest national priority, although it was just as unclear what this might mean in practice. Gardner was in a rage over the loss of the unique status for the ICBM, won with so many months of painstaking intrigue and labor, and tried several bureaucratic maneuvers to restore it, none of which succeeded. He blamed Engine Charlie rather than the president. Later denouncing the wastefulness of the parallel development of two IRBMs, Gardner mockingly said that Wilson regarded "competition in missiles . . . as desirable and necessary as it was in the automotive industry."

By the time Eisenhower signed the NSC memorandum on December 1, Schriever was nearly ready to begin the building of an IRBM. In August, as the pressure rose, he had instructed Ramo to have his people take a serious look at the contractor proposals Power had previously directed Bennie to solicit and to do some studies of their own. He had Hall assign a Navy missile specialist, Commander Robert Truax, to work with Ramo's people. They had heard of Truax and managed to have him seconded to the WDD staff. Power approved the design at the beginning of November and bids were solicited from contractors. Two days before Christmas, the airframe and missile assembly contract was awarded to the Douglas Aircraft Company of Santa Monica. A second race, a race against the Army, was on. Code designations for new aircraft or weapons last only as long as it takes someone to come up with a satisfactory name, and so it was with the Air Force's XSM-75 or WS-315A. The missile was soon dubbed Thor, for the Norse god of thunder. Schriever appointed Hall program director for the IRBM, although Hall retained his duties as propulsion officer for the ICBM project. Ramo in turn put his crew under the man he felt best qualified to manage Ramo-Wooldridge's engineering and technical direction side of the project, Ruben Mettler, his recently recruited star.

50.

THE TEAM OF METTLER
AND THIEL

"Rube" Mettler was to cap his career by taking a seat with the cardinals of the American aerospace industry as chairman and chief executive officer of TRW, Inc., the ultimate successor firm of Ramo-Wooldridge. At the beginning of 1956, however, he was just approaching his thirty-second birthday, an electrical and aeronautical engineer with a reputation for brilliance among the cognoscenti like Ramo, but yet to take on, let along succeed at, a project on the scale of what he was now being given. A split-rail figure of a man who seemed taller than the six feet he stood because he was so slim and erect, Mettler was a California boy and an example of what California was achieving with its institutions of higher technological learning. Born in the small town of Shafter near Bakersfield, he had grown up on a farm in the valley of the San Joaquin River just in from the mountains of the Coast Ranges in the southern part of the state. In the fall of 1941, he had enrolled in Stanford University, initially as a humanities and history student, but had then taken courses in calculus and chemistry after his academic adviser told him that a literate man also had to know some science and mathematics. The advice turned out to be fortuitous. When he joined the Navy at seventeen shortly after Pearl Harbor, a personnel officer took a look at his grades in calculus and chemistry and decided Mettler was a candidate for a special program to produce officer technicians. He was sent to Caltech, gained a B.S. in electrical engineering in eighteen months, and, after midshipman and radar schools, was dispatched to the Pacific to serve as a roving radar repair officer. He lived like an itinerant electrician, transferring from one ship to another as radar malfunctions were reported. The experience taught him that what appeared to be a complex technological problem often had a simple cause. One destroyer captain was so exasperated at the refusal of his electronic wonder to cooperate that he warned Mettler he was going to be confined to the ship until he fixed it. Mettler checked out the apparatus and found everything in perfect order, but the radar simply would not come on line. In desperation, he climbed the mast to examine the antenna, then came back down and asked for some razor blades. They were provided. When Mettler descended the mast a second time, the radar worked fine. Some sailor, wielding that implement in such constant use in the Navy to fight off corrosion from saltwater—a paintbrush—had slapped thick lead paint across the radar's window, effectively shutting it down.

Arriving at San Francisco in 1946 and expecting to be discharged, he was instead turned back to the Pacific on a mission that profoundly affected his outlook during the coming Cold War. Assigned to the naval task force supporting the first of the postwar nuclear tests at Bikini Atoll in the central Pacific, Mettler joined the team of officers who set up instruments to measure the effects. The horrendous sights of two atomic explosions, one a subsurface detonation that hurled a geyser of seawater into the air from which a mushroom cloud then emerged and the second a searing surface burst from a tower, led Mettler to vow that he would do all he could in future years to prevent weapons like this from being used against the United States. He returned to Caltech and in 1949 earned a Ph.D. there in electrical and aeronautical engineering. Ramo and Wooldridge, then transforming Hughes Aircraft into a high-technology powerhouse, were lecturing in courses at Caltech on the side as a way of spotting and hiring the best graduates. They signed up Mettler right away and put him to work on the airborne radar and fire-control computer for the Falcon air-to-air missile. When they left in September 1953 to form their own company, Mettler declined their invitation to join them. He was leader of the team that was mating the Falcon system to the F-102, the latest of the supersonic interceptors that were coming on line to protect the United States against Soviet nuclear bombers, and he wanted to finish the job.

Ramo lost out on recruiting Mettler again in early 1954 when Mettler too left Hughes. Donald Quarles, who had not yet succeeded Harold Talbott as secretary of the Air Force and was still assistant secretary of defense for research and development, pulled rank and brought Mettler to Washington as a special consultant. He was soon on a plane bound for SAC headquarters at Omaha with instructions from Quarles to find out why the new electronic navigation and bomb release system for the B-47 and B-58 bombers was failing so often, causing the bombers to miss their targets in practice exercises. LeMay had seen such techno wonder boys before and they had brought him scant benefit. He assumed Mettler was another of these useless geeks. LeMay paraded Mettler in front of his staff and asked him to explain precisely what he was going to do to help. Mettler didn't yet know what the problem was, never mind whether he could remedy it. He attempted to get off the hook by awkwardly explaining that he was headed for a SAC base in Texas where he would examine maintenance records, fly missions, and so forth. The Cigar proceeded to make fun of him. "He just shredded me to pieces," Mettler recalled. "He said this is the kind of nonsense we have to put up with. It was just awful."

Mettler left for Texas, studied records, and went out on several flights on B-47s and B-58s. He found nothing. Then on one flight, as if he were back on that destroyer in the Pacific, he suddenly noticed that the main electronic unit for the bomb-navigation system was housed in a closed metal cupboard. He put a hand on top of it. Intense heat burned his fingers. These were the days when electronic devices like this bomb-navigation system were still employing vacuum tubes, sealed glass tubes containing a near vacuum. The vacuum allowed free passage of electrical current to connect circuits. The tubes functioned reasonably well, but they were fragile compared to the tougher transistors to come and were especially prone to failure if subjected to excessive heat. When a vacuum tube failed, a circuit closed, and the electronic device malfunctioned. The Boeing engineers who had designed the B-47 and the General Dynamics designers of the B-58 obviously had no experience with electronics, nor were they systems engineers in Ramo's conception of designing an integrated whole. The electronics had merely been crammed into the planes as an afterthought, without any regard to what was needed to keep the system functioning. And all that was required in this case was some cooling air. Mettler had ducts cut in the metal cupboard and fans installed. Vacuum tube lifetime increased significantly and so did the performance of the bomb-navigation systems. LeMay ordered the fix copied in all SAC bombers. To his credit, he also apologized for his cruel behavior, awarding Mettler the Defense Department's Distinguished Public Service Medal in a ceremony back at SAC headquarters in Omaha. And this time, Ramo succeeded in recruiting Mettler for the missile program. In March 1955, as soon as Quarles was willing to part with him, he shifted back to California to confront the first great challenge of his career in Thor.

Mettler was fortunate to have someone experienced in rocketry to serve as his deputy—a forty-year-old Austro-German aeronautical engineer named Adolf Thiel, another veteran of the V-2 program and a refugee from the Redstone Arsenal. Although "Dolf" Thiel had come to the United States in 1946 with the original group of German rocketeers under the clandestine Operation Paperclip, he had never been part of the von Braun coterie. A slender man of medium height, with a prominent nose and thinning brown hair, Thiel had a friendly if intense manner that hid a quick temper. He had been born in Vienna and grew up there, but went to Darmstadt, just south of Frankfurt, for his higher education, because Darmstadt's university offered courses in aeronautical engineering. In 1940, right after he received his master's degree, he was put to work on the V-2 project. He did not, however, move to the rocket center at Peenemünde to join the rest of the V-2 team. Instead, under a contract the university negotiated with the German military, he did mathematical calculations for the Peenemünde group on flight mechanics, control systems, and guidance, traveling there frequently to obtain the team's requirements, then returning to Darmstadt to do his equations. In 1944, as part of his work for a Ph.D., he wrote a thesis on the control system for a ballistic missile, to be called the A-9, which was to have enough range to bomb New York. His Ph.D. project was aborted by the interregnum at the fall of Germany a year later and, fortunately for New York, the missile never got beyond the paper stage.

While not a genuine member of the Peenemünde club, his mathematical analyses attracted enough attention for him to be invited to join the group when it was transported to Fort Bliss, Texas, to conduct firings of the captured V-2s at the nearby White Sands Proving Ground in New Mexico. In 1952, after the German rocket men had been transferred to the Redstone Arsenal in Alabama, Thiel managed to break away from von Braun and received permission to form his own research group. All, with the exception of one German, were American missile technicians. The design of the Army's intermediate-range ballistic missile, XSM-68, emerged from their studies in 1955. It was to be named Jupiter after the chief god of the Roman state religion (Zeus was his equivalent in the Greek pantheon of gods), and like Thor was also associated with thunder and lightning. By this time, Thiel was an American citizen, eager to part with the Army and join a civilian firm. He began negotiations with Convair to work on the Atlas. Louis Dunn, former chief of Caltech's Jet Propulsion Laboratory and a member of the Tea Pot Committee, whom Ramo had persuaded to become his general deputy for the ICBM project, heard about the negotiations through the industry grapevine. Thiel, like Mettler, was just the sort of man they wanted. A phone call was made and Dunn convinced Thiel that Ramo-Wooldridge would prove a much more interesting organization to be part of than Convair. When Thiel's contract with the Army expired in March 1955, he left Huntsville for Los Angeles, soon to be pitted, as Mettler's second, against his former employer.

Although Hall was program director for the IRBM project, he did not attempt to micromanage it. He would not have been able had he wanted to do so. He was too busy advancing the North American engine and deciding on a source for the engine for the alternate ICBM, Titan. The Glenn L. Martin Aircraft Company of Baltimore, Maryland, was chosen to develop Titan in September 1955. Martin planned to build the missile at a new plant it was constructing on a 4,500-acre tract of land it had purchased near Denver, Colorado. Aerojet General

Corporation of California emerged as the best source for a second 150,000-pound-thrust rocket engine to power Titan. Hall left it to Commander Truax and Mettler and Thiel to design Thor. Thiel had thoughtfully brought with him to Los Angeles duplicates of the Army IRBM studies he had supervised at Redstone. It was thus not a coincidence, as Thiel pointed out in an interview years later, that Thor was essentially a copy of the missile that was to become the Army's Jupiter.

Jupiter stood 60 feet high. Thiel made Thor slightly higher at 64.8 feet. Diameter was approximately the same, 96 inches for Thor and 105 inches for Jupiter. Both missiles weighed in fully fueled for liftoff and fitted with their nose cones at about 110,000 pounds. The main body of the Jupiter was smoothly rounded all the way to the bottom. To make Thor look slightly different, Thiel tacked on fins that flared out at the base. The fins added nothing in the way of aerodynamic advantage. Each missile relied for its booster on a single one of Hall's North American Aviation engines and on both missiles the engines were attached to gimbals, the improved contrivances that enabled the engines to swing in any direction and thus steer the rocket with their thrust. In addition, Thor was equipped with two small rocket motors of just 1,000 pounds thrust, called verniers, attached to swivels and mounted on each side of the booster engine. They were kept burning after the main booster engine had been shut down and were used to make last-second adjustments in order to release the warhead at the precise angle required for it to hurtle through space to its target. These minor differences notwithstanding, Thor and Jupiter were, provided they flew as advertised, intermediate-range ballistic missiles of equal worthiness. The competitors now had to deliver on that question of whether and how each would fly.

51

JOHN BRUCE MEDARIS AND
WERNHER VON BRAUN

Schriever's opponent in this competition was Major General John Bruce Medaris of the U.S. Army Ordnance Corps. He was a man with visions of his own. A handsome, colorful figure to whom the art of promoting his cause seemed to come naturally, he was also an eccentric with a flair for showmanship. He sported a broad and bristling guardsman's mustache and was given to greeting visitors dressed in old-fashioned officer's riding breeches and boots, a short horse whip called a quirt tucked under an arm. To emphasize a point as he spoke, he would snap the quirt down and whack the side of a boot. He was also fond of the trappings of military authority. Anyone approaching his office was given notice that he was about to enter the precincts of an important man. He posted guards outside his door—military policemen in white gloves, spankingly pressed uniforms, and spit-shined boots. Yet for all these pretensions, Medaris was a highly intelligent officer with intiative and a talent for organization. Born in a small town in Ohio, he had joined the Marine Corps in 1918 at the age of just sixteen after the United States had entered the First World War and served as a rifleman in France. At Ohio State University in Columbus after the war studying for a bachelor's degree in mechanical engineering, he became cadet captain of the school's ROTC unit and won a commission in the Regular Army through a competitive examination. Bored by a couple of years of duty with infantry regiments, he had switched to ordnance, the branch of the Army that deals with the manufacture, storage, and supply of weapons, ammunition, and other military equipment. There he could exercise his engineering knowledge. But like many officers who found life in the shrunken, neglected Army between the wars too dull and underpaid to be borne, he had dropped out in the 1920s to go into business, retaining a connection through Reserve status.

In 1939, with the Army gearing up to take on the Nazis and the Japanese, he had been recalled to active duty and by 1944 was a full colonel and chief ordnance officer for General Omar Bradley's First Army in the Normandy landing and the campaign through France. Ten years later his career had flourished to the point where he wore the twin stars of a major general and was assistant chief of the Ordnance Corps at the Pentagon. In February 1956, he was sent to Redstone to form a new Army Ballistic Missile Agency out of the disparate guided missile activities there. He was granted special powers of decision and contracting similar to those Schriever had acquired in the Gillette Procedures. He had also been given a mission by a jealous Army, a mission to take the Army's aspirations in rocketry, which had no limit, just as far as he could.

Medaris's ace in the game of rocket poker that was about to be played was, of course, the Germans. They had "demonstrated capability as the best qualified group of ballistic missile engineers outside the Soviet Union, if not in the world," he was to boast. They represented, along with the American scientists and technicians who had worked under them in the 200-mile-range Redstone missile program at the Arsenal, "over 9,000 man-years experience in guided missiles and rockets." Their leader, Dr. Wernher von Braun, was a man of renown in the 1950s, regarded as the father of the V-2 (although the missile had, in fact, a number of fathers) and thus the leading rocket scientist of the day. Given his past, he naturally had his detractors. Thomas "Tom" Lehrer, the mathematician and satirical singer and songwriter, composed a ditty caricaturizing von Braun:

"Once the rockets are up, who cares where they come down?
That's not my department," says Wernher von Braun.

Lehrer was unfair to von Braun in one respect. Von Braun did care where his rockets came down. He was a professional. He wanted his rockets to hit the targets at which they were aimed. But Lehrer nonetheless touched the essential amorality of the man. Rockets in themselves did not fascinate Wernher von Braun. His real passion was the exploration of space. He dreamt of journeys to the moon and Mars. He saw the advancement of rocketry as the path that would one day enable man to roam that previously unreachable realm. "Space-

ships will eventually be used by everybody," he told Daniel Lang of
The New Yorker magazine in an interview in 1951. "All this military
application of rockets—it's only a part of the picture. A means to an
end," he said. In other words, it didn't matter to von Braun whether he
built rockets for Hitler or the Americans, as long as his endeavors led
into space.

An elegant German aristocrat, Wernher von Braun was the son of
a noble family that traced its lineage back to the 1200s in the east
Prussian region of Silesia. Almost all of the region's two provinces of
Upper and Lower Silesia and three neighboring German provinces
were erased at the end of the Second World War when Stalin carved a
slice off eastern Poland to move the border of Ukraine farther west.
Poland was awarded compensatory territory in eastern Germany along
the line of the Oder and Neisse Rivers. Virtually the entire German
population behind the river line in Silesia and the rest of the area,
about 12 million persons in all, was summarily expelled and driven
west into the remainder of Germany. Von Braun, born in 1912, was the
first engineer and scientist in the family. His father, Magnus Freiherr
von Braun, educated in law and economics, had been a high-ranking
civil servant, initially in the Prussian state and then, after the First
World War, in the fragile Weimar Republic that preceded the Nazis.
His mother, the daughter of another aristocratic family and an amateur
astronomer, started him on his quest for space by giving him an astro-
nomic telescope when he was thirteen. Stargazing with the telescope
aroused a passion for astronomy, which in turn led to dreams of space
travel. In 1930, when he was about to begin studies at the Technische
Hochschule (Technical University) in Berlin, von Braun made the acquaintance of Hermann Oberth, an early German space visionary and
rocket scientist. Oberth and his associates were conducting rocket experiments at a deserted government ammunition depot near Berlin.
During his spare time, von Braun pitched in to help. He had found his
life's endeavor.

By 1937, at the age of twenty-five, when most men are just starting
their climb, von Braun was technical director of the German army's
new rocket center on the island of Usedom in the Baltic. He had hundreds of men under him. There was an army general over him, but he
was an administrator. Von Braun reported to Major General Walter
Dornberger in Berlin, an army rocket pioneer who had become head of

all the Wehrmacht's missile projects. (That same year von Braun entered the Nazi Party, probably for career motives, as he does not seem to have been an active anti-Semite. He appears to have simply been indifferent to the regime's persecution of the Jews. Three years later he also accepted an officer's commission in the SS, once more apparently for career reasons.) The rocket center had been named Peenemünde after the little fishing hamlet that had previously been the only inhabited spot on the island. The site had, ironically, been suggested by the mother who had set him on his course. He had told her the army (he had joined the army's rocket section in 1932) was seeking a remote place to create a clandestine installation with plenty of room to fire rockets. She remembered that his father used to go duck hunting on Usedom. He then looked over the island himself. The expanse of the Baltic made for an excellent firing range. After he reported his findings to the military, the surveyors and engineers and bulldozers and concrete mixers arrived and the tiny fishing village and its island were tranquil no more.

With Hitler's invasion of Poland on September 1, 1939, and the outbreak of the Second World War, the center grew apace. Von Braun soon headed a staff of thousands. The führer initially seems to have regarded rockets as curiosities. He changed his mind in 1943 after the V-2, then still called the A-4 by the army, proved itself by flying its full course. The Luftwaffe was demonstrating its inability to stop the bombing of the Reich and the war in Russia was going against Hitler. He reached out desperately for anything he thought might help avert defeat. Suddenly Peenemünde had an unlimited budget and equivalent priority. Joseph Goebbels, Hitler's minister for propaganda, renamed the A-4 the V-2, for Vergeltungswaffe, Vengeance Weapon. (The subsonic cruise missile driven by a pulse-jet motor that was to become known as the buzz bomb to Londoners, developed by the Luftwaffe at a separate installation on Usedom, was named the V-1.) But the activity at Peenemünde attracted the attention of others besides the führer. The RAF struck the place with 600 four-engine Lancaster bombers on the night of August 17, 1943. Hitler ordered all production moved underground and put the SS in charge.

The precise number of slave laborers who died at the Mittelwerk, the V-2 factory burrowed into a mountainside in the Harz Mountains of central Germany for immunity against bombing, and at the nearby concentration camps that fed it, is unknown, but it was many thou-sands. Production began in the fall of 1943 and ran around the clock to satisfy the führer's demand. Jet engines for the new Messerschmitt 262 fighter, another miracle weapon that was supposed to turn the tide, and submarine components were also assembled there. To dis-courage sabotage, the SS erected a gallows and hanged suspected men on it in front of their assembled fellow prisoners. One month in the spring of 1945 they hanged 162. But the big killers were overwork, malnutrition, and disease from the appallingly filthy conditions in the camps, where sanitation was virtually nonexistent.

According to a sympathetic biography written by his close friend and fellow German rocketeer Ernst Stuhlinger and Frederick Ordway III, an American rocket historian, von Braun made frequent visits to Mittelwerk to solve manufacturing and testing problems. He told mem-bers of his staff back at Peenemünde whom he trusted that the sights he had seen there were "hellish," but said there was nothing he could do to alleviate the conditions. When he had protested to an SS guard he had been told to mind his own business or he would also be wearing a con-centration camp inmate's striped uniform. He said he then unsuccess-fully tried the tack with one of the senior SS officers that half-starved workers were turning out too many rocket parts of unacceptably poor quality. Heinrich Himmler, the chief of the SS, also put fear into von Braun by having him, his brother, Magnus Jr., who also worked in the V-2 program, and two of his senior engineers arrested and thrown into jail for two weeks in March 1944. The trumped-up charge was defeatist talk and hindering V-2 production by wasting time discussing the future of rockets in space exploration. There is considerable evidence, how-ever, that while von Braun may have found forced labor distasteful, he was perfectly willing to accept its employment to manufacture his rock-ets. And one would think that if he had been truly repelled at seeing the face of Nazism in all of its satanic horror at Mittelwerk, von Braun would have put on a cooperative exterior while quietly denying the regime his expertise in the continuing effort to perfect the V-2. Accord-ing to his friend Stuhlinger, he did just the opposite. Many of the Pee-nemünde laboratories and workshops had been scattered for safety to various places around Germany. Stuhlinger tells how, during the final months of the war, von Braun shuttled indefatigably by rail and auto-mobile from one to another of these, "often under most difficult circumstances because of the frequent air raids," attending meetings, encouraging everyone, striving to make the V-2 a better weapon. In December 1944, Hitler even approved awarding him the Knight's Cross of the War Service Cross, a high decoration that was the noncombat equivalent of the Knight's Crosses given for notable valor on the battlefield. One has to conclude that despite what he had witnessed at Mittelwerk, Wernher von Braun, like most Germans of his time, loyally served his mad, murderous führer to the end.

The mountain hell factory turned out about 5,800 V-2s before the end of the war. Of these, approximately 3,200 were launched against London, Paris, Antwerp, Brussels, and other civilian targets. The missile was too inaccurate to be of use against military targets and in no way delayed the end of the Third Reich. In all, the V-2s hurled roughly 3,000 metric tons of high explosive on urban centers, less than a third of the 10,000 tons that might be dropped by British and American bombers in a single big raid. But if the Allied bombers killed a lot more civilians than the V-2s could manage, the V-2s killed civilians nonetheless in the cause of one of the vilest regimes in human history.

Loyalty to Hitler did not prevent von Braun and his colleagues from simultaneously taking steps in the final weeks of the war to ensure their survival and that of their families once the fighting was over. Documents that they alone had the knowledge to reproduce were destroyed so that "we could make ourselves wanted as well as our work," von Braun said. "It all made sense," he explained to Daniel Lang of *The New Yorker*. "The V-2 was something we had and you didn't have. Naturally, you wanted to know all about it." Five trunks of plans and technical research material from General Dornberger's files were buried in an abandoned salt mine. The rocket specialists, and the SS men who were holding them as the end neared, possibly in the hope of ransoming the rocketeers to the Americans for their own survival, understandably wanted to avoid the Red Army. They moved south into small village resorts in the Bavarian Alps, the path of the American advance. "The hotel service was excellent," von Braun recalled. At the news of Hitler's suicide on April 30, the SS men disappeared. Two days later von Braun sent his brother, Magnus Jr., down the mountain on a bicycle to find the American forces. He encountered a PFC from an antitank company of the 44th Infantry Division, a German-American soldier from Wisconsin who shouted at him in good German, "Come forward with your hands up."

That contact began a chain of interrogations of von Braun and his fellows that led them to Colonel (subsequently Major General) Holger Toftoy, formerly head of the Army Ordnance Corps Rocket Branch in Washington and now chief of the Ordnance Technical Intelligence mission in Europe. Several of von Braun's engineers returned to the Mittelwerk plant with officers from Toftoy's team. Enough parts for about one hundred V-2s were assembled and loaded onto 300 railroad cars. The trains hauling these had to negotiate their way along the blasted and broken German railway network to the Belgian port of Antwerp, where the rocket components were shifted into the holds of sixteen freighters for transfer to the United States. The work went on into June. That month, just twenty-four hours before the Soviets were due to move into the Nordhausen area as part of their occupation zone, the five trunks filled with Dornberger's plans and research were retrieved from the abandoned salt mine and sent off to Antwerp.

Toftoy then instigated a clandestine project code-named Operation Paperclip. He and his team drafted a cable to Washington, which General Eisenhower signed, recommending that "100 of the very best men of this research organization be evacuated to US immediately." Cordell Hull, the secretary of state, whose consent was necessary under the law, approved. The number grew to 127 rocket specialists when Toftoy and von Braun selected those who were to come. By the end of 1945, all, including von Braun, were in the United States. The code name was inspired by the designator of selection, a paperclip attached to the individual's file. The Germans were given contracts granting them salaries and a per diem allowance for the room and board the Army would be providing. The hope of permanent residence and American citizenship was held out. Their families, they were promised, would follow at a later date. In the meantime, the families would be sheltered from the hardships that almost all other Germans were to undergo. They were billeted in a protected U.S. Army housing unit in Bavaria, fed, and furnished medical care. And when von Braun's Nazi Party and SS records were discovered, the information was suppressed by his U.S. Army patrons.

Initially, von Braun and his associates were disappointed by their lot in the United States. Sorting documents and firing assembled V-2s in experiments at the White Sands Proving Ground in the New Mexico desert were dull chores compared to the heady years at Peenemünde.

"At Peenemünde we'd been coddled," von Braun remarked to Daniel Lang. "Here you were counting pennies. Your armed forces were being demobilized and everybody wanted military expenditures curtailed." But there was nowhere else to go, and as the Soviet-American competition grew more intense and the funding for rocketry increased, life became more interesting. First came the shift to the Redstone Arsenal in 1950; then the building of the Redstone, the successful 200-mile-range tactical missile; now the creation of the U.S. Army Ballistic Missile Agency under a bold and eager general with the Jupiter IRBM project, which held the possibility of larger things to come. The von Braun team was back in business.

52.

THE CAPE OF THE CANEBRAKE VS. "MOOSE" MATHISON

The place where this competition between the Air Force and the Army was to take place had been, until barely a half dozen years earlier, 15,000 miserable acres of sand and swamp, interspersed with scrub brush and palmetto, which jutted out like an enlarged nose from the central coast of Florida. The Spanish, who discovered Florida in the early sixteenth century, had named it Cabo de Canaveral (Cape of the Canebrake) for the clumps of wild cane, with dense undergrowth, that also distinguished the protruding nose. They had never attempted to settle the Cape. Rather, they had destroyed the original human inhabitants, the Florida coastal Indians, by raiding their villages for slaves and transmitting European diseases like smallpox and typhus that decimated the Indians until the survivors fled to refuge inland. Yet Cape Canaveral had acquired an importance for the Spanish, if only as a navigation point, and is marked distinctly on sixteenth-century Spanish maps. The navigators of the galleons sailing up the Bahama Channel, with gold and silver from the mines of Mexico and Peru to sustain

Spain's economy and pay for its European wars, had known that at Cape Canaveral they could pick up the east wind that would carry them out across the Atlantic to the Azores and thence to Cádiz and the other ports of home. Galleons wrecked by the fickle storms of the Florida coast in the shallow seas around Canaveral made the region a favorite haunt for treasure hunters in the centuries to come.

On Cape Canaveral itself nothing really changed between the sixteenth century and the end of the Second World War. With the departure of the last of the coastal Indians, the sand and swamp and the scrub, palmetto, and canebrake had reverted to an abode of its natural inhabitants: cottonmouth water moccasins, diamondback rattlesnakes, an occasional black bear or cougar, and alligators, raccoons, and skunks. A few hardy squatters lived in shacks here and there and eked out a living hunting, trapping, and scavenging whatever might be available. The Coast Guard also manned a lighthouse out at the end of the Cape, but the small crew traveled back and forth by boat, not overland across the Cape itself.

Then, in October 1946, spurred on by the development of the V-2, the armed services decided they needed an adequate firing range for rockets and missiles. The desert range at the White Sands Proving Ground was 125 miles long and 41 miles wide on average, too cramped for what was envisioned. A two-year search settled on Cape Canaveral. It offered the security of remoteness because the neighboring central coast of Florida was only lightly populated at the time and the handful of squatters on the Cape would be easy to move out. Yet for all its remoteness, Canaveral was accessible by road, the coastal railway, and the Banana River, which ran behind it. Building materials, equipment, and rockets and missiles of any size could easily be transported there. The Caribbean and the South Atlantic Ocean beyond constituted a virtually limitless range. The British government was willing to negotiate agreements for the firing of missiles over the Bahamas and its other island colonial possessions beyond them and for the establishment of tracking stations on the islands. The abandoned Banana River Naval Air Station twenty miles south of the Cape, a wartime seaplane base for training and patrols to destroy Nazi U-boats preying on shipping, would also make an ideal airfield and headquarters base for the range. On October 1, 1949, the Defense Department established the Joint Long Range Proving Ground. Joint administration proved too cumbersome and so the Army and the Navy ceded everything to the Air Force, while reserving the right of use. By the time the contest between Thor and Jupiter approached, the old Banana River Naval Air Station had been renamed Patrick Air Force Base, in honor of Major General Mason Patrick, chief of the Army Air Service and its successor, the Army Air Corps, from 1921 to 1927, and the firing range at Cape Canaveral had become the Air Force Missile Test Center (AFMTC).

The first paved access road into the Cape was not laid down until 1950. Prior to Thor and Jupiter, the launch facilities constructed were also small and rudimentary. The missiles tested earlier, such as Redstone; the Matador, a jet-powered cruise missile with a range of 650 miles; and the long-range cruise missile, the Snark, also jet-powered, which was to be deployed briefly, did not require anything elaborate. The one substantial concrete structure built at the Cape in the early 1950s was a launch pad for the doomed supersonic cruise missile Navaho. (This was the impractical project Ed Hall had taken advantage of to create a rocket engine for Atlas and now Thor.) The Navaho was ridiculed at the Cape as the "Never-go Navaho" because of its repeated failures before it was finally canceled in 1957. Its launch pad was useless for the testing of Thor and Jupiter because its configuration did not fit their requirements. Big new concrete pads with wide troughs underneath, filled with water before launching to divert the flames of the igniting rocket engines so that they would not damage the missile before liftoff, had to be constructed for Thor and Jupiter. Rugged concrete blockhouses to shelter the launch control teams in the not unlikely event that a missile exploded had to be built. Storage tanks had to be installed for the rocket fuels—RP-1 (Hall's blend of kerosene) and liquid oxygen. Radio control and radar tracking facilities had to be erected, and paved access roads laid across the Cape on which to truck in these weighty missiles and the heavy equipment needed to test them.

And everything had to be done in a rush. Schriever, feeling the pressure of competition with the Army and Eisenhower's impatience for an IRBM, and wanting to get what he saw as a distinctly secondary task out of the way, had decreed that Thor was to be a double crash program. A cautious approach would have been to allot two years from inception to test launching. Bennie cut this in half. The first missiles were to be fabricated swiftly enough for test launching to begin by the end of 1956, one year from the formal signing of the contract on December 28, 1955. These first Thors were to be built with production tooling so that Douglas and the manufacturers of the subsystems could go into series production as soon the missile had been proven. Schriever was, in effect, laying a risky bet with one of those judgments on technological feasibility he had taught himself to make while running the Development Planning Office at the Pentagon. Whether what he was demanding would prove possible in this enterprise, considerably more complicated than anything he had dealt with before, was to be seen.

Lieutenant Colonel Charles Mathison, the officer sent to Patrick Air Force Base from Schriever's WDD organization to supervise the civilian contractors constructing the launch facilities at the Cape, could not have been a better choice. He had been nicknamed "Moose" in his cadet years because when he raised his voice it had the foghorn quality of a bull moose in rut, the result of an injury to his vocal cords when he was kicked in the throat while playing football at the Naval Academy. The nickname had a peculiar aptness in catching both the physique and the forceful personality of the man. He was six feet, two inches and 240 pounds of muscle and bone with a cannonball of a head. While boxing in the Marine Corps—he had joined at the age of seventeen and then won an appointment to Annapolis through competitive examination— he had hit an opponent so hard with a roundhouse right punch that he not only knocked the man out but sent him flying through the ropes as well, shattering his own wrist in the process. When not in a boxing ring, Mathison was a friendly, engaging man who delighted in his nickname because he understood how well it fit him. He never did become a naval officer. He had been attracted to Annapolis because of a desire to be a Navy flier. After the Navy barred him from flight training because of the throat injury, despite the fact that it had healed, he resigned from the academy, joined the Army, and after overcoming a number of vicissitudes, entered Flying School as an aviation cadet and won his wings and a second lieutenant's commission as a bomber pilot in the Army Air Forces. Although physically oriented and unintellectual, he was not unintelligent or uneducated. In the late 1940s the Air Force had sent him to the University of Maryland to obtain a B.S. in aeronautical engineering. And fortunately for Schriever, when unusual assignments came his way, as they seemed to do, Mathison did not shrink from them.

During the five years before coming to WDD, he had been assigned to the Special Weapons Command at Kirtland Air Force Base next to Albuquerque, New Mexico. One of his tasks there had been to figure out how to drop the first weaponized version of the hydrogen bomb, the 41,000-pound Mark 17, which exploded with a force of eleven megatons, from a B-36 without the plane itself being destroyed by the blast. The obvious answer was to attach a giant parachute to the bomb casing and so slow its descent while the plane got far enough away. Mathison set about calculating rates of descent against the size of parachute required and the time necessary for the bomber to get clear. He had to fly up to SAC headquarters at Omaha every month to brief LeMay on his progress. A test was going to be run with a SAC B-36 dropping a Mark 17 over a deserted atoll in the Pacific. The commander-in-chief of SAC, whose philosophy on weapons Mathison characterized as "the bigger the bang, the better the bomb," did not like the idea of parachutes on bombs. LeMay was afraid that Soviet fighters or antiaircraft guns might shoot up the parachute-dangling bomb before it detonated. He kept urging Mathison to make the parachute smaller and the bomb's descent faster. They reached a compromise. As a further precaution, Mathison had the bottom of the plane's fuselage painted with white enamel to reflect the heat from the thermonuclear blast. The painting was done while the B-36 was parked on a runway and its wheels down. The wheel well doors were thus open and the painters somehow missed them, leaving their silver aluminum surfaces bare. The compromise over the parachute was not quite compromise enough. Although the pilot took what evasive action he could by throwing the plane into what Mathison called "a screaming turn" down and away the moment the bomb was released, he did not have sufficient time to get clear. The extraordinarily intense heat burned away the unprotected wheel well doors and also scorched holes through the fuselage wherever oil had spewed on it from the six engines, but the pilot was able to land safely. Had Mathison not resorted to the white enamel paint as an additional safeguard, the B-36 and its crew would probably have been lost.

The task Mathison now faced was a daunting one, for he was under orders to build not just one, but four imposing concrete launchpads, and their related facilities, by the end of 1956, two for Thor and Jupiter and two for Atlas. Schriever wanted to make certain that if anything occurred to disable one of the pads during testing, there would be an alternate from which to continue launching. The first problem faced by Mathison and the civilian contractors was that the designated sites were swampy, the water table rising nearly to the surface. Ground like this was simply too soft to support massive concrete structures. They had to employ a dredging ship to scour millions of yards of sand from the bottom of the Banana River and pump it ashore at the Cape. Great earthmoving machines then scooped up the sand and hauled it four or five miles to the sites, where it was dumped and then spread and tamped down by rollers to fill in the swamps and create a firm soil base. To try to meet Schriever's deadline, Mathison had the contractors going in shifts around the clock, the nights eerie with the floodlights at the sites and the lights on the earthmovers shuttling back and forth. Just when they were ready to start mixing and pouring concrete, the workers at their major American cement supplier went on strike. (Concrete is a mixture of cement with sand and broken stone or gravel. As the water used to achieve the mix dries, the material hardens into stonelike consistency.) They overcame this obstacle by importing a shipload of cement from Belgium, which turned out to be cheaper than the American variety. The freighter was unloaded at the new Port Canaveral, a spot just south of the Cape that had been dredged out earlier precisely so that seagoing vessels could bring in bulky equipment or cargo.

The snakes and alligators and other critters of the Cape were intimidated by the earthmovers and floodlights and accompanying racket, but the mosquitoes were not. Vast swarms of them were a constant menace at Canaveral and all along the coast down past Patrick Air Force Base. The day Mathison arrived at Patrick he landed at dusk and got out of the plane wearing a short-sleeve shirt. A few minutes later he looked down at his arms and they were literally black with mosquitoes. After his family arrived, his six-year-old daughter was bitten so badly on the legs going to and from school that she caught a contagious and nasty bacterial skin infection with yellow crusty sores called impetigo. The contractors had to keep two large mosquito-repellent sprayers going at all of the sites in order to work their crews at night. Repellents, and covering as much of the body as possible, seemed to be the only solution. The Navy had sprayed so much DDT over the area to try to reduce the mosquito population during the war that a DDT-resistant strain had apparently mutated. The Air Force tried spraying with a different oil-based compound and it had some effect, but the number of bugs was not dramatically reduced. The coast below Cape Canaveral was one day to style itself the Space Coast and to be lined with motels, hotels, restaurants, and multistory beachside apartments. In 1955, the Cape was still mostly virgin wilderness and the coast below (there was only one motel at Cocoa Beach, about five miles south of Canaveral), sparsely populated stretches of sand. The mosquitoes had a paradise of swamps and low-lying stagnant water in which to breed.

Mosquitoes may swarm, but concrete hardens, and soon the launch emplacements, as the sites were formally known, began to take shape: the circular launch stand on which the missile would rest before its hoped-for flight; the flame troughs underneath on each side and in front; the formidable blockhouse for the controllers, its concrete resting on shock absorbers for additional protection, a good distance to the rear. Along with the RP-1 kerosene and liquid oxygen fueling tanks and other appurtenances of missile firings was a curious-looking multistory structure of steel beams called a service tower, or gantry for short, which could be moved on railroad tracks to and from the launch stand. The missile was hung in the middle of it for servicing and checks. When everything was ready, the tower would be wheeled over to the launch pad on its tracks and the missile transferred to the pad to stand there upright awaiting the command to rise. Spacious, hangar-like missile assembly buildings, also steel-framed, were erected near the launch emplacements. Missiles came to the Cape pretty well assembled, but the wide bays of these structures were convenient working spaces for the installation and changing of nose cones and other components and also provided shelter from the elements until launch time approached.

A FEW GRAINS OF SAND

Thor No. 101 arrived at Patrick Air Force Base through the wide front clamshell doors of a C-124 four-engine Globemaster transport from California on October 18, 1956, a record nine and a half months since the signing of the contract with Douglas. The Thor was numbered 101 in an attempt to fool Soviet intelligence into believing that the U.S. Air Force had a lot of these IRBMs near flight status, instead of just one. Mathison and the civilian contractors were approaching completion of one of the two launch emplacements for Thor and Jupiter and would have it ready in December. The second would not be finished until mid-1957. (The Atlas ICBM still held the highest priority as far as Schriever was concerned and so Moose had concentrated on completing the two launching stands for it by the end of the year, even though test firings would not begin for another six months.) One IRBM facility was enough for the moment and Mettler and Thiel had plenty of minor fixes to the missile and its various subsystems to keep them occupied until Mathison and the contractors were done. They had not had time to train a special launch crew for the blockhouse and so they formed a scratch one composed of themselves and other Ramo-Wooldridge engineers, a couple of Hall's officers, and Douglas personnel.

By January, a month behind schedule, all last-minute adjustments were done and they had the missile mounted on the circular launch pad. It was time to conduct several "captive" or "hold down" firings, also called "flight readiness firings." A rocket must be held upright on its launch pad by immensely strong steel latch mechanisms until the engine or engines swell to sufficient thrust to overcome the weight of the missile itself. At that point, the latches are thrown open and the missile lifts off into the air. If there were no latches to hold the missile in place, it would tip over before enough thrust had developed and blow up on the pad. The latch mechanisms permit the engineers, as part of the final flight readiness process, to further test the missile by igniting the engines, usually for short burns before they are shut down, without ever turning the rocket loose to fly. Mettler and Thiel had wanted to do this before coming to the Cape, but given the gallop to launch Schriever had imposed, there was no chance to construct concrete stands in California on which to lash down Thor for these captive firings. And so they were instead done using the latch mechanisms on the pad at Canaveral. All went well and January 25, 1957, was set as the launch date.

A countdown for a launch was (and still is) a complicated, tedious, and often exasperating procedure. Test missiles were instrumented with a myriad of sensors that served two purposes. Prior to the flight, they told the launch crew whether the missile's systems—propulsion, hydraulic steering controls, guidance, and others—were correctly connected and functioning well. During the flight, the same sensors monitored these systems to determine whether they actually did function as they were supposed to do. If something went wrong, the sensor detected what had gone awry so that the problem could be remedied before the next launch. In addition to sensors monitoring the main systems, there were many others that measured such factors as speed and angle of flight, the temperature on the surface of the missile at various points, and whether the engines were shutting down instantly at just the right moment to hurl the warhead accurately toward its target. The information provided by the sensors was called telemetry, a word sometimes used to refer to the sensors themselves. Once the missile took flight, the telemetry was transmitted to radio receivers on the ground through small transponders. The electrical power to operate these transponders was provided by batteries fitted into the Thor. (Later a more sophisticated power supply was devised by building a generator into the missile body.)

The interior of the blockhouse was brightly illuminated by fluorescents hung from the ceiling. Rows of consoles, their faces covered with instruments that gave off readings from the sensors, were arrayed around a table in the center. The instruments on a console encompassed the telemetry for a particular system of the missile, for example propulsion or hydraulic controls, or monitored some other aspect such as temperature or speed. A crew member of this pickup launch team sat in front of each console and called off the instrument readings as Mettler, who was acting as launch director, orchestrated the countdown from the table in the center. Thiel, as his deputy and the only man in the blockhouse with experience gained at White Sands and the Redstone Arsenal, moved from console to console, making certain they were getting correct readings and supervising anything else that required his expertise. If a malfunction is discovered during a countdown and it is a simple matter of something like a faulty electrical switch that needs only a few minutes to replace, then the countdown picks right up and marches on after it is repaired. But if the malfunction is substantial and requires longer to remedy, the countdown has to stop completely and resume again from the beginning, no matter how much time has been invested up to that point.

Despite all the prior testing and preparatory work by Mettler and Thiel and their colleagues, Thor 101 required several countdowns before they reached the critical and potentially perilous step of fueling the missile. The RP-1 was a stable element. The kerosene was pumped without much concern from the storage tank at the launching emplacement into its tank in the upper portion of the Thor. The liquid oxygen, or LOX as it was called, which burned the kerosene at the highest possible temperature to generate maximum thrust from the rocket engine, was an entirely different matter. A high-speed turbo-pump within the missile mixed the LOX and RP-1 before feeding them into the burn chamber of the rocket motor. LOX was highly volatile. To keep it from vaporizing, "boiling off," it had to be kept under cryogenic conditions—297 degrees below zero Fahrenheit—in an insulated storage tank that resembled a giant thermos bottle. To prevent or at least slow down vaporization of LOX after it had been pumped into the oxidizer tank in the lower section of the Thor, the first step in the entire fueling process was to cool down, "cold soak," the missile as much as possible by flushing both the RP-1 and LOX tanks with liquid nitrogen stored at the same cryogenic temperature as the LOX. Nitrogen is an inert gas that could be pumped into and out of the Thor's tanks without danger. The nitrogen also provided a means of checking for leaks, which had to be avoided at all cost, particularly where the LOX was concerned. Great care was imperative at every stage of its handling. The slightest spark would set it to burning fiercely once it began to vaporize. If it was contaminated in any way during the fueling process, instead of burning the kerosene in the rocket motor, it would explode.

But on this day, the fueling process went off without incident. The final steps in the countdown were completed. Mettler and Thiel and everyone else in the blockhouse felt their year of toil under unremitting pressure was soon to be rewarded with a ballistic missile sailing downrange across the islands of the Caribbean. "Everything looked just perfect," Mettler remembered. He turned loose the simple computer of the day that controlled the electrical firing sequence to ignite the engine. Roaring flames enveloped the launch pad, thrust built to the lifting point, the steel latch mechanisms holding down the missile were thrown open, and Thor 101 began to rise. It rose about eighteen inches and then suddenly fell back on the pad. With a deafening blast and a shock wave that was felt in the blockhouse, the missile blew up, not only tearing itself into pieces but also damaging the concrete launch pad seriously enough that Mathison's civilian construction crews needed two months to restore the pad to usable condition.

At the birth of Thor in 1955, Mettler had thought it both generous and daring of Schriever and Ramo to put a thirty-one-year-old engineer with no experience in rocketry in charge of the Ramo-Wooldridge technical direction team on a project this important. (He knew the decision had not been Ramo's alone because the two men conferred on everything that mattered.) When he later thought about that traumatic day in January 1957, he reflected that had they been different men they would have fired him right then, if only to satisfy the bureaucratic reflex to single out a scapegoat for such a catastrophe. They were waiting for him over at the motel at Cocoa Beach. They had flown to Patrick earlier in the day, checked into the motel, and had intended to watch the launch from there. Schriever was due in Washington the next day to brief the Joint Chiefs of Staff. Mettler drove over to the motel and told the two men he had no explanation for the failure. It was a mystery he and the rest of the Thor team would have to unravel. He could tell that Schriever and Ramo were disappointed, but neither man reproached him. "I expect things like this to happen," Schriever said. Mettler came away grateful and admiring of the courage of Schriever and Ramo in their willingness to risk giving him a second chance. He did not get off entirely lightly. Schriever took him along to Washington to join in the briefing the next day for the Joint Chiefs on the entire missile program. He had Mettler speak to the august body on the portion dealing with the Air Force IRBM. The chiefs, Schriever knew, would hold him and not Mettler responsible for the failure, but he seems to have reasoned that it would be best for them to hear the details from a man with firsthand knowledge.

For weeks, the explanation eluded Mettler and Thiel and their colleagues. They examined and reexamined the wreckage, checked and rechecked their instruments, went back over the countdown procedure again and again, always in vain. "The pressure came up, all the instruments were okay, and the damn thing was ready to go, and yet it didn't go," Mettler recalled of their bafflement. "In desperation, day and night we tried to find out what the devil was wrong." Finally, they turned to examining every photograph and every bit of film that had been taken of the launch. They were sitting in a hangar, "sort of bleary-eyed," as Mettler put it, watching a public relations film the Douglas company had made when all of a sudden they spotted the trail. The answer turned out to be not a complicated technological treatise, but once again an explanation as simple as the hot-box metal cupboards on the SAC bombers that had been destroying the vacuum tubes in the navigation and bomb release systems.

The film showed two technicians in white jackets, with "Douglas" printed in large letters across the backs, pulling a hose that was to be used to fill the oxidizer tank of the Thor with LOX. They were dragging one end of the hose, the end that was to be connected to the valve on the oxidizer tank, through sand. "Even a grain of sand in liquid oxygen under impact will explode," Mettler said. And here was the LOX hose picking up a good many grains. They searched through the wreckage again until they found and collected the remains of the valve on the tank to which the hose had been connected. Fitting the pieces together, they saw that the valve had been shattered "from the inside out," Mettler said. The probability that contamination from sand had caused the LOX to explode, rather than to burn, seemed certain, but to make sure they performed an experiment in the isolation of the Rocketdyne engine test grounds in Southern California. They set up a LOX tank with a fill valve identical to the one on Thor, contaminated the valve with sand while pumping in LOX, then closed it and ignited the LOX with an electrical charge. The valve immediately blew up. In the future, all hoses, valves, and other connections were kept in a state of pristine cleanliness that became known in the liquid-fueled rocket business as "LOX-clean."

54.

MEDARIS GOES FOR THE ICBM

On April 19, 1957, approximately two months and three weeks later, the launch pad had been repaired, several captive flight-readiness firings for the new missile had been completed, and the countdown was under way in the blockhouse for Thor 102. The atmosphere was particularly tense, not only because of the failure of Thor 101, but also because this was the second and possibly the third attempt (Mettler and Thiel could not remember precisely when they were interviewed many years later) to launch Thor 102. A twenty-four-hour limit had been established for launch attempts. It was feared that if countdowns had to be aborted and resumed over and over until the launch began to run more than twenty-four hours, the blockhouse crew would become so fatigued that someone would read an instrument incorrectly with disastrous results. Therefore, once twenty-four hours had been expended, the launch had to be canceled. This was precisely what had happened on the first, and the second, attempt to launch Thor 102. The countdowns had been repeatedly stymied by the discovery of mechanical problems. The countdown had to be stopped and restarted several times again on April 19, but matters went better on this day and Mettler at last pressed the button to start the electrical ignition sequence.

Thor 102 responded with fire and the percussive waves of its thunderous voice. When the hold-down latches on the launch pad were thrown open, the rocket rose, slowly at first, and then with quickening acceleration, beginning to fly up and out toward the sea. There was immense relief and exhilaration in the blockhouse until, just thirty-two seconds into the flight, the missile exploded. The range safety officer, housed separately in a central control bunker, announced that he had blown it up. Every missile launched at Cape Canaveral carried a packet of explosives hooked up to a radio-activated detonator. If a missile went awry and turned inland, the range safety officer pushed his destruct button to protect the lives and property of Florida's civilians.

Thiel was astonished. The instruments in the blockhouse had indicated that Thor 102 was doing fine, heading right out for the Caribbean. Some of his German friends and former colleagues from the Redstone Arsenal, who were at Canaveral for Jupiter launchings, had watched the launch from a building not far away. They told Thiel the missile had been flying perfectly and should not have been demolished. He and Mettler hurried to the control blockhouse. Unhinged by rage, Dolf Thiel dashed inside and confronted the range safety officer, an Air Force major. "You son of a bitch, why did you destroy the missile?" he shouted at the man. "You're nuts," he yelled, grabbing the major and cocking back his fist to punch the officer in the face. Mettler caught hold of Thiel's arm just in time. "Take it easy, take it easy," he said, calming his deputy.

It turned out that the mishap was the result of incompetence by a Ramo-Wooldridge technician and panic by the range safety officer. The range safety officer had three instruments with which to monitor the flight of a missile. One was an optical device with powerful magnification and a reticle with two parallel lines that enabled him to determine whether the missile was flying straight up, as it was supposed to do, or veering off to one side. The second was a standard radar tracking scope, referred to as a "skin radar" because the impulses of its transmitter were reflected back from the outer surface of whatever object it was tracking. The third was a different radar that had just been added to these first two monitoring instruments in the control center blockhouse at the instigation of someone on Mettler's staff. It was a Doppler Velocity and Position radar, otherwise known by its acronym, DOVAP. The Doppler radar tracked the Thor through a beacon installed in the missile and provided a more precise reading of the speed and position of the missile than the skin radar.

There was nothing wrong with this particular Doppler radar apparatus, but when the Ramo-Wooldridge technician installed it, he hooked it up backward. Instead of showing Thor 102 heading out to sea, the DOVAP showed it flying inland toward the city of Orlando. To make matters worse, someone from Ramo-Wooldridge had also advised the range safety officer to rely on the DOVAP as his principal monitoring instrument. The major had been understandably alarmed to see this IRBM streaking for inland Florida on the DOVAP scope. He should, however, have kept his head and followed commonsense procedure by looking at his two other instruments to be certain he was getting a correct reading. No electronic device is entirely dependable. A range safety officer is supposed to act with dispatch, but not to destroy lightly an expensive missile. Seconds counted, but he had seconds to spare. Instead, he had panicked and mashed the destruct button. He was transferred not long afterward to Alaska.

At least they knew now they had a missile that could fly, and on May 20, 1957, the countdown began in the blockhouse for Thor 103. It turned into a day of ill omens. Time after time they ran into problems that required them to stop the countdown and took long to remedy and they had to start the countdown over again. On through the night and into the next day the relentless process continued. By the morning of May 21 they had reached the twenty-four-hour limit, when the rules said they had to cancel the launch to avoid the chance of a grievous error from crew fatigue. But Thiel's blood was up and he did not want to quit on this third attempt to demonstrate that Thor could take to the air with the best of missiles. He was convinced that with just a bit more time they would achieve liftoff. The blockhouse had a direct Teletype line to the headquarters in California. Thiel persuaded Mettler to send an urgent message to Lieutenant Colonel Richard Jacobson, Schriever's overall chief of test facilities and operations, and ask for an exemption to continue. Jacobson's response was swift: "Negative. Approval is not granted. Terminate the test in accordance with standard operating procedures." Schriever and Ramo were late flying to Patrick and had just arrived at the motel at Cocoa Beach. Mettler and Thiel decided to go over Jacobson's head. Mettler telephoned Schriever at the motel and said the missile was nearly ready to go and asked permission to exceed the twenty-four-hour limit and launch it. Bennie's instinct was that Mettler and Thiel and the entire launch crew must be so exhausted by now from the interminable countdowns and from the stress they were all feeling that the wise thing to do was to stop and get a night's sleep. "Look, let's call this off and we'll start again tomorrow," he said to Mettler. But Mettler was insistent. They really wanted to go now, he said. "Well, I won't second-guess your judgment," Schriever said, relenting. "If you want to go, go ahead." He and Ramo walked out of their rooms to watch the launch. All of a sudden, the horizon over at the Cape was illuminated by a huge flash. "It lit up the sky," Schriever remembered.

The LOX tank of Thor 103 had ruptured, incinerating the missile on the pad, the intensely hot fire causing enough damage so that Mathison and the contractors again had to refurbish the pad. And crew fatigue and the loss of focus that accompanies it had been the cause. One of the earlier countdowns had reached the point where they had fueled the missile. Over the subsequent hours, as the countdown was repeatedly aborted and then resumed, enough of the volatile LOX vaporized so that the supply in the missile's oxidizer tank had to be topped off with more. A technician was assigned to make certain they did not overpressurize the tank in the process. The faces of the instruments of the time were the old-fashioned variety known as analog, not the brightly lit and colored numbers of the digital gauges that lay in the future. There were two pressure gauges for the oxidizer tank. One was a dial with a needle. The second was a drum on which was placed a round paper graph printed with lines to delineate levels of pressure. As the drum slowly rotated, an inking arm traced the amount of pressure in the tank. An investigation disclosed that while the technician might have kept looking at the gauge, he had lost so much alertness from exhaustion that he was no longer seeing it. Otherwise, he would have noticed that the needle had swung over into the red. The inked line on the paper delineated enough overpressure to burst the seal on the oxidizer tank and send Thor 103 to its fiery oblivion. Mettler was so embarrassed by what happened that he avoided seeing Schriever or talking to him on the phone for several days. He was not fired. Instead, Schriever removed Hall.

Bennie was in serious trouble. While he had nothing to show for Thor but three fiascoes, the Jupiter of his Army rival, Major General John Medaris, and of Medaris's prized team of Wernher von Braun and his German rocketeers, had been flying well. The first Jupiter, launched on March 1, 1957, approximately five weeks after Thor 101 exploded eighteen inches above the pad, had flown for seventy-two seconds before breaking up. The second, sent aloft on April 12, flew for ninety-two seconds before disintegrating. Telemetry disclosed that when the missile turned, fuel sloshed back and forth in the tanks with enough momentum to overcome the Jupiter's steering controls. A solution was rapidly worked out and adjustments made to the missile. On May 31, 1957, just ten days after the overpressurized LOX tank burst and Thor 103 perished in pyrotechnic wonder, a third Jupiter lifted off from Cape Canaveral. It sailed 1,610 miles down the Caribbean range, approaching the entire distance of 1,725 miles required for a full-fledged IRBM. Superior knowledge and skill acquired over years of hands-on experience were telling in the contest. For all their brain-power and engineering diplomas, with the exception of Thiel, Bennie's team was a pack of amateurs up against professionals. The difference was evident in a matter as simple as countdown times. Von Braun and his Germans did not engage in any attention-draining, twenty-four-hour countdown sessions. The countdown time for the first Jupiter ran an hour and fifty-five minutes, for the second two hours and fourteen minutes. The von Braun *équipe* got the third Jupiter, the one that flew nearly as far as needed, into the air in eight minutes. Von Braun had been able to find out quickly what had gone wrong on his first two launches because he instrumented Jupiter extensively. His missile carried sensors to transmit 150 points of telemetry. Thor was instrumented for less than a third of these. He also flight-tested components for Jupiter by launching them in Redstone missiles. In all, he was to stage twenty-nine Redstone firings at Canaveral for this purpose. It was no wonder that while Schriever was months behind schedule in Thor firings, Medaris was a bit ahead of schedule with Jupiter.

The previous year, Medaris had lost two important battles in the rivalry with the Air Force over ballistic missiles. On November 20, 1956, Secretary Wilson had issued a new "roles and missions" directive specifying that although the Army was building Jupiter, the Air Force would be responsible for its "operational employment." In other words, once Medaris and von Braun finished perfecting Jupiter, they would have to turn the missile over to the Air Force to deploy against the Soviets. Wilson had also decreed that in the future Army missiles would be restricted to a 200-mile range. The decisions, certainly approved by Eisenhower if not perhaps instigated by him, probably had as much to do with saving money by avoiding more duplication as they did with ruling that the Air Force was the logical service to control long-range missiles. But losing two battles did not amount to losing the war. If Thor was sufficiently discredited, Medaris could argue that it ought to be canceled on the grounds that the Air Force was incapable of building a satisfactory intermediate-range ballistic missile, at least within an acceptable period of time.

If he accomplished this, he could move on to the argument that since the Air Force had failed at the IRBM, how could anyone logically expect it to succeed at the far more difficult task of an ICBM? This need, so vital to the nation's security, should therefore be entrusted to his U.S. Army Ballistic Missile Agency and his superb German rocket builders, whose track record would assure success. Medaris had always had ambitions that went far beyond the intermediate-range Jupiter. He and von Braun had already discussed the possibility of a rocket big enough to carry men to the moon and in August 1958 would obtain approval from the Defense Department's Advanced Research Projects Agency to start designing it. Von Braun would also welcome the chance to move on from Jupiter to an ICBM because it would entail the creation of large rocket boosters, a sine qua non for space travel. Both men began denigrating Thor to anyone who would listen and also criticizing Atlas. The ingenious weight-saving concept Karel Bossart had first devised in the 1940s, a fuselage of thinly rolled steel that was inflated by the rocket's fuel, was "a balloon" that was unlikely to withstand the traumatic stresses of launching. While this scenario of the Army taking over the ICBM program because Schriever made a hash of Thor might seem far-fetched decades later, it was not far-fetched in 1957. Medaris had a trump he could play if Bennie gave him an opening. He had von Braun and von Braun's credibility in the making of rockets.

Schriever saw Medaris's game right away. Suddenly the minor project he had not wanted had turned into a nightmare threatening the major project that had become his life's ambition. He blamed Hall for what had occurred because the failures were not flaws in the missile itself. They were failures in the testing process and Bennie felt that Hall, as chief of propulsion for WDD and program director for Thor, should have been paying enough attention to avert them. The difficulty, as always, was Hall's personality. Hall was convinced that Mettler and the entire Ramo-Wooldridge contingent were unnecessary. They were interlopers. There was already enough technical expertise within the Air Force itself, Hall believed, for the service to act as its own prime contractor and systems engineer and to guide industry in the creation of both the IRBM and the ICBM. Schriever, who had good reason to believe otherwise and who was in command, was not about to jettison the partnership with Ramo. There was thus nothing Hall could do to change the situation, but he could not bring himself to accept it. And, as was to be expected with him, he did not hesitate to voice his resentment. As a result, he did not get along with Mettler and the rest of the Ramo-Wooldridge team assigned to Thor. Thiel was an exception, perhaps because Hall respected his knowledge, but Thiel in turn had decidedly mixed feelings toward Hall because of his behavior. On one occasion, when Hall had come to Canaveral to witness the launching of a Jupiter, he began calling out "Blow! Blow! Blow!" as the rocket rose. Some of Thiel's former German colleagues, with whom he swapped information and maintained cordial relations despite the rivalry, were sitting close by in the reviewing stands. He was embarrassed to the quick that they would see him associated with someone so lacking in politeness and protocol as to shout for their missile to blow itself up. "He was really a horrible guy . . . very arrogant," Thiel said.

Hall did fulfill his role of program director by participating in all of the working sessions in California. He was not, however, perhaps because of his antagonism toward Mettler, attending the launches at Canaveral, where he would have had the authority and responsibility as the senior Air Force representative to exercise supervision and control. Instead, he was delegating the task to a subordinate on his staff but was not giving the officer a charter to wield the same supervisory power he could have brought to bear. Because Schriever's management method consisted essentially of gathering around him men with outstanding aptitude for particular endeavors, or sharp-witted enough to grasp a new task swiftly, and then turning them loose to accomplish their roles while he surveyed all as a kind of high-tech ringmaster, Bennie had tolerated Hall. The lesson on how to get men to do what he wanted had been learned and practiced ever since, as a junior lieutenant, he had been given a Civilian Conservation Corps camp full of rambunctious boys to govern in Texas. "Talented people can be difficult," he once remarked. "You have to let them do things their way." But the tolerance was extended only as long as they produced for him and Hall was definitely not producing on Thor. Schriever had to find a replacement for him as soon as possible.

55

THE RELUCTANT RESCUER

A day or so after Thor 103 burned on the launching pad and while he was still on the East Coast, Schriever telephoned the lieutenant colonel who had so briskly instructed Mettler to abort the launch, Richard Jacobson, his chief of test facilities and operations. "Jake," he said, "I need you to take over the program." Jacobson had been warned by one of Schriever's deputies to expect the call and he had his answer ready. "General, I don't want it," he replied. "I really don't want it." He explained that he had striven hard to establish a reputation for performance in the Air Force and had too much to lose by getting involved with a sinking enterprise. "I can understand that," Schriever said, "but you know we're in a terrible competition with the Army, and if we can't make an IRBM work, the Army's going to say we can't make an ICBM work, and we're going to lose the whole guided missile program. You've got to make Thor work." The pressure on Schriever had become excruciating. One of his officers recalled long afterward that during a staff briefing on a Saturday, when Bennie had left orders he was not to be disturbed, his secretary had appeared at the doorway and said there was a call he had to take in his office. "That was Eisenhower," he said, as he walked back into the meeting, "and I'm not sure I'll be here on Monday."

Jacobson felt bad having to refuse Schriever anything because he had such respect for the man. The respect had been earned at the Pentagon one day back during the interregnum before the adoption of the Gillette Procedures. If they were to maintain schedule and proceed "to the maximum extent that technology would allow," as General White, the vice chief of staff, had directed in May 1954, they needed approximately $130 million for the next fiscal year. The launch complexes to be built at Canaveral, the downrange monitoring stations through the Caribbean, and other essentials, all had to be paid for. Yet they had so far been allotted only $38 million. Schriever arranged an appeal before a board of the Air Staff. Jacobson was awed by the galaxy of stars in the room. The chairman of the committee was a three-star general and all of its members had at least two and a couple of them three.

Schriever, followed by Jacobson and others from the WDD staff, briefed the committee on why they absolutely had to have the additional funds. The generals listened patiently and then discussed the matter among themselves. The three-star chairman turned to Schriever. "General, we have other high priority things and we don't have the funds," he said. "You're going to have to live with the $38 million and make your schedule." Schriever, as was his wont, had been sitting behind a table with his feet propped up on another chair. It was a favorite position because it was relaxing and solved the problem of what to do with his long legs. He took his feet off the chair and stood up, a conspicuous figure with the single star on his shoulder tabs before this multistarred committee. "Gentlemen," he said, "you can tell me what schedule you want me to make, in which case I'll tell you how much money you will have to provide. Or you can tell me how much money you will provide and I will tell you what schedule you will get. But you can't tell me both." Jacobson was astonished. A junior general running a program, no matter what the priority, was expected to salute and march off once his betters had rendered judgment. The program would then fall far behind schedule, or perhaps not get finished at all, but the requirements of seniority and protocol and budget would be satisfied. The committee had expected Schriever to behave accordingly. "My God," Jacobson thought, "these guys are going to eat him alive." The chairman broke the silence. "General, let us discuss it," he said. "We'll get back to you. Just wait outside." In about ten minutes they were summoned back into the room. "General," the three-star said to Schriever, "you're absolutely right. You've got your money."

Back in a bind again, Schriever was not about to relent with Jacobson. He pointed out that as far as he could tell, there was nothing fundamentally wrong with the missile. "All three errors have been because of the way in which they tested," he said. "And you, as director of tests, know more about how to get this thing done than anybody and I want you to do it." Jacobson tried again to wiggle away. "Boss, I got to tell you, I don't want my name on that goddamn program. You're going to lose that program." Jacobson was assuming that, with Jupiter flying so smoothly, should Thor run into much more trouble,

Secretary Wilson, if for no reason other than to please a president who was always seeking ways to reduce the military budget, would reverse himself and declare Jupiter the nation's IRBM. Schriever cut a deal with Jacobson. "I'll tell you what, Jake, I'll leave you as director of tests, but I'll make you acting program director of Thor," he said, underscoring the word "acting." "If you're concerned about it being on your record, it will never appear." Jacobson relented, partway. "Well, you've got a program director named Ed Hall," he said. "I'll get him out of your way," Schriever replied. And so he did, but not in a manner that would disgrace Hall and force his departure. Ed Hall was too gifted a man to lose. Schriever had in mind a new prospect appropriate to those gifts, one he knew Hall would take up with enthusiasm. He wanted to keep Hall around until matters matured enough for him to assign Hall to it. In effect, he suspended Hall while he shifted Jacobson into his job. He told Hall that although Jacobson would be taking over Thor, Hall would officially remain the program director. He was to wait in this holding pattern until Schriever could arrange an alternative worthy of him.

In Jacobson, Schriever had found a man who could rescue him from his predicament, for Richard "Jake" Jacobson was a man prepared to expend whatever energy and perseverance were required to achieve his ends. He was extremely intelligent, one of the smartest officers ever to serve Schriever. Enemies called him "Jake the Snake." The epithet was undeserved, a parting shot from officers angry at having been bested by him in some professional scrape. While he would resort to guile when necessary, Jacobson was no intriguer. He was normally as candid as he had been on the telephone with Schriever, his forthrightness reinforced by the cuss words that laced his language. The son of a prosperous family of Jewish ancestry in the ladies garment business in Birmingham, Alabama, he had grown up in a house with four African-American servants, including the chauffeur. His father steered him into business administration at the University of Alabama because it was assumed he would take up the family trade, but he found the subject boring and soon switched to his first intellectual love, mathematics, and developed an interest in flying.

By the fall of 1943 he was in England, a twenty-three-year-old captain in the U.S. Army Air Forces, piloting a C-47 transport in a troop carrier group. When a call went out for volunteers to fly a special

("special" being the military euphemism for "dangerous") mission, Jacobson raised his hand and found himself in a squadron that dropped
the first paratroops, the "pathfinders," during an airborne landing. He
was designated lead pilot of one of the three-plane flights, called "seri-
als," into which the squadron was organized. The pathfinders were
equipped with radio beacons to guide the subsequent waves of C-47s
with the mass of airborne infantry to the correct landing zones. The
trick was to drop the pathfinders on the right spot, always difficult in
those years of relatively primitive navigation instruments and particularly so at night, as had to be done for the Normandy invasion. In the
predawn hours of D-Day, Jacobson led his three-plane serial at fifty
feet over the English Channel, then up to 700 feet as they crossed Normandy's Cotentin Peninsula to gain enough altitude for the parachutes
of the pathfinder troops crowding the planes to open. He suddenly realized that his navigator had failed to alert him to a turn and he was off
course. He took his three C-47s back out to the Channel and up over
the Cotentin and into the German antiaircraft fire once more, so that
these parachutists would not fling themselves out the doors and into
battle in vain. He was awarded the Silver Star for Gallantry and later,
from Charles de Gaulle's Free French government, a Croix de Guerre.

A Silver Star and a Croix de Guerre were not all he had brought
home from the war. He had, in another instance of Jacobson persistence, won a brunette English beauty named Ethel Davies, called by
her nickname, Peg. She was as strikingly lovely as Jacobson was strikingly homely. He had a beak of a nose, large ears that stuck out, and
while still in his twenties, except for the hair on the side of his head,
which he kept clipped short in military fashion, he was bald. He spotted her on a railway platform in Nottingham in the East Midlands,
near the airfield where his squadron was stationed, and asked if he
could sit beside her on the train. "Well, I suppose so," she replied. "It's
a free country." She was in uniform. Britain drafted its women for noncombat duty during the war, and to avoid ending up as a secretary, Peg
Davies had joined the Royal Signals branch of the women's army organization, the Auxiliary Territorial Service. She was working as a
switchboard operator at a depot in the vicinity. Her stop was first and
by the time she got off, Jacobson had maneuvered the conversation
around to learning the name of the place and what she did there.

When he called the switchboard soon afterward to ask for a date, she told the other operators not to put him through. She had been struck on the train by his baldness and found it hard to believe he was as young as he claimed to be. The bald Englishmen she knew were in their fifties. He kept calling and she kept refusing to take the calls. Then one evening, right after she had finished washing her hair, a guard at the depot gate sent word to her barracks that an American officer was there asking to see her. She dressed, wrapped her damp hair in a big white towel, and walked down to the gate. It was Jake. She decided that if he was this persistent, he was worth at least one date. He courted her on a motorcycle filched from a British airborne outfit during a pre–D-Day practice drop, with Lucky Strike cigarettes, Hershey bars, and hefty No. 10 cans of grape juice, and he took her to dinners at a restaurant in Nottingham that still served steaks, locally reputed to be horse meat. He also stayed on active duty an extra year so that he could fly back to England and marry her at a registry office in Shropshire in 1946.

Foresight into the coming importance of guided missiles had led Jacobson to Schriever. He brought his English bride home to Birmingham and spent the next two years completing undergraduate studies for a bachelor's in mathematics. Although he had left the service, he was still enrolled in the Reserve. While attending some mandatory Reserve schooling, he was informed by a general he knew that if he applied for a Regular commission, the newly independent U.S. Air Force would send him to MIT for two years of graduate study under Charles Stark Draper, the god of inertial guidance. He would receive the full pay and allowances of the lieutenant colonel's rank he now held in the Reserve, along with tuition and any other expenses. He arrived at MIT's Instrumentation Laboratory, which Draper headed, on a Saturday morning and found the renowned professor in shirt sleeves sweeping the floor of the former shoe polish factory. Jacobson mistook him for a janitor until he asked directions to Dr. Draper's office and the great man introduced himself. Because of sundry delays between Birmingham and Cambridge, Massachusetts, it was 1952 by the time Jacobson received his master's degree in engineering from MIT. The question now was what to ask the Air Force to let him do with it. The Matador and Snark missiles were still in the development stage, but they caught his attention. Guided missiles, he decided, were in the Air Force to stay and he might one day want to command a missile unit.

Nuclear weapons were also obviously here to stay and so he thought it would be a good idea to learn how to mate nuclear warheads to missiles.

The same general who had urged him to go to MIT arranged his assignment to the guided missiles section of the Special Weapons Command at Albuquerque's Kirtland Air Force Base. He spent the next two years there, weaponizing nuclear devices from Los Alamos, first for missiles and then for bombers and fighters as well. His superior was Colonel Charles Terhune, whom Schriever had recruited as his second man, WDD's deputy commander for technical operations, while putting together his Schoolhouse Gang in Inglewood in the summer of 1954. A test pilot at Wright Field and fighter pilot in the Pacific during the Second World War, Terry Terhune had a deserved reputation within the Air Force as an engineer of consummate ability. Once at the Schoolhouse, Terhune began rounding up other officers with engineering prowess for Schriever. The Air Force personnel department had selected Jacobson for a term at the Naval War College after his assignment to Kirtland, a comfortable academic year in Newport, Rhode Island. Terhune warned him that, with Schriever's authority to put a hand on whomever he wanted, Jacobson was coming to Schriever's shop sooner or later, and, if he wanted a good position, he had better come sooner. He told Peg they would not be going to Newport and came sooner, near the end of 1954. Moose Mathison, who had become Jacobson's deputy at Kirtland, followed in 1955. It was Jacobson who, with Schriever's assent, had then sent him to Canaveral as WDD's delegate to oversee construction of the launch complexes there. "Colonel, do you have any experience in test operations?" Schriever had asked Jacobson on his arrival at Inglewood. "No, sir," Jacobson had replied. "Do you know anything about testing?" Schriever had probed. "No, sir," Jacobson said. "Good. You're my director of tests," Schriever announced. Terhune had assured him Jacobson was a quick study. Bennie had therefore assumed he would learn. And he did.

The first thing Jacobson did after taking over Thor was to send an officer he trusted to the Douglas plant at Santa Monica to find out why the company was not performing as it had promised and the original contract required. The Thors had been arriving at Canaveral with many parts missing. The unlaunchable missiles sat in one of the assembly buildings at the Cape until the parts arrived from California after long delays, and were installed. Even if Thor 101 had not blasted the pad so badly that repairs had taken two months, lack of parts would have delayed the launch of Thor 102, the missile the range safety officer mistakenly blew up, for an equivalent period of time. Jake's investigator found, as Jacobson recalled years later, that the manufacturing procedures at the Douglas plant were "in sad shape" and the engineers there "didn't seem to give a damn." Jacobson briefed Schriever on what he had learned and said he intended to wake up the slackers. "Boss, I'm going to close down Douglas Aircraft Company until they straighten out," he said. "I'm going to get their attention." Get it, he did. He telephoned one of the senior executives that he was cutting off all payments until Douglas began producing on time and up to quality standards. Three days later the Douglas executives were in his office with a plan of reform. Hall took umbrage at Jacobson's brusque methods and, his pride hurt because he was still officially the program director, went over to Santa Monica and told the engineers to ignore Jacobson. They immediately telephoned Jacobson and asked him what they should do. He said to put Hall on the phone, but Hall refused to talk to him. Jacobson called the Air Force security people and had them escort Hall out of the plant. The issue took months to square away and, while Jacobson relented after a time and allowed funds to flow again, the threat that he would once more stop the money was enough to keep Douglas on good behavior.

Jacobson's next move was to appoint Moose Mathison his deputy. Whenever he could not be at Canaveral to oversee work on a Thor and preparations for a launch, Mathison was to act as his delegate and to speak with equivalent authority. The same would hold true in the blockhouse during a launch. If he happened to be absent for any reason, Mathison was the man. Like Schriever, Jacobson understood how thoroughly dependent the Air Force was on Mettler and Thiel and their associates. He was determined, again among his first tasks, to impress on the staff of approximately eight officers he had inherited from Hall that in the future he wanted teamwork with the Ramo-Wooldridge men, not internecine warfare. Hall's staff were not an untalented bunch. One staffer was Sidney Greene, who, while a major at the Air Development Center at Wright Field back in 1952, had risked his career to divert $2 million to Hall for the prototype of the Rocketdyne engine that was powering Thor and would also power Atlas. But Jacobson discovered that instead of welding his staff into a team, Hall had each man doing his own thing with little interaction beween them. He decided that inviting them all to dinner at his house with their wives would be a good way to break down barriers and asked Peg to telephone the women and set it up.

In these years in the military, when the wife of your husband's boss called to invite the two of you to dinner, you said, yes, thank you. Peg was baffled and angered by the negative responses she got. She rang Jake back. "I'm not dealing with that bunch," she said. Jake convened a staff meeting. "Mrs. Jacobson and I are going to have a little affair Friday night, and we would like each of you to come with your spouse. We think you will enjoy it," he said. "It is not a command performance, but I will take the name, rank, and serial number of any son of a bitch who doesn't show up." Attendance was 100 percent and Jake began to transform his staff. He sat them down with Mettler and Thiel and their people and, making no attempt to hide the peril that Thor was in, said the project was doomed unless both sides learned to cooperate. Mettler in turn promised all the support he could muster from the Ramo-Wooldridge group. "Jake, you tell us what you want done and we'll do it," he said. They went over all their launch procedures and tightened up. There were to be no more foolish gambles with time and alertness. Instruments were checked and double-checked. There were to be no more backward-flying DOVAP radars.

Nearly three and a half months went by before they could get another Thor ready to launch, but this time, on August 30, 1957, Thor 104 flew downrange for ninety-six seconds before it blew apart. Jacobson's shaking up of Douglas now began to pay off in dramatically shorter launch intervals. Thor 105 was readied a lot faster and did a lot better on September 20. It lofted up and away, the engine shutting down instantly as it was programmed to do at 137 seconds and releasing the empty warhead, which flew on for 1,495 miles before impacting into the Caribbean. Twenty-one days later they crossed the finish line. On October 11, 1957, Thor 106 lifted off in a ballistic missile's storm of fire and thunder and tossed its warhead off down the full required 1,725-mile course along the islands of the West Indies chain to splash into the Caribbean off Venezuela.

56

THOR VS. JUPITER

The success Jacobson wrought came none too soon. That August, Eisenhower, as part of a renewed campaign to constrict the military budget, had instructed Wilson to end the absurd expense of two IRBM programs. Wilson had established a committee consisting of Schriever and Medaris, with Wilson's special assistant for guided missiles, William Holaday, as chairman, to decide whether the nation's IRBM was to be Thor or Jupiter.

Eisenhower and Wilson were not naive men and it is difficult to believe they thought that either Schriever or Medaris would consent to the cancellation of his own missile. The committee appears to have been structured as it was so that Holaday could permit each of the contestants to argue his case, examine the test results at Canaveral, and then render judgment for one side or the other. Disagree the two contestants did. On September 25, 1957, Medaris sent Holaday a lengthy, point-by-point memorandum, thickened with nine attachments, which extolled Jupiter as the superior missile, its worth demonstrated by its testing record and guaranteed by superior rocket makers under Werner von Braun. His recommendation was:

  a. The JUPITER be continued as the IRBM and,
  b. The THOR project be cancelled as expeditiously as possible.

Schriever countered in his brief that Thor was the better choice for the country because it could be fielded faster than Jupiter. The prototype Jupiters were being built individually at the Redstone Arsenal. The final design of the missile would subsequently have to be farmed out to industry for production. (Medaris intended to use the Chrysler Corporation, which was manufacturing Redstone.) In contrast, because the test model Thors were being created by Douglas on production tooling, the Air Force had the ability to move right into full production and then deployment as soon as the problems common to any new missile were solved. Furthermore, Schriever argued, the Army was building only a missile, not an IRBM weapon system that could be fielded. The Jupiter project lacked provisions for ground support equipment, such as tanks for the LOX and RP-1, shelters to protect the missile from the weather, and other equipment necessary for deployment. By the time the Army got around to furnishing this equipment, more delay would ensue.

Holaday, who submitted his report on October 8, 1957, after Jacobson had begun to rescue the test launches with Thor 105's 1,495-mile flight on September 20, decided not to place himself in the middle of a nasty interservice row. He beat a bureaucrat's retreat. He said that unless Thor showed marked improvement, "the spectacular success which has been achieved by the Jupiter test flights" might eventually force its choice. But he recommended that in the meantime the Defense Department "continue both programs until we have a better basis for resolving the various problem areas."

In his report he did, however, state "a firm requirement" that whichever missile might eventually be chosen must have the capacity for upgrading "to a 2,000 nautical mile [2,301 statute mile] range from the present design" of 1,500 nautical. Medaris claimed that while Jupiter could easily achieve 2,020 nautical miles (2,324 statute), Thor would never be able to fly more than 1,660 nautical (1,909 statute) because of its heavier reentry vehicle. Thor's reentry vehicle, designated the Mark 2, weighed 3,500 pounds and was the same RV designed for Atlas. In the hustle to put Thor together, it had been adopted without any remodeling to size it down for the smaller rocket. It was a heat shield, or "heat sink," type. Its nose consisted of a massive, conical shield of solid, machined copper, five eighths to three quarters of an inch thick and six feet in diameter. Behind the shield was a stainless steel compartment in which the one-megaton hydrogen bomb was to ride. The shield alone weighed more than a thousand pounds. As this blunt nose RV descended back into the atmosphere, the shield absorbed the extreme heat generated by the friction of the air and protected the bomb behind it. Because of its shape and the size of the shield, it was also aimed to enter the atmosphere at a shallow angle, thereby slowing itself down as it descended and reducing heat that way as well.

Jupiter's reentry vehicle, which weighed 3,000 pounds, was the one

technological advance the Army missile had over Thor. It was an ablative type, the first of its kind to be mounted on an American ballistic
missile and a tribute to the knowledge gleaned from experience by von
Braun's team. The word, originally a grammatical term for nouns or
pronouns indicating separation, later also denoted the removal of tissue by a surgeon, the melting of ice or snow, typically from a glacier, or
the erosion of rock by wind action. In this age of guided missiles coming into being, "ablative" referred to a reentry vehicle coated with a
compound of plastic and other heat-absorbing elements. As the RV
plunged back into the atmosphere and friction built up from the den-
sity of the air, the coating was enveloped by the red-hot abrasion and
progressively burned away, thereby diverting the heat that would otherwise destroy the reentry vehicle and the hydrogen bomb inside it.
Usually conical-shaped, or rounded like the nose of a torpedo (Jupiter's
was conical, if much smaller in diameter than Thor's), an ablative RV
had distinct advantages. It descended at a steep angle and retained its
speed, making it more accurate because it was less subject to deflection
from its course by the winds of the upper atmosphere. For this reason,
an ablative RV was later adapted for Atlas. In the case of Thor and
Jupiter, any minor difference in accuracy was largely academic, as both
were first-generation area-destroying weapons referred to as "city
busters" in the language of nuclear weaponry.

Thor was stuck with its 3,500-pound reentry vehicle, Medaris contended. There was no practical way to shave off the 500 pounds necessary for the missile to reach the required 2,000 nautical mile range.
"This would mean a complete nose cone redesign with attendant high
cost and extensive re-test programs," he wrote. What he did not calculate was that an IRBM, flying a far shorter distance than an ICBM, also
flew at considerably less than an ICBM's speed, about 10,000 miles per
hour. The higher the speed, the greater the heat generated on reentry.
Thus the warhead on Thor did not need anything approaching the heat
protection afforded by the copper heat shield designed for the Atlas,
which was six feet in diameter.

Jacobson, because of his knowledge of guided missiles, understood
this. When Schriever, who was in Washington at the time, passed the
word to Jake that he had to fly Thor 2,000 nautical miles, Jacobson responded, "Hell, that's easy." He instructed Mettler to trim hundreds of
pounds (later he could not recall the precise figure) off both the heat

shield and the bomb compartment behind it. When the engine of Thor
107 was ignited on October 24, 1957, the rocket flew flawlessly on
past the 1,725-mile mark and over the Windward Islands, the last of
the West Indies, to plunge into the Atlantic Ocean 3,043 miles from its
launching pad on Cape Canaveral. The issue was never raised again.
For some reason, Neil McElroy, the Procter & Gamble executive who
succeeded Wilson as secretary of defense that October, never enforced
Holaday's requirement to extend the reach to 2,000 nautical miles.
The 1,500-nautical mile range was retained. Jake flew the subsequent
Thors with the original Atlas heat sink reentry vehicle. There was no
necessity to fashion a lighter one. Holaday's recommendation to wait
and see turned into permanent hesitation. The Army and Air Force
went on duplicating money and effort as each continued to build its
own IRBM. Major General John Medaris had lost his power play. Bennie Schriever's ICBM program was safe.

57.

SPUTNIK

Permitting the Air Force and the Army the extravagance of duplicating IRBMs became the least of Eisenhower's concerns after
Sputnik, the Soviet surprise of October 4, 1957. Near the end of August, the Russians announced that they had flight tested an ICBM.
Sergei Korolev's monster R-7 rocket, the Semyorka, had flown a
4,000-mile course from its launching pad at the new Soviet test center at Baikonur, also known as Tyuratam, in Kazakhstan in Central
Asia all the way across Siberia to the Kamchatka Peninsula on the
Bering Sea. The test was not perfect. The reentry vehicle disintegrated
about six miles above the earth. No matter: the length of the flight
was what counted. The Semyorka (designated the SS-6 Sapwood by
NATO intelligence officers) was in reality the precursor of a Soviet
ICBM. Designed to carry a super-size 5.4-ton fission, or atomic, payload because the Soviet Union did not explode its first full-fledged hy-

drogen bomb until November 1955, let alone begin the process of downsizing one for an ICBM warhead, the rocket was so huge it weighed twenty-three metric tons with its tanks empty, meaning that it could be moved only by rail. The steps necessary to prepare it for flight and fuel it with LOX and kerosene took twenty hours, versus the fifteen minutes for which the Atlas was being designed. The Soviets were to deploy only four Semyorkas at another new launch center readied in 1959, Plesetsk, south of Arkhangelsk (Archangel) in the far north of western Russia. Khrushchev's son Sergei remembered that his father also recoiled at the cost, about half a billion rubles per R-7 site. "What will we do, we'll be without pants," Khrushchev complained to Korolev.

But if its bulk and long readiness time rendered the R-7 impractical as an ICBM, its power made it ideal for the launching of satellites. The trick to tossing a satellite into orbit was to burn the rocket engines long enough to gain sufficient velocity to escape the gravitational pull of the earth. The R-7 had plenty of capacity for that. The August announcement of an ICBM was played down by Wilson and Eisenhower and caused only ripples in Washington and in the country as a whole. The event of October 4 was another matter. That evening Baikonur time, Korolev, as the Soviet Union's leading rocket designer, watched through his personal periscope in the blockhouse as his Semyorka lifted off carrying in its nose cone a metal ball polished to a silvered finish. Reed-thin radio antennae for the small battery-powered transmitter within the ball trailed back to the sides. The whole weighed only 83.6 kilograms, 184.3 pounds. The voice of the launch controller called off the drama over the blockhouse's loudspeaker system as the rocket attained the required velocity and the nose cone separated and flew into orbit. The glistening ball was released and began circling earth, its little transmitter emitting a *beep, beep, beep* that told the world the Soviet Union, and not the United States, had inaugurated the Space Age.

The ball was named Sputnik, simply the Russian word for "satellite," and it provoked a national ordeal of soul-searching in the United States. However much Americans worried about the Soviet Union, they had always assumed it was technologically inferior, incapable of besting the United States in everything from kitchen appliances to rockets that would open space. Was America, proud America, now slipping into second place? What was overlooked in the furor was that the Soviet Union was a selectively superior nation. In the highly stratified and contorted society that Stalin had hammered into being, while most citizens suffered austere lives of deprivation, the state created and concentrated highly advanced science and technology in areas that interested it and rewarded those scientists and technologists who served it, as Stalin had rewarded Igor Kurchatov and those who had produced the atomic bomb for him, with comfort and privilege. Sputnik was a manifestation of this pattern.

The creation of the R-7 meant that the Russians had a lead, and as was to be proven, a quite temporary one, in long-range rocketry. With it, they had been the first to decide to launch a space satellite. Sputnik did not mean, as Khrushchev crowed, and as many Americans now were afraid, that the Soviet Union was the future. Its overall technological and economic strength, with wide gaps in its infrastructure, was immensely inferior to that of the United States. Eisenhower could have sent up a space satellite ahead of or virtually simultaneous with the Russians had he been willing to spend the money and had he thought it necessary. The secret U-2 flights over Russia were, he believed, keeping him reasonably well informed of Soviet military advances. (He could have eased the political pressure on himself by sharing this unique intelligence with the Democratic leadership of Congress, but he considered the photography too sensitive to do so.) A space satellite to conduct photographic reconnaissance after the U-2 had outlived its usefulness was in the secret planning stage. He saw no need to go to considerable expense to throw up some interim but militarily useless satellite. (And as Schriever and his associates were to learn, the real trick was not to hurl a satellite into orbit. It was to bring back to earth intact what you put into the satellite.)

Dwight Eisenhower was the last American president to believe that military spending which was not absolutely necessary was money wasted and that a well-founded economy was as important to the security of the country as armed might. His achievements during the Second World War also gave him confidence in his military judgment. He listened to his admirals and generals and then made up his own mind. He was caught unawares by Sputnik because he failed to foresee the psychological and political repercussions if he permitted the Soviets to get a space satellite up first. He had left it to the Navy to send a tiny satellite into orbit for the 1957–58 International Geophysical Year with an inadequately tested rocket called Vanguard, which blew up on its pad on December 6, 1957, two months after Sputnik, to the further embarrassment of the nation. It was to be Wernher von Braun, on January 31, 1958, approximately four months after Sputnik, and with the administration's belated support, who demonstrated that satellites were not a Soviet monopoly. Using Juno I, a multistage rocket derived from the Redstone, he lofted Explorer I, an eighteen-pound satellite, into orbit.

Few Americans, however, viewed Sputnik in this perspective. The Democrats, who had long been critical of the administration for its parsimony toward the military, went on the assault. The formidable Senate majority leader from Texas, Lyndon Johnson, accused Eisenhower of imperiling America by his obsession with balancing the budget. Senator Symington called for a special session of Congress, declaring that "unless our defense policies are promptly changed, the Soviets will move from superiority to supremacy." "Scoop" Jackson, the clandestine ally of Bennie and Trevor Gardner in obtaining the Gillette Procedures, urged observance of "a week of shame and danger." Johnson soon announced the opening in late November of lengthy hearings by the Preparedness Investigating Subcommittee of the Senate Committee on Armed Services, which he headed.

The hearings were to endure through January 1958 with dozens of prominent witnesses and to subject the administration to rising political pressure. Nor did it help when, on November 3, 1957, to celebrate the fortieth anniversary of the Bolshevik Revolution, Korolev, at Khrushchev's behest, launched Sputnik 2. It weighed 1,120 pounds, six times the heft of Sputnik 1 and sixty-two times the weight of von Braun's little Explorer I, and orbited the globe with a mongrel dog named Laika aboard. American animal rights activists protested after the poor creature died from overheating of the capsule, but the Soviet press pronounced Laika a martyr for the cause of space. The leadoff witness at the Johnson hearings was that genius of scaremongering Dr. Edward Teller. He warned that the Russians might beat Americans to the moon, that they might learn to control the weather and render the United States a second-class nation by restricting rainfall over the North American continent, and that within ten years they would have the best scientists in the world because Russian students were such math and science whizzes. Despite the ludicrousness of much of Teller's testimony, his appeal to undertake a major educational reform in the United States by raising the level of scientific and mathematical education, an appeal reiterated by a number of the witnesses to follow, was well taken. The National Defense Education Act of 1958, which provided federal funds for the teaching of math, science, and foreign languages, was the first harvest of these reforms.

Sputnik was definitely a blessing out of the blue for Schriever. He had first heard Quarles speak of the "Poor Man's" approach the secretary wanted the Air Force to adopt when, in the summer of 1956, Quarles had rejected Schriever's Fiscal Year 1957 missile budget and ordered a revision with substantial cost reductions. Quarles was reflecting pressure from Wilson, who was in turn reflecting it from Eisenhower, to rein in military expenditures in order to avoid raising the ceiling on the national debt, then running at approximately $275 billion. In testimony before a Senate committee that summer, Quarles had defended his severe reductions in the overall research and development budget of the Air Force with classic Eisenhower thinking: "I believe it both necessary and feasible to provide adequate military defenses and, at the same time, to preserve the sound economic foundations of the Nation." The Air Staff pointed out to General White that if Quarles's economies were accepted, the Air Force would not be obeying Eisenhower's September 1955 National Security Council injunction to field an ICBM force "at the earliest possible date." The president solved that conflict himself by issuing a new NSC directive in March 1957 that changed the attainment of an operational ICBM capability to "the earliest practicable date." Schriever had submitted to Quarles's "Poor Man's" edict in the fall of 1956 and produced another budget, this one for Fiscal Year 1958, of $1.335 billion, 20 percent lower than the previous one, scything down the number of planned ICBMs from 120 Atlas and Titan missiles to 80.

The Air Staff and General White endorsed Schriever's new plan and warned it was "as low as we dare go." But this was not low enough for Quarles and Wilson and the president. They also slashed the number of IRBMs to be deployed, from the original eight Thor and eight Jupiter squadrons totaling 240 missiles to four squadrons of each and 120 missiles in all. A draft agreement to base the Thors in England was signed by Wilson and Duncan Sandys, Britain's minister of defense, in January 1957 and ratified by Eisenhower and Prime Minister Harold Macmillan when they met at Bermuda that March. The Jupiters were eventually to be based in Italy and Turkey after agreements were later reached with both of those countries.

In May 1957, the blade of the economy guillotine fell once more, slicing another $200 million off the "as low as we dare go" missile budget of $1.335 billion. And again this was not enough. In July, Wilson, after he was chided at a National Security Council meeting for not being sufficiently ruthless, announced his intention to squeeze to $1 billion the annual missile costs of all three services, including those for a revolutionary submarine-launched ballistic missile named Polaris that the Navy had initiated. Schriever was nearly forced to eliminate overtime costs at the factories, to delay payments, and to slow down production. The existing program called for six Atlas, seven Titan, and six Thor missiles to come off the line every month. Wilson pressed the Air Force so hard that General White offered to take this down to four of each type per month, despite the delay this would have on deployment, but Wilson withheld agreement on the offer. He ordered the Air Force to study the repercussions of going down to a two-two-two production rate. Schriever did his best to keep the contractors who were building his missiles from becoming utterly discouraged. "There has been no change in national priority," he told the Convair and Douglas and other executives. What was occurring was "certain adjustments of key milestone dates" and "a logical stretch-out" of the program. And all of this was in vain. Despite reassuring words and soothing bureaucratic jargon, he could not prevent a deterioration in the morale of his contractors and within his own staff. They were supposed to be engaged in an enterprise central to the survival of the nation and this niggardly government was acting as if they were spendthrift schoolboys. Then Sergei Pavlovich Korolev sent his R-7 Semyorka aloft with Sputnik like a Space Age cavalry to the rescue.

THOR READIES FOR ENGLAND

A letter to Eisenhower on December 3, 1957, from his new secretary of defense, Neil McElroy, reflected the transformed political reality. McElroy told the president that the planned reductions in spending for ballistic missiles were "of historical interest" only. At an NSC meeting on January 30, 1958, the president gave in to the inevitable. He held firm on the number of Thor and Jupiter IRBM missiles that were to go to England, Italy, and Turkey, probably because he knew he could get away with this as they were to be deployed abroad. These IRBMs were to remain at four squadrons each for 120 missiles in all. The powerhouse ICBMs that were to be based in the United States were a different matter. The earlier total of approximately 120 was restored, divided into nine squadrons of Atlas ICBMs and four squadrons of Titans. A production target of six Atlas, six Titan, and eight Thor missiles per month, virtually the same as the old, was also instituted and restrictions on overtime were soon relaxed. Test launching at Cape Canaveral, which had never stopped despite the "Poor Man's" lament, was moving on.

The monitoring and tracking stations downrange through the Caribbean and into the South Atlantic had assumed increasing importance. The launches had been progressing from simple proofs of propulsion, steering, airframe worthiness, and capability for full distance flight into the more advanced testing necessary to make certain that each and every aspect of the weapon functioned as designed. To evaluate the entire performance of the missiles required a prodigious and far-flung array of monitoring and tracking stations. While Moose Mathison had been fighting off mosquitoes and supervising construction of the launch facilities at the Cape, Jake Jacobson had been busy making certain that this downrange network would be ready for Thor and then Atlas and Titan to follow. The Air Force had engaged Pan American Airways to build the stations with civilian construction crews and subsequently to take charge of the housekeeping chores. The

Radio Corporation of America was hired to provide the technicians who operated the radio and radar gear.

The missiles were initially picked up by a station at Jupiter Auxiliary Air Force Base on the Florida coast 110 miles south of Canaveral. The network then jumped seaward, following south and east along the islands that separate the Caribbean Sea from the Atlantic Ocean. The Bahamas led off with a station at Grand Bahama Island, then on down through the rest of the Bahamas to Eleuthera, to San Salvador, where Columbus made his first landfall in the New World, and to Mayaguana; then to Grand Turk Island in the Turks and Caicos Islands; then to the Dominican Republic on Hispaniola Island; on to Mayaguez Auxiliary Air Force Base on the American possession of Puerto Rico; to Antigua in the Leewards, 1,500 miles southeast of Cape Canaveral and far enough down the island chain to measure the range and accuracy of Jupiter and Thor. Next came a long leap to the island of Fernando de Noronha off the coast of Brazil, and after that a second leap to Ascension Island in the South Atlantic, midway between Brazil and Africa, approximately 4,500 miles southeast of Canaveral and 625 miles north of lonely St. Helena, where Napoleon was exiled to die. Ascension was to be the preliminary terminal point for Atlas and Titan. Twelve modified Second World War cargo ships, fitted out with appropriate gear, put to sea whenever there was to be a launch, filling in the gaps, particularly between Antigua and Ascension in the South Atlantic. Undersea cables tied many of the stations back to Cape Canaveral, providing instantaneous and secure communications.

The radar at the stations, while sophisticated and precise, fulfilled the relatively simple task of tracking the missile. The radio monitors had a more complicated job. They had to pick up and record the telemetry from the sensors fitted into the missiles. Atlas and Titan, before their testing was completed, were to carry sensors for 1,500 points of data during flight. All elements of the weapon, short of putting an actual hydrogen bomb into the warhead and exploding it, had to be proven by test. Not that the bomb was forgotten. A simulated bomb provided by the Los Alamos Laboratory with real arming devices and an actual fuse attached was placed in the reentry vehicle to be sure that the bomb would go off. The telemetry from the test said that it would. Near Antigua and Ascension was a bull's-eye, a circle of hydrophones a mile in diameter set in the water off the islands to measure accuracy.

The missile's reentry vehicle was aimed at the center of the circle. Precisely where it landed within the circle, or how far off it missed by landing outside the circle, was determined by instruments attached to the hydrophones. Moose Mathison, who was at Antigua and Ascension on several occasions, recalled the awe-inspiring display in the sky when a missile came in at night. The warhead, which had separated from the missile body, would arrive first, a blazing streak as it hurtled down from space into the atmosphere toward the waiting ring of hydrophones. Then the missile fuselage, its fuel tanks empty, its rocket motors spent, would appear trailing behind and plunge into the friction of the atmosphere in an even grander show of fireworks as it was incinerated.

The next phase of testing focused on determining the reliability and accuracy of the inertial guidance system that would govern the flight of the deployed missiles, or "war birds" as they were to be dubbed. For the initial testing, Jacobson had relied on the radio control arrangement Convair had invented for Atlas. A radio station on the ground transmitted commands to transponders attached to the steering and other controls of the missile. The weakness of radio was that an opponent could interfere with the signals and deflect the missile from its course. Installed within the missile itself, the inertial guidance mechanism was self contained and impervious to countermeasures. The inertial technique's history went back to the invention of the gyroscope in the 1800s, but it was not until the Second World War that major advances were made. Like those in rocketry, they were German. The V-2 was the first inertially guided missile. While it was too inaccurate to be effective for military purposes, the ability to fly a rocket of the V-2's size and range through an entirely internal guidance system was, nevertheless, remarkable for its time.

By the beginning of the 1950s and the return of that everlasting stimulus of innovation, the atmosphere of war in the competition with the Soviets, Dr. Draper of MIT was in the process of taking inertial guidance to its zenith. (Like John von Neumann, Charles Stark Draper gave of his genius to the needs of the U.S. military. When he retired, he chose as his successor to head his Instrumentation Laboratory at MIT a former pupil and one of Schriever's stars, Brigadier General Robert Duffy.) Schriever had put him under contract to design inertial guidance systems for all three of the Air Force's ballistic missiles, Thor,

Atlas, and Titan. Draper built a prototype for Thor at his laboratory. Copies were then reproduced on production tooling by the AC Spark Plug Division of General Motors, which had begun its existence making the little plugs that sparked off the gasoline in GM's piston engines and then graduated into the manufacture of precision equipment. Draper's inertial guidance mechanism was an ingenious contrivance of gyroscopes, accelerometers, and related controls. It calculated the missile's speed and course from the moment the rocket left the pad. The device instantly compared what it found with the correct course data stored in a computer that had also been installed in the missile. With Thor, the course data was basic. It consisted of an azimuth, or compass bearing, that pointed to the target and the distance of the target from the launch point. The inertial guidance mechanism then issued commands that took the rocket to the proper speed and angle, cut off the engines, and launched the warhead at the precise moment required for an accurate flight to its destination.

The greatest fear Jacobson and Mettler had before the first inertial guidance test was that the old-fashioned vacuum tubes, still being used for the circuit connections in the missile's primitive computer, might not withstand the stress of launch. Their worry may have been justified, because 107 seconds after Thor 112 lifted up and away from the pad on December 7, 1957, it suddenly lost stability, began to veer inland, and had to be blown up by the range safety officer. Two days later, they tried again and this time they could not have asked for a better outcome. The inertial guidance took Thor 113 aloft on a perfect flight and sent the warhead down the Caribbean island chain to splash unerringly into the ring of hydrophones near Antigua. To further test the guidance system and to be certain the fuselage of the missile was sturdy enough to withstand turbulent crosswinds if the crew had to launch during a storm, they programmed the computer to put the rocket through several violent maneuvers before the inertial guidance asserted itself for a smooth flight to the target. The test was a complete success, the sole casualties the two decorative fins Thiel had tacked on the base of Thor to distinguish it from Jupiter. Both were torn off by the whiplash turns of the rocket. Someone asked why they were bothering with fins anyway. There was no need for them and so Thiel's attempt at a distinctive feature for his rocket child was eliminated on future Thors coming through the Douglas production line.

After several more test launches in July and early August 1958, a decision had to be made. Was Thor ready to be deployed in England? Mettler and Thiel wanted to continue perfecting the missile. Jacobson said no. In this post-Sputnik era, just as Schriever felt pressure coming down from the White House, so Jacobson sensed the same pressure, if usually unspoken, from Schriever. The engine had been upgraded to 150,000 pounds of thrust. They had achieved a reasonable percentage of reliabilty and an average accuracy of about five eighths of a mile. "That's it," Jacobson remembered saying. "What we have is good enough. It performs its mission now. We don't need to do any better. Don't go fiddling with it." Schriever gave his assent and Jacobson ordered the rocket's configuration frozen. With the final changes from these tests, they had readied the IRBM that Douglas would now begin turning out on its production line for England. Test-launching continued through 1958 and 1959 and into early 1960, but these launches were made to retroactively fix flaws discovered in Thor after deployment got under way. The first Thor landed in Britain aboard a Military Air Transport Service (MATS) C-124 Globemaster on August 29, 1958.

59.

JAMIE WALLACE'S THOR SHOW

The officer most responsible for this alacrity was an Air Force major of short stature, Texas-size energy, and a modest, precisely clipped mustache named Jamie Walker Wallace. As his three quintessentially Scottish names (William Wallace, the hero of Scotland's first struggle for independence, was executed by Edward I of England in 1306) announced, his ancestry was hardly pacifist. Born in 1921 in Bolivar, a small town north of Fort Worth in north Texas, the son of two teachers, he had flown 209 missions as a fighter pilot in the Pacific, shot down three Japanese planes, and won three Distinguished Flying Crosses and numerous Air Medals. According to Jamie, no one could do anything finer for a man than to let him fly a fighter plane in combat. "Hell, we've already died and gone to Heaven," he would say with a laugh. After the war and a bachelor's degree in electrical engineering, he had gone into guided missiles, working on the Matador cruise type for several years. That experience had made him a marked man for Schriever. One day in the fall of 1955, Wallace was walking down the stairs at the Air Research and Development Command in Baltimore. He was assigned then to the Air Development Center at Wright-Patterson Air Force Base (still commonly referred to as Wright Field) in Dayton, engaged in further experimentation with the 650-mile-range Matador, and was at this senior headquarters in Baltimore on a related matter. He noticed a tall brigadier coming up the stairs with a shorter civilian walking beside him. Jamie recognized the civilian as Trevor Gardner from his photographs in Air Force publications. Wallace did not recognize the brigadier and later would never ask and so would never discover how Schriever had learned who he was. In those days, officers did not wear nametags on their uniforms. As they saluted and were about to pass one another, the general stopped him and inquired, "Are you Wallace?" He answered yes and was stunned by the general's reply. "Go back to Wright Field and report to me in California," Schriever said, and resumed his climb up the stairs with Gardner.

Wallace went into the office of a friend at the bottom of the stairs and asked who that brigadier was. The friend identified Schriever and asked Jamie what he was going to do. "I have the sneaking suspicion I ought to go to Wright Field, sell my house, and report to him in California," Wallace said. "Good boy," the friend advised. After he had returned to Ohio, Jamie found out that he had just been "selected" for reassignment to Schriever's operation and there was no way he could avoid the posting even had he wanted to do so. The house sold at a modest profit, which made Jamie's wife, Genevieve, a lively Texas woman who went by the nickname Gee, happy, and the Wallace family climbed into their sedan and set out for California. They arrived in January 1956, a few months after Bennie's expanding WDD organization had outgrown the Schoolhouse and shifted to a leased office complex called Arbor Vitae, which Ramo-Wooldridge had acquired near Los Angeles International Airport. The move had the advantage of placing both organizations together. Jacobson immediately snatched up Wallace for his test operations division and, after Schriever had to relieve Hall and draft Jacobson to rescue Thor, Jake tasked Jamie with putting together the ground support equipment they would need to field the IRBM.

This was a road familiar to Wallace. He had walked down it with Matador and this time he also had able help from Ramo's organization and Douglas. Everything was designed to be dismantled for transport by air and erection on site in England. The shelter to protect the missile from the corrosive English weather was brilliantly simple. It sat on railroad tracks. Its fore and aft sections could be rolled apart in a moment to uncover the weapon and permit the crew to raise the Thor erect into firing position with a hydraulically operated hoist. The concrete launch pad to be laid in England was modest. There was no necessity for a massive pad like those emplaced at Canaveral to withstand repeated firings, because if these missiles were fired in anger there would be one launch and that would be it. Tanks for the liquid oxygen and the RP-1 kerosene were each placed off to one side at a safe distance, with protective concrete blast walls to be erected around them in case of an accident. Fueling lines ran to the missile. A panoply of related equipment was arranged at spots where it would be needed. The launch control center, which housed the launch crew and the consoles of instruments for the countdown and firing, was just a trailer for a tractor trailer truck, so that it could be hooked up and hauled into place.

In October 1957, as Jacobson was beginning to get Thor to fly properly at Cape Canaveral, several officers working with him urged that he follow through with earlier plans to hold what is called a Development Engineering Inspection for the missile in California that December. Jake put Wallace in charge and Jamie turned the event into what might more aptly have been called "The Thor Show." The official purpose of a DEI is to gather everyone involved in the creation of a weapon system, from military project officers to contractors, and to lay out the entire project in order to make certain that all is ready and working. Inevitably, such events generate promotion for the new weapon within industry and the military community, and those officers recommending that Jacobson stage the inspection understood this. Wallace wanted something quite beyond the ordinary. He wanted promotion on a grand scale. He told Jacobson that if he could he would hold the DEI on the Twentieth Century–Fox soundstage in Hollywood. When Jacobson laughed at him, he said he was joking only because it was impossible.

He had to settle instead for the better part of a city block at a Douglas Aircraft facility in the west Los Angeles district of Venice. The place already had an auditorium that was perfect for the briefings. Jamie now proceeded to have a twelve-foot-high plywood fence put up around much of the block to create a large enclosure. Within it he set up a Thor launching site virtually the same as one that would appear when deployment occurred in England, if on a somewhat smaller scale. A real Thor missile was trucked in and installed on a hydraulic hoist to lift it erect as would be done for firing. There were the tanks for the RP-1 and liquid oxygen, naturally empty; a control center for the launch crew with instrument consoles; the whole nine yards.

The event was scheduled for three days, from December 10 to 12, 1957. It lasted two weeks. About 300 visitors were initially expected and about 3,000 showed up. In retrospect, the number was not surprising given the wideness of the net Wallace cast with Jacobson's and Schriever's approval. Invitations were sent to thirteen different institutions and commands, including the generals on the Air Staff at the Pentagon; the ARDC in Baltimore; SAC at Offutt Air Force Base; the Special Weapons Command at Kirtland; the Air Development Center at Wright-Patterson; the Air Matériel Command, also at Wright-Patterson; the Air University at Maxwell Air Force Base in Alabama; even the Alaskan Air Command. Wallace also sent invitations out to the scientific community and naturally to Douglas and the other firms like Rocketdyne and AC Spark Plug that were building Thor and had a serious role to play in the exercise. The VIPs were guided about in groups or, for those who wished it, driven in four-seater electric golf carts with a "Missile Express" sign on the front. An aging Theodore von Kármán was chauffeured over from Pasadena and reverentially received and briefed. After a while, Jamie stopped counting the two- and three-star generals. "We brought them in by the planeload," he said later with happy exaggeration. Tommy Power, who now wore four stars, having succeeded LeMay that July as commander-in-chief of SAC, led the lot. (LeMay had moved up to vice chief of staff under White.) Power posed for photographs with the nabobs of the aircraft industry who also came, such as Donald Douglas, Jr., the current CEO of Douglas Aircraft, and his retired father, Donald Sr., attired in a gray homburg and dark pinstriped suit as sveltely tailored as the fuselage of a new jet fighter plane. Even though Power had left ARDC he continued to regard Thor as one of his projects and it still was, because SAC would be responsible for manning the American element of the Thor sites once the missile was deployed to England.

With this many people coming and going, security was, in effect, thrown to the winds. While everyone who entered needed a security clearance and a pass, it would hardly have been difficult for a squad of Soviet intelligence officers to forge passes and wander about unnoticed among 3,000 people. Jamie didn't give a damn and neither did Jacobson and Schriever. If this was the price of attention, so be it. Wallace noted afterward that the only secrets worth keeping were in the nuclear warhead and he didn't happen to have one of those on the lot. It was impossible, in any case, to hide what was going on. One of Wallace's favorite circus tricks for the VIPs was to hoist the Thor straight up into its firing position, which put the 64.8-foot-high missile clearly in view from the street. The visitors seemed to particularly enjoy this and he estimated he must have had it raised and lowered fifty to sixty times. A group of little boys from the neighborhood noticed and began regularly pelting the Thor with pebbles every time it rose. Jamie went to the prettiest of the Douglas secretaries assigned to the DEI and asked her to get a paper bag of candy and go out and tell the boys she would give them a fresh bag every morning if they would leave the missile alone. The bribe worked.

Yet there were no inquiries from the news media. No one, other than the neighborhood boys, seemed to pay any attention. Jamie attributed this general lack of curiosity to the fact that they were holding the DEI in Los Angeles, the filmmaking capital of the world. In any other community, he was convinced, the sight of a twelve-foot-high fence around much of a city block with a tall missile going up and down inside and lots of uniformed men with stars arriving and departing in Air Force staff cars would have had reporters knocking at the gate and calling on the phone. "Not in Los Angeles," he said. "I'll make you a bet that most of the people thought somebody was running a goddamn movie set."

Most senior Air Force officers who accepted the invitation to the DEI probably did so out of curiosity, because Thor was the service's first ballistic missile. But what they saw, they seemed to like. Jamie got the impression that they had garnered some across-the-board support, not only for Thor, but for the missile program as a whole. While Power was a long-ago convert, they picked up several new high-level allies, the most important of whom was Lieutenant General Clarence "Wild Bill" Irvine, the deputy chief of staff for matériel. Irvine was a sturdy, broad-shouldered man. He probably had more time in service than any other general in the Air Force because he was a "mustang" who had clambered up from the ranks. He reached back to the First World War, when he had begun his career as a sergeant pilot while such noncommissioned flying positions still existed. Professionally, he was an effective air leader and a first-class executive. He had been one of LeMay's favorite wing commanders, picking up the boss's affectation of a stogie clenched between his teeth. In private, despite his passage into middle age, he remained a womanizing rogue who probably would have been drummed out of the no-hanky-panky Air Force of later generations. From Jake's and Jamie's point of view he became a friend of immense value, because as deputy chief of staff for matériel on the Air Staff, Irvine was in charge of procurement and had genuine clout. He told them to call him or to come and see him at the Pentagon whenever they had a problem.

The serious side of the DEI was not confined to winning high-placed benefactors. The auditorium was in constant use as representatives of all of the firms involved with Thor, Jake and Jamie and their Air Force colleagues, and Mettler and Thiel and the Ramo-Wooldridge team gave briefings and were briefed, examining and reexamining obstacles. Jamie's reproduction of a Thor launching site enabled them to examine physically—not just on paper—every element of the weapon system. Where a piece of equipment that was supposed to exist was missing, either because it had not yet been manufactured or because someone had forgotten to order it, a box was prominently marked and put in its place, so that an order would be issued and the piece installed. The same physical tracking procedure was followed for wiring connections, valves, pipes—everything. There was no time to lose.

60

THE BIGGEST AIRLIFT
SINCE BERLIN

The British were amenable to accepting Thor as soon as possible because a deterrent was needed against the increasing threat of Soviet medium- and intermediate-range missiles. Britain had its own IRBM, Blue Streak, in development, but the missile was five years in the offing. (It was canceled after the full deployment of Thor.) Britain was already under threat from the first Russian ballistic missile with an appreciable range, the R-5 (NATO: SS-3 Shyster), which had first achieved its full-scale flight of 800 miles in 1953 and been deployed with a nuclear warhead in 1956 and 1957. While classified as a medium-range ballistic missile (MRBM) and modest in reach by subsequent measurements, the R-5 had ample mileage to strike England across the North Sea from launching sites in Soviet-occupied East Germany. A much more substantial danger was the R-12 (NATO: SS-4 Sandal), the first of the Soviet intermediate-range ballistic missiles with a span of 1,250 miles. Deployed around 1958, it was intended to obliterate American and British air bases throughout the United Kingdom and Europe and, fired from the edges of the far-flung Soviet empire, those it could strike in the Middle East and Asia as well. And although its existence was not yet confirmed, the Soviets were in the process of readying a second and more formidable IRBM. This was the R-14 (NATO: SS-5 Skean), which could hurl its nuclear warhead 2,500 miles and would be deployed as early as 1960.

Not long after that first Thor landed in England on August 29, 1958, Jamie Wallace organized the biggest airlift since Berlin in 1948 to send over the other fifty-nine Thors and the related ground support equipment as fast as everything came off the production lines. With Wild Bill Irvine running interference and intimidating the Military Air Transport Service into scheduling the planes for him, Wallace virtually commandeered MATS for about three months, staging some 1,180 flights out of Long Beach Airport, then a semipublic facility that was actually the airfield for the Douglas Aircraft Company facility there. The racket of the MATS four-engine C-124 Globemaster transports landing and taking off day and night aroused so much protest from residents in adjoining neighborhoods that Jacobson and Wallace had to round up a passel of public relations types from Air Force detachments on the West Coast. They set the PR people to knocking on doors within ten miles of Long Beach Airport, explaining that the Air Force was engaged in flying vitally needed military equipment to Europe and their forbearance would be appreciated. As such assertions went unquestioned at the height of the Cold War, the good citizens of Long Beach were pacified.

Thor missiles and their ground support equipment were not all that had to be shipped to England. Jacobson decided that it made much more sense for Douglas technicians and engineers, by now thoroughly familiar with the system, to set up the missiles and gear on site in England than it would be to attempt the task with Air Force personnel. (Preparation of the sites with concrete pads and roads was the British share of the missile project.) A contract with Douglas was duly signed and Project Emily, as the company named the effort, duly launched. Then a new problem arose. About 1,200 people would be going to England, including families. How would they be housed? England was still recovering from the war and what spare housing existed was usually far below American standards. A Douglas pamphlet warned that "apartments, or 'flats' as the British call them . . . are usually old and sparsely furnished, in many instances consisting of an old house divided into separate living quarters; families frequently have to share bathrooms. Central heating is practically non-existent [and] the following items are not usually furnished: refrigerator, washer and dryer, pots and pans." The solution, Wallace decided, was to build trailer parks at points convenient to the missile sites. This required special permission from the British government because trailers, or "caravans" as the English call them, were considered unsightly and agglomerations of them forbidden by the local architectural authorities. The offense to the eye was overlooked in the interest of alliance. But Wallace still had to fly a lot of house trailers to England because so few were manufactured there. Snack bars and clubs were built for the newcomers out of more prefabricated unsightliness and the Douglas Company addressed sage words to its people: "The British are quiet, reserved, and do not intrude on one another's privacy. . . . They do not like to buy on credit. . . . The Briton . . . drives on the left side of the road and does not change his fork from his left to his right hand when eating. . . . Dress conservatively. Don't attempt to rush people." As it turned out, the proficiency of the Douglas technicians and engineers and the friendliness of the English brought all to a happy result.

Tommy Power, newly resplendent in his long-awaited position as commander-in-chief of SAC, could not resist a grab for control. He proposed that SAC man half of the missile batteries, the RAF the other half, and that SAC be in overall command. The British wouldn't have it. If a decision was ever to be made to trigger Götterdämmerung, the decision was going to be a joint one. At British insistence, a "two-key system" was devised. The RAF launch control officer on duty at a missile site would have a set of keys enabling him to unlock the missiles for firing after verifying a command from his higher authority. The SAC officer beside him would have a separate set of keys enabling him to arm the nuclear warheads, once he had received and verified an order through his own chain of command. But SAC did not give up easily. Squadron Leader H. Basil "Bas" Williamson was an outgoing twenty-seven-year-old flight lieutenant in the RAF when he came over in June 1959 with one of the first groups to be sent to the United States for training as a missile launch control officer. He had previously served two tours as a navigator in the back seat of a twin-jet Canberra bomber in England and Germany. He recalled that when they arrived at SAC's Davis-Monthan Air Force Base near Tucson for the initial phase of instruction, they were told that the SAC warhead officer would command the entire missile site. An RAF air commodore, the equivalent of a brigadier general, then showed up from the Ministry of Defence in London to square matters away. He gathered the RAF officers and NCO missile crewmen together and informed them in no uncertain terms that they were never to take orders from a U.S. Air Force officer, that they would respond to their chain of command and the SAC officer would respond to his. The issue, Williamson remembered, was never broached again.

61.

"ROY . . . I WANT YOU TO GET ME CAMP COOKE"

After several weeks of lectures in Arizona, the serious part of the four-month training course for the RAF launch crews got under way at the new Vandenberg Air Force Base on a sparsely populated stretch of the California coast near the town of Lompoc, about 170 miles northwest of Los Angeles. Schriever had acquired its 64,000 acres of sand and scrub brush, inhabited by rodents and the sidewinder rattlesnakes that fed on them, back in the fall of 1956 after long eyeing the place as an ideal West Coast base. The barren expanse belonged to the Army. It had been named Camp Cooke and used during the Second World War and the Korean War as a training ground for armored and infantry divisions. Schriever had several reasons to want it. Cooke's isolation and size—it was four times as big as Canaveral—made it perfect as a first operational base for the ICBMs and as a permanent training ground for launch crews, to include live practice firings out over the Pacific. Left unsaid, because the matter was considered so sensitive, but critical to Schriever's thinking nonetheless, was the fact that Camp Cooke lay along the one coastal area of the United States from which a polar orbit of a space satellite was most easily achieved. The earth rotates on its axis like a top spinning slowly on a table. If one removes the table in one's imagination and visualizes the top spinning by itself in the air, one can understand the importance of a polar orbit to spying from space. A photographic reconnaissance satellite circling around the ends of the top, the poles of the earth, can photograph any area of the globe's surface as the earth turns beneath it. Throwing such a spy satellite into polar orbit to photograph the Soviet Union's military installations and weaponry from on high, a secret project code-named WS (Weapon System)-117L, was on Schriever's agenda as soon as he had created a ballistic missile up to the task. Attaining a polar orbit from

Cape Canaveral was a perilous undertaking because the missile had to be launched over populated areas of Latin America with the possibility of diplomatic protests and a public relations disaster if anything went wrong and people were injured from falling debris. But from Camp Cooke, where the coast of California juts westward into the Pacific, there is, except for a few islands, nothing but open sea stretching all the way to Antarctica.

In the summer of 1956, Bennie had carefully observed the bureaucratic nicety of appointing a site selection board for an alternative ICBM operations and training base. The board had predictably recommended Camp Cooke. The Army didn't seem to have much use for it anymore, having abandoned the barracks and other buildings on Cooke to caretaker status after the end of the Korean War in 1953. Secretary Quarles was the obstacle. In those pre-Sputnik years, he was engaged in his "Poor Man's" program to please Eisenhower and didn't want to spend the money required. The estimates were that the cost of roads, buildings, and launch facilities would run $42 million in Fiscal Year 1957 and $400 million the following fiscal year. His attitude was that Schriever ought to make do with Cape Canaveral. Bennie, stubborn as ever when he believed something was really necessary, pressed the argument. The Air Staff supported him unanimously. A briefing was scheduled at the Pentagon, for the latter part of August, to decide the question. Bennie couldn't attend himself. Dora had become so upset over his neglect of her and the family that he had finally given in to her complaints by promising to take them on vacation to Hawaii at that time and he knew there was no way he could renege on his promise. And although he would have sat in the briefing room, prepared to respond to questions, he would in any case have delegated the actual task of rendering the briefing to his specialist in the art, Major Roy Ferguson, Jr.

Roy Ferguson was, like Jamie Wallace, a country boy type, born and raised in Tennessee. He was courageous, he thought for himself, and he was not intimidated by the opinions of others, regardless of how high the source of the opinion happened to rank. Thirty-five missions flown out of Italy in a B-24 bomber against German fighters and flak, during which he had twice been awarded the Distinguished Flying Cross along with four Air Medals, had undoubtedly reinforced these qualities. He also had a talent all his own, a talent the Irish call the gift of gab. He was a born persuader with a spectacularly retentive memory. In a night he could absorb enough facts on a subject of which he had previously known nothing to stand on a briefing platform the next morning and give a trenchant and convincing presentation. Of medium height, with a shock of dark hair combed back from his chiseled features, he also cut a good figure on a briefing stage. Ferguson was another example of Schriever's talent-oriented system of management. He had originally come out to the Schoolhouse from the Pentagon as the unit's operations officer, but as soon as Schriever had noticed his special gift, he had become WDD's command briefer. Whenever an important sell had to be put across, either in California or in Washington, Ferguson took a crash course in the subject and mounted the briefing stage.

"Roy, I'm going to Honolulu on vacation," Schriever said after he had summoned Ferguson to his office. "I want you to go up and brief the secretary and I want you to get me Camp Cooke. But don't you mention live firings from that facility." Schriever explained that saving money had become an obsession with Quarles and that the construction costs to transform Cooke into a suitable base were already an obstacle to acquiring it. Practice launching of missiles would cost more money. Training without launching was relatively cheap. Ferguson was to stick to training.

During the flight to Washington, Ferguson reflected on what Schriever had said and decided the boss was not making sense. Why would anyone give them such a huge and expensive piece of real estate if they were going to use it only for training that did not include launches? That could be done anywhere. The only cogent reason for possessing such an expansive base as Camp Cooke, and one on the sea at that, was to launch missiles from it, both for training and in war with the Soviets if it came to that. And so Ferguson made up two sets of charts. One set laid out the training argument Schriever wanted. An alternative set focused on the advantages of Cooke for live firing of missiles, in training and in war. The fact that he might have to disobey a direct order from the boss did not bother Ferguson. Schriever had said to get him Camp Cooke. If he didn't succeed in that, disobedience "would be the least of my problems."

Ferguson had assumed that a briefing for Secretary Quarles would be a high-profile affair, but he was astonished at the audience that began gathering and gradually filled the conference room. The secretary and Nathan Twining, still Air Force chief of staff, took their places in the front row. So did General White, the vice chief, and Tommy Power, then still commanding ARDC. Behind them were all the three-star generals who headed the various sections of the Air Staff and behind them their two-star deputies and sundry other major generals, including Major General John McConnell, then SAC's director of plans, who had flown in from Omaha for the occasion. (He was subsequently to succeed Curtis LeMay as chief of staff of the Air Force during the Vietnam War.)

SAC was interested in seeing the Air Force gain Cooke because of the foresight of a junior officer sitting in the back row. This was Captain Richard Henry. He had joined SAC in 1950 as a second lieutenant right after West Point and flight school to co-pilot a four-engine B-50 bomber, the advanced version of the B-29 fitted out to carry the first mass-produced atomic bomb, the Mark 3 Nagasaki-type plutonium weapon. Leningrad was their assigned target. SAC was short of tankers in its young years. Henry and the other members of the crew were told they would get a drink from a tanker on the way to Leningrad, but there would be no second drink to bring them home. Their one meager hope of survival after the plane ran out of gas would be to bail out and walk, through the snow if it was winter, into Finland. "We would still have flown the mission," he said. Henry had graduated in the upper 10 percent of his class at West Point. This induced the Air Force, after his tour in a B-50, to send him to the University of Michigan, where he earned not one but two master's of science degrees, in aeronautical engineering and in instrumentation engineering. The latter degree was particularly useful in the art of missilery and, on his return to Omaha, Henry was dispatched to Los Angeles in October 1955 as SAC's liaison officer to Schriever's organization.

LeMay had meant the appointment to be a gesture of contempt, conveyed by Henry's lowly rank of captain. "We had the last laugh," Schriever was later to say. "He ended up a lieutenant general in command of the place," which did occur in 1978. But not before Henry, in the years in between, had insisted on paying his dues as a combat airman by flying 200 missions in an F-4 Phantom jet fighter-bomber in Vietnam. Schriever had insisted that Captain Henry be shown every courtesy, and so when the site selection board had been created, Henry had been appointed to it as the SAC representative. He had immediately recognized the future usefulness to SAC of Camp Cooke. The Strategic Air Command was slated to take charge of all ICBMs once the missiles had been developed to the point where they could be deployed and no crew could be considered proficient until it had actually launched a missile in practice. Nor could crews be kept proficient without periodically retesting their skills with a live firing. Henry's report to SAC headquarters, pointing out how perfect Cooke was for all of this, had quickly caught the attention of the command and brought McConnell to the Pentagon on this day. His report may also have helped to achieve the unanimity among the generals on the Air Staff for obtaining Cooke and brought some of them to this briefing as well, as the influence of SAC was never to be underestimated. His position on the site selection board had, despite his mere captain's bars, entitled Henry to witness the briefing. A colonel who was sitting beside him at the back counted thirty-three stars in the room. He told Henry to look around. "Dick, this is a unique experience. You'll probably never have one like this again the rest of your career," the colonel said.

Brigadier General Osmond "Ozzie" Ritland, another technological innovator who had been detailed to the CIA as deputy director of the U-2 spy plane project and whom Schriever had recently recruited as his vice commander in California, introduced Ferguson to the gathering in a couple of sentences and then, as Schriever had instructed him, immediately sat down. Ferguson stepped up onto the low briefing platform, where his charts already rested on an easel, turned to his august audience, and began briefing exactly as Schriever had ordered him to do. He hewed strictly to the utility of Camp Cooke as a training base, saying nothing about money and nothing about missile launchings.

A pitchman of Ferguson's talent and experience develops an acute sense for the reaction of an audience. He watches their eyes. Ferguson didn't like what he was seeing. The eyes of this audience were dulling over. He was losing them. If he did not switch gears right away, the briefing was going to be a complete flop. He reached over to the easel, grasped the five live firing charts he had composed and put behind the training ones, and placed them in front. Ritland was sitting close enough to see what was on the new charts. His eyes grew large in surprise as he suddenly realized that Ferguson was about to defy Schriever. Not wanting to be unnerved, Ferguson shifted his gaze away from Ritland to the others and began briefing for all he was worth on the value of shooting missiles from Camp Cooke. He sensed the mood in the room change instantly. He had the attention of everyone now. He pressed on, exchanging charts as he led his audience through every category of live firing he had been able to think of the night before during the plane ride from California—testing new missiles, a graduation exercise for the training of a crew, the maintenance of proficiency that had concerned Henry, and the ultimate, the launching of war birds against targets in the Soviet Union or Communist China. He was silent only on the ease of achieving a polar orbit from Cooke, because the photoreconnaissance satellite project was such a closely guarded secret then.

The meeting came alive as the participants joined in with their own opinions. Tommy Power was interested primarily in the realistic training of launch crews and began holding forth on this point. He also focused on how suitable a base Cooke would be for the hurry-up deployment of the first few ICBMs as an initial deterrent to the Soviets, the "Ph.D. type" capability Trevor Gardner had spoken of two years earlier at the time of the Tea Pot Committee.

General White moved in to provide Ferguson with a four-star assistant and to steer the meeting where he wanted it to go. The range of the Atlas was 5,500 nautical miles (approximately 6,330 statute miles), wasn't it? he asked Ferguson. "Yes, sir," Ferguson replied. "Where does that go?" White continued. "From the northern tier of the United States, sir, it will cover about anything you need covered," Ferguson replied. White called for a map of the world, some string, and a grease pencil. He got up and walked over to the briefing stage, put the map up on the easel, measured off a length of string covering 5,500 nautical miles, tied the grease pencil to one end, held the other end on the approximate location of Camp Cooke, and then swung the grease pencil in an arc. Shooting across the North Pacific, they could strike all of China and most of the eastern Soviet Union, including Vladivostok, Russia's major Far Eastern port and naval base at the end of the Trans-Siberian Railroad on the Sea of Japan. "He's right," White announced to the room. "From the northern tier, we can." Tommy Power recovered to give Ferguson another opening. "What does that cost?" he asked, referring to practice live firings out over the Pacific. Ferguson knew that Power wanted him to say something playing down expenditures, and he obliged. "Well, keep in mind, sir, very little instrumentation," he said with assurance. He explained that since they would be launching over open water, they would not have to build expensive monitoring and tracking stations on islands, as they had in the Caribbean and South Atlantic, and could use Navy ships equipped with instruments instead.

Quarles had apparently heard enough. He turned to General Twining. "What do you think, Nate?" he asked. Ferguson was thirty-three years old at the time of the briefing, but Twining belonged to that First World War generation of Army Air Corps officers who still referred to a relatively junior officer as a "boy." He answered without hesitation. "The boy's right," he said. Quarles looked up at Ferguson: "Go home and tell Schriever he's got Camp Cooke." The budget-bound Quarles continued to have misgivings, but he did not renege on his word. When Ferguson and Ritland returned that evening to the Mayflower Hotel in Washington, where they were staying, they stripped down to their underwear so that they could completely relax, called for a fifth of whiskey, and did not have a great deal left in the bottle when they ordered something to eat. On November 16, 1956, Secretary Wilson transferred the 64,000 acres of Camp Cooke that Schriever wanted to the Air Force. Approximately two years later, on October 4, 1958, the place was renamed in honor of the late Hoyt Vandenberg, the Air Force's second chief of staff.

62

A TIE

By the time Basil Williamson and his contingent of RAF missileers-to-be arrived in the summer of 1959, desolation had given way to a panoply of permanent concrete launching pads, a network of roads connecting them, and housing and office blocks. SAC crews who had been trained on Thor by Douglas technicians were waiting to pass their knowledge on to their British allies. Months of lectures, demonstrations of the many parts of the weapon system, and practice countdowns followed. Graduation was a live firing. The SAC training team worked with the RAF men to be certain everything on the site was ready, but then, as soon as the actual countdown began, stepped back and let their pupils take the count through to the climax of flame and liftoff over the Pacific. In the England to which they returned in October 1959, ghost airfields from which the B-17s and the B-24s had once taken off to pummel the Third Reich had been pressed into a new mission. Down through the east of England, from East Riding in Yorkshire to the north, through Lincolnshire, and Norfolk, Suffolk, Cambridgeshire, and neighboring counties, the Thors were being arrayed. The RAF broke the sixty Thors down into batteries of three missiles each and formed a squadron of five launch control officers and forty enlisted technicians to man each battery, twenty squadrons in all. Four regular RAF airfields currently in use were selected as headquarters bases to provide communications and whatever other support was needed and the twenty squadrons were divided between them, five squadrons, or five three-missile batteries totaling fifteen missiles, assigned to each main base. One of the batteries was sited at the headquarters base. The other four were set up on abandoned airfields around it, many of these the Second World War American bomber bases. To disperse the missiles and prevent all from being knocked out in one blow, the airfields selected for the sites were roughly fifteen miles apart. From the air the whites and grays of the individual missile installations, emplaced in a one, two, three line, stood out starkly in the green of the English countryside.

Not all went well in the beginning. The missile itself was up to its mission, but the Douglas technicians had a lot of trouble making the ground support equipment function properly. For a time as much unusable equipment was coming home in the C-124s as new "modification kits" were going over. Although the first missiles ready to be launched against the Soviet Union theoretically went on alert at RAF Feltwell and its satellite installations in Norfolk in the spring and summer of 1959, the Thors there and at other installations rapidly organizing were, in fact, harmless. While the Soviets may not have known it, the Mark 2 reentry vehicles were empty. The RAF high command did not trust the system enough to allow the nuclear warheads to be mounted. The problem had not arisen because of Jamie Wallace's maximum speed philosophy. Had he not applied the blowtorch to move the ground support program along as rapidly as possible, more time would have been lost. The difficulty was that they were pushing the limits of technology with what was, for its era, a complex system. The failings could not be detected until Thor was actually being deployed. Jacobson solved the impasse by handing it to one of the most astute Air Force engineers of his time, Benjamin Bellis, then a thirty-five-year-old major.

Like Henry, Bellis was also eventually to wear three stars on his shoulder tabs and to oversee the creation of one of the most potent American fighter-bombers of the last quarter of the twentieth century, the F-15 Eagle. To stop the helter-skelter improvising that was occurring in the effort to make the Thor system function as advertised, Bellis instituted a procedure he called "configuration control." When a fix to a problem was achieved, the change was carefully recorded, applied universally, and coordinated with the production line of the manufacturer so that it would be phased into newly built ground support equipment. Bellis formed a committee, with himself, naturally, as its chairman, to supervise and enforce the process. To make certain there was an end to the confusion that had reigned prior to his arrival, no change in any equipment on site in England could be made without the permission of the committee. Within months, Bellis's engineering modifications and the forceful manner in which he applied them had the ground support gear working as it should. The achievement was not without casualties. Two Douglas technicians were killed in California by an accidental explosion while testing redesigned machinery to fuel the Thor's LOX tank. But in those years of Cold War urgency, such fatal accidents were a price everyone was prepared to pay. The RAF hierarchy was at last convinced it had a reliable IRBM. In May 1960, the one-megaton warheads were mounted on the Thors. All of the western Soviet Union, including Moscow and beyond to many of the industrial centers as far as the upper Volga, was within the fan of their 1,725-mile range.

Finding homes for the Jupiters among the other NATO allies was to prove a more difficult task. As a result, the Air Force, to the helpless rage of the Army's John Medaris at the Redstone Arsenal, reduced the number of Jupiters destined for NATO from sixty to forty-five. Charles de Gaulle had returned to power in Paris in 1958 as the only French leader capable of staving off the country's descent toward chaos and civil war because of the impending loss of Algeria after another fruitless colonial conflict. He was obsessed with restoring French pride and independence, regaining the international stature lost with the defeat by Nazi Germany in 1940, and creating France's own nuclear arsenal, his Force de Frappe. Although he privately admitted that Western Europe's security relied on American power, he was not about to publicly concede dependence on anyone by leaning on Washington's missiles. De Gaulle refused the Jupiters.

Italy was more forthcoming. It agreed to the stationing of thirty Jupiters under the two-key system of dual control worked out by the British. A headquarters was established at the air base at Gioia del Colle, in the heel of the boot formed by the bottom of the Italian peninsula. Italian air force launch crews were sent to Alabama for training at Redstone. In contrast to the Thors, which were laid on their sides within their shelters, the Jupiters, painted white with Italian air force markings, were emplaced in the open, erect for firing and ranged phalluslike across the southern Italian countryside in three-missile batteries. Turkey, also a NATO member, was short of skilled manpower to be trained as missile technicians, but more trusting of the United States. The fifteen Jupiters it accepted were entirely manned and controlled by U.S. Air Force personnel. The Turks simply provided security troops for the batteries. Again to prevent the missiles from being destroyed in a single preemptive strike, the batteries were widely dispersed through the rugged terrain inland from the port of Izmir, a once predominantly Greek city on the western end of the Anatolian Peninsula, known as Smyrna until the Turks expelled the Greek minority after the First World War.

From Turkey, the Jupiters could cover the entirety of European Russia and fly as far as Soviet Central Asia. The presence of American IRBMs in a nation right on the Soviet frontier was particularly unsettling to the Russians. It was, in fact, an act of provocation and should have been foreseen as such. The Soviets were upset enough to, on at least one occasion, send down a jet fighter on a photoreconnaissance mission. The plane crashed.

The dispatch of the Thors to England and the Jupiters to Italy and Turkey had effectively stymied the Russians. They had deployed their medium- and intermediate-range missiles earlier than Schriever and his comrades had managed to field their IRBMs, but not early enough to cause undue anxiety, because Britain's and Washington's other NATO allies had known that the American missiles were on the way. Schriever and those who labored with him had tied with their Soviet opponents in this first round of the race to deploy nuclear-armed ballistic missiles, and in the process they had learned some important lessons.

63.

BLACK SATURDAY

Bennie made the cover of *Time* magazine in the spring of 1957. The issue of April 1 displayed a profile shot in color of a handsome man in the dark blue uniform of an Air Force major general, silver braid on the brim of his cap, two silver stars on his shoulder tabs. "Missileman Schriever," the caption beside the photograph said, while in the background a ballistic missile lit a fiery trail above the clouds of earth as it streaked toward space. The cover photograph and the feature article inside that it advertised were a major public relations coup for Schriever, an indication that he and ballistic missiles were arriving. For months he had been pressing the Air Force hierarchy to raise some of the security curtains on the missile program in order to reap the public and congressional support that favorable publicity could provide, and this was the first, notable fruit of his effort. *Time,* which proclaimed itself "the Weekly Newsmagazine," was at the height of its influence in the 1950s as a newsmaker and fashioner of public opinion. Under the leadership of its co-founder and editor-in-chief, Henry Luce, who had heralded the twentieth as "the American Century," *Time* was a model of militant anti-Communism and brisk, upbeat reporting on the inevitably triumphant future of the United States. There was no hint in the article of the excruciating struggle Schriever, Gardner, and von Neumann, assisted by the intrigues of Vince Ford, had waged to set the ICBM enterprise in motion. "The history of the missile has little record of military unwillingness to accept it as the weapon that must be developed at top speed," *Time* said. "Defense Secretary Charles E. Wilson bulled the ICBM project through the National Security Council." Nor was there ever any doubt as to who was to lead the program. "Actually we didn't appoint him—Benny was born for this job," the magazine quoted an anonymous general in the Pentagon. "There wasn't another soul we knew who could handle it, so we just sort of nodded and said 'OK, now,' and Benny walked in and took over." (*Time* spelled Schriever's nickname as the sports reporters in the San Antonio of his youth had.)

The most factually accurate section was a warm account of Schriever's arrival in the United States in 1917 as a six-year-old from Germany with his mother and younger brother, Gerry, and of Elizabeth Schriever's heroic travail to raise her boys with housekeeping and the sandwich stand at the twelfth green of the Brackenridge Park Golf Course. But he was no longer San Antonio's boy wonder of golf who had achieved a mention in Ripley's *Believe It or Not* for three times driving a ball more than 300 yards onto the green and then sinking it with a single putt, quite a feat with the golf clubs of his youth. Now he was "hard-eyed Ben Schriever" pitted against the Soviets in "his destiny-sized race for an operational ICBM." The encomiums rolled on. "Ben Schriever, a tomorrow's man," had "the most important job in the country." He was a "discerning, thinking leader," an "outstanding and extremely tenacious manager." Not that much of the praise was unmerited, for Bennie was "a tireless, able, dedicated, imaginative officer" and in 1957 he was the man of the moment. And if much of the *Time* cover story was fiction, for a man who lived on the edge as Schriever did and who rarely strayed from a grasp on reality himself, fairy tales, as long as they were friendly, were welcome.

The fifteen men whom Schriever had gathered at the Schoolhouse when he had officially taken command of his fledgling Western Development Division on August 2, 1954, had metamorphosed into a ballistic missile and space satellite center. By the end of 1957, testing of Thor had been under way for virtually a year, Atlas launches had begun that June, and manufacture had started on Titan, the alternative ICBM in case Atlas should prove a failure. Planning for a photo-reconnaissance satellite under the WS-117L program was advancing. On June 1, 1957, in line with the same relaxing of security that had led to the *Time* cover story, the Air Force also peeled away the official disguise and redesignated the innocuously named WDD as the Air Force Ballistic Missile Division (AFBMD). Schriever had 485 Air Force officers and noncommissioned specialists and 222 civilian clerks, secretaries, and other auxiliary personnel at work in his new BMD. Employed alongside them to facilitate the processing of contracts was a special Ballistic Missile Office detachment from the Air Matériel Command at Wright-Patterson Air Force Base. It consisted of another 55 Air Force and 155 civilian employees. After Power took over from LeMay at Omaha, a decision was also made in late 1957 that SAC would take responsibility for the training and deployment of all ICBM units. A full-fledged SAC liaison office was created to work at Schriever's WDD. It was titled Office of the Assistant Commander-in-Chief, Strategic Air Command for Missiles, but it was known by its acronym, SAC-MIKE. Its head was Colonel William Large, Jr., a highly decorated B-24 veteran. He had won the Silver Star for Gallantry and twice been awarded the Distinguished Flying Cross for leading raids out of Italy against the notoriously perilous Ploeşti oil fields in Romania and other targets in east and south Europe. Co-located with all of these WDD components in the same but now much expanded Arbor Vitae complex of office buildings near Los Angeles Airport was a Ramo-Wooldridge organization that had mushroomed from 170 scientists and technicians in 1954 to 1,961 in 1957.

These numbers were paltry when compared to the tens of thousands at work in the offices and on the assembly lines of the firms building the missiles. The two ICBMs encompassed seventeen major contractors, like Convair and the Martin Company, which had the airframe and assembly contracts for Atlas and Titan, respectively, 200 subcontractors, and thousands of suppliers all over the United States. Nor were the profits small. Aerojet General, for example, had been given $400 million in Air Force orders to furnish the engines for Titan. Simon Ramo and Dean Wooldridge, whose products were the intangibles of technical expertise and brainpower, were not doing badly either with the simple cost-plus-fee arrangement Trevor Gardner had first pressed them into on the formation of the Tea Pot Committee in September 1953. By the close of Fiscal Year 1958, Ramo-Wooldridge had earned approximately $70 million.

While Schriever's primary management technique was and always would be selecting the right man and giving him the freedom and authority to accomplish a task, he had developed a second system for keeping track of all of these projects. It centered on a monthly briefing the staff referred to ruefully as "Black Saturday." The man Schriever chose to orchestrate this second system was Lieutenant Colonel Charles Getz III, tall and dark-haired, with round, friendly features. Getz had joined the Army Air Forces in May 1942 while he was still a senior in high school in Fort Wayne, Indiana, flew thirty-one missions against Germany out of England as a B-24 pilot in 1944, and then volunteered to fly a P-51 Mustang fighter in a special unit that scouted targets ahead of the bomber formations. The scouts would radio the bomber leader whether the target was sufficiently free of clouds to permit visual bombing, whether he would have to bomb by radar, or whether the cloud cover was so thick that the bombers would have to go on to their secondary target. In the course of an additional forty missions as a scout, Getz joined the tiny club of American aviators who shot down one of the new Messerschmitt 262 jet fighters. He spotted the German pilot descending for a landing, dove on him at full throttle, and opened fire with his six .50 calibers, the P-51 shuddering with the 400-mile-per-hour speed of the descent and the recoil of the guns. As he saw his tracer bullets striking, Getz got so excited that he forgot to take his finger off the firing button to shoot in bursts and burned out all six of his machine gun barrels.

After the war, to avoid being demobilized before he could obtain a

Regular commission, Getz took a course in statistical analysis that would qualify him for an unusual job classification, or Military Occupation Specialty as it was called, and was sent off to Japan for two years as a statistical control officer with the Far East Air Forces. A subsequent bachelor's degree in accounting and economics and a master's in industrial management made him precisely the man Schriever was seeking when he arrived at WDD in the latter half of 1955. Simon Ramo had decided to create a control room in the Ramo-Wooldridge Arbor Vitae office complex, where Schriever and his staff were shortly to move from the Schoolhouse in Inglewood. It was to serve as a focal point for management of the various programs. Schriever saw this as a move that could end with him becoming a captive of civilian managers. "I want to keep control," he told Getz when he summoned him to his office shortly after Getz's arrival. Getz was to assume responsibility for all management systems on Schriever's behalf. "Your job is to work with them [Ramo-Wooldridge], but you are in charge and take charge." To make the point to all that Getz spoke for him, Schriever assigned Getz directly to his office.

Getz proceeded to cast a reporting net that encompassed every detail of every enterprise in Schriever's little empire. For example, each month prior to the main briefing, the Air Force project officers and the Ramo-Wooldridge engineers working on a missile had to get together, reach agreement on the current status of all aspects—engines, guidance, warhead, and so forth—and then sign their assent on a chart that illustrated this. Milestones were established, such as a completion date for each stage in the testing of a missile. The milestones were often not met, of course, and when this happened, the charts had to indicate exactly how much slippage had occurred and why.

The Black Saturday briefing, held in the Arbor Vitae control room, became the major event of the month at headquarters. Getz was its maestro. Prior to arriving in California, his nickname had been "Bill," from his middle name of William. Soon, behind his back, he was being called "Cecil B. De Getz," after Cecil B. DeMille, the famous Hollywood producer and director of spectacular epics like *The Ten Commandments* and *Samson and Delilah*. Getz's productions began at 8:45 in the morning and extended until well after 5:00 in the afternoon, with ten-minute personal relief breaks at midmorning and midafternoon and an hour off between noon and 1:00 for lunch. He ran the sessions with ruthless efficiency, because he knew this was what Schriever wanted in order to pack as much as possible into a single day. A missile team would be allotted fifty minutes to make its presentation. If a briefer was starting to run over on his time, Getz would flash on a screen behind him a sketch of a hook pulling a man off a stage. The trick never failed to elicit laughter from the briefing room, but if the briefer ignored the message, Getz would abruptly inform him, even in the middle of a sentence, "Time's up!"

Schriever's subordinates had aptly dubbed the monthly briefing Black Saturday because "the Boss" was not interested in good news. At a time when the upper echelons of the American military were beginning to suffer from the disease of professional arrogance and lack of imagination, and the fare of a normal briefing was "Progress," Schriever took an opposite approach. He wanted to know the problems, on the not irrational assumption that if they were solved, success would take care of itself. "I don't like to be surprised," he would say. "Give me the bad news. I can take it. I will not fire you for giving me the bad news. I will fire you if you don't give me the bad news." The briefings thus tended to be succinct recitals of woe, with frequently tentative ideas on how a team was going to solve a problem that continued to baffle. The discussions that followed sometimes helped, sometimes not. The paperwork burden and the time consumed in team meetings to reach agreement on the status of every aspect of every project made Getz the most unpopular man in the command. Yet no one dared ignore him because they knew that Schriever wanted what he was demanding. And there was no revolt because all understood that the system enforced discipline and teamwork. Everyone was made aware of what everyone else was doing and thus could pitch in to assist. Most important of all, the focus stayed where it mattered—the gradual elimination of impediments to getting the job done.

64

THE TRIALS OF ATLAS AND A
CHRISTMAS SURPRISE

The launching of Atlas at Cape Canaveral began on June 11, 1957, with an ostensible failure, a left punch for Schriever to absorb after taking a right, as the disappointment came just twenty-two days after Thiel and Mettler incinerated Thor 103 on its pad by overpressurization of the LOX tank. In Atlas, an ICBM designed to hurl its warhead 6,330 miles, Bennie was dealing with a missile larger and more complicated than the intermediate-range Thor and thus considerably more prone to trouble. Atlas was approximately seventy-five feet long, ten feet in diameter, and had in excess of 40,000 parts. In firing position, it was as high as a seven-story office building. When fully loaded with fuel and a simulated hydrogen bomb in its reentry vehicle warhead, it weighed 243,000 pounds, in contrast to Thor's 110,000.

Where the 1,725-mile Thor could loft itself with one of Hall's booster engines, improved to 150,000 pounds of thrust, Atlas needed 360,000 pounds. To obtain it, three engines were lined up at the base of the rocket, two 150,000-pound boosters, one on each side, with a 60,000-pound sustainer engine set between them. Atlas was what is re-ferred to in the guided missile business as a stage and a half rocket. All three engines at the base fired simultaneously for liftoff, but two min-utes into the flight, after the rocket had long cleared the dense air of the atmosphere and was on its way to maximum speed, the two booster engines were cut off by a radio control signal from the ground during testing and by the onboard inertial guidance system after it had been deployed. Another signal fired a release mechanism on the framework to which the big boosters were mounted and they fell away back to earth. The 60,000-pound sustainer engine in the middle, separately at-tached to the bulkhead at the base of the fuel tank fuselage, was kept burning for close to another three minutes to bring the Atlas within a fraction of the 16,000 miles per hour necessary to hurl the warhead the full 6,330 miles. With a last signal, tiny "retro" rockets at the front of the fuselage blasted into life. They snapped the warhead free from the fuselage, sending it off on its curved journey upward through space, reaching a point more than 800 miles above the earth at the apogee, before arching down to its target. This, in any case, was how the Atlas was supposed to work. Getting it to do so was another matter now to be undertaken.

Because they were moving through uncharted terrain, everyone involved—Convair, the Ramo-Wooldridge group, and Bennie's project officers—had decided to test the Atlas in four stages. The Series A missiles would check out the functioning and air-worthiness of the fuel tank fuselage and the propulsion system. These missiles would be the lightest in the series at 181,000 pounds, as they would be equipped with only the two main booster engines, not the sustainer. They would also be flown the shortest distance, a mere 530 miles. The completeness of the missiles and the length of the flights would then gradually increase through Series B and C, until, in Series D, missiles identical to those that were to be deployed would be tested at the full range of 6,330 miles.

Atlas 4A, the first readied for flight (missile numbers often did not correspond to launch sequence because flaws would be discovered in preflight tests and another missile substituted), reached Cape Canaveral in late March 1957. It came, as all of its relatives would, by trailer truck on a 2,622-mile journey across the continent from the Convair plant at San Diego. Even with the nose cone removed and shipped separately to shorten it, the missile was still too long and bulky to fly to the Cape in a C-124 Globemaster. And so a special sixty-four-foot-long trailer was fashioned, a steel cradle on wheels, and the missile, wrapped in a canvas shroud, was loaded into it and the trailer hooked to a truck. The trip took nine days because, for safety reasons, driving was restricted to daylight. There were armed guards on the trailer truck and in accompanying vehicles.

At dawn on June 11, 1957, Atlas 4A stood on the launch pad, the stainless steel of its fuel tank fuselage section gleaming in the first washes of the sun rising over the Atlantic. The day of a missile launching at the Cape could no longer be kept hidden. There were too many leaks and giveaway signs of preparation, and so on this day thousands of spectators lined Cocoa Beach five miles to the south to watch America's first intercontinental ballistic missile soar in the inauguration of a new epoch. The countdown in the blockhouse had started earlier, at 5:00 A.M., half an hour before sunrise. The Atlas had passed months and months of preflight checks of the components in California and then of the assembled missile at the Cape, including a short, static firing of the engines on the launch pad. It was rigged out with telemetry sensors to monitor its performance during the flight. The care of the preparations was evident in the monotonous but confident manner in which the countdown unfolded for three hours and twenty minutes. There were only two hitches that paused it, both toward the end of the sequence. A joint in a line feeding LOX from a storage tank to the missile sprang a leak and had to be replaced. Then an electrical circuit breaker tripped, cutting off the connection between a control console in the blockhouse and the missile. A Convair technician walked out of the blockhouse to the electrical transfer room near the launch pad and the now fully fueled missile and reset the breaker. The blockhouse door was closed again and the last steps of the count completed. Little green lights flashed across the control panel of the Convair test conductor, who had led the countdown, as he pressed the button to start the ignition sequence.

To the relief and joy of those on the Cape so intimately involved and the bystanders on Cocoa Beach, Atlas 4A rose and began a magnificent flight, for twenty-four seconds. Then, all of a sudden, the engines lost thrust. The flare of rockets no longer lit the sky. Only orange smoke billowed from the engine nozzles. The Atlas flipped wildly through a loop-the-loop and fell back into its trail of fire. The voice of the range safety officer at Central Control came up on the blockhouse intercom: "Destruct." This time justifiably, he punched the button flashing a radio signal to the packet of explosives on the missile and scattered the Atlas in pieces of flaming debris. "That was a total waste," someone in the despondent blockhouse said. "Hell, no," replied Edward Doll, one of the Ramo-Wooldridge engineers, pointing out that what looked bad was actually good news. They had just watched the Atlas gyrate through a series of extreme contortions in the sky and the missile had not broken up from the stress. Karel Bossart's radical weight-saving design of the Atlas fuselage that doubled as its fuel tank had been a worry for everyone. John Medaris and Wernher von Braun had just been shown to be self-

serving Cassandras in predicting that the "balloon," as they had scorn-
fully referred to the Atlas, would crumple under the strains of liftoff and
flight. "We proved it could stand three G's," Doll said, engineer's short-
hand for three times the force of gravity. And Bossart was present at the
Cape that day to witness the vindication of his idea. Bennie could thus
console himself with a partial success, but he knew that the Pentagon
and the White House, like the spectators on Cocoa Beach, would see the
launch as another of Schriever's missiles gone down in flames or burned
up on the pad.

Partial success was certainly not enough after the second Atlas
launched, 6A, which took almost three and a half months to ready, put
in a virtually identical performance on September 25, 1957. The rocket
flew for thirty-two seconds before the failure of a LOX regulator, as
the telemetry would reveal, led to another loss of thrust and destruction. Jacobson's promising accomplishments with Thor provided some
diversionary comfort, but this vanished that October 4 with the shock
of Sputnik. The pressure on Schriever ratcheted up enormously. The
third Atlas, 12A, had to fly as promised and everyone involved, from
the launch crew in the blockhouse at Canaveral to those waiting at the
other end of the direct Teletype line at the Ballistic Missile Division in
Los Angeles, shared the unnerving suspense. The rocket's booster engines burned faultlessly for the full two minutes after liftoff on December 17, 1957, the fifty-fourth anniversary of the Wright brothers'
flight, sending the missile the 530 miles down the Caribbean range for
which the flight had been programmed. Eisenhower was in Paris,
where he could pass on the encouraging word to the other Allied leaders at a NATO meeting he was attending. Even Democratic Senate Majority Leader Lyndon Johnson, who was cranking up his Preparedness
Investigating Subcommittee to give the administration a thrashing, had
a compliment. "That is mighty good news," he said.

It was clear by this time that there was a major flaw in the 150,000-
pound-thrust booster engine, a flaw that had been responsible for the
loss of thrust on the original Atlas launch of June 11, 1957, and for
some of the failures in the Thor and Jupiter launches. The flaw was the
worst kind an engineer could face, because it appeared randomly, sometimes twice in a row but on average about every five or six launches.
The rest of the time the engines functioned fine. And to make the problem still more intractable, the engineers disagreed on where the flaw lay.

Thiel's former German colleagues on the von Braun team told him right away, and as it turned out correctly, that the defect was in the turbopump, which mixed the RP-1 and LOX together at extremely high speed as they were fed into the burn chamber of the engine. They were convinced that the force of liftoff caused the bearings within the pump to shift. The bearings were then seizing up in flight, stopping the pump and the flow of fuel to the engine and, if the pump overheated enough, causing it to blow up and take the missile with it. The answer, they said, was to put a restraining mechanism on the bearings to hold them in place. The Ramo-Wooldridge rocket engine specialist disagreed. He said the failures were being caused by a misalignment of the outlet from the fuel tank to the pump.

Ed Hall, who had been assigned by Bennie to develop a revolutionary ICBM with a solid-fueled rather than a liquid-fueled engine, was off on his own brainstorming and did not get involved. The argument endured for months with others injecting their guesses and no solution in view. Bennie, who had come to have a particular trust in Mettler, asked for a memo advising him what to do. Mettler urged him to keep firing missiles until they could sort out an answer because the failures were random and they were learning so much with each launch. Most Air Force generals, their careers at stake as Schriever's was, would have halted, focused on fixing the engine no matter how much time was lost, and then resumed testing. In his race with the Soviets, time was a commodity with which Bennie Schriever was unwilling to part. He took Mettler's advice and pressed on. The turbopump was not fixed until well into the fall of 1958.

After that first successful Atlas flight on the fifty-fourth anniversary of the opening of the aerial age, there were days of triumph and months of heartbreak, but the ultimate goal of an operational intercontinental missile force as a deterrent to a Soviet surprise attack was always in sight. On August 2, 1958, the second Atlas in the B Series, 4B, gave, on signal, a perfect rendition of the five prescribed steps of flight. The booster engines shut down after two minutes, the release mechanism jettisoned them, the sustainer continued to burn for nearly another three minutes until it too was cut off, the two diminutive vernier engines made the final corrections in speed and angle, and the miniature retro rockets then came to life and freed the warhead to take flight through space. On November 28, another missile in the B Series, Atlas 12B, became the first to fly the entire 6,330-mile course.

Then came a Christmas surprise thought up by Mettler and several Convair engineers. On December 28, 1958, Atlas 10B, fitted with a special aerodynamic nose cone, blasted off a pad at Cape Canaveral. Inside the nose cone were two battery-powered tape recorders fitted to two radio transmitters, a pair of each in case one of the devices should fail. Instead of being sent on the high looping course of an ICBM, Atlas 10B was directed along a lower course parallel to the earth, and instead of cutting off the booster and sustainer engines, they were kept burning until the entire missile reached the speed of 17,300 miles per hour, escaped the gravity pull of earth, and flew into orbit. Every 101 minutes, it completed a circle of the globe. On the thirteenth pass over the United States, another radio signal from Canaveral turned on the tape recorders and transmitters and the voice of Eisenhower broadcast Christmas greetings to the peoples of the earth. "Through the marvels of scientific advance, my voice is coming to you from a satellite circling in outer space," the president said. "My message is a simple one. Through this unique means I convey to you and to all mankind America's wish for peace on earth and good will toward men everywhere." Project Score, as the project had been code-named, lacked the shock of Sputnik, but it was still quite an accomplishment. Spent of its fuel, the Atlas had become a satellite weighing 8,800 pounds. It continued circling the earth for thirty-three days, traveling 12.5 million miles before falling back into the atmosphere near Midway Island in the Pacific on January 21, 1959, burning up in a fiery climax.

The next six months were the most heartbreaking time. Testing of the C and then the D Series, the model that was to be deployed initially, began with a string of failures. Only two of the eight missiles of both series launched during the first half of 1959 were truly successful. The other six did not just blow up on the pad, but neither did they meet most of their test objectives. The mid-1958 "Ph.D. type" operational capability that Trevor Gardner had dreamed of back in 1954 had proven impossible to meet, but so did the June 1959 deployment date that Schriever set. The testing did improve the accuracy of the missile during the first half of 1959, eventually attaining a consistent accuracy of 2.3 miles by substituting an aerodynamic ablative reentry vehicle for the blunt-nose Mark 2 heat shield type first designed for Atlas. As had happened with Thor, occasional random misses were occurring in the launches aimed at the circle of hydrophones off Ascension Island in the South Atlantic. And again as with Thor, analysis convinced the engineers that the high winds in the upper atmosphere were from time to time catching the heat shield of the Mark 2 and pushing it off trajectory. While Bennie had been willing to tolerate the flaw in Thor because it was an intermediate-range missile and he was in a rush to finish the project, he was unwilling to ignore it in America's first ICBM.

To obtain an ablative RV, they could not simply copy the one von Braun had pioneered for Jupiter, because the Atlas's nose cone would be reentering the atmosphere at the much higher speed of 16,000 miles per hour, thus generating a lot more heat. As the ablative type worked by coating the nose cone with a compound of plastic and other material that burned off on reentry—deflecting heat from the nose cone itself and the hydrogen bomb inside—the question was exactly how much and what composition of coating was required. At the suggestion of Simon Ramo, Schriever had commissioned Lockheed to create a three-stage rocket called the X-17, or Athena, for the precise purpose of mimicking the conditions under which an ICBM warhead reentered the atmosphere. A scaled-down model of the RV was mounted on the rocket and the first two stages launched it into space. The third stage was then ignited and fired the nose cone back down into the atmosphere. The X-17 turned out to be an example of the technologist outsmarting himself with gimmickry a bit too fancy for the moment. The X-17 declined to go fast enough on the downward leg to replicate the reentry heat of an ICBM warhead.

Major Prentice "Pete" Peabody used his imagination. A thoughtful man, Peabody had earned his B.S. in aeronautical engineering at Georgia Tech in 1936, when it was the only school in the South with a program in the subject. He instrumented prospective ablative warheads for Atlas (they looked like giant condoms, a long, tubular body extending back from a rounded nose), and put them on stands behind rocket engines Rocketdyne was testing. No one knew if the flame of a rocket generated the same heat a warhead would on reentry, but it was a reasonable comparison. In this fashion, Peabody worked out the amount and composition of coating required to keep the heat on the inside of the warhead within an acceptable limit for the hydrogen bomb. He had already tested the copper heat shield of the original Atlas RV in the same way. Ironically, years later Peabody was awarded a Legion of Merit for leading a team that redesigned the X-17 and gave it enough velocity to mimic the reentry of warheads for the Navy's submarine-launched ballistic missiles, Polaris and then Poseidon.

Launching of the D Series went much better during the second half of 1959 and that September the initial battery of three Atlas D missiles, manned by SAC crews, was declared operational at Vandenberg. Although the state of testing did not yet fully justify deployment, there was no choice but to go ahead.

65.

WHOSE MISSILE GAP?

A terrifying fairy tale called "the missile gap," which had the Soviets surging ahead of the United States in ICBM capability, was roiling Washington. The controversy was another example of the chronic American habit during the Cold War, partly from genuine fear but usually inspired as well by political and institutional motives, of seriously overestimating Soviet military power and technological capabilities. Khrushchev, whose solution to the carefully disguised military inferiority of the Soviet Union vis-à-vis the United States was boasting and bluff, had helped to foster it. In August 1957, approximately two months before the shock of Sputnik, he announced that Russia had ICBMs able to reach "any part of the globe." In November of the following year Moscow claimed to have begun "serial production" of ICBMs. That December of 1958, Khrushchev told Senator and future Vice President Hubert Humphrey, Democrat of Minnesota, who was on a visit to Russia, that the Soviets had a new rocket but no place to test it because it flew 9,000 miles. He asked Humphrey what his hometown was and then walked over to a map of the United States and drew a circle around Minneapolis. "That's so I don't forget to order them to spare the city when the rockets fly," Khrushchev said. On another occasion, he bragged that in Russia "missiles were being turned out like sausages from a machine."

The Soviet leader had a receptive audience in the United States for these lies. Aroused by Sputnik, Democratic Party leaders accepted the purported missile gap as real and accused the administration of allowing the United States to lapse into a position of strategic inferiority. One of those crying out the loudest was the Democratic senator from Massachusetts, John F. Kennedy, who was to make the missile gap one of the central issues in his victorious presidential campaign of 1960. Influential fearmongers like Paul Nitze and chronic alarmists in the press like the Alsop brothers, Joseph and Stewart, who shared a syndicated column, added to the presumed state of peril. Nor were the military services averse to exploiting the situation in order to force an increase in the Pentagon budget. The worst offender was the Air Force's assistant chief of staff for intelligence, Major General James Walsh. In November 1959, he predicted that the Soviets would have 50 ICBMs by mid-1960 and "an operational ICBM force of about 250 (185 on launcher) by mid-1961, 500 (385 on launcher) by mid-1962, and 800 (640 on launcher) by mid-1963." Eisenhower, who knew Khrushchev was lying from the U-2 photography and other intelligence, which, for security reasons, he refused to share with his opposition, attempted reassurance but was simply not believed. (To his credit, Schriever did not join in fostering the scare, although he naturally benefited from the loosening of the budget strings.)

The truth was that by 1959 there was a missile gap. The gap was widening steadily in favor of the United States, not the Soviet Union. Soviet rocket engineers like Sergei Korolev had been ahead through the mid-1950s with soundly constructed medium- and intermediate-range ballistic missiles. After Bennie Schriever and the Schoolhouse Gang got going in the summer of 1954, however, the key in the ignition had been turned and the motor started to reverse positions in the race once it reached the level of an ICBM. With the assurance of a 1,500-pound hydrogen bomb for the warhead by the time the missile was ready, Schriever and company could commence by designing a practical ICBM. They were not forced, as Korolev had been because the Soviet Union was three years later than the United States in acquiring the hydrogen bomb, to begin by designing a behemoth rocket capable of carrying a 5.4-ton fission, or atomic, warhead, and thus to produce a totally impractical ICBM. By mid-1960, when the Air Force's intelligence chief predicted that the Soviet Union would have fifty ICBMs, it had emplaced the only four of Korolev's R-7 proto-ICBMs it was ever to deploy at Plesetsk, 600 miles north of Moscow. Khrushchev was to admit years later that the R-7 had "represented only a symbolic counterthreat to the United States."

There were Soviet ICBMs comparable to the Atlas and its alternative, Titan, on the way in 1959, but they were still in the development stage. Korolev designed one called the R-9, first flight-tested in 1961. It did not find favor with the Soviet military and was never produced in substantial numbers. The missile that was to become the standard Soviet ICBM for much of the 1960s, the R-16, was created by Mikhail Yangel, Korolev's principal rival as a rocket designer. Its initial flight test on October 24, 1960, turned into the worst disaster in the history of rocketry. Marshal Mitrofan Nedelin, the commander of the Soviet Strategic Rocket Forces, came to supervise the launch. He was a career artillery officer, an impatient, bullheaded man who actually knew little about rockets. When there was a last-minute glitch, he refused to allow the launch crew to drain the fuel from the rocket as a safety precaution while making necessary fixes. One of the fuel's components was nitric acid, flammable and toxic, inflicting severe burns on contact with the skin. A technician accidentally ignited the engines and the rocket burst apart in a mammoth fireball, sloshing burning fuel all over the pad and the surrounding area.

A camera set up to record the launch instead recorded a horror movie of human torches, including Nedelin, futilely attempting to escape. Secrecy was clamped over the catastrophe and the exact number of victims is unclear. The toll of those incinerated was apparently somewhere in the neighborhood of a hundred. A Red Army newspaper reported in 1990, the year before the Soviet Union collapsed, that 156 perished. Nedelin's death was publicly attributed to a plane crash and a coffin supposedly containing his remains was buried with honors in the Kremlin wall. William Taubman, the Amherst College scholar whose splendid biography of Khrushchev won him a Pulitzer Prize, says there was nothing left to put in a coffin. All that remained of Nedelin, he writes, was "a marshal's shoulder strap and half-melted keys to his office safe." The calamity did not stop test launches of the R-16 and the ICBM was deployed in 1962. The Soviets were, however, still having trouble with the weapon in October 1962 when the Cuban Missile Crisis occurred and Khrushchev had a total of twenty operational ICBMs to the 160 Kennedy possessed. Preparations to fire the R-16 continued to require several hours rather than the thirty minutes Yangel had posited and that was eventually achieved. "Before we get it ready to launch," Kirill Moskalenko, a ranking Red Army marshal and friend of Khrushchev from Second World War days, warned in the midst of the crisis, "there won't even be a wet spot left of any of us."

66.

A VICTORY DESPITE THE BUGS

There was a hiatus of a year after that first symbolic deployment of Atlas D missiles at Vandenberg in September 1959, during which the test-launching continued at Cape Canaveral on the more advanced E and F Series models. They were equipped with an inertial guidance system, again designed by Charles Stark Draper of MIT, that was self-contained and immune to interference. The long pause was not voluntary. The same haste in deployment that had caused such havoc with Thor was now wreaking its pain on the Atlas program. The SAC launch crews in training at Vandenberg were having a difficult time learning how to handle the Atlas's complex LOX and RP-1 fueling system. One rocket blew up during fueling exercises there. No one was hurt, apparently because, in contrast to the R-16 incident in the Soviet Union, safety precautions were followed, but there was extensive damage to the pad and other launch facilities. Major Benjamin Bellis, the formidable young engineer who had worked a cure for Thor, was brought back to do the same for Atlas. "Mr. Configuration Control," as the wags on Schriever's staff referred to him, formed another committee, the Atlas Configuration Control Board, and once more, naturally, designated himself its chairman. He discovered maddening confusion between missile parts being turned out by Convair's assembly line and those altered on site by the engineers to get the weapons to fly. There was no procedure to note down the changes in order to replicate them in missiles still being manufactured or completed and awaiting launch. When an Atlas functioned properly, "we didn't have a record of how we made it successful," Bellis recalled. "So we were having random success, the worst thing that can happen to you because you know you got it right but you can't repeat it. It drives you wild."

To halt the chaos and stop the Convair and Ramo-Wooldridge engineers from tinkering, he had seals put on the doors of the missile compartments and on the electronic cabinets of the launch equipment. In a repeat of the decree he had issued for Thor, no one was allowed to make a single change until it had been cleared by the board and incorporated into the manufacturing system and the instruction manuals. Yet these complicated first-generation ICBMs had so many bugs in them that attempting to eliminate their flaws in a hurry was a truly challenging task. On September 2, 1960, at the end of the one-year pause, a second deployment, a squadron of six Atlas D models, was declared operational at Warren Air Force Base in Wyoming. Then there was another six-month pause while another round of fixes took place. At the beginning of March 1961 the deployments resumed with the installation of a second squadron, this time of nine D model Atlases, at Warren, and then at the end of the month a third squadron of nine at Offutt Air Force Base, SAC headquarters, in Nebraska. Troubles, however, were not at an end. That June a $20 million retrofit program was started to try to bring average reliability to between 50 and 75 percent. Schriever conceded to staff members of the Senate's Preparedness Investigating Subcommittee the same month that several more years of testing would be required before the missiles achieved an 80 percent reliability rate. Nonetheless, after a third halt of nearly six months, the deployments resumed in the fall of 1961 when three nine-missile squadrons of the more advanced E models went operational at Fairchild Air Force Base in Washington State, Forbes in Kansas, and again at Warren.

Once more, there was a halt for the better part of a year while everything possible was done to ready six twelve-missile squadrons of the last and most sophisticated of the Atlas series, the F models, the first to be emplaced in the protective underground silos that would house ICBMs of the future. With Schriever's organization, assisted by the Army Corps of Engineers, supervising construction of the silos and turning silos and missiles over to SAC to operate, the six deployments unfolded one after another through the fall of 1962—Schilling Air Force Base in Kansas, Lincoln in Nebraska, Altus in Oklahoma, Dyess in Texas, Walker in New Mexico, and Plattsburgh in northernmost New York State. Except for Plattsburgh, the sites were all in the middle and western half of the continent, chosen for a trajectory that would take the missiles over the northern Pacific, Canada, Alaska, and the Arctic. By December 20, 1962, when the twelve F model missiles became operational at Plattsburgh, the force was complete. A total of 132 Atlas ICBMs had been arrayed against the Soviet Union.

While all of this was happening, Titan, which had begun its existence as a fallback to Atlas, had gone on to become a second ICBM. It went through the same roller-coaster testing pattern at Cape Canaveral in 1959 and 1960, successful flights ultimately eclipsing failures. Although still a first-generation liquid-fueled rocket like Atlas, Titan was taller, at ninety feet, and a more sophisticated ICBM with two stages. A pair of 150,000-pound-thrust booster engines, produced by Aerojet General, powered the rocket through the first stage of flight until, as their flames died and they fell away, an 80,000-pound sustainer engine ignited in the air and propelled the rocket to near-warhead-release speed, when four vernier engines took over for the final burst.

The two-stage technique enabled Titan to lift a much heavier warhead and it was soon designated Titan I, as a second version, Titan II, was on the drawing boards. Titan II would unleash a warhead containing a hydrogen bomb of a terrifying nine megatons. On April 18, 1962, deployment began for six squadrons of nine Titan I missiles each at Air Force bases in California, Colorado, Idaho, South Dakota, and Washington State. The Titans were housed, as the Atlas Fs were, in underground concrete silos. By September 28, 1962, when the last of the six squadrons was declared operational, the Soviet Union was looking at another fifty-four American ICBMs.

How many of these Titan and Atlas missiles would fly if doomsday arrived and the command to launch was given, no one really knew. But Nikita Khrushchev and the other leaders of the Soviet Union could not afford to bet on percentages of reliability. All they could do was to count missiles. It was nearly nine years since, in March 1953, the vision of an ICBM had lit Bennie Schriever's mind while he listened to

John von Neumann and Edward Teller brief the Air Force Scientific Advisory Board meeting at Maxwell Air Force Base in Alabama. The goal of fielding the first generation of intercontinental rockets had just been achieved. As Schriever was to say years later to a reunion of those who had participated in the race against the Soviets: "We beat them to the draw." And the consummation of the victory, the fielding of the ultimate in ICBMs to emerge from the insight of Schriever and the creative genius of Edward Hall, had begun. The new missile was called Minuteman.

67.

MINUTEMAN: ED HALL'S TRIUMPH

When Schriever had relieved Hall as program director for Thor in the summer of 1957 after that missile's third failure and Hall's alienation of his co-workers, he had shrewdly avoided firing Hall from his staff and thereby losing his unique talents. Hall, in anger at his dismissal, had requested a transfer out of WDD. Schriever had refused. Instead, he had set Hall to work creating a second-generation ICBM. As all earlier liquid-fueled rockets had been descendants, in one form or another, of the German V-2, so this new guided missile was to be the progenitor of all rockets to follow. Hall's rocket was to be fueled by a solid substance rather than by RP-1 kerosene and the dangerous and highly volatile liquid oxygen that powered the first generation. If a solid-fueled ICBM could be devised, it would have a number of advantages over its liquid-fueled predecessors. It would be much smaller and far simpler in construction, thus making it more reliable and affordable for the United States to produce in many hundreds. It could be stored in full readiness for lengthy periods of time. And most important, it could be fired off on its journey through space in a minute or less.

Ed Hall had long had a yen to build a solid-fuel ICBM. Apparently understanding that this missile was the work for which he would be remembered, once over his pique about Thor, he dedicated himself to his task with a ferocious zeal. He had formidable obstacles to overcome. To begin with, he had to devise a solid fuel that would develop enough thrust, called "specific impulse" in the rocket business, to propel a warhead 6,330 miles. Hall had already dabbled in solid-fuel rocket work. At the beginning of the 1950s, he and his associates at the Wright-Patterson laboratories had improved on the small solid-fuel rockets Theodore von Kármán and his colleagues at the Guggenheim Aeronautical Laboratory at Caltech had invented during the Second World War to give aircraft a quick extra lift during takeoff. Hall's group had created a solid fuel potent enough to assist in getting a fully loaded B-47 aloft, but it did not approach what he needed now. He had also made considerable progress during a research study of solid-fuel engines Schriever had authorized at WDD in 1955 and 1956, but again a formula for the right fuel had eluded him.

The Navy, anxious to get into the strategic rocket business, had by 1957 also abandoned the batty idea of launching a Jupiter missile from the deck of a ship, a spectacular way to burn and sink the vessel if the liquid-fueled rocket malfunctioned, and was working up a solid fuel, submarine-launched missile that became Polaris. While the Navy was willing to swap ideas, its research was of little assistance to Hall. Polaris was to be an IRBM with a 1,380-mile range. Hall was searching for a solid fuel with a lot more thrust than Polaris would require. He selected the three firms he considered most promising, Thiokol Chemical Corporation, Aerojet General, and Hercules Powder Company, and began experimenting. Hall and the team working under him finally hit on a formula that provided the necessary power. It was a lot more exotic than liquid oxygen and kerosene. They used a chemical called ammonium perchlorate to provide oxygen for the rocket's flame, and as fuel aluminum additives and a combination with a long name, polybutadiene-acrylic acid. The whole propellant was compounded together and encased in a rubberlike wrapper that also burned.

One of the persistent problems in creating solid-fuel rockets was getting the fuel to consume itself evenly from the center to the outside casing of the engine, but without burning a hole through the casing and thereby destroying the integrity of the engine and causing an explosion. Ideas, particularly technological breakthroughs, have a way of traveling. In this instance, the Rocket Propulsion Department of Britain's

Ministry of Technology had discovered a solution earlier in the 1950s while experimenting with a solid-fueled antiaircraft rocket. If a star-shaped cut was made all the way down through the middle of the solid fuel, or the same thing was achieved by casting the fuel in a mold with a star shape at its center, then enough burning surface was obtained so that the propellant burned evenly from the center outward, consuming itself in the process and leaving the engine casing intact. The British never went beyond the laboratory with the technique because the missile was canceled. Thiokol was then a small company in Huntsville, Alabama, near the Redstone Arsenal. When the Air Force asked Thiokol to build a solid-fuel rocket of modest size to provide a preliminary boost for a jet-powered cruise missile of 700-mile range called the Mace, Thiokol helped itself to the British idea. The star-shaped cut turned out to be equally applicable to Hall's far more powerful solid-fuel engine.

The next hurdle was how to achieve instant shutdown of the engine, that absolute necessity for accuracy in a ballistic missile. This was not difficult with liquid fuels because the flow could just be cut off. But once a block of solid fuel had been set alight and was driving a rocket at thousands of miles an hour, how was one to extinguish it in flight? Some of the Ramo-Wooldridge engineers thought the problem insoluble. Hall came up with an elegantly simple answer. He designed an engine casing with shutdown ports. When the missile's control system flung these open with a signal, the pressure inside was reduced so swiftly that the propellant was snuffed out. Steering was to be achieved with equal simplicity, by swiveling the engine nozzles. Hall designated his creation, which had not yet been given its permanent name, Weapon System Q. He chose Q because he discovered that the majority of the remaining letters of the alphabet had already been co-opted by other departments, and projects of WDD and Q had an element of mystery and surprise for him. It called to his mind the Q-ships, merchantmen with disguised depth charge mounts and false sides that hid cannon, which the British navy had employed during the First and Second World Wars to lure and destroy German submarines. He believed that his new weapon and the plan he had conceived to employ it would also surprise.

By January 1958, he was ready to unveil it. He telephoned Schriever's deputy, Terry Terhune, and said that he needed several hours of Terhune's time to brief him. Colonel Terhune told Hall to come to his office right away and instructed his secretary to cancel his appointments. Hall held forth for two to three hours. He had a blueprint of the proposed new rocket and went step by step through its advantages over its liquid-fueled predecessors, as well as his plan on how to deploy it. Terhune was so impressed that he led Hall over to Schriever's office and said that he had to hear Hall immediately. Schriever in turn canceled his appointments and Terhune sat by while Hall launched into another two-to-three-hour briefing session. As soon as Hall was done, Bennie picked up the phone and called Lieutenant General Donald Putt, currently deputy chief of staff, development, at the Pentagon. He informed Putt that they wanted to come to Washington around the end of the month to brief him. He also asked Putt to set up briefings with the Air Force Council and with James Douglas, Jr., the new secretary of the Air Force, who had replaced Donald Quarles the previous May. In the meantime, Hall was to prepare charts and any other aids necessary for a full-scale presentation.

As Schriever and Terhune both had their families living in Santa Monica, they rode to and from work together each morning and evening when Schriever was not in Washington or at Canaveral. Terhune welcomed the custom as an opportunity to alert the boss to forthcoming problems, have him read over a proposal on which Terhune wanted his opinion, or just review the events of the day. Because Schriever was away so much and trusted Terhune completely, he had become, in effect, supervisor of the California end of their endeavor. With the Pentagon briefings in prospect, they thought it was time to give Q a catchier name, one that might help to sell the missile. Hall and others had already proposed three alternatives: Sentry, Sentinel, or Minuteman. Schriever and Terhune decided that the last most aptly caught the essence of the new rocket and so Minuteman went to Washington.

As matters turned out, the Pentagon briefings were postponed until the beginning of February. The first crucial briefing was on February 6, 1958, before the Air Force Council. Curtis LeMay was now vice chief and thus its chairman. They did not expect trouble from Thomas White, who had become chief of staff in July 1957 when Nathan Twining had moved up to become chairman of the Joint Chiefs, because White had been so supportive of the ICBM program from the outset. LeMay had remained unremittingly hostile to Atlas and Titan. "These things will never be operational, so you can depend on them, in my lifetime," he had predicted to Jerome Wiesner, the Tea Pot Committee veteran. Nevertheless, Schriever had felt it his duty, as the ICBMs would ultimately be turned over to SAC, to keep LeMay informed. He had always been rewarded with scorn. The Cigar had sat silently through one briefing on Atlas. At the end he had asked, "What is the biggest warhead you can put on that missile?" One megaton, he was told. "When you can put something on that missile bigger than a fucking firecracker, come and see me," LeMay replied.

If he reacted in the same fashion to Minuteman, they would have a fight on their hands, because, while White would, in the end, probably rule in their favor, he would be reluctant to just brush aside his subordinate's opinion. Schriever introduced Hall in a couple of sentences and then turned the briefing platform over to him and sat down. Terhune remembered the self-confidence with which Hall spoke and the skill with which he employed his blueprints and charts to illustrate his points.

Solid fueling had enabled Hall to shrink an ICBM. The Minuteman he described would be a small boy compared to an Atlas or a Titan. It would weigh, including its solid propellant, about 65,000 pounds at liftoff, compared to 243,000 pounds for Atlas, and would stand approximately fifty-five feet tall, in contrast to ninety feet for Titan. Yet he had sacrificed none of the reach and potency of the ICBM weapon. His rocket was a three-stage affair, each stage smaller and lighter than the last. Stage I, at 50,100 pounds, would provide liftoff and bring the rocket to initial velocity. As it shut down and fell away, the engine of Stage II would kick in and increase speed. Then as it too went silent and dropped off, the engine of Stage III, which weighed only 5,800 pounds, including the solid fuel, the missile's guidance system, and the ablative-type reentry vehicle at the nose with a one-megaton hydrogen bomb inside, would ignite and propel the rocket to terminal velocity for release of the warhead. Nor would there be any scrimping in range. Minuteman would throw its warhead the same 6,330 miles as Atlas and Titan with a CEP, circular error probable, of little more than a mile.

There was a proviso on warhead yield, Hall said. The nuclear weapons designers would have to size a one-megaton bomb down to 500 pounds. Given the rapidity with which the art of downsizing hydrogen weapons was progressing, Hall said, he did not doubt that this could be done by the time the first Minutemen began to flow to an operational squadron. Schriever and Terhune agreed. If the Air Force was willing to settle for a half-megaton warhead of 350 pounds, the Minuteman's range could be extended to a record 7,480 miles. (The nuclear weaponsmiths were indeed displaying an astonishing aptitude for miniaturizing their hellish contrivances. When deployed, Atlas and Titan I would both carry thermonuclear warheads yielding four times the one megaton Schriever had counted sufficient at the outset back in 1953, with no appreciable gain in weight beyond the 1,500-pound limit. The first 150 Minutemen were to be fitted with a one-megaton warhead and those that followed with a higher-yield bomb of 1.2 megatons.)

Hall's scheme for deploying Minuteman was as radical as the weapon itself. His design, he explained, was intended to deter the Soviets from ever resorting to a surprise nuclear attack on the United States. His plan was to build 1,616 Minutemen (the total included spares) by the end of calendar year 1965 and to deploy them in "missile fields" of one hundred or so. The rockets would be dispersed three miles apart, every one in an underground silo sufficiently hardened with concrete and steel so that if the Soviets hit the field with a five-megaton warhead, only one rocket would be lost. The silo covers would then slide open and the remaining Minutemen would be launched right out of the silos in retaliation. Because of their solid fuel, the rockets could be stored in the silos indefinitely. They would be checked constantly to be certain that every one was in working order and that the inertial guidance systems, internal to the missiles and therefore unjammable, were always up and running. If a malfunction was found, the missile would be removed from its silo and replaced by a spare until it could be repaired. Everything would be automated. Unlike the liquid-fueled ICBMs, which had to be launched individually after fifteen minutes of fueling, two or more remote control centers, also dispersed for survival, could fire individual Minutemen or salvo fifty at once, each with the coordinates of a different Soviet city cranked into its inertial guidance. The Russians would, of course, learn of the missile fields and the virtually instantaneous launch capability of Minuteman and draw the appropriate conclusion.

LeMay had written Twining back in November 1955 that he

would consider the ICBM "the ultimate weapon" worthy of inclusion in SAC's inventory when one could be created "with a capability of instantaneous launch and with acceptable reliability, accuracy, and yield." The conditions were technological pie in the sky at that time, an attempted stalling tactic, because LeMay knew that the technology of nearly instantaneous launch was years away, if ever, and at this moment in 1958 he continued to regard the bomber as the best of weapons. But he also turned out now to be as good as his word on what he required in an ICBM. Terhune remembered that after a short discussion at the end of Hall's briefing, LeMay swung around to the three-star deputy chiefs of staff sitting in the rows behind him and asked: "Do you agree it's a go?" They all did. Hall got the impression that what appealed most to LeMay was the massiveness of the scheme. The thought of hundreds and hundreds of rockets roaring out of silos was LeMay's vision of how to frighten the Russians and then to reduce the Soviet Union to cinders if it did come to nuclear war.

The briefing for Air Force Secretary Douglas was also a go, and on the morning of February 8, 1958, they faced the last hurdle: a briefing for Wilson's successor, Neil McElroy. LeMay came as well as Douglas and, to Hall's surprise, LeMay weighed in with comments underscoring Hall's briefing points. McElroy gave his assent. The meeting ended, Hall recalled, with the secretary turning to him and saying: "Now get out of here and go back to work." After they had returned to California, Terhune found himself astonished at what they had accomplished. They had been in Washington only a few days and had won approval for what would probably be the biggest rocket program the Air Force would ever undertake. "That was a world's record as far as I was concerned," he reflected years later. Schriever had Hall draw up a detailed development program and by the end of February they had formal approval and start-up funds of $25.9 million. Hall forged ahead toward a final design. By the latter half of July 1958, he had reached the point where the contractors who would build the missile had been selected.

68.

"YOU COULDN'T KEEP HIM
IN THAT JOB"

Then, that August, Schriever broke Ed Hall's heart by taking Minuteman away from him. The project was passing from the conception to the testing and production stage and it was impossible to leave him in charge. The task of managing a program on the huge scale looming ahead for Minuteman was beyond his gifts and prohibited by his personality. As he had with Thor, he would alienate too many people and make a hash of things. "We knew from our previous experience with him," Terhune, who admired Hall's fertile mind and aggressiveness, recalled, "that you couldn't keep him in that job." As Schriever put it in his comment as indorsing officer on Hall's last efficiency report under his command: "Col. Hall's inability to work harmoniously with persons with whom he disagrees seriously impairs his competence in the management area." Even Sidney Greene, Hall's friend now working for Jacobson, who had put his own future in peril back at the Wright-Patterson laboratories by shifting the $2 million to Hall for his pioneeering venture to devise the engine that would power Atlas and Thor, felt that Schriever had acted responsibly.

Hall, now intensely embittered toward Bennie, clearly could not remain in Los Angeles. He received orders at the end of August transferring him to Paris to start a project for a new solid-fueled intermediate-range ballistic missile that would be jointly produced by the NATO countries. Despite intra-Allied bickering and rivalry, he succeeded in getting the program started. His efforts eventually saw fulfillment in a French IRBM called the Diamant, but Ed Hall could not see much of a future for himself in the U.S. Air Force. Although he had been promoted to full colonel in February 1957, he was obviously not going to receive a star nor was he likely to get another compelling assignment. Twenty years of service, the minimum for retirement, would come due

for him in the fall of 1959. He returned to the United States to exchange his Air Force blue for a business suit that October 31, accepting a job offer as an engineer and assistant to the chief scientist of the
United Aircraft Corporation in East Hartford, Connecticut. Schriever
saw to it that his achievement was recognized. In January 1960, Hall
flew out to Los Angeles for a ceremony to award him his second Legion of Merit. It capped the first he had received as a first lieutenant in
England in 1943 for putting B-17s back into the air against Hitler's
Third Reich by inventing special tools to hasten repair of flak-damaged
fuselages. Terhune pinned on the medal with an oak leaf cluster, the
symbol of a second award. Hall would have spurned it from Schriever.

Bennie put one of his stalwarts from the Schoolhouse Gang, Colonel
Otto Glasser, an engineer and nuclear weapons specialist who had been
the original program director for Atlas, in charge of Minuteman until
the right officer could be found to guide it to fulfillment. (Glasser was yet
another of Schriever's crew to go on to win the three stars of a lieutenant
general before his career was over.) Terhune and Jacobson encountered
the man they needed during a trip to England in 1959 to assess the deployment of Thor. He was a straight-as-a-pencil young colonel named
Samuel Phillips, director of matériel for SAC's 7th Air Division in
Britain, temporarily assigned to help ready Thor installations for turn-
over to the RAF. He had participated in writing the Thor basing agreement with the British and was to receive a Legion of Merit for his
contribution. They were so impressed with him that they looked up his
background on return to Los Angeles. Phillips had graduated from the
University of Wyoming in 1942 with a degree in electrical engineering
and a Regular Army commission he had gained in a special ROTC competition. After flight training, he had done two tours as a fighter pilot in
Europe, and twice been awarded the Distinguished Flying Cross for
bravery, along with eight Air Medals and a Croix de Guerre from de
Gaulle's Free French. After the war, he had gone back to school for a
master's in electrical engineering from the University of Michigan, focusing on electronics, and then joined the laboratories at Wright-
Patterson for a gamut of assignments, including project officer on the
B-52. He arrived in Los Angeles in August 1959 as the new program director for Minuteman and proved to be a superlative manager of large-
scale enterprises. He also had plenty of help. Schriever had Ramo assign
Mettler to head the Ramo-Wooldridge team that worked with him.

By January 1961, when the time was approaching for the initial test firing at Canaveral, Phillips made up his mind to do something unprecedented for an opening launch. They would test the entire rocket—all three stages, the inertial guidance, a dummy warhead inside the ablative reentry vehicle—everything that would be on a deployed Minuteman except a real hydrogen bomb. General White had asked Schriever to trim a year off the deployment time and to field the first Minutemen in the fall of 1962, rather than in 1963 as earlier anticipated. There was no time to meet that deadline and follow the normal procedure of successive flight tests for individual components of the rocket. And so Phillips, who had confidence in the missile, decided on a gamble. He would risk what is called in the rocket trade an "all up" launch, never before attempted on a first try. Schriever agreed to the gamble, because there was no choice if they were to meet White's wishes, but not without considerable trepidation. If the missile failed, it was going to be a well-publicized fiasco. With Air Force permission about 150 reporters and television cameramen assembled at Canaveral on the morning of Wednesday, February 1, 1961, a fine clear day in Florida, to cover the event.

Ed Hall's rocket proved itself worthy of Phillips's confidence. At 11:00 A.M. the first Minuteman to fly lifted from its pad and rose, accelerating ever faster. At 65,000 feet the streak of flame and a long column of white smoke from the first-stage booster engine could still be seen, the missile now hurtling along at thousands of miles an hour. The countdown announcer in the blockhouse was calling off the telemetry readings the instruments in the missile were transmitting back:

"First stage burnout.
"Second stage ignition.
"Second stage burnout.
"Third stage ignition."

The range safety officer in the separate Central Control bunker announced over the circuit that his instruments showed the guidance system had released the warhead on a bull's-eye course for the center of the ring of hydrophones off Ascension Island in the South Atlantic. At that moment, a phone in the blockhouse rang. It was Schriever, who had been listening to all of this over a special communications hookup, calling from Washington to congratulate Phillips. The next day in East Hartford, Ed Hall received a telegram from Major John Hinds, a public affairs officer with the Ballistic Missile Division who had taken a particular interest in Minuteman from the time Hall's work had become general knowledge within the command. "Congratulations on fathering the most significant single missile and space event of the decade," the telegram said. "I thought of you as your brain child roared to life at Cape Canaveral." Phillips's reward was the star of a brigadier, the youngest general in the armed forces at forty years of age. He was subsequently loaned to NASA to run the Apollo program, which put astronauts Neil Armstrong and Edwin "Buzz" Aldrin on the moon on July 20, 1969, and then took on a series of senior Air Force commands, including the Space and Missile Systems Organization in Los Angeles, a later successor to Schriever's original WDD, which were to bring him the four stars of a full general.

Yet nothing that Ed Hall and Sam Phillips had ever done or would ever do would be more important than bringing Minuteman into existence. Schriever and his comrades had reversed the missile gap in favor of the United States with Atlas and Titan. The creation of Minuteman now put the United States so far ahead in the strategic missile competition that the Soviet Union was confronted not with a gap but with a chasm. Not until five years later, in 1966, did the Soviets acquire their first solid-fueled ICBM, designated SS-11 by NATO. By then the United States had 800 Minutemen waiting in silos in the Western and Midwestern states and the total would rise to 1,000 in April 1967 after 200 Minuteman II missiles, a larger and improved version that carried a still bigger warhead, were added to the force. Shortly after that first successful launch at Cape Canaveral on February 1, 1961, LeMay and Tommy Power at SAC proposed that the United States build and deploy 8,000 Minutemen. Robert McNamara, secretary of defense in the new administration of John Kennedy, who had assumed the presidency in January, decided that 1,000 was enough.

The advent of Minuteman put an end to the fear of a nuclear Pearl Harbor that had haunted Eisenhower. The Air Force organized the Minutemen into wings of 150 missiles, each wing composed of three squadrons of fifty, with five flights of ten comprising a squadron. Every flight was under a separate control center, housed in steel and concrete capsules placed well underground, with entry and exit through equally sturdy concrete shafts, and manned by two launch officers. Sufficient redundancy was built into the communications system so that if incoming Soviet missiles damaged it, any one of the control centers could fire all fifty Minutemen in the squadron. In practice it took more than a minute for the launch control officers to fire Minuteman. They needed two to three minutes. They had to verify the coded go command before each inserted a separate key into one of the two locks on the launch sequence control computer. Then they simultaneously turned the keys and in sixty seconds the missiles were gone. With the radar and other alert systems the United States possessed in 1961, and was to elaborate extensively in the years to come, this was certainly fast enough for hundreds of Minutemen to fly out of their silos before the Soviet missiles struck. And even if by some miracle the Soviets managed to hit first with everything they had, there would still be plenty of Minutemen intact in their steel and concrete shelters to doom Russia. No Soviet statesman with a vestige of sanity could risk a surprise attack.

BOOK VII

A SPY IN ORBIT AND A GAME OF NUCLEAR DICE

69

A WOULD-BE SPY IN THE SKY
GOES AWRY

Minuteman was not the only final accomplishment bequeathed by Bennie Schriever and his colleagues. There was another, Discoverer XIV, in its way a complement to Minuteman. On August 18, 1960, at Vandenberg Air Force Base, the first successful photo-reconnaissance satellite rose atop a Thor rocket to photograph, in a single mission, more of the Soviet Union from space than the U-2s had accomplished in all twenty-four flights over Russia during the four years before one was shot down just three and a half months earlier. "It was as if an enormous floodlight had been turned on in a darkened warehouse," said Albert Wheelon, a Stanford and MIT physicist who was part of the Ramo-Wooldridge team before becoming the CIA's first deputy director for science and technology in 1963. Schriever had taken charge of the Air Force's space satellite program, Weapon System 117L, back in 1955. It had originated with the Air Development Center at Wright-Patterson, but since he was eventually going to have to supply the rockets to lift the satellites into orbit, Schriever had reasoned that he ought to have control. Tommy Power, whose empire as commanding general of ARDC in Baltimore included the Wright-Patterson laboratories, agreed and gave the project to him. WS-117L encompassed a family of satellites to perform photographic, electronic, and infrared surveillance. One of the photographic satellites planned was a so-called readout version. The film would be developed aboard the satellite and then transmitted to earth. The second type envisioned a system whereby the camera would feed its undeveloped film into a capsule. Once full, the capsule would be ejected. An attached parachute would burst open after it entered the atmosphere and an aircraft trailing a trapezelike hook would catch the chute canopy or its lines and winch the capsule aboard.

Nothing of substance got done, once more because Donald Quarles was imposing his "Poor Man's" doctrine to hold down the military budget and please Eisenhower. Satellites had to be funded separately from the ICBM program and Quarles would not part with any meaningful amount of money for them. Sputnik and Eisenhower's concern about an eventual successor to the U-2 changed all that in the fall of 1957. Eisenhower created the position of special assistant to the president for science and technology and named James Killian, the president of MIT, to the post. Simultaneously, Killian became chairman of a reorganized Presidential Science Advisory Committee (PSAC). He and Edwin "Din" Land, the photography genius who had invented the Polaroid Land Camera and who also had entrée to the Oval Office, examined the WS-117L program. They decided that the technology involved in the capsule ejection system had the best chance of succeeding in the near term and convinced the president of this. In February 1958, Eisenhower authorized creation of the satellite, with the proviso that it was to be managed as the U-2 had been. The Air Force would provide the booster rocket and satellite vehicle and do the work, but the CIA would be in charge, even though the only hardware it would provide would be the camera. The agency would also exercise complete control over the intelligence derived from the film. Eisenhower knew how parochial the military services could be in intelligence matters, and in the CIA-run U-2 program he had a successful precedent to follow. The same two men who had brought it to fruition moved back into action. On the CIA side, Richard Bissell, Allen Dulles's special assistant for plans and development, was named overall manager, as he had been for the U-2, while Ozzie Ritland, who had been Bissell's deputy on that endeavor and was now Schriever's vice commander at the Ballistic Missile Division, headed up the Air Force team. Bissell, an economist by education, had displayed a gift for technological intelligence projects, and Ritland, who began his career as a test pilot at Wright Field, had a marked flair for technical improvisation. The arrangement did not let Schriever off the hook in the event of a fiasco. The official chain of command for the project listed him above Ritland: he was to keep a watchful eye and to take the blame if the Air Force failed to perform.

On the assumption that the series of launches involved could not be hidden entirely from the public, a cover story was concocted. Schriever announced that the Air Force was putting its rocket capability to the service of science and medicine with a new program called Discoverer. Its objective was to test the effect of the conditions of space—vacuum, weightlessness, and frigid temperatures—on everything from human bone marrow to corn seedlings, hence the need to recover the capsule in which these would be placed. In the meantime, the CIA had a second and secret code name for the enterprise, Corona, adopted by one of Bissell's subordinates from the brand of cigars he smoked. Lockheed had been chosen as contractor for the satellite vehicle for the WS-117L program and a decision was made that it could be used for Discoverer. The vehicle was called Agena and it was actually a combination second-stage rocket and satellite. After the Thor booster rocket had brought the Agena to near-orbital velocity and shut down and dropped away, the Agena's rocket kicked in to complete the flight. Once in orbit, the satellite characteristics of Agena came into play. The vehicle was fitted with small orientation rockets fired as needed by the inertial guidance system to keep the camera port pointing at the earth should the Agena begin to tip off kilter and aim the camera over the horizon. Retro rockets, ignited on radio command from the ground, were also mounted to slow down the satellite when the moment arrived for ejection of the film capsule.

Forrest McCartney, whose three-star career culminated in the directorship of NASA's Kennedy Space Center at Cape Canaveral, remembered how crude this first satellite was in comparison to what was to come. McCartney was a twenty-seven-year-old captain in early 1959 when he began to teach himself how to fly satellites at the nation's first satellite control center, set up for Discoverer in a motel in Palo Alto, California, just south of San Francisco. A nuclear weapons engineer by trade, McCartney had worked for Moose Mathison at the Special Weapons Center at Albuquerque's Kirtland Air Force Base. Schriever had put Mathison in charge of the satellite control center and Mathison was reaching out for younger officers smart enough to learn this new business, which he was also having to teach himself. They did not stay long in Palo Alto, soon moving to cramped quarters in Lockheed's facilities in nearby Sunnyvale. The "control room" was a twenty-foot-by-twenty-foot space with a table in the middle and folding metal chairs around it. There was a radio console on the table with which the operator on duty transmitted commands to the satellite. Facing him was a blackboard with various orbit parameters and instructions chalked on it. The "communications room" was an adjacent closet. In the closet Mathison had voice radio and Teletype hookups to the launching crew at Vandenberg and to the subsidiary monitoring and control stations on Kodiak Island, off Alaska's south coast, and in Hawaii.

The miniature computers with sophisticated microcircuitry that were to direct the satellites of the future did not exist in 1959. Nor did the solar panels that would be attached to satellites to provide plenty of electricity from their photovoltaic cells. Electrical power came from batteries. These limited the amount of time the satellite could be kept in orbit and their weight reduced the payload for camera and film. The Agena's control system resembled that of an old-fashioned player piano, which had a roll of paper with holes punched in it to trip the keys in accordance with the tune as the paper unwound. Agena's mechanism consisted of an electric clock timer hooked up to a motor that drove a long plastic tape with holes in it. The clock, either through pre-programming or on a radioed signal from the operator back on earth, told the motor when to start and stop. Metal fingers of different lengths, bent inward at the ends, reached out over the tape. When the tape arrived at the point where a hole lined up with the end of one of the fingers, the bent end dropped through the hole and completed an electrical circuit, thereby executing a command. Because of the primitiveness of the system, Agena was capable of only thirteen commands, such as the order to eject the capsule.

The test launches began inauspiciously. During the first attempt from Vandenberg, on January 21, 1959, the Agena nearly took off on its own from atop the Thor. Its systems accidentally turned on during a prelaunch check, the Agena's orientation rockets fired, the explosive bolts attaching it to the Thor also blew, and the Agena's main rocket engine might have ignited had the launch crew not managed to shut everything down, but not before there was serious damage to the satellite vehicle and some to the Thor. The crew decided the whole thing had been so farcical that they would not count this attempt as part of the series, labeling it Discoverer 0.

The president was not so dismissive. When Bissell, who had just been promoted to deputy director for plans, the CIA's euphemism for chief of clandestine operations, went to the White House to deliver a report, Eisenhower gave him a dressing-down. Discoverer I, the second launch, a bit over a month later, went fine. As far as could be determined, the Agena sailed up into the intended polar orbit from which, with the earth spinning sideways on its axis beneath, the whole of the Soviet Union would be exposed to photography. Attaining a correct orbit had been the main purpose of this mission, and so there had been no test of ejection and recovery of the capsule. Not so Discoverer II on April 13. Its liftoff launched Moose Mathison off into an adventure on the edge of the Arctic.

The Agena circled the earth every ninety minutes. Because of the limitations of battery power, the capsule had to be ejected on the seventeenth orbit, slightly more than a day in space at twenty-five and a half hours. As this terminal orbit approached, the Sunnyvale center instructed the subsidiary control station in Hawaii, the satellite's last point of contact before it headed back around the bottom of the world, to issue the ejection signals. "Commands going out," Hawaii replied. Unfortunately, the Hawaii controller's radio equipment was malfunctioning. An antenna to his receiver had become disconnected. He was supposed to get a sign on his console confirming that the commands had been transmitted to the Agena. When he saw none, he transmitted again. Again there was no confirmation and so he transmitted a third time and a fourth time and a fifth time before he realized he had better stop. Telemetry from the instruments on the Agena told the Sunnyvale center that the satellite had received all five transmissions.

This information precipitated a reaction that might charitably be described as extreme anxiety and more accurately as panic, because it meant that the Agena would eject its capsule somewhere far from the area in the Pacific approximately 380 miles northwest of Hawaii where the capsule was supposed to come down. A squadron of C-119 transports, their crews trained in the retrieval process and equipped with the trapezelike hooks that trailed behind in flight, was on alert at Hickam Air Force Base near Honolulu. The C-119 had wide clamshell doors at the rear through which the capsule could be winched after the hook snatched the canopy or rigging of its parachute. There was no way the Sunnyvale center could correct the problem, because they could no longer talk to the satellite. The designers of the Agena had outsmarted themselves. To prevent the Soviets from seizing control of their satellite in flight and also to conserve battery power, they had programmed its radar beacon and radio receiver to switch off as soon as the Agena was out of range of the Hawaii station. The beacon and receiver would not switch on again until the satellite had gone back around the earth and was approaching the Alaska station. By that time it would be too late to correct. An analysis concluded that the capsule was going to eject far from the Pacific, on the Norwegian island of West Spitsbergen. The island's northern end edges the Arctic Circle.

Not a man to abandon a prize wherever it might land, Mathison borrowed a C-54 at Edwards Air Force Base and flew it to the air base at Thule, Greenland, where he switched to a C-130 that he could land on the island's airfield. The Norwegian embassy in Washington was called and asked to have officials on Spitsbergen watch for the capsule's parachute. A friend in the Norwegian air force also arranged a welcome for Mathison from Odd Birketvedt, the governor of the island. The governor told Mathison a number of people had observed an object attached to an orange and white parachute and with a strobe light on it descend in an area where analysis had been posited that the capsule would land. When a search party reached the site, however, they had found nothing but tracks in the snow leading from and returning toward a coal mining concession the Soviet Union had held since the 1930s in northern Spitsbergen. The concession was regarded as under Moscow's sovereignty and the Norwegians did not venture there. Mathison was convinced the Russians had his capsule, but not even the undeterrable Mathison dared go any further. On the flight up a cautionary message from Schriever had also been relayed to him over the radio: "Tell Moose to stay out of Soviet territory."

The capsule contained nothing of military value to the Russians. A camera had not been mounted in the Agena and so the capsule's contents had only, in accordance with the cover story, consisted of "mechanical mice," electronic devices rigged to record biomedical effects. Mathison made a last try. He had the Norwegian governor send a telegram to the governor of the Soviet mining concession inquiring about the capsule. Many years later in retirement, Mathison had an English translation of the reply, sent to him by Governor Birketvedt, framed and hung on a wall of his bedroom in his home in Albuquerque. It read:

Dear Mr. Birketvedt: In connection with your telegram of 20th this month, of whether there was anybody of Russian population on Spitsbergen who saw a container of an American satellite, Discoverer II, I inform you that Russian population have not seen that container and we got no information about this. Yours sincerely, Ignat Shejko.

For the next year and four months, the Air Force program officers, their Lockheed counterparts, and the CIA officers involved were unable to land a capsule on Spitsbergen or anywhere else. Through ten more flights, something always went wrong: the Agena did not go into orbit, or the orbit was bad, or the retro rockets that were to slow down the satellite for capsule ejection did not fire, or some other misfortune occurred. "It was a most heartbreaking business," Bissell said later. "In the case of a recce [reconnaissance] satellite, you fire the damn thing off and . . . you never see it again. So you have to infer from telemetry what went wrong. Then you make a fix, and if it fails again you know you've inferred wrong. In the case of Corona [Discoverer] it went on and on." Pauses as long as two months in launching were taken to try to puzzle out the glitches. Specialists from the Ramo-Wooldridge team working on the missiles were summoned. When the launching resumed, success would again prove to be a mirage.

Eisenhower, who was briefed after each launch, began to complain with mounting asperity not only to Bissell, but also to Allen Dulles, Bissell's boss as the director of central intelligence. The presidential temper became yet markedly shorter after the U-2 was shot down on May 1, 1960. With the charges of a missile gap agitating Washington and stoking John Kennedy's presidential bid, Eisenhower had lost his one means of penetrating the sealed world of the Soviet Union. Schriever also caught the president's wrath. Bissell and Schriever did their best to shield the program team, but the men felt the increasingly less bearable pressure. Bissell's CIA officers began to lose heart and suggested abandoning the whole project and trying some other approach. One of the Air Force men, recalling the many bleak days with Thor and Atlas, remarked, in the words of the secret official history, declassified forty-seven years later, that "it was too early for a wake" and urged pressing on. Bissell agreed and press on it was.

70

MATHISON SNATCHES THE PRIZE

Schriever did not favor abandonment but, after the failure of Discoverer XII on June 29, 1960, he decided a new Air Force team was needed to take a fresh look and was about to clean house. He warned Mathison he would soon be relieved. Mathison replied that if Schriever gave them one more chance, "I'd put it [a recovered capsule] on his desk." Mathison's job running the satellite control center was on the periphery of the project's organization. He had never been admitted to the inner councils of the Air Force program office or briefed by the CIA operatives on the plan to turn a public Discoverer into a secret Corona. He was shrewd and resourceful enough, without sanctioned access, to discern what was going on and to keep abreast of progress being made and problems being encountered, which is why the private reports he made to Schriever were valuable to a boss to whom he was intensely loyal. Moreover, the experience he had acquired in the missile-building trials had given him perspective to judge when enough of the bugs had been removed so that a system would probably work. Mathison was convinced Discoverer was at that point.

Willis Hawkins, Lockheed's manager of space systems, had recently eliminated one of the most persistent bugs—the ejection of the capsule. To send the capsule straight down into the atmosphere, and not have it drift off into space on an orbit of its own, it had to be spun like a top as it emerged from the Agena. Then, after entering the atmosphere, the capsule had to be "despun," stopped from spinning, so that it would not tangle up the lines of the parachute released at that moment by small explosive charges. Finding the right type of miniature rockets and attaching them to the capsule to perform this spinning and despinning ballet had proved maddeningly difficult, but Hawkins had at last accomplished the task.

When Discoverer XIII lifted off from a pad at Vandenberg on August 10, 1960, Mathison waited through three circuits of the earth to be certain the Agena was in a correct orbit and then flew straight to

Hickam. The capsule ejected perfectly on the seventeenth orbit and came down exactly where predicted, over the Pacific Ocean 380 miles northwest of Hawaii. The C-119 from Hickam missed catching the parachute in midair because of confused communication with an RC-121 control plane and obscuring cloud cover. The capsule was fortunately sealed and buoyant and so bobbed in the waves, easily visible because of its trailing parachute. (There was no precious film to be lost. The flight had been designed to see if the ejection system jinx had at last been dispelled. The capsule held only instruments and an American flag.) A Navy recovery ship, the USS *Haiti Victory,* equipped with a helicopter, had also been stationed in the vicinity. It took a few hours, but the pilot of the C-119 guided the ship to the spot. The helicopter crew plucked the capsule from the water and delivered it safely to the *Haiti Victory*'s deck.

On the morning of Friday, August 12, Lieutenant Colonel Gus Ahola, the commander of the Hickam squadron, expected to meet the *Haiti Victory* at Pearl Harbor to accept delivery of the capsule. He learned to his surprise that Mathison had already helicoptered to the ship and taken charge. There was nothing Ahola could do to stop him because Mathison, a full colonel by this time, outranked him. To indicate that he would brook no attempt by the Navy to reap glory by hanging on to the space trophy, Mathison, who had a fondness for the dramatic gesture, arrived on the ship with a Colt .45 service pistol strapped to his hip. The ship's captain offered no resistance and Mathison was soon back in the helicopter, capsule secured, headed for Pearl Harbor. He had arranged by radio for General Emmett "Rosie" O'Donnell, Jr., the commander of the Pacific Air Forces, to meet him there for a photo opportunity with the capsule that was certain to generate headlines, as the photos would be distributed nationally and internationally by the wire services. ("Satellite Is Recovered off Isles in Perfect Condition," the headline in one Hawaii newspaper read.)

The publicity parade set in motion, Mathison shifted himself and the capsule to a C-130 for the long flight back to Sunnyvale, where he picked up Ritland and Lieutenant Colonel Clarence "Lee" Battle, Jr., an engineer with an indefatigable temperament whom Schriever had chosen as program director, and then flew on to Andrews Air Force Base near Washington. It was raining when they arrived on Saturday, but Schriever and General White, the chief of staff, were waiting to greet them. Both men were ecstatic at the success of the mission. One of the photographs shows the two generals beaming as Mathison held up the lines of the parachute still attached to the capsule and explained how the parachute was released by explosive charges after reentry. The capsule resembled a big kettle of shiny copper or brass, rounded at the bottom and flat on top where the cover was attached. That night and Sunday night as well, the capsule sat, as Mathison had promised, in a protective container in front of Schriever's desk in his new office at Andrews. (In April 1959 Schriever had received the third star of a lieutenant general and promotion to command of the Air Research and Development Command. Its headquarters had shifted to Andrews from Baltimore. Ritland had replaced him as commander of the Ballistic Missile Division in Los Angeles, while simultaneously serving as Bissell's deputy for Discoverer-Corona. His promotion did not relieve Schriever of any responsibility for Minuteman or any of the other missile programs or for the Air Force role in the photoreconnaissance satellite project. It merely widened and deepened that responsibility and he kept as close a watch as ever over it all.)

On Monday, August 16, they all went to the White House. Secretary of Defense Neil McElroy, the new secretary of the Air Force, Dudley Sharp, and LeMay, at the time still vice chief of staff, joined the group as General White removed from the capsule the Stars and Stripes that had circled the earth seventeen times and presented it to Eisenhower. Afterward, a clearly delighted president invited Schriever and Mathison, who had exchanged his gray pilot's coveralls for neat summer tan jacket and trousers, to join him for coffee in a small inner sanctum off the Oval Office. The meeting lasted fifteen minutes, a generous visit in a president's busy day. Schriever sat quietly while Eisenhower questioned Mathison closely about the details of the project. Then Schriever and Mathison were off to Capitol Hill to garner political support by displaying the capsule to such powerful men as Senator Richard Russell of Georgia, chairman of the Senate Committee on Armed Services, and Lyndon Johnson, the Senate Majority Leader. The capsule never went back to California. It toured the United States under Air Force sponsorship and years later came to rest in the Smithsonian Air and Space Museum in Washington. McCartney and the other young controllers named the capsule Lucky XIII.

None of this was supposed to happen. The CIA had worked out a cloak-and-dagger plan for surreptitious delivery of film-filled capsules to Eastman Kodak's photographic-processing facility at Rochester, New York. Although Discoverer XIII's capsule contained no film, its retrieval was going to be a dress rehearsal of the CIA scheme. At Hickam, Ahola was supposed to turn the capsule, in its protective container, over to an Air Force courier from BMD in Los Angeles. On the courier's arrival in California, probably by commercial air, a switch would be made. The container, emptied of the capsule, would go by some fairly obvious route to Lockheed, while the capsule, disguised by repackaging, would be sent east in an unmarked truck to Rochester. Then the bull moose had charged and scattered the plan.

The secret official history accused Mathison of possessing a "unique mix of creative anarchy and casual effrontery." Had Mathison known these qualities would be attributed to him, he would have been flattered. What Mathison had done was precisely what Schriever had wanted him to do, otherwise Schriever would have stopped him. Like Jacobson and several others, Mathison was a member of a small band of officers, spoken of within the Air Force, and not always in a friendly tone, as "Bennie's colonels." They were bold and clever men of initiative, who believed fervently in what "the Boss" was seeking to achieve, and were entrusted with tasks Schriever would not have delegated to anyone else. The venerable Air Matériel Command at Wright-Patterson was soon to be broken up into two functionial organizations. One, to be called the Air Force Systems Command, was to be an enlarged ARDC, responsible for research, development, and initial production of all the Air Force's aircraft, missiles, and other weaponry. (The other organization, a new Air Force Logistics Command, was to be concerned solely with supply.) Schriever was slated to head the Systems Command, a post he hoped to use to gain responsibility for all space satellites—a function, he believed, that belonged naturally with the Air Force. The struggle to get the ICBM program moving by briefing Eisenhower in 1955, and the lift provided by public relations coups like the *Time* cover story in 1957, had taught him how important political backing and enthusiastic publicity were to an undertaking. This was what Mathison's actions had been all about. In showing off the Discoverer XIII capsule, Schriever and Mathison stuck to the biomedical cover story, because they had to, but it is doubtful that this fiction fooled the Soviets or any other interested parties. The aviation industry press in the United States had been speculating that the Air Force was in the process of creating a photoreconnaissance system from space. Why else put up a satellite with an ejectable capsule except to fill it with film from a camera?

71.

DISCOVERER GOES "BLACK" INTO CORONA

No time was wasted getting Discoverer XIV up into space on August 18, 1960, just eight days after its predecessor had been launched. XIV was the real thing, with a Space Age panoramic camera called the Itek mounted in its port. The Itek had been specially created for satellite photography by a recently formed firm of the same name in Massachusetts. One of the company's founders was Richard Leghorn, an Air Force Reserve colonel who was a pioneer in high-altitude photoreconnaissance. He had worked for Schriever in earlier years as the reconnaissance specialist in the Plans and Programs Office at the Pentagon. A witty, iconoclastic man, Leghorn had been one of the instigators of the U-2 and of Eisenhower's Open Skies program. An idealist, he believed that the United States and the Soviet Union could coexist in peace if they dispelled fear by allowing free passage of each other's reconnaissance vehicles over any part of the globe. Discoverer XIV's orbit took in more than 1,650,000 square miles of Soviet territory. The camera exposed and spun into the capsule 3,000 feet of film, virtually all of the twenty pounds that had been stored in the Agena. Ejection and recovery went perfectly, the C-119 snatching the parachute in midair, and after Eastman Kodak had developed the film, the CIA photo interpreters pronounced the results "terrific, stupendous."

At least half of the frames were clear of cloud cover. The Itek camera was so exacting that from roughly 120 miles above the earth, it had taken photograhs with a resolution of fifty-five lines per millimeter.

Objects on the ground ranging upward from thirty-five feet in dimension were identifiable. Less than a week later Edwin Land unrolled a reel of developed film across the carpet of the Oval Office to Eisenhower's desk. "Here are your pictures, Mr. President," he announced. After viewing the take, as the developed film was called in the photographic intelligence business, Eisenhower was extremely pleased and extremely emphatic. The success of this spy satellite and all future ones was to be held in utmost secrecy. No photograph from space was ever to be released for publication, a policy retained for many years by his successors. What seemed to worry him most was that if the United States boasted of its intelligence triumph, Khrushchev would raise the same brouhaha he had over the U-2, whereas if all was kept quiet, the Russians might not react even if they did detect what the satellites were doing. He was also fearful that they might attempt to interfere with the satellites.

As it turned out, neither fear was justified. The Soviets intended to put up their own photoreconnaissance satellites once they acquired the technology, which they did in later years, and Forrest McCartney's "implied rules of engagement" during the Cold War applied as much to satellites as they did to other technological spy systems like the Turkish Radar. The Russians never attempted to interfere with or control an American satellite and the courtesy was returned. As McCartney phrased it: "You don't tinker with my satellites and I don't tinker with yours." Discoverer XIV's photography also discredited definitively the myth of a missile gap. As was the custom in 1960 for presidential contenders, Kennedy was given a top secret briefing. He stopped talking about a missile gap himself, but politics being a killer sport, he did not stop his supporters from talking about it, and Nixon suffered the consequences on election day.

The program now went "black" in the lingo of the intelligence community, Discoverer gradually disappearing into the darkness of Corona. The Air Force provided less and less detail about each subsequent launch until its press spokesmen would provide none at all. Eisenhower, who had always prided himself on restricting military spending to what he believed was necessary, had fostered creation of the means to perpetuate that policy through a constant flow of concrete information. Regrettably, not all of his successors were inclined to be guided by reality. Corona remained the nation's principal source of photographic intelligence until 1972, when it was retired and replaced by a more advanced system that remains secret. There were many failed launches and malfunctions of the satellite in the years to come, but they were far outweighed by the successes. Its capacity and sophistication moved ahead rapidly. McCartney recalled that within six to eight months the crude plastic tape with thirteen punch-hole connections was replaced by a mechanism called the Lockheed Orbital Decoder and Programmer. This gave the satellite sixty-four commands. The controllers could turn the camera on when the satellite was over areas of the Soviet Union they wanted to photograph, and then off, rather than just letting the film run. They could even load fresh film into the camera from the ground. By 1964, camera life in orbit had been extended to eight days. In 1965, the satellite was equipped with multiple cameras to obtain a stereoscopic effect for height and depth. By 1967 camera life was fifteen days. The ejection and retrieval systems became so dependable that between 1966 and 1970, twenty-eight capsules were launched and twenty-eight capsules were recovered.

Moreover, in addition to finding airfields, missile installations, nuclear weapons manufacturing facilities, and other targets in the Soviet Union, the Corona satellite greatly enhanced the power of the American deterrent by making it possible to determine the exact location of these targets. Prior to the existence of the satellite, targeting had to be done with maps and photography from the U-2, the occasional SAC penetration flight on the periphery of the Soviet Union, or even from Second World War Luftwaffe aerial reconnaisssance photos in the captured German archives. All of this involved a certain level of error. The targeting officers at SAC headquarters in Omaha always had to ask themselves exactly how far and on exactly what bearing was the center of Moscow or the Soviet missile complex at Plesetsk from an Atlas missile silo at Warren Air Force Base in Wyoming or from their own nearby runways at Offutt. An inertial guidance system in a missile or an inertial navigation system in a B-52 could perform only as well as the information cranked into it. With the coming of Corona, error was dispelled. It became possible, as McCartney explained, to "tie continents together." Because the parameters of the orbit were known and the satellite was fitted with a clock that recorded the time the photograph was taken, the precise distance and direction of the target from a known point in the United States or anywhere else in the world could be calculated. Even such factors as the curvature of the earth could be taken into account. That the missile would strike and the bomber would find its target became far more certain. As the Soviets built their own photoreconnaissance satellites, they would learn this and the knowledge would make them fear all the more the formidable deterrent they faced.

The CIA was to take credit for Corona, because Eisenhower had placed the agency in charge, but the dedication and skills of the organization Schriever built had put it into the sky. This first photographic reconnaissance satellite and its precious capabilities became the final brick in the foundation they laid for a nuclear peace.

72.

A HAREBRAINED SCHEME

By October 1962, the lofting of Discoverer XIV on August 18, 1960, had dispelled the darkness from the interior of the Soviet Union for more than two years, permitting an acccurate assessment of its strategic capabilities. Minuteman, the weapon that was to play such an important role in keeping the nuclear peace by safeguarding against the nuclear Pearl Harbor so dreaded earlier, was moving into deployment. The first flight of ten Minutemen went on alert in silos at Malmstrom Air Force Base in Montana on October 22, 1962. Yet that same month, in no small irony, the eternal curse of the human race, man's folly, brought the United States and Russia the closest they were ever to come to nuclear war. Nikita Khrushchev precipitated the crisis by shipping Soviet missiles to Fidel Castro's Cuba in a wild poker play to try to even the strategic odds. When Khrushchev was overthrown two years later in a conspiracy led by one of his principal subordinates in the Presidium of the Soviet Communist Party, Leonid Brezhnev, the Missile Crisis was cited as an example of his "harebrained scheming." It was not the only reason for his downfall. His colleagues had other complaints against him as well, but a harebrained scheme it certainly was.

The genesis of Khrushchev's Cuban gamble seems to have been a meeting in February 1962 of the Soviet Union's Defense Council, a gathering that included senior military commanders, leading missile designers like Korolev and Yangel, and members of the Presidium. Khrushchev was informed that it would take a number of years to provide him with a sizable force of reliable and accurate ICBMs. In the meantime, he would have to endure an American opponent in John Kennedy who possessed awesome nuclear superiority. By the end of the forthcoming October, for example, Khrushchev would possess a mere twenty unreliable ICBMs, along with a bomber force of fifty-eight Bison jets, limited to a one-way trip, and seventy-six Tu-95 turboprops, slow planes that were dead pigeons to the American jet interceptors and surface-to-air missiles. In contrast, Kennedy would flaunt ninety-six Atlas ICBMs, fifty-four Titans, ten Minutemen, forty-eight of the Navy's new Polaris submarine-launched IRBMs hidden on station in the depths, and SAC's bomber force of 1,741 B-47s, B-58s, and B-52s. Uncounted because of their joint control but also ready were the sixty Thor IRBMs in England, the thirty Jupiters in Italy, and the sixteen in Turkey.

Khrushchev saw a way around this dilemma. The Soviet Union possessed plenty of well-tested IRBMs. If a substantial number of these were slipped into Cuba, their presence 90 miles from Key West would, as he put it in his memoirs, equalize "what the West likes to call 'the balance of power.' " Soviet IRBMs this close would effectively neutralize much of SAC; there would be no time to get planes off the ground in the event of an attack. Besides, he had been particularly rankled by the Jupiters in neighboring Turkey ever since their deployment. "The Americans . . . would learn just what it feels like to have enemy missiles pointing at you; we'd be doing nothing more than giving them a little of their own medicine." The range of the first-generation IRBM, the R-12, had been extended by 1962 from 1,250 to 1,292 miles and its warhead blast increased from 700 kilotons to the eighty Hiroshimas of a megaton. The R-12 would hold hostage all Eastern cities through Washington to New York, which was 1,290 miles from Cuba, and those as far west as Dallas and Oklahoma City. (During the crisis, the CIA designated the R-12 a medium-range rocket, or MRBM, but rocket historians refer to it as an intermediate-range missile because of its 1,000-mile-plus reach.) The second-generation R-14, at 2,500 miles, would threaten the whole of eastern and much of western Canada and virtually the entire United

States out into Montana. The plan was to ship thirty-six R-12s to Cuba with twenty-four launchers for them and twenty-four R-14s with sixteen launchers. (Some of the rockets would be "reloads" for second firings.)

The question was whether the missiles could be transported and emplaced in Cuba secretly. Khrushchev planned to complete deploying them on the island in October and then to tell Kennedy they were there after the midterm congressional elections in November, when he assumed the American president would be under less political pressure and more likely to accept the rockets without too much of a fuss. Anastas Mikoyan, like Khrushchev another of Stalin's henchmen who had survived to be a better man in better days and was now Khrushchev's closest friend and adviser in the Presidium, urged him to abandon the scheme. It was too dangerous, Mikoyan said. They would get caught in the act and a crisis would ensue. Khrushchev's foreign minister, Andrei Gromyko, who had considerable experience dealing with the Americans, warned him that "putting missiles in Cuba would cause a political explosion in the United States. I am absolutely certain of that." Khrushchev heeded neither man. He seems to have had no conception that, however uncomfortable Russians might be over hostile missiles in adjacent Turkey, Russian sensitivities about Turkey were mild compared to those of Americans about Cuba and the Caribbean as a whole. Americans regarded the Caribbean as the Romans had regarded the Mediterranean. It was Mare Nostrum, Our Sea. Similarly, Cuba had come to be looked upon as an American possession and treated as American territory after the United States seized it from Spain in 1898. This was why there had been such an uproar when Castro had nationalized the American-owned businesses that virtually monopolized the island's economy and declared himself a Communist. It was bad enough to have the Red Menace now just across the Florida Straits from Miami. No American president could withstand the political firestorm that would ensue if he acquiesced in the positioning of Russian nuclear missiles on the island.

73

PALM TREE DISGUISES

At the end of May, a high-level Soviet delegation flew to Cuba on a clandestine visit to obtain Castro's assent. He had reservations but would not object if the Soviet leaders wanted to "buttress the defensive power of the entire socialist camp." One member of the delegation was Marshal Sergei Biryuzov, who had succeeded the unfortunate Nedelin as commander of the Strategic Rocket Forces. Attired in civilian clothes and carrying a false passport that identified him as Engineer Petrov, Biryuzov, who, according to Mikoyan, "wasn't very bright," scouted the island for likely missile sites. On the delegation's return to Moscow, he told Khrushchev that there wouldn't be any problem concealing them from American aerial reconnaissance. The missiles, he said, could be disguised as palm trees. Mikoyan ridiculed Biryuzov's leafy stratagem. Missile sites are extremely difficult to hide from aerial surveillance. Approach roads have to be cut out of the landscape, more earthmoving and the emplacement of a large concrete slab are required for the launcher, and the site is populated by a shelter tent for the missile, rows of tanker trucks with liquid oxygen and the Russian version of RP-1 rocket fuel, sundry other vehicles and equipment, and electrical cables running here and there. Mikoyan's assessment of Biryuzov's powers of intellect may have been correct, or Biryuzov may have decided to tell Khrushchev what Khrushchev wanted to hear. In any case, Khrushchev once more brushed aside Mikoyan's warning and serious planning for his Cuban adventure began.

At the time, the Soviet Union lacked an oceangoing fleet like the U.S. Navy, but the best was made of what it had. Between July and October, eighty-five freighters and passenger ships shuttled the thousands of miles, including 150 round-trips, between Soviet ports and Cuba with the missiles and with the men and the panoply of an elaborate task force to protect the rockets. Four motorized rifle regiments were dispatched, each with 2,500 men, thirty-four tanks, and associated arms and transport; three regiments of MK-6 surface-to-air missiles, the weapon that had brought down Francis Gary Powers's U-2 in 1960, arrived to ring the island with 144 launchers to shield the missile sites against air attack; a regiment of thirty-three helicopters; a squadron of seventeen Il-28 light bombers, seven equipped to drop atomic bombs, an eleven-plane transport and communications squadron, and much else also came. Altogether 41,902 Soviet officers and men were dispatched to Cuba before the crisis broke. The voyages took eighteen to twenty days in the stifling holds of the freighters, the men allowed up on deck only at night in small groups. All thirty-six of the R-12 IRBMs arrived, along with their twenty-four launchers, and the nuclear warheads for them. Just as ominously, so did the tactical nuclear weapons with which Khrushchev armed the task force: two FKR cruise missile regiments wielding thirty-six missiles with a range of one hundred miles and warheads of 5.6 to 12 kilotons, the equivalent of the Hiroshima blast, each capable of wiping out an entire American invasion fleet; twelve Luna missiles with a range of thirty-one miles and a two-kiloton warhead to obliterate a beachhead of landing troops; and eight atomic bombs for the Il-28s. Khrushchev reserved permission to fire the IRBMs to himself, but he gave his commanding general in Cuba, Issa Pliyev, a cavalryman who had served with him during the Second World War, leave to employ the tactical weapons at Pliyev's discretion against an American invading force.

It is astounding in retrospect that the movement of so many men and so much armament all the way from Russia to an island in the Caribbean went undetected. One reason was the pathetic state of the CIA spy network in Cuba, if network it can be called. This had already been demonstrated the previous year during the CIA-sponsored Bay of Pigs fiasco. The agency had predicted that a revolt would break out in the interior of the island as soon as the brigade of anti-Castro Cuban exiles it had trained landed there. Instead, nothing happened inland and all of the exiles were ringed around on the beach and captured by Castro. Since enduring the shame of that failure, John Kennedy and his brother and attorney general, Robert, had been exerting relentless pressure on the agency to do whatever was necessary to eliminate Castro. The Mafia was enlisted to assassinate him and there was a poisoning plot, all to no avail. The Soviets also took stringent security precautions. The officers and men were issued civilian trousers and plaid shirts. The Cuban population, which was not fooled, was told they were agricultural specialists. Radio silence was maintained, not only between Pliyev's headquarters and Moscow but also between it and units on the island. Messages had to be hand-carried to and from the countryside.

Another and critical reason for American ignorance was the temporary blinding of aerial reconnaissance. A U-2 on a routine twice-a-month spying mission at the end of August had photographed eight MK-6 surface-to-air missile batteries under construction in western Cuba. The presence of SAMs in Cuba was not in itself alarming. The Soviets had already given the antiaircraft missiles to allies like Nasser's Egypt, Sukarno's Indonesia, and Mao's China. But in early September a U-2 strayed accidentally into Soviet airspace and a second U-2 being flown by a Taiwanese pilot was shot down over China. To avoid another incident, the administration banned U-2 flights over the island for five weeks in September and October. The president; Robert Kennedy; McGeorge Bundy, the national security adviser; and a number of others at the top also simply did not believe that Khrushchev would be irrational enough to mount long-range missiles in Cuba.

74.

KEEPING THE MILITARY ON THE LEASH

Finally, Khrushchev got caught. A mounting controversy in Washington over precisely what the Soviets were doing in Cuba had reached the point where the administration had to authorize a resumption of flights by the U-2s, which had just been transferred from CIA control to that of SAC. On Sunday, October 14, a U-2 piloted by Air Force major Richard Heyser made a twelve-minute camera run over western Cuba and the game was up. The 4,000 feet of film his cameras took was delivered the next morning in eight cans to the

CIA's National Photographic Intelligence Center in the top four floors of a nondescript office building in downtown Washington. Every missile, by its measurements and other characteristics and the equipment needed to fire it, makes its own distinct fingerprint on the earth. From previous aerial photos of R-12 sites in Russia, the CIA photo interpreters knew exactly what they were looking at. Kennedy, who had been out of town, got the news on the morning of the 16th, when he was shown the photographs at the White House and they were interpreted for him. "He can't do that to me!" he exclaimed in his rage at Khrushchev. According to Max Frankel in his first-rate account of the drama, *High Noon in the Cold War: Kennedy, Khrushchev, and the Cuban Missile Crisis,* Robert Kennedy's reaction was more earthy. "Oh shit! shit! shit! Those sons of bitches Russians."

The president quickly got his anger against Khrushchev under control. He was also able to put himself in Khrushchev's place and see the situation from the Soviet leader's perspective. In the opening sessions of the ad hoc Executive Committee of the National Security Council, or ExCom as it came to be known, which he convened in secret session, he said it was clear that the sixteen Jupiters in Turkey would have to be one of the bargaining chips in any deal they made with the Soviet dictator to lever his missiles out of Cuba. He refused a unanimous recommendation from the Joint Chiefs of Staff, including his favorite general, Maxwell Taylor of the Army (Kennedy had brought him back on active duty as chairman of the JCS), and initially Robert McNamara as well, for immediate air strikes to take out the missile sites before the IRBMs could be erected on their launchers and nuclear warheads mounted. (McNamara conceded that the planes would miss at least 10 percent of the installations.)

Kennedy reasoned that as a great power, the Soviet Union could not accept having Russian missile crews killed without retaliating. That retaliation, he feared, would come in a move against isolated and vulnerable West Berlin, which Khrushchev had been repeatedly menacing. Even after the perceived danger of the Soviet missiles grew at midweek as CIA interpreters, going over now constant U-2 photography, detected evidence of sites under construction for the 2,500-mile R-14s, which could reach Canada and virtually the entire continental United States, Kennedy maintained his sangfroid. (As it turned out, the R-14s never got to Cuba. They were still aboard ship hundreds of miles away when the crisis broke.) He decided on a naval blockade to turn around any ship carrying missiles or other military equipment to Cuba. It was to be carefully controlled and selective, referred to as a "quarantine" in public to avoid having to invoke formal blockade rules, and only gradually tightened into a full blockade of the island should Khrushchev not respond. He intended to announce the quarantine in a nationally televised speech the forthcoming Monday, October 22. He would sound as menacing as possible to spook the Russians, threatening ultimate military action if the missiles were not removed, but set no timetable. What he would be setting was a table for a bargain.

When he met with his military chieftains on Friday to tell them of his decision, the meeting turned into a confrontation. They now wanted to hit the island with 1,000 air strikes by Air Force and Navy jets and to follow up the air assaults with a full-scale invasion by the Army and the Marine Corps. They scoffed at Kennedy's blockade and negotiations strategy as just "political action" and "talk." LeMay, who had succeeded to chief of staff after White's retirement in June 1961, was particularly belligerent. He took a directly opposing position to Kennedy's reasoning on Berlin. "If we don't do anything to Cuba," he said, "then they're going to push on Berlin and push real hard because they've got us on the run." He accused Kennedy of being another Neville Chamberlain, in short, a moral coward who, by his weakness, would bring on the war he was seeking to avoid. "This blockade and political action, I see leading into war. . . . It will lead right into war," LeMay argued. "This is almost as bad as the appeasement [of Hitler] at Munich." Kennedy responded that if the United States acted precipitately, "we'd be regarded as the trigger-happy Americans who lost Berlin." LeMay was undeterred. "You're in a pretty bad fix, Mr. President," he said as the argument continued. Kennedy asked him to repeat what he had said and seemed amused at LeMay's description of his predicament.

The president held fast. Generals and admirals, even those as bullying as LeMay could be, did not intimidate John Kennedy. He had proven his courage in battle as the skipper of a fast torpedo boat in the South Pacific. He was worried about Berlin and he was also worried about inadvertently triggering a chain reaction that would end in nuclear war. He had been reading *The Guns of August,* Barbara Tuchman's cautionary tale on how the statesmen and generals of Europe had bumbled their way into the First World War, and did not intend to become a central character in *The Missiles of October*. He had anticipated the reaction of his military leaders. Shortly before the meeting he remarked to his longtime retainer and political aide Kenneth O'Donnell that "these brass hats have one great advantage in their favor. If we listen to them, and do what they want us to do, none of us will be alive later to tell them that they were wrong."

75.

"USE 'EM OR LOSE 'EM"

Kennedy was more foresighted than he could know at the time. Had he displayed less strength of character and wisdom in this crisis and given in to his military, the world might well be a different place. The CIA and the military intelligence services believed that there were about 10,000 Russians on the island. They had no idea that the number was virtually four times that. It was assumed that the nuclear warheads for the missiles had arrived with the rockets, but the photo interpreters were unable to determine their location. It turned out that they were sitting in vans parked at the R-12 sites for quick mating to the rockets. No one on the U.S. side suspected the presence of the tactical nuclear weapons or knew that Khrushchev had given Pliyev authority to fire them at an American invasion force. (The secret would not come out until years later.) On October 18, Khrushchev restricted permission to fire the two-kiloton Lunas to "an extreme situation," such as when communication with Moscow was impossible, and then, on October 22, the day of Kennedy's blockade speech, when he had grown more alarmed, he ordered Pliyev not to resort to any nuclear weapons without his personal consent.

Khrushchev was still thinking in a crack-brained mode. He had committed the incredibly reckless act of placing a Soviet task force armed with nuclear weapons in a position of potentially extreme peril more than 6,500 miles from Moscow, with no hope of support or sustenance if attacked. Had the island been invaded, he would have lost control over the nuclear weapons and everything else he had in Cuba soon after the preliminary air bombardment began. Military communications in the early 1960s were not nearly as dependable as the space satellite relay systems that were to follow. They were mainly reliant on radio and so subject to atmospherics and blackouts. And among the first targets the planes would have struck, in addition to the missile sites, would have been suspected Soviet communications centers. (These can easily be located once they begin to transmit, if they have not already been spotted by the antennas at the sites.) With the horrendous destruction from the bombs of a thousand sorties crashing on his troops and installations, and Air Force and Navy fighter-bombers shooting up every vehicle caught out on a road, Pliyev in turn would probably have lost contact with many or most of his units. In the confusion, subordinate commanders would have been left to make their own decisions.

These were the officers and men of a proud army, the Red Army that had destroyed the mightiest host the vaunted German nation had ever fielded. However hopeless their position, it is unlikely they would have laid down their weapons meekly and trudged off to prison camps. With 42,000 of them on the island, they would have put up a fight. Regardless of what Khrushchev might ordain from the safety of Moscow, there is an old adage about soldiers resorting to any weapon they can get their hands on in the hair-trigger emotions of battle: "Use 'em or lose 'em," the saying goes. Years later, General Anatoly Gribkov, a senior General Staff officer detailed at the time to draw up the plans for the expedition, described the trepidation with which he had done so: "Would a desperate group of Soviet defenders, with or without an order from above, have been able to arm and fire even one Luna warhead . . . or one of the more powerful [cruise missile] charges? If such a rocket had hit U.S. troops or ships, if thousands of Americans had died in the atomic blast, would that have been the last shot of the Cuban crisis or the first of global nuclear war?"

76

LEMAY AND TOMMY POWER AS
THE WILD CARDS

Had Soviet action been limited to firing its tactical nuclear weapons to destroy an invasion fleet, it is probable that the American side, in shock and fury, would have reacted by escalating to its own tactical nuclear weapons and incinerating much of Cuba and its inhabitants and would-be Russian defenders. But far worse might have ensued because LeMay and Power would have become wild cards in the crisis. To exert maximum psychological pressure on Khrushchev, right after Kennedy's blockade speech on Monday, the 22nd, Army and Marine divisions were started on the move to assembly points in the Southern United States; a fleet, including eight aircraft carriers, began gathering in the Caribbean; and the president ordered SAC into Defense Condition 3 (DEFCON 3), two steps short of war. To ratchet up the pressure, he raised the alert to DEFCON 2, a single step short of all-out nuclear conflict, on Wednesday, October 24. Tommy Power announced the escalation himself in the clear over the radio circuits to be certain that the Russians monitoring them would hear it. All of SAC went to the highest possible state of readiness. Sixty-six of its B-52s, fully loaded with hydrogen bombs, took off in an airborne alert of unprecedented scale. They flew north to circle over Canada and the Arctic and east across the Mediterranean on the southern attack route to the Adriatic coast of Greece and Yugoslavia, holding just short of their points of no return, awaiting the go code to roar for their targets. When a B-52 had been on station for twenty-four hours and the crew was deemed exhausted, it returned to base to be replaced by a fresh bomber. The rest of SAC's 639 B-52s were put on strip alert, bombs aboard, planes cocked for takeoff. The 1,102 B-47 and B-58 medium bombers, also with bombs loaded, were dispersed to forty airfields, a lot of them civilian, across the United States to guard against loss should the Soviets attempt a surprise strike against regular SAC bases.

Their crews alternated between strip alert and necessary rest periods. Counting the Atlas, Titan, and Minuteman ICBMs, also now under Power's command and likewise at full readiness, SAC had approximately 2,800 megatons, 224,000 equivalents of the Hiroshima bomb, to launch at the Soviet Union, at Russian targets such as air bases in its East European possessions, and at Mao's China. The targeting scheme, the Single Integrated Operational Plan, or SIOP, estimated that 175 million persons would be killed outright.

Despite claims that he was an outlaw militarist, LeMay had always remained subordinate to civilian authority. Accusations that he had ordered reconnaissance flights over Soviet territory in violation of presidential restrictions were untrue. The flights had been secretly authorized by Truman and then by Eisenhower. Nor was he an advocate of preventive war like John von Neumann. But he was a firm believer in preemptive war. While commander-in-chief of SAC, he had said that if he was persuaded the Soviets were about to attack, he would strike first. Whether he would check to make sure the president agreed with him, LeMay did not say. If the Russian garrison on Cuba obliterated a beachhead with a two-kiloton Luna or the whole invasion fleet with a twelve-kiloton FKR cruise missile, these acts might have enraged him but not convinced him that the Soviets were preparing to assault the United States itself. If, however, amidst the mayhem, one of the Russian R-12 crews had decided to take as many of their opponents as possible with them into eternity, mounted a nuclear warhead on their IRBM, and fired it at an American city, one can say with some certainty that he would have been pushed over the edge. So would Power, who shared LeMay's mind-set on this issue.

One of the president's military aides carried a briefcase containing the go codes (it was called "the football" in a bit of gallows humor) wherever the chief executive went because, under the Constitution, he alone as commander-in-chief had the legal authority to decide on an act of such momentous consequences for the nation and humanity. But the generals had the ability to act on their own. That alternative had to exist in case the president was incapacitated or beyond reach. Knowing the characters of LeMay and Power, one can again conclude that had an order to launch not been quickly forthcoming from the White House, they would not have waited. They would have turned everything loose and, in their ignorance of atmospheric radioactive fallout, nuclear winter, and the other doomsday aftereffects of nuclear war, destroyed the entire Northern Hemisphere.

The recollection of a Russian officer who served in Cuba was that, if attacked, he and his comrades would have given LeMay and Power their opportunity. In October 1962, Viktor Yesin, who subsequently rose to colonel general and chief of staff of the Soviet Union's Strategic Rocket Forces, was an engineer lieutenant with an R-12 missile regiment stationed near Calabazar de Sagua, about 160 miles east of Havana. The regiment was armed with eight launchers and twelve missiles, for an initial barrage of eight rockets followed by four reloads. Its position was the optimal launching point for America's East Coast cities. Each night, when darkness hid them from the cameras of the U-2 spy planes, the crews would practice removing the one-megaton warheads from nearby vans, mounting them on the rockets, then transferring the nuclear-armed missiles to concrete launching pads and raising them into firing angle. Before dawn, all would be dismounted and hidden away. The crews knew what they wanted to hit. They had been issued targeting data for Washington and New York and other Eastern urban centers.

Decades later, Michael Dobbs interviewed Yesin in Moscow for his startlingly detailed account of the crisis, *One Minute to Midnight*. He asked Yesin how the Soviet missile regiment would have reacted had the United States suddenly launched the air assault the Joint Chiefs were proposing as the opening blow of an invasion. "You have to understand the psychology of the military person," Yesin replied. "If you are being attacked, why shouldn't you reciprocate?"

77.

AVOIDING GÖTTERDÄMMERUNG

To his credit, Khrushchev reversed course as soon as he realized his folly. By Thursday, October 25, he had made up his mind to remove the missiles from Cuba. "Once you begin shooting, you can't stop," he told his son Sergei. Humiliation was inevitable. What remained was to negotiate the most face-saving exit he could obtain from Kennedy. This turned out to be a public pledge by the president not to invade Cuba and a secret promise, conveyed by Robert Kennedy to the Soviet ambassador in Washington, Anatoly Dobrynin, to remove the Jupiters from Turkey within four to five months. Secretary of State Dean Rusk had warned the president that a public swap of the Jupiters for the IRBMs in Cuba would appear a betrayal of an ally, as Turkey was a member of NATO, and undermine the alliance. The Kennedy brothers were careful not to commit any mention of it to paper and Dobrynin was told that continued secrecy was a condition of its fulfillment, a stipulation Khrushchev scrupulously observed.

On Sunday, October 28, a week of excruciating tension ended when Khrushchev sent Kennedy a letter, broadcast over Radio Moscow so that no time would be wasted in transmission, signaling acceptance of all terms. An enraged Castro, who, as the crisis neared its climax, had urged Khrushchev to make the suicidal leap of a full-scale nuclear attack against the United States if the island was invaded, was not interested in mitigating his would-be protector's humiliation. He refused to allow United Nations inspectors on Cuban soil to either verify the dismantling of the missiles at the sites or the loading of dismantled missiles on board ships at dockside. The administration had demanded some form of verification and the United Nations had seemed the least offensive agency. Khrushchev was reduced to having the missiles loaded as deck cargo and then uncovered at sea so that they could be photographed by U.S. planes and helicopters. It was a moment of intense shame for the Soviet military. The scores of MK-6 surface-to-air missile batteries, the regiment of helicopters, and most of the men of the four motorized rifle regiments with their tanks and artillery and other accoutrements went home too. Kennedy lifted the quarantine on November 20, after Khrushchev also promised to remove the Il-28 light bombers within a month. Castro tried to hang on to some of the tactical nuclear weapons, but the Russians refused to hand them over and secreted them out of Cuba. All that was left behind of the 42,000-man task force was a lone brigade of 3,000 men. Its presence, a kind of protective trip wire, was meant to say that if the pledge not to attack the island was dishonored, the United States would have to contend with the Soviet Union. It became a forgotten brigade. Seventeen years later the administration of President Jimmy

Carter discovered to its amazement that a brigade of the Red Army was still on duty in Cuba.

Khrushchev actually gained little for an ungrateful Castro with the no-invasion pledge. As desperate as the Kennedy brothers were to get rid of Castro, they drew the line at invading the island, fearful that Castro would take refuge in the mountains and American troops would get tied down in a guerrilla war. Khrushchev also gained nothing he would not have soon gotten anyway from the clandestine commitment to take the Jupiters out of Turkey within four to five months. The deployment of Atlas and Titan and the fast coming on of Minuteman had made the Thors and Jupiters superfluous and the United States had already intended to remove them. McNamara had informed the British in May 1962 that the United States would cease logistic support for Thor when the basing agreement between the two countries expired in November 1964. As a result, the British decided to act sooner and the last Thor in England went off alert at RAF North Luffenham in the English Midlands on August 15, 1963. The Thors had by 1963 served their useful time. They had remained on fifteen-minute alert, 18.2 minutes' flight from their targets, for more than three years. The old bomber fields that hosted them became ghosts once again.

The day after the crisis ended, on Monday, October 29, 1962, McNamara did something he would have done in the near future in any case, but which he did now to keep the promise to Khrushchev. He signed a directive ordering the removal of the Jupiters from both Turkey and Italy by April 1, 1963. The deadline was more or less met for Italy. The thirty Jupiters there were all disassembled by April 23, 1963. In Turkey the dismantling went more slowly and the last of the sixteen there did not depart until July 26, 1963. What Khrushchev did salvage from his Cuban misadventure was the preservation of the Soviet Union from nuclear destruction and he owed that to John Kennedy, as the peoples of the Northern Hemisphere also owed their salvation to him.

BUYING TIME FOR THE
EMPIRE TO IMPLODE

The most intractable problems of the Cold War, such as the division of Germany, the uncertain status of a splintered Berlin, and Soviet domination of Eastern Europe and the Baltic states, could not be solved as long as a strong Soviet Union existed. Although no one could have foreseen it when Bernard Schriever assembled his small band at the Schoolhouse in Inglewood in the summer of 1954, their greatest achievement and that of all those who were to labor with them was to help buy the time needed for the Soviet Union to collapse of its own internal contradictions. Time was the only solution. A nuclear war was certainly not the answer. And until the coming of Mikhail Gorbachev, whose attempts at reform hastened the collapse, the leaders of the Soviet state regarded the post–Second World War status quo as nonnegotiable. But they could not evade the cumulative effects of time.

The Soviet society that Joseph Stalin fashioned was not sustainable. The three pillars of the state—the Communist Party, the military, and the secret police—were costly to maintain. The precise figure is difficult to arrive at, but a high percentage of total production went to the military. To urbanize and feed the workers in his new heavy industries, Stalin had utterly destroyed initiative in Soviet agriculture with his forced draft system of collective and state farms. Russia, once the breadbasket of Europe through its possession of Ukraine, no longer grew enough food to feed itself. Khrushchev's effort to revitalize agriculture, constrained as it was by this straitjacket of state control and centralized planning, failed, and he began the imports of American corn and wheat that were to continue under his successor, Leonid Brezhnev. The system produced no products that could be sold abroad to renew wealth that would offset such imports and help pay the costs of maintaining this expensive state. The Soviet Union's only exports were raw materials, such as petroleum and natural gas. Much of the latter two were wasted providing cheap energy to its East European possessions to try to keep their restive populations from rising as the Hungarians had in 1956, and in subsidizing client states like Fidel Castro's Cuba, which had its own unworkable Marxist economy. Once a source of power and prestige, the empire had become a costly burden.

The Soviet Union, as heir to czarist Russia, was the last of the great multinational empires. The restiveness of its many peoples extended from Ukraine in the west through Kazakhstan and the other former khanates of Central Asia in the east that the czarist army had sabered into submission. Stalin kept the ethnic tensions under control through terror, but his successors were less hard men and tensions grew with the years. The rot fully set in after Brezhnev's overthrow of Khrushchev in 1964. He and his associates were stand-still men who wanted to enjoy their perquisites, in Brezhnev's case young mistresses, a tame form of wild boar shooting, and a collection of expensive foreign cars.

"All that stuff about Communism is a tall tale for popular consumption. After all, we can't leave the people with no faith," he once said to his brother, Yakov, shocking his sibling, who was a firm believer in the Party line. One would have thought Brezhnev might have learned something from watching the American debacle in Vietnam. He did not. Instead, he demoralized his own army by sending it into a fruitless war in Afghanistan in 1979 to rescue Afghan Communist protégés who had seized power and provoked tradition-bound Muslim tribesmen into revolt against unbelievers. The Soviet empire was like a house whose beams have been consumed by powderpost beetles. From the outside, the beams appear sturdy. Yet when the point of a knife is thrust into one, the thin crust cracks open to reveal nothing but the powdered wood residue the beetles have left inside. Gorbachev's endeavors at reform during the latter half of the 1980s brought civil liberties, but also wrought a plunge in the already marginal living conditions of ordinary Russians as his tinkering made the sclerotic economic system worse. In 1989, in his desperate attempt to hold the Soviet Union together, he let Eastern Europe go and the Berlin Wall was torn down. Enraged, the old guard of the Party attempted to overthrow him in August 1991, in a coup that failed. Boris Yeltsin then led the Russian Republic out of the Soviet state and the empire that so many had for so long thought invincible broke into fragments.

In doing so much to foster a nuclear stalemate, Schriever and his associates contributed mightily to buying the time necessary for the Soviet Union to exhaust itself. By starting in the mid-1950s, before it was too late, and then winning the race for a practical ICBM, they warded off the possibility of blackmail that Trevor Gardner had so dreaded and also discouraged nuclear adventures by the Soviets. After Khrushchev's humiliation in the Cuban Missile Crisis, no Soviet statesman would ever again dare such a gamble. Nor could any Soviet leader hope to prevail in a surprise attack after the deployment of Minuteman in 1962 and the growing presence beneath the seas of the Navy's Polaris missile-firing submarines. The same dilemma applied to the United States once the Soviets reached parity with their own solid-fuel ICBMs and missile-firing submarines around 1970. No American leader could contemplate a first strike, as it was called, against the Soviet Union without knowing that enough of Russia's nuclear arsenal would survive intact to destroy the United States in turn. A nuclear stalemate was complete.

The strategists referred to the condition as Mutual Assured Destruction, or MAD. There was nothing mad about the grim equation. It made perfect sense by enforcing a nuclear peace. The arms race should have ended there. It was senseless to go on, but go on it did on both sides at the cost of trillions. Technology was in the saddle of a horse named Fear in a race of human folly. Minuteman went through two transformations into missiles always bigger and better. Minuteman II, with its range of 7,021 miles, a more powerful warhead, and accuracy to within a mile, was succeeded in 1971 by Minuteman III. It could fly 8,083 miles and was the first ICBM to carry multiple independently targetable reentry vehicles, called MIRVs. Its warhead was fitted with three MIRVs, each yielding 375 kilotons, the equivalent of thirty Hiroshima bombs, and each released at timed intervals onto a different target with an accuracy of 800 feet. The 1,000 of these third-generation Minutemen deployed by the United States thus became the equivalent of 3,000 rockets. The Soviets were always matching, and to humanity's ultimate good fortune always deepening the stalemate, until time could do its work.

Purchasing the time in which the Soviet Union could self-destruct was not the only accomplishment of Schriever and those he led. Their ICBMs became more than weapons, they became vehicles that opened the exploration of space. John Glenn, the first American to circle the earth in February 1962 in NASA's Mercury program, was lofted on an Atlas rocket and orbited and returned to earth in a modification of the same Mark 2 hydrogen bomb reentry vehicle used on Thor. The technology that applied to bringing a bomb back into the atmosphere without burning the bomb up made it possible to do the same with a man. The second-generation Titan ICBM, Titan II, was the lifting horse in Gemini, NASA's 1965 follow-on program in its progress to the moon. With a booster stage thrust of 430,000 pounds, this ICBM was able to hoist into orbit a spacecraft large enough for two men to perfect the rendezvous and docking operations in space that were a necessary precursor to the moon voyage. The venture that had been forced to rely on Simon Ramo to round up the technogical expertise needed because the American aircraft industry was an aerospace desert in the mid-1950s generated a vast aerospace industry that would carry the United States into the twenty-first century as the world's sole superpower. The question became not the quantity and quality of American military power, but whether the leaders of the United States would wield it wisely or foolishly, as the war in Iraq would so aptly illustrate.

Schriever was unable to obtain control of the space photoreconnaissance system for the Air Force after Discoverer succeeded and became the covert Corona. Again on the advice of Killian and Kistiakowsky, as well as that of Edwin Land, Eisenhower established a new ultra-clandestine office to jointly manage reconnaissance satellites with the CIA. Under President Kennedy, it was named the National Reconnaissance Office and kept so hush-hush that its very existence was secret. The NRO dwelt within the Air Force, was chiefly manned by Air Force personnel, and its head was the undersecretary of the Air Force, but it was not *of* the Air Force. The undersecretary reported directly to the secretary of defense on NRO matters and Air Force officers assigned to the NRO were forbidden to discuss anything they did with outsiders. The only Air Force officer who could be briefed on its activities was the chief of staff, and he could not tell anyone beneath him what he learned.

Robert McNamara, Kennedy's and then Johnson's secretary of defense, also canceled the manned space programs Schriever initiated. Manned space missions remained the sole prerogative of NASA. But the ICBM endeavor had led the Air Force to invest too much in the infrastructure of space operations at Cape Canaveral and Vandenberg and to educate too many officers in guidance and astronautical engineering to suppress the impetus to use space. And by the 1970s enough officers who were disciples of Schriever were attaining senior positions of influence to propel space operations forward. Whole families of satellites came into being. Weather satellites were sent aloft, initially to avoid wasting reconnaissance satellite film by attempting to photograph targets in the Soviet Union when they were obscured by cloud cover, then for general prediction of weather to assist military operations. Communications satellites, free of the interference caused by weather and other factors within earth's atmosphere, began sailing in space to provide command and control of ground forces, naval vessels, and aircraft. Intelligence satellites were developed that not only transmitted photographs but also eavesdropped on hostile communications. Midas, an early warning infrared satellite system first envisioned under the WS-117L program, circled the earth in a series known by the innocuous title Defense Support Program (DSP). The sensors on the satellites would be able to detect the flame of a Soviet missile the moment it was fired. (During the 1991 war in the Persian Gulf over Saddam Hussein's invasion of Kuwait the sensors picked up heat from the firing of one of his medium-range Scud ballistic missiles as soon as it was launched. The missile's course could then be quickly triangulated and people in the target area warned to take shelter.) The coming of Global Positioning System satellites has been an enormous boon to navigation and the accuracy of weapons. Whether it is a Tomahawk cruise missile fired over a 1,500-mile course or a 2,000-pound bomb dropped from a fighter-bomber overhead, a weapon can be guided either spot-on or to within one meter of the target, hardly a difference given the ensuing blast. As one of Schriever's professional descendants, Major General Franklin "Judd" Blaisdell, who began his career as a Minuteman missileer and rose to become the Air Force's director of space operations and integration, put it this way: "Space is the ultimate high ground."

These military satellite systems inevitably evolved into like systems for civilian use in communications, navigation, television broadcasting, and other fruitful purposes. The communications satellites, relaying voice, data, and televised images throughout the world, made globalization possible. By 2007 approximately 6,600 satellites of all types, military and civilian, had been sent up over the years. Of these,

850 to 920 were in active use in 2007, 568 for communications. The most common orbit is along the line of the equator about 22,000 miles above the earth. It is called geosynchronous because the satellites are given an orbital speed synchronized with the rotation of the earth. Viewed from earth, they appear to be motionless. The satellites are, in effect, parked in space at a point where they can most efficiently fulfill their function. So much that Schriever and his comrades pioneered would be taken for granted and go unremarked in daily life. For example, most people who slide their credit card into the electronic reader on a gas pump or an automated teller machine have no idea their card's validity is being checked via space, because it is cheaper to rent access to a satellite than to a phone line. And they assume, correctly, that if they have a GPS instrument in their car, they won't get lost anymore.

EPILOGUE: THE SCHRIEVER LUCK

79

JOHNNY VON NEUMANN FINDS
FAITH BUT NOT PEACE

The cruelty of John von Neumann's fate deprived him of seeing the fulfillment of his work. His left shoulder became painful in the summer of 1955 and that August he went to see an orthopedic surgeon at the Bethesda Naval Hospital. As a commissioner of the Atomic Energy Commission, he was entitled to government medical care. The surgeon X-rayed the shoulder and discovered what he described to von Neumann as a "giant cell" tumor. The tumor was probably benign, the doctor said, but surgery soon afterward revealed otherwise. Worse, the tumor itself was not the primary source of the malignancy. He had testicular cancer. The disease there had metastasized and the cancer was spreading throughout his system. At first, he continued going to his AEC office as usual, but it soon became apparent that this was no longer possible. He and his wife, Klari, disposed of their house in Georgetown and moved to an apartment at the Woodner, only a fifteen-minute drive to the Walter Reed Army Medical Center in Washington, where he went regularly for treatment and therapy. Their marriage had been a difficult one. She was given to depression and resentment over his neglect of her as a result of an obsession with his work and his absentmindedness and they had had ferocious rows. Yet once he became ill, she treated him with nothing but tenderness. The treatments did not help. His condition grew steadily worse. Cancer medicine was in its infancy in the mid-1950s. In April 1956, he entered Walter Reed as a full-time patient, never to emerge again, except by ambulance in a wheelchair, until his death.

Vince Ford was assigned to watch over von Neumann and to be of what assistance he could to Klari. He was immensely kind and caring to both. That February, with Johnny already mostly bedridden at home, Ford arranged through Lewis Strauss, the chairman of the AEC, for Eisenhower to award von Neumann the Presidential Medal of Freedom. He had to accept the honor in a wheelchair in the Oval Office, the president bending over to pin the medal on the lapel of his suit jacket, but it is evident from the smile on his face caught by the White House photographer that he was pleased. "I wish I could be around long enough to deserve this honor," he said to the president. Eisenhower attempted to ignore the finality. "You will be with us a long time," he replied. "We need you." At Ford's suggestion, Strauss also saw to it that the AEC presented von Neumann with the prized Enrico Fermi Award. Von Neumann tried to stay game. Out of respect and affection for him, his colleagues on the ICBM Scientific Advisory Committee held one of their meetings at Walter Reed, so that Johnny could still chair it. Then he passed the chairmanship to Clark Millikan of Caltech, but had himself driven by ambulance to the Pentagon where he attended meetings in his wheelchair until he was too weak to do even that. Again out of a unique respect, Millikan kept the word "acting" before his title of chairman until Johnny was gone.

The confrontation with eternity forced von Neumann to answer finally the question that had pursued him for so many years: was he a Christian or a Jew? He decided he wanted to be a Christian. He asked Ford, who was a Catholic, to find a priest who could instruct him in the Roman faith, warning Vince he needed one who was sufficiently intellectual to be compatible. Ford located the right man at the Benedictine priory in Washington, a scholarly priest named Anselm Strittmatter. He and von Neumann had long conversations and when Father Strittmatter concluded that von Neumann was ready, Johnny affirmed his faith, confessed, and received Communion. There was no need for him to be baptized, because he had already received that sacrament back in 1935 when his daughter, Marina, was baptized.

Von Neumann's new faith brought him little consolation. He was frightened to die. The doctors would not sedate him heavily until the final months and he was in pain and had terrible nightmares. His screams and shouts disturbed the other patients on the ward. Ford went to Strauss once more and through his influence von Neumann was moved to a private suite on Walter Reed's third floor, the same suite in which General John "Black Jack" Pershing, commander-in-chief of the American forces in France during the First World War and subsequent chief of staff of the Army, had spent his last years. The security people became concerned that his outbursts might reveal secrets to Soviet spies. The special phone installed in the suite to connect him with the AEC was disconnected. The other phones were monitored and the doctors, nurses, and corpsmen assigned to care for him were vetted for reliability.

No one could know for certain, but from fragments of what von Neumann said in his agony, it appeared that his nightmares did not arise from any Roman Catholic vision of the fires of Hell or Purgatory. Rather, they seemed to be provoked by the realization that his extraordinary mind, which he valued so much, was going to cease to exist. Death was cheating him out of the years of achievement that should have been opening before him. He seemed to fear as well that what he had accomplished would not outlive him, that he would become a forgotten man.

He died on February 8, 1957, at the age of fifty-three, after Father Strittmatter, who subsequently said a funeral mass for him in the Walter Reed chapel, had given him the last rites of the Church. Von Neumann had asked to be buried at Princeton, where the Institute for Advanced Study had been his home for so long. The bishop of Trenton refused him burial in consecrated ground there because he was a divorced man, despite the fact that it was his first wife, Mariette Kovesi, who had divorced him. The von Neumanns had previously purchased a family plot in a nondenominational cemetery at Princeton and on a clear, cold morning he was laid in it beside his mother and Klari's father, Charles Dan, who had committed suicide in despair after his exile from Hungary in 1939. Several of his former colleagues at the institute came to the burial, including Robert Oppenheimer in his trademark porkpie hat, grateful for von Neumann's valiant defense of him against the unjust charges of disloyalty. Six years later, Klari was buried next to her Johnny. She had remarried and the new marriage seemed a comfortable arrangement, but one evening in November 1963, after a cocktail party in La Jolla, California, she walked into the sea.

As the decades passed, von Neumann was sometimes forgotten when he should not have been. In 2005, Thomas Schelling, a professor emeritus at the University of Maryland, and Robert Aumann, also an emeritus professor at the Hebrew University of Jerusalem, received a Nobel Prize for their achievements in applying game theory to the deterrence of nuclear war, labor negotiations, and other conflict situations. A lengthy article in *The Washington Post* reporting the award neglected to mention that von Neumann was the inventor of game theory. In general, he retained a modest if shrunken fame. A postage stamp was struck in his honor in 2005. The *New Columbia Encyclopedia* and similar reference works carried short entries citing his invention of game theory and his work in quantum theory (also referred to as quantum mechanics) and in the development of high-speed electronic computers. The references usually do not mention his role in the building of the rockets and the consequences that flowed from their creation. The Air Force did not forget. In 1997, he was posthumously given the Air Force Space and Missile Pioneers Award and named to the Hall of Fame at Space Command Headquarters at Peterson Air Force Base at Colorado Springs.

80.

"THE SLOWEST OLD TREV HAS EVER GONE IN A CADILLAC"

The Roman candle that was Trevor Gardner flared out before he could help guide to fruition the extraordinary enterprise he had done so much to initiate. In February 1956, just as the building of the Atlas was gathering momentum, he resigned as assistant secretary of the Air Force for research and development. His resentment at the administration's economies had been growing for some time. He also felt betrayed by Wilson's acquiescence in Eisenhower's decision at the end of 1955 to assign the IRBM joint priority with the ICBM. Gardner was convinced that the lesser intermediate-range missile would drain the resources needed to create the big one that the nation had to have to survive. Matters came to a head in the winter of 1955–56 when Gardner demanded increases in Air Force research and development funding. He drew up a new budget and got Twining, who was still chief of staff, White, then vice chief, and others in the Air Force hierarchy, along with Jimmy Doolittle, to sign off on it with him. Quarles rejected it as "juvenile" in view of the stringencies mandated by Eisenhower. Gardner told Quarles the official budget "would simply guarantee us the second best Air Force in the future" and said he was going to resign.

He went to see von Neumann in his apartment at the Woodner and told him that he could no longer work with Quarles. By now the two men had become comrades in a common endeavor. The day Eisenhower pinned the Presidential Medal of Freedom on von Neumann, he telephoned Gardner afterward and said, "Today, I received your medal." Von Neumann received Gardner in his wheelchair. He did his best to dissuade his impetuous friend from quitting. Gardner's best hope to influence events over the long haul lay from within government, von Neumann argued. Once he dropped out of the administration, his influence would depart with him. "One does not leave a position of strength if one wishes to win the campaign," von Neumann said. "And your position of strength is crucial to winning." Gardner listened and, to the sorrow of his friend, remained adamant. There was a last-minute meeting with Wilson aboard his yacht off Miami, where he was vacationing. Wilson also wanted Gardner to stay, but he would not concede Gardner's price of an increase in research and development. And so Gardner submitted his formal letter of resignation on February 10, 1956. Events were to prove how right von Neumann's admonition was that they were engaged in a marathon, not a sprint. Twenty months later Sputnik I's *beep, beep, beep* from space as it circled the earth broke the padlocks on the budget coffers.

As so often behind the curtain in human dramas, there was more to Gardner's resignation than policy disagreements. His personality was disintegrating. His drinking, always heavy, had grown much heavier. The alcohol and the womanizing to which he was prone were destroying his marriage. (It ended in divorce in 1958 and his wife, the former Helen Aldridge, committed suicide afterward.) Vince Ford noted sadly how erratic his judgment had become. With the resignation, Ford later said, Gardner "had just shot himself down in flames by

his own hand." He returned to Pasadena to rebuild Hycon, his electronics firm there. Simultaneously, he began publishing a series of articles in *Life, Look,* and a semiofficial Air Force magazine contending
that because of confusion, bungling, and false economies at the top of
the Pentagon, the United States was losing the missile race to the Soviets. "With every tick of the clock, the Soviet Union is moving closer
to . . . knocking this country out. Intercontinental air power and missiles are the new double-edged sword of destruction, hanging by a hair
over us all," Gardner wrote in one article. If the Russians obtained
ICBMs first, and Gardner predicted that the Soviets might well have
them by 1960, "Pearl Harbor could seem like child's play." The articles
were the catalyst for the subsequent missile gap fright. Schriever tried
to convince him that things were not that dire, that despite its problems the ICBM project was essentially on course. Gardner would not
heed him. The articles made the task of rebuilding his business more
difficult because they brought retaliation in the form of military contracts he should have been given but was denied. Luckily for Gardner,
the retaliation was not severe enough to drive him out of business. His
security clearance was suspended for a time as well, purportedly because of the drinking but probably also as a backhand for the articles.
   Then Gardner got ahold of himself. He stopped drinking. He did
not go to Alcoholics Anonymous or any other organization that helps
addicts. He just stopped cold. "Do you have any coffee?" he would ask
one of the waiters during cocktails after a meeting in Washington or
elsewhere. Schriever kidded Gardner about his unaccustomed teetotal-
ing. "Since you've been drinking that stuff, you're no damn fun anymore," he would say with a glance at Gardner's cup full of coffee and
smile. His business began recovering and a month after his divorce he
married a Swedish woman, Carie Bjurling, whom he had met and apparently been courting during the divorce proceedings. With her, he
started a new family. Schriever and Ford encouraged him to get back
into government service. After Kennedy's election in 1960, he served
on a preinaugural space commission chaired by Jerome Wiesner and
the following year on an Air Force space commission convened by
Schriever. But he was barred from any position of substance. The problem was not that he had been a Republican. Schriever and Ford went
to Wiesner, who was appointed Kennedy's special assistant for science
and technology, and others within the new administration, urging that

Gardner's talents not be wasted. The answer was always the same: "He's too controversial."

On the morning of September 28, 1963, while he was shaving at a second home he had established in Washington, he died of a massive heart attack. He was forty-eight years old. Schriever, who had never lost his affection for the wild Welshman and his admiration for all that Gardner had done for the nation, knew that he would break down if he attempted to give the eulogy during the funeral service at the Andrews Air Force Base chapel. He delegated the task to Jacobson. Gardner's second wife, Carie, asked Schriever to ride with her in the back of the limousine behind the black Cadillac hearse that then carried an urn with Gardner's ashes to a mausoleum at the Fort Lincoln Cemetery in Washington. Ford recalled the sight of Schriever on the rear seat of the limousine outside the Andrews chapel before the cortege started, his long frame leaning back, his hands folded in his lap, his eyes staring off without seeing, the tears running down his face. Later, when the cortege got moving, Schriever turned to Carie and said, "Well, this is the slowest old Trev has ever gone in a Cadillac." As with von Neumann, the Air Force remembered and in 1997, Gardner also joined the roster at the Space and Missile Pioneers Hall of Fame at Space Command in Colorado.

81.

LOSING IT ALL
AND FORGIVING A BROTHER

John Bruce Medaris, the dashing Army major general in riding boots with a guardsman's mustache, who had attempted to steal the ICBM program out from under Schriever, lost everything himself. First came the loss of Jupiter to the Air Force. Then, at the urging of Killian and Kistiakowsky, Eisenhower decided that manned space flight should be for peaceful purposes and should be placed under a single civilian agency with the authority to levy manpower, expertise, and hardware from the military. Congress went along with his wishes and in the passage of the National Aeronautics and Space Act of 1958, the National Aeronautics and Space Administration (NASA) was born. Medaris opposed the creation of NASA in Senate testimony, but his voice had no more resonance than a whisper in a cathedral.

In October 1959, with a decree from Eisenhower in his hand, NASA's first administrator, Dr. T. Keith Glennan, stripped Medaris of approximately 2,100 engineers and other specialists engaged in rocket and space work at the Redstone Arsenal, including von Braun and his entire team of German experts. Simultaneously, Glennan confiscated a project that Medaris had been overseeing with von Braun for a giant booster rocket named Saturn. It would be designed to produce 1.5 million pounds of thrust in order to place large manned satellites in orbit and conduct lunar exploration. Medaris was deprived of everything but the tactical rocket business. Von Braun was delighted with the takeover. He had been urging it for two years. In November 1957, he and his friend and senior assistant, Ernst Stuhlinger, had distributed a paper advocating a National Space Establishment, an organization virtually identical to NASA, to conduct "scientific exploration and eventual habitation of space." Von Braun was appointed director of the George C. Marshall Space Flight Center, which NASA formed in nearby Huntsville, Alabama, and remained its chief until 1970. The ambition he had held while building V-2 vengeance rockets for Adolf Hitler had been realized happily at last. The huge Saturn V rocket that transported Neil Armstrong and Edwin Aldrin to the moon in 1969, much changed and improved over the original model ten years earlier, was von Braun's masterpiece. Medaris left the Army, took holy orders, and spent his retirement years as an Episcopal priest.

Ed Hall forgave his younger brother, Ted, for committing treason. There was something exquisitely ironic about the coincidence that the man who gave birth to Minuteman, the most formidable of American rockets, had a sibling who was the second most important Soviet atomic spy at Los Alamos. Because the FBI had never approached him about his brother's treachery, Hall had known nothing about it until 1996 when, five years after the collapse of the Soviet Union, the National Security

Agency released the Venona documents, the decoded intercepts of the Second World War radio traffic between Moscow and the KGB spy center at the Soviet consulate in New York. One of the messages, instead of referring to Ted Hall by his code name, Vlad, Russian for "Youngster," had carelessly used his real name. Although he moved to England in 1962 to take a post as a biophysicist at the renowned Cavendish Laboratory at Cambridge University when he thought the FBI might be close to unmasking him, no move was ever made to prosecute him. The NSA did not want the Soviet Union to know that it had broken Moscow's wartime codes. (Thanks to information obtained from his CIA friends by the infamous Kim Philby, who was a Soviet spy during his entire and highly successful career in the British Secret Service, the Russians had known all along about the code breaking.)

Ed confronted his brother about the spying during a visit he and Edith made to England in September 1997. The two men had not seen each other since Ted and his family had left the United States in 1962 and both were now looking at the setting sun. Ed was eighty-three at the time of the reunion. Ted was approaching seventy-two and had cancer, with only two years to live. He made no attempt to hide his spying from his brother. He said he had believed that in giving the Soviets the secrets of the bomb he was helping to preserve world peace, that if the Russians also possessed this most terrible of weapons, there would be a standoff and less likelihood of war. Ed Hall found he could not be angry at his brother's duplicity. Ted's motive had not been venal, nor had his intent been evil, and he ceased spying as soon as the Second World War was over. But Ed's lack of anger did not mean that he approved. "It was damned foolish," he said. He attributed his brother's espionage to youth's impetuousness and absence of wisdom. "It was idealism, misplaced idealism. He was only nineteen," Ed said.

Hall's capacity for forgiveness did not extend to Schriever for taking Minuteman away from him. He grew more bitter about it in his old age. But he knew cheerfulness and pride as well when, in 1999, he too was recognized with the Air Force Space and Missile Pioneers Award.

82

"ONLY IN AMERICA"

The post-ICBM years were an anticlimax for Bernard Schriever. He received the fourth star of a full general in July 1961 after he became responsible for shepherding all aircraft, missiles, and other weapons from research and development right into production as chief of the new Air Force Systems Command. Bennie and his younger brother, Gerry, had preserved their boyhood relationship down through the decades since San Antonio. Now they were united professionally. Schriever brought Gerry, who had retained the eagles of a full colonel that LeMay had awarded him on Iwo Jima in 1945, to work for him as his chief of personnel. There were no accusations of nepotism, but Schriever would not have paid any attention if there had been. He knew that he could count on his brother.

Four stars did not bring contentment. Schriever did not get along with Robert McNamara and the civilian "Whiz Kids" from the RAND Corporation whom McNamara brought into the Pentagon with him to organize a new Systems Analysis Division. These self-styled experts on military affairs had no respect for experience and considered seasoned senior officers like Schriever dinosaurs who ought to quietly fade into extinction. They claimed to base their decisions on statistical analysis and other mathematical factors. To Schriever's mind they acted from preconceived and untried notions that they packaged in statistical wrapping. He found himself being constantly harassed and overruled.

LeMay, who had risen to chief of staff in June 1961, never put his hand out in peace to Schriever. The two men stalked around each other. In one sour encounter, LeMay glanced at the four stars on Bennie's shoulder tabs and said, "You realize if I had had my way, you wouldn't be wearing those." Schriever said he understood that. Having come so far he could not help aspiring to be appointed chief of staff when LeMay retired at the beginning of 1965, but the Vietnam War was on and the airplane drivers argued that an operational type was needed. General John McConnell, who had worked for both LeMay and Power at SAC, got the job. On August 31, 1966, two weeks before his fifty-sixth birthday, Schriever retired in an elaborate ceremony near his headquarters at Andrews Air Force Base. He had served thirty-three years as a commissioned officer and could have held on for two more years until the mandatory retirement limit of thirty-five years, but it seemed pointless.

He decided he did not want to trade on his prestige and get rich by accepting a high position in one of the military industries. Somehow that did not accord with his self-image. Instead, he formed a consulting firm in Washington with another retired general, William "Bozo" McKee, who had been the first head of the Air Force Logisitics Command, the other half of the Air Matériel Command after the reorganization in 1961. They naturally availed themselves of their connections and prospered, but not to an unseemly extent. Schriever also accepted a number of directorships on corporate boards. His marriage to Dora, which had seemed to take a turn for the better after his retirement but never really recovered, went over the cliff in 1968 when Bennie began an affair with another woman. As a fervent Roman Catholic, Dora was opposed to divorce and so, after a failed reconciliation, they separated but remained friendly. Bennie made certain she did not suffer in a material way, buying her an apartment in Washington and deeding her his share in a house in Palm Springs, California. He settled into a reasonably satisfying Washington life, playing golf at Burning Tree, an exclusive club in nearby Maryland; promoting his consulting business, serving on several presidential commissions, and as a member of the President's Foreign Intelligence Advisory Board under Ronald Reagan. He especially enjoyed mentoring younger generals still on active duty who would quietly seek his advice when confronted with a problem.

Every year there were reunions of those who had participated in the ICBM adventure. At first these were big, lavish affairs sponsored by Simon Ramo's TRW, Convair, Lockheed, Boeing, and the other companies involved. After a time, Schriever got bored with them and the companies no longer saw much advertising value in paying for them. There was a lapse and then Jacobson, Jamie Wallace, and others who had been with him at the beginning suggested that they hold a modest annual gathering called the "Oldtimers Reunion," by invitation only, at some Air Force base willing to host them. There was never any difficulty finding a base, such as Patrick down in Florida next to

Cape Canaveral, or Vandenberg out in California, whose commander was pleased to welcome them, for Schriever had come to be recognized as the father of the modern, high-technology Air Force. The reunions were touching events. "Those were the best years of our lives," Bennie said, looking back. A visitor invited to participate could see how these men venerated "the Boss," as they invariably referred to Schriever. There would be dinners, a "staff meeting" on one morning to decide where to hold next year's reunion, briefings by the base's specialists on progress in missile and aerospace activities, and afternoons of golf.

In 1986, at a dinner at the home of a friend in Palm Beach, Florida, he met Joni James, who had been one of the biggest pop singing stars of the 1950s. The records of her hits, songs like "Why Don't You Believe Me?," "Your Cheatin' Heart," written by Hank Williams, and "How Important Can It Be?," had sold in the millions. In 1959, "America's Princess of Song," one of the appellations Joni had earlier gained in the heyday of her career, performed in New York's Carnegie Hall. She was accompanied by a thirty-voice choir and the renowned Arturo Toscanini's one-hundred-member Symphony of the Air radio orchestra, on this occasion conducted by her husband and manager, Anthony "Tony" Acquaviva, an accomplished musician who had studied under the maestro. In the 1960s popular music tastes changed rapidly. Acquaviva was acccidentally given an overdose of insulin for the diabetes from which he suffered and the effects made him so sick he could no longer work. Joni dropped out of the music world and devoted herself to nursing him. He died in 1986 and Joni's acceptance of the dinner invitation in Palm Beach was one of her first steps out of the cloister in which she had secluded herself.

After she and Schriever were introduced and Bennie seated beside her that evening, he said he was sorry but he knew nothing about her singing career. She was amused rather than irritated and said she knew nothing about the Air Force. A courtship began. She was drawn to him and decided he was good for her. He encouraged her to resume her career, which she did. There was no hope of regaining the glory days of the 1950s, but she still had a voice and made a go of it. She would have married him quickly, but Schriever stalled. His attitude toward women was one of his flaws. He was an old-fashioned sexist and, with the exception of his mother, did not appear to regard any woman as an equal. The one issue on which his former subordinates had mutinied and overruled him had been the question of whether they could bring their wives to the Oldtimers Reunions. He had argued to keep the occasions stag affairs and they had voted him down at a staff meeting. At Burning Tree, he had been one of the leaders in the fight to keep the place all male, even though continuing to bar women cost the club a hefty tax deduction the state of Maryland grants to golf clubs for the open space they maintain. He regarded a second marriage as an encumbrance. He had been exploiting the marital limbo with Dora to tell women with whom he had become involved over their eighteen-year separation that he could not marry them because Dora would not give him a divorce. She would have agreed to one, but he was careful not to ask.

He tried the tactic with Joni. They could live together in Washington, but for appearance's sake not at his house. He would buy a separate apartment for her so that everything would seem genteel. Becoming the mistress of a technically married man was a proposition Joni could not accept. She was also a practicing Catholic who had been born Giovanna (Italian for Joan) Babbo to a poor but respectable Italian-American family on the southeast side of Chicago. Her mother had been widowed young, while pregnant with her fourth child, and raised Joni and the three other children on her own. In the 1940s and 1950s entertainers with ethnic backgrounds usually changed their names to Anglo-Saxon ones. Tony Acquaviva had invented Joni's name for her. "That's not our way," she replied to Bennie's nonproposal. Because he was also a stubborn man, the courtship dallied for eleven years until Dora at last divorced Schriever. He called Joni and made a proper proposal. "I'll take you," she said. They were married on October 5, 1997. He was eighty-seven and she was sixty-seven, but Joni thought there was still time for some happiness.

Schriever had always been a lucky man. He had not perished flying through a snowstorm during the air mail fiasco of 1934 as twelve of his fellow fliers had. He had escaped being exiled to Korea by LeMay in 1953. He had prevailed in all the gambles he had risked to build the rockets. His last turn of good luck was Joni. Life-enhancing and compassionate, she dedicated herself to seeing to his wants. She transformed his house in the northwest corner of Washington, which had acquired an atmosphere of bereftness while he lived there alone, into a warm and comfortable place where she entertained his Air Force ac-

quaintances and other friends. She sang for the Oldtimers and their
wives at the reunions and performed on other occasions when Bennie
received some honor. He realized what a fool he had been not to have
married her earlier. "We should have done it years ago," he said one
evening not long after their wedding.

The honors had also been rolling in to console him as the afternoon lengthened into the evening. In 1994 a chair in astronautics had
been endowed in his name by Emerson Electric at the Air Force Academy near Colorado Springs. Then, in 1996, he had been given the
Smithsonian's National Air and Space Museum Trophy for Lifetime
Achievement. In June 1998 came the finest honor the Air Force could
bestow. Falcon Air Force Base, the center for the control of all satellites
a few miles from Colorado Springs, was renamed Schriever Air Force
Base. The Army had once named an airfield for a living person, but the
Air Force had never done so before. When a friend telephoned to congratulate him on this unprecedented laurel, Schriever's response reflected the gratitude, always within him, to the nation that had taken
him in and given him such extraordinary opportunities. "Only in
America," he said. "Only in America."

The annual reunions thinned as Oldtimers died or became too enfeebled to attend. Jake Jacobson passed away in mid-May 2001, just
two weeks from what would have been his eighty-first birthday. He
and Peg Davies, the English brunette beauty he had won with his persistence despite his prematurely balding head, had been married for
fifty-seven years. Vince Ford, who had long been retired in the Washington suburb of McLean, Virginia, went that fall. The last reunion
was held in April 2003 at Bolling Air Force Base across the Anacostia
River from the rest of the capital. General Richard Myers, an Air Force
officer who was chairman of the Joint Chiefs of Staff, General John
Jumper, the Air Force's chief of staff at the time, and General Lance
Lord, commander-in-chief of the Space Command, were among the
generals who came to dinner on the final evening in a gesture of
thanks, not only to Schriever, but also to the other Oldtimers present
like Jamie Wallace and Dick Henry. Shortly afterward, Jamie joined his
buddy Jake.

On May 25, 2005, General Lord flew in from Colorado and drove
to Schriever's home in northwest Washington to present him with the
new badge the Air Force had devised for members of the Space Com-

mand. The ceremony took place in a bright, cheerful sunroom off the house's living room. Bennie, unable to stand anymore, sat in a special lounge chair Joni had bought for him. The badge was mounted nicely behind glass in a small brown lacquered wooden frame. It was silvered, with a rocket superimposed on a globe representing the earth and satellites circling behind it. "This is the first one and we want you to have it," Lord said as he handed the framed badge to Schriever. A citation on a little plaque within the frame read: "Gen. Lance Lord to Bernard A. Schriever, General, USAF (Retired), the First Badge to America's First Space Operator." Lord then bent down and draped a blue-and-white checkered scarf the command had also just adopted as a new accoutrement to its uniform around Schriever's neck. Bennie smiled. He seemed to understand what was happening and to be immensely pleased.

Joni had refused to send him to a nursing home after he became too weak to take care of himself. She had a hospital bed brought into the house and organized a team of nurses to care for him, also tending to him herself. As the end approached, she leaned over the bed and told him that he didn't have to hang on, that he had done everything he had wanted to do, he could let go now. She didn't know whether he understood or even heard her, but he opened his eyes and looked at her and she thought he had. He died on Monday, June 20, 2005. He was ninety-four years old.

83.

A REUNION WITH HAP

Joni found the spot at Arlington National Cemetery for him—on a knoll about twenty paces from where Hap Arnold is buried. General Myers's wife, Mary Jo, helped her to find it. Joni had known Bennie wanted to rest near his first commanding officer and great mentor, whom he had admired so much, and she had appealed to the wife of the chairman of the Joint Chiefs for assistance. The head of the staff at Arlington had led them to the grave site and thrust a stave into the ground so that Joni could judge its distance from Hap Arnold's. He asked if that was close enough and Joni said yes, it was fine, and asked if there was room for her beside it. "That's the last one left, ma'am," the official said, but added that Joni's coffin could be laid on top of Bennie's and Joni said that would be fine too. That night, as Joni lay beside him in bed, she told Bennie what she had arranged. She heard him say "Ja," in a tone of approval. During the final months of his long life he often reverted to saying something in the language of his childhood.

The day before the Arlington funeral there was a special Roman Catholic service at the Cathedral of St. Matthew in Washington. Joni arranged that too as an additional tribute. Schriever had converted to Roman Catholicism after his marriage to her and the Church had made him a Knight of the Holy Sepulcher of Jerusalem, but it was the Arlington funeral, approximately three weeks after his death, that would have mattered to him. In his will, he had requested that he be buried with the full military honors due his four stars. General Jumper, the chief of staff, said that these honors were insufficient, that Schriever would go to his grave not simply as a four-star general, but with all the pomp and pageantry reserved for a chief of staff. And so on the morning of July 12, 2005, at Arlington, the Air Force spared no detail. Nine of the service's ten four-star generals, including Myers, would march behind the coffin. The generals had been holding a conference of four-stars down in Florida and had flown up to Washington early that morning, leaving their tenth colleague behind to tidy things up, while they paid homage to Schriever.

The original red-brick chapel at Fort Myer beside the cemetery gate has no air-conditioning and the day was typical for Washington in July. The temperature was at ninety-five degrees, with the humidity in the eighties. The large crowd of mourners therefore gathered in the newer modernistic chapel nearby to hear the funeral mass. There were hymns and prayers and readings from the Scriptures, but no eulogy during the service. Myers was to deliver the eulogy at graveside. Then the coffin of gunmetal gray, draped in the Stars and Stripes, was wheeled out. The honor guard, in parade dress uniform, came to attention as six of its members grasped the coffin and lifted it atop the old-fashioned field artillery ammunition caisson drawn by six horses. Five of the horses had riders from the honor guard. The saddle on the sixth horse was empty, as were the spurred boots placed in reverse in its stirrups. It seemed fitting that Schriever should be carried to his rest on this antique conveyance, as he had originally been commissioned a second lieutenant in the field artillery as an ROTC cadet at Texas A&M and would joke that he had been unsuited to be a gunner because his legs were too long for the stirrups. His alma mater sent a representative to the funeral. The handsome young man with close-cropped hair stood out because he was in an officer's uniform of the same vintage as the caisson—riding breeches and well-shined brown boots of the kind in which Schriever had once stood proud and which cadet officers at A&M still wear on ceremonial occasions.

The generals formed up in ranks behind the caisson, Jumper and Myers in the lead row. Behind the four-stars, two three-star generals formed a line. Then, standing all by himself at the end, like the woeful "tail-end Charlie" in a formation of aircraft, was a single major general, a tall, good-looking man with two stars on his shoulder tabs. Dick Henry, one of the few Oldtimers still well enough to attend the funeral, had been in that room at the Pentagon nearly fifty years earlier when men with thirty-three stars on their shoulders had gathered to decide whether the Army's old training ground of Camp Cooke would become one of the nation's missile centers. He had been told that day that he would never see the like again. Now he was seeing forty-four stars paying their respects to the Boss. They were doing so in the most uncomfortable circumstances possible. The generals were elegant in their blue uniforms, silver braid on the brims of their caps, their jackets tailored to fit close. It was difficult to imagine attire less suited to the ordeal that lay ahead of them, a half mile march to the grave site in this ferocious heat. One bystander remarked jokingly to a four-star that it was fortunate the modern Air Force required even its senior generals to keep fit, given the task they now faced. The general laughed and turned back into line. Michelangelo Acquaviva, Joni's adopted son, a specialist four, the equivalent of a corporal, in the Alabama National Guard, who had served in Iraq, had come to the funeral in his Army uniform. General Jumper, to whom Joni had introduced him, invited him to join the march. He stepped in on one side of the two-star tail-end Charlie, while the Texas A&M cadet stepped in on the other. The drum major at the head of the band in front of the horses raised his silver mace high in the air. He brought it down swiftly, the band broke into a marching tune, and the cortege set off for the knoll with the waiting grave. The mourners, sheltering in the air-conditioning of their vehicles, followed the generals in a long, slow-moving stream, with Joni at their head in a black limousine.

When the cortege reached the base of the knoll and the drum major halted it, white-gloved hands of the strong young airmen of the honor guard hefted the coffin from the caisson and carried it up the slope. A sergeant followed close behind, holding aloft Schriever's personal flag, its four white stars on a field of blue rippling in the faint breeze that was vainly attempting to lend a touch of coolness to the day. As the bearers laid the coffin on straps stretched across the open grave, straps that would be used to lower the coffin into the earth after the ceremony was over and all had departed, three jets in a horizontal line formation flew high overhead. The third jet was separated from the other two by a space wide enough for a fourth aircraft, the missing plane that would fly no more, the aviator's salute to a fallen comrade.

General Myers stepped forward to a lectern equipped with a microphone that had been set up off to one side of the grave. He praised Schriever as "a man of deep conviction, steady determination, bold vision . . . a man of action as well as a man of ideals." Schriever, he said, "had the vision to see beyond the limits of technology and politics, to see the role space and ballistic missiles could play in deterring our enemies and preserving peace. . . . And he had the courage to press forward despite all the technical challenges and the critics who said it couldn't be done." He was glad, he said, that Bennie had lived "to see the end of the Cold War . . . the Berlin Wall come down . . . millions of people enjoying free speech and electing their own governments. These are a part of his legacy." Myers moved to his conclusion. "At some future date the high court of history sits in judgment on each one of us . . . were we truly men of courage, were we truly men of judgment, were we truly men of integrity, were we truly men of dedication? History will record that General Bernard Schriever was such a man."

The chaplain, the Most Reverend Richard Higgins, Roman Catholic auxiliary bishop for the military services of the United States, resplendent in a pinkish-red skullcap and elegant robes, recited the graveside prayers for the dead. Brett Schriever walked to the lectern and read a short tribute to his father. Schriever's four-star flag was furled on its staff by the sergeant bearing it, assisted by another sergeant who slid a leather sleeve over the cloth. The band broke into a tune, then commands were shouted from where the firing party was stationed below the knoll and three rifle volleys crashed in the sultry air. A bugler played taps. A senior sergeant folded the Stars and Stripes that draped the coffin into a triangle with the stars showing in the deep blue field. He handed it to General Jumper, who had moved forward to receive it, saluting the general as he did so. Jumper walked over to where Joni was sitting in front of the coffin in the first of several rows of folding metal chairs set up for the family. She looked like a little Italian lady in mourning, her diminutive figure in a black dress with a filmy black scarf over her hair as dark as both garments. She stared at Jumper as he dropped to one knee before her. So much water was running off his face that she thought he was weeping. It was perspiration.

"This is a small token from a very grateful Air Force to the man who helped shape the Air Force we have today. All Americans are grateful to him and to you," he said, as he placed the flag in her hands and rose. Just then a figure in civilian clothes appeared from the back of the knoll. He bent over Joni for a few minutes with words of condolence while everyone watched in curiosity. The man was Donald Rumsfeld, secretary of defense since the outset of the administration of George W. Bush, doomed to a resignation in disgrace because of his fervid promotion of the catastrophic war in Iraq. In appearing at the funeral he was paying Schriever singular respect because of the level of his office, but afterward Joni, so familiar with the stage herself, could not help comparing his entrance to that of an actor "coming in from the wings."

The band played a recessional. Dora, Dodie and Ted Moeller's middle daughter, named after her grandmother, who had died four years earlier, had thoughtfully brought red roses for her grandfather. She distributed them to the family and these were laid on the coffin. Then Joni stepped forward with a different rose, a yellow rose for the song "The Yellow Rose of Texas," and placed it at the head of the coffin. The band and the honor guard marched away. Joni, the family, the generals, the friends all climbed into cars and drove to the postfuneral reception at the Officers' Club at Fort Myer. The ice sculptures that decorated the main table in the center of the room, customarily of swans and dolphins, were Atlas, Thor, and Titan missiles on this occa-

sion. Bernard Schriever was soon left alone in his place of honor near
Hap Arnold in Arlington National Cemetery. An engraver would soon
carve under his name and rank on the simple white granite tombstone:
"Father of the Air Force's Ballistic Missile and Space Programs."
Eighty-eight years before, had the six-year-old German boy, clasping
his mother's hand in the cavernous immigrants hall at Ellis Island, been
able to foresee what this new country held in store for him, he might
have smiled.

ACKNOWLEDGMENTS

This book is a work of history written for the lay reader. It seeks to convey the essence of the Cold War and the Soviet-American arms race through the human story of the men caught up in one of the Cold War's great dramas—the building of the unstoppable weapon, the intercontinental ballistic missile. To write the book required educating myself in unfamiliar subjects. Although I have spent the better part of my life writing of war and military affairs, my principal efforts have focused on the war in Vietnam. For me, missiles, space, and nuclear weaponry were sparsely explored terrain.

At the head of the list of those who educated me must come Bernard Schriever and the men who toiled alongside him in his extraordinary endeavor. They submitted to lengthy interviews with patience, never telling me I had run over my time, never showing irritation at questions that must have seemed simplistic to many of them.

I also owe a debt to a number of Air Force historians, particularly to Jacob "Jack" Neufeld, author of the definitive documentary history of the missile programs, *Ballistic Missiles in the United States Air Force, 1945–1960*. Over the years of research and writing, Jack never tired of answering questions about various aspects of the missile programs, and he provided me with a small library of Air Force biographical and historical publications, which proved invaluable. Mark Cleary, command historian of the 45th Space Wing at Patrick Air Force Base, generously shared with me his monographs on the history of Cape Canaveral and missile operations there; Dr. Jeffrey Geiger, chief historian of the 30th Space Wing at Vandenberg Air Force Base, did the same. Dr. Harry Waldron, chief, History Office, Space and Missile Systems Center, Los Angeles Air Force Base, a successor organization to Schriever's original Western Development Division, spared no effort to unearth source documents for me, including a chronology that straightened out conflicts in the memories of the participants. Robert Young, historian at the National Air Intelligence Center at Wright-Patterson Air Force Base, assisted me in locating retired technical intelligence specialists such as Col. James Manatt of the Turkish Radar episode. George "Skip" Bradley, command historian at Headquarters, Air Force Space Command, at Peterson Air Force Base in Colorado, repsonded to inquiries as to when major participants in the story were given the Space and Missile Pioneers Award and named to the Hall of Fame there.

Donald "Jay" Prichard gave me a sense of what it was like to stand next to a Thor missile on a launching pad and to sit through a countdown in a control bunker at the Space and Missile Heritage Center he founded and now directs at Vandenberg Air Force Base.

Col. Charlie Simpson, USAF (Ret.), executive director of the Association of Air Force Missileers, guided me to men who could answer questions about specific details of different missiles from their service with various missile units.

R. Cargill Hall, an Air Force historian who later became historian at the National Reconnaissance Office, facilitated my acquiring a copy of the declassified history of the Discoverer-Corona program.

Dr. John Lonnquest, chief of the Office of History of the U.S. Army Corps of Engineers, generously shared with me his 1996 Ph.D. dissertation, "The Face of Atlas: Bernard Schriever and the Development of the Atlas Intercontinental Ballistic Missile, 1953–1960," as well as additional details his research had uncovered.

Michael Baker, command historian at the U.S. Army Missile Command at the Redstone Arsenal in Alabama, passed along his observations of Maj. Gen. John Bruce Medaris, as well as copies of Medaris's monographs and other documents on the Jupiter-Thor competition.

Robert Norris of the Natural Resources Defense Council, the author of *Racing for the Bomb: General Leslie R. Groves, the Manhat-*

tan Project's Indispensable Man, gave me informative publications on Soviet and American nuclear weaponry.

Bill Burr, senior analyst at the National Security Archive at George Washington University, contributed additional declassified documents on the Cold War competition between the United States and the Soviet Union.

The late Mary Wolfskill and the staff of the Reading Room of the Manuscript Division of the Library of Congress were unfailingly helpful during my research into the LeMay, Twining, and von Neumann papers.

Much gratitude goes to Ms. Sandy Smith and other members of the protocol staff at Patrick Air Force Base for their hospitality during several Oldtimers Reunions held there.

Brig. Gen. Robert Duffy, USAF (Ret.), Lt. Gen. Richard Henry, USAF (Ret.), and Lt. Gen. Forrest McCartney, USAF (Ret.) graciously consented to read the manuscript for technical accuracy. Any errors that may remain, however, are my responsibility.

Fred Chase copyedited the manuscript with superb exactness.

Paolo Pepe, Tom McKeveny, and Bob Perini collaborated on the book jacket.

Caroline Cunningham is responsible for the pleasing design of the book.

Steve Messina guided the book through production.

Abby Plesser and Ben Steinberg, assistants to Robert Loomis, were ever helpful to me.

Joni James Schriever was unstinting in her hospitality.

Harold Evans, the legendary newspaperman and former president of Random House, made it possible for me to write this book. I hope it will not disappoint him after the long wait.

For the past thirty-eight years it has been my good fortune to work with two princes among men in the world of publishing, my agent, Robert Lescher, and my editor, Robert Loomis. Throughout those years Bob Lescher has stood with me in joyful times and difficult ones, always supportive, never the source of a harsh word, unfailing in his fine judgment. Bob Loomis has shaped this book as he did the prior three books of my career. It would not be the book it is without him. He has an extraordinary sense for narrative train, an exquisite ear for balance and tone, and the gentle persistence and capacity for friendship to guide a writer through revision after revision until the book is right.

And then there is Susan, always Susan, my wife, my lover, my friend. For more than forty-four years now we have critiqued everything written by each other. Through the long years of this book, she read and edited each section as it was finished, then read and edited each and every revision. When I was about to succumb to one of those bouts of dicouragement that afflict a writer, she cheered me with her love and gave me the courage to press on. There are miracles in marriage and Susan is mine.

INTERVIEWS

This book could not have been written without interviews. Fine histories have been composed on the basis of letters, diaries, memoirs, newspaper accounts, documents, and previously published books. But there is another and equally important dimension to history and that is human memory. It is the perishable dimension and must be captured from the participants before time washes it away. I am immensely grateful to those who shared their memories of the events chronicled in this book with me. Lapses in those memories brought about by the years between the occurrence of the events and the later recollection of them had to be corrected, where necessary, from the written record, but those memories were indispensable nonetheless. I am also grateful to those interviewed who were not participants in the events, but who added a further dimension from their knowledge of the subjects and the individuals involved. The rank and status given for military personnel are those held at the time of the initial interview. If the abbreviation for retired (Ret.) does not follow the name, the individual was still on active duty. The intensity of the interviews varied from the fifty-two I had with General Schriever over the years of research, to hours or days at the homes of participants around the country, to telephone sessions and conversations. The standing invitation General Schriever and his comrades extended me to attend their annual Oldtimers Reunion was also particularly helpful. The most important interviews were tape-recorded and transcripts made so that I could compare memories and do my best to arrive at the truth of an event, again with the assistance of the written record. I also accumulated forty-five stenographer pads of notes. Most of the interviewees listed here are not to be found in the narrative because mentioning them was not central to the telling of the events I chose to recount. This does not mean they were any less important than those I do mention. They gave me insights I would otherwise never have had and educated me in subjects in which I had sparse knowledge when the research and writing of the book began. All listed below contributed to the completion of this book, but any flaws that may lie in it are my sole responsibility.

Barbara Schriever Allan
J. Leland Atwood
Col. Langdon Ayres, USAF (Ret.)
Michael Baker
Naomi Baker
Lt. Gen. Benjamin Bellis, USAF (Ret.)
Victor Bilek
Maj. Gen. Franklin Blaisdell, USAF (Ret.)
Lt. Col. Benjamin P. "Paul" Blasingame, USAF (Ret.)
Lt. Gen. Devol Brett, USAF (Ret.)
Burton Brown
Dino Brugioni
Lt. Col. Frank Buzard, USAF (Ret.)
Samuel Cohen
Brig. Gen. Maurice Cristadoro, USAF (Ret.)
Maj. Gen. Richard Curtin, USAF (Ret.)
Maj. Dik Daso, USAF
James R. Dempsey
Lt. Col. Lucille Dion, USAF (Ret.)
Brig. Gen. John Dougherty, USAF (Ret.)
Brig. Gen. Robert Duffy, USAF (Ret.)
Gen. Howell Estes III, USAF
Dr. Foster Evans
Maj. Gen. Harry Evans, USAF (Ret.)
Lt. Col. Roy Ferguson, Jr., USAF (Ret.)
Brig. Gen. William Fiorentino, USA (Ret.)
Harry Fitzgibbons
Gen. Ronald Fogleman, USAF
Col. Vincent Ford, USAF (Ret.)
Dr. John Foster, Jr.
Maj. Gen. Ben Funk, USAF (Ret.)
Trevor Gardner, Jr.
Dr. Ivan Getting
Lt. Col. Charles Getz III, USAF (Ret.)
Dr. Stanley Goldberg
Col. Leroy Good, USAF (Ret.)
Michael Gorn
Sidney Graybeal
Col. Sidney Greene, USAF (Ret.)

R. Cargill Hall
Col. Edward Hall, USAF (Ret.)
Edith Shawcross (Mrs. Edward) Hall
Sheila Hall
Dr. Richard Hallion
Col. Joseph Hamilton, USAF (Ret.)
Air Marshal Sir Reginald Harland, RAF (Ret.)
William Harwood
Col. Vernon Hastings, USAF (Ret.)
Lt. Gen. Richard Henry, USAF (Ret.)
Maj. Gen. John Hepfer, USAF (Ret.)
Richard Holbrooke
Prof. David Holloway
Sir Michael Howard
Col. Charles Hughes, USAF (Ret.)
Ethel "Peg" Jacobson
Col. Richard Jacobson, USAF (Ret.)
Gen. John Jumper, USAF
Col. Francis Kane, USAF (Ret.)
Spurgeon Keeny, Jr.
Lt. Col. Michael Kelly, USAF
Chief Master Sergeant Raymond Kelsay, USAF (Ret.)
Brig. Gen. William King, Jr., USAF (Ret.)
Arnold Kramish
W. Anthony Lake
Col. William Large, Jr., USAF (Ret.)
Lt. Col. John Leber, USAF (Ret.)
Col. Richard Leghorn, USAF (Ret.)
Brig. Gen. William Leonhard, USAF (Ret.)
Julian Levine
Gen. Lance Lord, USAF
Col. James Manatt, USAF (Ret.)
Col. Charles Mathison, USAF (Ret.)
Lt. Gen. Forrest McCartney, USAF (Ret.)
Felix McKnight
Group Captain Peter McMillan, RAF (Ret.)
Dr. Ruben Mettler
Dr. Aubrey Michelwait
Dodie Schriever (Mrs. Theodore) Moeller
Col. Theodore Moeller, USAF (Ret.)
Gen. Thomas Moorman, USAF
Joseph Moriarty
Robert Muchmore
Gen. Richard Myers, USAF

Jacob Neufeld
Paul Nitze
Robert Norris
Col. Robert O'Brien, USAF (Ret.)
Col. Frederic Oder, USAF (Ret.)
Col. Peter Palmos, USAF (Ret.)
Col. Prentice Peabody, USAF (Ret.)
Thomas Pownall
Donald Prichard
Dr. Simon Ramo
Robert Reck
Maj. James Rosolanka, USAF
Col. Rob Roy, USAF (Ret.)
Lt. Col. Peter Schenk, USAF (Ret.)
Gen. Bernard Schriever, USAF (Ret.)
Col. Gerhard Schriever, USAF (Ret.)
Joni James (Mrs. Bernard) Schriever
Dr. Glenn Seaborg
Col. Ray Soper, USAF (Ret.)
Senior Master Sergeant Peter Standish, USAF (Ret.)
Sue Taskin
Dr. Edward Teller
Lt. Gen. Charles Terhune, USAF (Ret.)
Dr. Adolph Thiel
Françoise (Mrs. Stanislaw) Ulam
Nicholas Vonneuman, Esq.
Lt. Col. Jamie Walker Wallace, USAF (Ret.)
Paul Warnke, Esq.
Dr. Jacob Wechsler
Dr. Gary Weir
Col. Albert Wetzel, USAF (Ret.)
Dr. Albert Wheelon
Dr. Marina von Neumann Whitman
Squadron Leader Basil Williamson, RAF (Ret.)
Maj. Gen. John Zierdt, USA (Ret.)

SOURCE NOTES

BOOK I   ✦   BECOMING AN AMERICAN

Until I decided to write a book on the Cold War and the Soviet American arms race, I had never heard of Gen. Bernard Adolph Schriever. The subject is an immense one. I needed to distill this immensity into a human narrative that a reader could identify with and comprehend. One afternoon in the fall of 1993, while I was seeking the elements of such a narrative in the library of the Air Force Association just across the Potomac River from Washington in Arlington, Virginia, someone suggested that I look up Schriever. The first item in the library's file on him was an eight-by-ten photograph of a tall, handsome man in the uniform of an Air Force general with four stars, sitting on the edge of a table surrounded by models of rockets. The man and his creations looked interesting. Further research bore out the intimation. He turned out to be living in retirement only about six blocks from my own home in northwest Washington. I telephoned him and explained my hope to use his story as a framework around which to organize a larger tale. He agreed. We began the first of fifty-two interviews that lasted until, in the final few years of his life, he became too feeble for searching examination of the past. My visits then became conversations between friends, yet often still fruitful of history. His diary, which he allowed me to copy, likewise proved of inestimable value.

I do not use footnotes. What follows are summaries of the sources drawn on for the writing of each chapter. The summaries do not list all sources, only the main ones.

In this section and elsewhere in the book, conversations are rendered in quotation marks where there is a written record or the memory of the person or persons interviewed seemed precise enough to justify placing the words in quotes.

Chapters 1–3: Early interviews with General Schriever; scrapbooks he kept of his baseball and golf exploits with newspaper clippings and photographs; additional family photographs; documents such as a history of his maternal grandmother's family, the Klattenhoffs, which contained details of General Schriever's own family; Morningside Ministries of San Antonio, which runs the Chandler House and adjacent facilities as a retirement community, for biographical details of Edward Chandler and a history of the house. I am also in debt to General Schriever's younger brother, Col. Gerhard "Gerry" Schriever, USAF (Ret.). During a trip to San Antonio in 2001, he and his wife, Zada, took my wife, Susan, and me on a tour of the youthful haunts of the Schriever boys. They showed us the little house on the edge of the twelfth green of the Brackenridge Park Golf Course in which the boys had grown up. The house is now cut off from the course by an atrocity of a highway driven through by the city in the 1960s, but Elizabeth Schriever's sandwich stand, abandoned and crumbling, can still be seen beneath the overarching limbs of the antique live oak trees.

Chapters 4–8: Schriever interviews and scrapbooks of his year at Flying School and his first year of service at March Field in California. At my request, General Schriever obtained a copy of his entire service record from the Air Force. Here and later in the writing of this book, the file was invaluable in reconciling dates of his assignments with his memories of them, seeing how his superiors viewed him through his efficiency reports, and other details of his career. I am indebted in these chapters for historical background, the characteristics of aircraft of the period, and biographical information on such figures as Henry "Hap" Arnold to a number of Air Force historians whose works are cited in the Bibliography. For example, Maj. Gen. Benjamin Foulois's incredible assertion that the Army Air Corps of 1934 was proficient in night and bad weather flying is to be found on p. 132 of John Shiner's *Foulois and the U.S. Army Air Corps: 1931–1935*. Biographical information on the Air Force Web site, Air Force Link, was also helpful. Arnold's autobiography, *Global Mission,* and biographies of Carl Spaatz and Ira Eaker are also listed in the Bibliography. See DeWitt Copp's 1980 *A Few Great Captains* for colorful biographical data on all three men, particularly Arnold.

Chapters 9–10: John Toland's history of the Second World War from the Japanese perspective, *The Rising Sun,* and William Manchester's magnificent biography of Douglas MacArthur, *American Caesar,* were invaluable in providing the wider context of the war in the Southwest Pacific. George Kenney's autobiography, *General Kenney Reports,* provided grist for the air war against the Japanese and his relationship with MacArthur. The account of the harum-scarum dive-bombing in a B-17 is based on interviews with both General Schriever and Brig. Gen. John Dougherty. A copy of the written report on the incident submitted by Schriever and Dougherty at the time and preserved among Schriever's papers was also crucial in correcting lapses in their memories and in contributing more fascinating details. Chapter 10 was, as is obvious from the narrative, drawn mainly from General Schriever's memory, corrected and amplified by his service record.

BOOK II ✦ INHERITING A DIFFERENT WORLD

For a number of years after the collapse of the Soviet Union in 1991, until Vladimir Putin closed them again, the archives of the former Communist superpower were opened to Western scholars and open-minded Russian historians. The Woodrow Wilson International Center for Scholars in Washington launched the Cold War International History Project, funded by the John D. and Catherine T. MacArthur Foundation. For the first time, the world was able to learn what transpired in the secret councils of the Kremlin and the real motivations of Stalin and his successors. The research into these archives has contributed to all ten chapters of Book II. I am, for example, grateful to Kathryn Weathersby for her monograph on the origins of the Korean War and to Vladislav Zubok and Constantine Pleshakov for their comprehensive 1996 study, *Inside the Kremlin's Cold War: From Stalin to Khrushchev.*

Earlier work, however, has also been valuable. I drew on Daniel Yergin's 1977 book, *Shattered Peace: The Origins of the Cold War and the National Security State,* as well as on Samuel Williamson, Jr., and Steven Rearden's 1993 *The Origins of U.S. Nuclear Strategy: 1945–1953* for help with Harry Truman and James Byrnes's atomic diplomacy in Chapter 11.

Chapter 12: I drew principally on Joseph Albright and Marcia Kunstel's *Bombshell: The Secret Story of America's Unknown Atomic Spy Conspiracy* for Theodore Hall's spying at Los Alamos. I also consulted Richard Rhodes's magisterial *The Making of the Atomic Bomb* and his subsequent *Dark Sun: The Making of the Hydrogen Bomb,* along with David Holloway's *Stalin and the Bomb,* as well as sundry newspaper clippings.

Chapters 13–16: See Holloway, *Stalin and the Bomb;* Zubok and Pleshakov, *Inside the Kremlin's Cold War;* Rhodes, *The Making of the Atomic Bomb* and *Dark Sun;* Yergin, *Shattered Peace;* Dean Acheson's *Present at the Creation;* and James Chace's *Acheson: The Secretary of State Who Created the American World.* Also Dimitri Volkogonov's authoritative and immensely valuable 1988 biography, *Stalin: Triumph and Tragedy.* As a colonel general in the Red Army responsible for the army's political education and its publishing activities, Volkogonov had access to the most closely guarded archives, sources denied to other historians before the Soviet Union's fall. He also interviewed widely knowledgeable survivors of Stalin's reign. The extent of German cruelty and destruction in Russia and the preeminent role of the Soviet Union in the defeat of Nazi Germany, at a horrendous cost in human life, was long suppressed in the West by the atmosphere of the Cold War and the myths created in the self-serving memoirs of German generals like Heinz Guderian and Erich von Manstein. Alexander Werth's 1964 history, *Russia at War: 1941–1945,* was an attempt to set the past straight, but it was premature. The task was then successfully launched in 1975 by the English historian John Erickson, with the first volume of his massively documented history of the Soviet-German war, *The Road to Stalingrad*, followed in 1983 by his second volume, *The Road to Berlin*. The English historian Richard Overy contributed a brief but still useful history, *Russia's War: Blood upon the Snow*, in 1997. John Keegan, that most prolific of British military historians, documents the effects of the fighting on the Eastern Front on the German divisions awaiting the Allied landing in Normandy in his 1982 work, *Six Armies in Normandy: From D-Day to the Liberation of Paris*. I have leaned on all four historians in Chapter 15. For Chapter 16 see Acheson's memoir, Chace's biography of him, Yergin, and Zubok and Pleshakov.

Chapter 17: The U.S. Air Force has amply documented the Berlin Airlift in its 1997 two-volume history, *Winged Shield, Winged Sword: A History of the USAF*, edited by Bernard Nalty. See also a 1998 paperback by Roger Miller, *To Save a City: The Berlin Airlift, 1948–1949*, and Lt. Gen. William Tunner's 1964 memoir, *Over the Hump*.

Chapter 18: See Holloway, *Stalin and the Bomb*; Rhodes, *The Making of the Atomic Bomb* and *Dark Sun*; and Zubok and Pleshakov, *Inside the Kremlin's Cold War*.

Chapter 19: For the sad anecdote of Ho Chi Minh's prediction that the United States would not wage a war in his country, see Mieczyslaw Maneli's 1971 memoir, *War of the Vanquished*.

Chapter 20: Albright and Kunstel's *Bombshell*; Kathryn Weathersby's unpublished 1993 monograph, "Soviet Aims in Korea and the Origins of the Korean War, 1945–1950: New Evidence from Russian Archives"; and Zubok and Pleshakov, *Inside the Kremlin's Cold War*.

BOOK III + THE PERILS OF AN APPRENTICESHIP

Chapters 21–22: Interviews with General Schriever; his service record, including his efficiency reports; Michael Gorn's 1988 study of the *Toward New Horizons* project and the creation of the Air Force Scientific Advisory Board, *Harnessing the Genie: Science and Technolgy Forecasting for the Air Force, 1944–1986*; his further 1994 work on the project and its repercussions, *Prophecy Fulfilled: "Toward New Horizons" and Its Legacy*, and his 1992 biography of Theodore von Kármán, *The Universal Man: Theodore von Kármán's Life in Aeronautics*; Thomas Sturm's 1967 *The USAF Scientific Advisory Board: Its First Twenty Years, 1944–1964*; Maj. Dik Daso's 1997 *Architects of American Air Supremacy: General Hap Arnold and Dr. Theodore von Kármán*; sections of the *Toward New Horizons* project provided to me from Air Force archives; the von Kármán papers held at the California Institute of Technology; interview with Dr. Ivan Getting, brilliant radar designer at the MIT Radiation Laboratory, on his experience on the Scientific Advisory Board as well as his 1989 memoir, *All in a Life-*

time: Science in the Defense of Democracy. On the creation of the Air Research and Development Command: interviews with General Schriever, Col. Vincent Ford, Lt. Col. James Dempsey; Lt. Col. Peter Schenk; Air Force pamphlet, 1955, *The First Five Years of the Air Research and Development Command;* and Michael Gorn's 1985 monograph, *Vulcan's Forge: The Making of the Air Force Command for Weapons Acquisition (1950–1985),* Vol. 1 (narrative).

Chapter 23: I drew on two biographies of Curtis LeMay: *Mission with LeMay: My Story,* a collaborative effort published in 1965 between LeMay and the writer MacKinlay Kantor, a friend of the general, and Thomas Coffey's 1986 *Iron Eagle: The Turbulent Life of General Curtis LeMay.* The two-volume history of the Air Force *Winged Shield, Winged Sword* and Copp's *A Few Great Captains* contain further biographical information on LeMay. The fortieth anniversary official history of SAC, *The Development of Strategic Air Command, 1946–1986,* tracks well LeMay's buildup of his formidable force.

Chapter 24: Interviews with General Schriever and Ivan Getting; Curtis LeMay–Nathan Twining correspondence in the LeMay and Twining Papers in the Manuscript Division of the Library of Congress; Rhodes's *Dark Sun.* On LeMay's desire for a twenty-megaton hydrogen bomb, see Scientific Advisory Board to the Chief of Staff, USAF, Professor John von Neumann's Report on Nuclear Weapons, October 21, 1953, in the archives of the USAF Historical Research Agency at Maxwell Air Force Base, Alabama; for the bomber gap, see the USAF two-volume history, *Winged Shield, Winged Sword;* Fred Kaplan's *The Wizards of Armageddon;* and T. A. Heppenheimer's 1997 *Countdown: A History of Space Flight.*

Chapter 25: Research at the Rocket Museum in the Fortress of St. Peter and St. Paul in St. Petersburg during a trip to Russia in 2002; James Harford's 1997 biography of Sergei Korolev, the leading Soviet rocket designer, *Korolev;* Heppenheimer's *Countdown;* official SAC history, *The Development of Strategic Air Command.*

Chapter 26: Interviews with General Schriever; Nathan Twining correspondence in the Manuscript Division of the Library of Congress; *Atomic Audit: The Costs and Consequences of U.S. Nuclear Weapons Since 1940,* edited by Stephen Schwartz, 1998, pp. 123–26 and footnotes.

Chapter 27: Interviews with General Schriever; research at Rocket Museum in St. Petersburg; Frederick Ordway and Ronald Wakeford's 1960 *International Missile and Spacecraft Guide;* Col. Benjamin "Paul" Blasingame remembered vividly Maxwell facing down LeMay.

Chapter 28: The description of the experimental heavy bomber that was never built is drawn from the memories of General Schriever and Colonel Blasingame. Both also recalled the offshoot benefits from the project, such as the turbofan engine and its effect on both military and commercial aviation. The specifications of the B-70 are taken from the USAF's *Winged Shield, Winged Sword;* Marcelle Size Knaack's authoritative 1988 *Post–World War II Bombers;* and the official SAC history, *The Development of Strategic Air Command.*

BOOK IV + STARTING A RACE

Chapters 29–31: Schriever interviews; also interviews with Marina von Neumann Whitman and Françoise Ulam and their reminiscences at Hofstra University conference on von Neumann, May 29–June 3, 1988; interviews with Foster Evans and Jacob Wechsler; also Evans's lecture, "Early Super Work," published in the Los Alamos Historical Society's 1996 *Behind Tall Fences;* interview with Nicholas Vonneuman and his unpublished biography of his brother, "The Legacy of John von Neumann"; John von Neumann Papers in the Manuscript Division of the Library of Congress; Rhodes's *The Making of the Atomic Bomb* and *Dark Sun;* Herman Goldstine's 1972 *The Computer from Pascal to von Neumann;* Stanislaw Ulam's 1976 *Adventures of a Mathematician;* William Poundstone's 1992 *Prisoner's Dilemma;* Norman Macrae's 1992 *John von Neumann;* and Kati Marton's 2006 *The Great Escape: Nine Jews Who Fled Hitler and Changed the World.*

Chapter 32: Interviews with General Schriever, Col. Vincent Ford, and Trevor Gardner, Jr.; Colonel Ford's unpublished memoir on the building of the ICBM; Air Force Space and Missile Pioneers biography of Gardner.

Chapter 33: Interviews with Simon Ramo and General Schriever; Ramo's 1988 autobiography, *The Business of Science: Winning and Losing in the High-Tech Age;* Col. Vincent Ford's unpublished memoir.

Chapter 34: Interview with Simon Ramo; Col. Vincent Ford's memoir; Ramo's *The Business of Space;* John Chapman's 1960 *Atlas: The Story of a Missile,* for Karel Bossart's early experimental work; General Schriever's papers for copies of the declassified original correspondence, membership, and recommendations of the Tea Pot Committee; see also Jacob Neufeld's 1990 *Ballistic Missiles in the United States Air Force, 1945–1960* for Tea Pot Committee proceedings. Sidney Graybeal, the CIA's original specialist on Soviet guided missilery, helped explain how difficult it was to obtain reliable information in the early years. The hair-raising account of the attempt to conduct photoreconnaissance of the Soviet launching grounds at Kapustin Yar with an RAF Canberra in 1953 is recounted by R. Cargill Hall, an Air Force historian and an authority on spy overflights of the Soviet Union and satellite photographic reconnaissance, in the Spring 1997 issue of *MHQ: The Quarterly Journal of Military History.*

Chapter 35: Trevor Gardner's March 11, 1954, memorandum to Secretary Harold Talbott and Gen. Nathan Twining; Col. Vincent Ford's memoir; Schriever and Ford interviews; Neufeld, *Ballistic Missiles in the United States Air Force, 1945–1960;* interview with Col. Ray Soper, USAF (Ret.).

Chapter 36: Schriever interviews; Col. Vincent Ford's memoir.

BOOK V + WINNING A PRESIDENT

Chapter 37: Schriever and Simon Ramo interviews; Schriever diary; Col. Vincent Ford's memoir; Jacob Neufeld's *Ballistic Missiles in the United States Air Force,*

1945–1960, for Secretary Quarles's suggestion that the Ramo-Wooldridge team be integrated with Schriever's WDD organization.

Chapter 38: Edward Hall interviews; interview with Edith Shawcross Hall; Hall's unpublished autobiography; his entire military record, a copy of which was kindly obtained for me, with Hall's permission, by his daughter, Sheila Hall. Interview with Col. Sidney Greene on the $2 million diverted from Convair for a prototype ICBM rocket engine.

Chapter 39: Schriever interviews and Schriever diary—memo on July 17, 1954, meeting with Tommy Power.

Chapter 40: Schriever interviews and diary; background on Joseph McNarney from Air Force histories and Web site. Thomas Lanphier, Jr.'s, role in shooting down the bomber carrying Adm. Isoroku Yamamoto is taken from Toland's *The Rising Sun.* General Power's efficiency reports on Schriever from Schriever's service record.

Chapter 41: Schriever interviews and diary; Ramo's autobiography, *The Business of Science;* the circumstances of Harold Talbott's resignation are recounted in George M. Watson, Jr.'s, 1992 *The Office of the Secretary of the Air Force, 1947–1965.*

Chapter 42: Schriever interviews and diary.

Chapter 43: Interview with Dodie Schriever Moeller.

Chapter 44: Schriever interviews and diary; Col. Vincent Ford interviews and his memoir; an unpublished 1996 Ph.D. thesis by U.S. Army historian John Clayton Lonnquest, "The Face of Atlas: General Bernard Schriever and the Development of the Atlas Intercontinental Ballistic Missile, 1953–1960," sheds considerable light on this episode. Dr. Lonnquest, chief, Office of History, Headquarters, U.S. Army Corps of Engineers, most kindly shared his thesis with me.

Chapter 45: Dwight Eisenhower's 1963 *Mandate for Change: 1953–1956;* Charles Bohlen's 1973 *Witness to History: 1929–1969;* William Taubman's 2003 *Khrushchev: The Man and His Era;* Zubok and Pleshakov, *Inside the Kremlin's Cold War;* and Erickson, *The Road to Stalingrad* and *The Road to Berlin,* on Stalin's attitude toward Marshal Georgi Zhukov.

Chapter 46: Schriever interviews and diary; Col. Vincent Ford interviews and memoir.

Chapter 47: Schriever interviews and diary; the structure of the Gillette Procedures is explained well in Jacob Neufeld's *Ballistic Missiles in the United States Air Force, 1945–1960.*

Chapter 48: Interview with Burton Brown. Sidney Graybeal and Dr. Albert Wheelon, an original member of the Ramo-Wooldridge team who later became the CIA's first deputy director for science and technology, were very helpful in laying out the subsequently intense and largely successful program to track Soviet missile progress.

BOOK VI ✦ BUILDING THE UNSTOPPABLE

Chapter 49: Schriever interviews; Neufeld, *Ballistic Missiles in the United States Air Force, 1945–1960;* Nathan Twining Papers for excerpt from Gen. Maxwell Taylor's testimony before the Stuart Symington subcommittee.

Chapter 50: Interviews with Dr. Ruben Mettler and Adolf Thiel. Julian Hartt's 1961 *The Mighty Thor: Missile in Readiness* was also of assistance in the writing of this and subsequent sections on Thor. An unpublished July 31, 1972, monograph by W. M. Arms for McDonnell Douglas, "Thor: The Workhorse of Space—A Narrative History," was similarly helpful.

Chapter 51: The portrait of Maj. Gen. John Bruce Medaris is drawn from the observations of a number of people who worked with him, including his deputy, Maj. Gen. John Zierdt, USA (Ret.); Brig. Gen. William Fiorentino, USA (Ret.), project manager for the Army's Pershing II cruise missile; and Michael Baker, command historian at the U.S. Army Missile Command at Alabama's Redstone Arsenal. *Current Biography 1958* provided further biographical details. The profile of Wernher von Braun is drawn from a variety of sources, including his 1951 interview with Daniel Lang in *The New Yorker* magazine; Army Ordnance Satellite Program, unpublished November 1, 1958, historical monograph on the Army Ballistic Missile Agency by Paul Satterfield and David Akens; Ernst Stuhlinger and Frederick Ordway III's 1994 *Wernher von Braun: Crusader for Space,* and Michael Neufeld's definitive 2007 biography, *Von Braun: Dreamer of Space, Engineer of War.*

Chapter 52: Interview with Mark Cleary, command historian, 45th Space Wing, Patrick Air Force Base, and monograph he wrote on the history of Cape Canaveral; interview with Col. Charles "Moose" Mathison, USAF (Ret.), on the construction work for the test-launching of the missiles.

Chapter 53: Interviews with Dr. Ruben Mettler, Adolf Thiel, Simon Ramo, and Schriever.

Chapter 54: Interviews with Dr. Ruben Mettler and Adolf Thiel, Col. Richard Jacobson, USAF (Ret.), Schriever, Simon Ramo, Maj. Gen. John G. Zierdt; Michael Baker; September 25, 1957, memorandum with attachments from Maj. Gen. J. B. Medaris to W. M. Holaday, Special Assistant for Guided Missiles to the Secretary of Defense, Subject: Recommendations on the Selection of a Land-Based IRBM System; unpublished November 1, 1958, monograph by Satterfield and Atkins; unpublished December 1959 monograph, "Jupiter Story," from Major General Medaris to Secretary of the Army Wilber Brucker.

Chapter 55: Interviews with Col. Richard Jacobson and General Schriever.

Chapter 56: Interviews with Col. Richard Jacobson and Schriever; September 25, 1957, memorandum from Medaris to Holaday; October 8, 1957, memorandum from Holaday to Secretary of Defense Charles Wilson, October 8, 1957.

Chapter 57: Schriever interviews; Holloway's *Stalin and the Bomb;* Walter McDougall's 1985 *The Heavens and the Earth: A Political History of the Space*

Age; Harford's 1997 biography of Sergei Korolev, *Korolev;* Heppenheimer's 1997 *Countdown;* research at Rocket Museum in St. Petersburg; Jacob Neufeld's *Ballistic Missiles in the United States Air Force, 1945–1960,* for Donald Quarles's "Poor Man's" economies; *Inquiry into Satellite and Missile Programs,* Hearings Before the Preparedness Investigating Subcommittee of the Committee on Armed Services, United States Senate, Eighty-fifth Congress, First and Second Sessions, 1957–1958, for the testimony of Edward Teller and others before Lyndon Johnson's subcommittee.

Chapter 58: For details of the test range in the Caribbean and the South Atlantic I owe much to my interview with Mark Cleary and his 1991 monograph *The 6555th Missile and Space Launches Through 1970;* Schriever interviews; interviews with Ruben Mettler, Adolf Thiel, Cols. Richard Jacobson and Charles Mathison, and Brig. Gen. Robert Duffy, USAF (Ret.).

Chapter 59: Interview with Lt. Col. Jamie Wallace, USAF (Ret.). Colonel Wallace also provided me with a number of photographs of the DEI inspection. Also interviews with General Schriever and Col. Richard Jacobson.

Chapter 60: Humphrey Wynn's 1994 *RAF Nuclear Deterrent Forces;* Harford's *Korolev;* interviews with Lt. Col. Jamie Wallace, Col. Richard Jacobson, General Schriever, and Squadron Leader H. Basil Williamson, RAF (Ret.). Air Marshal Sir Reginald Harland, RAF (Ret.), who spent several years in the United States as a liaison officer on missile development, working with Schriever's organization, arranged my interview in England with Squadron Leader Williamson and was most informative on the British-American agreement on Thor and its deployment.

Chapter 61: Interviews with General Schriever, Col. Roy Ferguson, Jr., USAF (Ret.); Lt. Gen. Richard Henry, USAF (Ret.).

Chapter 62: Interviews with Squadron Leader Williamson, Air Marshal Harland, Col. Richard Jacobson, and Lt. Col. Jamie Wallace; Wynn's *RAF Nuclear Deterrent Forces;* interview with Lt. Gen. Benjamin Bellis, USAF (Ret.); Neufeld, *Ballistic Missiles in the United States Air Force, 1945–1960;* Medaris's "Jupiter Story" monograph.

Chapter 63: Neufeld, *Ballistic Missiles in the United States Air Force, 1945–1960; Space and Missile Systems Organization: A Chronology, 1954–1979,* monograph, Office of History (SAMSO was a successor to Schriever's WDD); interview with Lt. Col. Charles Getz III, USAF (Ret.), for Black Saturday.

Chapter 64: Schriever interviews; *Space and Missile Systems Organization;* Neufeld, *Ballistic Missiles in the United States Air Force, 1945–1960;* John Chapman's 1960 *Atlas: The Story of a Missile;* interviews with Dr. Ruben Mettler and Adolf Thiel on the faulty engine turbopump; interviews with Mettler and Brig. Gen. Maurice Cristadoro, USAF (Ret.), one of the Atlas project officers, on throwing an Atlas into orbit with a 1958 Christmas greeting from Eisenhower; interview with Col. Prentice Peabody, USAF (Ret.), for the X-17 rocket and the successful development of an ablative warhead.

Chapter 65: Schriever interviews; interviews with Sidney Graybeal and Albert Wheelon; William Taubman's *Khrushchev: The Man and His Era*; Harford's *Korolev*; Heppenheimer's *Countdown*.

Chapter 66: Schriever interviews; Neufeld, *Ballistic Missiles in the United States Air Force, 1945–1960*; interview with Gen. Benjamin Bellis.

Chapter 67: Schriever and Edward Hall interviews; Edward Hall's unpublished autobiography; interview with Lt. Gen. Charles Terhune, USAF (Ret.), Schriever's deputy at WDD; Robert Piper's 1962 unpublished monograph, "The Development of the SM-80 Minuteman," a secret history of the Minuteman program, written for the Historical Office of the Deputy Commander for Aerospace Systems of the Air Force Systems Command and subsequently declassified, with attachments, was a source of important details and helped to correct lapses in the memories of Schriever and Hall; General Terhune confirmed Curtis LeMay's positive reaction to Hall's briefing at the Pentagon and his support for Hall during the subsequent briefing for Secretary Neil McElroy.

Chapter 68: Interviews with Schriever, Edward Hall, Lt. Gen. Charles Terhune, Sidney Greene, Col. Richard Jacobson; Air Force biographical sketch of Gen. Samuel Phillips; Roy Neal's 1962 *Ace in the Hole: The Story of the Minuteman Missile,* which also provided more biographical information on General Phillips. Colonel Hall had preserved the telegram from Maj. John Hinds among his papers and gave me a copy.

BOOK VII + A SPY IN ORBIT AND A GAME OF NUCLEAR DICE

Chapters 69–71: Schriever interviews; interviews with Col. Frederic "Fritz" Oder, USAF (Ret.), Lt. Gen. Forrest McCartney, USAF (Ret.), Colonel Charles Mathison, and Richard Leghorn; *Space and Missile Systems Organization; The Corona Story,* the official history of the Discoverer-Corona project, completed in 1987 by Colonel Oder, James E. Fitzpatrick, and Col. Paul Worthman, USAF (Ret.), and declassified by the National Reconnaissance Office in 2007. R. Cargill Hall, who served as historian at the NRO for a time, kindly obtained a copy for me. Also *Forging the Shield: Eisenhower and National Security for the 21st Century,* 2005, chapter by Cargill Hall entitled "Clandestine Victory: Eisenhower and Overhead Reconnaissance in the Cold War."

Chapters 72–77: Neufeld, *Ballistic Missiles in the United States Air Force, 1945–1960*; Heppenheimer's *Countdown*; Zubok and Pleshakov, *Inside the Kremlin's Cold War*; Taubman's *Khrushchev*; Robert Kennedy's 1968 *Thirteen Days: A Memoir of the Cuban Missile Crisis*; Fred Kaplan's 1983 *The Wizards of Armageddon*; Anatoly Dobrynin's 1995 *In Confidence*; Aleksandr Fursenko and Timothy Naftali's 1997 *One Hell of a Gamble: Khrushchev, Castro, and Kennedy, 1958–1964*; *The Kennedy Tapes: Inside the White House During the Cuban Missile Crisis,* Ernest May and Philip Zelikow's 1997 editing of the tapes of the White House meetings during the crisis; Max Frankel's 2004 *High Noon in the Cold War: Kennedy, Khrushchev and the Cuban Missile Crisis*; Fursenko and Naftali's 2006 *Khrushchev's Cold War*; Michael Dobbs's 2008 *One Minute to Midnight: Kennedy, Khrushchev, and Castro on the Brink of Nuclear War;* the official SAC history, *The Development of Strategic Air Command;* Wynn's *RAF Nuclear Deterrent Forces.*

Chapter 78: Leonid Brezhnev's cynical remark to his brother is recounted in the 1995 memoir by his niece, Luba Brezhneva's *The World I Left Behind: Pieces of a Past.*

EPILOGUE ✦ THE SCHRIEVER LUCK

Chapter 79: The John von Neumann Papers, Manuscript Division of the Library of Congress; Col. Vincent Ford's memoir; Macrae's *John von Neumann;* Poundstone's *Prisoner's Dilemma.*

Chapter 80: Schriever interviews; Col. Vincent Ford's memoir; interview with Trevor Gardner, Jr.

Chapter 81: November 1, 1968, historical monograph on Army Ballistic Missile Agency; Edward Hall interview.

Chapter 82: Schriever interviews; personal attendance at annual Oldtimers Reunions as an invitee; interviews with Joni James Schriever.

Chapter 83: Interviews with Joni James Schriever; personal attendance at funeral.

BIBLIOGRAPHY

Abella, Alex. *Soldiers of Reason: The RAND Corporation and the Rise of the American Empire*. Orlando, Florida: Harcourt, 2008.

Acheson, Dean. *Present at the Creation: My Years in the State Department*. New York: W. W. Norton, 1969.

Aganbegyan, Abel. *Moving the Mountain: Inside the Perestroika Revolution*. London: Bantam, 1989.

Albright, Joseph, and Marcia Kunstel. *Bombshell: The Secret Story of America's Unknown Atomic Spy Conspiracy*. New York: Times Books, 1997.

Allred, John C., et al. *Behind Tall Fences: Stories and Experiences About Los Alamos at Its Beginning*. Los Alamos, New Mexico: Los Alamos Historical Society, 1996.

Alperovitz, Gar. *The Decision to Use the Atomic Bomb: And the Architecture of an American Myth*. New York: Alfred A. Knopf, 1995.

Ambrose, Stephen E. *Eisenhower: Soldier and President*. New York: Simon & Schuster, 1990.

———. *The Victors: Eisenhower and His Boys: The Men of World War II*. New York: Simon & Schuster, 1998.

———. *The Wild Blue: The Men and Boys Who Flew the B-24s over Germany, 1944–45*. New York: Simon & Schuster, 2001.

Arms, W. M. *Thor, the Workhorse of Space—A Narrative History*. Huntington Beach, California: McDonnell Douglas Astronautics Company–West, 1972.

Arnold, H. H. *Global Mission*. New York: Harper & Brothers, 1949.

Baar, James, and William E. Howard. *Combat Missileman*. New York: Harcourt, Brace & World, 1961.

———. *Spacecraft and Missiles of the World, 1962*. New York: Harcourt, Brace & World, 1962.

Ball, Desmond, and Jeffrey Richelson, editors. *Strategic Nuclear Targeting.* Ithaca, New York: Cornell University Press, 1986.

Beevor, Antony. *Stalingrad.* New York: Viking, 1998.

Beschloss, Michael. *The Conquerors: Roosevelt, Truman and the Destruction of Hitler's Germany, 1941–1945.* New York: Simon & Schuster, 2002.

Birdsall, Steve. *Flying Buccaneers: The Illustrated Story of Kenney's Fifth Air Force.* New York: Doubleday, 1977.

Blumberg, Stanley A., and Louis G. Panos. *Edward Teller: Giant of the Golden Age of Physics.* New York: Scribners, 1990.

Bohlen, Charles E. *Witness to History, 1929–1969.* New York: W. W. Norton, 1973.

Borkland, C. W. *Men of the Pentagon: From Forrestal to McNamara.* New York: Frederick A. Praeger, 1966.

Brezhneva, Luba. *The World I Left Behind: Pieces of a Past.* New York: Random House, 1994.

Broad, William J. *Teller's War: The Top-Secret Story Behind the Star Wars Deception.* New York: Simon & Schuster, 1992.

Brugioni, Dino A. *Eyeball to Eyeball: The Inside Story of the Cuban Missile Crisis.* New York: Random House, 1991.

Buderi, Robert. *The Invention That Changed the World: How a Small Group of Radar Pioneers Won the Second World War and Launched a Technological Revolution.* New York: Simon & Schuster, 1996.

Bussey, Lt. Col. Charles M., USA (Ret.). *Firefight at Yechon: Courage and Racism in the Korean War.* McLean, Virginia: Brassey's, 1991.

Chace, James. *Acheson: The Secretary of State Who Created the American World.* New York: Simon & Schuster, 1998.

Chapman, John L. *Atlas: The Story of a Missile.* New York: Harper & Brothers, 1960.

Cleary, Mark C. *The 45th Space Wing, Its Heritage, History & Honors, 1950–1995,* N.p.: 45th Space Wing History Office, 1996.

———. *The 6555th Missile and Space Launches Through 1970.* N.p.: 45th Space Wing History Office, 1991.

Clifford, Clark, with Richard Holbrooke. *Counsel to the President: A Memoir.* New York: Random House, 1991.

Coffey, Thomas M. *Iron Eagle: The Turbulent Life of General Curtis LeMay.* New York: Crown, 1986.

Cohen, Sam. *The Truth About the Neutron Bomb: The Inventor of the Bomb Speaks Out.* New York: William Morrow, 1983.

Condit, Doris M. *History of the Office of the Secretary of Defense,* Vol. 2, *The Test of War, 1950–1953.* Alfred Goldberg, general editor. Washington, D.C.: Historical Office, Office of the Secretary of Defense, 1988.

Copp, DeWitt S. *A Few Great Captains: The Men and Events That Shaped the Development of U.S. Air Power.* McLean, Virginia: EPM, 1980.

Daso, Dik A. *Architects of American Air Supremacy: Gen. Hap Arnold and Dr.*

Theodore von Kármán. Maxwell Air Force Base, Alabama: Air University Press, 1997.

Davis, Richard G. *Carl A. Spaatz and the Air War in Europe*. Washington, D.C.: Center for Air Force History, 1993.

Day, Dwayne A. *Lightning Rod: A History of the Air Force Chief Scientist's Office*. Washington, D.C.: United States Air Force, 2000.

Dobbs, Michael. *One Minute to Midnight: Kennedy, Khrushchev, and Castro on the Brink of Nuclear War*. New York: Alfred A. Knopf, 2008.

Dobrynin, Anatoly. *In Confidence: Moscow's Ambassador to America's Six Cold War Presidents*. New York: Times Books, 1995.

Dugan, James, and Carroll Stewart. *Ploesti: The Great Ground-Air Battle of 1 August 1943*. New York: Random House, 1962.

Eisenhower, Dwight D. *Mandate for Change, 1953–1956: The White House Years*. New York: Doubleday, 1963.

Emme, Eugene M., editor. *The History of Rocket Technology*. Detroit: Wayne State University Press, 1964.

Erickson, John. *The Road to Berlin: Stalin's War with Germany*, Vol. 2. New Haven: Yale University Press, 1983.

———. *The Road to Stalingrad*. London: Cassell Military Paperbacks, 2003.

Fitzgerald, Frances. *Way Out There in the Blue: Reagan, Star Wars and the End of the Cold War*. New York: Simon & Schuster, 2000.

Frankel, Max. *High Noon in the Cold War: Kennedy, Khrushchev, and the Cuban Missile Crisis*. New York: Presidio, 2004.

Frisbee, John L. *Makers of the United States Air Force*. Washington, D.C.: Air Force History and Museums Program, 1996.

Fursenko, Aleksandr, and Timothy Naftali. *Khrushchev's Cold War: The Inside Story of an American Adversary*. New York: W. W. Norton, 2006.

———. *"One Hell of a Gamble": Khrushchev, Castro, and Kennedy, 1958–1964*. New York: W. W. Norton, 1997.

Getting, Ivan A. *All in a Lifetime: Science in the Defense of Democracy*. New York: Vantage, 1989.

Goldstine, Herman H. *The Computer: From Pascal to von Neumann*. Princeton: Princeton University Press, 1972.

Goodwin, Doris Kearns. *No Ordinary Time: Franklin and Eleanor Roosevelt: The Home Front in World War II*. New York: Simon & Schuster, 1994.

Gordon, Theodore J., and Julian Scheer. *First into Outer Space*. New York: St. Martin's, 1959.

Gorn, Michael H. *Harnessing the Genie*. Washington, D.C.: Office of Air Force History, 1988.

———, editor. *Prophecy Fulfilled: "Toward New Horizons" and Its Legacy*. Washington, D.C.: Air Force History and Museums Program, 1994.

———. *The Universal Man: Theodore von Kármán's Life in Aeronautics*. Washington, D.C.: Smithsonian Institution Press, 1992.

———. *Vulcan's Forge: The Making of an Air Force Command for Weapons*

Acquisition (1950–1985), Vol. 1, *Narrative*. Andrews Air Force Base, Maryland: Office of History, Headquarters, Air Force Systems Command, 1985.

Greenspan, Nancy Thorndike. *The End of the Certain World: The Life and Science of Max Born*. New York: Basic Books, 2005.

Gustafson, Thane. *Capitalism Russian-Style*. Cambridge: Cambridge University Press, 1999.

Halberstam, David. *The Coldest Winter: America and the Korean War*. New York: Hyperion, 2007.

Hall, Edward N. *The Art of Destructive Management: What Hath Man Wrought?* New York: Vantage, 1984.

———. *"A Nation at Risk."* Unpublished autobiography, undated, spiral-bound.

Harford, James. *Korolev: How One Man Masterminded the Soviet Drive to Beat America to the Moon*. New York: Wiley, 1997.

Hartt, Julian. *The Mighty Thor: Missile in Residence*. New York: Duell, Sloan and Pearce, 1961.

Harwood, William B. *Raise Heaven and Earth: The Story of Martin Marietta People and Their Pioneering Achievements*. New York: Simon & Schuster, 1993.

Hastings, Max. *Armageddon: The Battle for Germany, 1944–1945*. New York: Alfred A. Knopf, 2004.

Heppenheimer, T. A. *Countdown: A History of Space Flight*. New York: Wiley, 1997.

Herken, Gregg. *The Winning Weapon: the Atomic Bomb in the Cold War, 1945–1950*. New York: Alfred A. Knopf, 1980.

Holloway, David. *Stalin and the Bomb*. New Haven: Yale University Press, 1994.

Hopkins, J. C., and Sheldon A. Goldberg. *The Development of Strategic Air Command, 1946–1986 (The Fortieth Anniversary History)*. Offutt Air Force Base, Nebraska: Office of the Historian, Headquarters Strategic Air Command, 1986.

Hubler, Richard G. *SAC: The Strategic Air Command*. New York: Duell, Sloan & Pearce, 1958.

Hughes, Dr. Kaylene. *Redstone Arsenal's Pioneering Efforts in Space*. Redstone Arsenal, Alabama: U.S. Army Missile Command, 1992.

Hughes, Thomas P. *Rescuing Prometheus*. New York: Pantheon, 1998.

Hunter, Mel. *The Missilemen*. New York: Doubleday, 1960.

Hutchings, Robert L. *American Diplomacy and the End of the Cold War: An Insider's Account of U.S. Policy in Europe, 1989–1992*. Washington, D.C.: Woodrow Wilson Center Press, 1997.

Hyland, William G. *The Cold War: Fifty Years of Conflict*. New York: Random House, 1991 (revised edition).

Kaplan, Fred. *The Wizards of Armageddon.* Stanford: Stanford University Press, 1983.

Keegan, John. *Six Armies in Normandy.* New York: Viking Penguin, 1982.

Kennedy, Robert F. *Thirteen Days: A Memoir of the Cuban Missile Crisis.* New York: W. W. Norton, 1973 (paperback edition with afterword by Richard E. Neustadt and Graham T. Allison).

Kenney, George C. *General Kenney Reports.* New York: Duell, Sloan & Pearce, 1949.

Killian, James R., Jr. *Sputnik, Scientists, and Eisenhower.* Cambridge: MIT Press, 1982 (first paperback edition).

Knaack, Marcelle Size. *Post–World War II Bombers.* Washington, D.C.: Office of Air Force History, 1988.

Koch, Scott A., editor. *Selected Estimates on the Soviet Union, 1950–1959.* Washington, D.C.: CIA History Staff, Center for the Study of Intelligence, 1993.

Leighton, Richard M. *History of the Office of the Secretary of Defense,* Vol. 3: *Strategy, Money, and the New Look, 1953–1956.* Alfred Goldberg, general editor. Washington, D.C.: Historical Office, Office of the Secretary of Defense, 2001.

LeMay, Curtis E., with MacKinlay Kantor. *Mission with LeMay: My Story.* New York: Doubleday, 1965.

Ley, Willy. *Rockets, Missiles, and Space Travel.* New York: Viking, 1957.

Lightman, Alan. *Dance for Two.* New York: Pantheon, 1996.

Lonnquest, John C. "The Face of Atlas: Bernard Schriever and the Development of the Atlas Intercontinental Ballistic Missile, 1953–1960." Ph.D. diss., Duke University, 1996.

Lonnquest, John C., and David F. Winkler. *To Defend and Deter: The Legacy of the United States Cold War Missile Program.* Washington, D.C.: Department of Defense Legacy Resource Management Program, Cold War Project, 1996.

Macrae, Norman. *John von Neumann.* New York: Pantheon, 1992.

Makhijani, Arjun, Howard Hu, and Katherine Yih, editors. *Nuclear Wastelands.* Cambridge: MIT Press, 1995.

Manchester, William. *American Caesar: Douglas MacArthur, 1880–1964.* Boston: Little, Brown, 1978.

Maneli, Mieczyslaw. *War of the Vanquished.* New York: Harper & Row, 1971.

Marchetti, Victor, and John D. Marks. *The CIA and the Cult of Intelligence.* New York: Alfred A. Knopf, 1974.

Marton, Kati. *The Great Escape: Nine Jews Who Fled Hitler and Changed the World.* New York: Simon & Schuster, 2006.

Matlock, Jack F., Jr. *Autopsy on an Empire: The American Ambassador's Account of the Collapse of the Soviet Union.* New York: Random House, 1995.

Maurer, Maurer. *Aviation in the U.S. Army, 1919–1939*. Washington, D.C.: Office of Air Force History, 1987.

May, Ernest R., and Philip D. Zelikow, editors. *The Kennedy Tapes: Inside the White House During the Cuban Missile Crisis*. Cambridge, Massachusetts: Belknap, 1997.

McDougall, Walter A. *The Heavens and the Earth: A Political History of the Space Age*. New York: Basic Books, 1985.

Mets, David R. *Master of Airpower: General Carl A. Spaatz*. Novato, California: Presidio, 1997.

Military History Quarterly 9, no. 3 (spring 1997).

Miller, Roger G., editor. *Seeing Off the Bear: Anglo-American Air Power Cooperation During the Cold War*. Washington, D.C.: Air Force History and Museums Program, 1995.

———. *To Save a City: The Berlin Airlift, 1948–1949*. Washington, D.C.: Air Force History and Museums Program, 1998.

Moody, Walton S. *Building a Strategic Air Force*. Washington, D.C.: Air Force History and Museums Program, 1996.

Morris, Edmund. *Dutch: A Memoir of Ronald Reagan*. New York: Random House, 1999.

Murray, Williamson, and Allan R. Millett. *A War to Be Won: Fighting the Second World War*. Cambridge, Massachusetts: Belknap, 2000.

Nagorski, Andrew. *The Greatest Battle: Stalin, Hitler, and the Desperate Struggle for Moscow That Changed the Course of World War II*. New York: Simon & Schuster, 2007.

Nalty, Bernard C., general editor. *Winged Shield, Winged Sword. A History of the United States Air Force*, Vol. 1 (1907–1950) and Vol. 2 (1950–1997). Washington, D.C.: Air Force History and Museums Program, 1997.

Neal, Roy. *Ace in the Hole: The Story of the Minuteman Missile*. New York: Doubleday, 1962.

Nelkin, Dorothy. *The University and Military Research: Moral Politics at M.I.T.* Ithaca, New York: Cornell University Press, 1972.

Neufeld, Jacob. *Ballistic Missiles in the United States Air Force, 1945–1960*. Washington, D.C.: Office of Air Force History, 1990.

Neufeld, Michael J. *Von Braun: Dreamer of Space, Engineer of War*. New York: Alfred A. Knopf, 2007.

Norris, Robert S. *Racing for the Bomb: General Leslie R. Groves, the Manhattan Project's Indispensable Man*. South Royalton, Vermont: Steerforth, 2002.

Norris, Robert S., and Thomas B. Cochran. *US-USSR/Russian Strategic Offensive Nuclear Forces, 1945–1996*. Washington, D.C.: Natural Resources Defense Council, 1997.

Oder, Frederic C. E., James C. Fitzpatrick, and Paul E. Worthman. *The Corona Story*. Sunnyvale, California: National Reconnaissance Office, 1987.

Ordway, Frederick I., III, and Ronald C. Wakeford. *International Missile and Spacecraft Guide*. New York: McGraw-Hill, 1960.

Overy, Richard. *Russia's War: Blood upon the Snow*. New York: TV Books, 1997.

Parton, James. *"Air Force Spoken Here": General Ira Eaker and the Command of the Air*. Bethesda, Maryland: Adler & Adler, 1986.

Perret, Geoffrey. *There's a War to Be Won: The United States Army in World War II*. New York: Random House, 1991.

———. *Winged Victory: The Army Air Forces in World War II*. New York: Random House, 1993.

Poundstone, William. *Prisoner's Dilemma*. New York: Doubleday, 1992.

Power, General Thomas S. *Design for Survival*. New York: Coward-McCann, 1965.

Powers, Thomas. *The Man Who Kept the Secrets: Richard Helms and the CIA*. New York: Alfred A. Knopf, 1979.

Ramo, Simon. *The Business of Science: Winning and Losing in the High-Tech Age*. New York: Hill & Wang, 1998.

Ransom, Harry Howe. *The Intelligence Establishment*. Cambridge: Harvard University Press, 1970.

Rearden, Steven L. *History of the Office of the Secretary of Defense*, Vol. 1, *The Formative Years, 1947–1950*, Alfred Goldberg, general editor. Washington, D.C.: Historical Office, Office of the Secretary of Defense, 1984.

Reed, Thomas C. *At the Abyss: An Insider's History of the Cold War*. New York: Ballantine, 2004.

Remnick, David. *Lenin's Tomb: The Last Days of the Soviet Empire*. New York: Random House, 1993.

———. *Resurrection: The Struggle for a New Russia*. New York: Random House, 1997.

Rhodes, Richard. *Dark Sun: The Making of the Hydrogen Bomb*. New York: Simon & Schuster, 1995.

———. *The Making of the Atomic Bomb*. New York: Simon & Schuster, 1986.

Schell, Jonathan. *The Abolition*. New York: Alfred A. Knopf, 1984.

———. *The Fate of the Earth*. New York: Alfred A. Knopf, 1982.

Schwartz, Stephen I., editor. *Atomic Audit: The Costs and Consequences of U.S. Nuclear Weapons Since 1940*. Washington, D.C.: Brookings Institution, 1998.

Schweibert, Ernest G. *A History of the U.S. Air Force Ballistic Missiles*. New York: Frederick A. Praeger, 1964.

Schweizer, Peter. *Victory: The Reagan Administration's Secret Strategy That Hastened the Collapse of the Soviet Union*. New York: Atlantic Monthly Press, 1994.

Shambroom, Paul. *Face to Face with the Bomb: Nuclear Reality After the Cold War*. Baltimore: Johns Hopkins University Press, 2003.

Sherwin, Martin J. *A World Destroyed: The Atomic Bomb and the Grand Alliance*. New York: Alfred A. Knopf, 1975.

Shiner, John F. *Foulois and the U.S. Army Air Corps, 1931–1935*. Washington, D.C.: Office of Air Force History, 1983.

Shurcliff, W. A. *Bombs at Bikini: The Official Report of Operation Crossroads*. New York: H. W. Wise & Co., 1947.

Smelser, Ronald, and Edward J. Davies II. *The Myth of the Eastern Front: The Nazi-Soviet War in American Popular Culture*. New York: Cambridge University Press, 2008.

Space and Missile Systems Organization: A Chronology, 1954–1979. Los Angeles: Office of History Headquarters, Space Division, n.d.

Steury, Donald P., compiler. *Estimates on Soviet Military Power, 1954–1984: A Selection*. Washington, D.C.: History Staff, Center for the Study of Intelligence, Central Intelligence Agency, 1994.

————, editor. *Intentions and Capabilities: Estimates on Soviet Strategic Forces, 1950–1983*. Washington, D.C.: History Staff, Center for the Study of Intelligence, Central Intelligence Agency, 1996.

Strauss, Lewis L. *Men and Decisions*. New York: Doubleday, 1962.

Stuhlinger, Ernst, and Frederick I. Ordway III. *Wernher von Braun: Crusader for Space*. Malabar, Florida: Krieger, 1994.

Sturm, Thomas A. *The USAF Scientific Advisory Board: Its First Twenty Years, 1944–1964*. Washington, D.C.: Office of Air Force History, 1986 [reprint of the February 1967 edition originally issued by the USAF Historical Division Liaison Office].

Taubman, Philip. *Secret Empire: Eisenhower, the CIA, and the Hidden Story of America's Space Espionage*. New York: Simon & Schuster, 2003.

Taubman, William. *Khrushchev: The Man and His Era*. New York: W. W. Norton, 2003.

Teller, Edward, with Allen Brown. *The Legacy of Hiroshima*. New York: Doubleday, 1962.

Thomas, Shirley. *Men of Space: Profiles of the Leaders in Space Research, Development, and Exploration*, Vol. 2. Philadelphia: Chilton, 1961.

Toland, John. *In Mortal Combat: Korea, 1950–1953*. New York: Morrow, 1991.

————. *The Rising Sun: The Decline and Fall of the Japanese Empire, 1936–1945*. New York: Random House, 1970.

Tolstoy, Nikolai. *Stalin's Secret War*. New York: Holt, Rinehart & Winston, 1981.

TRW, Inc. *Space Log, 1996*. Redondo Beach, California: TRW, Inc., 1997.

Tunner, William H. *Over the Hump*. Washington, D.C.: Air Force History and Museums Program, 1998 [reprint].

Udall, Stewart L. *The Myths of August: A Personal Exploration of Our Tragic Cold War Affair with the Atom*. New York: Pantheon, 1994.

Ulam, S. M. *Adventures of a Mathematician*. New York: Charles Scribner's Sons, 1976.

U.S. Congress Senate Committee on Armed Services. *Inquiry into Satellite and Missile Programs, Part I.* Washington, D.C.: United States Government Printing Office, 1958.

Volkogonov, Dmitri. *Stalin: Triumph and Tragedy.* New York: Grove Weidenfeld, 1988.

———. *Trotsky: The Eternal Revolutionary.* New York: Free Press, 1996.

Vonneuman, Nicholas A. "John von Neumann as Seen by His Brother." Meadowbrook, Pennsylvania, 1992, revised edition [typed and privately printed in spiral-bound form].

Warner, Michael, editor. *The CIA Under Harry Truman.* Washington, D.C.: CIA History Staff, Center for the Study of Intelligence, Central Intelligence Agency, 1994.

Watson, George M., Jr. *The Office of the Secretary of the Air Force, 1947–1965.* Washington, D.C.: Center for Air Force History, 1963.

Watson, Robert J. *History of the Office of the Secretary of Defense, Vol. 4, Into the Missile Age, 1956–1960.* Alfred Goldberg, general editor. Washington, D.C.: Historical Office, Office of the Secretary of Defense, 1997.

Weiner, Tim. *Legacy of Ashes: The History of the CIA.* New York: Doubleday, 2007.

Werth, Alexander. *Russia at War, 1941–1945.* New York: E. P. Dutton, 1964.

Williams, Beryl, and Samuel Epstein. *The Rocket Pioneers: On the Road to Space.* New York: Julian Messner, 1958.

Williamson, Samuel R., and Steven L. Rearden. *The Origins of U.S. Nuclear Strategy, 1945–1953.* New York: St. Martin's, 1993.

Wynn, Humphrey. *The RAF Strategic Nuclear Deterrent Forces: Their Origins, Roles and Deployment, 1946–1969.* London: Her Majesty's Stationery Office, 1994.

Yergin, Daniel. *Shattered Peace: The Origins of the Cold War and the National Security State.* Boston: Houghton Mifflin, 1977.

Zubok, Vladislav, and Constantine Pleshakov. *Inside the Kremlin's Cold War: From Stalin to Khrushchev.* Cambridge: Harvard University Press, 1998.

INDEX

ABOUT THE AUTHOR

NEIL SHEEHAN was a Vietnam War correspondent for United Press International and *The New York Times* and won a number of awards for his reporting. In 1971 he obtained the Pentagon Papers, which brought the *Times* the Pulitzer Prize gold medal for meritorious public service. His landmark book *A Bright Shining Lie* won the National Book Award and the Pulitzer Prize for nonfiction in 1989. Sheehan lives in Washington, D.C.

ABOUT THE TYPE

This book was set in Sabon, a typeface designed by the well-known German typographer Jan Tschichold (1902–74). Sabon's design is based upon the original letter forms of Claude Garamond and was created specifically to be used for three sources: foundry type for hand composition, Linotype, and Monotype. Tschichold named his typeface for the famous Frankfurt type-founder Jacques Sabon, who died in 1580.